I0605616

# Greater Philadelphia and the World

A NEW HISTORY FOR THE TWENTY-FIRST CENTURY

VOLUME 3

# GREATER PHILADELPHIA AND THE WORLD

Edited by

Andrew Heath

PENN

University of Pennsylvania Press
Philadelphia

The University of Pennsylvania Press gratefully acknowledges funding support for the print version of *The Encyclopedia of Greater Philadelphia* from the Philadelphia Funder Collaborative for the Semiquincentennial, a philanthropic partnership of the Connelly Foundation, the William Penn Foundation, the Neubauer Family Foundation, the Pew Charitable Trusts, the Hamilton Family Charitable Trust, and Comcast; and from the members of the External Board of Advisors of the University of Pennsylvania Press.



Published by
University of Pennsylvania Press
Philadelphia, Pennsylvania 19104-4112, USA

www.pennpress.org

EU Authorized Representative: Easy Access System Europe
Mustamäe tee 50, 10621 Tallinn, Estonia, gpsr.requests@easproject.com

Printed in the United States of America on acid-free paper

10 9 8 7 6 5 4 3 2 1

Hardcover ISBN: 978-1-5128-2738-5

A catalogue record for this book is available from the Library of Congress.

Cover and Book Design by Shubhani Sarkar, sarkardesignstudio.com

Front cover—*Top: Migrant Imaginary* © 2019 City of Philadelphia Mural Arts Program / Layqa Nuna Yawar & Ricardo Cabret, 1902 South 4th Street. Photo by Steve Weinik. Reprinted by permission. *Bottom:* The Delaware River viewed from the West Jersey Ferry Terminal in Camden, New Jersey, in 1876. Free Library of Philadelphia.

Back cover—*Top:* View of Centennial Hall at the Centennial Exhibition, 1876, Library Company of Philadelphia. *Middle:* Advertisement for H. P. and W. C. Taylor, 1851, Library of Congress. *Bottom:* Geno's Steaks, Ninth Street and Passyunk Avenue, Philadelphia, 2019, Carol M. Highsmith Archive, Library of Congress.

50

Published in association with
*The Encyclopedia of Greater Philadelphia*

EDITOR-IN-CHIEF
Charlene Mires

Mid-Atlantic Regional Center for the Humanities
(MARCH)
at Rutgers University—Camden

*The Greater Philadelphia Region*

EDITED BY
Howard Gillette, Jr. AND Carolyn Adams

*Greater Philadelphia and the Nation*

EDITED BY
Charlene Mires AND Jean R. Soderlund

*Greater Philadelphia and the World*

EDITED BY
Andrew Heath

GENO'S
STEAKS
THE
Best
GENO'S STEAKS
CHEESE FRIES
ROAST PORK
STEAKS
BEST
GENOS

# Contents

Chapter 6

## ENVIRONMENT



Chapter 7

## EPIDEMICS AND PUBLIC HEALTH



Chapter 8

## NETWORKS OF KNOWLEDGE, SERVICE, AND ACTIVISM

## Chapter 9

## COMMERCE, INDUSTRY, AND LABOR



## Chapter 10

## WORLD AT WAR

# Preface

We all exist in place and time. Place may seem easy enough to visualize, starting with the room where you are reading this book, your home, street, and neighborhood. Beyond that immediate view, though, you might need a map to see your town, county, or the route you travel to and from work—and a more extensive map or even a satellite view to find your place within a wider region, the nation, and the world. While existing in those many dimensions, you also inhabit a place in time, marked by a date within the narrative of your personal experience. But this, too, extends and entwines with multiple layers of time, from family lineage and cultural heritage to flows of social, political, and economic history. Compounding matters, none of us stands still. We constantly move in place and time, interacting with multiple communities as visible as a stadium filled with fans or as virtual as a network of users of a data stream.

How are we to fathom this complex web of existence and history, to see not only ourselves but our neighbors and common interests? How can we know what has gone before and prepare for what may come next? How can we sort through and assess the avalanche of information produced moment by moment in a digital age? These are some of the needs that the editors seek to address with this book, one of a set of three published simultaneously by the University of Pennsylvania Press: *The Greater Philadelphia Region*; *Greater Philadelphia and the Nation*; and *Greater Philadelphia and the World*. This book and its companions derive from more than a decade of collaboration among hundreds of writers, editors, research assistants, and civic partners who took up the challenge of advancing knowledge of Philadelphia and the surrounding region. Their findings first appeared digitally, one topic at a time, in *The Encyclopedia of Greater Philadelphia*. However, these books are not a print replica of the *Encyclopedia*, which at the time of the books' publication exists online at https://philadelphiaencyclopedia.org/ as a project of the Mid-Atlantic Regional Center for the Humanities (MARCH) at Rutgers–Camden. The books are, instead, curated and updated collections of essays on selected topics. They are arranged thematically, highlighting connections that may not become apparent from casual Internet searching, and framed with new essays that illuminate the rich patterns of the region's experience. The goal is to draw insights from the encyclopedia's many parts, to create a different reading experience and deeper understanding of the region's reach and history.

By happy coincidence, the digital *Encyclopedia of Greater Philadelphia* grew at a pace that enabled publication of these thematic books for 2026, the nation's 250th anniversary. It is a fitting time to reflect on Philadelphia's impact and reach across the region, the nation, and the world. Drawing upon recent generations of scholarship, and often advancing new knowledge, these books convey to the general reading public an up-to-date, diverse history of Philadelphia in its many dimensions. They are milestones that offer starting points for the next generations who take up the challenge of understanding this dynamic region, whether they are pursuing personal knowledge, insights for news reporting or tourism, local information for teaching, foundations for new research, or background for developing public policy.

Philadelphians have not often paused to assess the deep history of their city and the surrounding region. The first attempt came in the 1820s, while memories of the colonial and Revolutionary eras remained. To preserve those memories, John Fanning Watson, a banker, collected oral histories for his *Annals of Philadelphia*, published in multiple editions beginning in 1830. Decades passed before the three-volume *History of Philadelphia, 1690–1884*, appeared as one of many such massive histories published in the years following the nation's centennial. Its lead author, J. Thomas Scharf, a Baltimore-based author of similar histories of his home city and St. Louis, teamed with Philadelphia journalist Thompson Westcott to produce the work. A generation later, in 1912, the prolific biographer and history writer Ellis Paxson Oberholtzer published *Philadelphia: A History of the City and Its People, a Record of 225 Years.* Journalist Joseph Jackson compiled a four-volume *Encyclopedia of Greater Philadelphia* during the 1930s, but the next deep dive into the city's history did not come until the multiple-authored *Philadelphia: A 300-Year History*, which finally appeared in 1982 after many years of effort shepherded to conclusion by historian Russell F. Weigley.

In contrast to these earlier works, this book and its companions encompass not only the city but also a "Greater Philadelphia" extending across eastern Pennsylvania, southern New Jersey, and northern Delaware. "Greater Philadelphia" is a phrase with resonance for Philadelphia dating at least to the 1890s, an era of growth, annexation, and aspiration for cities in the United States. Philadelphia accomplished its greatest leap of annexation earlier, in 1854, when the city's limits extended to the boundaries of Philadelphia County. But in the last decade of the nineteenth century, as electric streetcars brought outlying towns into urban orbits, Philadelphia joined other cities in imagining a "greater" region of cities and suburbs. The phrase "Greater Philadelphia" (or uncapitalized "greater Philadelphia") became common during the period bookended by Chicago's 1889 vote to annex 126 square miles, which allowed it to surpass Philadelphia in population, and the consolidation of the five boroughs into "The City of Greater New York" in 1898. During the 1890s, the reach of the streetcar lines also inspired boosters of "Greater Camden" and "Greater Wilmington" to imagine orbits of influence centered on their cities and converging with more populous Philadelphia. As the Wilmington *Evening Journal* editorialized in 1895, "In a few years the great metropoli of Pennsylvania and Delaware will be connected by a chain of residences, and then may come a greater Philadelphia."

More than a geographic term, "Greater Philadelphia" at the turn of the twentieth century signaled superiority and aspiration. Philadelphia politicians invoked the phrase as early as 1894, when Samuel H. Ashbridge campaigned for mayor on the platform "A Greater Philadelphia." By this he meant that an already "great" city could be made greater through improvements such as better port facilities on the Delaware River. Subsequent mayoral candidates, both Democrats and Republicans, championed Greater Philadelphia as a shorthand for their commitment to progress. By the time John E. Reyburn served as mayor, between 1907 and 1911, the Greater Philadelphia envisioned by his comprehensive planning committees included projects such as the diagonal parkway between city hall and Fairmount Park, a convention hall, and modern subways.

Philadelphia businesses also adopted and propelled "Greater Philadelphia" into common usage. In the wake of the economic panic of 1893, for example, the Wanamaker & Brown and William H. Wanamaker stores celebrated their survival in business with ads published in three states proclaiming, "Greater Philadelphia recognized our courage and sound judgment by flocking into our stores." Newspaper ads for the larger Wanamaker's department store regularly described its scope of business as "Greater Philadelphia," and Gimbel Brothers ran "Greater Philadelphia Sales." Reaching out to the wider region, the J.B. Van Sciver Company of Camden proclaimed itself "The Furniture Center of Greater Philadelphia." During the First World War, shipbuilding on the Delaware River helped to define a "Greater Philadelphia" industrial region uniting the three states of Pennsylvania, New Jersey, and Delaware.

By the 1920s, organizations and businesses ranging from sports clubs to real estate firms adopted names starting with "Greater Philadelphia" to associate their activities not only with the city but also its suburbs. The phrase reached greatest prominence in the middle of the twentieth century, when business leaders formed a Greater Philadelphia Movement to reform the city's corrupt politics and redevelop Center City, but it echoed through organizational names into the twenty-first century. While indicating scopes of interest connecting the city and its suburbs, the phrase continued to infer aspirations to greatness.

This book adopts "Greater Philadelphia" in its geographic sense to indicate a regional scope. Like earlier uses, the term as used here is not limited by a fixed geographic boundary but rather refers to the interdependence between the city and its periphery across parts of three states: southeastern Pennsylvania, southern New Jersey, and northern Delaware. Embedded in this region are flows of people, cultures, ideas, and products that connect the Philadelphia area with the nation and the world. Each topic developed for *The Encyclopedia of Greater Philadelphia*, the source for many of the essays in this book, represents a focused investigation into the region's scope and impact. The extent of the region emerges differently by topic and across time, but patterns are evident and revealing.

To highlight connections among topics, section introductions and conclusions in this book were written by the volume editor, Andrew Heath. Numerous editors of *The Encyclopedia of Greater Philadelphia* had a hand in developing the selected essays, and they are listed in the acknowledgments that follow the text. For the chapter on world religions, Randall Miller served as a contributing editor, with Andrew Heath. Also important to production of this manuscript were managing editor Hillary S. Kativa, who coordinated the illustrations; copy editor (and website managing editor) Donald D. Groff; copy editor Tamara Gaskell; editorial assistants Gina Torres, Luke Hoheisel, and Elizabeth Eimer; and our editor Robert Lockhart of the University of Pennsylvania Press. In keeping with the goals of *The Encyclopedia of Greater Philadelphia*, we hope that the collective effort to create this book serves to connect the past with the present, to build community, and to create a legacy that benefits the Philadelphia region.

**CHARLENE MIRES**

Editor-in-Chief,
*The Encyclopedia of Greater Philadelphia*

# Chapter 1

# Atlantic World

Evan Rothera

Philadelphia's nearest ocean has left a profound imprint on the region's politics, economy, and culture, but the relationship between the Delaware Valley and the Atlantic basin has passed through several distinct phases. From its beginnings as a European settler colonial city, Philadelphia matured into an important Atlantic node, serving as a commercial hub, an immigrant entrepôt, and a center of revolutionary conflict over liberty and enslavement. Over the course of the nineteenth century the region became an industrial dynamo whose workshops and factories persuaded emigrants to brave the Atlantic crossing and helped the United States challenge European power. As Greater Philadelphia's relationship to other parts of the globe grew in the later twentieth century with new patterns of trade and immigration, the relative importance of the Atlantic to regional fortunes diminished, but collective memory of ties to Europe and Africa remained central to civic identity. Atlantic World trends and connections have shaped the city and the region, just as ideas, people, and goods from Philadelphia shaped the Atlantic World.

## Colonial Connections

Philadelphia's connections with the Atlantic predated William Penn's founding of the city in 1682. Imperial rivalries among European powers in the seventeenth century made the Delaware Valley a site of colonization, conflict, and diplomatic wrangling. In 1638, the powerful Swedish monarchy established the colony of New Sweden in the area that later became portions of Delaware, Pennsylvania, and New Jersey. The colony survived until 1655, at which point the Dutch Republic conquered it and incorporated New Sweden into New Netherland. Less than ten years later, in 1664, the English took over New Netherland (renaming New Amsterdam as New York in the process), although the Dutch recaptured the colony during the Third Anglo-Dutch War (1672–74). The Treaty of Westminster (1674) relinquished New Netherland to the English. Such contests among European monarchies and republics gave the Delaware Valley a cosmopolitan hue. Before Penn arrived, Lenape people lived alongside Swedes, Dutch, Finns, and Germans; enslaved African people have been documented around the Delaware region from 1639.

Within a few decades of the city's founding, Philadelphia had become a bustling port city and a center of transoceanic trade. Commercial networks bound Philadelphia to the Atlantic World. By the 1750s, Philadelphia had outgrown Boston to become the busiest port in British America. Its shipping carried flaxseed exports to Ireland and sugar grown by enslaved people in the Caribbean for refining along the Delaware waterfront. Philadelphia, in other words, quickly became integrated into the dense web of connections stretching across the Atlantic and beyond. From the beginning, pirates took advantage of these connections as they preyed on vessels. William Penn discovered to

ATLANTIC OCEAN &c.
SHEWING THE COMMUNICATION
BETWEEN
EUROPE, NORTH AMERICA
AND THE
PACIFIC.
The Ocean Currents are represented by shading thus
and the Arrows shew their direction.
The different Routes proposed for a Pacific Railway are shewn thus
and the existing Trunk Lines to which they join, thus
Atlantic Telegraph Cable shewn thus
HUDSON'S BAY
BRITISH AMERICA
CANADA
UNITED STATES
MEXICO
NORTH PACIFIC OCEAN
GULF OF MEXICO
CARIBBEAN SEA
SOUTH AMERICA
CENTRAL AMERICA
Longitude West 60 from Greenwic

**FIGURE 1.** *Atlantic Ocean*, showing connections between the United States and Europe, ca. 1873. LIBRARY OF CONGRESS.

his dismay in a 1699 visit to his city that pirates thrived in Philadelphia, where they received significant support from some of the city's well-to-do residents and royal officials, and from whence they ventured to target Muslim pilgrims in the Indian Ocean.

Transatlantic migration peopled early Philadelphia and its surroundings. Irish, English, Welsh, and German Quakers accompanied Penn across the ocean, drawn—like other dissenting groups—by Penn's promise of the religious freedom denied to them in the Old World. Other newcomers in the eighteenth century, frequently from the British Isles and Germany, flocked to the rich agricultural land to the west of the city. Their small farms offered better economic opportunities than could be found in Europe, giving the region a reputation as "the best poor man's country."

But that land belonged to other people and, consequently, European immigration to the Delaware Valley assumed a settler colonial character marked by diplomacy and conflict. Negotiations between Lenape people and Europeans in Greater Philadelphia became an important, if much mythologized, part of the early history of the region. Some Native Americans appear to have preferred dealing with pacific Quakers and established productive relationships with them. At least in the beginning, Penn and Quakers seemed to negotiate in good faith. However, as time passed, more and more Europeans arrived in the region, eyed Native American lands covetously, and plotted to appropriate further territory for themselves. By the mid-eighteenth century, Scots Irish settler colonials to the west of Philadelphia blamed the colony's Quakers for checking further conquest. In 1763, a marauding band known as the Paxton Boys massacred the residents of a Susquehannock settlement in Lancaster County that had been on good terms with the colony. Such instances reveal how voluntary European migration across the Atlantic led to the violent expropriation of the lands of the region's Native peoples.

Not all passages across the ocean, though, were voluntary. Indentured servitude and African enslavement—the first a temporary form of unfree labor, the second a permanent one—also crossed the Atlantic. Some European immigrants could pay their fare, but those who could not traded up to seven years of their future labor for passage to the Americas. Conditions indentured servants experienced varied widely across different times and places, but most did not have easy lives. The German schoolmaster Gottlieb Mittelberger sought to discourage such emigration from his homeland. His *Journey to Pennsylvania* (1756), based on his voyage from Rotterdam to Philadelphia and his subsequent sojourn in Lancaster County, did not pull any punches about the misery and exploitation that indentured servants and other immigrants often faced.

Trafficked African people, assigned by their captors with the inheritable status of enslavement, also arrived in Philadelphia, sometimes on ships outfitted in the city. In the early years of the colony most came from the Caribbean. However, when that supply became more fraught, as it did during Seven Years' War, Philadelphian traffickers turned to direct importation from Africa. At the beginning of the American Revolution, Philadelphia contained roughly seven hundred enslaved people, who brought with them elements of African and Caribbean culture like pepper pot soup. Philadelphia and its hinterland—where enslavers held over two thousand more people as property—never developed the export-oriented plantation economy that flourished in Virginia, the Carolinas, and the Caribbean. That said, enslaved people served in households, craft industries, and aboard ships. Furthermore, Philadelphians who did not enslave people themselves often purchased the products of enslaved labor, invested in slaving voyages, and facilitated the buying and selling of their fellow human beings.

## The Revolutionary Atlantic

A region scarred by Black enslavement became a cradle of white liberty over the middle decades of the eighteenth century. As the foremost port in British North America, Philadelphia played a critical role during the Seven Years' War, the imperial crisis, and the American Revolution. Each of these upheavals had Atlantic origins and ramifications. The struggle between Great Britain and France in Europe reverberated in the Americas. Similarly, events that occurred in the Americas, like George Washington's military encounter with Joseph Coulon de Jumonville in Fayette County, Pennsylvania, rippled across the Atlantic as well. For Philadelphians, the backdrop of conflict among great powers intensified existing transatlantic connections and created opportunities for new ones. Benjamin Franklin spent considerable time in Great Britain in the 1760s and 1770s trying to prevent war between Great Britain and the thirteen colonies, as well as securing jobs for his friends and associates. Franklin had long been an Atlantic celebrity, and his growing disillusionment with Great Britain represented the fraying political and intellectual links between Parliament and its American possessions.

Over these years Philadelphia and its surrounding region became a key battleground in the age of Atlantic revolutions. Between 1770 and 1833, violent upheavals transformed France, Haiti, and vast colonized regions of North and South America into republics. In 1776 the Second Continental Congress, composed of delegates who were often born and educated in Europe, met in Philadelphia to sign the foundational document of the new United States. The Declaration of Independence reverberated across the ocean and reflected the influence of transatlantic thought. Its authors presented facts to the candid world and addressed a much broader audience than the residents of the thirteen colonies. The draft of Thomas Jefferson also revealed the western drift of Enlightenment ideas. He adapted, for instance, the claim of the seventeenth-century English philosopher John Locke that men had the right to "Life, Liberty, and the Pursuit of Property." But the declaration, and the new republic it announced, were also shaped by Atlantic World slavery. As scholars have demonstrated, ideas about white freedom and liberty developed in tandem with racialized ideas about Black enslavement and submissiveness. Jefferson's initial draft of the declaration placed the onus for slavery solely on Great Britain. From London, it prompted the lexicographer Dr. Samuel Johnson to wonder why the loudest cries for liberty emanated from the mouths of enslavers.

The imperial crisis and the American Revolution severed links to Britain. For some in the Delaware Valley the divorce proved hard to imagine. By no means all residents in the region flocked to the Patriot cause and "Loyalists" who wanted to maintain relations with the mother country could be found among both the economic elite and ordinary people. The Delaware Valley's Atlantic merchants confronted a difficult dilemma. Ties to the British Empire granted local merchants access to imperial markets, not least in the Caribbean, where food grown in Philadelphia's fertile hinterland had been exchanged for sugar and cash crops. War cut off such long-established trading routes and led to the questioning of loyalties. Quaker merchants like Henry Drinker often had deep ties to Great Britain. Drinker and his wife, Elizabeth, faced the challenge of trying to thread the needle between making concessions to Revolutionaries while maintaining their Atlantic connections. Revolutionaries eventually arrested him for treason, imprisoning him in Virginia, while Elizabeth navigated life in British-occupied Philadelphia during 1777–78. After regaining control of the city, Patriots held 638 "Tory" collaborators as suspected traitors. The Drinkers, embedded in Atlantic World networks, suffered as they attempted to navigate the complex politics of the Revolutionary era. Other Philadelphian merchants turned their gaze west, looking for new markets in China and the Pacific.

The Revolutionary War, like the Seven Years' War before it, recalibrated Atlantic relations in other ways, too. At Valley Forge in 1777–78 the Prussian officer Baron von Steuben helped to drill George Washington's army. The British evacuated Philadelphia in June 1778 and retreated to New York. Around three thousand Philadelphian Loyalists left the city with the British military forces, joining a wider exodus of Tories and their allies (including enslaved Black Americans who had been promised freedom in exchange for military service) to Canada and Britain. Von Steuben's work at Valley Forge helped Washington fight the British to a draw at Monmouth. A few months before Patriots retook Philadelphia, Benjamin Franklin, having been dispatched to Paris, steered the rebel colonies into a crucial alliance with France that helped to determine the outcome of the war. The decision to use Franklin as a diplomat proved a sound one. He fascinated the French, who saw him as the premier example of American genius, and he played his role with aplomb.

In the decades following the American Revolution, Philadelphia remained closely connected to the political currents of the Atlantic World. The ideas of the American Revolution were carried east and south. Revolutions erupted elsewhere—in France, in other parts of Europe, in Haiti, and in Spanish America. The career of Thomas Paine indicates their entangled paths. Paine, who was born in Norfolk, England, had

**FIGURE 2.** *The Reception of Benjamin Franklin in France*, 1888. Franklin used his status as an Atlantic World celebrity between 1776 and 1778 to secure French support for the Patriot cause. LIBRARY OF CONGRESS.

been convinced by Franklin to go to the Americas. Arriving in Philadelphia in late 1774, his influential pamphlet *Common Sense* made the case for revolution in plain language that appealed to a wide readership. In the doldrums of 1776, Paine's *The American Crisis* helped buoy Patriot morale. After the American Revolution ended, Paine traveled to France and served as a member of the National Convention, where he narrowly avoided the guillotine after falling out of favor with leading Jacobins. Paine's career as an Atlantic revolutionary, with Philadelphia at its center, demonstrates how ideas easily crossed oceans.

As a major port city and an Atlantic World hub, Philadelphia often welcomed revolutionaries like Paine, while selectively supporting revolutions elsewhere. French minister Edmond-Charles Genêt, also called Citizen Genêt, arrived in Philadelphia to a rapturous welcome in 1793. Genêt angered George Washington by attempting to subvert Washington's proclamation of U.S. neutrality in the brewing conflict between Great Britain and France. Another figure to become embroiled in partisan battles of the early republic was the Polish nobleman Tadeusz Kościuszko. Having fought with the colonials during the American Revolution and then for Poland against Russia and Prussia, in 1797 he returned as a political exile to the United States, where he lived briefly in Philadelphia until leaving for Europe in 1798. Kościuszko wrote a will, which named Thomas Jefferson as the executor, that dedicated his estate to purchasing the freedom of enslaved people and providing them with education.

Whether as a place of refuge from revolution and reaction or as a source of support for insurgents, the Delaware Valley became enmeshed with tumultuous upheavals across the Atlantic. When revolution erupted in Saint-Domingue (later Haiti) in 1791, French masters fled the colony, forcing many of the people they enslaved to join them. The exiles who arrived in Philadelphia brought firsthand accounts of the hemisphere's first Black-led revolution, which energized both abolitionist and anti-abolitionist politics. Another Francophone uprooted by revolutionary wars was Joseph Bonaparte, who fled to the United States after his brother Napoleon's defeat at Waterloo. Following a short sojourn in Philadelphia he moved out to an estate in nearby Bordentown, New Jersey, where he spent most of his remaining years. Supporters of the Greeks in the Greek War of Independence from the Ottoman Empire raised money for the cause and even tried to persuade the United States to intervene. And in 1848, citizens gathered on Independence Square to welcome the proclamation of a new French Republic. People did not always like the direction foreign revolutions took, but Philadelphians, both Black and white, recognized their city's place in a revolutionary Atlantic World.

## Battles over Abolition and Immigration

Black Philadelphians insisted that those Atlantic revolutions had to reckon with enslavement—the cry of liberty rang hollow if new republics were built on the back of forced labor. Finding allies, however, did not prove easy; abolitionism was never more than a minority sentiment among white people in the eighteenth century. That said, some of the region's Quakers, African Americans, and other friends of liberty raised their voices in favor of ending enslavement and emancipating enslaved people. Connections to the Caribbean and Europe shaped antislavery activism in the Delaware Valley. An extraordinary individual named Benjamin Lay, a Quaker immigrant, became one of the region's earliest abolitionists. Born in England the same year as Philadelphia's founding, Lay spent years traversing the Atlantic as a sailor, left for Barbados, and from there migrated to Philadelphia. Lay's abolitionism sprang from his ardent Quaker faith, as well as his experiences in Barbados, where he witnessed enslavement's brutality firsthand. While in Barbados, Lay and his wife, Sarah, held meetings at their house and served meals to enslaved people, which infuriated white slaveholders. After he and Sarah relocated to Philadelphia, Lay tried to convince fellow Quakers in the region to emancipate enslaved people. While some Friends had rejected enslavement before Lay's arrival, his activism led to his disownment, and he retreated to a cave he converted into a cottage in Abington, Pennsylvania. From there Lay continued to urge the region's Friends to acknowledge Atlantic enslavement as apostasy.

By the end of Lay's life more Quaker voices in the region had begun to proclaim the abolitionism gospel, including the New Jersey merchant John Woolman, a member of the Chesterfield Friends Meeting, who died in Britain on an antislavery mission, and the French-born religious refugee Anthony Benezet, who played an important role in founding the Society for the Relief of Free Negroes Unlawfully Held in Bondage in 1775. The first abolition society in the Americas, it was later reorganized as the Pennsylvania Society for Promoting the Abolition of Slavery and for the Relief of Free Negroes Unlawfully Held in Bondage (usually referred to as the Pennsylvania Abolition Society) in 1789.

In the decades that followed, Black abolitionists in Philadelphia built institutions and cultivated connections that reached across the Atlantic. By doing so they recognized that the struggle against enslavement in the United States was part of a wider battle for rights that extended to Europe, the Caribbean, and Africa. Richard Allen, building on his efforts in establishing Philadelphia's Free African Society in 1787 and Mother Bethel Church in 1794, founded the African Methodist Episcopal Church in 1816 and became the church's first bishop. AME churches subsequently sprang up all over the globe. By the end of the nineteenth century they had reached Bermuda, West Africa, and South Africa. An African American institution that began in Philadelphia therefore shaped the global spread of Black Christianity. Bishop Allen supported abolition, as did James Forten, a self-made sailmaker who after an initial flirtation with the idea of "colonizing" formerly enslaved Americans in Africa or Haiti became a fierce opponent of such schemes and an ardent advocate of an immediate end to enslavement. But the Atlantic connections of Philadelphia's Black abolitionists are perhaps most evident in the career of Robert Purvis. Born free in Charleston, South Carolina, to parents of British, Moroccan, and Jewish roots, Purvis migrated to Philadelphia, where he helped found the American Anti-Slavery Society. Like many of his fellow abolitionists, Purvis sought to rally support in the United Kingdom, which had put enslavement on the path to extinction in its own colonies, and he traveled back and forth across the Atlantic Ocean on fundraising missions while corresponding with prominent British figures in the antislavery movement. When, on August 1, 1842, Black abolitionists marched through the southern wards of the city to mark the eighth anniversary of abolition across the British Empire, a rampaging white mob threatened to burn down Purvis's house.

The Lombard Street Riot of 1842, as it became known, proved just one of a series of riots that pitted rival immigrant and racial groups against one another in the 1830s and 1840s. Tensions over religion, enslavement, and politics that reached across the Atlantic Ocean played out on the streets of Philadelphia. Immigration from Europe continued in the decades after the Revolution, with British, Germans, and Irish (especially after the beginning of the Potato Famine in the 1840s) the most heavily represented. Old World experiences shaped their politics. British Chartists, veterans of the struggle for the vote in the United Kingdom, welcomed the political rights denied to them in their country of origin. Irish Catholics gravitated toward the Democratic Party, in part due to the hostility of prominent Democrats like Andrew Jackson toward Britain. Indeed, the frequency with which Irish Catholics participated in anti-abolitionist violence owed something to their equation of abolitionism with support for the British Crown. Germans, on the other hand, often backed the new antislavery Republican Party in the 1850s, and many of them saw the fight against enslavement as a continuation of the revolutions of 1848 in Europe. Catholic immigration in particular met a nativist backlash. The Philadelphia nativist riots of 1844, which saw the county placed under martial law, sprang from rumors that Irish newcomers wanted to replace the Protestant King James Bible in the city's public schools. Philadelphia became a battleground in a conflict that stretched back to the English colonization of Ireland and break with Rome.

**FIGURE 3.** Robert Purvis, ca. 1840–49. BOSTON PUBLIC LIBRARY.

## Atlantic Crossings in the Long Nineteenth Century

Movement across the ocean brought epidemics as well as people. Diseases rarely remained within the borders of one country; they spread rapidly across an increasingly connected world. Philadelphia's status as an Atlantic port increased its vulnerability. A yellow fever epidemic in 1793, possibly carried on ships transporting French enslavers fleeing the Haitian Revolution, killed at least five thousand Philadelphians and sent tens of thousands fleeing from the city. Yellow fever recurred on a less destructive scale for decades. After the epidemic in 1793, the city decided to build new waterworks and engaged British-born architect Benjamin Latrobe to design them. Latrobe built the waterworks in a neoclassical style that evoked Athens. Cholera too crossed the Atlantic

**FIGURE 4.** *Joan of Arc*, by Emmanuel Frémiet, Twenty-Fifth Street and Kelly Drive, 2011. Commissioned at the instigation of Philadelphia's French community to mark the centenary of the 1789 Revolution and placed on the eastern end of the Girard Avenue Bridge before its relocation in 1948, the bronze sculpture of the patriotic heroine duplicated one standing in the Place des Pyramides in Paris. WIKIMEDIA COMMONS.

and caused epidemics in 1832, 1849, and 1866. By the late nineteenth century, Philadelphia's sanitarians were learning from the hygiene measures that had begun to control such diseases in Europe.

Such exchanges of knowledge had long been a feature of the region. The arts and sciences flourished in eighteenth- and nineteenth-century Philadelphia. Benjamin Franklin and John Bartram's establishment of the American Philosophical Society in 1743 marked the first of many efforts for Philadelphians to demonstrate leadership in the arts and sciences. Philadelphia was the first city to lay claim to the mantle of the "Athens of America," although some people later argued that Boston also deserved the title. The Academy of Natural Sciences of Philadelphia was founded in 1812, in part to impel the creation and diffusion of knowledge about the sciences and in part to place science in the United States on a par with its status in Europe. While Atlantic

World rivalries proved important, the flourishing of the arts and sciences in Philadelphia also sprang from cultural exchange and connection, with leaders in fields as diverse as medicine (Benjamin Rush), botany (John Bartram), and history (Henry Charles Lea) all maintaining close links through either education or correspondence to their European counterparts. The French, in particular, had a powerful influence on the city, not least through the career of the merchant Stephen Girard, an immigrant who became one of the richest men in the United States and left most of his estate to his adopted city. Such figures cultivated and affirmed Atlantic World relationships.

If Philadelphia's intellectual connections to the Atlantic remained a constant across the eighteenth and nineteenth centuries the region's significance to the transoceanic economy eventually started to wane in the 1800s. In contrast to Washington, D.C., which foreign observers and even many people in the United States derided as a miasmic swamp or a sleepy, provincial village, Philadelphia remained an Atlantic financial hub well into the 1830s. The second Bank of the United States, based on Chestnut Street and boasting a federal charter from its foundation in 1816 to 1836, maintained transatlantic financial ties between the United States and Europe, particularly Great Britain. Its demise at the hands of President Jackson strained those relations, which suffered further when Pennsylvania defaulted on its debt payments to European creditors in 1842, prompting the English Lake poet (and self-styled "surly creditor") William Wordsworth to rail against the commonwealth's "degenerate Men." Furthermore, Philadelphia lost ground to New York City as an Atlantic port, as the Erie Canal (among other factors) fueled Manhattan's ascent as the financial capital of the United States. The source of Greater Philadelphia's wealth shifted from commerce to manufacturing, as the Athens of America transformed into the workshop of the world, which increased local support for high protective tariffs to protect home industry. These higher tariffs, however, made it harder for the city to cultivate European markets. Some Philadelphians nevertheless found overseas clients. Joseph Harrison Jr., for example, built locomotives for Russia, and Czar Nicholas I awarded him a gold medal for completing the St. Petersburg–Moscow Railway. After his return to Philadelphia, Harrison amassed an impressive art collection, which he displayed at his mansion off Rittenhouse Square. Harrison, like some of his contemporaries, remained connected to the Atlantic World and prioritized connections and cultural exchange.

## Philadelphia and the Atlantic After 1900

Philadelphia's reputation as an Atlantic center of politics, finance, and commerce may have declined over the course of the nineteenth century but its links to its nearest ocean persisted in other respects. Immigration, which had slowed during the Civil War, accelerated again in the decades that followed. These arrivals increasingly came from eastern and southern Europe—especially Italy—rather than the western and northern reaches of the continent. Their children and grandchildren then often made the Atlantic crossing in reverse to fight in that continent's wars. U.S. intervention in European conflict left a marked impact on the region's economy and society. World War I and World War II stimulated ship production along the Delaware. During the latter, the Philadelphia Naval Shipyard employed over fifty thousand workers, whose labor made Philadelphia a vital part of the "Arsenal of Democracy." Europe and Africa continued to exert an influence in art, design, and politics, too. Jacques-Henri-Auguste Gréber, a French landscape architect, designed and built the Benjamin Franklin Parkway. Marcus Garvey, the founder of the Universal Negro Improvement Association and a proponent of Pan-Africanism, had a following in Philadelphia. Garvey is not the only example of Philadelphia's connections to Africa. After the loosening of federal restrictions on immigration in the 1960s, Ethiopians, Ghanaians, Liberians, and Nigerians were prominently represented in the new African diaspora of the late twentieth and early twenty-first centuries to Philadelphia.

Philadelphia's Atlantic connections remained evident in spaces and civic life of the twenty-first-century region. The Irish Memorial near Penn's Landing, dedicated in 2003, sought to remind visitors about the migrants who built the city. The Mummers Parade could trace its roots back to older immigrant traditions from England, Germany, and Sweden. Annual Columbus

Day celebrations testified to both the strength of Italian American pride and the contested legacy of European colonization. Founders of the ODUNDE Festival, held the second Sunday in June, sought to celebrate the history and heritage of African peoples around the globe and created one of the longest-running and largest African American street festivals in the United States. Philadelphia's historical connections to the Atlantic—forged in cultural exchange, revolutionary conflict, and the movement of peoples and revolutionary ideas—helped make the twenty-first-century city a mecca for tourists. Yet such connections have sometimes underpinned a resurgent nativist politics that echoed an earlier era, as some residents used the region's European cultural heritage to question the place of new immigrants from the Americas and Asia in the city. Philadelphia connections by the twenty-first century were global rather than primarily Atlantic. But the ocean the Delaware River empties into made the city a political and economic hub and the links it enabled remained lodged in civic memory.

NORRIS BROTHERS
PHILADELPHIA
1850
COPIAPÓ

Chapter 2

# The Americas

Molly Nebiolo

PHILADELPHIA HAS OCCUPIED A CENTRAL place in the history of the Western Hemisphere. While the Atlantic provided a lifeline to the region's early European residents, connections to the north, south, and west proved critical, too. Philadelphia served as a refuge for exiles and migrants from across the Americas while also providing a launching pad for Anglo-Americans who sought to survey and subdue its territories and peoples. The Delaware Valley, shaped by great power rivalry, became a political, intellectual, and cultural capital of New World republics. From the nineteenth century onward, it transformed into an industrial behemoth that drew migrants to its factories and sent out to American markets the goods they produced. And in the twenty-first century, with Spanish as its second most spoken language, the region maintained its strong hemispheric connections.

## Early Colonization and Migration

Philadelphia's early history tied it closely to the Atlantic World, but from the earliest days of English colonization, the city became a center for expansion into the interior and a node linking different places in the Americas. Eighteenth-century Philadelphia became a vital port town that connected the North American region with Caribbean and Atlantic world goods and people. In the early years of Philadelphia's settlement, the government welcomed English and European migrants who, having first sought out fortune in the West Indies, found Pennsylvania, with its temperate climate and good soil, a more attractive place to settle. Ships from the Caribbean stopped frequently in Philadelphia, bringing rum, sugar, coffee, news, and knowledge to the city. Sometimes those vessels carried enslaved people, who brought to the Delaware Valley elements of Caribbean culture like the fiery Philadelphia pepper pot stew. The shops and taverns that clustered around Front Street gave Philadelphians a chance to drink coffee from South America, taste sugar from Barbados, and hear information brought from the South that included medical information about tropical diseases, price standards for materials, or news of escaped enslaved laborers from plantations.

The Seven Years' War (1754–63) solidified Philadelphia's status as a major continental center. When great power rivalries spilled over into war in the Great Lakes and Mississippi Valley, Philadelphia—despite its large population of Quaker pacifists—provided men and materiel for the British in their struggle against the French. Desperate for more men, the British asked the Lenape to fight for them in exchange for lands in the Ohio River valley. The Treaty of Easton in 1758 resulted in another wave of displacement for the remaining Indigenous populations in the Philadelphia region. Even though Philadelphia stood far removed from the front lines, the struggle for control of North America profoundly affected the city, which served as a launchpad for Brigadier General John Forbes's assault on

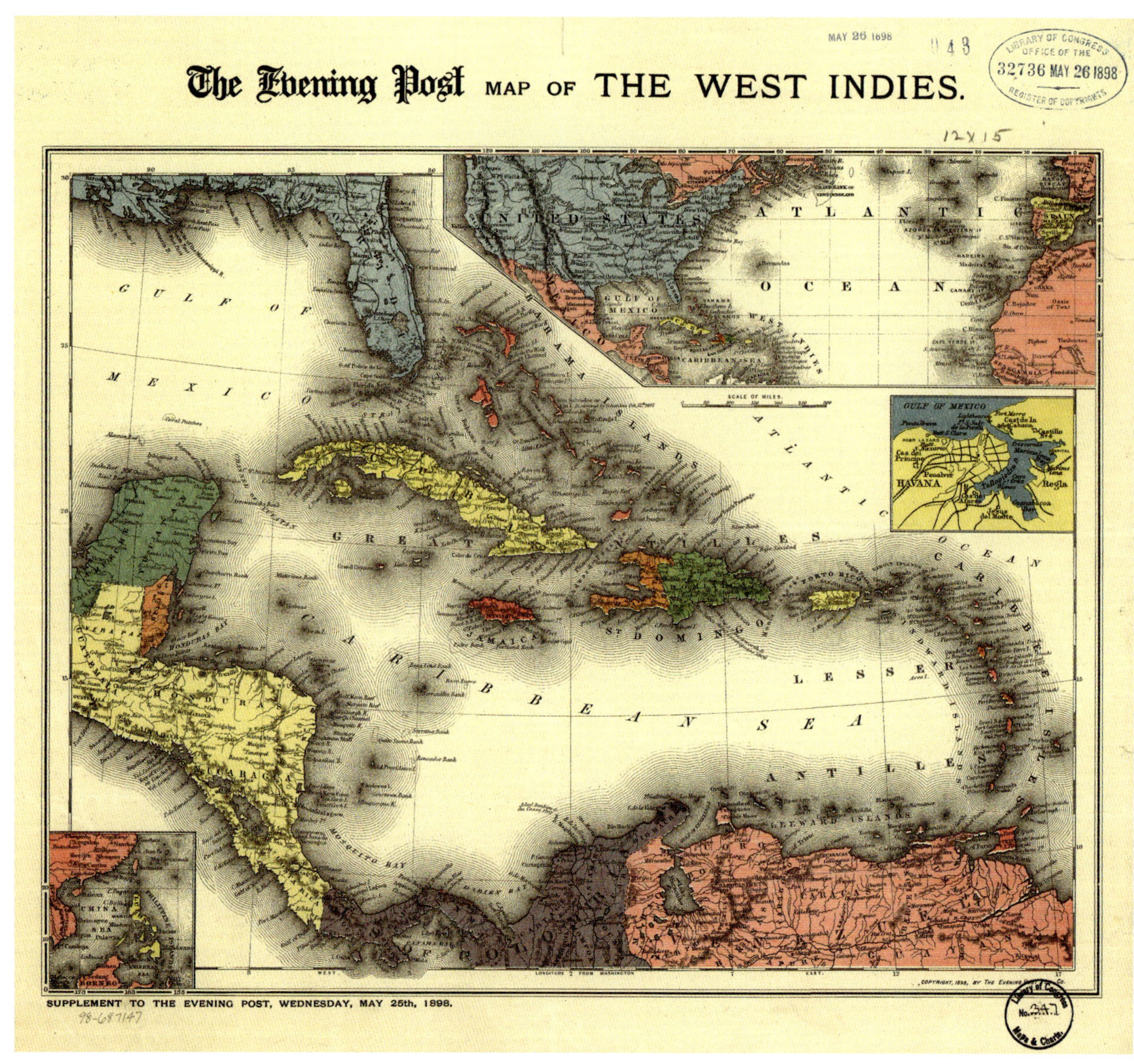


**FIGURE 5.** Map of the Caribbean, 1898. Trade with the sugar islands of the Caribbean enriched the Philadelphia region. U.S. independence cut off access to British colonial markets, but Spanish Cuba (yellow, left center) and the French colony of Saint-Domingue remained important links. When free Black and enslaved people on Saint-Domingue launched a revolution of their own in 1791, it culminated in the creation of Haiti (orange, center) and French planters fled to Philadelphia. LIBRARY OF CONGRESS.

Fort Duquesne in 1758 and gave the British control over the Ohio Valley. Amid the fighting between European empires and Native American nations, the city became a home to displaced people. In 1755, the British expelled the French Acadian population that lived in what is now Nova Scotia. About 450 Acadians fled to Philadelphia. Confined to "French houses" at Sixth and Pine Streets, the Acadians in the city unnerved the British colonial residents. New arrivals also came from western Pennsylvania, where the war had pitted Native American allies of the French against Protestant settler colonials. After France's surrender, Indian nations continued to resist British American settlement in the backcountry, leading to a conflict in which Scots Irish Presbyterians known as the Paxton Boys massacred a Conestoga community in Lancaster County before marching on Philadelphia. William Penn's earlier hope of peacefully settling the portion of the continent allocated to him by the English Crown had given way to murderous violence.

Philadelphians did not just see the Americas as an arena for geopolitical struggle; the hemisphere also provided them with a laboratory. Influenced by Enlightenment ideas, Philadelphians pursued an interest in natural philosophy, or science, of the world around them. Founded by Benjamin Franklin and a handful of associates in 1727, the Junto, or Leather Apron Club, provided a forum for discussion of such matters. From this foundation local scientific societies like the American Philosophical Society (established in 1743) supported efforts to map and classify the continent. Taking advantage of trade routes to the Caribbean, South America, and Canada, naturalists and botanists like John Bartram traveled the world to study, label, and collect plant and animal species. Franklin, Charles Willson Peale, and others acquired specimens and knowledge from across the Americas, and institutions such as the University of Pennsylvania Medical School became centers of learning that over the course of the nineteenth century drew students from distant parts of the hemisphere. The Cuban physician Juan Guiteras, for instance, completed his training in Philadelphia in 1873 before becoming a leading figure in the Pan-American Medical Congress twenty years later.

If education linked early Philadelphia to the Americas, so too did enslavement. The sugar trade in the eighteenth century brought Delaware Valley merchants into close contact with Caribbean enslavers. About one in five vessels from foreign ports during the 1790s came from the island of Saint-Domingue, which up to that point had been a French colony. Stephen Girard, a French-born merchant who became one of Philadelphia's most generous benefactors, had spent time on the island, where he claimed ownership over an enslaved woman called Hannah. Despite Pennsylvania's gradual emancipation law, Hannah remained his property after he relocated to Philadelphia, and she only secured her freedom on Girard's death.

## The Revolutionary Americas

Hannah's arrival in the 1780s presaged a much larger exile from Saint-Domingue. When, taking advantage of the dislocation caused by the French Revolution, enslaved people launched a revolt on the island, white planters sought refuge in Philadelphia. An influx of refugees, often with the men and women they enslaved in tow, arrived in the summer of 1793, mere weeks before the infamous yellow fever outbreak plagued the city that autumn. While the enslaved people were forcibly relocated and integrated into the region's growing Black population, the Haitian planters brought with them warnings of servile insurrection. Yet in 1798 an emissary from the revolutionary leader Toussaint

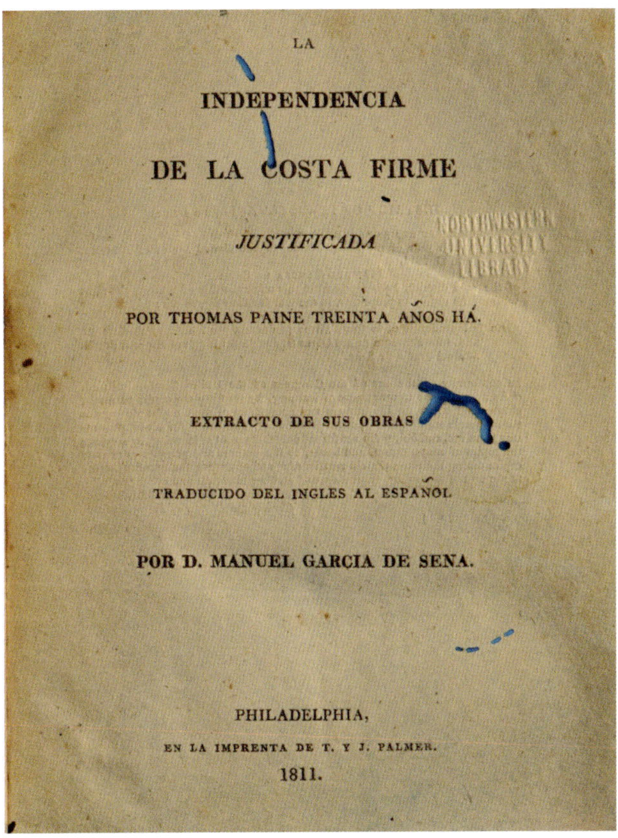
LA

INDEPENDENCIA

DE LA COSTA FIRME

*JUSTIFICADA*

POR THOMAS PAINE TREINTA AÑOS HÁ.

EXTRACTO DE SUS OBRAS

TRADUCIDO DEL INGLES AL ESPAÑOL

POR D. MANUEL GARCIA DE SENA.

PHILADELPHIA,

EN LA IMPRENTA DE T. Y J. PALMER.

1811.



**FIGURE 6.** *Independence of the Costa Firme Justified by Thomas Paine Thirty Years Ago*, 1811. A generation after U.S. independence, revolutionaries in Spanish America looked to Philadelphia for legitimacy. Thomas Paine, whose pamphlet *Common Sense* radicalized opinion in Philadelphia in 1776, influenced the Venezuelan translator Manuel Garcia de Sena. NORTHWESTERN UNIVERSITY VIA HATHITRUST.

L'Ouverture traveled to Philadelphia to meet leading figures in the administration of President John Adams, laying the groundwork for three years of strong relations between the United States and Saint-Domingue's insurgent leadership before the Virginian, President Thomas Jefferson, reversed course. The Haitian Revolution, which established a Black republic in the Western Hemisphere, invited Philadelphians to ponder the limits of their own revolutionary tradition: Were the "self-evident" truths Jefferson enunciated in the Declaration of Independence universal?

Revolutionaries elsewhere in the hemisphere thought so. Over the following decades, the Philadelphia region's role in a struggle against the Crown made it a beacon for other Americans battling for autonomy. The success of the United States in breaking with Britain inspired leading figures in Spanish American independence movements between 1808 and 1833. Restless subjects of the Spanish Empire found inspiration and support on the banks of the Delaware River. As the Napoleonic wars weakened Spain's grip on its American possessions, Philadelphia sheltered political exiles from its colonies, published books by leaders of independence struggles, and became a site where Spanish Americans could see republicanism in action. By 1811, a Peruvian had published the first Spanish translation of Tom Paine's *Common Sense*, an anti-monarchist pamphlet written in Philadelphia that had electrified the colonies in 1776.

Yet over the following decades, learned Philadelphians assembled evidence they had gathered from encounters with Indigenous, Black, and Spanish people from across the Americas to suggest that liberty had strict racial limits. White Philadelphians, who maintained connections to regions of the Americas that depended on enslaved labor, also used the continent's peoples to develop a pseudoscientific understanding of race. Samuel G. Morton, a scientist with ties to the Academy of Natural Sciences, became a prolific collector of human remains from across the continent. His 1839 publication, *Crania Americana; or, A Comparative View of the Skulls of Various Aboriginal Nations of North and South America*, used craniology to categorize the hemisphere into a hierarchy of peoples. His theory that humanity divided into several subspecies—known as polygenism—provoked fierce debate in a Delaware Valley divided over slavery. Published five years after enslaved people had won their freedom in the British West Indies, Morton's book seemingly showed that Black Americans stood as both separate and unequal from the white race, thus providing an intellectual rationale for their subjugation. Abolitionists in the Philadelphia region, like their counterparts elsewhere in the Union, rejected polygenesis and emphasized the common origin of humankind. Morton's work nevertheless acquired wide influence among proslavery theorists eager to justify the South's "peculiar institution" at a moment in which U.S. slavery seemed increasingly an outlier in the hemisphere.

## Violence and Disorder in the Nineteenth Century

While Philadelphians boasted of their city's contribution to liberty, they often endorsed schemes for western expansion. The Louisiana Purchase of 1803, which doubled the territory claimed by the United States, prompted efforts to bring the Mississippi Valley and its inhabitants under U.S. control. Just a year after the acquisition from France, the American Philosophical Society sponsored an expedition led by Merriwether Lewis and William Clark, who set out to survey the natural history of the territory and demonstrate U.S. sovereignty. Near the mouth of the Mississippi River, 280,000 acres of Louisiana Purchase land came into the hands of the French-born Philadelphia merchant Girard, who left a share of it to the municipal government in his will, ensuring his adopted city would profit from the expansion of U.S. plantation slavery in the vicinity of the Gulf of Mexico.

Just as in the Seven Years' War, the question of land rights that resulted from attempts to survey and subdue the South and West led to bloodshed, this time pitting white American colonizers against Indigenous communities and Mexicans. The Mexican-American War (1846–48), which concluded in the annexation of California and the Southwest to the United States, became one of the most controversial in American history and divided opinion in the Philadelphia region. Philadelphians of abolitionist and antislavery leanings warned that the conflict threatened to expand an empire for slavery. Nativists hostile to immigration cautioned against bringing a large Catholic population into the republic. Nevertheless, pro-war sentiment in the age of Manifest Destiny proved strong, too, and Pennsylvania sent six regiments to the conflict. Even the utopian socialist Philadelphia novelist George Lippard celebrated the continental conquest in his *Legends of Mexico* (1847), a paean to the war hero and future president General Zachary Taylor.

The conflict overlapped with Philadelphia-sponsored projects to tie the continent together under U.S. sway. Irish Catholics in the region sometimes supported efforts to make the British provinces in Canada part of the American republic. The Irish Republican Brotherhood movement, better known as the Fenians, held a convention in Philadelphia in 1865 that heard calls for the invasion of the nation's northern neighbor as part of a wider strategy to liberate Ireland. A year later Fenians launched a failed assault on Canada, which strengthened support for the creation of a Canadian confederation in 1867. The Fenians' military adventurism had little support outside the region's Irish Catholic population, but Philadelphians looked for other ways to extend American power. Soon after the conclusion of the Mexican war, ships began to leave the Delaware waterfront for the arduous passage through the Magellan Straits to newly acquired and mineral-rich California. They returned with gold that contributed to the economic prosperity of the early 1850s. By then Philadelphians regularly imagined that their city would serve as the eastern depot of a railroad that would traverse the North American continent and avoid the

**FIGURE 7.** South America's first locomotive, photographed in 2008. Built by Philadelphia's Norris Locomotive Works in 1850, the *La Copiapó* carried passengers and freight in Chile. WIKIMEDIA COMMONS.

time-consuming sea voyage. As the nation went to war with Mexico in 1846, Philadelphians secured a charter for the Pennsylvania Railroad, which would provide an unbroken rail link to the Ohio Valley at Pittsburgh, the first chain in "iron bonds" that some anticipated would soon reach the Pacific. The Pennsylvania Railroad grew over the following decades into a corporate behemoth and the largest private enterprise in the world. Its post–Civil War president, Thomas Scott, briefly ran the Union Pacific, which linked eastern railroads to the Pacific and sparked further conflict with Native Americans over whose land it trespassed.

The steam power that enabled the United States to conquer the continent also accelerated Philadelphia's industrial transformation. Opportunities for employment in manufacturing and the search for markets for the region's goods forged new hemispheric links. While nineteenth-century migration from the Americas to Philadelphia did not approach European levels, a small Spanish American community established itself in the late nineteenth century, with exiles from war-torn Cuba particularly prominent. The tobacco and sugar trades that linked Philadelphia and the Caribbean in the colonial period provided a long-established connection to entice migration. Cubans often found work in cigar manufacturing, where they were numerous enough to have a Spanish-speaking labor union in 1877. Immigrants sometimes labored in the oil and coal industries, too, while the city's locomotive-building companies employed workers from Cuba, Puerto Rico, and other Latin American communities. Spanish-speaking communities coalesced in the Northern Liberties, Spring Garden, and Southwark areas of Philadelphia. There, Cubans especially often joined the fight for independence from Spain. Cigar makers became active in the Partido Revolucionario Cubano (PRC) that organized in Tampa, Florida, in 1892 and called for autonomy for their homeland and the nearby Spanish colony of Puerto Rico. Six PRC clubs organized in Southwark alone prior to the Spanish-American War.

Goods as well as revolutionary politics fanned outward from Philadelphia across the Americas in the nineteenth century. The Philadelphia mint produced coins for Panama. Steam engines went to Brazil and Chile, the latter purchasing South America's first train from the Norris Locomotive Works in 1850. Seven years later, the Baldwin Locomotive Works at Broad and Callowhill responded to depressed domestic demand by trying to drum up business in Cuba, where despite the antislavery politics of its founder Matthias W. Baldwin, its engines were employed in transporting sugar cane grown by enslaved people. After 1885, when the same company distributed marketing materials to Spanish-speaking countries in the Americas, it enjoyed some success in eroding Britain's near monopoly in the region. The nineteenth-century industrial revolution—along with the U.S. victory in the Spanish-American War of 1898—expanded Philadelphia's influence and reach. Philadelphia produced goods for export to Central and South America while offering work and shelter to the region's mobile population.

## Twentieth and Twenty-First Centuries: Sanctuary and Opportunity

Following war with Spain in 1898, which solidified the military and economic ascendancy of the United States in the Americas, thousands of Caribbean and South American families sought out Philadelphia. By 1923 it was possible to talk of a "Spanish colony" in Southwark that housed many of the five thousand or so Spanish-speaking residents. Two of the five major cigar factories were found in that part of the city. Like other immigrant groups, Spanish speakers established benevolent associations and sought out places of worship. The first recorded church service in Spanish in the city dates to 1909, and three years later, Spanish speakers started to attend La Milagrosa, a Catholic chapel at 1903 Spring Garden Street, initially led by a priest from Barcelona. The goods immigrants produced in Philadelphia's factories and workshops were sometimes exported to Latin America, while Central and South America and the Caribbean shipped foodstuffs to the Delaware Valley.

Immigration restrictions between 1924 and 1965 made it much harder for Europeans to migrate to the region, which offered Latin American communities more opportunities to find a home in the United States. Puerto Ricans, who came under direct U.S. control after 1898, became the largest Spanish-speaking community in the Philadelphia area. The push of periodic economic crises in Puerto Rico and the pull of work in the Delaware Valley's industries and farms drew islanders to the region. The two world wars proved a particular impetus as factories looked for labor to meet heightened demand. During World War II, the federal government's War Manpower Commission encouraged employers to turn to Puerto Rico for labor. Campbell Soup Company in Camden recruited workers from the island, and although some of those who responded to its call returned home in peacetime, many remained in the region. The rapid wartime growth of the region's Puerto Rican population put down a foundation for further migration over the second half of the twentieth century to Philadelphia and Camden especially. World War II also brought Mexicans to Philadelphia to work in agriculture and for the Pennsylvania Railroad. Other Latinos fled due to revolutionary turmoil. After Fidel Castro secured power in Cuba in 1959, Cuban refugees arrived in the Delaware Valley, often via Florida.

Amid these upheavals, Latinos played an active civic role in the region. Philadelphia's Pan American Association, created by University of Pennsylvania academics in league with prominent figures of the city's Latino community, formed in 1940 and sought to promote harmonious relations across the hemisphere. It fostered economic and cultural ties between Philadelphia and the Americas while also providing a forum for discussing diplomatic relations. Efforts to improve the lives of local Latino residents also gathered pace. Concilio—also known as the Council of Spanish Speaking Organizations—was founded in 1962 as a Pan-Latino advocacy group that also provided social services. Puerto Ricans in Camden started what became an annual San Juan Bautista Parade, named for the patron saint of their island, in 1957. Just over a decade later some young Puerto Ricans in Camden made common cause with Black Power activists by joining sit-ins and protesting police mistreatment.

Immigration from the Americas accelerated as the twentieth century entered its twilight years. As Cold War fears led the United States to interfere in the affairs of several Central and South American countries, Philadelphia remained attractive to emigrants for its economic opportunities and as a place of sanctuary from conflicts in Guatemala, El Salvador, and Nicaragua. Agriculture in the region drew considerable numbers. Chester County, which by the early 1990s produced about a quarter of the nation's mushrooms, relied heavily on an estimated four thousand Mexicans who made up about 90 percent of the workforce. Economic and political instability in Central and South America also pushed migrants to the Philadelphia region. The North American Free Trade Agreement in 1994 catalyzed a new wave of Central and South American immigration into the United States. By the twenty-first century, a strong Latino presence ran from long-established communities in South Philadelphia and Northern Liberties all the way up to Olney in North Philadelphia, roughly following SEPTA's 47 bus route. In 2003, Spanish speakers could hear a mass in their own language at twenty-one parishes in South Jersey and thirty-four in southeastern Pennsylvania. Two decades later, Spanish and Portuguese were the most common languages other than English used in the city.

A steady growth in Latino population allowed for a continuous, long-standing trade route that drew the produce of the hemisphere to the Delaware Valley. Into the 2000s, the ports of the Delaware River remained major importers and exporters of agricultural goods, including fruits from tropical latitudes such as pineapples and bananas. In 2011, Chile, Costa Rica, Guatemala, Colombia, Brazil, and Argentina were among the top nine origin countries for traffic in food and related goods, while Puerto Rico and Venezuela were two of the biggest three agricultural export markets. The United States' northern neighbor, Canada, also remained an important trading partner, accounting for 27 percent of Philadelphia's exports in 2018.

After its late seventeenth-century founding as a colonial port city, Philadelphia provided a home for displaced French Canadians, enslaved Haitians, and exiled Spanish American revolutionaries, while offering a market for the commodities the continent produced. As Philadelphians accommodated newcomers, they also sought to extend their influence across the Americas through conquest, trade, and the pursuit of knowledge. Hundreds of years later, Philadelphia continued to attract migrants from all over the hemisphere, who could be easily seen when walking down any street. The presence of diverse migrants remained evidence of continental connections that run north, south, and west, rather than merely east across the Atlantic.

CHAPTER 3

# PACIFIC WORLD

Lawrence H. Kessler

FROM THE EIGHTEENTH CENTURY ONWARD, Philadelphia has forged distant but significant connections with the Pacific World—the lands in western North America and South America, Oceania, Australia, and Asia that circle the Pacific Ocean. Exchanges throughout the Pacific—primarily but far from exclusively with China—of industry, people, and ideas helped make Philadelphia the city it became. Philadelphians became active participants in trade with the Pacific after the American Revolution. Early national Philadelphia became a center for shipbuilding and a shipping industry that played a crucial role in connecting the city to the Pacific. In 1784, Robert Morris, the Philadelphia financier active in the Revolution, partnered with a New York merchant to launch the *Empress of China*, the first American ship to trade with Canton. They hired John Green of Philadelphia to captain the vessel. That same year the *United States* sailed from Philadelphia and became the first American ship to trade with India. By 1800, forty ships owned in and launched from Philadelphia engaged in the China trade.

In the early nineteenth century, when the Napoleonic Wars cut Philadelphia off from its established trade routes and markets in the Caribbean, the city's traders and merchants such as Stephen Girard increased investment in commerce with China. These traders were not only instrumental to bringing Chinese goods to Philadelphia, but also to connecting dispersed parts of the Pacific region to each other. Because China offered little market for goods from the United States, Philadelphia merchants plied complex trade routes that moved furs from the Pacific Northwest of North America, hides from Chile, sandalwood from the Hawaiian Islands, and metals from the region later known as Indonesia into China. Return voyages brought silks, tea, and porcelain to the Philadelphia region and the nation.

## RESOURCES FUEL COMMERCE

Over the course of the nineteenth century, Philadelphia's growth as an industrial and financial center and the Greater Philadelphia region's natural resources helped to further connect the nation to the Pacific World and fueled commerce between the city and regions throughout the Pacific. Just as the shipyards had established commercial ties between Philadelphia and the Pacific, railroads extended this commerce. In 1837, Austrian artist Francis Martin Drexel established in Philadelphia the banking house Drexel & Co. The bank provided a transcontinental financial link between Philadelphia and San Francisco during the California Gold Rush. Following the Civil War, Francis's son Anthony Joseph Drexel founded Drexel, Morgan & Co. (renamed J.P. Morgan & Co. in 1893), which was a major financier for U.S. railroad companies. The Baldwin Locomotive Works, established in 1835 at Broad and Spring Garden Streets, became the leading U.S. locomotive manufacturer by the 1880s, creating

**FIGURE 8.** Map of China in a Philadelphia-published atlas, 1804. LIBRARY OF CONGRESS.

opportunities for commerce and transit between Atlantic and Pacific regions through the transcontinental railroad. Baldwin also exported its locomotives around the world, including to Australia, which experienced its own nineteenth-century transportation revolution through the spread of railways. Similarly, the Edge Moor Iron Company, incorporated in Delaware in 1869 by Eli Garrett and the Philadelphia engineer William Sellers, exported iron and steel bridges to Australia and South America.

In 1897, University of Pennsylvania botanist William P. Wilson opened Philadelphia's Commercial Museum as a center for information on international trade. Entrepreneurs from the Philadelphia region came to the museum to learn about foreign markets and goods. This coincided with the city's rise as an industrial power and its adoption of the nickname "Workshop of the World." Philadelphia's industrial and manufacturing productivity joined the city to a global economy that included the Pacific both as a source for raw materials and as a market for finished products. This dominance, however, was short-lived. By the 1920s, the U.S. Department of Commerce began providing much of the information that the Commercial Museum once did, and Philadelphia lagged behind other cities and ports in industry and trade.

While the Great Depression dramatically reduced Philadelphia's industrial and economic output, World War II provided an opportunity for military production that buoyed Philadelphia but brought the city into violent contact with Japan. Philadelphia's Navy Yard became a center for ship and aircraft construction; the Navy Yard also contributed to the development of atomic weapons, and the Frankford Arsenal produced arms and conducted munitions research. This military production ended along with World War II but experienced a brief resurgence in the 1950s during the Korean War.

Notwithstanding the increase in war-related industrial activity, following World War II Philadelphia's industries suffered from increasing globalization and competition from industrial manufacturers in the Pacific region. The second half of the twentieth century was a period of general deindustrialization and economic contraction in Philadelphia. Improved shipping technology, standardization of production machinery, and increased use of synthetic fabrics helped Asian manufacturers to undercut Philadelphia's many textile and clothing firms. Similarly, in the 1970s the increase in imports of Japanese automobiles contributed to the decline of Ford, GM, and Chrysler factories in Greater Philadelphia.

## Impact of Intellectual Curiosity

The pursuit of knowledge has spurred Philadelphians toward interest in the Pacific since the Revolutionary era. The American Philosophical Society, founded in 1743 by Benjamin Franklin and John Bartram, was the first notable organization for the study of natural history in the city, but others followed, notably the American Society for the Promotion of Useful Knowledge in 1768, Charles Willson Peale's Philadelphia Museum in 1786, and the Academy of Natural Sciences in 1812. These institutions made Philadelphia a center for scientific knowledge, publishing papers, housing collections, and promoting exploring expeditions of importance for the study and development of natural history in the United States. Through such organizations, Americans on the Atlantic coast learned about the Pacific World, a distant region that few would see for themselves.

Several scientific projects connected Philadelphia to the Pacific. The American Society for the Promotion of Useful Knowledge emphasized in its manifesto that European plants did not thrive in North America and that the colonies should instead be considered more environmentally and agriculturally similar to China. The society noted that Philadelphia stood at the same latitude as Beijing and that plants such as mulberry, persimmon, ginseng, and tobacco grew well in both North America and China. They proposed introducing more plants from China to promote North American agriculture and economy. The Corps of Discovery expedition, better known by the names of the expedition leaders, Meriwether Lewis and William Clark, sought to connect Philadelphia and the Pacific geographically. American Philosophical Society member Thomas Jefferson, who launched the expedition while president of the United States, held an abiding interest in the exploration of the North American continent and research into a continental route to the Pacific Ocean. Lewis, who studied at the University of Pennsylvania and consulted with several key figures in Philadelphia's learned societies, organized much of his expedition from the city. Upon the expedition's completion, Lewis and Clark gave many of the specimens they collected to the American Philosophical Society and the Philadelphia Museum.

These institutions helped establish Philadelphia as a center for scientific knowledge and exploration of the Pacific World. Charles Willson Peale's legacy extended to his children, who carried on their father's interest in natural history to bring to Philadelphia greater knowledge of the Pacific. Titian Ramsay Peale, the sixteenth of Peale's children, became a naturalist and explorer for several expeditions, most notably the 1838–42 United States Exploring Expedition to the Pacific Northwest, Oceania, and Australia. Titian Peale specialized in collecting animal specimens, bringing back 2,150 bird, 134 mammal, and 588 fish specimens. Other notable Philadelphia naturalists on the expedition included Charles Pickering from the Academy of Natural Sciences and William Brackenridge, a Scottish-born horticulturist. The ornithologist John Cassin, who became curator of the Academy of Natural Sciences in 1842, helped revise Titian Peale's official report on the zoology he observed, helping to spread knowledge of distant species to American naturalists.

Others connected with the China trade also helped spread knowledge about this remote region and its cultures. The Dutch merchant Andreas Everardus van Braam Houckgeest, who became a U.S. citizen in 1784 and thus claimed the record for the first American to visit China, introduced Philadelphians to a better understanding of Chinese material culture. When he settled in Philadelphia in 1796, van Braam built a country home called China's Retreat that held mementos from his travels and was staffed by Chinese servants. Van Braam also published an account of his visit to China's emperor, further disseminating information about the Qing Empire to Americans. From 1818 to 1831, the merchant Nathan Dunn collected many Chinese artifacts and housed them in his summer home known as his Chinese Cottage. By 1838, Dunn chose to open a Chinese museum at Ninth and George (Sansom) Streets in Philadelphia, in the same space as the Peale Philadelphia Museum. Often known as the museum of Ten Thousand Chinese Things, Dunn's collection educated and entertained the Philadelphia public. Dunn's museum reflected great interest in Chinese culture: in its first year of operation, it attracted one hundred thousand visitors. This interest, however, or at least enough interest to be profitable, did not last long. By 1842, Dunn moved his collection to London.

Three decades later, the 1876 Centennial Exposition featured exhibits from Japan, China, Hawaii, and Australia, as well as the Latin American Pacific nations from Mexico to Chile. Out of the eleven nations that erected their own buildings for the exposition, only Japan represented the Pacific. This was, however, a significant step in educating Americans about the culture of Japan, which had been closed to the West until 1853. The Japanese exhibit included the first Japanese garden to be constructed in the United States. The site of the original Japanese exhibit, located in Fairmount Park, continued in the twenty-first century to feature a Japanese garden and host cultural activities.

## Artifacts and Controversy

Interest in art and artifacts from the Pacific found an outlet in Philadelphia's cultural institutions. The Philadelphia Museum of Art, established from the art gallery of the Centennial Exhibition, collected Japanese and Chinese art, including ceramics, metalwork, and textiles, which were displayed in prominent exhibits in the late nineteenth and early twentieth centuries. Founded in 1887, the University of Pennsylvania Museum of Archaeology and Anthropology (more familiarly known as the Penn Museum) demonstrated strong interest in collecting ethnographic artifacts and material culture objects from Oceania, insular Southeast Asia, and Australia. The Penn Museum sponsored several expeditions to the Pacific and also purchased items from international dealers, housing them in a permanent Oceanian section of the museum.

The practice of collecting artifacts and specimens sometimes led to controversy over the appropriation or theft of important cultural objects. In 1924, the Penn Museum purchased a large collection of ceremonial items from a Tlingit clan from coastal Alaska. In the early twenty-first century, Tlingit groups sought the return of these items but met with resistance from the museum. In 2016, the federal repatriation review committee, under the auspices of the Native American Graves Protection and Repatriation Act, determined the items must be returned to Alaska.

In addition to the collection of artifacts, literary arts connected the Philadelphia area to the Pacific World. Through their work, Philadelphia-area authors introduced Americans to life and culture in the Pacific. Pearl S. Buck settled in Bucks County after spending the first forty years of her life in China. Buck's experiences with peasant life in China led her to publish *The Good Earth* (1931), which won the 1932 Pulitzer Prize for the novel. Buck published several other works of fiction about life in Asia and translations of Chinese fiction, including *East Wind: West Wind* (1930), *Sons* (1933), *All Men Are Brothers* (1933), *A House Divided* (1935), and *The Big Wave* (1948). Doylestown native James A. Michener provided many Americans with a compelling, though often romanticized, view of Polynesia and Alaska through his prolific writing. Michener, who was stationed in the South Pacific Ocean as a naval historian during World War II, used his observations to write *Tales of the South Pacific* (1947), which won the 1948 Pulitzer Prize for fiction and was adapted by Richard Rodgers and Oscar Hammerstein into the Broadway musical *South Pacific* (1949). Michener later published many other short stories and novels about the Pacific World, including *Return to*

**FIGURE 9.** The Japanese Garden, Fairmount Park, ca. 1900. Constructed around 1898 near the site of the Japanese bazaar at the 1876 Centennial Exhibition, the garden reflected growing American interest in East Asia. Atlantic City also established a Japanese garden in the same period. A later Japanese House and Garden, given to the United States after World War II, moved from New York to Fairmount Park in 1958. LIBRARY OF CONGRESS.

*Paradise* (1950) about the South Pacific, *The Bridges at Toko-Ri* (1953) about wartime Korea, *Sayonara* (1954) about cultural conflict in postwar Japan, and *Hawaii* (1959) and *Alaska* (1988), two epic novels about each places' long history and experience with U.S. colonialism. Buck and Michener both went on to become philanthropists and activists after achieving fame through their writing. Buck promoted cross-cultural understanding and humanitarianism through the Welcome House adoption agency (1949) and Pearl S. Buck International (1964), and Michener helped found the James A. Michener Art Museum (1988), all located in Bucks County.

In the late twentieth and early twenty-first centuries, Philadelphia remained a center for the study of Euro-American and European exploration in the Pacific and its history. In 1969, the Academy of Natural Sciences led a team to search Australia's Great Barrier Reef for artifacts discarded from Captain James Cook's HMS *Endeavour* when, in 1770, the ship struck a reef and nearly sank. One of the *Endeavour*'s ten-pound cannons

**FIGURE 10.** Philadelphia's Chinese community members wearing buttons to mark them apart from Asian Americans of Japanese descent after Japan's attack on Pearl Harbor, 1941. SPECIAL COLLECTIONS RESEARCH CENTER, TEMPLE UNIVERSITY LIBRARIES.

became part of the academy's collections. The *Endeavour* cannon, recovered from a shipwreck that occurred as Philadelphia was beginning to take interest in the Pacific, can serve as a reminder of the complex networks of economic and cultural exchange that have tied the city to a distant ocean. University-based programs focused on areas of the Pacific also proliferated throughout Greater Philadelphia's institutions of higher education. Princeton University became a leading center for East Asian studies, and its East Asian Library and Gest Collection assembled a large body of rare books and archival material from China, Japan, and Korea.

## Immigrants from the Pacific

Philadelphia's population of immigrants from Pacific nations was small but significant. Throughout the nineteenth and twentieth centuries, Philadelphia's rate of immigration from foreign countries was lower than that of many other U.S. cities, and most of the city's immigrants came from Europe. Nevertheless, communities from the Pacific World, particularly China, did much to shape Philadelphia's modern history. Philadelphia became home to a growing population from the Pacific World in the late nineteenth century. In the 1870s, in the face of anti-Asian hostility, Chinese migrants made their way east from the railroads and gold mines of the North American West. The migrants first settled around Ninth and Race Streets, near what was then Philadelphia's Skid Row.

This small community established Philadelphia's Chinatown. At first, Chinese residents of the city were restricted to working in domestic service, laundries, or small groceries; small eateries and community associations served as places for cultural and social cohesion. By the turn of the twentieth century, the neighborhood's "chop suey joints" gained notice from non-Asian Philadelphians. Flavors of the Pacific expanded the already diverse food culture, which had been shaped since colonial times by the city's shipping industry and cosmopolitan upper class.

The Asian and Pacific Islander population of the city remained below two thousand during the first half of the twentieth century, after the federal Chinese Exclusion Act of 1882 restricted new immigration. During World War II, the Greater Philadelphia region experienced an increase in its Asian population through the relocation of Japanese Americans from federal concentration camps. Seabrook Farms, located in southern New Jersey's Cumberland County, was a major supplier of vegetables to the U.S. military and a beneficiary of Japanese American workers employed through a program of the War Relocation Authority. Between 1944 and 1946, 2,700 Japanese Americans came to work at Seabrook. Following World War II, new immigration contributed to a significantly larger and more diverse Pacific population. Cultural institutions such as the Holy Redeemer Chinese Catholic Church at Tenth and Vine Streets, which served not only as a religious center but also as an organizing point for Chinese involvement in city politics, helped immigrants create new communities.

Meanwhile, armed conflicts in the Pacific region impacted Philadelphia and its population. Philadelphians in the military who deployed to the Pacific returned home with greater knowledge of the region, while antiwar activists sought to bridge cultural differences to mount resistance to the war in Korea and, later, Vietnam. In the aftermath of the Vietnam conflict, Southeast Asian refugees began settling in Philadelphia. Often placed in areas already suffering from racial and economic conflict, they frequently became targets of violence. Nonetheless, Vietnamese and Cambodian communities persisted and grew; Philadelphia became home to some of the largest Vietnamese and Cambodian populations on the East Coast.

The Philadelphia region's many universities fostered not only education about the Pacific but also the exchange of people between the two regions. In 1982, Temple University became the first American university to establish a campus in Japan. In the early twenty-first century, the universities of the Philadelphia area attracted a large number of students from the Pacific region, with the majority of foreign students originating from China.

While Philadelphia's geographic position places it firmly in the Atlantic World and on the United States' Eastern Seaboard, intercourse with the Pacific has nonetheless been a significant factor in the history of the Delaware Valley. Connections to Pacific people and places helped Philadelphia develop commerce and industry, grow into a center for the exchange of knowledge and ideas, and become home to a diverse and multicultural population.

Chapter 4

# Immigration and Culture

## Introduction

"On the whole," the humorist W. C. Fields reputedly remarked when asked for an inscription for his gravestone, "I would rather be living in Philadelphia." His fictional epitaph rang true for the millions of immigrants who arrived from afar to make the Delaware Valley their home. In successive waves, they came from across the Atlantic, the Americas, and the Pacific, peopling the city and its environs and contributing to a diverse regional culture visible in the built environment, audible in the over eighty languages spoken in the twenty-first-century metropolis, and tasted in a local cuisine that reflects centuries of global influence.

Migration shaped the region prior to the founding of Philadelphia as an English settler outpost in 1682. Approximately fifteen thousand years ago, the ancestors of Indigenous Americans likely crossed a land bridge from Asia to North America, arriving in the Delaware Valley about three thousand years later. From the seventeenth century onward, the Lenape people, who lived in small communities close to freshwater, began to encounter Europeans with increasing frequency, as the English, Dutch, Swedish, Finnish, and French settlers all established small footholds in the future states of Pennsylvania, Delaware, and New Jersey. Prior to the 1680s, though, these newcomers did not dominate. Until the English arrived in larger numbers and began to force Indigenous people farther west, the Delaware Valley remained "Lenape country."

When William Penn established Pennsylvania in 1681, he envisaged it as a place of sanctuary. As a member of a proscribed sect in his native England, he pictured his province as a place of refuge for religious dissenters. Some of his fellow Quakers, indeed, had already settled in parts of New Jersey over the preceding decade, drawn in part by the friendly reputation of neighboring Lenape villages. From its early days, then, Pennsylvania and its surroundings drew immigrants escaping persecution. Quakers, Catholics, and others whose faith brought them into conflict with the churches and crowns of the Old World flocked to the region. They were joined by economic migrants drawn to Philadelphia's rich agricultural hinterland (whether as free farmers or indentured servants) and enslaved people for whom immigration never presented a choice. Later, in the nineteenth century, the region drew displaced people from European revolutions, Irish exiles fleeing famine and British rule, and Cubans eager to overthrow their island's Spanish overlords. Into the twenty-first century Philadelphia retained its reputation as a sanctuary city with the region offering shelter to those taking flight from conflict. In the early 2020s refugees from recent wars in Iraq, Afghanistan, and Ukraine found repose in the Delaware Valley.

The city of refuge, however, has also stood at the center of an American nativist creed resolutely hostile to newcomers. As the birthplace of the United States, Philadelphia nurtured citizens who saw it as their duty to guard the Revolutionary tradition from foreign threats. Their exclusionary definition of what it meant to be American, rooted most often in Protestantism and whiteness, inspired calls at various points to relocate the region's free Black population to West Africa and bar immigrants from citizenship. When translated into local action it led to mob action against African Americans and the burning of Catholic churches during the so-called Bible Riots of 1844: one of the most notorious instances of anti-immigrant violence in U.S. history. Yet like their twenty-first-century successors, the nineteenth-century nativists who became a major political force in the city during the 1840s and 1850s did not see themselves as bigots. Rather, they imagined themselves as guardians of the republic, ever vigilant to the threat posed by subversive outsiders. More often than not they failed in their mission: The Civil War did far more to slow the pace of immigration than nativists ever managed prior to the 1880s. But first with Chinese exclusion in 1882 and then with the Johnson-Reed Act of 1924, national anti-immigrant forces succeeded in curbing new arrivals, and only in 1965 did immigration to the region take off again, this time from parts of the developing world like Asia and Africa. A resurgent nativism, sometimes cheered on by descendants of reviled nineteenth-century immigrant groups, reemerged in the Philadelphia region by the early 2000s. At various points—often in times of conflict when the threat of internal or external subversion seemed real—the region's immigrants have been scapegoated and threatened.

Americanization offered an alternative to exclusion. Immigrants who reached the Delaware Valley were welcomed provided they remade themselves into model citizens. In its more liberal form, Americanization involved subscribing to the civic creed forged in the city between 1776 and 1787. From the early national era, indeed, Philadelphians with roots abroad made important contributions to the region's public life as voters, elected officials, militiamen, volunteer firemen, and later police officers. Others would become "American under fire" by proving their patriotic mettle on the battlefields of Mexico, the South, the Spanish Empire, and Europe. Through this process, once despised groups like Irish Catholics won grudging acceptance that transformed over the first half of the twentieth century into celebrated white ethnic status. With their Americanness no longer questioned, Irish Americans could proudly hang green, white, and orange tricolors alongside the Stars and Stripes above the front doors of Philadelphia's row homes. But Americanization could also take the form of a project to safeguard Protestant white America. The philanthropic work Progressive Era reformers undertook with southern and eastern Europeans, for example, undoubtedly alleviated the material hardships immigrants faced. But it also marked an effort to acculturate newcomers to the values of a self-styled Anglo-Saxon elite.

Often, however, the process of Americanization worked both ways. As Philadelphia's immigrants became American, they reshaped what America meant. The region's foodways exemplify this exchange. Whether in the form of German pretzels, cheesesteaks created by Italians, or the spicy pepper pot sold from market stalls by free and unfree Black people who had carried the dish with them from the Caribbean, Philadelphia's distinctive regional cuisine reflects the paths taken by immigrants and the improvisations they made in their new home. Meanwhile cultural traditions that trace their roots back to far-flung continents have been carried to the Delaware Valley and given new meaning. Perhaps the best known is the New Year's Day Mummers Parade: an echo of earlier European customs that became a way for Philadelphians to mock authority and mark ethnic pride.

Immigration, so central to the region's culture, has also shaped the Delaware Valley's geography. Early Philadelphia's gridiron layout initially checked the growth of ethnic neighborhoods. The foreign-born poor often dwelt in narrow courts and alleys behind the town houses that lined the main thoroughfares rather than in distinct quarters. But as the nineteenth century progressed new patterns began to emerge. Either side of what is now South Street, Irish Americans lived alongside Philadelphia's free Black population, with whom they frequently came into conflict. In North Philadelphia, Kensington became another district with a distinct Irish presence while Germans flocked to Brewerytown. Such neighborhoods, often close to places of work where immigrant groups had carved out a niche, were neither homogeneous nor particularly well defined, but they sustained ethnic businesses, institutions, and cultural life.

By the early twentieth century adventurous Philadelphians could have seen many of the world's cultures inside a couple of hours. Starting at the Italian Market around Ninth Street and Washington Avenue, they might have proceeded on foot to Fourth Street to the German and eastern European Jewish garment district known as Fabric Row then meandered north and west to the launderettes and restaurants of Chinatown along Race Street. If they felt like venturing farther, they could have ridden a trolley to watch a quintessentially English game of cricket in Chestnut Hill, taken a ferry across the Delaware to visit the burgeoning Polish community in Camden, or caught a train to Trenton to see Chambersburg, the New Jersey capital's "Little Italy."

It is easy to assume that the growth of suburbia from the mid-nineteenth century onward divided urban immigrant neighborhoods from the wealthier, "waspy" enclaves beyond. But the wider region too has been shaped by immigration, from the Welsh Quakers who named Main Line townships after places in the principality they had left behind to the Irish Americans who worked in the Dupont gunpowder mills on the Brandywine Creek. Some migrants, such as the Amish from Germany who eventually settled in rural Lancaster County and the Holocaust survivors who wound up as chicken farmers in postwar South Jersey, bypassed cities entirely. Low-paid agricultural work such as fruit picking and mushroom growing drew laborers from the likes of Mexico and Puerto Rico after 1945. Over the closing years of the twentieth century and into the twenty-first, Greater Philadelphia's suburbia too became more diverse, and symbols of new immigration—Buddhist temples, Sunni mosques, Korean churches—sprang up.

Meanwhile old immigrant neighborhoods in the city changed in character as new immigrants arrived. The eastern end of Washington Avenue, once the terrain of Italians and Jews, became Mexican and Southeast Asian, with the hoagie and cheesesteak increasingly rivaled by the burrito and banh mi. Such transformation, much like the Irish immigration of the 1840s, was not without its tensions, but Philadelphia emerged stronger for it. Indeed, after the ravages of deindustrialization the urban population began to grow once more in the early 2000s. Neighboring cities like Camden have also been bolstered by new migration from Latin America especially.

For all this, Greater Philadelphia has rarely been regarded as an archetypal immigrant metropolis. Since the early 1800s, the region has not rivaled the likes of New York in its proportion of foreign-born residents. And memories of its nativist politics and Quaker provincialism do little to bolster the image of a vibrant multicultural metropolis. Yet from the city's beginnings as a place of sanctuary for religious refugees, its culture and spaces have been regularly remade by immigrants from different parts of the globe. Wherever they have come from, they have shown they would rather be in Philadelphia.

## Colonial Immigration and Migration

**Marie Basile McDaniel**

European settlement of the region on both sides of the Delaware River dates to the early seventeenth century. The population grew rapidly after 1682, when Pennsylvania's policy of religious tolerance and its reputation as the "best poor man's country" attracted people from all walks of life during the colonial era. By the time of the American Revolution, Philadelphia was the largest city in colonial America. With a population above thirty-two thousand, it was noticeably larger than the next two largest cities, New York (twenty-five thousand) and Boston (sixteen thousand). Its size was almost entirely the result of migration from Europe, Africa, and other American colonies.

Settlers—both voluntarily and involuntarily—came to Philadelphia and the surrounding region from England, Wales, Ireland, Scotland, German-speaking lands in the Holy Roman Empire, France, Holland, Spain, Sweden, the west coast of Africa, New York, New Jersey, Massachusetts, Delaware, Maryland, Virginia, and the Caribbean. They were Quakers, Presbyterians, Lutherans, German Reformed, Baptists, Anglicans, Catholics, Jews, possibly some Muslims, and others from a variety of smaller religious sects. Some were wealthy, many more arrived as artisans, laborers, small farmers, or servants hoping to make their fortunes, and many came unwillingly as enslaved Africans. Philadelphia even had its share of pirates.

In many ways the founder of Pennsylvania, William Penn, designed the province to be socially and

**FIGURE 11.** Trade between Swedish colonizers and Indians in the Delaware Valley, 1702. HISTORICAL SOCIETY OF PENNSYLVANIA.

economically diverse. He envisioned a utopian society, one in which differences of opinion and background would naturally create a stable and tolerant society. In his 1670 *The Great Case of Liberty of Conscience*, Penn articulated these beliefs on the necessity of a religiously tolerant society. A few years later, in 1675, Penn noted in his *England's Present Interest Considered* that the suppression of religious dissent created disorder, while religious diversity and freedom enabled a more ordered, peaceful society. To that end Penn invited persecuted religious groups from other nations to settle in Pennsylvania. He made voyages to continental Europe in 1671, 1677, and 1686 in part to recruit settlers. He wrote four works specifically intended for Dutch and German prospective settlers that were later translated and circulated. Penn recruited the mistreated to Pennsylvania to ensure a wide range of religious and ethnic interests to meet his societal goals.

By the time of Penn's arrival in Pennsylvania in 1682, the inhabitants included Native Americans as well as some six hundred Swedes, Finns, Dutch, and Germans—including some who had settled as early as 1638, when the west side of the Delaware River belonged to New Sweden. When New Sweden became incorporated into New Netherland in 1655, the number of Dutch increased. The European population then remained stable and their relations with Native Americans limited until Penn received his charter for Pennsylvania in 1681. Seventeen years earlier, the Duke of York gave the east side of the Delaware River (what is now New Jersey) to Lord Berkeley and Sir George Carteret; the former sold his plot to Quaker John Fenwick. In the late 1670s under Penn's guidance, more than one thousand Quakers from London, Kent, and Yorkshire settled West New Jersey and established towns in Salem and Burlington.

Penn arrived on the ship *Welcome* on October 27, 1682, with about one hundred other Quakers. On the west side of the Delaware they joined another one hundred recently settled Quakers who had established two meetinghouses near what would be Philadelphia. These Quakers were of English, Welsh, Irish, and German descent and quickly took over the establishment of government in the new Pennsylvania. In addition, Penn sold plots of land to wealthy Quaker investors, mostly of English descent. A few Welsh Quakers bought forty thousand acres of land on the other side of the Schuylkill River, historically known as the "Welsh Tract," and established the towns of Haverford, Merion, and Radnor. Other Quakers established the towns of Darby, Chichester, and Concord west of the city, all in the early 1680s. Penn also authorized the naturalization of the preexisting Dutch, Swede, and Finnish inhabitants, some of whom took him up on the offer.

In the first decades under Quaker leadership, Philadelphia became a major port city and a booming trade center, which encouraged migration by merchants and tradesmen coming from England and Wales. By 1700, central Philadelphia grew from a small collection of Swedish homesteads to a population of approximately 2,000 concentrated in a half-mile-wide stretch along the Delaware River that extended four blocks inland. Pennsylvania as a whole grew from 680 to 18,000

**FIGURE 12.** Gloria Dei, S. Water Street, Philadelphia, ca. 1936–41. Built at the end of the seventeenth century as a place of worship for Swedish Lutherans, Gloria Dei is the oldest church in Pennsylvania. LIBRARY OF CONGRESS.

European residents; West New Jersey grew from 1,000 to 14,000 Europeans; and the lower counties on the Delaware (later the state of Delaware, also controlled by Penn) grew from about 200 to 2,500 Europeans by 1700. As trade increased, skilled craftsmen, mostly Quakers, migrated to Philadelphia to do the work of construction, shipbuilding, masonry, carpentry, and other service needs of the growing city. Opportunity also attracted farmers, weavers, and millers, who moved to the available hinterland.

The mercantile possibilities of Philadelphia attracted poor, single young men and some women in search of their fortunes. Some signed contracts for between one and four years of service in exchange for their voyages. Even more signed indentured servant contracts, which bound them to up to seven years of service. Some arrived with their masters as part of the family. If they served out their term, they gained fifty acres of land, some tools, and another set of clothing. However, as historian Sharon Salinger noted, four men migrated for every woman, leading to a very uneven gender ratio in seventeenth-century Pennsylvania.

Philadelphia's demographics changed drastically in the first half of the eighteenth century. Immigrants from western Europe arrived in search of land and religious freedom. Migrants from other colonies came in search of greater, or perhaps just the next, opportunities. Philadelphia experienced exponential growth through the influx of thousands of Germans, Scots Irish, English, and hundreds of enslaved and some free Africans. In 1710, at the start of the influx, Philadelphia contained 2,684 residents. By 1740 that number more than tripled to 10,117, and by 1775 the population tripled again to 32,073. As historical demographer Susan Klepp's research shows, Philadelphia's white population had a modest 10 to 15 percent increase from 1700 to 1710. Then from 1710 to 1740, Philadelphia's white population grew about a third each decade. In an era of high mortality and low birth rate, most of this increase was due to migration and immigration.

More than ten thousand new settlers arrived annually into the port of Philadelphia. Most moved on to land in Lancaster, York, Berks, and Bucks Counties, while only 10 to 20 percent remained in the city. While migration made the city more crowded and diverse, many surrounding towns remained relatively ethnically and religiously homogeneous in cases in which whole towns from Europe migrated en masse. Philadelphia quickly became a city in which no group, including the English, had a majority but the same could not be said for all of the mid-Atlantic. For instance, as Stephanie Grauman Wolf has shown, Germantown was 80 percent German even though it included a diversity of other settlers.

Migration was a part of colonial American life. Eighteenth-century American colonists searched for better opportunities, especially from land-crowded New England and religiously troubled Maryland and Virginia. Boston-born Benjamin Franklin is possibly the most famous example of such a migrant. Other Americans wandered (mostly walked) into Philadelphia and other parts of Pennsylvania in search of their fortunes. As historian James Lemon noted, nearly half of the population of Philadelphia, and other surrounding towns, migrated every ten years. Of those migrant Philadelphians whose origins in North America (including English Caribbean colonies) between 1700 and 1740 have been firmly established, approximately 17 percent originally arrived in Maryland, 17 percent in Virginia, 11 percent in New York or New Jersey, 17 percent in New England, and 38 percent in the Caribbean. Although migrants often moved several times in their lives, records rarely exist for those multiple transitions. The brief appearances of migrants in the records reveal a general migration toward cities, then continually westward.

Transatlantic immigrants to Philadelphia left from the ports of Belfast, Derry, Larne, Portrush, and Newry, in Ulster, and Cork and Kinsale in southern Ireland; London, Portsmouth, and Plymouth in England; Rotterdam and Amsterdam in the Netherlands. Although colonial migration records are incomplete, historians Marianne Wokeck and Sharon Salinger examined the port records in North America and in Europe that listed ports of origin, and from that information determined the probable ethnic breakdown for most of the European migrants arriving in Philadelphia between 1710 and 1769. Immigrants in this period were mostly from German-speaking areas, although in the 1710s and 1720s English immigrants dominated, and in the 1720s and 1760s waves of Scots Irish and Irish temporarily altered earlier immigration patterns.

The ethnic breakdown on European immigration into the port of Philadelphia suggests the white ethnic diversity of the mid-Atlantic region. However, the population of the city of Philadelphia did not match the demographic composition of the arrivals to its port. Only a small percentage of the total arrivals settled in Philadelphia; the city's population remained steadily English until the 1730s, when the Irish and German-speaking immigrants became a majority of the population.

Most migrants traveled to Pennsylvania during periods of European crises. The biggest migration years—1709, 1717, 1727, 1738, and 1749—related to external events. For instance, as historian Marianne Wokeck noted, the end of the War of Austrian Succession in 1749 correlated with a sharp increase in migration from the regions affected by the war. Further, Pennsylvanian booster literature encouraged German-speaking religious groups to migrate. These promoters emphasized material advancement and a ready welcome to migrants.

During the 1710s through the 1730s, immigrants sometimes traveled in family groups or followed earlier arrivals and settled with them to get help in establishing households in the new colony. Wokeck noted that at least 35 percent of German-speaking migrants traveled in family groups. This chain migration revealed the strong desire of colonists to draw in others from Europe. In a process called redemption, immigrants signed contracts for ship passage in exchange for either labor or payment at the end of the voyage. They hoped a friend or kin would pay for the voyage upon their arrival. Germans often redeemed other German-speaking migrants, even strangers.

Despite the prosperity that migrants brought to Pennsylvania, Philadelphians, especially those in positions of wealth and authority, distrusted these new, non-English arrivals. In 1717, Governor William Keith recommended to the Provincial Assembly to not "lose any Time in securing yourselves, and all the People of this colony, from the inconveniences which may possibly arise by the unlimited Number of Foreigners that . . . have been transported hither of late." The governor believed that migrants would cause harm to Philadelphians. In 1718, James Logan declared that "we are resolved to receive no more of them." In 1727, the assembly asserted that "the great Importation of Foreigners into this Province . . . who are subjects of a foreign Prince, and who keep up amongst themselves a different Language, may, in Time, prove of dangerous Consequence to the Peace." To the assembly, foreign migrants were not symbols of a prosperous economy, but a danger. The Provincial Council tried to assuage elite fears by controlling migration. In 1717, the Provincial Council imposed a tax on all incoming Palatines. In 1718, the Provincial Council requested that ship merchants list their passengers and that all foreigners swear an oath to the king—a requirement not always faithfully observed. These two acts did not curtail migration from Europe.

The other major migrant groups to settle in Philadelphia after 1710 came from Ireland. Although most of these migrants were Presbyterian, they also included Anglicans, Baptists, Quakers, and Catholics. Those from northern Ireland were Scottish Presbyterian transplants to Ireland labeled "Scots Irish" or "Ulster Scots." Those from southern Ireland were mostly Catholic and labeled simply "Irish." Altogether, approximately 7,500 Scots Irish and Irish migrants arrived in Pennsylvania before 1740, among about 20,000 in the American colonies as a whole. Only about 20 percent of these migrants resided in Philadelphia. The rest continued to rural Pennsylvania, founding the town of Carlisle, for instance, in the 1750s. Between 1710 and 1740, Philadelphia's Irish and Scots Irish population grew from 600 to over 2,600 residents, consisting of between 20 and 27 percent of the total population. As historian Patrick Griffin noted, this population grew so much because Scots Irish and Irish migrants reported cheap, plentiful, and bountiful land to their friends and family in Ireland. It was also desirable because Pennsylvania lay on a major trade route, needed weavers and linen workers, and housed the only Presbytery in North America.

Elite Pennsylvanians initially welcomed Scots Irish and Irish migrants in the hope that they would move to the countryside, creating a buffer between Native Americans and the already settled Pennsylvanians. However, they also worried that Irish and Scots Irish behavior could destroy peaceable relations with the Delaware Indians. In the city, elites blamed recent Irish and Scots Irish migrants for drunken disorderliness.

Surprisingly, little is known about eighteenth-century English migration into Pennsylvania. Nearly fourteen thousand English migrants sailed into the port of Philadelphia. Unlike the German, Irish, or Scots Irish migrants, English arrivals did not concern Pennsylvania's residents. No one complained of an indentured servant or a recent migrant as English. On the other hand, no one extolled the virtues of English migrants, either. One-third of these London-embarked migrants traveled as indentured servants. Most of the travelers, servants or not, did not originate from London, but from the far-flung countryside, many from Wales and the north of England, constantly looking for new opportunities.

Nearly 2,700 enslaved Africans had arrived in the port of Philadelphia by the eve of the American Revolution. Quakers eagerly bought the first group of enslaved people directly from Africa in 1684, totaling nearly 150 souls for clearing and building the city. By 1705, nearly 7 percent of families were enslavers. Many of the early enslaved arrivals (apart from the first 150) came from the Caribbean, but by midcentury they increasingly arrived straight from Africa. Most arrived in Philadelphia in two peak periods, from 1732 to 1741 when 510 enslaved people arrived, and from 1757 to 1766 when a further 1,290 did so. Importations increased when arrivals of indentured servants decreased and vice versa. As historians Gary Nash and Jean Soderlund have shown, the strength of European indentured servitude in the eighteenth century slowly eroded the importance of imported enslaved labor. In 1710, enslaved people constituted 10 percent of the population, but only 3 percent by the time of the Revolution. Yet in the twenty years before the Revolution, they constituted between two-thirds and three-fourths of unfree labor in the city. Philadelphians of all socioeconomic levels bought human property, and two-thirds of those held in slave status in Pennsylvania lived and worked within the city. White Philadelphians bought enslaved people to work in the household, but also as help in crafts and aboard maritime ships. The few enslaved people outside of Philadelphia were often bought as status symbols for a country estate. Rarely did farmers use enslaved labor, preferring to use European servants.

By the time of the Revolution, Philadelphia and the surrounding counties, Berks, Bucks, Cumberland, York, and parts of New Jersey, were ethnically, religiously, and economically diverse. But they were also continually changing. Migrants who had the freedom to do so moved frequently in search of greater opportunities. This movement, despite the fears of some settlers, created an environment of acceptance for white people in the region. While no one would call it a pluralistic society (because the term was not common), people of multiple ethnicities and religions lived as neighbors and enjoyed relative peace and prosperity.

## Philadelphia Pepper Pot

**Theresa Altieri Taplin**

Philadelphia pepper pot, a spicy stew-like dish comprised of tripe, other inexpensive cuts of meat, vegetables, and an abundance of spices and hot peppers, is related to the pepper pot soup of the Caribbean region. By the early nineteenth century, the dish had developed characteristics making it uniquely Philadelphian. Philadelphia pepper pot became popular throughout the country before declining in favor in the early twenty-first century.

Enslaved Africans most likely brought an indigenous version of pepper pot (also known as "pepperpot" or "pepper-pot") based on callaloo to the Philadelphia area in the mid-eighteenth century from the Caribbean, at that time connected with the city through trade. A hybrid of Spanish and West African food traditions, pepper pot was a communal dish that had no specific recipe, only general guidelines. By the late eighteenth century, pepper pot had become well known in the American colonies. A recipe for "A West-India Pepper Pot," clearly indicating the popular belief about the dish's origins, appeared in the first cookbook produced in America for an American audience, *The New Art of Cookery*, published in Philadelphia in 1792. The recipe

**FIGURE 13.** *Pepper-Pot: A Scene in the Philadelphia Market*, 1811. Artist John Lewis Krimmel, a newcomer to Philadelphia who had emigrated from Germany a year earlier, shows a free Black woman serving the spicy stew to her white clientele. PHILADELPHIA MUSEUM OF ART.

called for a variety of meat and vegetables, simple dumplings made of flour and water, and spices including all-spice, cloves, and mace. One of the last steps was to "season it very hot with Cayan pepper and salt," emphasizing the heat associated with the dish.

Pepper pot became more prominent and characteristic of Philadelphia by the early nineteenth century. *The Cries of Philadelphia*, published in 1810, included a woodcut illustration titled "Pepper Pot, smoking hot," and described the "numerous Black women" who sold a "pleasant feast" of pepper pot in markets and on street corners. In 1811, *Pepper-Pot* by the genre painter John Lewis Krimmel showed an African American woman selling pepper pot to a diverse group of customers. These images documented Black women's work as entrepreneurial street vendors, an alternative to domestic work when options for employment were limited.

Philadelphia pepper pot became well known throughout the country. By the late nineteenth century, advertisements for restaurants serving "Philadelphia" pepper pot as well as recipes appeared throughout Pennsylvania, the Midwest, New Orleans, and Hawaii. An account written in 1894 by a New Yorker visiting Philadelphia described pepper pot as a regional dish unique to Philadelphia, much like scrapple, and commented that anyone asking for it in other cities "would be looked upon as a candidate for an asylum."

As pepper pot reached new markets in the twentieth century its roots in Black enslavement and freedom were forgotten. The first canned version of Philadelphia pepper pot appeared in the early 1900s as one of the original soup offerings sold for twelve cents a can by Camden-based Campbell Soup Company. By 1927, Campbell's advertised it as the same version "served at the favorite club of Philadelphia's early Colonial aristocracy," despite the dish's origin as a street food. Although the dish dipped in popularity over the following decades, it resurged around the United States' bicentennial celebration in 1976 because of a supposed connection between pepper pot and the Revolutionary War. Legend had it, incorrectly, that pepper pot had been invented to nourish the troops at Valley Forge.

By the late twentieth and early twenty-first centuries, Philadelphia pepper pot fell out of favor, although it continued to be made by home cooks. It could be found consistently in just a few locations, such as the colonial-themed, reconstructed City Tavern, which advertised its West Indies Pepperpot Soup as "a spicy colonial classic." Philadelphia pepper pot originated in the West Indies and migrated to Philadelphia with enslaved Africans, providing them and their free descendants with an inexpensive meal and a ware to sell in markets. For more than a century, Philadelphia pepper pot was both a popular street food and a specialty dish at high-end restaurants.

## Scrapple

**Mary Rizzo**

Scrapple, which came to the Philadelphia region from Germany, is a loaf of cooked pig parts thickened with cornmeal or buckwheat usually spiced with sage and pepper. Once cooled, the loaf is sliced, fried, and served as a breakfast side dish, often with syrup. Not just a culinary transplant, scrapple exists because of the interplay of Old and New World traditions and ingredients.

As a rural tradition during hog-butchering time, scrapple dates to the sixteenth century in Germany, where it was called panhas, *pawnhos*, or *pan haas*, meaning "pan rabbit." While parts of the pig became sausages or bacon, the rest, "everything but the oink," was collected for scrapple and for black or blood puddings, of which scrapple is a variant. The German product did not include cornmeal, which was unavailable in Europe.

German immigrants to Pennsylvania, mistakenly called Pennsylvania Dutch, shared their culture with English settlers, who had similar food traditions. The English influence can be seen in the shift in the product's name. No longer called panhas, except in rural communities, it became scrapple (or Philadelphia scrapple) by the 1820s—at least in print. Food historian William Woys Weaver has argued that scrapple was a conflation of the German word *panhaskroppel*, which literally meant slice of panhas, and the English word scrapple, which referred to leftovers and to spade-shaped kitchen implements. Others have said that English speakers came up with the name scrapple as they conjured up images of a product made with leftovers that were otherwise suspect. The "scrap" in scrapple, however, does not mean low-quality parts, but merely what had not been used in making other foods, like sausage.

In the Civil War era, production of scrapple industrialized to meet the needs of a nation at war and a growing urban population. In 1863, Joshua Habbersett opened Habbersett Pork Products in Middletown Township, Delaware County, Pennsylvania, the first company to mass produce scrapple. Nevertheless, cookbooks and newspapers offered home cooks advice on making the dish. *Domestic Cookery*, published in 1869 by Elizabeth Ellicott Lea, detailed the culinary culture of Pennsylvania Germans and the Tidewater South for "young housekeepers." Its scrapple recipe was a basic one: "Take eight pounds of scraps of pork that will not do for sausage; boil it in four gallons of water; when tender, chop fine, strain the liquor and pour it back into the pot; put in the meat; season it with sage, summer savory, salt and pepper to taste; stir in a quart of corn meal; after simmering a few minutes, thicken it with buckwheat flour very thick."

Although cooked and thickened loaves of pig parts can be found throughout the United States, scrapple has retained its deep connection to the Philadelphia region. In the early twenty-first century, festivals celebrating scrapple took place in Bridgeville, Delaware, and at the Reading Terminal Market in Philadelphia. The locavore movement, with its celebration of regional cuisine, showed signs of making scrapple popular again as an edible artifact of the region's rural roots.

## Immigration, 1790–1860

**James M. Bergquist**

The revival of immigration to Philadelphia and its surrounding region in the early nineteenth century was one of the most powerful elements in reshaping the city's society. After a decline in immigration during the wars of the French Revolution and the Napoleonic era, the growing industrialization of the Philadelphia region began to attract streams of newcomers. The main flow of these migrants still came, as in colonial days, from northern Europe, especially Ireland, Germany, and Britain. But four decades of relatively low migration during and after the American Revolution led to an ethnic society considerably different from what had existed in colonial days. The growing number of Catholic newcomers thereafter gave rise to conflict between nativists and immigrants. Immigrants became a persistent issue in the politics of the Philadelphia region and of the nation. The newer immigrants began to find their place in the economic and geographical structure of the city and began to develop their own separate cultures. By the time of the Civil War, immigration had transformed the city.

Over the nearly four decades from the beginning of the American Revolution in 1776 until the fall of Napoleon in 1815, the flow of immigrants to the United States fell drastically. The Revolution itself, followed by the European wars that began during the French Revolution, served as discouragement to immigrants traveling from the familiar sources in northern Europe. In the 1790s, Ireland provided the largest source of immigrants to the United States; an unsuccessful rebellion there in 1798 sent many exiles seeking asylum in America. The smaller number of refugees from revolutionary France acquired more notoriety; they raised suspicion among Federalist Americans because they were thought to be politically dangerous and to support radical Jeffersonian views. In 1798 a Federalist Congress (meeting in Philadelphia, then the nation's capital) passed the Naturalization Act, one of the Alien and Sedition Acts. This law raised the waiting period for acquiring citizenship to fourteen years; it was reduced to five years in 1802, after Jeffersonians gained control of the government.

Over these years, the Philadelphia port of entry played a dwindling role in the movement of immigrants into the United States. In colonial times, the Delaware Valley had provided a convenient entryway for the many German and Scots Irish migrants who were heading into the hinterland of Pennsylvania and the backcountry of Maryland, Virginia, and the Carolinas. From 1799 onward those arriving via this maritime route had to pass first through a quarantine station known as the Lazaretto, located on the Delaware River about eight miles south of the city. But by the time of the Lazaretto's completion, New York had emerged as the preeminent port of entry for immigrants, in part due to its closer proximity to northern Europe. New York, which had become the foremost port for transatlantic commerce after the War of 1812, became the favored gateway into the interior of the United States when the Erie Canal, opened in 1825, allowed easy transportation between the Hudson River and the Great Lakes. Manhattan also had many ship lines operating frequent service from Liverpool, the point of departure of many transatlantic immigrants. Philadelphia had fewer regular scheduled services. Thus immigration through Philadelphia's port declined even as the number of foreign-born in the city increased. During the 1820s, around 12 percent of the total of new immigrant arrivals nationally entered through the Philadelphia port; by the 1850s, that figure had dwindled to 4.5 percent. Immigrants intent upon staying in Philadelphia often arrived in New York and made the overland trip via railroad or canal to Philadelphia.

In 1815, at the end of the Napoleonic Wars, immigration began to revive but remained relatively low throughout the 1820s because of the economic recession after the Panic of 1819. The principal arrivals settling in the Philadelphia region were, as before the Revolution, Germans, Irish, and British. Increasingly the Irish immigrants outnumbered the Germans. More importantly, Irish Protestants and Catholics became more distinguishable, and hostility between the two communities sometimes spilled over into the streets. In 1831, as Irish Catholic immigration gathered pace, a riot broke out in Philadelphia between the two groups. When Protestant Irish began to parade in celebration of the 1690 Battle of the Boyne (in which William of Orange defeated the Catholic James II on Irish soil), Catholics came out in opposition. The affair signified the separation of Irish Catholics from Irish Protestants in the social makeup of Philadelphia. Increasingly after that point, the Irish would be divided into two separate and often conflicting religious groups, with the Catholics increasingly outnumbering the Protestants.

The period from 1830 to 1860 saw a great increase in the flow of immigrants to Philadelphia, as in the nation generally. The forces determining the rise and fall of the flow of immigrants are usually described as "pushes" and "pulls." The pushes included the conditions in Europe: increasing pressures of population upon the limited supply of land, poor conditions of the new urban masses, and political unrest. The pulls often worked to bring new immigrants to Philadelphia, especially the availability of work in the new industrial environment that was developing there. There were, of course, rises and declines in the rate of immigration, often determined by the state of the economy. In the United States the depressions that occurred after 1837 and 1854 sharply reduced the flow of immigrants. Between those lulls, the years 1847 to 1854 saw the largest increase in the annual rate of immigrants. The Irish Potato Famine, the political uprisings on the European continent in 1848, and the diminishing conditions of the European worker moved many to come to the United States. At the same time, the American economy was booming, inspired by the gold rush in California and the expansion of the country after the Mexican War.

Philadelphia, with its burgeoning industrial economy, offered those in need of work numerous opportunities, especially in terms of the unskilled jobs that many Irish immigrants filled. Irish woman often found work in domestic service. Textile mills and iron factories proliferated in the region; mill sites in Delaware County attracted Irish and English newcomers; the building of canals along the Schuylkill and Delaware Rivers enlisted the labor of Irish and other immigrants; and immigrants were attracted to new canal towns such as Conshohocken, Norristown, and Bristol. In 1832 a new route to the West opened in the form of the Philadelphia and Columbia Railroad, a part of the state-sponsored Main Line of Public Works, a system of canals and railroads stretching across the state. Much of it was built with Irish labor, and immigrants followed into the new towns being opened up in Chester and Lancaster Counties. In New Jersey, similar transportation developments brought new immigrant laborers. In 1834, the first railroad line in the state, the Camden and Amboy Railroad, was opened for its entire route between New York harbor and Camden, where passengers could catch a cross-river ferry to Philadelphia. This made Camden and Bordentown centers of transportation development, attracting immigrant railroad and dockworkers. New industries soon followed. Since much of the agricultural land in the immediate Philadelphia region was already occupied by 1800, new immigrants intent upon pursuing an agricultural livelihood often made their

**FIGURE 14.** *National Memorial to An Gorta Mór (the Great Hunger)*, Front and Spruce Streets, Philadelphia, 2023. Erected in 2002 at Front and Chestnut Streets, the bronze sculpture commemorates the Irish who died in the famine of 1845–50 and those who crossed the Atlantic to make new lives in the United States. In 2023 the monument temporarily moved to this location, nearby Foglietta Park, while work took place on Interstate 95. PHOTOGRAPH BY DONALD D. GROFF.

way toward western Pennsylvania and Ohio, or to the southwest through the Cumberland and Shenandoah Valleys into western Virginia and the Carolinas.

The population of Philadelphia, which had been around 100,000 in 1815, grew to 400,000 in 1850 and, following the annexation of the outlying county in 1854, to 565,000 in 1860. The great influx of immigrants in the period 1847–54 contributed largely to that growth. In 1860, Irish-born Philadelphians numbered about 16.7 percent of the total population and German-born numbered about 7.5 percent. As the city grew, immigrant settlement tended to follow the pattern of the "walking city," where individuals lived within walking distance of their workplace. That brought together people of various ethnicities and classes within one neighborhood. While some neighborhoods might harbor many of the immigrant churches and voluntary societies, one group did not dominate in any neighborhood. German institutions in the colonial period had arisen in the area to the northeast of the center of Philadelphia; in the nineteenth century, the heaviest concentrations of Germans were still seen north of Market Street, but many Germans, more upwardly mobile than the Irish, found residences throughout the city. By 1860, a neighborhood of German Jews formed just to the southeast of the center of the city.

Traditionally the Germans in Philadelphia and the surrounding region had been of many different backgrounds, given their religious diversity and the variety of provincial origins in a European region not yet united into one nation. The Germans found many reasons to disagree, not only in religion but in cultural matters as well. The complex divisions among Germans made it hard for them to unite politically for

HIBERNIA
HIBERNIA
HIBERNIA

any cause (other than opposition to prohibition laws). When immigration from Germany revived after 1815, it became clear that there were considerable differences between those whose arrival dated to the eighteenth century and those who came later. Some of the differences were generational: younger people, many of them of the second and third generations, began to question the exclusive use of German in the churches and other institutions. Controversy over language in the Lutheran churches led to an acrimonious court battle in 1815. The German Society of Pennsylvania, perhaps the most venerable of German institutions, made English its official language in 1818; it did not return to the use of German until the 1860s, after new generations of immigrants had taken over the society. Catholic Germans took pride in the fact that a German-speaking immigrant, John Nepomucene Neumann, became bishop of Philadelphia in 1852. Until he died in 1860, he labored to serve all elements of his multiethnic diocese.

The region's Irish population was even more widely distributed, although South Philadelphia and industrial suburbs like Kensington housed larger numbers. By the mid-nineteenth century, the group was heavily Catholic, and the church served as the center of the Irish institutional life. Irish saloons also developed as seedbeds of social and political life. Overwhelmingly working-class Irish immigrants found themselves subject to the fluctuations of the economy. Nativist riots in 1844, directed particularly at Irish workers, left a notable mark on the Irish immigrant population. Competition among ethnic groups in the labor market especially affected the mostly unskilled Irish; Philadelphians of German and English extraction had more of a niche in middle-class occupations, where competition for jobs proved less intense. Growing numbers of free Black people also contended with the Irish in the labor market. Their numbers grew after the passage of Pennsylvania's gradual emancipation law in 1780. The internal migration of free Black Americans across the Mason-Dixon Line also increased after Congress closed the international slave trade in 1808; many came to southeast Pennsylvania in that northerly migration.

**FIGURE 15.** *Hibernia Fire Engine Company*, No. 1, 1857. Prior to the professionalization of Philadelphia's fire department in the 1870s, firefighting relied on volunteer companies. By 1850, many of these companies had organized along ethnic lines. Despite their undoubted heroism, the companies often participated in the urban violence of the era and wound up fighting one another as often as they battled the city's frequent infernos. HISTORICAL SOCIETY OF PENNSYLVANIA.

Newcomers from the British Isles were a distant third in the flow of immigrants from Europe. Having no language problems, they could easily blend into American life and institutions, and they had no need of founding separate churches. The development of Philadelphia as an Italian American city was just beginning before the Civil War. In 1852, Bishop Neumann recognized the mostly northern Italian group (numbering 417 in the 1860 census) by establishing a parish, St. Mary Magdalen de Pazzi, especially for them. The city's Italian residents were already concentrated in South Philadelphia.

By 1860, Philadelphia had emerged as the model of the new industrial and ethnic city. Such a development would never have occurred had it not been for the great number of immigrant workers flocking into the region in the early nineteenth century. The presence of these newcomers fostered nativist reaction, which would remain in the society for a long time. Yet no one could possibly call for the exclusion of these elements now embedded in the city's economy. While the city and its surrounding region were still in control of native white elements, the immigrants had become a force to be dealt with in its economic and political life.

## Lazaretto

**Lance Eisenhower**

Situated roughly ten miles south of Philadelphia, in Essington, on the west bank of the Delaware River, the Lazaretto is considered to be the oldest and last surviving quarantine station in the United States. Throughout most of the nineteenth century, the Lazaretto was the first stop for immigrants and merchants on incoming ships whose passengers and cargo had to be quarantined until passing a health inspection. The Philadelphia Board of Health commissioned the Lazaretto in 1799, largely in response

**FIGURE 16.** Philadelphia Lazaretto, Essington, Delaware County, 2005. LIBRARY OF CONGRESS.

to the yellow fever epidemics that plagued the city in the late eighteenth century. They chose the site for its strategic location near the mouth of the Delaware River, whereby all incoming ships, passengers, and cargo attempting to dock in Philadelphia and other northern ports were required to be quarantined pending inspection. The ten-acre Tinicum Lazaretto complex opened in 1801. Once docked, ships were searched for sick passengers, infested cargo, or the bodies of those who died during the voyage. Any sign of contagion would result in sterilization and fumigation of the clothing and baggage and quarantine of the passengers at the Lazaretto hospital for a period of days or weeks, and sometimes for months. The hospital could accommodate five hundred persons.

During the summer of 1800 the old quarantine station on Province Island, the predecessor to the Lazaretto, housed more than 170 enslaved Africans after the USS *Ganges* captured two U.S. ships engaged in illegal trafficking off the coast of Cuba. The captives were brought to Philadelphia, where the ships were held during condemnation proceedings. Since many of the enslaved people were sick or starving, they were held at the hospital for a month before being released to the Pennsylvania Abolition Society, whereupon the survivors among them became part of the Philadelphia-area free Black population.

The Lazaretto operated under the authority of the Philadelphia Board of Health until 1893, when the state took over and ran the quarantine station through to its closure in 1895. By then, most of the screening had passed to the Delaware Breakwater Quarantine Station, a national quarantine station, near Lewes, Delaware, established in 1884, or the station at Reedy Island, forty-five miles below Philadelphia. In 1913 state authorities consolidated screening procedures at a facility at Marcus Hook.

## Colonization Movement (Africa)

John Saillant

The African colonization movement, dedicated to resettling North American free Black people in West Africa, caused heated debates in Philadelphia in the early nineteenth century. Proposals to remove free Black individuals from North America date from the 1770s, but the heyday of African colonization occurred between 1818 and 1865. Often described as a "return to Africa," the resettlement plans actually focused on free Black people who had never set foot on African soil. Colonization is better described as a semivoluntary expatriation than as a return to a homeland.

White Americans were the most active in promoting colonization, but many Black people desired opportunities outside North America in places that appeared to offer greater self-determination and economic gain. The first colonizationists, Black and white, envisioned various territories for expatriates including Haiti and Sierra Leone. By the early 1820s, American colonizationists focused on Cape Mesurado in Africa, where Monrovia was established in a territory soon called Liberia (after the Latin word for freedom). Some also proposed removing free Black people to the American western frontier, where they might be distant from white Americans as well as useful as a buffer against Native Americans.

Although often considered an American colony, Liberia was a territory initially purchased by American settlers from African rulers in several transactions in the 1820s with financial support from the American Colonization Society, a national organization founded in Washington, D.C., in 1817. In 1847, when settlers declared independence, it was home to about three thousand Americo-Liberians, a number sufficient to establish political dominance over native Africans but far fewer than the number of free Black individuals that colonizationists had hoped to resettle from the United States.

In Philadelphia, members of the Pennsylvania Abolition Society discussed colonization in the 1810s as a response to the growing number of freedpeople or runaways coming to Philadelphia from southern states. At that time, leaders of Black Philadelphia including Richard Allen and James Forten endorsed colonization. But soon, in Philadelphia and elsewhere, colonizationist sentiment was attacked from several angles. In 1817 a gathering of Black Philadelphians at Mother Bethel Church denounced colonization as an insult to African Americans and a forced removal hidden behind a thin veil of voluntary emigration.

Allen and Forten modified their earlier views although at times they articulated lukewarm support for colonization. Allen declared: "This land which we have watered with our tears and our blood, is now our mother country, and we are well satisfied to stay where wisdom abounds and the gospel is free." Similarly, in an 1818 address to white Pennsylvanians, Forten stated the desires of free Black persons to remain in their homes and to assist in the abolition of slavery and the improvement of Black life in the United States. In 1818, the Pennsylvania Abolition Society moved firmly against colonization, but it expressed the belief that resettlement might be salutary in some circumstances.

Despite these mixed opinions, the American Colonization Society enjoyed strong support in the Greater Philadelphia region. Robert Finley, who led the committee that established the American Colonization Society, was born in Princeton, New Jersey. Like most states beginning in the 1820s, Pennsylvania, New Jersey, Delaware, and Maryland had local colonization societies that identified likely settlers and drummed up financial support for travel and the needs of the Liberian settlements.

Even after the Pennsylvania Abolition Society condemned African colonization in 1818, Philadelphians were involved in the movement of free Black people to Liberia. Episcopal Bishop William White became a vice president of the American Colonization Society in 1819. Philadelphia Quaker Roberts Vaux became a colonizationist in the 1820s, when he decided that a Liberian settlement would help suppress the African slave trade as well as provide a home for victims of the slave trade (known as recaptives) who were seized by the American government, sometimes at sea, from illicit slave traders. Other Quakers including Joseph Hemphill and Sarah Moore Grimké adopted the colonizationist cause. Philadelphia luminaries such as Mathew Carey and Elliott Cresson also supported colonization.

The Pennsylvania Colonization Society formed in 1828 to promote Black emigration from Pennsylvania as

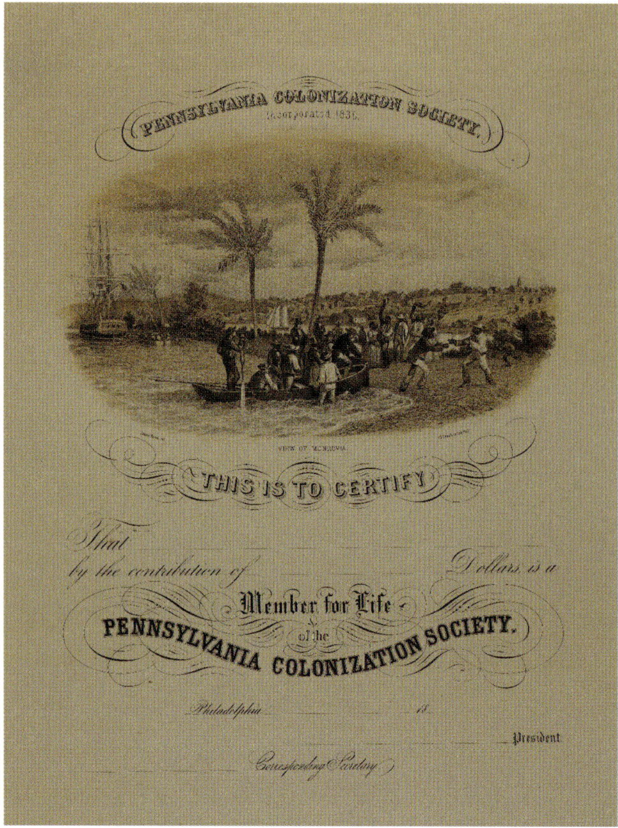


**FIGURE 17.** Membership certificate for Pennsylvania Colonization Society, showing Monrovia, Liberia, ca. 1855. Colonizationists proposed the emigration of Black Americans to Liberia as an alternative to enslavement. While the idea found considerable support among white Philadelphians, the region's Black community overwhelmingly rejected such designs. HISTORICAL SOCIETY OF PENNSYLVANIA.

well as to fund transportation of freedpeople from other states to Liberia. It was followed in 1834 by the Young Men's Colonization Society of Pennsylvania (absorbed into the American Colonization Society in 1838), which, in cooperation with the national society and the Colonization Society of the City of New-York, funded the travel of 126 freed Afro-Virginians from Norfolk to a new settlement in Liberia called Bassa Cove. In 1835 this settlement was attacked by the dominant local slave trader, King Joe. Although the new settlers were routed in the first battle, they were able, with the assistance of the Monrovian settlers, to force King Joe to cede territory to the United Colonization Societies of New-York and Pennsylvania.

A Philadelphia Ladies' Liberia School Association formed in 1832 under the leadership of Quaker Beulah Biddle Sansom. The Young Men's Colonization Society of Pennsylvania had been calling for women to support the work of colonization, and in the early 1830s Philadelphia women began raising money to support schools in Liberia. Such charitable support was part of a larger pattern of middle-class women's Christian benevolence in antebellum America. The enthusiasm of the Ladies' Liberia School Association remained high throughout the 1830s, as its members funded construction of schoolhouses and selected teachers for its schools in Liberia, though it struggled for funds in the 1840s as the growth of the anti-colonizationist American Anti-Slavery Society dimmed the association's Liberian hopes.

Some of the early Americo-Liberian settlers were Black Philadelphians. By 1822, about fifty-four Black Philadelphians had emigrated to Liberia (a tiny number compared to about ten thousand free Black individuals in Philadelphia, but significant in the settlement). One of the folk heroes of early Liberia was Matilda Newport, a young woman who emigrated from Philadelphia in 1820 around age twenty-five and, according to the legend, stood her ground singlehandedly with a rifle in a battle with local people in 1822.

Both Black and white residents of the Philadelphia region thus participated in a resettlement effort that would have momentous implications in the modern world. Although colonization's advocates and its foes expressed mixed sentiments about the resettlement, and Philadelphians' initiatives were mostly limited to the 1820s and 1830s, the repercussions of colonization both in the United States and in West Africa made it a crucial phase in Philadelphia's history.

## Nativism

**James Kopaczewski**

While Philadelphia has not been alone in experiencing sharp undercurrents of nativism, virulent rhetoric and periodic waves of violence aimed at the foreign-born have often wracked the city. Clashes between nativists and immigrants between the 1720s and the 1920s helped to set the boundaries of the city as well as define the limits of American citizenship. A renewal of nativism in the Philadelphia region in the early twenty-first century rested upon a long history of misunderstanding and exclusion.

William Penn founded Pennsylvania on principles of tolerance, and the earliest settlers of Philadelphia included English, Scots Irish, and German immigrants, among others. By the early eighteenth century, however, the influence of German-speaking peoples, settled primarily in and around Germantown, provoked the antagonism of Philadelphia's English elites. Comprising nearly one-third of the region's population, German voters became a vital political bloc courted by both Quaker and Anglican politicians. Germans allied politically with Quakers, who conducted business with German merchants and shared pacifist views. With their failure to sway German voters, Anglican politicians, led by William Allen, initiated a wave of Election Day violence in 1742 to prevent Germans from voting. A large group of Anglican-affiliated sailors verbally and physically assaulted German voters, but the Quakers, with their German allies, won in a landslide.

Leading city figures, including Benjamin Franklin, harbored some of the most virulent anti-German sentiments. In his *Observations Concerning the Increase of Mankind*, Franklin argued that Germans were of inferior intellectual and biological stock. He asked, "Why should Pennsylvania, founded by the English, become a Colony of *Aliens*, who will shortly be so numerous as to Germanize us instead of our Anglifying them, and will never adopt our Language or Customs, any more than they can acquire our Complexion?"

In the early republic new threats from abroad loomed large in nativist imaginations. Fears of immigrants heightened in the 1790s as thousands of men, women, and children fled from the French Revolution. Philadelphia, then serving as the nation's capital, and its surrounding region became home to a robust French community that included radicals exiled from Paris, sparking Federalist concerns of internal subversion. During the first half of the nineteenth century, though, nativist focus shifted to Irish Catholics, then immigrating to the Philadelphia region in increasing numbers. In the early 1840s, Bishop Francis P. Kenrick's efforts to allow Catholic students to use their Douay Bible in the city's public schools metastasized both nativist and anti-Catholic feelings, and organizations such as the American Protestant Association and the American Republican Party targeted a wide range of immigrant groups, including German Americans. The conflict turned to violence in 1844 in two murderous riots that pitted Catholics, Protestants, and the militia against one another.

In the aftermath of the riots, nativist candidates swept to significant victories in the election of 1844. Philadelphians elected Lewis C. Levin and John Hull Campbell, both members of the nativist American Party, to the United States House of Representatives. Levin, the editor of the *Daily Sun*, became a vigorous proponent of extending the naturalization period for citizenship to twenty-one years as well as banning immigrants from holding elected office. The American Party's success in Philadelphia politics solidified with Levin's reelection in 1846 and 1848. With nativist politicians in office across the Northeast, especially in Boston and New York City, the American Party nominated Daniel Webster as its candidate for president in 1852. When Webster died a few days before the election, nativists threw their support behind a Philadelphian, Jacob Broom. Although Broom received less than 1 percent of the popular vote, he recovered to win election to the U.S. House of Representatives in 1854 from Pennsylvania's Fourth Congressional District.

The election of 1854 was a watershed moment for nativists in Philadelphia city politics. Robert T. Conrad, a playwright and former editor of the *North American*, was elected mayor with the backing of a coalition of the Whig Party and the nativist Know Nothings. Conrad implemented the Consolidation Act of 1854, which extended the city's jurisdiction over significant Irish Catholic districts like Moyamensing and Kensington. Conrad used the patronage of his office to fill city positions, especially the Philadelphia Police Department, with his nativist supporters. Under Conrad, the city government became an instrument through which nativists could surveil and police immigrant communities.

The years that followed saw nativism decline as an independent political movement while finding support in established parties. After 1856, nativists often defected to the fledgling Republican Party, which actively courted their vote. While many Republicans, especially abolitionists, were uncomfortable with nativist rhetoric, the party subsumed much of the nativist vote. Following the Civil War, anti-Irish and anti-German politics diminished as these groups became "old stock," but traces of animosity remained. The Loyal Orange Institution, a Protestant Irish fraternal order that spread across the United States after the Civil War, organized marches for its Greater Philadelphia "Orangemen" to celebrate William of Orange's victory over Catholic forces at the Battle of the Boyne in 1690 well into the post-1945 era. Hatboro, in Montgomery County, still had an Orange march in 1987, though one participant ruefully remarked, "The only thing that stinks about it is it keeps getting smaller and smaller."

By the 1880s, though, nativists had begun to target immigrants from Asia, particularly in the western United States. The Page Act of 1875 barred Chinese women from entering the country, and in 1882, the Chinese Exclusion Act made all immigration from China illegal. Assaults on Asian communities drove Chinese immigrants in the West to escape to northeastern cities, including Philadelphia. A small but vibrant Chinese community formed along the 900 block of Race Street. With limited job opportunities, Chinese workers established laundries, grocery stores, and restaurants. Their shops became targets for police who periodically raided Chinatown under the guise of preventing immorality. After the Philippine-American War from 1899 to 1902, the Philadelphia chapter of the American League argued that imperialism threatened to open the door to waves of Filipino immigrants.

Millions of Italians, Jews, Poles, and Slavs migrated to the United States during the late nineteenth and early twentieth century, generating intense fear and hatred of immigrants among many Americans. Responding to nativists who demanded limits on the number and national origins of immigrants, in 1924 Congress passed the Johnson-Reed Act, which implemented a rigid quota system. Russian, Polish, and Italian immigrants were particularly targeted by the Johnson-Reed Act, which slowed immigration from southern and eastern Europe to a trickle.

The immigration laws of the 1920s remained in place until 1965, when the Immigration and Nationality Act redistributed the quota system to allow for a greater diversity of immigrants. From the mid-twentieth century into the twenty-first century, Philadelphia received increasing numbers of immigrants from South Asia, Africa, and the Caribbean. In the 1990s, Philadelphia became a "sanctuary city," preventing the deportation of undocumented immigrants who had not been charged with a crime, without a warrant. Nevertheless, while new immigrant communities carved out niches in the region's economy and culture, nativism remained an acute issue. In the first decades of the twenty-first century, vandals targeted mosques and Jewish cemeteries. In December 2015, a severed pig's head was found outside the Al Aqsa Islamic Society in Kensington. Amid a national wave of anti-Semitism in early 2017, the Mount Carmel Cemetery in the Wissinoming section of Philadelphia was desecrated. In response to these ethnically motivated attacks, Muslim and Jewish activists banded together to raise funds for the restoration of holy sites. With renewed waves of violence, immigration relief organizations, such as the Nationalities Service Center and Welcoming Center for New Pennsylvanians, remained newly arrived immigrants' best option for sound legal and employment advice.

The historical trajectory of nativism in Philadelphia paralleled that of the rest of the country. In periods of political turmoil, Americans often resorted to nativist rhetoric to defend their position in society. Despite Philadelphia's reputation as the Cradle of Liberty and the City of Brotherly Love, at times the city repulsed its newest residents. Nativism in Philadelphia served as a reminder of the tensions between American ideals and American actions.

## Nativist Riots of 1844

**Zachary M. Schrag**

In May and July 1844, Philadelphia suffered some of the bloodiest rioting of the antebellum period, as anti-immigrant mobs attacked Irish American homes and Roman Catholic churches before being suppressed by the militia. The violence was part of a wave of riots that convulsed American cities starting in the 1830s. Yet even amid this tumult, they stand out for their duration, itself a product of nativist determination to use xenophobia for political gain. In the aftermath of the riots, shocked Philadelphians began debating new methods of maintaining order, a discussion that contributed to the consolidation of Philadelphia County in 1854.

Ethnic and religious antagonism had a long history in the city. Since the 1780s, Irish textile workers had come to Philadelphia after losing their jobs to mechanization in the British Isles. As early as 1828, when an off-duty watchman was killed after disparaging "bloody Irish transports," Catholic presence had provoked anxiety among American- and Irish-born Protestants. In 1831, Irish Catholics battled along Fifth Street with Protestants celebrating the anniversary of the Battle of the Boyne.

Anti-Catholic agitation increased in the early 1840s, organized in part around a perceived threat to the Bible in the public schools. Catholic Bishop Francis Patrick Kenrick, an Irish immigrant himself, objected to Protestant teachers' leading students in singing Protestant hymns and requiring them to read from the King James Bible. Nativists used Kenrick's complaints to gain followers. In 1842, dozens of Protestant clergymen formed the American Protestant Association to defend America from Romanism. In 1843, editor Lewis Levin made the *Daily Sun* an organ for attacks against Catholicism and Catholic immigration. In December of that year, like-minded Protestants founded a nativist political party called the American Republicans.

**FIGURE 18.** *Death of George Shifler*, 1844. John L. Magee's lithograph turned a nativist rioter into a martyr to American Protestantism. LIBRARY OF CONGRESS.

In 1844, the Bible controversy intensified in the district of Kensington, a suburb to the northeast of Philadelphia City and home to many Irish immigrants, both Protestant and Catholic. In February, Hugh Clark, a Catholic school director there, suggested suspending Bible reading until the school board could devise a policy acceptable to Catholics and Protestants alike. Further inspired by a victory in the New York mayoral election, nativists rallied by the thousands in Independence Square. On May 3, 1844, they rallied in Kensington itself but were chased away.

The first serious violence broke out three days later. On May 6, the nativists reassembled in Kensington, provoking another fight, during which a young nativist named George Shiffler was fatally shot. By day's end, a second man was dead and several more nativists were wounded, two mortally. The next day, the First Brigade of the Pennsylvania Militia, commanded by Brigadier General George Cadwalader, responded to the sheriff's call for help. The troops faced little direct resistance, but on May 8, mobs torched several private dwellings (including Hugh Clark's house), a Catholic seminary, and two Catholic churches: St. Michael's at Second Street and Master and St. Augustine's at Fourth and Vine. Only a flood of new forces—including citizen posses, city police, militia companies arriving from other cities, and U.S. sailors and marines—ended the violence by May 10.

The city remained superficially calm for the next eight weeks, but both nativists and Catholics anticipated further violence. In Southwark—an independent district south of Philadelphia City and a seat of nativist strength—a Catholic priest's brother began stockpiling weapons in the basement of the Church of St. Philip de Neri on Queen Street. On Friday, July 5, a crowd of thousands gathered to demand the weapons. When the crowd reassembled the following day, the sheriff requested militia troops, and Cadwalader led about two hundred into Southwark. Saturday ended without bloodshed, but the situation remained tense, with a small group of militiamen—some of them Irish Catholics themselves—guarding the church and a group of nativist prisoners inside it.

On Sunday, July 7, the crowd reassembled, and this time it armed itself with cannon. Egged on by nativist speakers, the crowd forced the militia to surrender the church and its prisoners. Cadwalader returned to Southwark about sunset at the head of a column and tried to clear the area around the church. When the crowd attacked the militia with bricks, stones, and bottles, the militia fired on them, killing at least five and wounding more. Starting around 9 p.m., the crowd counterattacked. For the next four hours, rioters and the militia battled in the streets of Southwark, with both sides firing cannon. By morning, two militiamen and probably a dozen rioters were dead or dying, along with many more wounded. Southwark's aldermen negotiated the militia's withdrawal from their district, but hundreds of militia troops from other parts of the state arrived to patrol the city of Philadelphia.

The 1844 riots were extreme in their severity and duration. While some of the violence had been spontaneous, the ambitions of the nativist newspapers and political party in an election year likely sustained nativist fury through the spring and summer. Though the riots were more than the simple transplantation of anti-Catholic violence from northern Ireland, they echoed the deliberate provocation seen there.

The riots did not resolve the place of the Irish in the city though they did spur changes in metropolitan governance. While few Philadelphians were willing to endorse publicly the attacks on Catholics, in the October elections, amid the heaviest turnout in the city's history, Levin and another nativist won congressional seats and other nativists took lesser posts. Meanwhile, Philadelphians began discussing plans for a stronger police force to deter future riots. In April 1845, the State legislature passed a law requiring each major city and district of Philadelphia County to support at least one police officer for each 150 taxable inhabitants, and in 1850 it created a new Philadelphia Police District to cover the entire metropolitan area, including the outlying districts of Kensington and Southwark. Though not the sole cause, these steps contributed to the consolidation of Philadelphia County into a single city government in 1854.

## Immigration, 1870–1930

**Barbara Klaczynska Schmidt**

During the national explosion of immigration that took place between 1870 and the 1920s, the Philadelphia region became more diverse and cosmopolitan as it was energized by immigrants who indelibly changed the character of the places where they settled. With its reputation as the "Workshop of the World," Philadelphia attracted immigrants to jobs in industry, construction, and its vibrant port. Immigrants spread through the city and region, but they were more likely to organize in small clusters drawn to centers of employment, churches and synagogues, schools, shops, friends, and families. The upsurge lasted until the United States government enacted unprecedented restrictions on immigration in 1924.

By the 1870s, Philadelphia's diverse population included the descendants of earlier immigrants, including the English, Swedes, Germans, and Dutch. The city also had one of the largest African American populations of any northern city and overflowed with the first and second generation of Irish immigrants whose numbers had increased dramatically with the 1840s' Potato Famine. Into this already-diverse region new waves of immigrants from eastern and southern Europe, China, Latin America, and the Caribbean arrived. Philadelphia neighborhoods changed in response to the increasing numbers of arriving immigrants as particular ethnic groups came to dominate areas that had once been mixed. Nevertheless, Philadelphia was marked by the scattering of ethnic groups throughout the city and the region; for example, the city had eight different Polish parishes in different neighborhoods.

Philadelphia is commonly described as a "low immigration city" because its proportion of foreign-born residents lagged behind other cities. While New York had a 40 percent foreign-born population between 1870 and 1920, and Buffalo, Cleveland, Detroit, Milwaukee, Minneapolis, and Chicago had even higher proportions, Philadelphia reached its peak of 27 percent foreign-born

**FIGURE 19.** Members of the Killers street gang, 1848. As battles over enslavement and immigration raged in the 1840s and 1850s, young men flocked to street gangs. The names attributed to the gangs offer clues to their ethnic and religious loyalties: The Kerryonians, Orangemen, and Molly Maguires, for instance, hint at longstanding divisions between Irish Protestants and Catholics. Others, like the Garroters, the Bleeders, and the Bloodtubs, suggest a fondness for violence. The Killers, who allied with Irish Catholics in the southern suburb of Moyamensing, acquired the greatest notoriety, thanks in part to the efforts of the popular Philadelphia novelist George Lippard, who turned their attack on a tavern owned by an interracial couple in 1849 into a sensational work of urban gothic fiction. Gang violence subsided with the organization of a professional police in the 1850s, though this owed much to the tendency of city mayors to reward loyal gangsters for the muscle they provided around election time with a police badge. LIBRARY COMPANY OF PHILADELPHIA.

in 1870. In 1910 Philadelphia, with a population of more than a million and a half, had a foreign-born population of about 25 percent, still well below the median that year for all major cities (29 percent). Still, at the turn of the twentieth century Philadelphia was the third-largest city in the United States and the total number of immigrants surpassed most other American cities. In addition to newcomers from abroad, the grandchildren and great-grandchildren of earlier immigrants sustained distinct religious and cultural traditions. Philadelphia became a home for immigrants fleeing political turmoil, persecution, and drastic poverty who came to places where they could find relatives, countrymen, churches, synagogues, and agencies able to understand and in some cases welcome them. They found employers who spoke their language and needed workers with their skill sets, such as leatherworkers from Poland, lace makers from Ireland, and cigar makers from Puerto Rico. The push and pull combined to make Philadelphia a receptive immigrant destination.

The number of foreign-born in Philadelphia grew steadily between 1870 through 1920, even though the percentage of foreign-born dropped from 27 percent in 1870 to 22 percent in 1920. Census figures illustrate how new migrations changed the ethnic composition of the city and region. In 1890 the largest group of immigrants in Philadelphia was the Irish, numbering 110,935 or 41 percent of the foreign-born population. German immigrants numbered 74,971 and made up 27.8 percent of the total foreign-born population. By 1920, Philadelphia's foreign-born numbered 400,744 with the leading groups being Russians (95,744), Irish (64,500), Italians (63,723), Germans (39,766), Poles (31,112), English (30,866), Austrians (13,387), Hungarians (11,513), Rumanians (5,645), and Lithuanians (4,392). Most of the Russians and many other eastern Europeans were Jews who fled persecution.

By 1930, more than two-fifths of all foreign-born residents in the city of Philadelphia were Russian Jews (22.5 percent) or Italians (18.3 percent). These two groups made up almost as much of the larger region's foreign-born residents (Italians, 19.7 percent, and Russians, 18.4 percent). By 1900, only 5.5 percent of Philadelphia's immigrants were German, but as the city was at that time the third largest in the United States, there were more German-born residents than in traditionally identified German strongholds in Buffalo, Cincinnati, Milwaukee, and St. Louis. In 1901, Philadelphia activists founded the National German American Alliance, which served as a key organization to encourage resisting assimilation. As historian Russell Kazal has shown, lively German immigrant communities along Girard

**TABLE 1. ORIGINS OF PHILADELPHIA'S FOREIGN-BORN POPULATION, 1920**

| | |
|---|---|
| Russia | 95,744 |
| Ireland | 64,590 |
| Italy | 63,723 |
| United Kingdom | 40,284 |
| Germany | 39,766 |
| Poland | 31,112 |
| Former Austrian-Hungarian Empire | 16,726 |
| Scandinavia | 5,764 |
| Romania | 5,645 |
| Lithuania | 4,392 |
| Canada | 4,244 |
| France | 3,886 |
| Caribbean | 2,181 |
| Switzerland | 1,889 |
| Greece | 1,814 |
| Armenia | 1,393 |
| Low Countries | 1,044 |
| Spain and Portugal | 895 |
| China | 709 |
| Central and South America | 667 |
| Middle East | 544 |
| Mexico | 485 |
| Turkey | 283 |
| Albania | 260 |
| Australia | 184 |
| Africa | 140 |
| Japan | 105 |
| India | 66 |
| Bulgaria | 47 |

SOURCE: U.S. Census.

Avenue, which included churches, shops, and social clubs, helped sustain that identity. Kensington in eastern North Philadelphia became a place where German immigrants lived along with Irish, Polish, and other native-born and immigrant groups who found work in the local mills.

Immigrant communities placed their indelible marks on Philadelphia's neighborhoods and the city as a whole. The immigrants established social clubs (such as the Venetian Club for Northern Italians in Chestnut Hill), fraternal organizations for men and women that provided insurance and social opportunities (such as the Union of Polish Women in America), and banks throughout the city. They operated bakeries, groceries, restaurants, travel agencies, and shipping services originally designed to cater to their fellow immigrants but in some cases serving the entire communities where they were located. The Jesuit priest Father Joseph Barbelin established Saint Joseph's Hospital on Girard Avenue as a hospital to serve Irish immigrants while other ethnic groups developed health services for their populations in the twentieth century. The Drueding family brought an order of German sisters to America to operate their North Philadelphia workers' infirmary, which developed into the Holy Redeemer Health System.

Immigrant groups settled throughout the region. Germans and Poles who were farmers in their homeland moved onto small farms across the metropolitan area. Immigrants also were attracted to mill towns and smaller industrial cities including Camden, Chester, Norristown, Pottstown, and Trenton, where men, women, and children could find work. African Americans migrating from the South arrived in some of these places, including Camden and Chester, in large numbers at the same time, drawn by employment opportunities and family networks.

Initially, many of the immigrants lived in the inner core of the city but by the early twentieth century many German, Irish, and other European immigrants moved along with native-born citizens to the suburbs. It is possible to trace the mass movements of ethnic groups to the near and, later, far suburbs of the city. For example, Germans and Jews from North Philadelphia moved to Elkins Park and Melrose Park north of the city; Italian, Polish, and Jewish residents of the river wards crossed the river into South Jersey; and Irish residents of West Philadelphia took a foothold in Delaware County suburbs.

The immigrant groups of this period significantly changed the cultural and religious landscapes of the metropolis. To serve the influx of newcomers, Roman Catholic ethnic parishes took up entire city blocks with churches, school buildings, convents, and rectories. Within four blocks on Allegheny Avenue in Port Richmond, three massive Roman Catholic parishes converged, each created to carry out liturgies in different languages and cultures. Throughout the region, national parishes developed to serve the needs of immigrant groups. These included many operated by the Archdiocese of Philadelphia, such as Sacred Heart Parish in Clifton Heights, Delaware County, and Sacred Heart Church in Swedesburg, Montgomery County, for Polish populations, and Saint Ann's Parish in Bristol, Bucks County, for Italian parishioners. New synagogues served immigrant founders from Russia and Germany. Among Protestant denominations, churches and traditions harked back to German and Swedish origins. Orthodox churches reflected Greek, Russian, Ukrainian, and Armenian traditions.

During this period, South Philadelphia resembled New York's Lower East Side as large numbers of immigrants arrived right off the boat from Europe or by train from New York or Boston. Philadelphia's Little Italy was the second largest in the country—surpassed only by New York's. The unification of Italy between 1861 and 1871 and the unsettling changes that followed prompted many to leave for other parts of Europe, South America, and North America. As scholars Richard Juliani and Stefano Luconi have documented, Philadelphia's largely Ligurian colony in 1870 expanded to encompass arrivals from northern Abruzzi, Molise, Campania, Puglia, Basilicata, Calabria, and Sicily. Subnational colonies of Italians developed throughout the city and region. Immigrants from the province of Catanzaro, in the Calabria region, lived along Ellsworth Street, while the territory around Eighth and Fitzwater Street was home primarily to people from Abruzzi. These settlers split into even smaller districts in which specific streets had settlers from specific towns in Abruzzi. Italians lived in enclaves of row houses in South Philadelphia and in clusters in West Philadelphia, North Philadelphia, Nicetown, Mayfair, Manayunk, Germantown, Chestnut Hill, and Southwest Philadelphia as well as outside the city in Norristown,

**FIGURE 20.** Jewish Philadelphians march against Nazi anti-Semitism following Adolf Hitler's rise to power in Germany, Fifth Street and Washington Avenue, 1933. SPECIAL COLLECTIONS RESEARCH CENTER, TEMPLE UNIVERSITY LIBRARIES.

Bristol, Strafford, Chester, Conshohocken, Coatesville, Marcus Hook, Narberth, Ardmore, and Bridgeport, and in Camden, New Jersey.

While many Italians came through an elaborate recruitment system of contract labor, immigrants generally were drawn to Philadelphia by their ties with friends and relatives already living in the region and work opportunities in manufacturing and construction. Stonemasons came from Friuli to help build the homes and estates of Chestnut Hill and established an ongoing presence in that area, where their descendants continued to live. Italians worked in the textile and clothing industry, building trades, and railroads. In the clothing industry Italian men and women worked in the shops, but the largest numbers of Italians were found in the contracted homework until passage of the National Industrial Recovery Act in 1933 shut down this business. In the 1890s, Italians owned 110 contract clothing workshops out of a total of 600 citywide. Italians often came as temporary workers with the intention of returning their wages and eventually themselves to Italy once money had been made. However, when they were not able to save the money needed to make the return trip home or once home failed to establish themselves and their families they often chose to remain in or to return to the United States.

A majority of Italian immigrants and their offspring were Catholic, with distinct parishes for northern and southern Italians. In 1852, the first Italian parish established in the United States, Saint Mary Magdalen de Pazzi near the Ninth Street Market in South Philadelphia, served the early Italian settlers from Liguria and Piedmont in northern Italy. When southern Italians began to arrive in the 1890s they were discouraged from attending Saint Mary Magdalen and instead were directed to Our Lady of Good Counsel, Philadelphia's second Italian parish founded in 1898, a few blocks east. By 1930 sixteen parishes served Italians in various parts of the city.

Philadelphia's Jewish population dated to the colonial era, but in the late nineteenth century Russian Jews became the largest foreign-born group in the city. Jewish immigrants from Russia, Poland, and other parts of eastern Europe arrived at the Christian Street wharf and in many cases walked a few blocks to the homes of relatives and countrymen. The Jewish population of South Philadelphia grew from fifty-five thousand in 1907 to one hundred thousand in 1920. Even though a Philadelphia Housing Association survey reported continuing decreases in South Philadelphia, it remained the most populous Jewish neighborhood in the city, numbering close to fifty thousand, according to Rakhmiel Peltz.

North Philadelphia, with fifty thousand Jewish residents in 1930, was the fifth-largest Jewish section in the city. It developed as a center for Jewish institutional life with social associations, two Jewish colleges, and the Jewish Publication Society. Synagogues began to follow central and eastern European, or Ashkenazi rituals in response to new immigrant groups, and to adopt Reform practices. A vibrant shopping area on Marshall Street around Girard Avenue became a major hub operated by Jewish merchants and patronized by Polish and German Christian customers who shared common languages and tastes.

A variety of organizations addressed the needs of Jewish workers in Philadelphia. Poor working conditions and the presence of Jewish anarchists and socialists made the community a center for labor organizing, leading to workers associations and unions for a variety of occupations including bakers, men's clothing tailors, and ritual slaughterers who worked in kosher butcher plants. Synagogues, based on the ethnic background of their membership and the types of services performed, included the first Russian synagogue in Philadelphia, B'naa Abraham; Kesher Israel; and the Romanian American Synagogue. Jewish institutions included a labor lyceum formed by nine branches of the Workmen's Circle and the Downtown Jewish Orphanage. The Neighborhood Settlement Center was started at Fifth and Bainbridge to serve Jewish families and stayed there until 1948, when it moved to North Philadelphia, where it again served as an important hub of Jewish life.

Another Jewish community, New Jerusalem in the Port Richmond section of the city, became a destination for Russian Jews who met with discrimination by more established and prosperous Jews of German descent. In New Jerusalem, residents worked as peddlers and rag pickers and began to translate work they had done in the Russian shtetl to occupations such as shoemakers, horseshoers, water carriers, coopers, tailors, leatherworkers, cigar makers, umbrella repair men, horseradish vendors, and eventually hardware merchants, dealers in glass, grocers, and dry goods merchants. New Jerusalem established Orthodox synagogues, and the Hebrew Education Society opened

**FIGURE 21.** St. Joseph's Polish Catholic Church, Camden, 1942. Polish families living in Camden came together to form St. Joseph's parish in 1892. In 1914, they moved to the building shown here. St. Joseph's History Society of South Camden. PHOTOGRAPH BY WILLIAM LANG.

a school to teach children English and marketable skills including carpentry, cigar making, and sewing. By 1908, New Jerusalem had four thousand residents and they remained an important component of this multiethnic community through the 1970s, when the last of the merchants left the area. Russian Jews also moved into North Philadelphia, where they replaced an earlier population of German Jews, who by the early 1900s had begun a migration from their original enclaves to other parts of Philadelphia including Logan, Parkside, Southwest Philadelphia, Strawberry Mansion, and Wynnefield.

As historian Caroline Golab has shown, Polish immigrants clustered throughout the city in small communities in Nicetown, Port Richmond, Bridesburg, and Manayunk, as well as in Conshohocken and Camden. In each of these communities they quickly constructed churches, parochial schools for their children, and networks of institutions and businesses. Many Polish immigrants who arrived in Philadelphia did not remain, but instead quickly traveled to other regions. With little experience in the type of work available in Philadelphia's textile and clothing industries, they often headed to places offering work they had done in Poland, such as coal mining in central and western Pennsylvania or labor in the steel mills, iron foundries, sugar and oil refineries, leather tanneries, and slaughterhouses in Chicago, Buffalo, Milwaukee, Cleveland, and Pittsburgh.

Although the vast majority of immigrants came from Europe during this period, the Chinese Exclusion Act of 1882 resulted in violence and intimidation in the western United States that drove Chinese immigrants to eastern cities, including Philadelphia. The beginnings of the city's Chinatown date to this era, when laundries and later restaurants and stores clustered in the area of Ninth and Race Streets. Newcomers also came from the Caribbean, although in fewer numbers than from Europe. In the 1890s immigrants from Cuba and Puerto Rico arrived on the same boats that carried sugar and tobacco grown in the islands, according to historian Victor Vázquez. These immigrants worked as cigar makers for firms including Bayuk Cigars, the largest manufacturer of cigars in the area. The Cubans who arrived in the 1890s brought with them experience and interest in the Cuba Libre movement that was working toward Cuban independence and set up political clubs to support the effort. Cigar making continued to offer employment opportunities in Philadelphia through the 1950s and drew additional newcomers as the industry declined in Florida, Cuba, and Puerto Rico.

Spanish speakers clustered in Northern Liberties, where they worked at the local small cigar factories and shopped at Marshall Street. The neighborhood resembled South Philadelphia and New York's Lower East Side in its density, ethnic diversity, economy, and civil society. To serve Spanish speakers, the Catholic Church established the Mission of the Miraculous Medal at Old Saint Mary's Church on Fourth Street as a place of worship and the home for weddings, baptisms, and holy communions. This and other community organizations would help receive the larger migration of Puerto Ricans and other Latino groups that followed after World War II.

Immigrants encountered increased hostility, prejudice, exploitation and violence in America in the early twentieth century. For example, Philadelphia newspapers once committed to praising the Italian immigrants increasingly criticized immigrants in the period leading to the restriction laws in 1924. Italians faced growing prejudice during the prohibition years when they came to represent organized crime and various "families" came to control narcotics rings, prostitution, bootlegging, and numbers writing in South Philadelphia. The Ku Klux Klan in Philadelphia boasted the third-largest number of initiations in any American city in the interwar years (thirty-five thousand) and targeted Italian immigrants because they were Catholic, foreign-born, and former or current subjects of a totalitarian regime. While upper-class nativists such as Henry Cabot Lodge drew distinctions between northern and southern Italians, the Klan attacked all Italians without discernment.

The Immigration Restriction Act of 1924, which exempted migrants from the Western Hemisphere, created opportunities for increased migration from Cuba and Puerto Rico. Cubans and Puerto Ricans found jobs and housing in working-class neighborhoods of Southwark, Spring Garden, and Northern Liberties, mixing with other ethnic groups who had been in these communities for generations. Latin American and Caribbean migrants of the early and mid-twentieth century also settled temporarily in the region for seasonal

TABLE 2. **PERCENTAGE OF FOREIGN-BORN POPULATION OF PHILADELPHIA, 1860–2020**

| YEAR | PERCENTAGE |
|---|---|
| 1860 | 28.9% |
| 1870 | 27.2% |
| 1880 | 24.1% |
| 1890 | 25.7% |
| 1900 | 22.8% |
| 1910 | 24.8% |
| 1920 | 22.0% |
| 1930 | 19.1% |
| 1940 | 15.1% |
| 1950 | 11.5% |
| 1960 | 8.9% |
| 1970 | 6.5% |
| 1980 | 6.4% |
| 1990 | 6.6% |
| 2000 | 9.0% |
| 2010 | 11.6% |
| 2020 | 14.3% |

SOURCE: U.S. Census; Pew Charitable Trusts.

agricultural work, often brought by labor recruiters. Some also traveled in the summer to Hammonton and other New Jersey farms to pick berries, tomatoes, and other crops.

Between 1870 and 1930, what had been a city and region of mainly northern Europeans and African Americans became a far more diverse metropolis of residents from eastern and southern Europe, Asia, Latin America, and the Caribbean. While anti-immigrant acts and sentiments persisted, immigrants and migrants, including African Americans from the South and Puerto Ricans, found ways to live and work together. Although statistically Philadelphia had a smaller percentage of immigrants than other cities, it is clear that the immigrant groups left an indelible imprint, which long continued to influence the region's people, places, and institutions.

## Italian Market

**Helen Tangires**

The Italian Market, in the Bella Vista neighborhood of South Philadelphia, became the popular name for the food shops and curbside stands on Ninth Street between Fitzwater and Wharton Streets, where merchants sold fresh produce, prepared foods, imported products, goods, and equipment for both household and commercial consumption. The market evolved as the principal food shopping hub for the Italian immigrants who began to settle South Philadelphia in large numbers at the end of the nineteenth century. Existing row houses on Ninth Street, formerly occupied by Irish, German, and Jewish residents, provided building stock of contiguous structures that were easily modified for family businesses, with stores at ground level and living spaces for relatives and boarders on the upper floors. Ninth Street grew rapidly as the commercial catalyst for the Italian community, as waves of new immigrants in the early twentieth century found the neighborhood to be a familiar cultural, architectural, and linguistic setting in which to live, work, and shop.

The commercial character of Ninth Street was secured in 1915, when the community's leading businessmen (second-generation Italian Americans with ancestral roots in central and southern Italy and eastern Sicily) formed the South Ninth Street Business Men's Association, whose mission was to promote commercial development on Ninth Street between Catharine and Federal Streets. The association received the privilege of incorporation from the Commonwealth of Pennsylvania in exchange for ensuring cleanliness, illumination, paving, and police protection within the boundaries specified in its charter. Ninth Street became an official curb market at a time when fear of food shortages and the high cost of living stimulated their popularity nationwide. Vendors sold from pushcarts, wagons, trucks, or sidewalk stands arranged in a linear fashion along a designated street. They offered an immediate and economical outlet for food products and related merchandise, without the need for specialized market buildings or intermediaries in the distribution process.

Formal establishment of the Ninth Street curb market was timely and progressive, for it secured a year-round market for fresh produce, imported goods, quick meals, restaurant supplies, processed foods, and household goods, all within close proximity to purveyors and customers. Customers remained devoted to the market's traditional character and product offerings, and during World War I the market helped to counter high food prices and shortages. As with other curb markets around the country, the relationship between the storekeepers and street vendors ranged from mutual cooperation to occasional hostility over territory, street cleaning, and trash removal.

By the 1940s commerce on Ninth Street was commonly known as the Italian Market, owing to the dominance of Italian-owned businesses and clientele. Merchandising proved central to its success. The linear arrangement of contiguous businesses with awnings appended to storefronts provided an uninterrupted covered sidewalk. The awnings, sometimes decorated with colorful patterns, protected buyers, sellers, and merchandise from the elements and created an attractive atmosphere where vendors could conduct open-air business through the year. Over the course of the twentieth century the Italian Market became a popular destination for street foods such as cheesesteaks, hoagies, pizza, Italian ice, and soft pretzels.

After World War II, following the broad pattern of assimilation and dispersion of other ethnic groups in the United States, the character of the Italian Market began

**FIGURE 22.** The Italian Market, S. Ninth Street, Philadelphia, n.d. PHOTOGRAPH BY R. KENNEDY FOR VISIT PHILADELPHIA.

to change. The traditional practice of living above one's shop disappeared, as subsequent generations dispersed and settled in other parts of the city, the suburbs, or in southern New Jersey. They either commuted to their shops or maintained their market real estate as landlords. The availability of commercial space for rent attracted new immigrant groups as tenants, marking a change in the ethnic composition of merchants. In 1983 the Italian Market introduced its first Korean-owned establishment at 1000 S. Ninth Street, and over the following decades a significant number of Vietnamese, Korean, Chinese, and Mexican businesses joined the traditional Italian shops. Some establishments featured their own ethnic cuisines, such as Korean barbecue and Vietnamese pho (noodle soup), while others catered to local residents with specialty gift shops and services.

In 2000 the city Planning Commission certified the S. Ninth Street area including the Italian Market as blighted. As a result, the Italian Market was slated for redevelopment in 2006, and the city and business community joined in a commercial revitalization initiative to improve sanitation and to rehabilitate the market stalls and awnings. The storefronts were maintained to reflect the individual tastes, trends, and upkeep of the vendors, with varied facades of red brick, yellow brick, faux stone, aluminum siding, and stucco. By the early 2000s the area built on the popularity of outdoor shopping, sidewalk dining, specialty food shops, and ethnic street festivals. Patrons included a varied clientele of local shoppers, gourmet cooks, restaurant suppliers, and tourists, all of whom were attracted to its special product offerings and ambience. It maintained its integrity as a commercial district with independent but interrelated businesses that shared similar merchandising strategies and a common identity as a place dedicated to Philadelphia's evolving food landscape.

## Chinatown

Kathryn Wilson

Settled by Chinese migrants in the 1870s, Philadelphia's Chinatown grew over the course of the twentieth century from a small ethnic enclave on the outskirts of Skid Row to a vibrant family community in the heart of Center City. Threatened by urban renewal in the 1960s and 1970s, Chinatown residents marshaled the redevelopment process to rebuild and expand their community over the course of the late twentieth century. This legacy of activism continued to inform struggles against gentrification and for affordable housing, education, and community self-determination. While Chinese and other Asian immigrants dispersed throughout the greater Philadelphia area, Chinatown remained as a central touchstone for Asian life in the region.

Philadelphia's Chinatown had its roots in the "great driving out" of Chinese from the American West in the 1870s and 1880s, when Chinese migrants fled racist backlash and violence. During these decades Chinese merchants and laundry men established a small enclave along the 900 block of Race Street, on the outskirts of the central business district. Excluded from the region's industrial worksites, Chinese immigrants were restricted to domestic service, laundry work, and small commercial ventures such as groceries and, later, restaurants.

Life in Chinatown at the turn of the twentieth century was structured around the spaces of shops, restaurants, communal boarding houses, and common rooms (or *fongs*). Social life largely focused on the many family and business associations, later consolidated under the umbrella of the Chinese Benevolent Association. Restrictive U.S. immigration laws such as the Chinese Exclusion Act of 1882 prevented all but merchants from bringing families, creating a hierarchical "bachelor society" of men living as single in extended kin arrangements. From the 1910s to the 1940s Chinese Americans expanded their presence around 900 Race, occupying adjacent blocks amid a multiethnic population, making a home amid the city's Skid Row to the east and "Tenderloin" district to the west. This community publicly manifested its ethnic character in enactments of Chinese identity such as funeral processions, political demonstrations, and New Year celebrations, all of which provided exotic spectacle for non-Chinese Philadelphians. On the other hand, Chinatown also gained visibility as a "nuisance" and deviant vice-ridden area. It was frequently raided by police in the early 1900s during the so-called "tong wars." Tongs were traditional Chinese associations adapted to serve business and social needs in America,

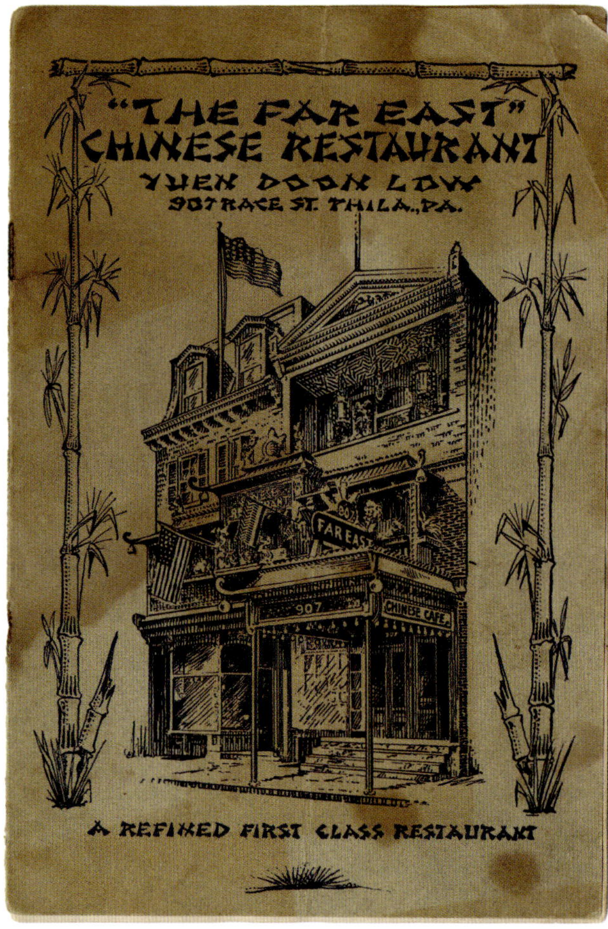


**FIGURE 23.** Menu for Yuen Doon Low restaurant, Ninth and Race Streets, Philadelphia, ca. 1920. A home for Chinese immigrants from the 1870s onward, Philadelphia's Chinatown introduced the wider community to the likes of Oolong tea and chicken chow mein. LIBRARY COMPANY OF PHILADELPHIA.

but they gained a criminal image informed by negative Orientalist stereotypes.

Liberalized immigration policies after World War II allowed Chinese Americans to bring wives from China. This initiated a new wave of immigration to Philadelphia that transformed Chinatown into a family-oriented community. Churches, businesses, and social/cultural organizations were established to improve neighborhood life, preserve Chinese culture, and provide services to the growing number of new immigrants. Holy Redeemer Chinese Catholic Church at Tenth and Vine Streets dates to this period, as does the Chinese Christian Church and Center at Tenth and Spring Streets. From 1940 to 1980, the boundaries of Chinatown expanded greatly north to Wood Street, south to Arch Street, and east-west from Eighth to Twelfth Street as this area became more or less exclusively Asian in character.

This growth of Chinatown coincided with emerging city plans, as early as 1945, for a crosstown expressway and other urban redevelopment projects in and around the neighborhood core. From the mid-1960s through the 1980s, urban renewal projects laid waste to each of Chinatown's borders. An expansion of Independence Mall closed off the eastern boundary, the Gallery/Market East mall the southern. Later in the 1980s the construction of the Convention Center occupied a western border on Eleventh Street. Most significantly, in 1966, Chinatown residents learned that the construction of an expressway along Vine Street would entail the destruction of the beloved Holy Redeemer Chinese Catholic Church and School. A young widow, Cecilia Moy Yep, began organizing residents to fight the expressway plan. With George Moy, Yep founded the Philadelphia Chinatown Development Corporation (PCDC) in 1969. PCDC was joined in the fight by the more traditional Chinese Benevolent Association and a radical student group, Yellow Seeds, whose Maoist and Black Power-influenced activism embraced the fight to save Chinatown as well as providing community services including a health clinic, newspaper, and breakfast programs. Yellow Seeds' slogan, "Same Struggle, Same Fight," linked the fight in Chinatown to the struggles of "Third World peoples" throughout the city and worldwide.

A turning point in the expressway battle came in July 1973, when a group of young people defied the demolition cranes and climbed up onto a pile of rubble at Tenth and Winter Streets to protest the destruction of houses in their neighborhood. The incident drew the attention of the local media (one television reporter joined the youth atop the pile). Using a variety of tactics, activists delayed the project for over a decade, allowing for modifications of the plan. Their success saved the church and launched new and more inclusive leadership in Chinatown.

The fight against the expressway also transformed Chinatown's relationship with the City of Philadelphia. In the mid-1970s PCDC collaborated with the City

Planning Commission on a study for Chinatown (the Chadbourne Report) that outlined redevelopment activities including new housing, streetscape improvements, and a senior center. Working through private/public partnerships from the 1970s to the present, PCDC completed various housing and mixed residential-commercial structures and an "authentic Chinese" Friendship Gate. Under the leadership of Reverend Yam Tong Hoh, of the Chinese Christian Church and Center, the community created On Lok House, a senior citizen residence and center. PCDC projects articulated a vision of a "living community" that emphasized housing, family, and community institutions "beyond the restaurants" and the neighborhood's status as a tourist destination.

To protect this vision of a "living community," Chinatown residents and supporters continued to mobilize against urban renewal schemes. In 1993, residents pushed back against a proposal for a federal prison near Holy Redeemer. In 2000, a complex coalition that included Asian and non-Asian Philadelphians organized to oppose a proposal for a baseball stadium at Twelfth and Vine Streets. This opposition aimed to protect Chinatown housing and community spaces adjacent to the stadium site and reaffirmed the cultural and historical significance of the neighborhood for the region as a whole.

The stadium fight also highlighted the importance of the area north of Vine Street—dubbed "Chinatown North"—for Chinatown's future. Chinatown North emerged as a site of neighborhood expansion beginning in the late 1990s, when PCDC located its offices and a housing development on Ninth Street north of Vine. The Chinese Christian Church and Center opened a new congregation on Vine Street in 2005. Other organizations such as Asian Americans United and the Asian Arts Initiative located their facilities north of Vine Street. Also in 2007, Asian Americans United opened the Folk Arts and Cultural Treasures Charter School, or FACTS, the first public school in Chinatown, in an empty factory at 1023 Callowhill Street. Chinatown North continued to be home to small-scale manufacturing and product warehousing ventures, serving as a "back end" for the Chinatown retail and restaurant sectors. Plans called for a new high-rise community center, known as Eastern Tower, for the historic corner of Tenth and Vine Streets, solidifying the historical significance of this area for the Chinatown community.

Chinatown continued to be a destination and launching point for new immigrants. After the Immigration and Nationality Act of 1965, which removed restrictions on immigration from Asia, the Greater Philadelphia area incorporated ongoing waves of immigration from China and other Asian nations. An influx of immigrants from Hong Kong led to the growth of Chinatown in the 1970s. In the 1980s, resettled refugees from Vietnam, many of them ethnic Chinese, diversified the population of Chinatown and created many new businesses. Most of the newcomers to Chinatown after the 1990s were Mandarin- or Fujianese-speaking immigrants from Fujian. Differences of language and custom presented challenges for local churches and organizations but the recent arrivals reanimated traditional customs and celebrations such as Chinese New Year and the Mid-Autumn Festival, celebrated each year in Chinatown. A new annual parade for the Hoyu Folk Culture Festival honored the founder of Fuzhou, the capital of Fujian Province in southeastern China.

In the twenty-first century, Chinatown embodied a pan-Asian identity, serving as a central touchstone for a larger cultural community of Asians around the greater Philadelphia area. Organizations such as Asian Americans United and the Asian Arts Initiative reflected this new pan-Asian focus. Chinatown remained predominantly Chinese American but had a significant population of Indian, Korean, Vietnamese, Filipino, and Japanese heritage, with smaller numbers of Indonesian, Malaysian, Cambodian, Pakistani, and Burmese residents. While Chinatown remained a primary entry point for arrivals from East and Southeast Asia, though, far more now lived across the wider region. New immigrants used Chinatown as a base, traveling to and from New York's Chinatown, an important source of labor and migration for greater Philadelphia. Local and regional immigrants from New Jersey and Pennsylvania came to Philadelphia's Chinatown on the weekends to shop, dine, attend events, and, on Sundays, go to church. Family banquets and other significant gatherings continued to occur in Chinatown, and a majority of traditional family, regional, and business associations remained located there. But Chinatown's workforce extended beyond those of Asian origin. Many restaurant workers, for example, hailed from Mexico or Central America.

Chinatown's small size and strong sense of history and community made it resilient. Nevertheless, the community remained vulnerable to larger outside forces. In the twenty-first century, gentrification presented an ongoing threat. New condominium developments occurred at a brisk rate, adapting old hotels and factories and leading to a dramatic threefold increase in home values. Renewed efforts to build a stadium in the vicinity also posed a challenge. Chinatown's residents and advocates continued to draw on a legacy of activism and struggle to develop the community and secure a future "beyond the restaurants."

## Fabric Row

**Danielle Podwats D'Amelio**

A textile and garment district emerged during the late nineteenth and early twentieth centuries on S. Fourth Street, between Catharine and Bainbridge Streets in South Philadelphia, as immigrants transformed the neighborhood into a Jewish quarter. Fabric businesses survived the Great Depression and remained prosperous for more than a century, employing generations of garment workers. Some shops continued to be active in the twenty-first century in the district that became known as Fabric Row.

In the 1880s, as part of a widespread and varied wave of immigration to the United States, Philadelphia became home to a large number of eastern European Jewish newcomers. The Jewish population increased significantly in 1905, when nine thousand Russian Jews arrived in Philadelphia following renewed pogroms against them in Russia. Moving into areas that later became known as Queen Village and Society Hill, these waves of immigrants created a Jewish quarter extending from Spruce Street in the north to Christian Street in the south, between Third and Sixth Streets. Fourth Street became the core of the Jewish community, while the perpendicular South Street became a diversified hub for immigrants of other ethnicities. Starting in the late nineteenth century, Fourth Street became known as "Der Ferder," meaning "the fourth" in Yiddish, and began to fill with fabric- and garment-related trades.

Initially, many immigrants worked as tailors or seamstresses in sweatshops or did sewing work at home, but during the first half of the twentieth century they also transitioned to peddling fabrics, dry goods, and produce from knapsacks or at curbside stands made from boards and sawhorses. The most prosperous peddlers sold goods from pushcarts, for which licenses could be purchased for $5.00 from city hall. By 1906, immigrant entrepreneurs operated hundreds of pushcarts on S. Fourth Street between Lombard and Carpenter Streets. Peddlers who could not afford to buy pushcarts had the option to rent them from wealthier businessmen who purchased licenses in bulk and rented them out for 25¢ per day or $1.50 per week.

Many fabric businesses on Fourth Street started as curbside stands or pushcarts, then moved into storefronts. Families played important roles in establishing and sustaining these businesses for decades. For example, Abraham Marmelstein, a Polish immigrant, entered the fabric industry in 1919 as a peddler selling needles and thread door-to-door. Eventually, he purchased a pushcart and, later, in 1937, a three-story row house on Fourth Street where he lived and ran his business with his wife, Dora, and family. The business passed down to succeeding generations, remaining in operation until 2015. Other family businesses—Paul's, Maxie's Daughter, and Albert Zoll's, among others—followed a similar pattern. S. Fourth Street became dominated by fabric- and garment-related trades (textiles, bridal, drapery, wallpaper) but also included kosher butcher shops and other grocery-related food shops (vegetable and fruit stands, fish and meat markets). The Famous Fourth Street Delicatessen, which opened in 1923 at Fourth and Bainbridge Streets, became a symbol of Jewish culture and prosperity, featured in films such as *Philadelphia* (1993) and *In Her Shoes* (2005).

As it grew, the Fourth Street business community weathered and responded to world events. In 1905, thousands of people marched on Fourth Street in mourning for the victims of the pogroms against Jews in Russia. In 1918, the worldwide influenza epidemic hit densely populated areas like Fourth Street especially hard. Many businesses voluntarily closed and helped distribute food and supplies to the needy. During the

Great Depression, fabric businesses on Fourth Street remained prosperous because people who could no longer afford to buy ready-made clothing from department stores purchased fabric to sew their own garb. Nevertheless, in 1933 merchants formed the South Fourth Street Business Men's Association to promote continued trade and address issues such as street sanitation, police security, and hours of operation. That same year Jewish Americans in the neighborhood came together to protest the anti-Semitism of Germany's new National Socialist regime.

The Second World War and its aftermath brought new challenges to Fourth Street. During the war, merchants found it difficult to keep their stores stocked as manufacturers constantly supplied the armed forces. To conserve electricity, all stores on Fourth Street closed early on Tuesdays and Thursdays. After the war, postwar trends of consumerism and movement from cities to suburbs added to the challenge. As demand for fabrics shifted to décor for new suburban homes, Fourth Street merchants adapted their merchandise to offer goods such as ready-made curtains. Some of the merchants themselves moved to the suburbs, still running their businesses on Fourth Street but no longer living above the store. With the increase of automobiles and demand for parking spaces, in 1955 a city ordinance brought an end to an era by banning pushcarts from Philadelphia streets.

Fabric Row adapted to such changes. Some Fourth Street businesses expanded to the wholesale market, while others extended their sales nationally. Internationally, Samuel Goldberg, of Sam Goldberg's Fabrics, traveled from the streets of Philadelphia to Europe, Latin America, and Asia to handpick fabric choices for his clients. Goldberg's personal touch and stylistic eye attracted the business of public figures like Jacqueline Kennedy and couture designers like Christian Dior. Nevertheless, Philadelphia's fabric businesses declined during the 1960s' controversy over the proposed Crosstown Expressway, which would have run through South and Bainbridge Streets. Shop owners and customers fled from Fourth Street to the suburbs in anticipation of demolition, and many of the businesses closed in the process.

In 1996, seeking to generate new publicity, businesses on S. Fourth Street formed a merchants association called Shops of Fabric Row, which led to the City of Philadelphia officially designating S. Fourth Street as "Fabric Row." By the early decades of the twenty-first century, however, fabric stores that had been open for generations, including Marmelstein's and Albert Zoll's fabric store, closed their doors. In 2018, eleven fabric stores remained open on Fabric Row, including Fleishman Fabrics and Supplies, Maxie's Daughter, and Valentia Fabrics. Over the course of its history, Fabric Row has been a culturally dense and rich center that has married history with innovation.

## Octavia Hill Association

**Anne E. Krulikowski**

The Octavia Hill Association of Philadelphia was founded in 1896 to provide clean dwellings at reasonable rents to some of the city's poorest residents, who were often exploited by profit-hungry landlords. Influenced by reformers abroad, and catering to immigrant and African American communities, the organization responded to changing conditions and housing needs in a fast-growing metropolis.

Despite Philadelphia's reputation as a "city of homes," by the late nineteenth century many back alleys and courtyards were overcrowded with two- and three-story dwellings. Such poor conditions, particularly in the Southwark vicinity of South Philadelphia, drew the attention of Progressive Era reformers who wanted to assist African American and immigrant residents. Hannah Fox and Helen C. Jenks, both members of the newly organized Civic Club of prominent women interested in the arts and social service, founded the Octavia Hill Association after attending a talk on slum conditions. These women, inspired by English reformer Octavia Hill, raised funds to purchase and renovate dwellings to be rented to families.

The two most important leaders of the association during its first several decades were Hannah Fox and her friend and cousin Helen Parrish. Both women were connected to the white, upper-class, and Quaker Parrish-Wharton family, which had a long tradition of social service. Fox and Parrish personally encountered the overcrowded and distressing conditions in South Philadelphia in the 1880s when they worked with Susan

**FIGURE 24.** Germantown Cricket Club, 1892. Brought over by English immigrants in the middle decades of the nineteenth century, cricket caught on in Philadelphia, and the region produced world-class players into the early 1900s. As baseball superseded the game in popularity, the Delaware Valley's Anglophile elite turned their cricket clubs into country clubs, but the game received a new lease of life in the twenty-first century with immigration from the Caribbean and South Asia. Boasting a new fan base, Philadelphia secured its first professional cricket franchise in 2021, and an estimated forty to fifty clubs played recreationally in the region. LIBRARY COMPANY OF PHILADELPHIA.

Parrish Wharton, founder of the St. Mary Street Library Association (1884). Susan, another of Helen's cousins, was the daughter of Susanna Wharton, a social activist and friend of Octavia Hill.

Following Hill's model, in 1888 Fox purchased two houses on St. Mary's Street (now Rodman Street) and with Parrish refurbished and rented them to African American families. That same year, Parrish visited Hill in London for six months to observe her methods. Two decades earlier, with the encouragement of social critic John Ruskin, Hill had purchased several London houses to rent at fair prices to poor families. She established the pattern of housing reform known as "five percent philanthropy" (sometimes described as "four percent philanthropy"), combining philanthropy with limited profit to investors. Hill, who believed in the power of the physical environment to shape human values and attitudes, hoped that purchasing and renovating clusters of dwellings would create a sense of community and provide an example to surrounding neighborhoods. "Friendly rent collectors" would visit tenants each month to instill thrift and responsibility.

The Philadelphia reformers who named their association for Octavia Hill shared her belief in the power of environment and example; like her, they also rejected public subsidies (as noneducative) and, at first, multifamily housing. In 1911, Parrish argued that the single-family home in the form of the small row house was the "better method of housing, the only method that ultimately will offer a solution of the great housing problem." To both purchase and renovate was expensive, so the association also renovated and managed properties for other owners. Tenants were expected to contribute both rent and their own effort to maintain the renovated dwelling. The Philadelphians were not as rigid as Hill about tenants meeting rent payments, but some workers attempted to intervene in their tenants' behaviors. Contrary to Hill's recommendations, some settlement workers rented accommodation from the association and often served as "friendly rent collectors" themselves.

The association's first properties were located in densely inhabited neighborhoods either side of South Street that ran from the Delaware to the Schuylkill. This included the Seventh Ward, with a population that was about 30 percent African American by the 1890s, which W. E. B. Du Bois made famous in his study *The Philadelphia Negro* (1899), and the crowded Third Ward, predominantly inhabited by Italian immigrants. The growing housing problem and the high costs of purchase and renovation prompted association members to reconsider the use of multifamily dwellings and undertake the management of Casa Ravello. This four-story tenement, located on Seventh Street between Catherine and Fulton Streets, housed thirty-three Italian families.

The Octavia Hill Association soon expanded its activities to other areas of the city, including Germantown, Kensington, and Manayunk. In 1915, a new division, the Philadelphia Model Homes Company, built a group of one- and two-family courtyard town houses in Port Richmond. By 1929, the association owned or managed a total of 450 housing units.

From its founding, the association worked closely with settlement houses, the School of Social Work at the University of Pennsylvania, and the Philadelphia Housing Commission (later Association, then the Housing Association of the Delaware Valley) to pursue a common goal of improving living conditions in the city. Although mainly focused on day-to-day property management, the association also commissioned Emily Wayland Dinwiddie to study housing conditions in three South Philadelphia wards. Detailed information from this 1903 survey allowed association members to move beyond friendly visiting and piecemeal reform to fight for effective housing legislation. One success was the Tenement Inspection Law of 1907.

The scope of the association's activities changed in the twentieth century as municipal regulation increased, the federal government became involved in public housing projects, and immigration restrictions in the 1920s led to a decline in the city's foreign-born population. These factors, combined with problems meeting stockholder dividends, spurred a change of direction: after World War II, the Octavia Hill Association incorporated as a real estate management company that managed both luxury and affordable housing in many areas of the city. In the last two decades of the twentieth century, the Octavia Hill Association built housing in North Philadelphia and Point Breeze, some for ownership rather than for rental.

## Settlement Houses

**Rosina McAvoy Ryan**

The settlement house movement, a phenomenon of the Progressive Era with origins in London, spread to Philadelphia in the 1890s as a large influx of needy immigrants and unsanitary conditions in the city attracted the attention of middle-class, college-educated reformers. Living among the poor in South Philadelphia, Kensington, and other neighborhoods, settlement house residents sought to improve area living conditions. In the process, they also created new roles for women in a changing society.

The settlement house movement began in London in 1884 when Samuel Barnett and his wife, Henrietta Barnett, opened Toynbee Hall "to live as neighbors of the working poor." The volunteers who settled in the neighborhood and lived in the settlement house differentiated the movement from a mission or a school. Stanton Coit brought the movement to New York City's Lower East Side in 1886. Three years later, Jane Addams and Ellen Gates Starr established what would become the nation's most well-known settlement, Hull-House in Chicago. These were among the first of hundreds of social settlements established in the United States during the Progressive Era.

Settlement residents were typically middle-class college graduates. Many were inspired by the Social Gospel movement, which emphasized Christian responsibility for addressing urban problems. The

**FIGURE 25.** Women in a settlement house feeding young Jewish immigrants, ca. 1900. SPECIAL COLLECTIONS RESEARCH CENTER, TEMPLE UNIVERSITY LIBRARIES.

headworker was salaried; other residents paid room and board. Men participated in the movement, but women comprised the majority of settlement workers. Female settlement residents were "new women" who revolted against the prevailing values of domesticity by gaining independence and finding personal satisfaction through "municipal housekeeping"—improving conditions outside the home.

Between 1870 and 1920, a period of high immigration, Philadelphia's population doubled with many of the newcomers confined to crowded, unventilated row homes that lined putrid streets. Responding to those conditions, the St. Mary Street College Settlement opened in 1892, changing its name in October 1893 to the College Settlement of Philadelphia. Motivated by the housing reform efforts of the Octavia Hill Association, members of the St. Mary Street Library Executive Committee, including the prosperous philanthropist Susan P. Wharton, contacted Vida Dutton Scudder, the Wellesley English professor who was the main impetus behind the College Settlements Association (CSA). Wharton and her associates offered the house at 617 St. Mary Street, near South Street, and agreed to cosponsor a settlement with the CSA. As the first settlement in Philadelphia, the College Settlement became known as "the Settlement."

Scudder intended that CSA houses would enable women college graduates to apply the knowledge learned in economics and sociology classes while interacting with the urban poor. Consequently, the College Settlement offered graduate-level courses in economics and sociology and training in social work prior to the 1898 opening of the New York Summer School of Philanthropic Work, the first recognized school for social work education in the United States. Located in one of the oldest and most destitute African American neighborhoods in Philadelphia, the College Settlement was established exclusively to aid African Americans. In 1896, the settlement house, encouraged by Wharton, collaborated with the University of Pennsylvania to sponsor sociological studies of African Americans in the Seventh Ward by W. E. B. Du Bois and Isabel Eaton. Arriving in August 1896, Du Bois and his wife, Nina, lived in the College Settlement's kitchen and coffeehouse/library building at 701 Lombard Street for one year while he conducted his research.

When the city demolished all of the houses on the 600 block of Rodman Street (formerly St. Mary Street) in 1899 to expand Starr Garden Playground, College Settlement was forced to move. Instead of heading west across Broad Street and remaining with African Americans, it moved east to 431 and 433 Christian Street because Scudder and the CSA encouraged relocating to a more ethnically diverse neighborhood. College Settlement's "Visiting Nurse Report for October 1899 to October 1900" indicated that diversity. The 489 patients included 216 native-born Americans, 105 Italians, 70 Russians, 57 Germans, 19 African Americans, 9 Irish, 7 Polish, 2 Hungarians, and one from each of the following: England, France, Scotland, and Wales. Opposed to the move to Christian Street because of her life-long dedication to African Americans, Wharton resigned from College Settlement and opened Starr Centre at what had been the settlement's kitchen/library building at Seventh and Lombard. She later opened Whittier Centre for Black people in North Philadelphia. Renamed the Susan Parrish Wharton Settlement after her death in 1928, the settlement continued in the twenty-first century as the Wharton Centre at 1708–10 N. Twenty-Second Street.

By 1911, Philadelphia had twenty-one settlements. Most were in South Philadelphia, but others opened in other neighborhoods, including two in Kensington: The Lighthouse, founded in 1893 at 153 W. Lehigh Avenue, and the Lutheran Settlement House founded in 1902 at 1340 Frankford Avenue. In addition to collaborating to alleviate squalid living conditions among the poor, the settlements supplemented public school Americanization efforts with programs in citizenship, civics, and hygiene. Classes for adults included literacy, cooking, childcare, nutrition, housekeeping, and carpentry.

**FIGURE 26.** Florence Kelley, ca. 1910–16. The Philadelphia-born daughter of Radical Republican congressman William Darrah Kelley, Florence Kelley became an internationally renowned social reformer. On her travels to Europe, she befriended Karl Marx's collaborator Friedrich Engels and translated his *Condition of the Working Class in England* into English in 1887. After returning to the United States, she enlisted in the settlement house movement and fought for women's suffrage, Black civil rights, and better working conditions. In Philadelphia, she helped found the New Century Guild (headquartered at Thirteenth and Locust Streets from 1907), which aimed to improve conditions for working women. Kelley then became a founding member of the National Association for the Advancement of Colored People (NAACP) in 1909. LIBRARY OF CONGRESS.

The settlement movement declined after World War I as more career and employment opportunities opened to women college graduates, and settlement houses that continued to operate abolished the residency requirement. Social work became professionalized, and settlements achieved many of the reforms they had worked for, such as kindergartens, playgrounds, truant officers, juvenile courts, visiting nurses, maternity and childcare, and street cleaning and paving. Despite these changes, the organizations left a strong institutional legacy, and the Lighthouse, the Lutheran Settlement, and the College Settlement—alongside several neighborhood centers with roots in settlement work—remained active in the city and region into the twenty-first century. With its late nineteenth-century origins across the Atlantic, the settlement movement became a long-serving provider of American social services in Philadelphia and its surroundings.

## Mummers

Christian DuComb

The Mummers Parade, an institution in Philadelphia since 1901, brought together many of the loosely organized groups of folk performers who roamed the streets each year between Christmas Eve and New Year's Day. Known variously as mummers, shooters, belsnickles, fantasticals, and callithumpians, these masqueraders traced their roots to immigrants from England, Sweden, and Germany who introduced mumming to prerevolutionary Philadelphia. Throughout much of northern Europe and colonial North America, groups of mummers roved from house to house during the Christmas season, entertaining their hosts and expecting food, drink, or a small tip in return. Mumming and belsnickling in southeastern Pennsylvania persisted into the 1800s, not only in Philadelphia but also in smaller cities like Easton, Lancaster, Pottstown, and Reading.

Most nineteenth-century mummers were young, working-class men, and their street-side antics could be raucous. According to the *Philadelphia Public Ledger*, New Year's Day 1876 witnessed impromptu parades by men dressed as "Indians and squaws, princes and princesses, clowns . . . [and] Negroes of the minstrel hall type." Philadelphia's new, central police force eventually cracked down on unruly holiday celebrations, and H. Bart McHugh—a newspaper reporter and theatrical agent—led the effort to bring the mummers to Broad Street for an organized parade, with prizes funded by the city. In 1901 the City of Philadelphia sponsored the first official Mummers Parade, and the *Public Ledger* reported that "three thousand men and boys in outlandish garb frolicked, cavorted, grimaced, and whooped while the Mayor and members of Councils, Judges, and other officials, State and municipal, looked on." From the beginning, most mummers clubs specialized in comedy, music, costume, or dance, leading to an elaborate structure for judging a varied assortment

**FIGURE 27.** An unidentified reveler in the Mummers Parade, 1924. Tracing its origins to Christmas festivities of northern Europe and colonial North America, the New Year's Day Mummers Parade, which first took place in 1901, became a raucous, burlesque day of celebration for the region's white ethnic residents. HISTORICAL SOCIETY OF PENNSYLVANIA.

of parade performances that included clowning, string bands, elaborate costumes, burlesque impersonation (the "wenches"), and Broadway-style staging and choreography. Until World War II, a plurality of mummers hailed from South Philadelphia, especially from the neighborhood's Irish American and Italian American enclaves. Kensington and Port Richmond were also well represented in the early twentieth-century Mummers Parade, and beginning in the 1950s, mummers clubs sprang up throughout the region, especially in Northeast Philadelphia and the New Jersey suburbs.

African American mummers regularly competed for prizes on Broad Street between 1901 and 1929, and African American composer James Bland wrote the parade's unofficial theme song, "Oh, Dem Golden Slippers." However, the mummers in later years developed a reputation for racial insensitivity. Many mummers marched in blackface makeup until the city banned the practice following civil rights protests organized by Cecil B. Moore and the Philadelphia chapter of the NAACP in 1963. In the early decades of the twenty-first century, blackface still appeared at the nighttime party on "Two Street" after the official parade, and both the burlesque wench costume and the mummers' strut (the signature dance step of the parade) originated on the minstrel-show stage. In 2013 the Joseph A. Ferko String Band celebrated the mummers' connection to minstrelsy with a controversial parade routine titled "Bringin' Back Those Minstrel Days," performed in brown rather than black makeup to avoid censure by the judges.

Despite its troubled racial history, the Mummers Parade grew considerably more diverse and inclusive after 1963. In the 1970s most mummers clubs began admitting women as performers for the first time. Women had long worked behind the scenes, helping to stitch the mummers' costumes, and one woman—a newspaper reporter named Laura Lee—snuck into the parade in 1929. In 1984 the Goodtimers Comic Club, with an African American president and hundreds of minority members, started competing in the parade. And in 1992 a group of Cambodian American artists and students teamed up with the Golden Sunrise Fancy Brigade to stage a Khmer dance drama on Broad Street. At the behest of the Philadelphia Human Relations Commission, the 2016 Mummers Parade included a new, noncompeting unit called the Philadelphia Division, organized with the explicit goal of making the parade more diverse. Participants included a Mexican American carnival organization, an African American drill team, a Puerto Rican bomba group, and a brigade of drag queens. Although most mummers clubs embraced the growing diversity of the parade, reports of individual marchers using racist and homophobic slurs along the parade route complicated efforts to make the Mummers Parade more inclusive.

Despite challenges from cuts to public funding and the closure or consolidation of clubs, the mummers maintained a strong record of resilience into the new millennium. Since 1901 the Mummers Parade has been canceled only thrice, in 1919, 1934, and due to the COVID-19 pandemic in 2021. To adapt, though, the parade route has changed at various points. In 2015, for instance, it reversed course to begin at the city hall judging stand and proceeded southward along Broad Street. (The wenches opted out of this route change, insisting on a traditional northward march). This literal change in direction reduced the gaps between performances at popular viewing spots in Center City, boosting the size of the crowds and demonstrating the mummers' willingness to adapt to the evolving tastes—and shortening attention spans—of the twenty-first century.

## Immigration, 1930 to Present

**Daniel Amsterdam AND Domenic Vitiello**

For most of the decades since the United States' immigration restriction acts of the 1920s, Philadelphia was not a major destination for immigrants, but at the end of the twentieth century the region reemerged as a significant gateway. Beginning with changes in U.S. law in 1965 and accelerating by the 1990s, immigration added large, diverse groups of newcomers to the city and suburbs. Immigrants and refugees dramatically altered the region's economic, social, and political life and its geography of race and ethnicity. While the city and region remained more Black and white than the global cities of New York, Los Angeles, or Miami, newcomers from Asia, Latin America, the Caribbean,

Africa, and eastern Europe significantly diversified the population of Greater Philadelphia.

During and after World War II, with limited foreign migration, internal migrations transformed the city and region. From the 1940s through the '80s, two major demographic trends—the Second Great Migration of African Americans and mass suburbanization of the region's white population—were joined by a third smaller, but significant, development: the Great Migration of Puerto Ricans. Between 1940 and 1980, the nine-county region's Black population grew from 330,000 to more than one million. The Puerto Rican population expanded from 3,000 in 1950 to almost 55,000 in 1980, and by 2010 to more than 120,000, the second-largest Puerto Rican population in the country, behind only New York. As U.S. citizens, Puerto Ricans are not an immigrant group, but as migrants to the mainland they became the largest group of newcomers to Philadelphia since the 1920s whose first language was not English.

Puerto Ricans and African Americans settled mainly in the old row house neighborhoods in Philadelphia, Camden, and working-class suburbs like Norristown, places earlier immigrants and their children left in the post–World War II era. Unlike earlier generations, however, the new migrants entered a region whose manufacturing economy crashed in the 1950s through the '80s, as the jobs that had sustained these communities disappeared. Socially, economically, and spatially, in this period the region became a different destination for new immigrants. Although the federal government reopened the borders with new immigration regulations in 1965, immigrant settlement in Philadelphia intensified and diversified only after 1980 and to a greater extent after 1990. New immigrants came from a much wider range of countries outside of Europe, with large numbers of Indians, Mexicans, Southeast Asians, Africans, Chinese, and Koreans in the city and suburbs. They entered a new regional economy, with the bulk of jobs dispersed in the suburbs, including high-paid posts in service and scientific sectors like health care, higher education, finance, computers, and pharmaceuticals. These jobs attracted well-educated immigrants, while working-class immigrants found employment in food and domestic service and other low-wage jobs. Such trends marked significant changes in immigration to the region and nation, as the newcomers of the post-1965 era were far more diverse socially and economically than the working-class immigrants from Europe that preceded them a century earlier.

Immigrants to late twentieth-century Philadelphia entered a low-immigration region struggling with deindustrialization and racial polarization. When new immigrants began to arrive in sizable numbers in the early 1980s, they did not immediately follow local jobs to the suburbs. Instead, most initially settled in the old, economically debilitated urban core. They found a city divided sharply between Black and white with a small but growing Latino population, primarily Puerto Rican, and an old Chinatown struggling to survive urban renewal. Almost exclusively white suburbs encircled the city. Yet many of the less upwardly mobile descendants of old immigrants remained in the city, vying, sometimes violently, with Blacks for power, turf, and the political upper hand. For new immigrants, the precipitous fall in the city's population that coincided with deindustrialization provided readily available housing, but often amid racial and economic tension.

Such was the case for the many Southeast Asian refugees resettled in Philadelphia after the Vietnam War. The resettlement agencies tended to find open housing in borderland areas, where the combination of gentrification and job loss had already pushed lower-income residents out. Vietnamese, Cambodian, and other Southeast Asian refugees in Philadelphia often found themselves wedged between struggling African American communities and significantly wealthier neighborhoods. Settled in West Philadelphia, in North Philadelphia's Olney and Logan sections, and in South Philadelphia, refugees struggled to make an already difficult cultural adjustment amid existing Black-white racial animosity and economic tension. The consequences of life in these borderlands were harsh. According to the Philadelphia Commission on Human Relations, Asian Philadelphians comprised roughly a quarter of the victims of interracial violence reported in the city in the late 1980s; at the time, Asians comprised only 3 to 5 percent of the city's total population. A small group of Hmong refugees from Laos resettled in Philadelphia faced such adversity that they fled the city, mostly for established Hmong settlements in Minnesota

**FIGURE 28.** Worshippers entering Muhahideen Mosque, 1914 W. Columbia Avenue, 1973. African Americans accounted for most of Philadelphia's Muslim community in the decades after World War II, but increasing immigration from the Middle East spurred the establishment of new mosques across the region. SPECIAL COLLECTIONS RESEARCH CENTER, TEMPLE UNIVERSITY LIBRARIES.

and Wisconsin. Yet most Southeast Asian refugees in Philadelphia persisted, increasingly leaving West Philadelphia for South Philadelphia and East Camden, where working-class Cambodians and Vietnamese began to concentrate. Middle-class Vietnamese families more often moved to suburbs like Upper Darby and Cherry Hill.

By 1990 Koreans also made up a sizable proportion of Asian immigrants in Philadelphia, illustrating different conditions of migration but also some similarities in settlement experiences. Middle-class Koreans, frustrated with opportunities in their own country, took advantage of the 1965 immigration law's skills-based employment preference system. Others obtained professional training in the United States and remained in the area. Once settled, Korean immigrants sponsored their relatives' visa petitions, a broad pattern shared with other immigrants. Many Koreans with high levels of education struggled to transfer their credentials or to overcome an initial language barrier and hence gravitated toward small business ownership rather than professional jobs, often experiencing considerable downward mobility for a time.

Korean entrepreneurs helped sustain commercial districts in North Philadelphia, West Philadelphia, Germantown, and the old streetcar suburb of Upper Darby. In each of these areas, Korean store owners did business with the region's working-class, especially African American, populations. And like in other cities, where Black-Korean tensions boiled over into violence, conflict sometimes defined relations in Philadelphia. Yet the relationships between Korean store owners and their clients, as elsewhere, were most often defined by tolerance and civility. In addition to these store owners, a considerable number of working-class Koreans also migrated to the city, often through family sponsorship. Most worked in the local garment industry, in laundries, or in small stores, frequently employed at Korean- or Chinese-owned enterprises. Many remained in the city, but more moved to the suburbs of Delaware County, Cheltenham, or North Wales and nearby towns in central Montgomery County. From the 1990s onward, Dominicans and Arabs bought and ran a large portion of Koreans' inner-city stores.

Also fueling the growth, diversification, and suburbanization of the immigrant population in Philadelphia, a diverse mix of immigrants and refugees arrived from Africa, hailing from over thirty countries, with Liberia and Nigeria the largest groups in the region. Highly educated Africans began arriving soon after the 1965 immigration law was passed, and many went on to sponsor the migration of family members. Beginning in the 1980s and continuing in the new millennium, first Ethiopian and Eritrean refugees, and then people displaced by wars in Liberia, Sierra Leone, Somalia, and Sudan, settled in the metropolitan area. Most came from large African cities and settled in West and Southwest Philadelphia, Delaware and Newcastle Counties, Trenton, and later Northeast Philadelphia.

Black immigrants and refugees further illustrated the complexity of newcomers' diversity of experiences. Although African immigrants to the United States had the highest educational attainment of any other immigrant group, many struggled to transfer their credentials to the United States. Africans in Philadelphia established employment niches in nursing homes, home health care for elders, parking lots, and taxi service. African and Caribbean immigrants and refugees largely settled in Black neighborhoods, suffering most of the same ill effects of segregation and discrimination as their African American neighbors. Many Liberians, Sierra Leoneans, and Haitians were periodically granted temporary protected status, meaning the U.S. government expected them to ultimately return to their countries, adding to an already diverse range of legal statuses. Pan-African organizing and civil society, however, succeeded in forging a politics of shared prosperity by the early twenty-first century, partly in response to violence between young native and immigrant Blacks.

Joining Black immigrants in reinforcing Black-white segregation were eastern Europeans who settled in the 1980s and '90s especially in the predominantly Jewish sections of Northeast Philadelphia and surrounding suburbs. Many arrived as refugees from the USSR, Russia, and Ukraine. Poles settled in the old Polish enclave of Port Richmond. Albanian Muslims were resettled in Fishtown and South Kensington, overlapping a small Palestinian enclave that had formed after the Yom Kippur War in 1973.

In the 1990s, Indian and Mexican immigrants finally supplanted Italians and Germans as the largest foreign-born groups in the region, as Greater Philadelphia experienced more substantial and diverse immigration that continued into the early twenty-first century. Mexican settlement in South Philadelphia and Norristown provided labor for the downtown and suburban service economies, including the Center City restaurant scene and regional construction boom. The region's South Asian population, predominantly Indian, mostly came for middle-class jobs and higher education, settling in Northeast Philadelphia, King of Prussia, and other suburbs. Some working-class Indians and Bangladeshis also settled in West Philadelphia and Millbourne, a tiny borough in Delaware County and the first majority-Indian municipality in the United States. Chinese immigration in this era also included both professionals and members of the working classes, who lived in the historic downtown Chinatown and "satellite Chinatowns" in Cherry Hill and South and Northeast Philadelphia. Like Africans, these groups illustrated the bifurcation of immigrants' economic and residential experiences in the late twentieth century.

By 2000, the map of foreign-born population in the region illustrated major centers and corridors of settlement. Higher-income immigrants clustered along the Route 202 corridor with its concentration of jobs in pharmaceuticals and other technology sectors, running from the suburbs of Trenton west across

**FIGURE 29.** Baptism at the Ethiopian Orthodox Church, Southwest Philadelphia, 2000. The Delaware Valley's Ethiopian community grew in the 1970s and 1980s, and by 2000 about four thousand to five thousand lived in the region, especially in West Philadelphia and Upper Darby. HISTORICAL SOCIETY OF PENNSYLVANIA. PHOTOGRAPH BY VERA VIDITZ-WARD.

Bucks and Montgomery Counties, and turning south through Chester County to the suburbs of Wilmington in Newcastle County. Super-diverse, "global neighborhoods" had emerged in South and Upper North Philadelphia and in Upper Darby just west of the city. Since the 1980s a Mexican community helped sustain Kennett Square in southern Chester County as the world capital of mushroom production, as well as agriculture in Bridgeton, Vineland, and other parts of South Jersey.

The 2010 census revealed Philadelphia had gained population for the first time since the 1950s, propelled mainly by immigration, which also helped reverse population loss in Norristown and other older suburbs and towns. According to a Brookings Institution report of 2008, among similar metropolitan areas Philadelphia had "the largest and fastest growing immigrant population," with 9 percent of the region's people foreign-born. Many immigrants moved to the area after originally having settled elsewhere in the United States, especially the New York region. They often chose Greater Philadelphia because the price of property and opportunities for starting businesses compared favorably to other major urban centers. Demographic growth continued into the 2010s.

In the early twenty-first century, Greater Philadelphia also became a national center of immigration debates and movements. Beginning

**FIGURE 30.** Good Friday procession, St. Thomas Aquinas Catholic Church, Seventeenth and Morris Streets, Philadelphia, 2003. Reflecting the diversity of its South Philadelphia neighborhood, the church in the early 2020s held services in English, Spanish, Vietnamese, and Indonesian. HISTORICAL SOCIETY OF PENNSYLVANIA.

in spring 2001 the city had a "sanctuary" policy of protecting unauthorized immigrants by forbidding local police from asking for immigration papers. In 2003, Norristown passed a law recognizing the Mexican consular identification card for access to municipal services and banks. On February 14, 2006, Independence Mall was the site of the first "Day Without an Immigrant" rally of mainly Mexican restaurant workers. By that spring, headlines juxtaposed large immigrant-rights marches against disputes over an "English only" sign in the storefront window of the city's famous Geno's Steaks. That summer and fall, first the town of Hazleton in the Poconos, then Riverside, New Jersey, and then Bridgeport, Pennsylvania, passed "illegal immigration relief acts" to punish landlords and employers of unauthorized immigrants. Riverside repealed its act when it saw people leave, local businesses suffer, and the township receive negative national press. Anti-immigration activism continued into the 2010s.

In some ways such dynamics of newcomer settlement and debates over immigration recall the era of mass European immigration a century earlier, though much about the new immigration of the 1990s onward was indeed new. For example, the experiences of Mexican immigrants resembled those of earlier generations of Italians, from their roles as low-paid laborers in booming food and construction industries to the fear they encountered among receiving communities about housing overcrowding and integration. Yet the legal status of many new working-class immigrants was quite different, partly since immigration restrictions barely existed for Europeans prior to 1924. Receiving communities' politics of immigration remained fragmented and polarized, yet their responses took new forms. Moreover, newcomers of the early twenty-first century settled in a region with new geographies and structures of opportunity. Finally, the newest immigration was more diverse than older eras of immigration, in every way. It began to push Philadelphia and many of its suburbs beyond the Black-white binary of their twentieth-century population and neighborhood identities.

## Cheesesteaks

**Dianna Marder**

A cheesesteak is a sandwich unlike any John Montagu, the fourth Earl of Sandwich, might have encountered. Made up of thin bits of frizzled beef served on a locally made Italian roll, usually topped with fried onions and Cheez Whiz, the Philly cheesesteak offers insights into how immigration and its opponents have shaped the city and contributed to a national American cuisine.

Cheesesteaks originated in 1930 as steak sandwiches, the cheese part coming later. The undisputed creators, Harry Olivieri and his brother Pat, ran a hot dog stand in South Philadelphia. One day, weary of eating their own dogs for lunch, they grilled some sliced beef with onions instead. Before either could take a bite, a passing cab driver offered five cents for the sandwich and declared it better than their hot dogs.

The brothers Olivieri did not make the steak sandwich their main attraction until 1940 when they opened Pat's King of Steaks on Passyunk Avenue, where it intersects with Ninth and Wharton Streets. They did not initially add cheese because many of their customers in the neighborhood were Jewish and dietary laws barred them from eating meat and cheese together. But after Kraft introduced Cheez Whiz in 1952, Pat Olivieri realized he could simply take the lid off the industrial-size can, put the whole can on the grill to cook, and add cheese to some steaks without tainting the grill for his kosher customers. When Joey Vento opened Geno's across the street from Pat's in 1966, he acknowledged the Olivieris invented the cheesesteak, but insisted he made it better. The sandwich spread across the city, but the intersection of Ninth, Wharton, and Passyunk remained the center of the cheesesteak universe. The Philly cheesesteak made national news in 2005 when Geno's owner Joey Vento fed the national debate on immigration by posting a sign telling customers, "This is America—When Ordering Speak English." The open-air food market that ran north from Vento's store, known for decades as the Italian Market, had by then attracted newer immigrants from Southeast Asia and Latin America. While Vento appeared on national television programs hosted by conservatives Glenn Beck and Lou Dobbs, the Philadelphia Commission on Human

GENO'S
STEAKS
THE
Best
GENO'S STEAKS
CHEESE FRIES
ROAST PORK
STEAKS
GENOS

**FIGURE 31.** Geno's Steaks, Ninth Street and Passyunk Avenue, Philadelphia, 2019. CAROL M. HIGHSMITH ARCHIVE, LIBRARY OF CONGRESS.

Relations charged him with discrimination. Vento ultimately was exonerated of the antidiscrimination charge and said at the time that if his family took the trouble to learn English, recent arrivals should as well. He passed away in 2011, and under the ownership of his son, the sign was removed in 2016, around the time Donald Trump ate there during his presidential campaign. He was not the first candidate for the White House to pay homage to the iconic sandwich. The 2004 Democratic nominee John Kerry faced ridicule after he ordered a cheesesteak with Swiss rather than the acceptable Whiz, American, or provolone at Pat's.

The city's claim to cheesesteak fame is recognized nationwide. Some high-end steakhouses developed gourmet versions of the lowly cheesesteak. In 2004, restaurateur Stephen Starr introduced a Kobe beef version at his Barclay Prime restaurant priced at an even one hundred dollars. Starr later replaced that version with a Wagyu ribeye beef cheesesteak topped with foie gras, truffles, and fontina on a ciabatta roll. Even if those stylized versions are tasty, they miss the crucial point politicians reach for when they order a Philly cheesesteak. It is about connecting with everyday people.

## Nationalities Service Center

**Andrew McNally**

The Philadelphia branch of the International Institute, renamed the Philadelphia Nationalities Service Center in 1963, opened in June 1922 and initially operated under the auspices of its sponsor, the Young Women's Christian Association (YWCA). Like the four to five dozen other International Institute branches in operation by the 1920s, the Philadelphia organization aided immigrant women in learning English, developing employment skills, and navigating the naturalization process. In the 1930s, the group incorporated independently of the YWCA and expanded its focus to include men and families. After World War II, the branch increasingly turned its attention to fostering and moderating community discussion about race and culture and helping to resettle thousands of refugees to the Greater Philadelphia area.

Often compared with settlement houses, which shared similar aims and originated at similar times, the International Institutes were founded in 1910 in New York City by social worker Edith Terry Bremer. Historian Kristin Hoganson has argued that the institutes represented a part of the "immigrant gifts" movement in which, like settlement houses, nonimmigrant whites appropriated the folk traditions of immigrants to celebrate a vision of pluralism and acculturation. Institute branches sponsored folk festivals, internationality dinners, and other programming that celebrated immigrant folk traditions (and, to some degree, the modern scientific and cultural innovations that immigrants contributed to the United States).

While the institute began as a social organization for immigrant women, it soon offered courses in English and, with the advent of restrictive immigration quotas under the National Origins Act of 1924, began casework assisting young immigrant women in understanding and completing the naturalization process. Such efforts were not without the paternalist assumptions of almost all Progressive Era, white-organized immigration services. But by 1929, the institute had caseworkers who spoke Russian, Czech, Armenian, Italian, Polish, and German; by 1933, staff and volunteer interpreters spoke over a dozen languages, including Hindi, Armenian, Portuguese, Polish, Arabic, and Greek.

Immigrants came to the International Institute to develop employment, social, and naturalization strategies. Institute caseworkers also often aided them in navigating legal and bureaucratic obstacles. For example, the institute helped a young man born in Turkey secure permanent residency after he faced deportation because his father's marriage, and therefore his own citizenship, had been declared illegal. In performing its work, the institute frequently collaborated with Jewish, Catholic, Quaker, and Protestant social service agencies in the city, but it claimed to be the first nonsectarian organization of its type to serve Philadelphia.

During the Second World War, the U.S. government commissioned the Philadelphia International Institute to help immigrants comply with the Smith Act (Alien Registration Act) of 1940. When Pennsylvania prevented immigrants who had not declared their intentions to naturalize from obtaining welfare, the institute offered funds for immigrants to initiate the naturalization process. Similarly, naturalized immigrants needing documentation to work for defense contractors frequently came to the organization to help.

Before and after the war, immigrants (and nonimmigrants) also used the organization to build community within and across ethnic groups, and second-generation youngsters came to the institute to socialize with children outside their own ethnic groups and to reconnect with their heritage. Immigrants took classes in English, Spanish, and other languages. Affiliated organizations of immigrants and nonimmigrants—like the Polish KOP Club, the Japanese American Citizens' League, the Women's International Council, or the American Indian Society—held events in the organization's space. From the 1920s through the 1950s, an annual Internationality Dinner celebrated different national foods, and Sunday Teas and Starlight Balls in the 1950s and 1960s offered opportunities for immigrants of different national origins to socialize. Between 1956 and 1984, the organization sponsored a folk festival, which at its peak attracted tens of thousands of visitors over three days and represented more than five dozen nationalities.

Under the federal Displaced Persons Act of 1948 and the Refugee Relief Act of 1953, the organization became increasingly involved in refugee and displaced person resettlement. Its most high-profile effort involved refugees fleeing the fallout from the Hungarian and Cuban revolutions, and in the 1970s the Nationalities Service Center (NSC) helped thousands of refugees from Southeast Asia resettle in Philadelphia. The group's role in resettling refugees varied. In the late 1940s and early 1950s, caseworkers primarily helped displaced persons from Europe find employment. During the resettlement of about one hundred Cuban families in the early 1960s, it communicated with the International Rescue Committee in Miami to select families, plan their well-publicized "Freedom Flights" to Philadelphia, and identify southeastern Pennsylvania families to sponsor them (usually through religious groups). The institute helped refugees with work, clothing, housing, and English classes, while connecting them to Cubans living in Philadelphia already.

Resettlement efforts were rarely without complications, and new Philadelphians who resettled with the NSC's help repeatedly advocated for improved access to adequate resources. Refugees who had been highly skilled workers and professionals raised concerns that they were overqualified for the unrewarding jobs found for them. At one point, a group of nine recently resettled Cuban families wrote to the NSC requesting better treatment and considered reporting inadequate conditions to the newspapers. Refugee communities proved resilient, entrepreneurial, and resourceful: a thirty-three-year-old Cambodian man named Kim Hort Ou helped Cambodian arrivals who resettled with the assistance of the NSC to secure better lodging and fix heat and gas utilities that would not turn on. With his own money, he purchased a van to take community members to English lessons, teach them to drive, purchase groceries, and wash clothes at the laundry.

The institute's name change to Nationalities Service Center in 1963 signaled a broadening of the organization's scope during the 1960s and 1970s to include services and engagement for nonimmigrants. The institutes' umbrella organization also changed its name, from the Institute for Immigrant Welfare to the American Council of Nationalities Service. Beginning in the second half of the 1960s—pushed by the accomplishments of freedom and civil rights movements and a growing understanding of the intertwined dynamics of immigrant life and racial justice—the organization attempted to influence broader conversations about race, ethnicity, and cultural understanding. During the 1960s and 1970s, the center sponsored conferences on subjects like bilingual education and affirmative action and held cultural workshops and training. It secured a grant in 1968 to fund the "Nationality Race Community Relations" project. Partly driven by concern about rising racism among ethnic whites in Philadelphia, the project produced a World Cultures curriculum taken by sixty-three Black and white students from William Penn High School and John Hallahan Catholic Girls School. The project director, Dr Jay Jaipaul, and school officials later testified at congressional hearings that led to the passage of the 1974 Ethnic Heritage Studies Act.

Some projects were brief and troubled. Starting in the mid-1960s, the center expanded its outreach to Puerto Rican Philadelphians, culminating in 1971 with the creation of "El Centro," a Spanish-language satellite center in North Philadelphia intended to build connections with Spanish-speaking Philadelphians. The program was short-lived, however. Puerto Rican community leaders in Philadelphia asked that services for their community be designed and administered by Puerto Ricans.

As the numbers of highly skilled immigrants grew in the 1960s, the NSC responded to shifting demands. Its work in assisting relatives in coming to the United States, for example, became increasingly important. In the mid-1970s, the NSC continued its important role in resettlement by aiding thousands of Vietnamese, Cambodian, Laotian, and Hmong refugees. In addition to helping to secure housing and offering classes in English language and practical skills, the NSC in this period employed bilingual mental health workers to provide counseling, chaired a refugee task force, and partnered with other organizations to coordinate medical care.

After 1980, the NSC continued to grow and worked in coalitions to advocate for immigration reform and continued refugee resettlement, helping political refugees resettle from Albania, Kosovo, the Congo, Eritrea, Bhutan, Nepal, Iraq, Syria, and elsewhere. In the late twentieth and early twenty-first centuries the organization's work expanded to include refugee health care, legal services for unaccompanied minors, initiatives opposing human trafficking, and legal advocacy. As anti-immigrant politics of the 2010s restricted the number of refugees for resettlement, the Nationalities Service Center faced new challenges, including hiring freezes and staff layoffs. But as the city's first nonsectarian organization dedicated to assisting in the naturalization process, the Nationalities Service Center had a record of welcoming thousands of new Americans as they sought to make their homes in Philadelphia.

## ODUNDE Festival

**Christina Afia Harris**

The ODUNDE Festival, held in South Philadelphia each year on the second Sunday in June, celebrates the history and heritage of African people around the globe and serves to instill and encourage cultural pride. Taking its name from the word meaning "Happy New Year" in the Yoruba language (placed in all capital letters by the festival founders for emphasis), the event celebrates the coming of another year for Africans in America and throughout the diaspora. From its origins in 1975, the festival became the largest and longest-running African American street festival in the United States.

The festival grew from an idea conceived by South Philadelphia resident Lois Fernandez with the help of her friend Ruth Arthur after a trip to Nigeria, West Africa, in 1972. Her concept drew from African cultural heritage, specifically the Oshun festival of the Yoruba people in Nigeria. The first event (originally called the Oshun Festival) in 1975 was made possible by a $100 grant from Philadelphia's Southwest Center City Community Council and the support of Fernandez's neighbors. In 1976, Councilman John Anderson awarded a $5,000 grant. After two years, propelled by the cultural movement sweeping the nation in the wake of the civil rights struggle, the festival grew explosively and began to draw people from around the region. "Our neighborhood needed something," Fernandez said. "We didn't have anything to connect to. The whites have the Mummers, Now we have ODUNDE."

While the Black community embraced the festival, increasing gentrification in South Philadelphia led to opposition by some new occupants of the neighborhood. In 1984 a group of residents collected signatures and petitioned city hall to remove the festival, stating that it had grown too large for the neighborhood. The city offered Fernandez a subsidy to move the event to Penn's Landing, but because of the racial undertones of the complaints and the tradition of using the South Street Bridge to present offerings to Oshun, she refused. Over the years other residents and neighborhood groups also tried suing to stop the event, but with the support of the Black community, Fernandez succeeded in keeping the festival in its original South Street location and responded to the opposition by expanding.

By 2015, the festival had grown to attract many thousands of celebrants and more than one hundred vendors over the space of twelve city blocks. Sponsored and hosted by ODUNDE Inc., a South Philadelphia–based cultural organization established in 1983 to provide cultural enrichment for African American people, the festival sustained a communal, familial, and spiritual atmosphere through the efforts of several hundred volunteers and a board of directors, Fernandez (the organization's president), and her daughter, Oshunbumi Fernandez (executive director). One veteran

FIGURE 32. ODUNDE Festival celebrants move along South Street en route to the Schuylkill River to present offerings to the Yoruba deity Oshun, 2016. PHOTOGRAPH BY DONALD D. GROFF.

attendee, Junious Stanton, wrote in 2003 that "being at Odunde is like a mystical baptism. The festival there immerses you in a vibratory sea of Blackness. You get dipped into a positive spirit of being African and come up revived, energized, and feeling good."

The festival has officially begun with a procession from Twenty-Third and South Streets to the Schuylkill River to honor the Yoruba *orisha* (deity) Oshun, the goddess of the river, who is associated with love, beauty, femininity, and fertility. Participants usually wear white clothing or traditional African attire and make their pilgrimage to pour libations, offer prayers and incantations, and give offerings of honey, fruit, flowers, or money while accompanied by drumming and dancing. The procession has then made its way back from the river to the festival area, a vibrant recreation of an African marketplace. In the streets packed with participants, vendors from all over the African diaspora sell African and Caribbean food, crafts, clothing, art, and jewelry.

In 2011, Oshunbumi Fernandez created ODUNDE 365 to build a cultural movement beyond the festival. This organization promoted the principles of the festival year-round through African drumming and dancing classes for children, African arts courses, a self-esteem program for young girls called "I AM BUMI" (Beautiful, Unique, Magnificent, Individual), and a program called "My Story," which promoted success through local, influential professionals sharing their stories with young people. In 2013 the organization collaborated with Philadelphia music legend Kenneth Gamble to create Kwanzaabration, an event to educate children and adults about Kwanzaa and the holiday's seven principles.

Although it started from humble beginnings, ODUNDE evolved into a prominent community staple and celebration of the cultural heritage of African people around the globe. Seeking to instill and encourage cultural pride throughout the year, the festival demonstrates the impact that committed individuals have had on their local, national, and international communities.

## EXPLORE MORE

Neighborhoods shaped by immigrant communities can be found across the region. Not much of colonial Germantown remains, but Wyck House, at 6026 Germantown Avenue, was first owned by a seventeenth-century German immigrant, Hans Millan, of Quaker and Mennonite descent. Vernon Park, meanwhile, has a statue of Germantown's founder, Franz Daniel Pastorius, which was erected in 1920 to honor not just Pastorius but also later immigrants.

The imprint of nineteenth- and early twentieth-century emigration to Philadelphia is more visible. While the Irish presence has faded from old centers like Kensington, the *National Memorial to An Gorta Mór (the Great Hunger)*—the famine of the 1840s that brought so many Irish people to North America—is located near Penn's Landing. The Italian Market on Ninth Street around the intersection with Washington Avenue and the old Jewish garment district of Fabric Row on S. Fourth Street are now diverse neighborhoods, but still bear traces of their roots as ethnic enclaves. Chinatown, which stretches roughly from Eighth to Eleventh Street between Vine and Arch, remains a center of East and Southeast Asian culture and community. Some of the immigrants who arrived in the Delaware Valley in this era passed through the Washington Avenue Immigration Station, which though long gone, is remembered via a historical marker at the intersection with Christopher Columbus Boulevard. The building that housed its successor, which closed after World War II, can still be seen at 101 S. King Street, Gloucester City, N.J.

Twentieth- and twenty-first-century ethnic neighborhoods stretch across the city and into suburbs. El Centro de Oro (the Golden Block) centers on N. Fifth Street at Lehigh Avenue, while Olney, also in North Philadelphia, has a strong Hispanic and Korean presence. An Ethiopian community—part of the "New African Diaspora"—has grown up around Forty-Fifth Street and Baltimore Avenue in West Philadelphia. Such examples offer just a small sample of how the metropolitan geography has been molded by immigration.

Museums and archives that explore the immigrant experience in the region are numerous. The American Swedish Historical Museum, in Franklin Delano Roosevelt Park, Philadelphia, provides an introduction to one of the earliest European groups to arrive in the Delaware Valley. City institutions open to the public include the Weitzman National Museum of American Jewish History, 101 S. Independence Mall East; the History of Italian Immigration Museum, 1834 E. Passyunk Avenue; and the German Society of Pennsylvania, founded in 1764, at 611 Spring Garden Street. The Balch Institute collection at the Historical Society of Pennsylvania (1300 Locust Street) documents American ethnic history. Beyond Philadelphia, two places to explore immigration are the New Jersey State Museum at 205 W. State Street, Trenton, and the Delaware History Museum, operated by the Delaware Historical Society, at 504 N. Market Street, Wilmington.

The literature on immigration to the region is vast. On the relationship between migration, neighborhood, and work, a good place to start is Sam Bass Warner Jr., *The Private City: Philadelphia in Three Periods of Its Growth*, 2nd ed. (University of Pennsylvania Press, 1987). For the Delaware as a port of entry, see Fredric M. Miller, "Immigration Through the Port of Philadelphia," in *Forgotten Doors: The Other Ports of Entry to the United States*, ed. M. Mark Stolarik (Balch Institute Press, 1988). The essays in Allen F. Davis and Mark H. Haller, eds., *The Peoples of Philadelphia: A History of Ethnic Groups and Lower-Class Life, 1790–1940* (Temple University Press, 1973) cover a variety of communities from the eighteenth to the early twentieth centuries, while Ayumi Takenaka and Mary Johnson Osirim, eds., *Global Philadelphia: Immigrant Communities Old and New* (Temple University Press, 2010) moves from the late nineteenth century to the early 2000s.

On colonial immigration to the region, see James T. Lemon, *The Best Poor Man's Country: A Geographical Study of Early Southeastern Pennsylvania* (Johns Hopkins University Press, 1972); Sharon V. Salinger, *"To Serve Well and Faithfully": Labor and Indentured Servants in Pennsylvania, 1682–1800* (Cambridge University Press, 1987); and Edwin Wolf II, *Germantown and the Germans* (Library

Company of Philadelphia and Historical Society of Pennsylvania, 1983).

Irish immigration and the nativist reaction it met are explored in Dennis Clark, *The Irish in Philadelphia: Ten Generations of Urban Experience* (Temple University Press, 1973); Harry C. Silcox, *Philadelphia Politics from the Bottom Up: The Life of Irishman William McMullen, 1824–1901* (Balch Institute Press, 1989); and Zachary Schrag, *The Fires of Philadelphia: Citizen-Soldiers, Nativists, and the 1844 Riots over the Soul of a Nation* (Pegasus Books, 2021). The colonization movement that saw Black emigration as a path out of enslavement is documented in Beverly C. Tomek, *Colonization and Its Discontents: Emancipation, Emigration, and Antislavery in Antebellum Pennsylvania* (New York University Press, 2011).

Other nineteenth- and early twentieth-century immigrant groups are covered in Friederike Baer, *The Trial of Frederick Eberle: Language, Patriotism and Citizenship in Philadelphia's German Community, 1790 to 1830* (New York University Press, 2008); Jordan Stanger-Ross, *Staying Italian: Urban Change and Ethnic Life in Postwar Toronto and Philadelphia* (University of Chicago Press, 2009); Russell A. Kazal, *Becoming Old Stock: The Paradox of German-American Identity* (Princeton University Press, 2004); Stefano Luconi, *From Paesani to White Ethnics: The Italian Experience in Philadelphia* (State University of New York Press, 2001); Rakhmiel Peltz, *From Immigrant to Ethnic Culture: American Yiddish in South Philadelphia* (Stanford University Press, 1998); and Victor Vázquez, "Tobacco, Trains, and Textiles: Philadelphia's Early Spanish-Speaking Enclaves, 1920–1936," *Pennsylvania Legacies* 3, no. 2 (November 2003): 12–15. Progressive Era settlement houses are treated in Lucy Perkins Carner, *The Settlement Way in Philadelphia: The Settlement Movement in Philadelphia* (Delaware Valley Settlement Alliance, 1964), and Richard N. Juliani, "Social Reform Through Social Service: The Settlement Movement in South Philadelphia," *Pennsylvania Legacies* 7, no. 2 (November 2007): 22–29.

On twentieth- and twenty-first-century immigration, see Kathryn E. Wilson, *Ethnic Renewal in Philadelphia's Chinatown: Space, Place, and Struggle* (Temple University Press, 2015); Carmen Teresa Whalen, *From Puerto Rico to Philadelphia: Puerto Rican Workers and Postwar Economies* (Temple University Press, 2001); Jae-Hyup Lee, *Dynamics of Ethnic Identity: Three Asian Communities in Philadelphia* (Garland Publishing, 1998); Domenic Vitiello, *The Sanctuary City: Immigrant, Refugee, and Receiving Communities in Postindustrial Philadelphia* (Cornell University Press, 2022); Leigh Swigart et al., *Extended Lives: The African Immigrant Experience in Philadelphia* (Balch Institute Press, 2001); Howard Gillette Jr., *Camden After the Fall: Decline and Renewal in a Post-Industrial City* (University of Pennsylvania Press, 2005); Henry Bischoff, *A New Wave of Immigration in New Jersey: Diversity and Vitality, 1940–2009* (New Jersey Historical Commission, 2010); and Seth Stern, *Speaking Yiddish to Chickens: Holocaust Survivors on South Jersey Poultry Farms* (Rutgers University Press, 2023).

On the region's foodways and cultural history, see Mary Anne Hines, Gordon Marshall, and William Woys Weaver, *The Larder Invaded: Reflections on Three Centuries of Philadelphia Food and Drink* (Library Company of Philadelphia and Historical Society of Pennsylvania, 1987); Carolyn Hyman, *The Great Philly Cheesesteak Book* (Running Press, 2009); and Stephen M. Highsmith, *Philadelphia Mummers* (Arcadia Publishing, 2017). These works demonstrate in different ways the lasting cultural imprints of immigration on the Delaware Valley.

Chapter 5

# World Religions

## Introduction

Although it has been widely known as the "Quaker City," Philadelphia has a religious history that extends far beyond the Society of Friends, and since the region's European colonization it has had a deserved reputation for religious diversity. William Penn's provision for freedom of conscience opened Pennsylvania to religious refugees from the wars and persecutions of Europe. Philadelphia, and the surrounding region, therefore offered a haven for dissenting groups and faiths that flocked to its environs. From the earliest days of English settlement, and in some cases before, Protestants, Catholics, and Jews found sanctuary in the Delaware Valley. Over the following centuries, they would be joined in greater numbers by followers of other world religions who, just as early colonizers had done, adapted their beliefs and practices to the environment they encountered.

Over the course of the eighteenth century the religious landscape of the region remained diverse, with no single sect predominating. Pluralism marked out the mid-Atlantic region as a whole. In contrast to Congregationalist Massachusetts and Anglican Virginia, the colonies of Pennsylvania and New Jersey, as well as the three counties that later formed Delaware, did not have established churches prior to the American Revolution, and if local Church of England ministers could count on more official support from over the Atlantic than their counterparts, they too had to compete for converts. Often they lost out to soul-stirring itinerant preachers who traipsed across the region in the Great Awakening of the 1700s, the first in a series of evangelical revivals that imbued American Christianity with fervor and mission.

Immigration brought a multitude of beliefs to the city. Some were more visible than others. It is likely that enslaved African Muslims and Hindu and Sikh sailors either resided in or visited early Philadelphia, though their presence is hard to trace with certainty. The nineteenth century saw Catholicism surge, particularly due to Irish immigrants, who were later followed by Italians and Poles. The liberalization of U.S. immigration laws in 1965 diversified the religious landscape further. With increasing numbers of Asian people forging a new life in the Delaware Valley, Buddhism, Hinduism, and Sikhism emerged as major faiths. Islam too grew with greater migration from parts of Africa, the Middle East, and Southeast Asia. These faiths sometimes drew converts from longer-established populations. The Nation of Islam, for example, found Black followers despite its deviation from Sunni orthodoxy, while elements of Buddhist and Hindu beliefs and practices like meditation and yoga resonated with American-born residents seeking alternatives to the perceived materialism of postwar mass culture. World religions in this manner have taken on distinctly local characteristics.

Faith communities have shaped the region's geography too. Those with the resources to do so have built upward toward the heavens. Christ Church on N. Second Street may not have rivaled the scale of Europe's Gothic cathedrals, but for the city's early history it stood as its tallest building, its steeple providing a visible symbol of the Church of England's place as first among equals in an outpost of the British Empire. The twenty-first-century Mormon Philadelphia Pennsylvania Temple, a neoclassical edifice located just off the imposing Benjamin Franklin Parkway, provides a more recent example, as does the Hindu Temple of Delaware in Hockessin, with its five-tiered monumental entrance tower known as a Rajagopuram. But even where places of worship are hidden behind storefronts or in strip malls, their presence has had a marked impact on communities. The tendency of faith groups to cluster together is evident from early settlements like predominantly Lutheran Germantown and Moravian Bethlehem. By the mid-nineteenth century, the Catholic Church played a crucial role in the life of urban neighborhoods, providing social services as well as a place of worship to congregations. The diocese proved quick to respond to changing demographics. When Italians began to settle in South Philadelphia in the 1850s, for example, the bishop of Philadelphia established the church of Mary Magdalen de Pazzi, which in turn drew further immigrants to the vicinity. This pattern continued after 1965, with Buddhist, Hindu, and Sikh temples in the city and suburbs serving as magnets for newcomers. As the religious needs of communities changed, places of worship have often been repurposed, with pews once reserved for Protestants providing seats to Orthodox worshippers and Buddhists burning incense in buildings in which Jews had once read the Torah. The region's religions have often built on the foundations of their predecessors.

Yet religious pluralism has not necessarily meant peace. Sectarian tensions, especially between Protestants and Catholics, occasionally erupted into violence. In the 1844 nativist riots, militant Protestants marched onto Irish Catholic turf in Kensington, reenacting on American soil the post-Reformation struggles that brought so much bloodshed to Ireland. When Catholics fought back, Protestants torched several of their churches. A few years later, as devout Philadelphians began to venture overseas to propagate the gospel, evangelicals also established "home" missionary outposts in supposedly "heathen" suburbs to preach to the immigrant poor. One early missionary remembered being pelted with dead animals by unimpressed Catholic residents. Similar conflicts played out in battles over sacred texts, with the 1844 Protestant outrage over the proposed use of the Catholic Bible in public schools mirroring legal controversies a century later over school prayer. Whether in the streets or in the courtroom, Philadelphians have waged their own holy wars.

These conflicts reflect the common human aspiration to shape the world according to one's own belief system. Especially in Philadelphia's early history, Protestant groups felt the evangelical urge to convert others and build a "Godly kingdom" on earth. Preachers during the Great Awakenings of the eighteenth and nineteenth centuries instilled a sense of divine mission in their followers, inspiring social reform movements such as temperance and antislavery. Other faith traditions, including Quakers, Buddhists, and Muslims, have also endeavored to make Philadelphia and the world conform to their visions of an ideal society. Whether possessed of this missionary impulse or not, though, the region's faith communities have provided spiritual and material nourishment for believers. From its founding with the principle of freedom of conscience to its twenty-first-century tapestry of faiths, Philadelphia has provided a fertile ground for religious belief to flourish and adapt.

## Society of Friends (Quakers)

**Isaac Barnes May**

Much as New England was shaped by its Puritan heritage, the history of Philadelphia and the Delaware Valley intertwined heavily with the Religious Society of Friends. Philadelphia gained one of its nicknames, "The Quaker City," from its founding and settlement by the Friends, colloquially known as Quakers, a Christian religious sect that emerged during the English Civil War (1642–51). Although less influential in Philadelphia after the eighteenth century, the Religious Society of Friends remained a vital part of the city's religious landscape.

Quakerism grew out of the ministry of George Fox, a shoemaker's apprentice who believed that Jesus "had come to teach his people himself" and that this occurred in the form of an "inward light" that was present and accessible to human beings. By gathering together in silence with other believers, Quakers believed that individuals might be directly influenced by God to offer vocal ministry. One of the notable features of this new religious group was its relative egalitarianism. While early Quakers did not seek to abolish all earthly hierarchies, they spurned established custom by addressing everyone (including those of higher social status) using the informal plain speech of "thee" and "thou," language that was normally reserved for intimates. Quakers also adopted "plain dress," unadorned clothing designed to defy the custom of having fashion signify social status, and did not doff their hats to their social superiors. This concept of equality also extended to the idea that both sexes were equal in spiritual matters. Early Quakers believed that women had the same authority to preach in meeting as men did, and, like their male counterparts, women often traveled in their ministry. Within and among local congregations (Quakers called these "meetings"), committees of women known as "women's' meetings" were supposed to be of equal value to the governance provided by the "men's meetings."

The Quakers' understanding of Christianity distinguished the group from its neighbors in other ways. They professed a "peace testimony," which called on their members to avoid violence and warfare. Quakers also refused to swear oaths, arguing that Jesus had forbidden the practice in the New Testament. Because of these differences and their belief that they alone correctly practiced Christianity, Quakers only married within their own group and expelled members who married non-Quakers.

**FIGURE 33.** Quaker meetinghouse and burial ground, Jordans, United Kingdom, 1853. The founder of Philadelphia, William Penn, was laid to rest in a humble Quaker grave in his native England. Efforts to disinter his remains and relocate them to a tomb at the foot of Philadelphia's new city hall came to naught in the 1880s, partly owing to opposition from Friends in England and America. WIKIMEDIA COMMONS.

## WILLIAM PENN'S "HOLY EXPERIMENT"

Because of their distinctive religious practices and their rejection of the established Anglican Church, the Quakers endured significant persecution in England where thousands faced fines and imprisonment. By the 1670s Quakers had begun to consider the possibility of emigrating to North America to escape religious oppression. In 1680 William Penn, a prominent leader with the Quaker movement, received a land grant for a new colony from English monarch Charles II as a payment for a debt that the king had owed to Penn's father, Admiral Sir William Penn.

Penn saw the colony as a "holy experiment" and designed the laws of the new colony with Quaker beliefs in mind. No oaths were required in courts or to hold public offices, Quaker-style marriage ceremonies were made the legal form of marriage, and because of past Quaker experiences with persecution, Penn extended religious liberty to all monotheists.

Philadelphia became the site of Philadelphia Yearly Meeting (PYM), an aggregation of Quakers in the Philadelphia region. PYM comprised several quarterly meetings, which in turn were composed of multiple monthly meetings (similar to congregations). While PYM remained technically separate from the civil government, important Quaker men tended to be elected to fill leadership roles in both bodies. Though other yearly meetings existed in New England, Maryland, and North Carolina, PYM soon became the most influential grouping outside of London.

## WAR, PEACE, AND ABOLITION

By the 1750s Quakers' involvement with Pennsylvania politics began to conflict with their commitment to nonviolence. In 1754 when the French and Indian War began, the British government instructed Pennsylvania to equip an army to prepare to fight. Many Quakers in the colonial legislature complied initially. However, after Catherine Payton, a visiting English Quaker minister, exhorted them to adhere to Quakerism's peace testimony, many reconsidered. When the assembly voted to go to war regardless, Quakers resigned en masse, and their political influence rapidly waned thereafter. Over the next several centuries, only a small number of Quakers served in elected positions.

The issue of Quaker participation in war arose again during the American Revolution. Most Quakers refused to take part, causing persistent accusations of British loyalties. Quaker meetings disowned or expelled some Friends for serving with the American army. These included a small group that founded a splinter denomination, the Free Quakers, which existed into the early nineteenth century.

By the early eighteenth century some Quakers had become increasingly skeptical about the compatibility of slavery with their religious convictions. By the early 1700s, the PYM and other yearly meetings began exhorting Quakers not to import enslaved people, and in the ensuing years they put out a number of pronouncements advising Friends to avoid enslaving. Influential Quaker members of the PYM, particularly John Woolman and Anthony Benezet, stressed the immorality of enslavement and its tendency to lead masters into such sins as haughtiness, laziness, and violence.

Beginning in the 1690s, individual members' arguments against enslavement became increasingly vocal and insistent, though significant numbers of the region's Quakers held people in slave status themselves. After arriving in the region in 1732, the English-born Quaker abolitionist Benjamin Lay, who had witnessed the horrors of slavery in Barbados, denounced apostate enslavers at monthly meetings and PYM, but found himself excluded from the gatherings as a result. Yet by the 1770s, PYM's constituency had become mostly united behind the policy that any Quaker who bought, sold, or held people in slave status should be barred from membership. In subsequent years PYM helped to coalesce the national efforts to petition Congress to end the slave trade entirely.

Philadelphia Quakers' distain for enslavement led them to help found the nation's first abolitionist organization in 1775, when seven Quakers were among the ten men who gathered at the Rising Sun Tavern on Second Street and created the Society for the Relief of Free Negros Unlawfully Held in Bondage. This society brought a number of lawsuits to secure the freedom of African Americans who had been kidnapped into slavery or whose rights had otherwise been breached. In 1787 (after slavery had been outlawed by the 1780 state legislation) the group expanded to include more non-Quakers and renamed itself the Philadelphia Abolition Society, also expanding its mission to include enslaved people. The next generation of Pennsylvania Quakers included several leading abolitionists such as noted Quaker minister Lucretia Mott; these radicals spearheaded the creation of the Philadelphia Female Anti-Slavery Society in 1833.

## REFORM AND DIVISION

Enslavement was not the only social issue about which Philadelphia Quakers were vocal. In the late eighteenth century they often became pioneering reformers, creating a number of organizations designed to improve life for their neighbors. Quaker women in particular proved active in establishing Philadelphia's first philanthropic and charitable societies. The Female Society for Relief of the Distressed, founded in the 1790s, sought to minister to the "Inner Light" in every individual by clothing, feeding, and providing nursing care to the poor, while the Aimwell School provided primary education to poor girls.

Prison reform also concerned Philadelphia Friends. In the 1770s a group of Quakers founded the Philadelphia Society for Relieving Distressed Prisoners, which helped to develop the Walnut Street Jail, the first "penitentiary" in the United States. The new institution's emphasis on quiet reflection and repentance drew partially from Quaker religious practices. These concepts, first implemented at Walnut Street, became the prototype for the construction of Eastern State

Penitentiary and the basis for the widely adopted "Pennsylvania System" of prison management.

To outside observers early nineteenth-century Quakerism must have seemed to be a harmonious success story. Friends built a new meetinghouse on Arch Street in 1804, and the Quakers membership rolls were high. Yet just a few years later Quakerism broke into several rival branches. Though each faction laid claim to being the "true" Quakers, many factors led to the split between what would be known as Orthodox and Hicksite factions. Among these issues, the Orthodox claimed that the followers of Elias Hicks, a popular Long Island Quaker preacher, overemphasized belief in the Inward Light while underemphasizing the Bible. Hicks's followers accused the Orthodox of abandoning traditional Quaker teachings on these subjects. In 1827 this conflict reached the breaking point during the gathering of PYM, when both factions tried to assert their rights to leadership.

The Hicksites stormed out of the Arch Street Meetinghouse and built their own meetinghouse on Race Street. Over the following decades, Quaker yearly meetings in other regions of the United States experienced similar splits. The schism meant there were now two Philadelphia yearly meetings, one Hicksite and one Orthodox, with each side refusing to recognize the legitimacy of the other. By the 1830s, the Orthodox had established an all-male school outside the city, which would eventually become Haverford College. Hicksites founded coeducational Swarthmore College in 1864, a few miles from Haverford. Decades later, in 1885, the Orthodox helped establish Bryn Mawr College to educate women.

By the 1840s, in other yearly meetings, the Orthodox faction had further divided into separate groups, the evangelically inclined Gurneyites and the more traditional Wilburites. The Orthodox Philadelphia Yearly Meeting tried to avoid taking sides and essentially sealed themselves off from the rest of Quakerism. The Hicksites meanwhile battled over how vigorously to pursue abolition and women's rights. A short-lived group, the Philadelphia Yearly Meeting of Progressive Friends, even broke away from the Hicksite Yearly Meeting; for several decades they gathered at a meetinghouse in Longwood.

Over the course of the nineteenth century Quakers in Philadelphia from both groups became receptive to liberal theological ideas, such as the idea that the Bible was the product of a particular ancient historical era, or the truth of the theory of evolution. By the early twentieth century Quakers had given up most of the peculiarities of dress and speech that separated them so visibly from the rest of the population and began to intermarry with non-Quakers. Religious leaders like Haverford professor Rufus Jones pioneered a new understanding of Quakerism as a mystical religion uniquely suited to the modern age.

In the effort to reunite the divided parts of Quakerism, Jones and other influential Quakers helped to develop the American Friends Service Committee (AFSC), a Philadelphia-based organization intended to unite Quakers through a common interest that would transcend the Hicksite-Orthodox theological separation by focusing instead on relief, peace, and charitable work for others. In 1947 the AFSC shared the Nobel Peace Prize.

## QUAKERISM AFTER WORLD WAR II

These shared efforts helped facilitate a reunification of the fractured PYM in 1955, which was part of a similar reunion undertaken by many of the other Quaker factions in the United States. Subsequent decades saw Philadelphia Friends trying to uphold their denomination's traditional testimonies of equality and peace by supporting the civil rights movement. In the 1960s, PYM tried to assist minority communities, undertaking community development projects in Chester, Pennsylvania, and establishing the Minorities Economic Development Fund to fund similar projects around Philadelphia. Pennsylvania Quakers also harshly criticized the Vietnam War. In 1967 PYM expressed its support for a group of Quaker activists who illegally sent medical supplies to North Vietnam in the ship *Phoenix*, an action prompted by both humanitarianism and a desire to protest the ongoing conflict. Gay and lesbian issues were a third area of concern; in 1973 PYM publicly voiced its support for gay rights, and by 1991 it offered a guide for same-sex couples that wanted to be married in Quaker ceremonies. Increasingly, the majority of Quakers in the Philadelphia region identified themselves as politically liberal, and many saw these beliefs as intertwined with their religious identities.

Quaker populations became substantially older in the twentieth century, causing many local meetings to focus on providing retirement care. By the early 2020s many Quaker-inspired retirement communities operated near Philadelphia, such as Foulkeways (opened 1967), Kendal (opened 1973), and Pennswood Village (opened 1980). Often, they originated of nonprofits at the prompting of members of local meetings. These communities often boasted well-attended Quaker meetings, though only a fraction of their residents were Quakers.

From the mid-1970s PYM gathered at the Friends Center, a building at Fifteenth and Cherry Streets built in 1974. Statistics from 2010 indicated that the PYM then had 11,800 members spread across the Philadelphia region among 106 monthly meetings, a precipitous drop from more than thirty thousand members in 1775 or even the fifteen thousand recorded members in 1925. Although declining membership became a source of concern for the denomination, the PYM's central role in Quaker history meant that it continued to be an influential body within American—and indeed international—Quakerism.

## Protestantism

**R. Scott Hanson**

In the century after Martin Luther began the Protestant Reformation in Germany, William Penn's "holy experiment" in the Delaware Valley became perhaps the most important American beacon for religious freedom and a haven for the Society of Friends and other persecuted Protestant denominations and religious minorities from Europe. Protestant denominations proliferated in the eighteenth and nineteenth centuries due to aggressive recruiting by colonizers, unsettled conditions in Europe, and the absence of an established church. Philadelphia Protestantism continued to be shaped by religious revivals, patterns of immigration, and tensions with rival creeds and advocates of secularism into the new millennium.

### EARLY PROTESTANTISM IN PHILADELPHIA FROM THE SEVENTEENTH TO EIGHTEENTH CENTURY

Although the beliefs and practices of sects differed considerably, Protestants rejected the authority of the pope in Rome yet often found themselves at odds with non-Catholic rulers too. The Philadelphia region provided them with a place to build churches without state interference. Like Roger Williams's "lively experiment" in Rhode Island colony, liberty of conscience gave rise to the religiously diverse mid-Atlantic colonies. The area became what historian of American religion Randall Balmer has called a "proving ground for pluralism" that differed markedly from the Puritan Massachusetts Bay Colony, Catholic Maryland, and primarily Anglican Virginia, the Carolinas, and Georgia.

Dutch, Swedes, Finns, and other English settlers had been a presence along the rivers that came to be called the Delaware and Schuylkill, where they had established farms, log houses, and forts since 1609. In 1677 Swedish Lutherans, who had already established a presence in New Jersey, built a church in Philadelphia and recruited Rev. Jacobus Fabritius, an ordained Dutch Lutheran, to be their inaugural pastor until a native Swede, Rev. Andreas Rudman, arrived. The first wooden church lasted until 1698 when construction of a new one made of brick began. Dedicated in 1700, Gloria Dei (Old Swedes' Church) survived in the early twenty-first century as the oldest religious building in Philadelphia.

Other Protestants followed in the footsteps of the Swedes. In 1683, Dutch Quakers and followers of the Anabaptist preacher Menno Simons called Mennonites, who came from Krefeld (Crefeld), Germany, established Germantown, a village in rural Philadelphia County, and built a meetinghouse in 1686. German Lutherans led by Francis Daniel Pastorius joined them. Incredulous to learn that many Friends enslaved people, Pastorius and three like-minded Quakers in 1688 drafted the Germantown Protest, the first abolitionist document in America. Near Germantown, along a bank of the Wissahickon Creek, the German millennialist Johannes Kelpius brought Rosicrucianism, named for its symbol of a rose on a cross, to America. He lived communally with his followers in caves awaiting the Second Coming, which they expected to arrive in 1694. German Lutheran and Reformed congregations formed and built churches in both Germantown and Philadelphia, including St. Michael's Church under the leadership of Rev. Henry Melchior Muhlenberg in 1746.

The Moravian Brethren also settled in Philadelphia, and later, in the Lehigh Valley, they founded Bethlehem, which became the center of Moravian religious and educational life, and Nazareth. The Amish, a more conservative branch of Mennonites who followed the stricter teachings of Swiss-born Jakob Ammann, began arriving from Alsace-Lorraine and the German Palatinate from the late 1720s into the 1740s and settled first in Lancaster County, Pennsylvania. Similar German Pietist groups such as the Dunkers, Ephrata Community, and Schwenckfelders also migrated during this time.

Despite Pennsylvania's Quaker roots, the Church of England sought to confirm its primacy across the empire and provided for the speedy creation of an Anglican church. Christ Church, which occupied a wooden building after its founding in 1695 at Second and Market Streets, was rebuilt in brick from 1727 to 1744. After it added a towering steeple in 1754, it stood as the tallest building in North America until the nineteenth century and asserted Anglican ambitions to be recognized as the predominant faith in a city of many religions. Despite Anglicanism's association with the British Crown, many notable figures of the Revolutionary era attended the church and were later buried within its walls or—like Benjamin Franklin—in its burial ground.

During the eighteenth century the Philadelphia area also became a center of American Presbyterianism. The Calvinist Dutch Reformed Church, which had benefited from state sponsorship in the days of the New Netherland colony, remained prominent in the north of the province after the English wrested control from the Dutch in the second half of the seventeenth century. While Quakers established a stronghold in West New Jersey (the name given to the southern part of New Jersey), provisions for religious freedom allowed other sects to flourish, and Trenton's first Presbyterian congregation organized in 1712.

In Pennsylvania, Scots Irish immigrants began arriving in large numbers in the 1720s and by midcentury outnumbered the Quakers and other English colonists. Philadelphia became the site for the first American presbytery in 1706, which later represented both the "Old Lights" and "New Lights," the latter associated with more emotional forms of preaching and conversion during the Great Awakening of the 1730s. Presbyterians built a simple meetinghouse called Old Buttonwood in 1704 on High (Market) Street at White Horse Alley (Bank Street), which expanded several times before being replaced in 1794 by a Neoclassical Revival structure. A number of Scots Irish Presbyterians also settled on the Pennsylvania frontier in Paxtang, or Paxton (later a suburb of Harrisburg). During the Seven Years' War, when the Quaker-controlled Pennsylvania Provincial Assembly failed to defend settlers on the colony's borderland, the Scots Irish Presbyterians decried Quaker pacifism and turned on Native Americans whom they regarded as "savages." In 1763, the so-called Paxton Boys were responsible for the Conestoga massacre of Susquehannock Indians that marked the end of what William Penn had called his "Peaceable Kingdom."

## THE GREAT AWAKENING, DENOMINATIONAL GROWTH, AND REVOLUTION

During the mid-eighteenth century many colonists turned to a more emotional form of Protestantism during the revivals known as the Great Awakening. Congregationalist minister Jonathan Edwards reported early stirrings in Northampton, Massachusetts, in late 1733–34. The son and son-in-law of ministers, Edwards honed his sermons into powerful jeremiads. News of his success spread and by the end of the decade reached England, where Oxford men George Whitefield, John Wesley, and Charles Wesley had left the Church of England to found Methodism. Traveling extensively throughout England and the American colonies in the late 1730s, these early evangelicals embraced a fervent style of preaching, which they used to persuade the throngs who gathered to hear them to be born again in Christ. Whitefield became something of a colonial celebrity and visited Philadelphia repeatedly from 1739 to 1740 to preach to several thousand at a time, first at Christ Church (which he noted in his journal did not yet have a roof) and then at outdoor revivals. Reports indicated that ten thousand to fifteen thousand people gathered to hear him. At one meeting, a curious Benjamin Franklin tested, and confirmed, whether such a crowd could hear Whitefield's voice.

Revivalism, however, divided Old and New Light Presbyterians. The Old Lights, who valued ritual and hierarchy over the exuberance of itinerant preachers, had a stronghold in Philadelphia's First Presbyterian Church. The New Lights, led by William Tennent and his sons, established the so-called Log Cabin College in 1727 in Warminster, Pennsylvania, which educated many revivalist ministers. Old Lights clung to the principle that only the established institutions of Harvard, Yale, and Europe could prepare students for the ministry. The Log Cabin seminary moved across the Delaware River in 1745, and many of the New Lights associated with it supported the creation of the College of New Jersey, the forerunner to Princeton University. Meanwhile the schism between Old Lights and New Lights, which had led to the creation of two separate synods in 1745, ended in 1758, helped in part by the College of New Jersey offering a sanctioned route for evangelicals into the ministry.

As Presbyterians divided and reunited, Protestantism in the Delaware Valley continued to diversify. Baptists, who shared evangelical ties with Methodists but differed in their eponymous conversion technique, met in a series of temporary spaces for services as early as 1698. In 1707, a group formed the Philadelphia Baptist Association, the first of its kind in America, and took over a meetinghouse abandoned by the early abolitionist George Keith, who was at turns a Presbyterian, a Quaker, and then an Anglican. The congregation of Methodists grew in Philadelphia in the 1760s under former British army officer Thomas Webb who had been converted by John Wesley, and in 1769 they built St. George's Church on N. Fourth Street. With notable leaders like Francis Asbury, who preached there in 1771 and went on to become the nation's first Methodist bishop, it came to be regarded as the "cradle of American Methodism." Richard Allen, a Methodist convert born into slavery who had purchased his freedom, received a license to preach from St. George's in 1784. Allen was among the first Black members of the congregation, but after being asked to vacate pews reserved for whites, he and his followers left to establish Bethel African Church in 1794. In 1816, it took the name Bethel African Methodist Episcopal Church, with Allen as its first bishop. Camp meetings, meanwhile, carried the Methodist creed to other parts of the region, notably the Delmarva Peninsula, where in 1805–6 thousands of people in the vicinity of Dover, Delaware, converted.

**FIGURE 34.** Mother Bethel African Methodist Episcopal Church, S. Sixth Street, Philadelphia, 1829. Mother Bethel became the cradle of the African Methodist Episcopal Church, which spread to Africa and the Caribbean by the late nineteenth century. LIBRARY OF CONGRESS.

The Revolutionary era saw a spiritual as well as political break with Britain. Anglican clergy in New Jersey, who had taken an oath of allegiance to the monarch, tended toward loyalism. But in Philadelphia most Anglican ministers sided with the Patriots, and William White, the rector of St. Peter's and Christ Church, served as chaplain to the Continental Congress. White helped to reorganize the new United States' embattled Anglicans into a new Episcopal Church, which maintained links with fellow believers in England while abandoning all ties to the Crown. Well into the nineteenth century, Episcopalians remained prominently represented among Philadelphia's wealthy white residents, but they could also be found among the city's Black community. Absalom Jones, born into slavery in Delaware, established a Black Episcopal congregation in 1794 and joined the Methodist Allen in calling for abolition and African American mutual aid.

## RELIGIOUS FREEDOM, IMMIGRATION, AND CONFLICT IN THE NINETEENTH CENTURY

By the nineteenth century, state constitutions and the free exercise clause of the First Amendment had extended colonial ideas of liberty of conscience present in the region's lively experiment in pluralism to the nation at large. These changes coincided with another wave of revivals in the so-called Second Great Awakening of the 1830s and what historian Nathan O. Hatch has called the "democratization of American Christianity." They led to the further growth of Protestant denominations and churches. Philip Schaff, the German Reformed minister and theologian who taught at Mercersburg Seminary at Marshall College (later Franklin & Marshall) in Lancaster, Pennsylvania, called the United States in 1855 "the phoenix grave . . . of all European churches and sects." By this he meant all persecuted religious groups in the Old World could be reborn on U.S. soil.

Philadelphia did not escape the trend. While the region did not experience the same fervor of evangelical awakenings that "burnt over" parts of New York in the early nineteenth century, Protestantism nonetheless grew larger and more variegated. Pioneering evangelists like Presbyterian Rev. James Patterson preached the gospel to the burgeoning working-class population. Bringing a new wave of revivals to the city in 1816, he transformed the First Presbyterian Church in the Northern Liberties into the largest in the union over the following years, also establishing Sunday schools. Institutional growth took place across Philadelphia. Tract societies spread Protestant moral teachings, gospel lessons, and accounts of conversion, and the American Bible Society published Bibles and sent out itinerants to sell them and encourage conversions. Church building grew apace. By 1825, Philadelphia had roughly fifty Protestant congregations across a dozen denominations. On the eve of the Civil War, the number of churches approached three hundred, and the number of denominations had more than doubled, reaching twenty-nine. Wealthy citizens like locomotive builder Matthias W. Baldwin displayed their piety by funding church construction. New neighborhoods soon boasted places of worship for Protestants, while millenarian movements like the Millerites, who anticipated the world's end on October 22, 1844, attracted converts.

While Protestant churches flourished in the Philadelphia region in the eighteenth and early nineteenth centuries, immigration in the 1840s led to anti-Catholic nativism. In 1842 in Philadelphia, over fifty clergy from different denominations formed the American Protestant Association as an antidote to popery, and two years later the Kensington Bible Riots, which stemmed from a battle over the place of the King James and Catholic Douay bibles in public schools, concluded in the torching of several Catholic churches. Nativist tensions abated in the late 1850s as issues of slavery extension and threats of southern secession consumed political interests. At the same time, Protestant churches were wracked by internal divisions over questions of the extent to which churches should engage directly in public issues and openly align with political parties and interests.

## SOCIAL REFORM AND PROTESTANTISM

Philadelphia Protestants enlisted in movements to cleanse the city, republic, and world of sin, although their degree of commitment to the cause of moral reform varied. Albert Barnes, the New Light minister of First Presbyterian and president of the Philadelphia Bible Society, was among a host of antislavery Protestants in the city, although his attacks on the South's "peculiar institution" primarily took the form of intellectually refuting proslavery arguments. The Unitarian William Henry Furness proved less restrained in his abolitionism and vociferously attacked enslavers from 1839 onward. But like the national story of sectional strife that led Baptists, Methodists, and Presbyterians to break up into northern and southern organizations, the city's Protestants divided on slavery. One Episcopalian rector had to resign after parishioners objected to his criticism of the South Carolinian congressman Preston Brooks, who had violently attacked the antislavery senator Charles Sumner in the U.S. Senate in 1856. Some Baptist preachers returned to their native South when secession and the threat of civil war loomed. During the Civil War, Protestant churches argued over support for the war, provided aid to soldiers and their families, including working with the U.S. Christian Commission

**FIGURE 35.** St. Andrew's Russian Orthodox Cathedral, N. Fifth Street, Philadelphia, 1946. The congregation, which first met in 1897, received a boost a year later when Russian sailors waiting on warships to be constructed at the Cramp shipyard began to attend services. After buying a lot in 1902, worshippers constructed the building shown here in 1911. As immigration from eastern Europe increased, other Orthodox churches sprang up in the Philadelphia region. Divisions over the Russian Revolution led some St. Andrew's parishioners to break away and form St. Nicholas Eastern Orthodox Church in 1917, and the new congregation found a home in a former Dutch Reformed church in the Northern Liberties. Saint George's Greek Orthodox Cathedral took over a neoclassical Episcopalian church on S. Eighth Street in 1922. Suburbanization and new immigration sustained the Orthodox tradition in the second half of the twentieth century. Saint Thomas's Greek Orthodox Church first met in Cherry Hill, N.J., in 1967, while Orthodox Christians of Ethiopian heritage established a church in West Philadelphia in 1996. SPECIAL COLLECTIONS RESEARCH CENTER, TEMPLE UNIVERSITY LIBRARIES.

and the U.S. Sanitary Commission, and lobbied for emancipation or against it.

Others preferred to crusade against local evils or establish institutions to educate and uplift the masses. Prison provided one place for reformers to redeem wayward souls. One major experiment in rehabilitation was Eastern State Penitentiary (the term deriving from penitent), which opened in 1829. Inmates held in single isolated cells were visited by a Protestant moral instructor, although accommodations were later made for Catholics and Jews. Temperance also proved a popular cause among Protestants. Their achievements included Methodists establishing the Bedford Street Mission in the impoverished (and Catholic-leaning) district just south of South Street.

Protestant women played a prominent role in such benevolent work. The vast majority of Protestant sects in the nineteenth-century United States barred female ordination, but evangelical Protestantism's emphasis on the individual's relationship with Christ, and its stress on spiritual equality before God, created space for women to enlist in holy work. In middle-class Protestant culture the home became a sanctified space, where the moral influence of wives and mothers would radiate outward to purify the republic. For women eager to move beyond a purely domestic sphere, the prospect of reforming the nation in preparation for Christ's return proved enticing. Women-led organizations, like the Female Baptist Benevolent Society and the Philadelphia Female Anti-Slavery Society, stood alongside associations in which women played an important role as auxiliaries and fundraisers. Protestant women did not have a monopoly on such work—similar Jewish and Catholic organizations also existed—but they were prominently represented in the "benevolent empire" of the nineteenth-century region.

Following the Civil War, Protestants found other ways to extend their influence. In 1869, Methodists created the beachside camp meeting community of Ocean Grove in Monmouth County, New Jersey, which drew thousands of visitors from Philadelphia and New York. Asbury Park, named after the Methodist bishop, followed two years later. Both communities prohibited the sale of alcohol, and Ocean Grove restricted access to the beach on the Sabbath into the twenty-first century. Back in the region's urban centers, Protestant reformers came to articulate the values of the Social Gospel, which emphasized social outreach and moral reform as instruments of conversion and uplift. Philadelphia's Lutheran Settlement House, founded in 1902, marked one denomination's effort to uplift (and ideally convert) new immigrants. And Protestants from several denominations sought to reform education by establishing private religious schools, including Ursinus College in Montgomery County, Pennsylvania (German Reformed Church and later United Church of Christ), and Temple University (Baptist). Confronting industrial conflict and immigration from primarily Catholic and Orthodox parts of Europe, the region's Protestants found new ways to maintain their presence and proselytize to potential converts.

## PROTESTANTISM IN THE TWENTIETH CENTURY TO THE PRESENT

Reflecting trends in the United States, myriad factors shaped Protestantism in the Philadelphia region from the twentieth century to the early 2000s. The rise of Protestant fundamentalism and Pentecostalism, the Great Migration of African Americans from the South, and new immigration after 1965 all led to changes in the region's religious demography and landscape. Traditional mainline Protestant denominations like the Episcopalians and Quakers declined in influence and evangelical churches gained ground, not least in the expanding and increasingly diverse suburbs. Churches took stands in some of the leading battles of the period that saw Americans divide over civil rights and the proper boundaries between church and state. Internally, denominations divided over the role of women in the ministry and the place of LGBTQ+ people in the ministry and even in congregations. And newcomers to the region, like Korean Americans and people from Latin America, augmented Protestant ranks. At the same time, the use of radio and then television for purposes of evangelism spread gospel messages and Protestant influence, with the Philadelphia area having national prominence due to its radio Bible hour broadcasts and other programs.

In the early twentieth century, the city incubated a new fundamentalist Protestantism. Rejecting evangelicals' desire to prepare the world for Christ's return through moral reformation, some believers anticipated an imminent Second Coming and sought to ready the world for the End Times. William L. Pettingill, pastor of a Wilmington, Delaware, Baptist church, helped to establish the Philadelphia School for the Bible, which won funding from local businesspeople, sponsored urgent efforts to convert the globe, and propagated the belief that World War I and the collapse of Ottoman control over Jerusalem heralded the End of Days. Although the conflict ended without Armageddon, six thousand delegates from the United States and overseas gathered in Philadelphia for the World Conference on Christian Fundamentals in 1919, which historian Richard Kent Evans argues marked the birth of fundamentalism. Pettingill and his associates built a base from the city for fundamentalism to emerge as a powerful international Protestant movement.

The new fundamentalism that sprang from the 1919 Philadelphia World Conference turned away from Pettingill's interest in prophecy and emphasized biblical literalism instead. This set the stage for conflict. Just as the Enlightenment coincided with the Great Awakening centuries before, science and secularism in the twentieth century collided with Protestant efforts to maintain influence over society and education. These battles played out in court battles over the First Amendment and pitted politically organized fundamentalist Protestants against liberals. The 1963 case *Abington v. Schempp* tested the boundaries of church and state. The case originated when eleventh-grade student Ellery Schempp, whose family was Unitarian, chose to read the Qur'an instead of listening to verses from the King James Bible on November 26, 1956, at Abington High School in Montgomery County. The U.S. Supreme Court ruled that the requirement in Pennsylvania for mandatory Bible reading and prayer at school violated the Constitution's Establishment Clause. Fifty years later, in 2005, the Pennsylvania State Supreme Court revisited debates over Darwin and creationism in public school from the Scopes "Monkey Trial" of 1925 when it ruled in *Kitzmiller v. Dover Area School District* (in Delaware) that an attempt by the local school board, controlled by a majority of fundamentalist Christians, to have "intelligent design" taught alongside Darwin's theory of evolution was unconstitutional because it was religion, not science.

As these battles raged, the demographics of Protestantism in the Philadelphia region began to change. Over the middle decades of the twentieth century, the second wave of the Great Migration increased the city's African American population from 13 percent in 1940 to 37 percent in 1980, and Black churches became vital institutions where their congregations found support, solidarity, and a sense of belonging in a city often marked by racial segregation and discrimination. Older churches were joined by many storefront churches (there were ninety-three places of worship along Germantown Avenue alone by 2009), including the Church of Prayer Seventh Day founded by Mother Brown, who came to Philadelphia from Virginia in 1914. Pentecostalism, which had roots in an early twentieth-century Black-led revival in Los Angeles and stressed the direct connection of its followers with God, also flourished. So, too, did older Protestant sects. Zion Baptist Church, established in 1882, emerged as a pillar in the community during the civil rights movement under the leadership of Rev. Leon H. Sullivan, who was called to pastor from West Virginia in 1950 until his retirement in 1988. Sullivan used his ministry to demand the expansion of Black opportunities in employment and fight discrimination at home and abroad.

The Immigration and Nationality Act (or Hart-Celler Act) signed by President Lyndon B. Johnson in 1965 ended the immigration restrictions from the 1920s and opened the doors wider to immigrants from across the globe. Immigrants to Greater Philadelphia from Asia, Africa, and Latin America, many of them Protestants, revitalized old and new churches just as the many non-Protestants coming to the region redrew its religious profile. Among Protestants, Korean Protestants were particularly well represented, as the Korean American Presbyterian Church, for instance, was formed at Westminster Theological Seminary in Philadelphia in 1978.

Amid the religious pluralism of the twenty-first century, Protestants remained heavily represented in the region, albeit as one faith community among many. As of 2020, the Greater Philadelphia area had over one hundred African Methodist Episcopal congregations, over two hundred Baptist churches, over 50,000 Episcopalians, and over 70,000 Lutherans. Evangelical churches, numbering over seven hundred, claimed over 280,000 members. Scattered across multiple denominations and congregations, Protestantism endured as a dynamic religious tradition capable of reinventing itself and drawing new converts.

## Catholicism

**Elizabeth Hayes Alvarez**

Philadelphia's first Catholic Mass was heard in 1708. Despite English law prohibiting Catholic worship, broad religious tolerance had been laid out that year in the Pennsylvania Charter of Privileges by William Penn. The resulting legal tension came to a head in 1733 when a complaint about the "Romish chappell," Saint Joseph's in Willing's Alley, prompted the Pennsylvania Provincial Council to affirm that the colony's religious freedom took precedence over the laws of England. Jesuit priests at Saint Joseph's continued to hold Masses for forty or so English, Irish, and German parishioners. From this modest beginning, the Roman Catholic Church grew over the centuries to become the single largest denomination in the Philadelphia region, and Catholics became integral to civic life and the ongoing struggle for full religious freedom.

### ESTABLISHING A COMMUNITY

Philadelphia's early toleration of Catholic worship enticed migrants from Europe and from other American colonies and increased Philadelphia's Catholic population to 1,400 by 1757. To serve this growing community, a second Catholic church, St. Mary's Church, opened on S. Fourth Street in 1763. Catholic and Protestant leaders in Philadelphia congratulated themselves on their tolerant city, where a new and enlightened friendship promised to supplant the religious enmity of the Old World. During the American Revolution most of Philadelphia's Catholics were patriots with no love for the English Crown, France's and Ireland's longtime foe, and a particular dislike for King George III. Their support won favor with the Continental Congress, whose members attended the first public religious commemoration of the Declaration of Independence on July 4, 1779, at St. Mary's. Two years later, General George Washington, an Anglican, heard a Solemn Mass of Thanksgiving at St. Mary's for victory over the British. And on February 22, 1800, several Protestant members of Congress joined the Catholic community in a Solemn Mass memorializing Washington after his death. This was remarkable because, at the time, a Catholic priest could face life imprisonment for saying Mass in England.

After the American Revolution, as the Catholic Church found its footing in the new republic, many Catholics hoped for a similarly democratic American church. John Carroll, a Jesuit and the first Catholic archbishop of the United States, argued that Catholics' success in America hinged on their independence from Rome, writing that "the only connexion they ought to have with Rome is to acknowledge the pope as the Spiritual head of the Church." Carroll's convictions were shared by many of Philadelphia's lay Catholics, who attempted to retain control of the churches they built and financially supported through a practice known as "lay trusteeism." The Vatican, however, did not support a new church polity or expect the American church to be significantly divided from the global Catholic communion. This played out in a struggle that marked early Catholic life in the city and elsewhere, as laymen attempted to call and dismiss their pastors and factions broke out in support of competing clergy.

The fledgling Catholic community faced other challenges as well. The 1791 Haitian Revolution brought boatloads of Catholic refugees—both former enslavers and the formerly enslaved—to Philadelphia, while the 1793 yellow fever epidemic caused the deaths of roughly five thousand Philadelphians, around 10 percent of the city's population. The church met the challenges of resettling refugees and of caring for the victims and orphans of the epidemic by rapidly deploying priests and religious women caregivers and developing an infrastructure of makeshift hospitals and settlements.

In addition to these challenges, the multilinguistic and multicultural nature of American Catholicism also caused difficulties. German Catholics began lobbying for their own church. In 1784, approval was given for Holy Trinity Church to open as the first "national parish" in the United States, built for German-speaking Catholics. This opened a tension between maintaining a unifying geographic parish system and developing immigrant-supporting, ethnolinguistic churches that continued in Philadelphia and other American cities.

### CREATING A DIOCESE, CONFRONTING NATIVISM

In 1808 the Diocese of Philadelphia, encompassing Pennsylvania, Delaware, and southern and western New Jersey, was created to support the nearly thirty thousand Catholics then residing in the region (until 1808 this area was part of the Diocese of Baltimore). After the young diocese's first two bishops struggled to control lay trustees and the centrifugal force of a multinational Catholic populace, Pope Pius VIII appointed Irish-born Francis Kenrick as bishop, with a mandate to create stability and order. Kenrick inherited a range of other problems as well. Growing anti-immigrant nativism threatened the region's Catholics. During the 1830s, Philadelphia endured repeated outbreaks of anti-Catholic violence, culminating in the rise of the American Republican Party (and its various "Know Nothing" cousins) and the 1844 Bible Riots (also known as Nativist Riots), which resulted in the deaths of between twenty-five and forty people and the destruction of dozens of Catholic homes, a firehouse, two churches, and a convent. The riots were precipitated by Kenrick's request that Catholic students be allowed to read the Catholic Douay version of the Bible in Philadelphia's public schools. His request was not honored, nor were any Protestant nativists held legally liable for the violence and destruction of the riots. Kenrick also faced repeated cholera outbreaks among poorer Catholics in overcrowded neighborhoods and large waves of Catholic immigration due to the 1848–49 German revolutions and the 1845–52 Irish Potato Famine.

An able manager and institution builder, Kenrick secured the foundations to see the church through these troubles. He closed the prestigious St. Mary's Church until its lay trustees handed over their keys and their power to call priests. He acquired all Catholic property on behalf of the institutional church. He established Philadelphia's first diocesan newspaper, the *Catholic Herald*, and its first Catholic hospital, St. Joseph's Hospital at N. Sixteenth Street and W. Girard Avenue under the direction of the Sisters of Charity. He founded the Catholic seminary, St. Charles Borromeo, and established Villanova College (Augustinian) and St. Joseph's College (Jesuit). By the time he was created archbishop of Baltimore in 1851, the Philadelphia archdiocese had ninety-two Catholic churches and over 170,000 Catholics. Kenrick also moved to give Catholics a firmer institutional and pastoral foundation in South Jersey, in 1848 appointing the first priest assigned primarily to the area, though Jesuit, Redemptorist, Augustinian, and diocesan clergy from Philadelphia continued to serve the sparsely settled region on missions there. In 1849 Kenrick blessed the first parish church in South Jersey, the Church of St. Mary in Gloucester.

After Kenrick's tenure, Philadelphia-area Catholics continued to build the cocoon that would shelter them from nativism and create solidarity among immigrants of varied backgrounds. Key to their success was the development of the parochial school system and the proliferation of popular religious devotionalism that brought them together as a community and brought the pride of the community out onto the streets. Saints' parades, May devotions honoring Mary, and first Holy Communion processions of children in white suits and dresses showed the devout side of Catholic life. The raucous mummers (belsnickles) hailing from the Irish and Italian Catholic neighborhoods of South Philadelphia displayed their rowdier creativity and culture in sporadic, impromptu performances later supplanted by an established parade route.

In this mid- to late-nineteenth-century period of growth and expansion, Bohemian-born bishop John Nepomucene Neumann brought to the diocese his deep spirituality, formed among the Redemptorists (the Congregation of the Most Holy Redeemer community of priests and brothers). Mastering six languages to speak to his multilingual flock in their native tongues, and visiting every parish in the archdiocese each year, Neumann offered a more pastoral style of leadership. But, like his predecessor, he built institutions too, establishing over two hundred parochial schools and constructing new churches at the rate of almost one per month. He supported new immigrant communities by creating the Beneficial Bank to protect their savings and, in 1852, established an Italian-language national parish, St. Mary Magdalen de Pazzi at 712 Montrose Street. During this time of church growth, Neumann also requested that New Jersey be formed into a separate diocese, and in 1853 the church created the Diocese of Newark, which encompassed all of New Jersey. Canonized in 1977, Neumann became the first American male saint, with his

**FIGURE 36.** Bomb damage at Our Lady of Victory, Fifty-Fourth and Vine Streets, Philadelphia, 1919. A series of anarchist bombings across the United States in the spring and summer of 1919 fueled the first anti-communist Red Scare and led to a wave of arrests and deportations. Our Lady of Victory, the only church anarchists targeted, still managed to hold two masses the day after the explosion. SPECIAL COLLECTIONS RESEARCH CENTER, TEMPLE UNIVERSITY LIBRARIES.

shrine at St. Peter the Apostle Church at 1019 N. Fifth Street, Philadelphia.

During these years, the African American Catholic community grew as well. Black Catholics were the descendants of Haitian and other Afro-Caribbean immigrants, transplants from New Orleans and other southern cities, and converts in Philadelphia. They were initially segregated into separate "Negro Masses." Over time, four Black Catholic parishes were established in Philadelphia: St. Peter Claver (1886), St. Ignatius of Loyola (1893), St. Catherine of Siena (1914), and Our Lady of the Blessed Sacrament (1887). In 1892, the *Journal* newspaper was founded to serve Philadelphia's growing African American Catholic community. African American men who, due to white racism, were denied admission into the Catholic Knights of Columbus fraternity, joined the Black-led Knights of Peter Claver, an international Catholic brotherhood for fellowship and mutual support. The Oblate Sisters of Providence, a Baltimore-based Black congregation of women religious, served African American children in Philadelphia. Black Catholics also found a patroness in Katharine Drexel, the Philadelphia heiress who donated her large fortune to the church and founded the Sisters of the Blessed Sacrament in 1891 to serve underprivileged Native American and African American communities. While aspects of Drexel's legacy have been contested due to Native American cultural erasure, she and the Sisters of the Blessed Sacrament provided education for African Americans in Philadelphia and throughout the United States, founding the only historically Black Catholic college, Xavier University in New Orleans, Louisiana. In 2000 Drexel became the second Philadelphian to be canonized.

## CATHOLICISM AFTER 1900 IN THE DELAWARE VALLEY

The twentieth century saw the emergence of Philadelphia Catholics from their cocoon. While the parochial school system continued to flourish and expand, Catholics were also well represented in the public schools, the police force, political offices, and all aspects of Philadelphia's professional and cultural life. Dennis Joseph Dougherty led the church into this period of cultural dominance. Installed as archbishop in 1918, and created cardinal in 1921, his decisive and confident leadership inspired Catholics to boldly proclaim their faith. Known as "God's bricklayer," Dougherty aggressively expanded the church's presence across the Philadelphia area, establishing 112 parishes, 145 parochial schools, 53 high schools, 12 hospitals, and other institutions and encouraged Catholic homeownership as a foundation for parishes with Catholic savings-and-loan banks providing needed capital. He also drew upon the economic power of the city's Catholics to enact a boycott against movie theaters until the film industry stopped depicting immoral content. This flexing of power closed dozens of theaters.

Rapidly changing demographics in Philadelphia in the early to middle twentieth century challenged urban parishes and led to increasing Catholic populations in the suburbs. White Catholics who resided in increasingly Black neighborhoods and other areas of the city joined in the white flight to the Philadelphia and South Jersey suburbs, moves encouraged and facilitated by the church's rapid establishment of new parishes there. City parishes began to include many more Black Catholics, whose presence shaped these communities in new ways. They also began to seek converts among and offer charitable relief to their new African American neighbors. Some parishes continued to segregate Black Catholics or treat them as second-class members. Others, such as St. Malachy's on N. Eleventh Street, committed themselves to the work of racial integration, community service, and civil rights. In cities such as Philadelphia, Camden, and Chester, the parochial school system increasingly served the most vulnerable and marginalized children, offering high quality, generally affordable private religious education to Catholic and non-Catholic children alike. At the same time, better-endowed parochial and private Catholic schools grew in the suburbs across the region, adding to the appeal of such places for white Catholics wishing to escape changing cities.

Catholic parishes in Philadelphia-adjacent suburbs grew rapidly during this period, establishing new churches and parochial schools. As Catholics moved to the suburbs, old ethnic divisions between English, German, Italian, Irish, and other European Catholics began to lose their salience and were subsumed under the racialized label "white." In most suburbs, Catholics were a minority and banded together to create thriving communities of support. While some ethnocultural differences persisted, especially in inner-ring suburbs such as Upper Darby and Lansdowne, in Delaware County, many Catholics sought and gained social acceptance through the process of suburbanization and ethnic homogenization.

In the twenty-first century, the Catholic population had grown such that the original area of Philadelphia Archdiocese was served by eleven separate dioceses, while it served five Pennsylvania counties: Philadelphia, Bucks, Chester, Delaware, and Montgomery. However, like Christianity more broadly, American Catholicism began losing members in these decades. In the Northeast, the Catholic share of the population decreased nine points from 36 percent to 27 percent between 2009 and 2019. The church also faced challenges related to the priest sex-abuse scandal, which was widely covered by the media. While the majority of American Catholics surveyed in 2019 said that the Vatican was handling the scandal well and that the problems were not unique to their church, financial settlements in abuse cases cost the Philadelphia Archdiocese and the Camden Diocese millions of dollars. This, coupled with a declining population and aging buildings, stressed Philadelphia's Catholic infrastructure. Parishes closed, cemeteries were leased to private companies, and parochial schools merged or shifted to the control of a nonprofit, Independence Mission Schools. At the same time, a rapidly declining number of priests, and an aging clerical population generally, created staffing problems for churches across the region.

Still, Philadelphia continued to support a thriving Catholic community. While 85 percent of the Archdiocese of Philadelphia's Catholics were non-Hispanic whites in 2015, the church welcomed new waves of immigrants from Asia, Southeast Asia, the Caribbean, Mexico, and Latin America and a growing Puerto Rican community. In 2018 the archdiocese counted roughly twenty-two thousand registered Spanish-speaking Catholics. Drawn from across Puerto Rico, Mexico, the Caribbean, Central America, and South America, they brought many popular religious traditions and expressions to the archdiocese, which the church tried to respect by allowing festivals and recognition of particular religious icons from each group while also supporting an annual archdiocesan celebration of Our Lady of Guadalupe as an appeal to a common "Hispanic" identity. In southern New Jersey, Latino migrants and workers added to the ethnic mix of the larger Catholic population. Ministries such as the Catholic Social Services of the Archdiocese of Philadelphia and the Aquinas Center gave practical and legal support to immigrants, refugees, and migrants. In response to these later demographic shifts, the archdiocese moved away from the national parish model to support multilingual, multiethnic parishes with distinct but overlapping congregations attending services in different languages in one church.

In September 2015, Philadelphia hosted the triennial World Meeting of Families that brought over twenty thousand attendees from all over the world. During the event, Pope Francis concluded his six-day United States visit with a two-day pastoral visit to Philadelphia and an open-air Mass attended by over one million people. His visit acknowledged and celebrated the vital role that Catholics have played and continue to play in the Philadelphia region.

Two years later, Bishop Nelson J. Perez became the first archbishop of the diocese with Hispanic heritage. He had previously served as episcopal vicar for Hispanic ministry and as bishop served on the Bishops' Standing Committee on Cultural Diversity and the Pontifical Commission for Latin America. During the COVID-19 pandemic, which began shortly after Bishop Perez's installation in February 2020, he suspended all public Masses but moved rapidly to continue to support Catholic community, worship, support, and outreach in the city, declaring, "the Catholic Church in Philadelphia is not closing down. It is not disappearing, and it will not abandon you."

Despite many changes and challenges, Catholics continued to shape life in the Delaware Valley well into the twenty-first century. As of the early 2020s, over two hundred parishes made up the Philadelphia archdiocese. The Diocese of Camden, which the church erected in 1937, consisted of sixty-two parishes covering the counties of Atlantic, Camden, Cape May, Cumberland, Gloucester, and Salem. Philadelphia remained indebted to its Catholic citizens who have contributed to all aspects of the city's life and continued to provide resources, cultural, and religious contributions to the diverse life of the city.

## Judaism

**Reena Sigman Friedman**

From their arrival in the Delaware Valley during the colonial era to the twenty-first century, Jews in the greater Philadelphia area participated in, and contributed to, many aspects of the region's life. American Jews have always observed religious practices along a spectrum from the most to the least traditional. The Reform movement in America began in the 1820s and gained strength in the mid- to late nineteenth century; Orthodoxy and the Conservative movement developed over time and became more clearly defined in the interwar period; and the Reconstructionist movement had roots in the 1920s and became a separate movement in the late 1960s. All of the movements were represented in Philadelphia.

## FROM THE COLONIAL ERA TO THE CIVIL WAR

Pennsylvania's Quaker roots, dating to the 1680s, promised a favorable environment for minority religious groups that sought economic opportunity and freedom of worship. Although a few Jews had passed through Philadelphia earlier, an organized Jewish community took shape in 1737, with the arrival of Nathan Levy and his brother, Isaac, from New York. Nathan Levy purchased land on Spruce Street for a Jewish cemetery, and people began gathering for worship in rented quarters during the 1740s. They called their congregation, the first in the city, Mikveh Israel ("Hope of Israel"), a phrase from the biblical book of Jeremiah. Though the congregation formally organized in the 1760s (a draft "constitution" dates from about 1770), a synagogue building (on Cherry and Third Streets) was not dedicated until 1782.

An estimated three hundred Jewish persons lived in Philadelphia in 1775. The early settlers included Jews of both Spanish/Portuguese (Sephardic) and central/east European (Ashkenazic) origin. Many of these Jews worked as merchants, shopkeepers, and craftsmen, and some had connections with Jewish merchants in other ports in the colonies, Britain, and the Caribbean. During the American Revolution, most of the 1,000 to 2,500 Jews in the British colonies supported the patriot cause; some 100 Jews served in the Continental army or local militias. Philadelphia Jewish merchants signed the Non-Importation Resolutions against Britain, and some Jews provided supplies for the Continental army or secured critical loans to support the cause. Haym Saloman, a Polish-born exile and escapee from New York, gained respect and renown as a broker and fundraiser for the Articles of Confederation government. Philadelphia also became a haven for many Jewish refugees fleeing British-occupied cities.

In the early years of nation building, Jews continued to be active in civic affairs. Jonas Phillips, a prominent Jewish merchant who had served in a company of Philadelphia militia during the Revolutionary War, succeeded in getting the new Pennsylvania state constitution of 1790 to remove a stipulation requiring that individuals seeking public office affirm their belief in the "divine inspiration" of the Old and New Testaments. In gratitude for similar provisions for religious liberty in the new constitution, Jews jubilantly joined in the Grand Federal Procession in Philadelphia on July 4, 1788. They enjoyed kosher refreshments at a separate table at the end of the parade.

Philadelphia's Jewish population increased markedly in the early nineteenth century from about five hundred in 1820 to four thousand by 1848, due largely to an influx of central European immigrants. As early as 1802, a second congregation—Rodeph Shalom—formed to meet the liturgical needs of the new German-speaking congregants. Thus, Philadelphia became the first American Jewish community to boast more than one synagogue. By 1858, there were seven congregations in the city. As Philadelphia's Jewish population grew in the nineteenth century, prominent Jewish families often took the lead in establishing charitable organizations. The Gratz family proved especially active. Brothers Barnard and Michael Gratz, successful merchants and pillars of Mikveh Israel and the Philadelphia Jewish community, promoted civic improvement and charities. Michael's daughter, Rebecca Gratz, was an influential philanthropist and educator. She helped organize the Female Association for the Relief of Women and Children in Reduced Circumstances (1801), a nonsectarian organization that assisted the city's poor. She (often alongside other Jewish women) also helped to establish and run the Female Hebrew Benevolent Society (1819), the Hebrew Sunday School (1838), the Jewish Foster Home (1855), and the nonsectarian Philadelphia Orphan Asylum (1815).

Philadelphia Jews also played important roles in defining American Judaism and building Jewish cultural and educational institutions during the nineteenth century. Among them, Isaac Leeser, chazan (cantor) of Congregation Mikveh Israel from 1829 to 1850, established the first American Jewish Publication Society (1845), Hebrew high school (1849), rabbinical school (Maimonides College, 1867–73), and a successful American Jewish newspaper (*Occident and American Jewish Advocate*, 1843–69), in which he forcefully defended the separation of church and state in the United States.

By 1860, some eight thousand Jews lived in Philadelphia, and Philadelphia Jewry was becoming more engaged in the city's civic and political life. Some Philadelphia rabbis took public positions supporting abolition and the Union. But anti-Jewish scapegoating rose markedly amid the tensions of the Civil War. Jews

**FIGURE 37.** *Rebecca Gratz*, by Thomas Sully, 1830. One of the most prominent Jewish American women of the nineteenth century, Gratz moved to Philadelphia from Lancaster and played a leading role in several charitable organizations in the city, including the Female Hebrew Benevolent Society (established 1819). Legend has it that she served as the inspiration for Sir Walter Scott's Jewish heroine Rebecca of York in his wildly popular romance, *Ivanhoe*. DELAWARE ART MUSEUM, GIFT OF BENJAMIN SHAW II, 1971.

nevertheless gained significant rights during this time. The service of Philadelphian Michael Allen as an unofficial chaplain in the Sixty-Fifth Regiment of the Fifth Pennsylvania Cavalry (although he was forced to resign) led to Congress's revision of the military code to permit non-Christians to serve as military chaplains in July 1862. Philadelphia's Jewish women also played an important role on the home front through organizations like the Ladies' Hebrew Association for the Relief of Sick and Wounded Union Soldiers. In 1865, Jewish Philadelphians mourned Abraham Lincoln, who had countermanded the 1862 order by General Ulysses S. Grant that expelled Jews from his military department. In sharing in the nation's grief, they reminded everyone that they were part of that nation.

## IMMIGRATION, CULTURE, AND INSTITUTIONS, 1865–1945

Between 1880 and 1924, 2.5 million Jewish immigrants, mostly from eastern Europe, arrived in the United States. These immigrants were generally Ashkenazic, though some 50,000–60,000 Eastern Sephardic Jews arrived in the United States during the same period. Philadelphia's Jewish population mushroomed from about fifteen thousand in 1880 to around two hundred thousand in 1920. Most of the newcomers settled in South Philadelphia, on Fourth and Fifth Streets south of Pine; others lived in the neighborhood north of Market Street and in Port Richmond. Like Jewish immigrants in other cities, many worked in the growing garment industry, became peddlers and shopkeepers, or pursued other callings. Optician Siegmund Lubin, for example, became a pioneer in the motion picture industry.

Philanthropic Jews established a variety of organizations and institutions to assist the newcomers, including the United Hebrew Charities, Jewish Hospital, Hebrew Education Society, and Home for the Jewish Aged. Jewish women launched charitable ventures too, like the Young Women's Union, which operated educational programs for immigrants and a settlement house. When they were able to do so, immigrants created their own charitable, educational, and cultural institutions, such as synagogues, newspapers, and mutual aid and fraternal organizations. The city's first Russian Jewish congregation was B'nai Abraham, established in South Philadelphia in 1883.

The relationship between more established American Jews and the eastern European Jewish immigrants proved complex. Jewish philanthropists provided critical services for the newcomers yet sought to Americanize the immigrants as rapidly as possible to reduce growing anti-Semitism. For their part, the recent immigrants benefited from the charity of the so-called uptowners, while often resenting them. Most of the established Jews belonged to Reform congregations, while most of the newer immigrants, though not all Orthodox (as is often assumed), preserved their ethnic identities and some traditional religious practices, but were not necessarily fully observant. Over time, the differences between the two groups blurred through Americanization and intermarriage.

Other key cultural and educational institutions of the Philadelphia Jewish community emerged at this time as well. The city's major Anglo-Jewish newspaper, the *Jewish Exponent*, began publication in 1887. In 1895, Gratz College, the first independent college of Jewish studies in North America, was founded, and in 1907, Dropsie College for Hebrew and Cognate Learning opened. After a series of name changes and mergers, the latter became the Herbert D. Katz Center for Advanced Judaic Studies at the University of Pennsylvania in 2008.

As the Jewish population of Philadelphia expanded, more Jews began to settle in neighboring geographic areas. The Jewish community in Wilmington began to take shape in the late nineteenth century, with the formation of the Moses Montefiore Mutual Aid Society (1879) and Delaware's first congregation, Ohabe Shalom (1880). Another congregation, Adas Kodesch (formed in 1885), built the first synagogue in the state on Sixth and French Streets in 1898. The city's Jewish population grew to about four thousand by 1920. In South Jersey, the first Jews came to the city of Camden around 1890, and some founded the (Orthodox) Sons of Israel Congregation in 1894 and a YMHA in 1907.

While most Philadelphia-area Jews were city dwellers in the late nineteenth and early twentieth centuries, a significant number became farmers at the urging of Jewish leaders. In 1882, a group of Russian Jews, with the help of the Alliance Israélite Universelle (a French Jewish organization), founded Alliance, a farming community in South Jersey. Alliance was followed by Woodbine (established in 1891 by the Baron de Hirsch Fund; it included an agricultural school), as well as Rosenhayn, Vineland, and Carmel (South Jersey), and Toms River, Farmingdale, Lakewood, and Freehold (central New Jersey). Some Jewish families farmed in southern Delaware as well. These communities raised fruits, vegetables, and chickens, and often had manufacturing components. They welcomed European Jewish refugees during the 1930s and, later, Holocaust survivors.

In the late nineteenth and early twentieth centuries, a remarkable group of Jewish leaders emerged in Philadelphia. Often described collectively as "The Philadelphia Group," they included Rabbi Sabato Morais, Mayer Sulzberger, Solomon Solis-Cohen, Cyrus Adler, and Rabbi Bernard Levinthal. Morais, religious leader of Mikveh Israel, spoke out in support of striking garment workers in 1890. He was also a founder and first president of the Jewish Theological Seminary (JTS, the Conservative movement's rabbinical seminary). Sulzberger, a respected attorney and judge of the Court of Common Pleas, helped to found, and was the first president of, the American Jewish Committee (created in 1906 to combat anti-Jewish persecution and defend Jewish rights). Solis-Cohen, a physician and a longtime member of the Philadelphia School Board, supported the Philadelphia Young Men's and Young Women's Hebrew Association and the Jewish Publication Society. Adler, a Semitics scholar and for a time librarian at the Smithsonian Institution, served on many boards of non-Jewish, Philadelphia-based organizations and also, at one point in his life, headed five major Jewish institutions or organizations simultaneously. Rabbi Bernard Levinthal was widely recognized as the Orthodox unofficial "chief rabbi" of Philadelphia; he also held leadership positions in Agudat Harabbanim (the Orthodox rabbinical organization), Yeshiva University, the American Jewish Committee, the Federation of American Zionists, and Mizrachi (the religious Zionist organization). The prominence of such men reflected the rising influence of Jews in Philadelphia's intellectual, civic, educational, and social life, as well as their place among power brokers in the city.

By the 1920s, the Philadelphia Jewish community was the third largest in North America. Many of the city's Jews moved to new neighborhoods, such as Logan, Strawberry Mansion, and West Philadelphia. Significant numbers worked in business (especially retail stores), radio broadcasting, public school teaching, and filmmaking. Quite a few Jewish business leaders and professionals emerged as prominent public figures and philanthropists in the interwar years and beyond. These included attorney and judge Horace Stern, paper box manufacturer Frederic Mann, media giant Walter Annenberg, and real estate magnate Albert Greenfield. Among their many accomplishments, Stern served as chief justice of the Pennsylvania Supreme Court; Mann supported the Philadelphia Orchestra and the outdoor music amphitheater in Fairmount Park; Annenberg became editor and publisher of the *Philadelphia Inquirer*, *Philadelphia Daily News*, and other publications; and Greenfield played a leading role in Philadelphia city planning and urban renewal.

Even as they benefited from socioeconomic and residential mobility, and continued to build their communal institutions, Jews during the interwar period experienced discrimination in admission to large law firms, major banks, insurance companies, colleges and universities, medical and dental schools, social clubs and other organizations, resorts, and certain neighborhoods. Philadelphia Jews responded by creating their own law firms, clubs, and associations. By the 1930s, the city's Jews, like Jews in other American cities, confronted a sharp rise in anti-Semitism; they were often scapegoated by Americans suffering as a result of the Depression. The broadcasts of Detroit-based "radio priest" Charles Coughlin, replete with anti-Semitic stereotypes, became popular among segments of the city's population, and the German American Bund, a Nazi-style organization in the United States that terrorized American Jews, had a strong local presence.

By 1940, about 245,000 Jews lived in Philadelphia, and many served in the American armed forces during World War II. Significant numbers on the home front protested Nazi persecution of the Jews and raised funds to assist European Jewry. These difficult years witnessed some other important developments in the Philadelphia Jewish community. Akiba Hebrew Academy was founded in 1946, the country's first pluralistic Jewish secondary day school, not affiliated with any religious movement; several other Orthodox and Conservative Jewish day schools were established over the next two decades. There were also networks of Folkshulen (Labor Zionist schools, conducted in Hebrew and Yiddish) and Workmen's Circle Yiddish schools. While many Philadelphia Jews supported the Zionist cause (to create a Jewish national state in Palestine), a group of Reform rabbis and laypeople founded the anti-Zionist American Council for Judaism in the Philadelphia area in 1942.

## JEWISH LIFE IN THE REGION AFTER WORLD WAR II

In the post–World War II decades, Philadelphia's Jewish residents worked in clothing, supermarket, cigar-making and tobacco, electronics, entertainment, liquor, communications, and real estate businesses. Many others found work in public school teaching and public service, among other sectors of the economy. Some employment discrimination persisted into the early 1960s but lessened markedly by the end of the century. Quite a few formerly urban synagogues, following their congregants, relocated to new suburban buildings, including Adath Jeshurun (Elkins Park, 1964) and Har Zion (Penn Valley, 1971). Congregation Beth Sholom, founded in 1918 in the Logan section of Philadelphia, moved to suburban Elkins Park in 1951 and in 1959 dedicated its new building, designed by renowned architect Frank Lloyd Wright. The postwar period witnessed an all-time high in synagogue affiliation and religious school enrollment for American Jews. Conservative congregations drew the most adherents in those years, but Reform congregations (such as Rodeph Shalom, Keneseth Israel, and Beth David in Wynnefield) also thrived. Beginning in the 1960s, significant numbers of Orthodox Jews moved to Northeast Philadelphia, Wynnefield, Overbrook Park, and the western suburbs (especially Bala Cynwyd and Wynnewood), leading to the establishment of more Orthodox synagogues and schools in those areas.

Many Philadelphia-area Jews became activists for civil rights, working through the Fellowship Commission (established by Maurice Fagan in 1941), a unique organization that brought together Blacks and whites, Jews and Christians to advocate for fair treatment for Black workers and for civil rights legislation throughout the 1940s and 1950s. Significant numbers of Jews also participated in the civil rights marches, sit-ins, and freedom rides of the early 1960s. Despite these sustained cooperative efforts, tensions increased between Black and Jewish communities in the 1960s, as in other cities, due to poverty, racial discrimination, and inequality in housing and employment. A flashpoint for tension was North Philadelphia, which had been predominantly Jewish and retained Jewish-owned businesses, even though by 1960, most of its residents were Black. Members of the Philadelphia Jewish community turned to other forms of activism during the turbulent 1960s and beyond. Working through the Philadelphia Soviet Jewry Council, from the 1960s through the 1980s, many played key roles in the movement to free Soviet Jews. Philadelphia-area Jews sponsored Soviet Jews' immigration to the region. In June 1967, Jews throughout the Philadelphia area rallied and raised substantial sums in solidarity with Israel during the Six-Day War.

Philadelphia also became the birthplace of a fourth denomination in American Jewish life when the Reconstructionist Rabbinical College opened in North Philadelphia in 1968; the college moved to Wyncote in 1982. The Jewish Renewal movement, led by Rabbi Zalman Schachter-Shalomi and others, emerged in Philadelphia's West Mount Airy neighborhood in the 1970s. Reconstructionism is based on the philosophy of Rabbi Mordecai Kaplan, who described Judaism as "an evolving religious civilization." Jewish Renewal characterizes itself as a "transdenominational approach to revitalizing Judaism" that emphasizes spiritual experience, meditation practices, and creative prayers.

By 1970, most of Philadelphia's Jews lived in Center City, the Greater Northeast, the Old York Road suburbs, West Oak Lane/Mount Airy, Wynnefield, and the Main Line suburbs, as well as in Levittown and Norristown. In Camden, Parkside had been the city's foremost Jewish neighborhood, but during the 1950s and 1960s Jews joined the movement of white residents to suburban areas in South Jersey. Over the next few decades, Cherry Hill and Voorhees in Camden County, and Mount Laurel, Medford, Moorestown, and Marlton in Burlington County, emerged as prominent Jewish communities. In Delaware, by the end of the twentieth century more than half the state's Jews remained in Wilmington, about a third could be found in the Newark/Hockessin area, and a smaller fraction in southern Delaware.

In the last few decades of the twentieth century, and into the twenty-first century, a number of Delaware Valley Jews assumed prominent positions in city, state, and national politics. The success of Jewish political candidates in winning citywide and statewide offices indicated an acceptance of Jews, despite some undercurrents of anti-Semitism that surfaced during political campaigns. Milton Shapp served as the first Jewish governor of Pennsylvania (1971–79); Arlen Specter became the first Jewish U.S. senator from Pennsylvania (1981–2011); Edward G. Rendell was the first Jewish mayor of Philadelphia (1992–2000) and later governor of Pennsylvania (2003–11); and Josh Shapiro also won election to the Pennsylvania governorship in 2023.

By 2019, the Jewish Federation of Greater Philadelphia reported that an estimated 351,200 Jews lived in Philadelphia, Montgomery, Bucks, Delaware, and Chester Counties. Even as Jews in the Philadelphia region participated actively in the life of the larger community, they retained their own identity. Although some expressed concerns about the secularization of Jewish life and the impact of increasing intermarriage between Jews and non-Jews, Jews continued to express themselves through their religious practices, social and cultural organizations, foodways, and historical memory.

## Islam

**David M. Krueger**

Islam, a religion founded by the Prophet Muhammad in the early seventh century in the Arabian Peninsula, has had a presence in the Greater Philadelphia region since the colonial era, but the number of Muslims locally did not grow significantly until after the 1960s. By the 2010s, when Muslims in the United States numbered more than three million, the Philadelphia region had the second-highest concentration of Muslims among American metropolitan areas, behind only Detroit. Area Muslims have represented a wide variety of religious orientations (Sunni, Salafi, Shiʿa, Sufi, and more) and races and ethnicities including African American, Asian, and Arab. Reflecting national trends, Muslims have ranked among the fastest-growing religious groups in the region.

### FROM THE COLONIAL ERA TO THE EARLY TWENTIETH CENTURY

In 1682, William Penn founded Pennsylvania as a colony that welcomed religious diversity. This diversity no doubt increased in 1762 when ships carrying nearly five hundred enslaved individuals from West Africa, including from areas known to have significant Muslim populations, arrived in the Delaware Valley. Little knowledge about Muslims during the colonial era has survived, but scholars have estimated that as many as 10 to 30 percent of enslaved persons brought to North America during the slave trade were Muslim. In Philadelphia persons of African descent were known to partake in traditional drumming, singing, praying, and burial rituals in the area later known as Washington Square. If the Islamic call to prayer was ever sung in colonial Philadelphia, it might have been there.

**FIGURE 38.** The Algerian Bazaar (top left), the Egyptian and Syrian Bazaar (bottom left), and the Morocco Building (center) at the Centennial Exhibition, 1876. More than 1,600 Arab traders and artisans exhibited at the Fairmount Park event, which introduced many Philadelphians to the Islamic world. HISTORICAL SOCIETY OF PENNSYLVANIA.

The first Muslims of non-African descent began to arrive in the late nineteenth century, mostly from the Ottoman Empire. The 1876 Centennial Exhibition held in Philadelphia drew exhibitors from all over world, including over 1,600 Arab traders and artisans who came to sell Tunisian coffee, olivewood rosaries, and various other trinkets from the Holy Land. The event sparked a wave of immigration to the United States from the Arab world. A small Lebanese community began to form in South Philadelphia in the 1880s, although the majority were not Muslim but Maronite Catholic. Immigration from the Middle East slowed to a trickle with the U.S. immigration restrictions implemented in 1924.

## AFRICAN AMERICANS AND ISLAM

The first known Muslim missionary to the United States was Mufti Muhammad Sadiq, who arrived in Philadelphia in 1920. Sadiq was born in India and was a devotee of Mirza Ghulam Ahmad, who had claimed to be the most recent prophet of God. A charismatic speaker, Sadiq earned several hundred converts, both white and Black, in cities throughout the United States, including at least nineteen while imprisoned at an immigration center in Gloucester, New Jersey.

Religious innovation and experimentation increased during the early twentieth-century Great Migration of African Americans from the rural south to America's urban North. Philadelphia, Chester, Camden, and Trenton all experienced rapid increases in the number of African Americans, many of whom were drawn to factory work during the First and Second World Wars. These changing cities became fertile ground for Islamic ideas and practices to take root. The Islam-inspired Moorish Science Temple (MST) movement originated in Newark, New Jersey, in 1913, but also had a presence in Philadelphia. Founded by the Prophet Noble Drew Ali, MST aimed to disconnect African Americans from the legacy of slavery and define their identity not as "Negroes," but Moorish Americans. Ali established communities around the country, including Philadelphia, where he founded Temple #11 in 1928. Temples frequently operated with the direct support of businesses, many of which were operated by women. The neighborhood of Twentieth and South Streets in Philadelphia was an early center of the movement, but Temple #11 later moved to N. Fifth Street.

Traditional Sunni Islam began to take root among Philadelphia's African Americans in the 1940s. Former MST member Muhammad Ezladeen, founder of Addeynu Allahe Universal Arabic Association (AAUAA), co-led one of the first national gatherings of African American Sunni Muslims in 1943 in Philadelphia. Around this time, AAUAA established an Islamic agrarian community in Hammonton, New Jersey. In 1949, Imam Nasir Ahmed, leader of the Hammonton community, founded the International Muslim Brotherhood in South Philadelphia, the first mosque in the region. The mosque later moved to West Philadelphia's Lancaster Avenue and opened the Quba Institute, which became an early center for Islamic education.

It was the nonorthodox, non-Sunni, Nation of Islam (NOI), however, that became the most visible expression of Islam among the region's African Americans during the 1950s and 1960s. The NOI traced its origins to Detroit and the teachings of Wallace D. Fard and his successor, Elijah Muhammad. They taught a mythology of Black supremacy, which appealed to many disenfranchised African Americans who suffered under Jim Crow segregation and other forms of racial discrimination. The NOI established Temple #12 in Philadelphia after a 1954 visit by Malcolm X, who converted to NOI in prison. Five other temples were opened in the following years.

Shortly before he was killed in 1965, Malcolm X rejected the racial mythology of the NOI and converted to traditional Sunni Islam after his pilgrimage to Mecca. Others followed his lead, including Warith Deen Muhammad, the son of Elijah Muhammad, who in 1975 dismantled the Nation of Islam and called its adherents to embrace mainstream Sunni Islam, which emphasized racial equality. By 2017, there were more than two dozen Sunni Islam mosques that catered primarily to African Americans in the Greater Philadelphia region, including Masjid Freehaven in Lawnside, New Jersey, and Masjidullah on Philadelphia's Limekiln Pike.

Only a small percentage of American Muslims embraced the conservative Salafi tradition popular in Saudi Arabia, but by 2017 there were eight such mosques in the region, including the Germantown Masjid. Most Salafi Muslims were African American and tended to eschew political involvement and focus on individual religious obligations understood to conform to the practices of the earliest followers of Islam. Salafi Islam gained popular currency and support through proselytization efforts in local prisons and jails.

## ISLAM IN THE REGION AFTER 1965

Although African Americans made up the largest number of Muslims in the United States in the mid-twentieth century, the dynamics changed after 1965 immigration reform opened the door to immigrants from Asia, Africa, and the Middle East. As of 2011, approximately 33 percent of Muslims in the United States were South Asian, 27 percent Arab, and 24 percent were African American. The Philadelphia region gained from the new immigration. By 2020, an estimated 140,000 Muslims lived in the Greater Philadelphia region.

In Philadelphia itself, African Americans continued to make up the largest proportion of area Muslims, but the Muslim profile was changing. A handful of Palestinian immigrants arrived in Philadelphia following the Arab-Israeli War in 1948, but larger numbers immigrated to the region in the 1970s following the Yom Kippur War. Imam Hatip Jemali, an Albanian Muslim, brought his family in 1966 and founded a mosque on Girard Avenue in 1974. Palestinian immigrants formed a small Muslim enclave in Philadelphia's Lower Kensington neighborhood and founded the Al-Aqsa mosque in 1992. Palestinians, along with Egyptians and North Africans, formed enclaves in Philadelphia's Feltonville neighborhood and along Bustleton Pike in Northeast Philadelphia. As of 2010, approximately thirty to fifty thousand Arab Americans lived in the Greater Philadelphia region. The newest arrivals from the Arab world were refugees driven from conflicts in Iraq and Syria and were predominantly Muslim.

Muslims also came to the region from Asia and Africa. Immigrants from Bangladesh started arriving in significant numbers after the country gained independence in 1971. The Bangladesh Association of Delaware Valley was established that same year. Bangladeshis settled throughout the region but especially in West Philadelphia and the small Delaware County community of Millbourne. South Asians, including those from India and Pakistan, constitute most Muslims residing in the region's suburbs. Although most of the estimated fifteen thousand Indonesians in the region were Christian, according to the 2010 census, approximately 10 percent were Muslim, some of whom were affiliated with a mosque near Seventeenth and Tasker Streets in South Philadelphia. Conflicts in Liberia, Sierra Leone, Somalia, and Sudan brought immigrants in the 1980s and 1990s. The newcomers tended to settle in West and Southwest Philadelphia, Delaware County, and Trenton. As of 2017 five Shiʿa mosques in the area attracted both Farsi-speaking Iranians and Urdu speakers from India and Pakistan. The Imam Ali Masjid in Pennsauken, New Jersey, was frequented by Iranians and the Tri-State Bab-ul-ilm Islamic Center of Delaware served South Asians in Wilmington.

Immigrant communities also established Sufi Muslim communities such as the Bawa Muhaiyaddeen Fellowship in the Overbrook section of Philadelphia. M. R. Bawa Muhaiyaddeen came to Philadelphia in 1971 from Sri Lanka and formed a diverse community of spiritual seekers who practiced a Sufi ritual known as dhikr, or the recitation of the ninety-nine names of God. In 1984, the fellowship constructed a mosque. When Bawa Muhaiyaddeen died two years later, a shrine was constructed near Coatesville, Pennsylvania. Although many traditional Sunnis consider Sufi shrines forbidden, the Bawa shrine became a pilgrimage site.

Institutions and businesses supported the Delaware Valley's Muslims. By 2020, the Greater Philadelphia region contained nearly eighty mosques, which were quite diverse in architectural styles. Many occupied converted spaces that once served as churches, synagogues, or even former warehouses. The Bait-Ul-Aafiyat Mosque in North Philadelphia, on which construction began in 2013, provided a purpose-built place of worship designed in accordance with traditional Islamic architecture. Mosques took the lead in providing social services, spurring community development, and fostering political engagement. They also played important roles in interfaith initiatives such as the political organizing group Philadelphians Organized to Witness, Empower, and Rebuild, which formed in 2011. Al-Aqsa mosque was central in establishing the annual Philadelphia Interfaith Walk for Peace and Reconciliation in 2004. It became an annual event, drawing several hundred participants, including Jews, Muslims, and Christians. As of 2017, dozens of markets, restaurants, and even food carts in the region specialized in halal food that met Islamic dietary law. Mainstream supermarkets increasingly offered halal options during the 2010s.

Schools and colleges also provided services to the Muslim community. One of the earliest pioneers of Islamic education in the United States was Sister Clara Muhammad, wife of Elijah Muhammad, who founded one of her schools next to a West Philadelphia square later named in her honor. As of 2017, several Islamic schools operated in the region: Al-Aqsa Islamic Academy, the Islamic School of Trenton, and even a Montessori school located on Villanova University's campus. Students in these schools followed standard academic topics as required by state guidelines with Islamic teaching incorporated. At the higher education level, Muslim Student Associations (MSA) formed at universities and colleges throughout the region starting in the 1960s. The chapter at the University of Pennsylvania, established in 1963, provided dedicated prayer spaces for Muslim students, chaplain services, and opportunities to educate the broader public about Islam. One of the Philadelphia area's most famous Muslim voices was the Temple University scholar Ismail Faruqi, who was murdered in 1986. The Palestinian-born Faruqi, who drew criticism for his anti-Zionist politics and his Wahabist interpretation of Islam, argued that immigrant Muslims had an obligation to spread the Islamic values of justice in the American public square.

After the terrorist attacks on 9/11 in 2001, U.S. law enforcement put Muslims across the country under closer scrutiny. In 2011, attacks took place at Muslim and Islamic sites, but after one such incident in 2015, when someone placed a severed pig head in front of the door of a Philadelphia mosque, many neighbors rallied in support of Muslims in their midst. Some in the Arab Muslim community proactively built positive relations with the police. The Muslim American Society began an annual breakfast for area police officers.

Several local entities, including the City of Philadelphia's office of Immigrant Affairs and Human Relations Commission, sought to support and protect Muslims and, particularly, Muslim immigrants. The Nationalities Service Center and HIAS Pennsylvania assisted refugees and immigrants to meet the challenges of adapting to American life. The Center for American-Islamic Relations (CAIR) established a Philadelphia branch in 2004 with the aim of advocating for the civil rights of Muslims and challenging stereotypes about Islam in the media.

In the Philadelphia region, several Muslims reached high levels of government leadership, including being elected to the Pennsylvania State Senate in 2016, serving as Philadelphia's police commissioner from 2002–8, and taking office as a Philadelphia city councilman in 2008. The political influence of local Muslims became clear in 2016 when Muslim leaders successfully persuaded the Philadelphia School District to recognize two Muslim holidays, Eid al-Fitr at the end of Ramadan, and Eid al-Adha after the hajj pilgrimage.

After 9/11, many non-Muslim Americans came to view Muslims in a more positive light. However, the number of anti-Muslim hate groups in the United States increased, with several such groups active in the Philadelphia region. Philadelphia has a long history of welcoming religious minorities from around the world, but it has also experienced outbursts of xenophobia. Although William Penn's vision of a "holy experiment" where diverse religious groups might live together in harmony has never been perfectly implemented, Muslims have sought its promise in settling in the region and practicing their own faith.

## Buddhism

**Tehyun Ma**

By the early twenty-first century Greater Philadelphia had become a significant center of the Buddhist religion in North America, with the region dotted with temples and community organizations providing for believers' spiritual needs. Buddhism emerged in India from the teachings of Siddhartha Gautama (mid-sixth century BCE to late fifth century BCE) before becoming a major faith in East and Southeast Asia over the course of the first millennium. It arrived in the Philadelphia region through mercantile connections with China, periodic bursts of interest in Asian spirituality, and above all immigration from across the Pacific. Separated into several strands, and often practiced in syncretic form, Buddhism is an ethical system in which the individual seeks release from materialistic delusions and suffering, pursuing a state of "enlightenment" or "nirvana." As such, American converts sometimes found in it an antidote to what they saw as their own competitive and combative culture.

Philadelphians' interest in Asian religion has long roots. When British markets became inaccessible as a result of the American Revolutionary War, the city's merchants forged commercial links with East Asia. The China trade of the late eighteenth and early nineteenth centuries inspired a vogue for Chinese art and culture. Although Philadelphia's dominance of the trade did not last long, it left a marked impact, and in the 1830s the Canton merchant and sinologist Nathan Dunn opened his short-lived Chinese Museum at Ninth and George Street. Described as "China in miniature," it became one of the first places in the United States to put Chinese art on display, although its accompanying catalog proved scornful of Buddhism, denying its faith community entitlement "to any portion of our respect." Rather than embrace Buddhism as a belief system, Americans began to send missionaries over the Pacific with the aim of winning converts to Protestantism, which they associated with "progress" in contrast to supposed "Oriental" stagnation.

A few decades later, the 1876 Centennial Exhibition at Fairmount Park spurred another surge of interest in East Asian design with the popularity of the Japanese exhibit influencing taste across the United States. Buddhism, which some scholars argued had influenced the meditative ideas of transcendentalist and theosophist philosophers over the middle decades of the nineteenth century, began to draw occasional American converts. By 1901, Philadelphia even had its own Buddhist temple, albeit one on display at what would later become the University of Pennsylvania Museum. The immersive exhibit came from the collection of the Egyptologist Maxwell Somerville, who had toured Japan over the preceding years. Such interest fit with a wider culture of American Orientalism that saw East Asia as spiritual and enervated. The Haverford College librarian and Quaker Albert J. Edmunds, in contrast, sought to place Buddhism on an equal footing with Christianity through his widely read comparisons of their sacred texts.

**FIGURE 39.** Buddhists at Freewood Acres, Monmouth County, N.J., 1963. Kalmyk Buddhists, who established the Lamaist monastery at Freewood Acres in 1955, had fled Stalin's Soviet Union. SPECIAL COLLECTIONS RESEARCH CENTER, TEMPLE UNIVERSITY LIBRARIES.

## IMMIGRATION'S KEY ROLE

The main driver of a Buddhist presence in the Philadelphia region came in the form of immigrants from East Asia. The U.S. acquisition of the Pacific West after the Mexican-American War, dislocation in China prompted by the Taiping Rebellion (1851–64), and demand for labor in California led to Chinese migration to cities like San Francisco. Facing intense hostility from white Americans, Chinese immigrants formed Chinatowns, which offered sites for shelter, business, and mutual aid. Philadelphia's first Chinese business did not appear in the Race Street vicinity until 1871, but by the late nineteenth century a recognizable community had formed. Although many early Philadelphian Chinese would have been practicing Buddhists, likely combining their faith with Confucian and Taoist beliefs and practices, the community lacked the resources to establish permanent temples and support monks, so devotion took on more ad hoc forms. The Chinese Exclusion Act of 1882, which placed stringent limits on immigration from the Qing empire, made institutional growth harder still.

With Japan not covered by the anti-Chinese immigration restrictions, and the Japanese presence in Hawaii and the West Coast growing rapidly in the late nineteenth century, its Buddhist culture became more visible in the region. In 1868 Japan embarked on a program of rapid modernization known as the Meiji Restoration, which brought the previously isolated empire into much greater contact with the rest of the world. As it sent emissaries and emigrants abroad, its culture began to permeate North America. Japanese gardens, shaped by the meditative ethos of Zen Buddhism, became popular across the United States. The Meiji-era impresario Kushibiki Yumindo established a tea garden in Atlantic City in the late 1800s. Fairmount Park acquired a Japanese garden around the same time. And the Compton estate (later the University of Pennsylvania's Morris Arboretum) in Chestnut Hill bore Japanese elements. Such destinations, though sometimes placed on a commercial footing, offered oases of serenity in a rapidly industrializing society. Japan also sponsored the same kind of missionary work that marked European empires. In 1900, for instance, a Japanese Buddhist mission to the United States visited Philadelphia in search of converts. One of its English-speaking leaders, who stayed at the Bellevue-Stratford Hotel on Broad Street, told local newspapers that the protection of religious freedom on American soil made it a fertile ground for proselytizing.

Such efforts, however, appear to have made little headway among Philadelphians outside the small Asian American community. Beyond profit-making ventures like tea gardens, Buddhism's institutional footprint remained largely confined to the West Coast, which by the turn of the century had hundreds of temples catering primarily to Chinese and Japanese communities. Despite the well-publicized presence of a Theravada Buddhist at the Chicago Columbian Exposition's "World's Parliament of Religions" in 1893, there were none on the East Coast.

Twentieth-century global conflicts brought Buddhists to the Delaware Valley. During World War II Japanese Americans in the West faced internment on the orders of the federal government. In 1944, around 2,500 Japanese Americans were relocated from multiple camps in the central and western United States to work in a food-processing plant in Seabrook, New Jersey. With many of the transplanted workers remaining after the conflict, in 1945 the Japanese American community established a temple, which became one of the first permanent sites of worship for the region's Buddhists. Kalmyks, another group of displaced people, also settled in Greater Philadelphia. Descended from Mongolian Buddhists, the Kalmyks had migrated to Russia and eastern Europe, where they faced persecution and uprooting. After years as refugees, the Kalmyks secured admission to the United States in the early 1950s, and they soon established a temple at Freewood Acres in New Jersey's Monmouth County. Postwar rapprochement between Japan and the United States, meanwhile, led to another wave of Japanese garden building. The Shofosu Garden in Fairmount Park, for instance, opened in 1958.

## APPEAL OF A HARMONIOUS MESSAGE

In an age in which the threat of nuclear annihilation loomed large, some Philadelphians found in Buddhism a message of peace and harmony that gave the belief system an appeal outside the region's Asian American communities. The countercultural Beat movement, meanwhile, saw Buddhism as an antidote to the materialism of modern American life. By the 1970s and 1980s this led to a particular interest in the meditative strand of Zen Buddhism and later the religion's Tibetan strands, too. The Philadelphia Buddhist Association, based in Bryn Mawr, formed in 1986, and the Chenrezig Tibetan Buddhist Center, spiritually led by the Venerable Losang Samten, who had fled Tibet in 1959 and served the Dalai Lama, followed five years later. These organizations, with their active program of talks and opportunities for meditation, provided focal points for Philadelphians to find their own meanings in Buddhist practice.

As in the 1870s, though, new channels of migration played a much bigger role in boosting the Buddhist presence in the Philadelphia region. The relaxation of immigration restrictions in 1965 brought a wave of East and Southeast Asian newcomers to Philadelphia, many of whom practiced Buddhism. Like their nineteenth-century predecessors, few had the resources to build temples, and devotion often took place in the home in the form of prayer and burning incense. In keeping with other growing faith communities such as Hindus and Sikhs, Buddhists improvised, often repurposing houses and later buying churches and synagogues in neighborhoods once occupied by immigrants from Europe. In the mid-1980s, Cambodian American Buddhists in South Philadelphia initially rented a storefront at Seventh and Jackson Streets that served as a makeshift temple. In 1987, they purchased a former Presbyterian church at 240 Greenwich Street. Almost two decades later, in 2003, the Cambodian Preah Buddah Rangsey Temple in Mifflin Square took over a disused Lutheran church, with temple-goers soon moving into a vacant synagogue across the street.

Permanent temples took longer to reach Chinatown, with the Pu Men Temple—the first to be purpose-built in the historical center of the region's East Asian community—not opening until 1992. Others became tied to particular communities and branches of Buddhism in ethnically diverse suburbs. In Glenside, Pennsylvania, the Won Buddhist center, established in a former church, set out to cater to Korean Americans living nearby. Bensalem's Wat Mongkoltepmunee, established in 1986 and growing into a 13.5-acre complex built in the Thai style by the early 2020s, sprang from the initial effort of Thais in the Greater Philadelphia region to invite a monk. Buddhists have also provided charitable services to local Asian American communities. The Tzu Chi Philadelphia Service Center, part of a Taiwan-based Buddhist organization, in 2012 secured a home in Chinatown where it began to offer assistance to local residents.

From Philadelphian sinologists' and collectors' early, sometimes dismissive, awareness of Buddhism, the faith established itself in the region through the improvisations of immigrants from East and Southeast Asia, its ability to win converts from outside Asian American communities amid industrialization and war, and, from the 1980s onward especially, a wave of temple building. Multiple strands of Buddhism, reflecting the diversity of the belief system, flourished by the early twenty-first century. These included Mahayana (primarily among Chinese and Vietnamese Americans), Theravada (primarily among Southeast Asian Americans), Vajrayana (primarily among Taiwanese and Tibetan Americans), and Zen (especially among non–Asian American Buddhists). By the early 2020s, a belief system that had once been seen as an aesthetically pleasing relic of a supposedly stagnant civilization had become a dynamic element of Philadelphia's religious landscape.

## Hinduism and Sikhism

**Saanika Jeet Dhillon**

The presence in the Greater Philadelphia region of people who practice Hinduism and Sikhism—two of the major world religions to hail from South Asia—likely goes back to the circulation of people and ideas in the eighteenth-century British Empire, but the establishment of larger faith communities is more a later twentieth-century story, tied to the increase of South Asian immigration after 1965. From that point, and especially from the 1990s onward, Hindus and Sikhs in Greater Philadelphia built institutions and temples to sustain a communal religious life, contributing to the growing religious diversity of the Delaware Valley in an era of new migration.

Hinduism, which dates to ca. 1500 BCE, is one of the world's oldest religions, with about 1.2 billion followers in the early 2020s. At the beginning of that decade, about 2.5 million Hindus resided in the United States. Hinduism is a diverse belief system that draws on several different traditions from South Asia. With monotheistic and polytheistic strands, it can involve the worship of several deities in an act known as puja, which occurs in the household, or in temples called mandirs. In contrast, Sikhism, which emerged in the Punjab region of India, is a younger religion founded in the fifteenth century by Guru Nanak. In the early years of the 2020s, around 25 million Sikhs extended across the globe, with five hundred thousand living in the United States. The holy scripture, the Guru Granth Sahib, is central to all Sikh temples, known as gurdwaras, and worship is conducted around the hymns and teachings it contains.

### EARLY PRESENCE

Early examples of Hindu and Sikh presence in the Greater Philadelphia region have been difficult to track with any certainty. Sources referring to people from the Indian subcontinent often collectively categorized them as "Hindoos," erasing any Sikh or Muslim presence. For example, a petition from the Pennsylvania Abolition Society highlighted the case of James Dunn, an eight-year-old boy who was indentured from Calcutta, while the organization's archive indicates merchants enslaved South Asians. The heritage or religion of the individuals concerned, however, remains elusive. It therefore remains uncertain how many Sikhs and Hindus immigrated to the United States before the twentieth century, though the numbers are likely to have been small.

By the late nineteenth century Hindu migration to the region becomes easier to discern. Students counted heavily among the Indian immigrants of the era. One of those students, Anandibai Joshee, reputedly the first documented Hindu woman in the United States, secured admission to the Woman's Medical College of Pennsylvania in 1883. Ten years later, the arrival of the Hindu monk Swami Vivekananda at the Chicago World's Fair in 1893 influenced wider U.S. perceptions of Hinduism, as he expounded on Vedanta philosophy to an intrigued American audience. But South Asians lacked the numbers or wealth to establish a stronger foothold for their faith. When, in 1920, an almost complete Hindu temple—acquired by Adeline Pepper Gibson during a visit to India some years earlier—was installed in Fairmount Park's Memorial Hall, the original home of the Pennsylvania Museum of Art, the assembled dignitaries did not include a single South

Asian person. A pageant to celebrate the arrival of the sixteenth-century place of worship, previously a shrine to the goddess Lakshmi, featured Brahma, Shiva, and Lakshmi's consort, Vishnu—the triad of Hindu deities—played by white Americans. In 1940, the temple moved to the Philadelphia Museum of Art, where it still resided a century after its arrival in the United States. By then, restrictive immigration laws limited emigration from the subcontinent.

## HINDUISM AND SIKHISM AFTER 1965

With immigration restrictions in place, and the numbers of Hindus and Sikhs in the region small, temples for the use of the region's South Asian communities took much longer to arrive. But in 1965, Congress passed the Immigration and Nationality Act, which reduced restrictions on entry to the United States and spurred the immigration of highly educated Indians in particular. Between 1820 and 1960, only around 13,600 documented Indian immigrants arrived in the United States, yet by the 1980 census, the number had increased to 387,223, with most of the newcomers holding bachelor's degrees or higher. Among those who found a home in the Philadelphia region were Keralan nurses, 14 percent of whom were Hindus. In the 1980s and 1990s, these initial arrivals sent for family members to join them, growing the Sikh and Hindu communities and diversifying employment into small businesses and the service industry.

Religious identity, scholars have argued, mattered more in the United States than in India, for it proved crucial in building networks and creating community. As the region's Hindu and Sikh populations grew in the mid- to late twentieth century, believers congregated in houses for religious festivals and for prayers, until their numbers swelled to a point that they could establish dedicated places of worship. The front rooms of houses and local school buildings offered improvised spaces for devotional practices prior to the establishment of temples. When temples arrived, they then provided an impetus for community growth.

The experience of the region's Sikhs after 1965 provides an example. Early Sikh immigrants to Greater Philadelphia often settled in the suburbs of Delaware and Montgomery Counties. Millbourne, a township in Delaware County, developed a significant Sikh population that rose after the Philadelphia Sikh Society established a gurdwara in 1990. One of the organization's founding members remembered being the only Sikh in Upper Darby when he arrived in 1981, and he spent several religious festivals in friends' living rooms. By 2000, Millbourne had become the first municipality in Pennsylvania with a majority South Asian population.

Similarly, the Hindu community gathered at houses to pray until it became possible to establish mandirs. In the early 2000s Philadelphians of Bangladeshi heritage founded the Upper Darby Hindu Temple, Sree Sree Sanatan Shangho, planning it with the help of other Hindu families in the area. Such community support for temples proved a common story in the development of Hindu society in Greater Philadelphia. The Hindu Temple of Delaware, for example, opened in 2002 after the Hindu Temple Association of Hockessin raised money to buy the land. The temple building efforts followed from families gathering at local churches and schools to celebrate festivals, which had drawn other Hindus to the vicinity.

Building mandirs and gurdwaras contributed to nurturing a wider sense of belonging and encouraged further Hindu and Sikh emigration to parts of the Greater Philadelphia area. But these efforts built on the work of the first wave of post-1965 South Asian immigrants, who fostered a strong community spirit wherever they could. Beliefs were not solely contained within ornate buildings of worship, but within each other.

The increasing presence of South Asians in the region paralleled the growth of primarily white Americans' interest in aspects of Hindu practice. By 1966 the *Philadelphia Inquirer* was carrying advertisements for books like *Yoga, Youth, and Reincarnation*, which took aspects of Hindu spiritual practice and sold them to American consumers with the promise of youth and vigor. From its inception that same year, the International Society for Krishna Consciousness (ISKCON), better known as the Hare Krishna movement, became part of an American counterculture. By 1973, an ascetic community of twenty devotees had established a Krishna temple in Germantown, drawing the notice of a bemused *Inquirer* correspondent who referred to "those kids with the pale robes and shaved heads" peddling "their literature and incense to help finance their ascetic religious life." While few Philadelphians joined the Krishnas, the movement helped concepts such as meditation, reincarnation, and karma enter the American mainstream, and the establishment of a permanent home for ISKCON in Mount Airy in 1974 provided new immigrants from India who had not yet established their own temples with access to priests. In the 2020s, the Mount Airy temple continued to spread the teachings of Krishna consciousness, teach yoga and Bhakti scriptures, and facilitate voluntary work.

After 2000, the Hindu and Sikh communities in Greater Philadelphia grew in prominence. By 2020, the region had an estimated twenty-four thousand Hindus worshipping at fifteen temples and four places of worship for Sikhs. As a result, the region's states and municipalities granted these faith communities greater recognition. In September 2021, New Jersey aligned with the World Hindu Council to declare October as Hindu Heritage Month, and Millbourne and Upper Darby hosted an annual Guru Nanak parade organized by the Philadelphia Sikh Society. Temples and gurdwaras began to offer volunteering programs, youth lessons, lectures in a range of topics, as well as dances, art, and yoga, and the communities stepped up multiple times to support their wider cities and towns.

Furthermore, the celebration of festivals such as Diwali secured a place in Greater Philadelphia's social calendar, with the City of Philadelphia's Office of Arts, Culture, and Creative Economy sponsoring celebrations at Cherry Street Pier, dance performances and Indian art, and food at Reading Terminal Market. Such changes showed how faiths that were once confined in the region to sojourning South Asian students became more widely practiced across Philadelphia as immigration increased from the Indian subcontinent.

## EXPLORE MORE

Even amid the skyscrapers and strip malls of twenty-first-century Greater Philadelphia, the mark left by faith communities on the metropolitan landscape is hard to miss. A good guide is Roger W. Moss, *Historic Sacred Places of Philadelphia* (University of Pennsylvania Press, 2005). The essays in Elizabeth Hayes Alvarez, ed., *Religion in Philadelphia* (Temple University Press, 2016) are also a useful introduction.

Colonial churches still dot the region. Examples include Gloria Dei, Philadelphia's oldest building, at 916 S. Swanson Street; Christ Church, once the home of the Church of England in the city, at Second and Market Streets; St. George's United Methodist Church, Fourth and New Streets, which dates to 1769; and Germantown Mennonite Meeting, at 6133 Germantown Avenue, dating to 1770. Congregation Mikveh Israel, Philadelphia's first synagogue, has roots in the 1740s, but its current building at 44 N. Fourth Street is modern. Its eighteenth-century cemetery, however, is at 831 Spruce.

As the city expanded in the 1800s and early 1900s, so too did its places of worship. Philadelphia's Black population often established their own congregations. Mother Bethel AME Church, at 419 S. Sixth Street, has late eighteenth-century roots, with the current building (which also houses a museum) dating from the late nineteenth century. The Friends Meeting House at 320 Arch Street, built in 1804, still hosts the Philadelphia Yearly Meeting. Catholic churches from the era include the Cathedral Basilica of Saints Peter and Paul on Logan Square; St. Augustine's Catholic Church, at Fourth and New Streets, which was rebuilt after its torching in the 1844 Bible Riots; and St. Philip Neri, another flashpoint in 1844, at 218 Queen Street. Eastern European worshippers gathered at St. Andrew's Russian Orthodox Cathedral on 707 N. Fifth Street.

The wider Delaware Valley is similarly blessed with older sites of devotion. Holy Trinity Church (Old Swedes), built 1698–99, stands on E. Seventh and Church Streets in Wilmington, Del. Trinity Episcopal Old Swedes Church, in Swedesboro, N.J., dates from 1783. Among the many fine Catholic churches in the region, the Romanesque Revival St. Nicholas of Tolentine in Atlantic City stands out for its architectural merit.

Churches, mosques, and temples from the post–1945 era onward include Debre Genet Kidus Amanuel Ethiopian Orthodox Tewahedo Church, at 7100 Woodland Avenue; Masjid Quba, Philadelphia's first mosque, at 4637 Lancaster Avenue; the Bait Ul Afiyat Mosque at 1215 W. Glenwood Avenue; and the Masjid Muhammad Abdul Wahab mosque at 1032 Spruce Street, Camden. Buddhist temples include Fo Shou Temple at 1015 Cherry Street, Philadelphia; Wat Mongkoltepmunee, in Bensalem, Pa.; and Seabrook Buddhist Temple in Bridgeton, N.J. Among a growing number of Hindu places of worship are the Sree Sree Sanatan Hindu temple in Upper Darby, Pa.; and Hockessin's Hindu Temple of Delaware, inaugurated in 2002. The Philadelphia Sikh Society has a gurdwara (place of worship) in Millbourne, Pa.

Religious history can be explored in various heritage sites and archives. The Treasury of Faith Museum, operated by the Ukrainian Catholic Church in the United States, is located at 810 N. Franklin Street. Libraries and collections include the Catholic Historical Research Center of the Archdiocese of Philadelphia, 6719 Calvert Street; the American Catholic Historical Society, 263 S. Fourth Street; the Presbyterian Historical Society, 425 Lombard Street; the Friends Historical Library, at Swarthmore College; the Friends Historical Association, at Haverford College; the Philadelphia Jewish Archives Center, at Temple University Libraries; and the Jewish Historical Society of Delaware, 515 N. Market Street, Wilmington.

The literature on the religious history of the Delaware Valley is vast. Studies of individual congregations and faith communities include Deborah Mathias Gough, *Christ Church Philadelphia: The Nation's Church in a Changing City* (University of Pennsylvania Press, 1995); John M. Moore, ed., *Friends in the Delaware Valley* (Friends Historical Association, 1981); James F. Connelly, ed., *The History of the Archdiocese of Philadelphia* (Archdiocese of Philadelphia, 1976); Dennis C. Dickerson, *The African Methodist Episcopal Church: A History*

(Cambridge University Press, 2020); and Toni Young, ed., *Delaware and the Jews* (Jewish Historical Society of Delaware, 1979).

For the colonial era up to the end of the nineteenth century, see Melvin Endy Jr., *William Penn and Early Quakerism* (Princeton University Press, 1973); Katherine Carté Engel, *Religion and Profit: Moravians in Early America* (University of Pennsylvania Press, 2009); Fred J. Hood, *Reformed America: The Middle and Southern States, 1783–1837* (University of Alabama Press, 1980); Dale B. Light, *Rome and the New Republic: Conflict and Community in Philadelphia Catholicism Between the Revolution and the Civil War* (University of Notre Dame Press, 1996); Richard S. Newman, *Freedom's Prophet: Bishop Richard Allen, the AME Church, and the Black Founding Fathers* (New York University Press, 2008). Philadelphia's Jewish presence in this era is covered in Edwin Wolf and Maxwell Whiteman, *The History of the Jews of Philadelphia from Colonial Times to the Age of Jackson* (Jewish Publication Society, 1957); Dianne Ashton, *Rebecca Gratz: Women and Judaism in Antebellum America* (Wayne State University Press, 1997); and Murray Friedman, ed., *Jewish Life in Philadelphia 1830–1940* (Institute for the Study of Human Issues, 1983).

For the twentieth-century religious landscape, see Murray Friedman, ed., *Philadelphia Jewish Life, 1940–2000* (Temple University Press, 2003); Wendy Cadge, *Heartwood: The First Generation of Theravada Buddhism in America* (University of Chicago Press, 2004); Gurinder Singh Mann, Paul David Numrich, and Raymond Brady Williams, *Buddhists, Hindus, and Sikhs in America: A Short History* (Oxford University Press, 2001); and Kambiz GhaneaBassiri, *A History of Islam in America* (Cambridge University Press, 2010).

On world religions in the twenty-first-century region, see Randall Balmer and Mark Silk, eds., *Religion and Public Life in the Middle Atlantic Region* (Altamira Press, 2006); and Katie Day, *Faith on the Avenue: Religion on a City Street* (Oxford University Press, 2014). The last of these charts the dozens of places of worship that line Germantown Avenue, where immigrants and older residents practice different faiths. The region of the early 2000s, like its colonial predecessor, remains a place of religious diversity.

HAPPY NEW YEAR
HAPPY NEW YEAR
DON'T CLOWN WITH POLLUTION

# Chapter 6

# Environment

## Introduction

Greater Philadelphia has been built from the earth. Its wealth has come from water tumbling down from mountains, trees cut from the ground, minerals hauled from its substratum, and crops nourished in its soil. Formed over three hundred million years ago in the Carboniferous period, the anthracite coal that warmed homes and powered factories came from deposits buried deep beneath the Schuylkill and Lehigh Valleys; the food sustaining the region's workforce was often grown on local farms. As miners and farmers pulled life-sustaining energy from the ground, the environmental costs became apparent in polluted rivers, poisoned air, and a changing climate. For residents of a "private city" (in the words of its historian Sam Bass Warner Jr.) that tended to privilege the pursuit of profit over common needs, Philadelphians struggled to reconcile wealth and communal well-being. Yet over the course of its history the region has sustained conservationist and environmentalist movements that have called, in different ways, for a more harmonious relationship with nature.

The mid-Atlantic region has enjoyed what its nineteenth-century boosters liked to call "natural advantages." Philadelphia and its surroundings are subject to neither the harsh winters of New England nor the subtropical summers of the Deep South. The city's hinterland, especially Lancaster County, offered fertile soil, which drew European settlers to what one early German immigrant called the "best poor man's country in the world." Even unpromising local ecosystems for agriculture, like South Jersey's Pine Barrens, provided resources such as iron and charcoal. With Philadelphia a safe distance from major fault lines, seismic activity has not threatened to level the city, and although the New Jersey and Delaware shores stand in the front line of hurricanes and tropical storms—which present a greater threat with rising sea levels—the main urban centers of population have been sufficiently inland to avoid the worst of the devastation. Temperate, stable, and sheltered, Philadelphia has stood well placed to prosper.

What have Philadelphians done with this seemingly providential situation? There is a risk of romanticizing the Lenape people, whose presence in the region preceded European colonization. They too manipulated the environment, though often in ways that enhanced biodiversity. But rapid changes in the land came with the influx of English and German settlement in the late seventeenth and eighteenth centuries. While William Penn strove to deal peaceably with the Lenape, settlers' sense that property rights could be justified through "improving" the ground spurred the accumulation of wealth, bringing with it a host of associated problems.

Penn's capital Philadelphia, envisaged by its founder as a "greene Country Towne," rested on a design that paid little heed to the natural environment. Gridiron streets ignored the route of meandering streams and rivers. Some, like the creek that ran through modern

Dock Street, became open sewers before being covered as culverts, invisible to those treading over them. Efforts at environmental transformation extended to the Delaware River itself. When islands that stood between Philadelphia and Camden got in the way of the region's domestic and international trade, business interests lobbied successfully for their removal. Channels for commerce, like land for sale and settlement, had to be opened up.

Manufacturing has left an even greater environmental footprint. As one of the first regions in the world to experience industrialization, the Delaware Valley burnt through resources, alchemizing mineral wealth into a vast array of manufactured goods while paying little heed to the often-poisonous byproducts of this process. Renewable sources of energy have sometimes powered Greater Philadelphia's mills and manufactories. Early industry often ran on waterpower in the fast-flowing creeks that tumbled down from surrounding hills and mountains into the region's major rivers. As steam engines developed, however, the region came to depend on coal, especially the cleaner-burning anthracite variety, reserves of which northeast Pennsylvania had in greater supply than anywhere else in the world. First as a domestic fuel, then as an industrial one, anthracite hauled down the Schuylkill or over the tracks of the Reading Railroad coursed into the city. While much was exported, a good deal fueled local homes and factories. As Philadelphians turned the earth under their feet into energy the region's air suffered.

Pollution therefore came hand in hand with prosperity. The chemical and oil industries, which made Du Ponts and Rockefellers multimillionaires while employing thousands across the Delaware Valley, added to the toxic mix. So too did the runoff from the fertilizers used to enrich the soil of the region's farms. Water as well as air suffered. The marine life that once flourished in the waters of the Delaware River withered during the region's industrial heyday. In 1892 the Schuylkill River even caught fire. Meanwhile the extent of the region's urbanization raised its own set of problems: how to deal, for instance, with the volume of waste such an immense agglomeration of people generated. Dumping the region's detritus in landfills and rivers gave way to emptying out to sea or exporting trash to wherever proved desperate enough accept it. The long, futile voyage of the city's garbage on the vessel the *Khian Sea* became an odyssey for the late twentieth century. Efforts to export the city's unwanted material to far-flung corners of the globe, though, hardly diminished local impacts. Like epidemics, pollution has not affected the region evenly. Neighborhoods close to or downstream from industry have tended to suffer more. These have invariably been poor, working-class districts where people lived close to their workplaces. Even when the jobs have gone—as in a postindustrial city like Camden—the pollution has often remained, toxic compounds continuing to impact health long after the machinery has stopped humming.

Local environmental challenges have been compounded by global ones. The burning of fossil fuels in the region, when replicated worldwide, led to climate change. Global warming, a term that began to appear in the region's press by 1980, has presented a grave existential threat. Scientists predicted that heatwaves, deadly to the poor and aged in urban centers, would appear with increasing frequency. So too would tidal surges that threatened to inundate homes. By the twenty-first century, a host of apocalyptic threats loomed for residents of the Delaware Valley: epidemics of mosquito-borne infections, the submersion of Jersey shore beneath rising sea levels, and greater risks of extreme weather like hurricanes and droughts. In the face of such threats the region no longer appears so sheltered, and the risks posed by climate change have inspired residents to take action. Climate protesters, demanding action locally, nationally, and globally in pursuit of sustainability, repeatedly took to the streets of the twenty-first-century city and region. Whether in strikes by school children, resilience plans drawn up by municipal governments, or research undertaken in the region's universities, the threat has not been ignored.

Such activities only mark the latest chapter in a longer history of environmental engagement in the Delaware Valley. Inquiries into the workings of nature date back to colonial times when "natural philosophers" like John Bartram and Benjamin Franklin explored the botany and meteorology of the hemisphere. Later research in the region, often driven by concerns over pollution, has sometimes led to intervention and regulation. The 1972 Clean Water Act, which (together with the region's deindustrialization as dirty industry relocated to other parts of the globe) breathed life back into the Delaware River.

At other points, especially in the conservation movement of the early twentieth century and the environmental movement of the 1970s onward, residents of the region have called for a reconfiguring of the relationship between humans and the natural world. They have injected a romantic sense of nature into an industrial region through the creation of Fairmount Park and its extension into the Wissahickon and fought for the improvement of public squares as the "lungs of the city." And they have enlisted in campaigns that seek to fight for environmental justice locally while addressing problems like climate change that threaten humanity as a whole. In doing so, the people of the Delaware Valley continue to actively shape the world around them.

## Earthquakes

**Megan C. McGee Yinger**

Recorded earthquakes in the Philadelphia region have been relatively few and small in magnitude. Nevertheless, southeastern Pennsylvania has had the most seismic activity of all regions in Pennsylvania, perhaps emanating from stress on the North American tectonic plate that remained after the breakup of the continents about two hundred million years ago. Some earthquakes felt in Philadelphia may have occurred along the Ramapo fault in New York, New Jersey, and Pennsylvania. Hard bedrock beneath eastern North America, allowing large transfers of energy, has caused quakes to be felt far from their places of origin.

The Philadelphia region experienced a number of quakes between 1737 and 1889, according to sediment analysis. These have been difficult to confirm through written records, which noted possible explosions, mine collapses, or quake-like events with no known epicenter. As an indication of the severity of a potential quake, some records noted that people fell down. New Jersey's largest earthquake occurred during this period, in November 1783. This quake had an estimated magnitude of 5.3 on the Richter scale, and its aftershocks were felt in Philadelphia. In 1812, the region felt the effects of a series of severe quakes with epicenters in New Madrid, Missouri. The quake of January 23, 1812, which was estimated to be between 7.3 and 7.6 on the Richter scale, was strong enough for Philadelphians to observe items in their homes swaying and perhaps falling off the walls or shelves. Other earthquakes originated locally but had less severe effects. A quake in Wilmington, Delaware, on October 10, 1871, knocked over chimneys and caused other structural damage throughout the region, but a magnitude was not determined. In March 1889, an earthquake felt from Harrisburg to Philadelphia and Reading caused minor damage.

Other minor quakes occurred in January 1954 in Sinking Spring, Berks County, and in December 1961 in the Philadelphia suburbs and southern New Jersey. Several other quakes occurred on the New Jersey side of the Delaware Bay and River, the largest on February 28, 1973 measuring 3.8 on the Richter scale. In Pennsylvania, Montgomery County experienced a series of quakes during three months in 1980, the largest centered in Abington at magnitude 3.7 on March 11. The quakes—located around the Huntington Valley fault, running through Glenside, Abington, and Jenkintown—began on March 2, 1980. Because of the fault's proximity to the Montgomery-Philadelphia county line, the city felt the larger quakes. The activity prompted Penn State University and the Lamont-Doherty Earth Observatory of Columbia University to place monitoring stations around the area. After the sequence ended, Temple University students distributed surveys to local residents to help determine the perceived intensity of the quakes.

Pennsylvania's largest earthquakes occurred outside the Philadelphia area. The largest in southeastern Pennsylvania occurred in January 1994 west of Reading at magnitude 4.6, and it was preceded by a 4.0 foreshock. In September 1998, the largest earthquake in Pennsylvania occurred when a 5.2 earthquake struck the Greenville-Jamestown area in Crawford County, in the state's northwest corner. Hard bedrock beneath eastern North America made it possible for residents of the Philadelphia region to feel the August 23, 2011, earthquake that emanated from Mineral, Virginia, and registered magnitude 5.8. The seismic waves of that event could be felt as far south as Georgia and as far north as Canada. In Philadelphia, it caused minor damage, mainly in the form of broken windows. The region experienced another seismic event on November 30, 2017; the 4.1 earthquake was located northeast of Dover, Delaware and was the largest known earthquake in the state's history. On April 5, 2024, the Philadelphia region experienced more shaking when a 4.8 magnitude earthquake struck New Jersey's Tewksbury Township, the effects of which were felt throughout New York, New Jersey, and Pennsylvania. Neither the 2017 nor the 2024 quake caused significant damage.

Seismic research has suggested that the Philadelphia region has the potential for larger earthquakes, but the extent is largely unknown. A Penn State University study estimated that 99 percent of seismic activity in the commonwealth came from blasting, mining, and other man-made sources. One source of concern has been the increase of hydraulic fracturing for natural gas extraction, which coincided with significant increases in seismic activity in other states, notably Oklahoma (where fracking injected wastewater into wells, triggering quakes). Geophysicists and other seismic researchers believe that Pennsylvania experienced its first man-made earthquake (measuring between 1.8 and 2.3 on the Richter scale) in 2016 as a result of natural gas extraction near the Ohio border. As the Philadelphia region became more densely populated, more people lived in areas with elevated earthquake hazard.

## Hurricanes and Tropical Storms

**Megan C. McGee Yinger**

The Greater Philadelphia area's position near the Atlantic Ocean has made it vulnerable to hurricanes and tropical storms, especially along the Delaware and New Jersey shores, and to flooding from storm surges along the Delaware River. The majority of storms that have hit the region have been tropical storms, because hurricanes have tended to weaken over the colder waters of the North Atlantic.

Atlantic hurricanes and tropical storms, part of the family of rotating storms that also includes cyclones and typhoons, rotate around a central "eye" and create high winds and heavy rains. During the Atlantic hurricane season, primarily from June through November, these storms typically have formed off the western coast of Africa (near Cape Verde) and have moved with the trade winds toward the Caribbean and the eastern United States. Since 1973, meteorologists have classified the storms as tropical depressions, tropical storms, or hurricanes based on sustained wind speeds, with hurricanes ranging from Category 1 (74–95 miles per hour) to Category 5 (157 miles per hour or higher).

The history of hurricanes that have hit the region is well documented because of early interest in the sciences. In 1644, the Reverend John Campanius created the first American weather records at Swedes' Fort near Wilmington, Delaware. Benjamin Franklin studied the forward or "progressive" movement of hurricanes during the Eclipse Hurricane of 1743, the first storm to be measured with scientific instruments. Scientists also have found evidence of the strength of storms during this era through geological markers, such as changes in sediment. The Great Storm of 1693 was strong enough to alter the coastline of the Delmarva Peninsula.

The increased professionalization of the sciences in the nineteenth century produced clearer and more consistent records of notable storms. The Snow Hurricane of 1804 made landfall in Atlantic City in October, although the snow did not fall until the storm reached New England. The Norfolk and Long Island Hurricane of 1821 made landfall in Cape May, New Jersey. Equivalent to a Category 4 storm (130 to 156 mph), it affected much of the Philadelphia area with high winds and storm surge. In 1846, the Havana Hurricane caused storm surge throughout the Delaware Valley and caused extensive damage to Philadelphia wharfs.

In 1851 the National Oceanic and Atmospheric Administration started keeping hurricane records, which increased knowledge about storms during the second half of the nineteenth century. The Expedition Hurricane of 1861, a late-season storm, coincided with the American Civil War. The storm delayed a naval expedition on its way to the Battle of Port Royal and damaged some ships. The storm's damage to New Jersey rail lines hampered the Union war effort. Another storm of this era, the Gale of 1878, was no longer a full-fledged hurricane by the time it reached the mid-Atlantic region, but it caused extensive flood damage in Delaware and New Jersey (which had not yet fully recovered from damage to riverbanks from the San Felipe Hurricane

**FIGURE 40.** Police and the Red Cross visiting flooded homes in Eastwick, Southwest Philadelphia, following the Chesapeake-Potomac Hurricane, 1933. SPECIAL COLLECTIONS RESEARCH CENTER, TEMPLE UNIVERSITY LIBRARIES.

two years earlier). High winds injured church steeples in Pennsylvania. In addition to the effects of the Atlantic ridge of high pressure, climate variations known as the Atlantic Multidecadal Oscillation (AMO) have caused storm activity to vary in increased and decreased annual activity over cycles of twenty to thirty years. Following the inactivity of the early twentieth century, hurricane seasons became especially active again during the 1950s. In 1953, the World Meteorological Organization began giving the storms female names, a system aimed to improve communication with the public and standardize storm tracking. The system changed in 1979 to alternate names between male and female. In mid-October 1954, Hurricane Hazel came ashore in North Carolina and affected inland areas of Pennsylvania as a Category 1 storm, causing flooding and uprooting trees before moving into Canada. In August 1955, Hurricanes Connie and Diane struck the area within a week of one another. Connie caused flooding throughout the Greater Philadelphia region, but the drought conditions at the time in Delaware decreased the level of destruction. However, record flooding occurred in the Poconos and along the Delaware River when Diane hit the same areas of the region only five days later.

In the 1980s and 1990s, the mid-Atlantic region experienced a few major storms, primarily tropical storms or depressions. Hurricane Gloria in 1985 produced high winds, including a peak gust of 81 miles per hour in Ocean City, New Jersey, and caused extensive flooding throughout the Delaware Valley. Tropical Storm Floyd (1999) started out as a strong Category 4 hurricane in the Caribbean. Although it weakened as it traveled up the Eastern Seaboard, the storm caused widespread flooding and power outages across New Jersey and much of central and eastern Pennsylvania. Tropical Storm Allison (2001) formed in the Gulf of Mexico, hitting Texas and Louisiana before heading toward the mid-Atlantic region on a rare overland path. Despite never evolving into a hurricane, Allison was especially destructive. The Philadelphia area saw extensive flooding, including in Bucks County, where the Neshaminy Creek crested at almost seventeen feet. In Montgomery County, flooding caused a gas explosion that killed six.

Hurricanes Irene (2011) and Sandy (2012) struck the Jersey Shore unusually hard. On August 28, 2011, Hurricane Irene made landfall on Brigantine Island and caused extensive flooding throughout New Jersey, Massachusetts, and Vermont. It also spawned tornadoes and caused a storm surge along the New Jersey coast. Sandy made landfall at Brigantine, New Jersey on October 29, and exceeded most officials' expectations in its destructiveness. Ignoring evacuation orders, many residents stayed behind and risked the floods, winds, and storm surge. Because Sandy occurred late in the season, many people simply had not prepared for a hurricane, and the storm caused 1.2 million power outages in Pennsylvania alone. In 2020, Tropical Storm Fay caused chaos in the region, while the remnants of Hurricane Ida a year later led to flooding along the Brandywine Creek in Delaware.

Such storms suggested that climate change could be affecting the strength and frequency of strong hurricanes hitting the mid-Atlantic region. During the period from the 1970s through the second decade of the twenty-first century, the number of Category 4 and 5 storms approximately doubled. Although rotating storms strengthened around the world, the North Atlantic appeared to be more affected by the increase in ocean temperatures. Higher sea levels have created an increased risk of destructive storm surge, and as populations became denser in coastal areas, more people in the greater Philadelphia region stood at risk of being in the path of a hurricane or tropical storm.

## Meteorology

**Jessica Linker**

Philadelphians have pursued significant scholarly and popular interests in meteorology, the study of the atmosphere, since the eighteenth century. Pioneering individuals and scientific societies tracked meteorological data, short-term weather forecasting became possible with technological innovations, and by the twenty-first century, television viewers gained familiarity with the science through broadcast meteorology.

A number of Philadelphia's early meteorological discoveries resulted from the work of Benjamin Franklin, who became interested in tracking storms in the 1730s. In 1743, a lunar eclipse led Franklin to discover the nature of their movements. Franklin had hoped to observe the start of the eclipse from Philadelphia, but a storm with unusually strong northeasterly winds rolled in an hour prior and obscured his view. Later, Franklin learned that the eclipse had been visible in Massachusetts, where the storm arrived long after the eclipse started. Because the winds blew from the northeast, Franklin had assumed that the storm had traveled from Boston toward Philadelphia, but in fact it had traveled in the other direction. After researching storms with northeasterly winds, he discovered that storms begin to the leeward (the direction in which the winds are blowing) and move windward (against the wind). These and other scientific observations appeared on a 1749 map of the mid-Atlantic colonies published and drawn by Lewis Evans.

Throughout the eighteenth and nineteenth centuries, a pervasive culture of meteorological observation developed as Philadelphians recorded atmospheric and weather data in almanacs, diaries, and journals. These ranged from simple descriptions of whether it was sunny, cloudy, or rainy each day to sophisticated measurements of air pressure and temperature. During the 1820s, Reuben Haines, corresponding secretary of the Academy of Natural Sciences, maintained a meteorological register at Wyck House in Germantown. His data, which included mean temperatures, total snow- and rainfall, wind directions, and barometric readings, was incorporated into other scientific studies, including medicine. Diseases had seasonal patterns that

**FIGURE 41.** *Franklin and the Kite*, by Godefroy Mayer, after an original by Benjamin West, 1900. PHILADELPHIA MUSEUM OF ART.

doctors sought to explain by marrying knowledge of epidemics to meteorological data. Physicians John K. Mitchell and John Bell, writing to the *North American Medical and Surgical Journal* in 1826, used Haines's data to assess regional and temporal differences in smallpox outbreaks that had occurred in 1823 and 1824.

Local scientific institutions soon began to understand the necessity of keeping detailed weather data. In 1837, the Pennsylvania legislature funded the Joint Committee on Meteorology of the American Philosophical Society and the Franklin Institute of Pennsylvania. This committee issued various reports in the *Journal of the Franklin Institute* in addition to instructions for taking meteorological data. This was no simple job; calculations had to be taken at set times each day, and data takers had to be sensitive to the contingencies of storms. At Delaware County Institute of Science in Media, Delaware County, Joseph Edwards and Sarah L. Miller recorded weather data in the 1840s and 1850s. For several years, they spent a significant portion of their days compiling meteorological data. Such data was chiefly used to track long-term patterns. Meteorological data sets taken over the course of many years could be averaged to forecast weather for the coming year. By the mid- to late nineteenth century, as telegraphs allowed meteorological data to be shared more quickly, scientific societies increasingly used this information to generate short-term forecasts. Atmospheric phenomena could be tracked as they moved across the country; as a storm passed through particular outposts, for example, meteorologists could telegraph ahead to the next station in advance of the storm. New uses of meteorological data demanded a rigorous reassessment of standards; the Franklin Institute's meteorological records after 1872 were so thorough that the National Weather Service later used this historical data in assessing climate change.

In addition to the use of telegraphs, meteorological technology in Philadelphia improved in other ways between the late nineteenth and early twenty-first centuries. A number of Philadelphia companies, such as McAllister & Brother, sold meteorological instruments for use at home, school, and in professional settings. Illustrated catalogues from the mid- to late nineteenth century depicted finely made hygrometers, which measure moisture content; barometers, which measure atmospheric pressure; and rain gauges.

One of the more significant technological advances in meteorology came about by accident during World War II: Doppler radar, which an experimental radar station in Lakehurst, New Jersey, used to detect the Great Atlantic Hurricane of 1944, felt along the mid-Atlantic coast. During the war, the United States used airplanes equipped with Doppler radar units to detect enemy ships but realized that the radar was also picking up images of various weather events. Scientists adapted this technology to track weather systems; the Great Atlantic Hurricane was the first such storm in North America detected by a Doppler system. Pulse-Doppler, developed in the 1950s and 1960s, further improved radio and television forecasting and was later complemented by satellite technology. Local news stations often referred to their systems in colorful ways—for example, WPVI-TV ABC 6's "Stormtracker 6," which in the era of smartphones, also became available as an app that allowed users to track storms in real time.

By the late twentieth century local broadcast forecasting relied on information from the National Weather Service, which, in the 1980s, developed an S-Band Doppler system known as "NEXRAD" that was capable of more sophisticated Doppler velocity readings, among other advantages. NEXRAD was rolled out to the region in 1993, but the Philadelphia station was moved to Westampton near Mount Holly (designated as Philadelphia/Mount Holly). For hurricane data, local broadcast journalists used data from the National Hurricane Center.

Collaboration between local broadcasters and national meteorological institutions combined with improved technology gave the region more advance warning of impending major weather events. ABC 6's Cecily Tynan and NBC 10's Glenn "Hurricane" Schwartz, a former hurricane chaser for the Weather Channel and graduate of Penn State's prestigious meteorology program, provided copious scientific context for 2012's Hurricane Sandy. Seeking to engender the same scholarly enthusiasm that he brought to his own show, in 2005, Glenn Schwartz founded Hurricane's Outreach Program to Educate Scientists (HOPES), an academic program to increase minority participation in the fields of meteorology and earth science.

By the twenty-first century, the discipline of meteorology had dramatically changed. Eighteenth-century people could only make long-term predictions by averaging or manipulating data sets. By the early 2000s, Philadelphians benefited from meteorological communications ranging from CBS KYW's News Radio to Philly.com's NBC10 First Alert Weather widget to receive current and urgent atmospheric data.

## Pollution

**Stephen Nepa**

In its various forms, pollution immeasurably shaped the history and geography of Greater Philadelphia. For nearly four centuries, contamination of the region's air, land, and water reflected the civic and economic ambitions of people, businesses, and communities. Yet such contamination also compelled individuals, groups, and elected officials to address environmental and public health concerns while at times laying bare cases of discrimination and injustice.

Although Native Americans farmed, hunted, and erected structures in the Delaware Valley prior to European colonization, their methods generated little pollution in the modern sense. With the establishment of Philadelphia in 1682, founder William Penn hoped to avoid the filthy conditions of European cities by arranging the street plan as a spacious, orderly grid. Despite his intentions, in the early 1700s fetid alleyways developed between major streets. Residents threw garbage directly outdoors, a practice that attracted feral pigs, wild dogs, and vermin. Without paved roads, foot and carriage traffic soiled the air with dust, or, depending on the weather, mud made travel impossible. Such conditions prompted Benjamin Franklin to call for trash collection and street paving. Performed by enslaved people and servants, garbage collection began in 1757, with trash hauled downstream and dumped directly into the Delaware River. Street paving commenced in 1762. Initially using brick, it largely depended upon property owners, who after contributing funds, were reimbursed by the colonial assembly.

Early industry and commerce posed threats to the environment across the region. In Wilmington, Delaware, waste from textile shops, papermakers, and flour mills polluted stretches of the Brandywine River. Philadelphia's butchers, slaughterhouses, and breweries discharged carcasses and runoff into Dock Creek, a tributary of the Delaware River that became the city's de facto trash dump. Petitions argued for moving tanneries, which lined the creek, to the hinterlands. Backyard privies held human waste as well as household debris. Working after dark, collectors transferred the "night soil" to holding pits outside of town for use in fertilizer. But in heavy rains, privies flooded into gutters, eventually reaching Dock Creek. In 1763, the tainted creek sparked Philadelphia's first environmental laws, which imposed fines for illegal dumping and inadequate storage of refuse. Regulations also targeted unburied animal remains, littering in public spaces and squares, and obstructive signage. Hoping to minimize noise and uncleanliness, some residents in 1773 opposed extending High Street's crowded market stalls westward. When their lawsuit failed to materialize, they vandalized a nearby lime house in protest. New Jersey banned the burning of oyster shells to create "quicklime," a material used in mortar. Burning shells generated a thick, acrid smoke and the law, passed in 1775, was one of the region's first air pollution measures.

Pollution received heightened attention after independence. By 1784, Dock Creek had been covered to its mouth at the Delaware River. A major crisis came with Philadelphia's 1793 yellow fever epidemic, which killed more than four thousand people. Many theories suggested the disease emanated from contaminated streets, foul privies, or rotting cargo in the city's port. In response, Mayor Matthew Clarkson ordered the cleanup of market stalls and streets. Still others believed dirty water led to the fever's spread. Franklin bequeathed to Philadelphia funds for constructing a municipal water system. Designed by Benjamin Henry Latrobe, the first waterworks commenced operation in 1801. Using steam technology, the system delivered clean water to homes and businesses, reducing the need for private wells. A second, more powerful waterworks, built at Fairmount on the Schuylkill River between 1812 and 1815, garnered international attention and became an obligatory stop for foreign visitors to the region such as Charles Dickens. Despite these innovations, leading intellectuals such as Thomas Jefferson questioned the need for urban environments, which they saw as degrading to health and morals. And since colonial times, the region's affluent classes tended to own country houses, providing respite from increasingly toxic cities and their civic obligations to address such toxicity.

With expanding industries and transportation networks in the 1800s came new forms of pollution. To blunt the effects of water contamination, Philadelphia in the 1820s began acquiring private estates along the Schuylkill River for the establishment of Fairmount Park; in subsequent decades, the park's boundaries grew to maintain a buffer between the growing industrial city and its wooded hinterlands. Effluent from coal heaving in Manayunk, gunpowder making in Wilmington, and iron founding in Philadelphia entered creeks and rivers. Ferry passengers and operators routinely threw their waste overboard. Trains, running at street level, contended with pedestrian and equestrian traffic. Locomotives emitted noxious black smoke and were prone to explosions. In 1838, Philadelphia banned them from all streets, necessitating the construction of train stations beyond the then two-square-mile city limits. Meanwhile thousands of work horses augmented travel and transport. On average, each animal generated twenty pounds of manure and several gallons of urine per day, and cities found it difficult to secure the resources needed to keep pace with cleanup. Adding to water pollution were the refineries built along the Schuylkill River adjacent to Philadelphia's Fairmount Park after the discovery of oil in 1859 at Titusville, Pennsylvania. The first refinery, Belmont Petroleum, opened in 1865 just upriver from the Fairmount Waterworks. In 1870, to curb toxic runoff, the city purchased Belmont's land, prompting its relocation downriver to Point Breeze.

Following the Civil War, with rapid population growth and industrialization, contaminated water ranked among the region's most serious problems. Although flush toilets had come into use, early models were connected to privies, which overwhelmed municipal systems. Raw sewage, coal ash (from homes and businesses), industrial runoff, and household items were deposited directly into the Schuylkill and Delaware Rivers. Wilmington's Brandywine River, that city's main water source, also was heavily polluted. Outbreaks of cholera and typhoid fever occurred in the 1880s, prompting the building of reservoirs, a modern sewer system in 1890, and, in 1909, Wilmington's first water purification plant. Philadelphia City Council in 1900 approved funding for a municipal filtration system, which nearly eradicated typhoid.

In crowded neighborhoods populated by European immigrants and migrating African Americans the threat posed by epidemics proved particularly concerning. Progressive Era reformers and sanitary officials called for the likes of housing reform and asphalt paving. Personal hygiene and pollution became intertwined when, in 1897, Philadelphia's Women's Protective Health Association posted signs throughout the city warning of the dangers of public spitting, which many believed transmitted disease. In 1905, Dr. Lawrence Flick, a Jefferson Medical College graduate who made strides curing tuberculosis, further condemned the practice in *On Spitting*, a pamphlet he distributed to grocery stores, taverns, and passersby.

Despite earlier efforts to combat it, water pollution continued to pose significant problems into the twentieth century. Although some municipalities had banned releasing sewage into waterways, many continued to do so. Human waste was blamed for typhoid outbreaks in Trenton, New Jersey, and for high mortality rates among the poor, whose dwellings lacked flush toilets or indoor plumbing; in 1913 alone, 1,800 Philadelphia children succumbed to gastrointestinal ailments, with many linked to sewage-contaminated water. The following year, fears of bubonic plague launched the Philadelphia Bureau of Health's "kill the rats" campaign. The city offered advice on trapping and pledged five cents for those captured alive and two cents for those dead. Concerns also mounted over worsening air quality due to coal burning, factory emissions, and steam trains. In 1902, the *Philadelphia Inquirer* compared the city's sooty atmosphere to that of London. Across the river, Camden City Council in 1910 heard petitions against the Pennsylvania Railroad, whom citizens accused of "befogging" downtown with locomotive smoke. Automobile emissions in the early twentieth century added to the region's already bad air, prompting Philadelphia journalist Christopher Morley to describe in 1919 a "haze that is part atmospheric and part gasoline vapor."

As the middle of the twentieth century approached, the Delaware River's sections at Philadelphia were some of the country's most contaminated. From the city south to Marcus Hook, Pennsylvania, the river effectively was

**FIGURE 42.** Antipollution float in the Mummers Parade, 1972. SPECIAL COLLECTIONS RESEARCH CENTER, TEMPLE UNIVERSITY LIBRARIES.

a dead zone. Fish kills were common, and in summer months bacteria caused oxygen levels in the river to plummet. Pilots received warnings about the river's odors as they flew overhead while some ship captains, due to the smell, refused to dock. Chemical production in Wilmington and Newport, Delaware, led portions of the Brandywine and Christina Rivers to suffer similar fates. Although Philadelphia began upgrading its sewage treatment system in 1947, manufacturing waste continued to flow freely into rivers and creeks. At the time, no legislation required factories to limit waterborne pollutants, and without air monitors in use, atmospheric contamination also faced little scrutiny. During his mayoral tenure, Richardson Dilworth targeted Philadelphia's open trash dumps, eventually forcing them to close in 1957. Incinerators then handled solid waste, emitting hazardous fly ash particles. By 1960, the area's largest, on the Delaware River at Philadelphia's Spring Garden Street, processed six hundred tons of garbage per day. In 1961, Pennsylvania's governor, David L. Lawrence, convinced President John F. Kennedy to create the Delaware River Basin Commission (DRBC), the country's first federal river compact to address pollution. Yet one million pounds of waste still entered the river daily in 1964.

Concerns over pollution reached a national crescendo in the 1970s, as many Americans embraced environmentalism and the federal government enacted laws for resource and wilderness protection. At the local level, the health of the Delaware River and solid waste disposal remained intractable problems. The Environmental Protection Agency (EPA) declared the river "unfishable" in 1973, citing the disappearance of once-plentiful shad and striped bass populations.

Although sewage treatment plants had yet to meet standards mandated by the DRBC, the Clean Water Act of 1972 imposed federal restrictions on wastewater and pollutants. In addition, the region's widespread loss of factory jobs, while leaving behind contaminated properties, over time minimized industrial discharge into the river. By the early 1980s, local fishermen reported improved conditions and greater visibility. Although Philadelphia's trash incinerators complied with federal emissions standards, beginning in 1971 lawsuits accusing the city of air pollution forced their closure. Until the mid-1980s, New Jersey stood as the primary recipient of Philadelphia's trash. By then, a number of regional landfills, such as Lipari in Pitman, New Jersey, and Tybout's Corner in Wilmington had been shuttered and declared Superfund sites. The struggle to rid itself of garbage earned the city the unflattering nickname "Filth-adelphia," a source of national embarrassment.

By the 1990s, an environmental justice movement had begun to make gains, but the disproportionate impact of pollution on poor and marginalized communities remained apparent. This became especially evident in Chester, which in 1996 the *New York Times* labeled "the waste-processing capital of Pennsylvania." Already polluted by decades of steelmaking, shipbuilding, and heavy manufacturing, the impoverished, Black-majority city's waste plants handled all of Chester County's trash and 85 percent of its sewage. While surrounded by affluent suburban towns, the EPA declared the city had the state's highest infant mortality rate while the Centers for Disease Control found excessive lead levels in more than half of the city's children. Lead poisoning also threatened low-income families in North Philadelphia, Bridesburg, and Kensington. In Camden, New Jersey's most impoverished large city, officials beginning in the 2010s spent nearly $5 million annually to remediate illegal dumping sites while groups such as South Camden Citizens in Action brought lawsuits against smelting, cement grinding, and gasoline station operations. The city's Covanta Energy Recovery Center, a massive incineration plant adjacent to Newtown Creek, discharged more than 350 pounds of lead into the air each year.

Greater Philadelphia confronted myriad sources of pollution in the early twenty-first century. Many cities contained Superfund sites in various stages of remediation and brownfields in need of development, with notable successes at Wilmington's Justison Landing, Trenton's Waterfront Park, and Philadelphia's Reading Viaduct Rail Park. Yet the region continued to witness dangerous cases of pollution. In 2012, a Conrail freight train derailment in Paulsboro, New Jersey, caused thousands of pounds of vinyl chloride to spill into the air, leading to eye and lung ailments among residents. Five years later, the notorious "El Campamento," an illegal squatter camp populated by victims of Philadelphia's opioid crisis, was forcibly cleared from a Conrail-owned underpass in Kensington. Nearby residents had long complained of human waste, discarded syringes, and debris littering the area. That same year, greater Philadelphia ranked as the second-worst northeastern metropolitan area (behind Washington, D.C.) for smog contamination. And in June 2019, a massive explosion and fire at the Philadelphia Energy Solution Oil Refinery terrified nearby residents with worry over airborne pollutants.

As one of the largest metropolitan areas in the country, Greater Philadelphia continued to cope with pollution and its many sources. Although attempts to monitor and limit contamination began during the colonial period and intensified with subsequent generations, the region continually confronted threats to the air, land, and water.

## Garbage Barge (*Khian Sea*)

**Mark Jaffe**

During the 1980s, as regional landfills closed, it became increasingly difficult for Philadelphia to find places to put its trash and the ash from burning that trash. This dilemma became a global odyssey when the city loaded about fifteen thousand tons of municipal ash on a ship, the *Khian Sea*, and sent it off to the Bahamas in August 1986. The voyage proved to be only the first step in a long journey for the ash and the "garbage barge."

Philadelphia's disposal problem began in 1984 after Gloucester County, New Jersey, blocked outside dumping from its Kinsley Landfill, which had been taking more than 40 percent of the city's trash. Ash from Philadelphia's two municipal incinerators started piling up after another landfill, near Baltimore, failed to meet Maryland environmental standards and closed. When Philadelphia loaded the ash aboard the *Khian Sea*, it was to be taken to the Bahamas and used as fill. Before the ship reached its destination, however, concerns raised by environmental groups about the toxicity of the ash scotched the plan. With the ash still aboard, the *Khian Sea* embarked on a two-year journey across eleven countries and four continents. The ship was turned away at gunpoint at two ports, the crew almost mutinied, and its engineer threatened to scuttle the vessel and was also tossed into jail. Ultimately, the *Khian Sea* dumped two thousand tons in the remote Haitian port of Gonaives before being ordered out of that country. When the ship, renamed the *Felicia* in the hope of escaping the *Khian Sea*'s notoriety, arrived in Singapore in November 1988, its cargo had mysteriously disappeared.

The pariah ship changed its name several more times—to the *Pelicano*, then the *San Antonio*—by the time it was detained by federal officials in October 1989. In a 1993 federal court case the ship's captain, Arturo Fuentes, testified that the crew used a front-end loader to dump the ash from Philadelphia overboard, part of it in the Atlantic Ocean and part in the Indian Ocean. Two Annapolis, Maryland, businessmen, who operated the ship, were convicted of perjury for lying to a grand jury investigating the case and went to jail.

The local firm contracted by Philadelphia to haul the ash, Joseph Paolino & Sons, which had been blocked from disposing of the waste in landfills in West Virginia and South Carolina before turning to the *Khian Sea*, was eventually acquired by Waste Management Inc. of Houston, Texas. Waste Management repatriated

**FIGURE 43.** Philadelphia sludge barge leaves for the ocean, 1971. As the region grew, so too did the waste it produced. Disposing of the Delaware Valley's urban detritus presented environmental dilemmas. SPECIAL COLLECTIONS RESEARCH CENTER, TEMPLE UNIVERSITY LIBRARIES.

the last remnant of the *Khian Sea*'s cargo—the ash pile—in Gonaives, Haiti. The federal Environmental Protection Agency and the Pennsylvania Department of Environmental Resources both tested the ash pile and ruled it nonhazardous. The 2,345 tons of ash were moved to a hopper barge in Stuart, Florida, and sat there for two years. When it appeared that a Waste Management landfill in Louisiana might be the ash's final resting place, the Louisiana State Senate passed a resolution, 25–1, calling for banning the ash from the state. In the spring of 2002, the ash was shipped by rail to Hagerstown, Maryland, and then trucked to the Mountain View Reclamation Landfill in south-central Pennsylvania. "There is no happy ending to the story," said Lisa Finaldi, national coordinator of the toxic campaign of the environmental group Greenpeace. "Hopefully there was a lesson learned from this and we can do better at managing household waste in this country." Philadelphia taxpayers never had to pay the $630,000 to dispose of the ash because the contract required it to be disposed of legally.

By 1990, Philadelphia had closed its municipal incinerators and instituted a citywide recycling program to cut the volume of landfill waste. In response to the tight market, new landfill capacity opened in Pennsylvania easing the city's problems. Among big cities Philadelphia's problem was not unique. After New York City closed its Fresh Kills Landfill in 2001, it had to ship its solid waste to landfills in Pennsylvania, Ohio, Virginia, and South Carolina. While Philadelphia did find places to put its trash, the costs of disposal between 2000 and 2014 doubled to $140 per ton.

## Environmental Movement

**Alexandra L. Straub**

With its industrial past and expanses of natural resources, the Greater Philadelphia region teemed with activity during the environmental movement of the late twentieth and early twenty-first centuries. In the years following World War II, people across the United States began to demand new measures to assure their health and safety. The resulting environmental movement, a diverse yet collaborative effort on the local and national levels, sought to protect the natural environment from the harmful effects of industrialization, new technologies, and suburbanization.

Philadelphia's smelting plants, chemical producers, and oil refineries contributed to the region's economic prosperity, but these industries and other manufacturing interests generated a large amount of air and water pollution. It was not uncommon to see chimneys bellowing smoke and heaps of discarded coal around Philadelphia. Reflecting the extent of the problem, in 1970, two Bridesburg homemakers posted a sign posted outside of the Philadelphia Coke Company that read "Welcome to Pollutionburg."

The regional nature of the pollution problem spurred regional responses in the form of both federal initiatives and grassroots organizing. The federally mandated Delaware River Basin Commission (DRBC), founded in 1961, sought to abate water pollution in the Delaware River, especially in the eighty-five miles between Trenton and Wilmington, and to protect wildlife. A nonprofit organization founded in 1958, the Pennsylvania-New Jersey-Delaware Metropolitan Project Inc., also tackled environmental problems regionally by offering environmental research grants in the eleven-county area from Trenton to Wilmington. For example, a 1961 grant to Drexel Institute of Technology supported the study of air pollution in all three states. Regional action at the grassroots level included the 1967 founding of the Delaware Valley Citizens' Council for Clean Air by the Pennsylvania, New Jersey, and Delaware Tuberculosis and Health Associations. Seeking a regional solution to air pollution, Philadelphia's city government sponsored pollution awareness events like Cleaner Air Week throughout the 1960s and 1970s.

In keeping with the development of ecological science (the study of interactions among organisms and their environment), local universities and scientific institutions played vital roles in Philadelphia-area environmentalism. For example, Academy of Natural Sciences limnologist Ruth Patrick was a pioneer in environmental ecology. Her work in freshwater ecosystems promoted scientific understanding of pollution's effects on streams and helped to promote further pollution research. Chestnut Hill resident Ian Lennox McHarg incorporated the study of ecology into the curriculum of the University of Pennsylvania's

**FIGURE 44.** Philadelphia's first Earth Day rally, Belmont Plateau, Fairmount Park, 1970. The speaker pictured, Ira Einhorn, fled the United States eleven years later on the eve of his trial for the murder of his girlfriend. SPECIAL COLLECTIONS RESEARCH CENTER, TEMPLE UNIVERSITY LIBRARIES.

Department of Landscape Architecture and Regional Planning during his tenure as chair (1954–86). His lecture series Man and the Environment helped to publicize the scientific exploration of the human relationship with nature, and his book, *Design with Nature*, had a far-reaching influence on ecological sensibility.

McHarg also influenced a generation of ecologically conscious students. In 1970, students in McHarg's department spread the idea of an environmental consciousness by joining in a nationwide environmental teach-in, Earth Day. Not satisfied with just one day, students planned an entire week of activities and called this Earth Week. Earth Week focused on ecological awareness, involvement, and action. Activities at Philadelphia-area universities included an environmental teach-in committee of Temple University and speakers at Swarthmore College, Villanova University, and the University of Pennsylvania.

Students and universities in the region played an important role in spurring public consciousness about ecological issues before, during, and after Earth Week. In February 1970, the Philadelphia Ecology Action Group sponsored a daylong environmental teach-out at Drexel University. During Earth Week, student members of the organization helped with a "pollution trail" bus tour that carried more than five hundred tourists on ten buses to see the region's biggest polluters, smelting plants, and the Philadelphia incinerator. Students from Philadelphia College of Art created ecological-awareness art for the event. Although not as large as the 1970 event, Earth Week continued to educate people about the environment into the 1990s, and Earth Day continued to be observed in the region in the twenty-first century.

In the decade following the first Earth Week, additional environmental organizations formed throughout the region. In New Jersey in 1974 citizens in Logan Township, Gloucester County, formed Citizens Organization for Logan Township Safety to oppose a proposed liquefied natural gas terminal. Stating safety as their main concern, the local citizen group, along with state agencies in New Jersey, Pennsylvania, and Delaware, staunchly opposed the terminal until the plan stalled in the second half of the 1970s. Not all groups met with success. In the winter of 1973 a Montgomery County, Pennsylvania, environmental group, Stop the Oil Pipeline Society, tried but failed to halt the construction of an eighty-mile pipeline that would run through Chester, Montgomery, and Bucks Counties. In 1974, Open Space Inc., a group based in New Hope, Bucks County, lobbied the state to stop aerial spraying of pesticides to combat gypsy moths because of the harmful health effects of the pesticide DDT. Although unsuccessful in halting spraying, Open Space helped to publicize the controversy over harmful pesticides like DDT.

Many community-based environmental groups opposed industrial dumping of hazardous waste. The Eastern Pennsylvania Group of the Sierra Club, the loudest adversary of the improper disposal of hazardous waste in Philadelphia throughout the 1970s and 1980s, continuously fought to reduce dumping of toxic chemicals that could infiltrate public water sources. In South Jersey, the Stop Ocean Dumping Association engaged in legal action to stop Pennsylvania industries from dumping waste in Cape May County. The group argued the dumping not only spoiled the scenic beauty of the area but also adversely affected the fishing and tourism industry.

In the 1980s, landfills, especially those that were dumping grounds for industrial waste, proved the biggest offender to environmental sensibility. Throughout the 1980s and 1990s, the Environmental Protection Agency (EPA) assisted in the effort to clean up hazardous waste in the area, designating more than two hundred Superfund sites in the Greater Philadelphia region. Examples of these sites include the Lipari Landfill in Pitman, New Jersey; Strasburg in Coatesville, Pennsylvania; and Moyer's in Eagleville, Pennsylvania. The EPA also designated brownfields, contaminated sites less severe than Superfund sites, that still warranted support in cleanup work.

Environmental groups were also concerned with the nuclear industry. One of the earliest antinuclear environmental groups in Philadelphia was a local chapter of the national movement Women Strike for Peace. Formed in the early 1960s, the Philadelphia chapter lobbied against the adverse health and environmental effects of nuclear weapons testing. In the 1970s, antinuclear activists changed their focus to the dangers of nuclear power plants. In the Philadelphia region, the group Keystone Alliance led the charge to temporarily halt construction of a nuclear power plant in Limerick, Montgomery County. Joined by the groups Limerick Ecology Action and the Environmental Coalition on Nuclear Power, the action stopped construction until an environmental impact study could be completed. Although one nuclear power plant was constructed in Limerick, another planned plant was discontinued.

In the 1970s, following the post–World War II boom of new suburban housing tracts, shopping malls, and highways, local organizations mobilized to protect the environment and remaining open spaces, including local watersheds. Philadelphia activists formed the Save the Wissahickon Committee and the Pennypack Watershed Association. In Delaware County, residents formed the Concerned Area Residents for the Protection of Tinicum Marsh in 1972 and secured congressional legislation to protect the largest remaining freshwater tidal wetland in Pennsylvania, which became the nation's first urban wildlife refuge, the John Heinz National Wildlife Refuge at Tinicum.

In South Jersey in 1977, local, state, and national conservation groups including the Audubon Society and the West Jersey Group of the Sierra Club organized under the umbrella of the Pine Barrens Coalition. Backed by expert testimony, including soil experts from Rutgers University, the coalition successfully lobbied in Trenton and Washington for the passage of the Pinelands Protection Act. The act restricted development within the complex ecosystem. The Pine Barrens Coalition (later the Pinelands Preservation Alliance) served as a watchdog to ensure the act was enforced and the Pine Barrens preserved.

New Jersey had a history of commitment to preserving open spaces, exemplified in the passage of the Green Acres Program in 1961. From 1961 to 1995, New Jersey voters approved $1.4 billion in Green Acres bonds to protect open spaces. Support for these programs was clear in 1998 when voters approved a referendum to use tax revenues to protect natural landscapes for the next thirty years. By 2017, the Green Acres Program had protected more than 650,000 acres of open space in New Jersey.

Throughout the 1980s, people began to realize that hazardous environmental conditions disproportionately affected predominantly poor and minority communities. Efforts to correct these injustices took the form of campaigns for environmental justice, characterized by collaboration between community members and legal advocates, to ensure that environmental regulation would apply to all people regardless of race, national origin, or income.

The Public Interest Law Center of Philadelphia, founded in 1969, became involved in many environmental justice cases in the region, including two high-profile cases in Chester, Pennsylvania, and Camden, New Jersey. Both locales had predominantly low-income minority communities and disproportionate numbers of hazardous waste facilities compared to their surrounding counties. In Chester, residents complained that the white residents of Delaware County unfairly used their community as a "toxic wasteland." In 1993, the Public Interest Law Center worked with Chester Residents Concerned for Quality Living to challenge a proposed infectious medical waste sterilization facility on the grounds of civil rights, the first case to do so. In 1995 the Pennsylvania Supreme Court forced the plant to close.

In Camden, the 686-acre Waterfront South neighborhood alone was home to four junkyards, numerous heavy industrial companies, and a petroleum coke transfer station. In 2001, South Camden Citizens in Action, with the help of the Public Interest Law Center in Philadelphia, took legal action against St. Lawrence Cement. They won an injunction halting construction of a cement plant that would have caused extensive pollution. Although the injunction was overturned and the plant eventually built, the case raised awareness of environmental injustices suffered by communities like Camden. Community groups like the Center for Environmental Transformation, founded in 2005, continued to work closely with residents and organizations as agents of environmental justice.

The fight for environmental justice continued into the twenty-first century. In 2012, the Public Interest Law Center collaborated with the Eastwick Friends & Neighbors Coalition in Philadelphia to stop development of an apartment complex that would have adversely affected the health and safety of the neighborhood. The groups successfully convinced the developers to work toward a project with community-based planning. In 2016 PennEnvironment, a statewide citizens' environmental advocacy organization, released a study publicizing the disproportionate threat posed to low-income communities in Philadelphia from the pollution and potential derailments of oil trains. Dangerous derailments in the region in 2014 and 2015 brought the issue to the forefront.

The Greater Philadelphia region typified citizen engagement with diverse environmental issues after World War II employing regional, grassroots, and institutional approaches. The expansion of an environmental consciousness continued into the twenty-first century. While some groups focused on familiar issues like pollution, green spaces, and waste, the turn of the century also brought new concerns over climate change and hydraulic fracking. Advocacy groups such as PennEnvironment and the Pennsylvania Environmental Council approached these issues at a statewide level.

Others focused on the grass roots, especially as awareness of the threat posed by climate change grew. In 2012, students at Swarthmore College and the University of Pennsylvania were instrumental in starting a national movement toward fossil fuel divestment. Philadelphia-based Earth Quaker Action Team, founded in 2009, called attention to the devastating effects of mountaintop-removal coal mining and the Keystone XL Pipeline, while also calling on asset funds to divest from greenhouse gas–producing industries. The national Sunrise Movement, which formed in 2017, organized a Philadelphia chapter that demanded local food security, recreational spaces, and a Green New Deal. Climate protests became commonplace in Center City, and in 2023 schoolchildren across the region joined a strike demanding action to protect the globe. Amid this new wave of activism, many organizations active during the earlier environmental movement endured, expanding their goals to face new problems.

## EXPLORE MORE

Traces of the region's environmental engineering are sometimes hidden, sometimes visible. Many of the city's waterways are long-since buried underground. Dock Creek, once an open sewer, gives its name to the eponymous street that winds its way in a southeasterly direction from near the intersection of Third and Walnut Streets. Others found protection in the form of generous benefactors and municipal government. The Schuylkill River and Wissahickon Creek became part of the Fairmount Park system, which expanded from the 1840s onward as Philadelphians looked for a site of recreation and a safeguard of the city's water supply. Brandywine Park in Wilmington, Del., and Cooper River Park in Camden County, N.J., similarly run alongside rivers. Like Brandywine Park, Trenton's Cadwalader Park reflects the influence of Frederick Law Olmsted, the internationally renowned nineteenth-century landscape architect who prescribed cathartic (if often contrived) natural environments in the heart of sprawling metropolitan centers as a medicine for urban woes, most famously in New York's Central Park. Less picturesque are the coal waste piles that dot the anthracite fields of the Schuylkill Valley. Pennsylvania as a whole has an estimated 220 million cubic yards of detritus from the mining industry spread across 9,000 acres. The Anthracite Heritage Museum, at 22 Bald Mountain Road, Scranton, Pa., offers insights into the history of coal in the region.

Philadelphia museums and collections that cover knowledge of and action around the environment include the Science History Institute at 315 Chestnut Street; the Franklin Institute on Logan Square; the American Philosophical Society, adjacent to Independence Hall on Fifth Street; and the Independence Seaport Museum on S. Christopher Columbus Boulevard. The New Jersey Maritime Museum, in Beach Haven, documents life on the front line of the hurricanes and tropical storms that have battered the region.

On natural disasters in the region, see Karl F. Nordstrom et al., *Living with the New Jersey Shore* (Duke University Press, 1986); Cherie Burns, *The Great Hurricane: 1938* (Grove Press, 2005); Kathryn Miles, *Superstorm: Nine Days Inside Hurricane Sandy* (Dutton, 2014); Abigail Perkiss, *Hurricane Sandy on New Jersey's Forgotten Shore* (Cornell University Press, 2022); and John Nese and Glenn "Hurricane" Schwartz, *The Philadelphia Area Weather Book* (Temple University Press, 2002). Efforts to understand weather and climate are chronicled in J. D. Cox, *Storm Watchers: The Turbulent History of Weather Prediction from Franklin's Kite to El Nino* (John Wiley, 2002); and James Delbourgo, *A Most Amazing Scene of Wonders: Electricity and Enlightenment in Early America* (Harvard University Press, 2006).

The city's environmental past and future is considered in Brian Black and Michael J. Chiarappa, eds., *Nature's Entrepôt: Philadelphia's Urban Sphere and its Environmental Thresholds* (University of Pittsburgh Press, 2012) and, from the perspective of cultural history, in Alan C. Braddock and Laura Turner Igoe, eds., *A Greene Country Towne: Philadelphia's Ecology in the Cultural Imagination* (Pennsylvania State University Press, 2016). Though not by any means a conventional environmental history, Sam Bass Warner Jr., *The Private City: Philadelphia in Three Periods of Its Growth* (University of Pennsylvania Press, 1968) remains valuable for its powerful critique of the tendency to place profit ahead of communal needs. More specialized work on Philadelphia's environmental history includes Charles S. Olton, "Philadelphia's First Environmental Crisis," *Pennsylvania Magazine of History and Biography* 98, no. 1 (January 1974): 90–100; David Contosta and Carol Franklin, *Metropolitan Paradise, the Struggle for Nature in the City: Philadelphia's Wissahickon Valley, 1620–2020* (Saint Joseph's University Press, 2010); Elizabeth Milroy, *The Grid and the River: Philadelphia's Green Places, 1682–1876* (Pennsylvania State University Press, 2016); and John Frederick Lewis, *The Redemption of the Lower Schuylkill* (City Parks Association, 1924).

For a regional focus, Ellen Stroud, "Dirt in the City: Urban Environmental History in the Mid-Atlantic," *Pennsylvania History* 79, no. 4 (Autumn 2012): 428–39 provides a guide. Noteworthy contributions include Diane Sicotte, *From Workshop to Waste Magnet: Environmental Inequality in the Philadelphia Region* (Rutgers

University Press, 2016); Howard Gillette Jr., *Camden After the Fall: Decline and Renewal in a Post-Industrial City* (University of Pennsylvania Press, 2005); Thomas Dublin and Walter Licht, *The Face of Decline: The Pennsylvania Anthracite Region in the Twentieth Century* (Cornell University Press, 2005); and Gerald J. Kauffman Jr. "The Delaware River Revival: Four Centuries of Historic Water Quality Change from Henry Hudson to Benjamin Franklin to JFK," *Pennsylvania History* 77, no. 4 (Autumn 2010): 432–65. The final piece, which charts the return of fish species to a cleaner waterway, offers a degree of cautious optimism. However dirty and discontented the Delaware Valley has been, its residents have, at points in its history, found ways to comprehend and conserve their environment.

# Chapter 7

# Epidemics and Public Health

## Introduction

When William Penn's surveyor, Thomas Holme, laid out Philadelphia in the late seventeenth century, he sought to avoid the misfortunes that had befallen London over the previous decades. Penn's "greene Country Towne," where houses would sit amid verdant surroundings on wide gridironed streets, promised to ensure the airflow required to prevent infernos and disperse foul odors. The causes of great fires and bubonic plagues, which had wreaked such devastation on London's crowded streets, would be blown away by the breeze. But if Philadelphia's original design sought to protect the city against natural disasters, the city did not develop as Penn and Holme hoped. While the grid survived, the greenery did not, as settlers clustered into blocks close to the Delaware River. By the 1790s, one of the built-up parts of the city's few green spaces, Washington Square, had become a potter's field used to bury victims of yellow fever. Those who had the means to do so fled to the surrounding countryside when such epidemics struck.

The oceanic links that brought commerce and people to the Philadelphia region also brought waves of sickness. Microbes cross borders, and the diseases they cause have often acquired names reflecting their purported place of origin, casting aspersions in the process on the populations associated with them. "Asiatic" cholera, the "Spanish" flu, and the "China" virus, as some called COVID-19, have all taken their toll in the Delaware Valley. The most deadly imports, though, surely came with the first European settlers. With no immunity to diseases endemic in Europe, the indigenous Lenape people saw their numbers dwindle by an estimated 90 percent over the course of the seventeenth century. By the time of the Seven Years' War in the mid-eighteenth century, British troops fighting in western Pennsylvania used smallpox-infected blankets as a form of biological warfare against the Lenape. But European settlers and their descendants also proved vulnerable as heightened global connections and the patterns of living in a rapidly industrializing and urbanizing society created ripe conditions for the spread of disease.

At various points in the region's history, public health officials have tried to stop epidemics from crossing borders, albeit with limited success. The first quarantine station on the Delaware River opened in the 1740s, while during the height of the COVID-19 pandemic the United States blocked many foreigners from entering the country. Invisible microbes, though, have circumvented such lines of defense. As a result, diseases have exacted a deadly toll on the region. Philadelphia lost 10 percent of its population in the yellow fever epidemic of 1793. Later epidemics never approached such a catastrophic scale, but about 1 percent of the city perished in the influenza pandemic of 1918–19, where the spike in the death rate after a well-attended parade near the end of World War I served as a stark lesson on how not to slow the circulation of a lethal pathogen. Soldiers who had survived the trenches of Flanders succumbed in droves to the flu. Over eight hundred servicemen died at Fort Dix in Burlington County, New Jersey.

Mortality rates for the city and region only tell part of the story. The diseases that have ravaged the Delaware Valley have done so unevenly, hitting some communities harder than others. Epidemics are not just natural disasters; their impact is shaped by patterns of human behavior, settlement, and inequality. Waterborne and airborne diseases disproportionately struck crowded immigrant and working-class neighborhoods, where poor sanitation, confined quarters, and poor underlying health created vulnerabilities. Wealthier people who lived in affluent suburbs or who could retreat to country estates, proved less likely to get sick. In the yellow fever epidemic of 1793, for instance, one-third of Philadelphians fled the city. Other diseases, like HIV, disproportionately hit marginalized communities, often leading to fear and stigmatization.

In the face of such threats, people in the Delaware Valley took action. Often at great risk, residents tended to the sick. When yellow fever struck in 1793, Black residents stayed behind to bury the dead and look after the infected. By then, the region was fast becoming the center of medical learning in the Western Hemisphere. From the nineteenth century onward, Philadelphia's medical colleges drew students from around the world to learn from eminent physicians. Not all the theories they taught withstood the test of time. For instance, Benjamin Rush, a Revolutionary era doctor and signer of the Declaration of Independence, theorized that Blackness was a symptom of disease and that epidemics spawned from rotting matter. But in halting steps, Philadelphians helped make life-saving breakthroughs. Philadelphia's pharmaceutical industry, while hawking plenty of quack medicines, provided Union forces in the Civil War with quinine, an effective prophylactic against malaria; a century and a half later, scientists in the region's biotech labs played a critical role in developing the mRNA technology that saved millions of lives worldwide in the COVID-19 pandemic of 2020–22.

Though the pursuit of public health has occasionally shut the region off from the rest of the world, it has also created connections, as developments across the globe have shaped practice in the Delaware Valley. After the catastrophic yellow fever epidemic of 1793, Philadelphia developed a waterworks that, after moving to a new site on the Schuylkill River in the early nineteenth century, impressed European visitors such as Charles Dickens and lessened mortality for waterborne diseases. Its elegant neoclassical buildings, which evoked the grandeur of Athens and Rome, indicated its creators' intent to build a lasting monument of American civilization. At other points, officials and medics have borrowed from innovations elsewhere, such as the epidemiological work in mid-nineteenth-century Britain that traced cholera to the water supply. Inspired around the same time by pleasure grounds in European cities, the city created Fairmount Park, with a view to both protecting the purity of the Schuylkill and providing fresh air and verdant grounds for recreation. Perhaps the most dramatic example of imitation came in the COVID-19 pandemic when Pennsylvania, Delaware, and New Jersey all followed the precedent set by China (and endorsed as an emergency measure by the World Health Organization) in ordering citizens to stay at home to slow the spread of the virus.

While the region's public health has often been shaped by international events and ideas, epidemics have provoked intensely local conflicts. The threat of disease has fueled nativism and homophobia, with newcomers and afflicted groups cast as a threat to the region's health. Calls for the exclusion, criminalization, and reform of the region's vulnerable communities have grown louder when epidemics have loomed. In response, affected communities have often fought back. When, amid the cholera epidemic of 1866, the city proposed to use Moyamensing Hall as a temporary hospital, neighboring Irish Americans burned it to the ground. In the late twentieth century, AIDS activists took to the streets demanding greater support for HIV-positive people.

The scars left by epidemics remain etched into the civic memory of the region. Designed to withstand the waves of disease that claimed so many lives in seventeenth-century London, Philadelphia never proved quite as resilient as its founder wished. But through innovations in medicine and public health and the efforts of its people, the Delaware Valley has thrived despite the microbial threats that have menaced it.

## Yellow Fever

Simon Finger

For more than a century beginning in the late seventeenth century, sudden outbreaks of yellow fever sowed death and panic throughout Philadelphia and its environs. With medical science seemingly powerless against it, yellow fever was a terrifying and mysterious threat that rivaled any disease of the era in its capacity to take lives and disrupt society.

Yellow fever is a flavivirus that spreads among humans via the bite of *Aedes aegypti* mosquitoes. Once introduced to a human host, the virus begins replicating in the lymph nodes. Initial symptoms include aches and pains, fever, nausea, and dizziness lasting several days before receding. In serious cases, the symptoms return with renewed intensity as the disease spreads to the liver, inducing jaundice, delirium, and internal hemorrhaging. The victim begins bleeding from the ears and nose, retching up a blend of gastric contents and blood known as the "coffee grounds" or "black vomit." In the terminal phase, the victim falls comatose as his organs and circulatory system begin to fail, usually expiring as the liver or kidneys finally give out, some seven to ten days after the relapse. Those who survived the ordeal acquired immunity to the disease, but any population composed largely of unseasoned newcomers provided a fertile environment for an outbreak.

Epidemiological evidence suggests that both the virus and its vector originated in Africa. They crossed the Atlantic by the slave trade, becoming endemic in

**FIGURE 45.** Stephen Girard depicted helping the sick in the 1793 yellow fever epidemic, 1871. Girard, one of the city's merchant princes, organized a fever hospital, but the image ignores the assistance provided by the city's Black population in combating the deadly disease. UNIVERSITY OF CALIFORNIA LIBRARIES VIA INTERNET ARCHIVE.

the sugar islands of the West Indies. Once established there, it was only a matter of time before the fever spread to North American ports. From its earliest days, Philadelphia carried on a bustling trade with the Caribbean, and a "Barbados distemper" struck the city in 1699, felling 220. For almost a century, yellow fever was an erratic visitor, abruptly appearing after long intervals of relative inactivity. Significant outbreaks appeared in 1741, 1747, and 1762, but major episodes were too uncommon and unpredictable to have a broader impact until the 1790s, when the fever began striking with greater frequency and fury.

After some three decades absence, yellow fever returned to Philadelphia with a vengeance in 1793, during the period that it served as the capital of both Pennsylvania and the United States. It began with a cluster of infections near the Delaware waterfront, possibly introduced by French enslavers fleeing the revolution in Saint-Domingue, where the pathogen was endemic. The fever then spread rapidly through the summer and autumn, fueling panic throughout the city. Those who could fled the city to destinations in the healthier countryside, like Germantown and Gray's Ferry, an exodus numbering in the thousands. Among those who remained, the fever claimed an estimated five thousand lives. Other American cities embargoed the nation's capital, fearful that traffic from Philadelphia could introduce the infection.

Officers of federal, state, and municipal government vacated the city, leaving management of the crisis to Mayor Matthew Clarkson and a committee of volunteers led by merchant Stephen Girard, who organized a fever hospital at Bush Hill, the mansion built by Andrew Hamilton. Black Philadelphians served in disproportionate numbers, owing to a widely held belief that they were immune to the fever, and their heroic service as nurses, porters, and inspectors is widely regarded as a formative event in the history of Black Philadelphia. When printer Mathew Carey published an account of the crisis impugning the conduct of African American volunteers, Black church leaders Absalom Jones and Richard Allen responded by publishing a powerful rebuttal of the charges, forcing Carey to amend later editions of his tract.

The epidemic also set off a wide-ranging debate over the cause of the fever and the best means of controlling it. Philadelphia's College of Physicians contended that it was both contagious in nature and foreign in origin, while a faction led by Benjamin Rush, the city's most celebrated doctor, argued that only domestic environmental factors were to blame. Incorporating insights from both parties, Pennsylvania established a new Philadelphia Board of Health in 1795 to enforce both quarantine and sanitary regulations.

Notwithstanding the new measures, the fever returned seven times in the following twelve years, and 1793 set the model for how Philadelphians responded to subsequent outbreaks. Each episode spurred similar patterns of evacuation, isolation, and scapegoating and stoked the ongoing controversy within the medical community while motivating broader, though futile, efforts to ameliorate the effects of the disease. Nursing may have offered some comfort, but only winter frost—and its extermination of the mosquitoes—brought an end to each fever year.

The ordeal of fever had a profound effect on the city and the country. It was one of several factors in Philadelphia's decline relative to rising ports like New York City. It inspired literary and journalistic development as writers and printers discussed, described, and debated the disease. The urban nature of the fever fueled the agrarian romanticism of the Jeffersonian era. And throughout the country, and the broader Atlantic World, medical men struggled to understand a foe that thwarted their best efforts.

Yellow fever struck Philadelphia and other northern ports only sporadically after 1820, but it remained a persistent problem in the American South until the turn of the century, when researchers like Carlos Finlay and Walter Reed unraveled the etiology of the disease and formulated effective measures to control it.

## Cholera

**John B. Osborne**

The cholera epidemics that struck Philadelphia in 1832, 1849, and 1866 provided a catalyst for transforming the health and hygiene standards of the city. Asiatic cholera, endemic to India, escaped the subcontinent in 1817. It reached western Europe in 1831 and was carried to North America in 1832 aboard immigrant ships, breaking out in Philadelphia in July of that year.

The disease is characterized by extreme pain and dehydration from violent diarrhea and vomiting, often leading to death.

The prestigious College of Physicians of Philadelphia, dominated by sanitarians, presumed it was not a new disease but an "epidemic phase" of indigenous summer diarrhea caused by miasmic vapors emitted from the ever-present filth in nineteenth-century cities. Rejecting the theory that cholera was spread by contagion, the fellows of the college believed predisposing conditions made the poor, the profligate, the immoral, those with weak constitutions, and especially certain ethnic groups the most likely victims of the disease. To combat the epidemic, they advised the Board of Health to clean the city of filth, set up local hospitals, and educate the populace to avoid dangerous foods and habits they believed led one to be susceptible to the disease. These recommendations were put into effect when cholera broke out in the city in July 1832. Meanwhile, to help the afflicted, private charity and church groups provided nurses and places for recovery. The Catholic Church especially responded to the challenge of aiding the Irish and other Catholic immigrants, with some nuns coming from as far away as Emmitsburg, Maryland, to meet the crisis. By mid-September the epidemic had run its course, leaving a death toll of 935.

Particularly hard hit were the state-owned Arch Street Prison and the city almshouse where inmates suffered from overcrowding, appalling hygienic conditions, and generally poor health, which the fellows of the College of Physicians saw as proof of the validity of their theory of the etiology of the disease. In an attempt to stop the carnage at the prison, the authorities released inmates who had not been convicted of major crimes. Many fled to Chester, Berks, Lancaster, and other neighboring counties, spreading cholera as they went. Citizens fleeing the city also spread cholera to surrounding areas.

Philadelphia's death rates were one-quarter those suffered in New York City and one-twelfth those of Montreal. Medical authorities attributed the city's good fortune to the use of water from the Fairmount reservoir to cleanse filth from the streets, inspiring cities such as New York and Boston to create municipal water supplies modeled on that of Philadelphia. Unbeknownst to the medical profession, the disease was caused by a bacterium and was spread primarily through feces-contaminated drinking water. It was not clean streets but drinking water from the reservoir, uncontaminated by the cholera bacilli, which accounted for the city's low death rates. In the Black and Irish districts south of South Street, the death rate from cholera was three to four times greater than in the city. While the College of Physicians attributed these deaths to the poverty and "racial" character of the population, in reality these areas had very limited access to Fairmount drinking water and consequently suffered far more affliction than those with such resources.

Cholera returned to Philadelphia in 1849. Despite a 50 percent increase in population, only 747 people died from the disease. Medical officials again concentrated on eliminating filth and building neighborhood hospitals, but in fact this radical reduction in the death rate from cholera was due primarily to the expansion of the Fairmount water system. Again, the largest concentration of deaths was in the almshouse, where approximately 228 died.

Although fellows of the College of Physicians continued to advocate the miasma theory at midcentury, doctors trained in the city were challenging its validity. In Columbia, Lancaster County, seventy-five miles west of the city, cholera broke out in September 1854, killing at least 127 people. Immigrants traveling west from Philadelphia on the railroad brought the disease to the city. Dr. T. Heber Jackson of Philadelphia attended victims and concluded that transmission of the disease was best explained by contagion, not miasma. He also questioned the prevailing belief in predisposing causes, pointing out the disease had struck rich and poor, Black and white alike.

Philadelphia-trained Dr. John Atlee of Lancaster reinforced this criticism. He observed that an outbreak of cholera in Lancaster in the summer of 1854 had not developed spontaneously but had been brought to the city by infected people and spread by contagion. His discovery of microscopic particles in the effluvia of the Lancaster cholera victims gave credence to the germ theory that soon became medical orthodoxy. The analyses of these two physicians mirrored the research linking cholera to polluted water being done by Dr. John Snow of London.

Lesser cholera outbreaks occurred in 1866, 1891, and 1899. While many in the city's medical community still advocated the miasma theory in 1866, they had come to believe that the disease was also spread by contact with fluids emitted by the victims. The Board of Health's use of disinfectants greatly reduced deaths during that epidemic and marked another major step toward the acceptance of the germ theory of medicine. Typhoid epidemics and recurrences of cholera in the 1890s led the Board of Health to install water-filtration systems for the city. No subsequent outbreaks of cholera occurred after the city expanded and improved sewage disposal and water treatment in the twentieth century.

## Typhoid Fever and Filtered Water

**Steven J. Peitzman**

Philadelphia in the late nineteenth century stood shamefully high among large American cities in rates of death from typhoid fever (also known as enteric fever). Caused by a type of salmonella bacterium, the disease had become common in Philadelphia and other cities with crowded populations, inadequate disposal of human waste, and lack of water treatment. Local outbreaks and the knowledge that they might be prevented by improving the water supply spurred physicians, activists, and organizations to press Philadelphia's city government to improve water quality with a filtering system. After a decade of delay and fumbling, a massive apparatus installed between 1900 and 1910 largely ended deaths from typhoid fever.

By the last decades of the nineteenth century, the Philadelphia region no longer suffered from massive epidemics of yellow fever, cholera, or smallpox—though the horrific influenza pandemic of 1918 lay in the future. Typhoid fever, meanwhile, had become both endemic (common) and given to outbreaks or local epidemics. Philadelphia endured outbreaks in 1876 (probably relating to the crowds coming to the city for the Centennial Exhibition), 1888–89, 1899, and 1906—but the disease was always present. During the 1890s, more than 5,400 deaths from typhoid fever occurred. More died from tuberculosis, but the means existed to prevent typhoid. The symptoms of typhoid include high fever, headaches, a subtle rash, vomiting, and sometimes diarrhea; complications such as bowel perforation or hemorrhage can cause death. The microbe spreads through the "fecal-oral" route and was transmitted via contaminated milk, asymptomatic carriers, and most importantly, impure water. Before antibiotics, treatment consisted of a "mild" diet (milk, eggs, beef broth), bed rest, and cold baths, the latter much loathed by patients. Surgery could occasionally save patients who had bowel perforations.

In a time of industrial growth and population increase, typhoid was a regional problem, but no regional framework existed to deal with it. In the nineteenth century, as in the twenty-first, Philadelphia drew its water from the Schuylkill and the Delaware Rivers, into which both the city and upstream districts discharged all manner of industrial and human waste. The creation of Fairmount Park in the nineteenth century lessened the city's contribution to the Schuylkill's considerable defilement, but pollution from upstream industrial towns remained.

As one response to this menace, in the 1880s the Philadelphia Bureau of Water built an "interceptor sewer," a sort of bypass channel that drained waste from Roxborough, Manayunk, and Falls of Schuylkill (East Falls), diverting it from the river. The city also created larger reservoirs to allow the sedimentation of particulate contamination. The rate of death from typhoid declined into the early 1890s, but more preventative measures seemed to be needed. In 1889, the influential Germantown physician and author Henry Hartshorne argued for filtration of the water supply. Hartshorne cited recent experience in Europe, where cleansing of municipal water through "slow" filters of layers of sand and crushed coal had become an accepted technique.

Into the 1890s, a variety of lay and medical groups in Philadelphia campaigned for clean water and particularly for a system of filters. These included the Woman's Health Protective Association of Philadelphia (founded in 1893), the College of Physicians of Philadelphia, the Civic Club, and beginning in 1896 a broadly based City Organizations' Filtration Committee. The councils (then bicameral) took up the issue, but political factionalism, unclear authority to borrow large funds, and an extreme diversity of opinion delayed approval of funding. For example, while some members of council favored filtration, Thomas Meehan,

**FIGURE 46.** Department of Public Health representatives testing water for typhoid in Fairmount Park, 1931. SPECIAL COLLECTIONS RESEARCH CENTER, TEMPLE UNIVERSITY LIBRARIES.

the "dean of American horticulturists" and a locally prominent Germantown resident, dismissed its value and may have doubted the germ theory of infectious disease. In addition, the chief of the Bureau of Water, a capable engineer named John Cresson Trautwine, deplored the waste of water more than the waste in it and so persistently urged the metering of water (then not in effect) more than the filtering of it. In addition, several proposals to bring pure water from either the Pine Barrens of New Jersey (suggested in 1891) or from unpolluted realms of the upper Schuylkill (1889, 1897) episodically competed for attention.

A particularly vicious outbreak in 1898–99 (which some alleged related to the movement of soldiers into the city at the time of the Spanish-American War) resulted in 948 deaths in 1899 and finally provoked progress. The city councils approved the request of Mayor Samuel Ashbridge for a $12 million bond issue to build the system of sand filter beds. Construction began in 1901 and 1902 at the reservoirs and pump stations in Roxborough, ("upper" and "lower"), West Philadelphia (Belmont), and Torresdale. The end of the decade saw the last filter beds completed, at the Queen Lane location. Numerous photographs made by the city show the enormity of these vast undertakings, probably then the largest municipal projects in Philadelphia's history. The plan included laying massive pipes interconnecting the several water facilities. The entire effort ended up

**FIGURE 47.** The Eleventh U.S. Cavalry at a Victory Loan parade, Broad Street, Philadelphia, April 1919. A similar event the preceding September led to a deadly spike in influenza cases in the city. SPECIAL COLLECTIONS RESEARCH CENTER, TEMPLE UNIVERSITY LIBRARIES.

costing an estimated $26 million to $28 million.

Typhoid fever rates eventually fell by more than 90 percent with the advent of filtered drinking water—which was also, at least sometimes, clear and free of odor, something new to Philadelphians. A serious outbreak occurred in 1906, but it was mainly limited to areas not yet receiving filtered water. In 1909 chlorination was added to further combat waterborne bacteria. In the 1910s and 1920s typhoid immunization came into wide use, but until vaccines made most of the population resistant to the disease, occasional small outbreaks still occurred; one in 1911 resulted from a rupture of a large main supplying the Roxborough plant. By 1935, however, rarely did a Philadelphian die from typhoid fever, although the disease remained a major killer well into the twenty-first century in countries without the infrastructure to deliver safe drinking water to all their inhabitants.

## Influenza Pandemic, 1918–19

**Thomas Wirth**

As World War I drew to a close in November 1918, the influenza virus that took the lives of an estimated fifty million people worldwide in 1918 and 1919 began its deadly ascent. The United States had faced flu pandemic before, in 1889–90 for example, but the 1918 strain represented an altogether new and aggressive mutation that proved unusually resistant to human attempts to curb its lethality. The devastating effects of the virus, known today as H1N1, were first felt in late summer 1918 along the Eastern Seaboard in a military encampment outside of Boston. From there, influenza propagated ruthlessly across the country, claiming nearly seven hundred thousand lives before running its course in the spring and summer of 1919. Globally, estimates place the toll of the pandemic as high as fifty million, with young children and adults especially vulnerable.

The pandemic hit Philadelphia exceptionally hard after sailors, carrying the virus from Boston, arrived at the Philadelphia Navy Yard in early September 1918. In a city of almost two million people, half a million or more contracted influenza over the next six months. Over sixteen thousand perished during this period, with an estimated twelve thousand deaths occurring in little more than five weeks between late September and early November 1918. Historians and epidemiologists have identified several critical factors that shaped the peculiarly rapid and catastrophic spread of disease in Philadelphia.

First, a severe shortage of medical personnel rendered the city partially defenseless against the pandemic. More than 25 percent of Philadelphia's doctors, some 850 total, and an even greater share of its nurses were occupied with the war effort. In 1917 and 1918, three-quarters of the staff of Pennsylvania Hospital at Eighth and Spruce Streets were stationed at the Red Cross Base Hospital 10 in Le Tréport, France. The absence of vital medical support made the difficult task of containing the flu and healing the sick even more challenging once the virus migrated from the military camps—including the Navy Yard, Camp Dix in New Jersey, and Camp Meade in Maryland—to the civilian population in late September.

The increased demand for labor during the war also compounded matters. While Philadelphia enjoyed a boom in employment in its shipbuilding, munitions, and steel industries, overcrowding turned the city's housing deficiencies into a legitimate public health crisis. As African American migrants from the Jim Crow South and immigrants from eastern and southern Europe searched for a better life, many found the opportunities gained in Philadelphia came at the price of their health and safety. Cramped, dilapidated, and unsanitary living quarters in places like the Seventh Ward rendered these districts a fertile source for influenza.

If the city's execrable living conditions and depleted medical corps made suppressing influenza difficult, its unabated proliferation in the fall of 1918 likely had its origins in the response of city health officials who drastically underestimated the flu's potency. On September 21, just days after six hundred sailors at the Navy Yard fell ill and the first civilian flu cases were confirmed, Philadelphia's major newspapers reported that Dr. Paul A. Lewis of the Henry Phipps Institute at the University of Pennsylvania had determined the cause of the disease—a bacteria known as Pfeiffer's B. influenzae. The *Philadelphia Inquirer* wrote that Lewis's findings had now "armed the medical profession with absolute knowledge on which to base its campaign against the disease."

The city's top health administrators concurred and yet promptly contradicted their own best advice for staving off the grippe: avoid crowds. With virtually no resistance from the city's leading public health officials at the Department of Public Health and Charities, a rally for the Fourth Liberty Loan campaign brought two hundred thousand Philadelphians together into the city's streets on September 28. A concert at Willow Grove Park featured the music of John Philip Sousa, stoking patriotic fire. Within three days of the event, 635 new civilian cases of influenza signaled the beginning of the most deadly period of pestilence ever recorded in the city's history. Restrictions belatedly followed as officials in Harrisburg, Philadelphia's city government, and boards of health in New Jersey and Delaware closed churches, saloons, and schools in early October.

Despite the belated restrictions, influenza tore through Philadelphia at a ferocious pace in October and early November. During the second week of October, around 2,600 people succumbed to the flu, and the following week saw that number nearly double. The city's immigrant poor suffered particularly hard. Those born of foreign parents in the Russian, Hungarian, and Italian communities, among others, died at a higher rate, with some 1,500 more total deaths than those born to American mothers. In a wartime atmosphere on the eve of the Red Scare, immigrants were the primary target of inflamed nativist sentiment. Public health officials and private citizens alike scrutinized the personal hygiene habits of the foreign-born and often linked insalubrious tendencies to the supposedly questionable morals associated with "alien" cultures. One "disgusted woman" wrote to the *Public Ledger* in October 1918 demanding that "don't-spit signs be placed in our post-office building in all languages necessary, to reach all foreign men, and with fines for violations." The city set fines for spitting at $2.50 and in one day, October 23, the *Evening Bulletin* reported 114 arrests.

As death stalked the city, bodies piled up by the dozens in a lone morgue at Thirteenth and Wood Streets. The extreme circumstances of the pandemic also meant, however, that many bodies simply rotted for days in the streets. Eventually five makeshift morgues, including one at a cold-storage facility on Cambridge and Twentieth Streets, were established to meet the deluge of corpses. Cemeteries lacked the space and manpower to adequately bury the dead, too. At Holy Cross Cemetery in Lansdowne seminarians-turned-gravediggers took in an average of two hundred bodies a day in October and deposited hundreds of coffins into a large common grave. "On one occasion," recalled Rev. Thomas C. Brennan of St. Charles Borromeo Seminary, "the students worked on this task until 10:30 p.m. by the light of the October full moon, the long rows of coffins in the trench presenting a weird and impressive picture in the moonlight."

Those attempting to care for the living at Philadelphia General Hospital on Thirty-Fourth Street faced similarly overwhelming circumstances. Already at its capacity of 2,000 patients when the virus struck, the hospital had to find room for 1,400 more people as it peaked in mid-October. With hospitals inundated and facing a shortage of medical staff, volunteers were culled from religious organizations, civic associations, and, most prominently, the city's medical and nursing schools. Across Philadelphia these men and women turned parish houses and armories into temporary emergency hospitals, but on the whole extra assistance remained scarce. As one volunteer recalled, "If you asked a neighbor for help, they wouldn't do so because they weren't taking any chances. . . . It was a horror-stricken time." And yet just as quickly as the horror arrived did it also depart. When ten thousand dosages of a flu vaccine finally arrived in Philadelphia on October 19, the virus was already in the beginning stages of a rapid decline. By the second week of November, deaths caused by influenza and pneumonia were less than a quarter of what they were the week prior, and by the end of the month the death toll had dipped under one hundred for the week for the first time since early September. Still, the city's death rate from influenza, officially recorded at the time as approximately 407 per 100,000 people, exceeded that of all other American cities in 1918. A subsequent estimate has revised that figure upward to 748 per 100,000.

Statistics such as these provide a tangible sense of the staggering loss of life that occurred in Philadelphia during this short period, though they tell us next to nothing about how influenza inflicted widespread fear and distress across the city. Perhaps the words of the renowned cardiologist Isaac Starr, a third-year medical student at the University of Pennsylvania at the time of the outbreak, came closest to encapsulating the ordeal of late 1918 when he noted simply that it was as if "the life of the city had almost stopped."

## Legionnaires' Disease

**Dan Royles**

The outbreak of a mysterious pneumonia-like disease in the Philadelphia region in the summer of 1976 puzzled doctors and public health officials. Many of the sick had attended an American Legion convention at the Bellevue-Stratford Hotel, giving the new illness the name "Legionnaires' disease." Months later, doctors discovered that bacteria in the hotel's air-conditioning system had caused the outbreak. By then, 34 of the 221 people who fell ill had died, and the Bellevue-Stratford Hotel had closed its doors for lack of business.

The outbreak occurred during the bicentennial of the Declaration of Independence. After returning home on July 24 from the three-day American Legion meeting in Philadelphia, several of the legionnaires began to fall ill with chest pains, high fevers, and lung congestion. By August 2, twelve had died. Doctors initially suspected that swine flu might be the culprit. If so, it was feared that Philadelphia could become the epicenter of an influenza pandemic, on the order of the 1918 "Spanish" flu that had killed as many as one hundred million worldwide. In this light, Pennsylvania state health director Leonard Bachman considered a quarantine of the city. Bachman held daily press conferences—sometimes twice a day—to update the public on the progress of the epidemic, while the City of Philadelphia set up a hotline to take reports of potential new cases.

Meanwhile, the numbers of sick continued to grow: by August 6, 25 had died, with 112 others hospitalized. However, tests for known viruses, bacteria, and fungi that might cause similar symptoms all came back negative. Moreover, the disease showed no evidence of secondary infection; that is, the sick did not seem to pass the illness to those with whom they came into contact. There would be no deadly pandemic, but the question remained: what was killing the legionnaires?

To find out, a team of local and state health officials distributed a survey to the ten thousand people—legionnaires and their families—who had attended the meeting. Through computer analysis of their responses, epidemiologists determined that the sick had all been inside the Bellevue-Stratford Hotel, although some had stayed elsewhere. Moreover, several attendees of the International Eucharistic Conference, which took place at the hotel shortly after the American Legion meeting, also became ill with the same mysterious pneumonia. On August 14, epidemiologists added presence at the Bellevue-Stratford to the case definition of the new disease.

In the absence of a clear infectious agent, doctors turned their attention to chemical toxins like nickel carbonyl. Researchers also tested the pesticides and

**FIGURE 48.** Bellevue-Stratford Hotel, Broad and Walnut Streets, Philadelphia, ca. 1933–70. In 1976, the hotel became the epicenter of an outbreak of a mystery pneumonia that led to the identification of *Legionella pneumophila*, the bacteria commonly responsible for Legionnaire's disease. LIBRARY OF CONGRESS.

cleaning products used in the hotel. Although answers remained elusive, the number of new cases of "legion disease" dropped off. By the end of August, officials announced that the epidemic had ended. Nevertheless, business at the Bellevue-Stratford declined precipitously. The hotel's rate of occupancy dropped from 80 percent to 3 percent at its lowest point, while the once-bustling restaurant, bar, and coffee shop were all nearly deserted. In November, the hotel's owners announced that the Bellevue-Stratford would have to close its doors. (It reopened in 1979, after a major renovation, under new management.)

In January 1977, researchers finally pinpointed the source of the legionnaires' pneumonia: a bacterium from a previously unknown genus, subsequently named *Legionella* after the first recognized outbreak. Researchers thereafter realized that *Legionella* bacteria thrive in large central air-conditioning systems, such as that used by the Bellevue-Stratford. They also concluded that outbreaks had occurred going back to 1965 in hospitals and large office buildings but had escaped detection at the time. Although more recent outbreaks in places such as Spain, Portugal, and Dubai indicated Legionnaires' global reach, the names of both the disease and the bacteria remained linked to the initial outbreak in Philadelphia. A 2002 outbreak of the disease at a Jewish nursing home in suburban Horsham, Pennsylvania, killed two and sickened eight others. In 2005, two attendees of the Pennsylvania American Legion convention in King of Prussia were sickened with Legionnaires', reviving memories of the 1976 crisis, although both men survived. Since the discovery of the *Legionella* bacillus, doctors have been able to treat cases of the disease with antibiotics.

## AIDS and AIDS Activism

**Dan Royles**

Doctors in Philadelphia diagnosed the first local case of what would later become known as AIDS (acquired immune deficiency syndrome) in September 1981, just months after the Centers for Disease Control first reported unusual diseases in otherwise healthy young men. Researchers later discovered the cause of AIDS to be the human immunodeficiency virus (HIV), which replicates in the human body by killing cells that are vital to immune function.

Although the number of new cases in New York City, Los Angeles, and San Francisco multiplied quickly over the first two years of the epidemic, at first the number of people with AIDS in Philadelphia rose slowly. Within the first year, only seven cases were reported locally, but by early 1983 trends in Philadelphia seemed to be catching up to the rapidly growing epidemic witnessed in New York and California. The disease also appeared in New Jersey, particularly in the urban corridors between Philadelphia and New York and between Philadelphia and Atlantic City, and in Delaware.

As gay men watched their friends and lovers die in increasing numbers, they organized in response. Philadelphia Community Health Alternatives (PCHA, later known as the Mazzoni Center), a health clinic founded in 1979 to serve the local lesbian and gay community, formed the Philadelphia AIDS Task Force to provide social services to those affected and offer information about AIDS and other sexually transmitted diseases through a local hotline. Meanwhile, social clubs like the Gay Men's Chorus and Girlfriends Motorcycle Club joined forces to raise funds for PCHA's education and prevention efforts.

By the middle 1980s public health authorities recognized that the AIDS epidemic had grown beyond the communities of gay men in which doctors first identified the disease. Researchers in the United States and France had identified HIV as the cause of AIDS in 1983 and thus definitively determined that the disease could be transmitted through blood-to-blood contact. At the same time, in cities around the country, reports showed the growing incidence of HIV and AIDS among African Americans and Latinos, particularly within networks of intravenous drug users and among their sexual partners and young children. Although those in this "second wave" of new cases had likely been infected for some time, their low access to medical care combined with the long latency period of HIV initially masked the prevalence of AIDS within communities of color.

In Philadelphia, by 1985 African Americans made up almost half of all reported AIDS cases and the majority of cases among people under twenty-five years old. David Fair, a longtime local gay activist and

**FIGURE 49.** ACT UP demonstrators on City Avenue, Bala Cynwyd, demanding more state funding for fighting AIDS, 1988. Police arrested ten protesters for blocking a road. JOHN J. WILCOX LGBT ARCHIVES OF PHILADELPHIA.

secretary-treasurer of a local predominantly Black health care workers' union, and Rashidah Hassan, a nurse who had worked with PCHA and its AIDS Task Force, became dissatisfied with the groups' failure to effectively reach out to African Americans at risk of contracting HIV. To stem the rising tide of new infections in Philadelphia's Black community, in 1985 they founded Blacks Educating Blacks About Sexual Health Issues (BEBASHI), one of the nation's first Black AIDS service organizations. Perceiving that the AIDS Task Force's efforts to reach out to the Black community had been undercut by its reputation as an all-white organization, BEBASHI representatives worked through existing social institutions like African American churches so that their education and prevention messages would resonate with Black audiences. In New Jersey, Project IMPACT (Intensive Mobilization to Promote AIDS Awareness through Community-based Technologies) also reached out to African American leaders in urban areas.

In 1987, as the AIDS community nationwide became frustrated with the dearth of effective treatments and President Ronald Reagan's reticence on the epidemic, grassroots AIDS politics took a radical turn. In March, a group of New York activists founded the inaugural chapter of the AIDS Coalition to Unleash Power (ACT UP), an organization whose protest actions became the public face of AIDS advocacy in the United States during the late 1980s and early 1990s. The group quickly spawned a network of chapters in cities across the country and abroad, including in Philadelphia, South Jersey, and Delaware.

Members of the Philadelphia branch of ACT UP began staging theatrical "die-ins" and other dramatic demonstrations to highlight the human cost of high prescription drug prices and inadequate public health policy. To protest the Catholic Church's opposition to condom use, in May 1991 around one hundred ACT UP Philadelphia members interrupted a prayer service for people with AIDS conducted by Archbishop Anthony Bevilacqua and tried to place wrapped condoms near his hands and feet, shouting, "These will save lives—your morals won't." In addition to public protests, ACT UP became well-known for creating memorable visual messages to both educate people about AIDS and mobilize those affected by the epidemic. In this vein, during one holiday season the Philadelphia chapter circulated stickers featuring an HIV-positive Santa Claus with the tagline "If only Reagan and Bush had told the truth, Santa wouldn't have to die from AIDS."

During the mid-1990s, ACT UP declined in national prominence as the white gay men who filled much of the organization's ranks passed away, grew tired of activism, or gained access to the highly effective (but expensive) class of new antiretroviral drugs that became available due to advances in HIV treatment research. The Philadelphia chapter, however, remained vital due to the recruiting efforts of a core group of members who reached out to lower-income people of color, among whom the nationwide AIDS epidemic continued to grow fastest. The changing membership in turn shaped the direction of the group's activism, as it increasingly focused on affordable housing, HIV prevention in prisons, and access to medications for impoverished people in the United States and throughout the developing world. Working with Health GAP (Global Access Project), a coalition of AIDS activists and allied organizations, Philadelphia ACT UP members pressured the White House to move forward with a coordinated response to the worldwide AIDS pandemic. This effort, supported by numerous AIDS action groups in Philadelphia and the Cooper Early Intervention Program in Camden, culminated in 2003 with President George W. Bush's announcement of the President's Emergency Program for AIDS Relief (PEPFAR), a five-year, $15 billion commitment funding HIV prevention and drug access programs in Africa. In 2008, Congress reauthorized the program through 2013 and expanded its funding to almost $48 billion.

As the epidemic entered its third decade, the Philadelphia Department of Public Health estimated that 1.3 percent of the city's population was living with HIV or AIDS, about three times the national average. Despite the city's relatively large percentage of people living with HIV and AIDS, local trends reflected patterns of infection for the United States as a whole, inasmuch as the epidemic in Philadelphia disproportionately affected African Americans and, in particular, men who had sex with men and women, among whom the disease was growing fastest.

In light of these realities, activists reignited the search for an AIDS cure. In 2009 a group of veteran Philadelphia activists, many of whom had been part of ACT UP chapters around the country during the organization's heyday, founded the AIDS Policy Project to advocate for funding and scientific research on treatments to not only slow the spread of HIV within a patient's system, but eliminate it altogether. By the early 2020s, breakthroughs in medical science led to growing optimism over vaccines and new treatments. But AIDS remained a grave burden in the region. Around eighteen thousand Philadelphians lived with an HIV diagnosis, and Delaware and New Jersey had the thirteenth and fifteenth highest prevalence of the virus adjusted for population in the United States. In the face of an ongoing threat, residents of the Delaware Valley sought to lead the way to the end of the AIDS epidemic once and for all.

## Coronaviruses

**Timothy Kent Holliday**

Two major coronavirus epidemics in the early twenty-first century left their mark on the Greater Philadelphia region. The second of these epidemics, beginning in 2019, caused considerable loss of life; prompted major restrictions on education, social life, and the area's economy; and exposed urban inequalities. Vaccine research undertaken in Philadelphia, however, played a critical role in limiting the death toll across the world.

Coronaviruses, so-called because of their resemblance under a microscope to a crown, are a group of viruses that can infect a diverse array of mammals and birds, leading to an equally diverse array of symptoms and prognoses. The origin story of coronaviruses stretches back almost three hundred million years, when the most recent common ancestor of all modern coronaviruses began to differentiate into distinct viruses. But only in the 1930s—just a few decades after the Russian biologist Dmitri Ivanovsky discovered viruses in 1892—did humans become aware of coronaviruses, first in chickens, then in mice, and later in humans and other animals.

Coronaviruses became a topic of worldwide significance following the November 2002 report of an outbreak of severe acute respiratory syndrome (SARS) in Guangdong Province, China. Between its first identified appearance and July 2003, roughly eight thousand cases of SARS were confirmed globally, mostly in China. Of the twenty-seven cases identified in the United States, at least eleven came from Pennsylvania and five from New Jersey. Although the first probable case in Greater Philadelphia likely came from exposure in Toronto, the virus's association with East Asia hit business owners in Philadelphia's Chinatown, who reported income declining by as much as 60 percent in April 2003. Philadelphia International Airport screened new arrivals, and some individuals wore masks to curb spread. Limited human-to-human transmission made containment possible both locally and globally.

Sixteen years later, a more transmissible coronavirus proved far harder to contain. In December 2019, epidemiologists and local health officials noticed a mystery pneumonia in Wuhan, China. By examining patients' airway cells, a team of Chinese researchers identified a novel coronavirus—which they dubbed 2019-nCoV—as the cause of the outbreak. The virus—later named COVID-19 by the World Health Organization—spread rapidly, affecting more than two dozen countries by mid-February 2020.

In the Philadelphia area, officials from the city's public health preparedness program and similar programs in suburban counties urged preparation over panic. The *Inquirer* noted in early February 2020 that the flu remained "more dangerous" than "the scary new virus." Despite such attitudes, on March 11, 2020, the World Health Organization declared the novel coronavirus a pandemic, which recognized the virus's international spread. In the wake of the World Health Organization's announcement, disease control specialists increasingly advocated "social distancing," or the restriction of physically close interpersonal contact, as well as mandated mask wearing and shutdowns, despite concerns that some such mitigation strategies could violate individual human rights. Public health experts in the United States and elsewhere often pointed to Philadelphia's erratic implementation of such measures during the city's catastrophic 1918 flu epidemic to make the case for restrictions.

In late March 2020, Philadelphia experienced its first COVID-19 death. The number of confirmed cases in the Philadelphia area grew rapidly between March and May 2020. In response, federal, state, and local authorities adopted emergency measures to slow transmission. On March 12, the city government barred gatherings of over a thousand people; on March 16 it closed public schools and nonessential businesses; and on March 22 it issued a stay-at-home order. The switch to work from home and closure of cafes and restaurants left downtown streets deserted. Other jurisdictions adopted similar restrictions. The governor of New Jersey, Phil Murphy, ordered residents to stay at home on March 21, while his counterpart in Delaware, John Carney, did so a day later. On March 23, Governor Tom Wolf of Pennsylvania followed suit, with an executive order that covered Philadelphia and nearby counties. Soon after the announcement of the first COVID-19 death in Philadelphia, local hospitals prepared for a surge of patients that could overwhelm their capacity. By the end of March lockdowns extended across the Greater Philadelphia region.

The widespread shutdowns in the spring of 2020 spurred debates about weighing individual liberties against the greater good. However, public health experts at Drexel University's Urban Health Collaborative estimated that the first forty-five days of shutdown in the city prevented 6,200 deaths. Other measures also attempted to slow transmission. In June Philadelphia mayor Jim Kenney signed a mask mandate for indoor and busy outdoor locations and by September, eighty contact tracers—including a group of thirteen Community College of Philadelphia students—worked to curb the virus's spread. Even with such measures, COVID-19 strained the region's health care system. As more and more victims succumbed to the disease in mid-April, one local hospital resorted to transferring body bags to the

Medical Examiner's Office in the back of a pickup truck. Recognizing the traumatic impact of the pandemic on the region, historians, librarians, and archivists in Greater Philadelphia urged members of the public to document their experiences for use by future historians.

COVID returned after its deadly first wave. Cases spiked again in November and December 2020, with over 7,000 testing positive in the city during the week after Thanksgiving. A smaller surge followed in the Spring of 2021. By mid-August 2021, the city had reported over 160,000 positive COVID tests, and a month later the death toll stood at 3,800. Some groups—notably people of color, prison inmates, and undocumented workers—struggled to access testing, care, and financial support. Additionally, COVID-19 hospitalizations and deaths tended to cluster in neighborhoods with larger minority and low-income populations, following a pattern seen in epidemics that stretched back to the eighteenth century. This data had prompted the Philadelphia Department of Public Health to craft a racial equity plan in July 2020 to improve access to testing and care, with the ambitious long-term goal of reducing the disparate impact on communities of color by preventing chronic health conditions that increased the risk of severe COVID-19 infection.

Vaccines, which rested in part on a revolutionary discovery by Philadelphia scientists, offered a more immediate route to limiting the death toll. In December 2020, approximately two dozen Philadelphians received their first doses of a COVID-19 vaccine, which markedly reduced the likelihood of serious illness. The rapid development of a vaccine owed much to the research of University of Pennsylvania–affiliated biochemists Katalin Karikó and Drew Weissman, whose work in the 1990s and early 2000s established how to modify messenger RNA (mRNA) to "teach" the human immune system how to resist infections. The mRNA vaccines produced by Pfizer-BioNTech and Moderna became by far the most widely used vaccines in the United States, Europe, and parts of Africa and the Americas, while by 2023, China too had embraced the technology in its fight against the virus. Locally, almost two-thirds of Philadelphia residents were fully vaccinated against COVID by June 11, 2021, when the city "reopened" by relaxing restrictions, although schools did not welcome back students fully until August. In 2023, Karikó and Weissman won the Nobel Prize in Medicine for their medical breakthrough.

Although vaccines provided strong protection against serious illness, they proved less effective at blocking the virus's spread. The emergence of the BA.2 subvariant in the spring of 2022 led to another dramatic shift in pandemic response, as well as to renewed confusion. Effective April 18, 2022, Philadelphia reinstated its indoor mask mandate, becoming the first major U.S. city to do so. Later that day, U.S. District Judge Kathryn Kimball Mizelle of Florida struck down the federal mask mandate for public transportation. Mizelle's decision prompted transit agencies SEPTA and PATCO to rescind their own mask mandates, despite Philadelphia's new mandate coming into effect the same day.

Vaccines and immunity acquired from infection made these later waves of COVID far less deadly than the initial surges of 2020–21. Nonetheless, the regional toll of the virus proved chastening. As of July 2023, COVID had claimed the lives of over 5,600 Philadelphians and over 8,000 in adjacent Pennsylvania counties. By then, almost 1,700 had also succumbed to the disease in New Castle County, Delaware, with 4,500 New Jerseyites in Burlington, Camden, Gloucester, and Salem Counties dying. According to the team of Chinese researchers who first identified the virus that causes COVID-19, though, the risks of future spillover events involving coronaviruses remained.

## EXPLORE MORE

Some of the region's early efforts to promote public health still survive. The Pennsylvania Hospital, one of the first public institutions of its kind in what became the United States, is at 800 Spruce Street. The main building dates to 1756. Not far away lies Washington Square, part of William Penn's design for a sylvan city, but by the end of the eighteenth century a potter's field used to inter victims of yellow fever. The College of Physicians, founded in 1787, is at 19 S. Twenty-Second Street, a home it shares with the Mütter Museum, which has collections on anatomy and medical science. A little farther out of Center City the Fairmount Water Works, with its interpretive center and elegant neoclassical buildings, overlooks the Schuylkill River at 640 Waterworks Drive. The Lazaretto, at 97 Wanamaker Avenue, Essington, Pa., provides an insight into attempts to halt the spread of disease into the United States.

Efforts to improve public health gathered pace in the nineteenth century as sanitarians and municipal reformers developed better understandings of disease. Fairmount Park, intended as the lungs of the city and the protector of its water supply, amounts to one of their most ambitious efforts. On a smaller scale, drinking fountains intended to provide pure water and keep men out of taverns dot the city. The "First Fountain," erected in 1854, stands at Forbidden Drive in Wissahickon Valley Park. Additional examples can be found at 615 S. Washington Square and 312 Arch Street. Laurel Hill Cemetery contains a monument to the sixty volunteer nurses from the city who traveled to Virginia in 1855 to fight yellow fever. Fifteen died in the outbreak.

Other sites provide reminders of failure. Broad Street not only hosted the September 1918 military parade that led to a deadly spike in influenza infections, but also marks the location of the first documented outbreak of Legionnaires' disease, at the Bellevue-Stratford Hotel (200 S. Broad Street) in 1976. Duffy's Cut in Malvern, Chester County, is the site of a mass grave of Irish American railroad workers who died during the 1832 cholera epidemic, either of the disease, or, as archaeological evidence suggests in some cases, from gunshots and blunt force trauma. A historical marker in East Whiteland Township is close to the spot.

On the region's public health up to the end of the nineteenth century, see Simon Finger, *The Contagious City: The Politics of Public Health in Early Philadelphia* (Cornell University Press, 2012); J. Worth Estes and Billy G. Smith, eds., *A Melancholy Scene of Devastation: The Public Response to the 1793 Philadelphia Yellow Fever Epidemic* (Science History Publications, 2013); David Barnes, *Lazaretto: How Philadelphia Used an Unpopular Quarantine Based on Disputed Science to Accommodate Immigrants and Prevent Epidemics* (Johns Hopkins University Press, 2023); Charles E. Rosenberg, *The Cholera Years: The United States in 1832, 1849, and 1866* (University of Chicago Press, 1987); John B. Osborne, "The Lancaster County Cholera Epidemic of 1854 and the Challenge to the Miasma Theory of Disease," *Pennsylvania Magazine of History and Biography* 133, no. 1 (January 2009): 5–28; Michael P. McCarthy, *Typhoid and the Politics of Public Health in Nineteenth-Century Philadelphia* (American Philosophical Society, 1987). Accounts of success and failure in the era are given in Elizabeth Milroy, *The Grid and the River: Philadelphia's Green Places, 1682–1876* (Pennsylvania State University Press, 2016), and Sam Alewitz, *"Filthy Dirty": A Social History of Unsanitary Philadelphia in the Late Nineteenth Century* (Garland Publishing, 1989).

Twentieth- and twenty-first-century epidemics are covered in Thomas Wirth, "Urban Neglect: The Environment, Public Health, and Influenza in Philadelphia, 1915–1919," *Pennsylvania History* 73, no. 3 (Summer 2006): 316–42; Laura Spinney, *Pale Rider: The Spanish Flu of 1918 and How It Changed the World* (Jonathan Cape, 2017); Jon Zonderman and Laurel Shader, *Legionnaires' Disease* (Chelsea House, 2006); James Gillett, *A Grassroots History of the HIV/AIDS Epidemic in North America* (Marquette Books, 2010); Jonathan Engel, *The Epidemic: (A Global History of AIDS)* (Harper Collins, 2006); Dan Royles, "Taking It to the Streets: AIDS, Race, and Protest in Philadelphia," *Pennsylvania Legacies* 16, no. 1 (Spring 2016): 26–31; Tor Chaykin, *Photo Pandemica: The Face of Covid-19 in the City of Brotherly Love* (BlinkArtStudio, 2021); Joe Miller, *The Vaccine: Inside the Race to Conquer the COVID-19 Pandemic* (Welbeck Publishing, 2021). Such literature documents the toll epidemics have taken on the region and the efforts the people of the Delaware Valley have made to combat them.

Troops in the Army Reserve Urban Augmentation Medical Task Force prepare for deployment from Joint Base McGuire-Dix-Lakehurst in Burlington County, New Jersey, as they join the fight against COVID-19, April 8, 2020. U.S. DEPARTMENT OF DEFENSE. PHOTOGRAPH BY STAFF SGT. SHAWN MORRIS.

BILLINGTON, HUTCHINSON & CO.
Insurance
TUESDAY
2
JULY
30

CHAPTER 8

# NETWORKS OF KNOWLEDGE, SERVICE, AND ACTIVISM

## INTRODUCTION

IN 1811, THE ARCHITECT BENJAMIN HENRY LATROBE expressed his hope that Philadelphia would "become the Athens of the Western World." The ambition to turn the Delaware Valley into a center of artistic, cultural, and scientific learning that would mirror the influence of its ancient Greek counterpart ran deep at a time when the United States sought intellectual as well as political independence from Europe. Drawing on the city's religious and secular traditions, institutions and individuals in Philadelphia took up the challenge. However, Latrobe and his generation—like those who preceded and followed them—never aimed solely to serve as an example to the rest of the world. The flow of people, goods, and knowledge in and out of the region led its residents to repurpose old ideas and generate new ones. In this way, Philadelphia became a place where the world was understood, manipulated, and reimagined in myriad ways.

Eager to mirror developments in Europe, colonial institution builders made intellectual innovation possible in the Delaware Valley. Connected by travel, correspondence, and the city's extensive publishing trade to Enlightenment centers of learning like Paris and Edinburgh, Philadelphia became the knowledge capital of the Americas by the time of the Revolution. Benjamin Franklin and his associates established a club, the Junto, which led to the creation of the first of the Delaware Valley's scientific societies, the American Philosophical Society, in 1743. This provided a springboard for a host of later organizations such as the Academy of Natural Sciences (established in 1812) that exerted their influence well into the modern era and acquired an international reputation. Scientific societies proliferated beyond the city as men and women in Philadelphia's outlying counties enlisted in the pursuit of knowledge. The importance of the learned institutions Franklin and his imitators helped to build only grew in the new republic, where an educated citizenry was considered crucial to prevent the new nation from falling apart.

Those educated citizens would also be forged in the region's institutions of higher learning. Even before the Revolution ended, the forerunners of the University of Pennsylvania, Princeton, Rutgers, and the University of Delaware had been established, as had the hemisphere's first medical college. Over the nineteenth and twentieth centuries, dozens of other colleges joined these early starters, focusing on theology and the liberal arts on the model of their European antecedents or aspiring to the status of the research universities that had originated in post-Napoleonic Prussia. By the early 1900s, such sites of higher education had begun to supplant scientific societies as hubs for knowledge production, drawing scholars and students from across the globe. Over the first half of the twentieth century college classrooms became platforms for debating ideas like Pan-Africanism and developmental economics.

Philadelphia's influence around the world, though, probably owed more its Revolutionary association than its institutions. In the years that followed American independence, the struggle for liberty rooted in the Delaware Valley inspired imitators elsewhere. Thomas Paine, who had popularized the fight against monarchy in Philadelphia in 1776, carried the torch to revolutionary France, nearly losing his head in the process. His ideas later then found favor among Spanish American revolutionaries who sought sanctuary and support in the Delaware Valley. And at the end of World War II the Vietnamese revolutionary Ho Chi Minh drew on the opening lines of the Declaration of Independence to sever his nation's ties with France. Words penned in Philadelphia thus echoed around the world. Around the same time, as the new United Nations searched for a permanent home, Philadelphians embarked on a serious if ultimately unsuccessful bid to establish their city as the capital of a postwar world. In the middle of the "American Century" the nation's birthplace made symbolic sense as the headquarters for an organization committed to international cooperation.

Yet despite their city's association with liberty, Philadelphians have tended to offer the world practical solutions rather than abstract ideas. The pursuit of "useful knowledge," as Franklin called it, persisted long after the passing of the Revolutionary generation. Scientific management, forged in Midvale Steel by Frederick Winslow Taylor, provided a blueprint for making the labor process more efficient. As Taylorism spread in the early twentieth century, it not only reshaped the rhythms of work in Delaware Valley factories, but also left its mark as far afield as China, whose nation builders came to see its promise of a disciplined and productive citizenry as a pathway out of colonial domination.

To say Philadelphia has been a site of intellectual innovation is not to say it has always been a force for good. Taylorism, it is worth remembering, provoked fierce resistance from workers who resented being reduced to an engineering problem. Well-meaning prison reformers, whose designs for the Walnut Street Jail and Eastern State Penitentiary drew inquiring minds from across the Atlantic, drove inmates to insanity rather than cleansing their souls. The city's role in the development of racial theory is another reminder that bad ideas can travel too. The Academy of Natural Sciences provided a platform for the Edinburgh-educated Samuel George Morton, whose skull collection, amassed from across the hemisphere, gave the imprimatur of science to Black subordination. Yet Philadelphians could draw on evidence from around the world to challenge Morton's work. Black residents of Philadelphia, for example, questioned his claim that Africans had never sustained a great civilization by pointing to the glory of ancient Egypt.

In challenging proslavery science, African Americans showed that networks of knowledge and activism flourished beyond exclusive colleges and scientific societies. Black-led movements, like Bishop Richard Allen's African Methodist Episcopal Church and Father Divine's International Peace Mission (initially based in Harlem but moving to Philadelphia in 1942), implanted roots in the region before spreading their influence elsewhere. Both movements spurred efforts to improve the lives of local people through mutual aid, self-help, and religious devotion. From their Philadelphia base they expanded globally in a way that connected faith and civil rights in the Delaware Valley to struggles for freedom and equality elsewhere. The work of the Reverend Leon Sullivan also exemplifies this trajectory. His efforts to fight job discrimination in Philadelphia through consumer boycotts achieved impressive local results from World War II onward, while his Sullivan Principles, first set down in 1977, became an important weapon in the fight against apartheid on the international stage.

The influence of faith leaders like Allen, Father Divine, and Sullivan highlights the religious inspiration behind many Philadelphians' efforts to reshape the world. While the Quaker voice in politics diminished after the Seven Years' War, the Society of Friends' commitment to peace found expression in social movements, including abolitionism. The American Friends Service Committee, a recipient of the Nobel Peace Prize, is a notable twentieth-century legacy of this commitment. Other faith communities have sent missionaries abroad to spread the gospel. But activism has also had a strong secular strand, dating back to Benjamin Franklin's insistence that the future University of Pennsylvania, unlike other colonial colleges, would be nonsectarian. Whether in search of sacred or profane ends or driven by grand ideas or the pursuit of useful knowledge, the people of the aspiring Athens of America have drawn on ideas from across the globe and nourished world-changing designs of their own.

# Scientific Societies

Jessica Linker

Since the eighteenth century, Philadelphia-area scientific societies have promoted scholarship and innovation, increased access to scientific knowledge, and played an important role in the professionalization of various disciplines. Longstanding institutions, including the American Philosophical Society (1743), the Academy of Natural Sciences (1812), and the Franklin Institute (1824), have garnered national and international accolades, while many smaller or shorter-lived societies vitalized scientific study in specific localities or became outlets for women's participation.

Eighteenth-century scientific societies in Philadelphia were eager to establish America's role in a global scientific network. The colonies lacked a pan-colonial entity on par with the Royal Society of London to evaluate and promote scientific innovation. The American Philosophical Society, Philadelphia's first and longest-lived scientific society, emerged as an early contender for this role, balancing pursuit of transatlantic prominence with service to Philadelphia and, especially by the late eighteenth century, to Americans at large. First organized by members of the Junto, which included Benjamin Franklin, and active between 1743 and 1746, then revived in 1767, it merged with the American Society, Held at Philadelphia, for Promoting Useful Knowledge in 1769. The society attracted widespread attention in Europe for its work documenting the 1769 transit of Venus, notably through the efforts of astronomer David Rittenhouse. In 1771, the American Philosophical Society, in emulation of the Royal Society of London, published the first volume of its *Transactions*, which reported on the society's activities and recent discoveries and innovations. By the early republic, the American Philosophical Society acted as a quasi-umbrella organization in America, corresponding with a variety of individuals and scientific societies that had emerged in the United States and also in Europe.

In the early republic and into the nineteenth century, Philadelphia-area scientific societies took steps toward acting as professional bodies by establishing prizes and holding exhibitions, sponsoring scientific ventures or smaller institutions, and publishing journals and

**FIGURE 50.** Print of a Prussian embroidery pattern sheet showing the founder of the American Philosophical Society, Benjamin Franklin, ca. 1842–52. LIBRARY OF CONGRESS.

scientific literature. Prize contests could be narrowly defined, seeking solutions stemming from local problems, or more substantial, such as the Philosophical Society's Magellanic Premium (established 1786) for work in navigation, astronomy, or natural philosophy, or the Franklin Institute's Benjamin Franklin Medals (established 1824) for engineering. In these early years, scientific societies sought to reward practical use of science.

A number of Philadelphia-area scientific societies encouraged women to participate, although they often stipulated that women's participation should be congruent with prevailing gender norms. Similar to the way societies encouraged men to use science to enhance artisan trades and businesses, they imagined women's scientific knowledge as an extension of their labor and sensibilities. The 1820s and 1830s saw a proliferation of local societies and cabinets in surrounding counties, including Chester, Bucks, and Montgomery, some of which were open to women's contributions. Thought to be more attuned to beauty in nature, women often collected and donated specimens despite not having full access to other society activities. The Cabinet of Natural Science of Montgomery County's first annual report from 1832 claimed that Hannah Corson had single-handedly collected the five hundred native and naturalized plants that made up its herbarium.

Although some societies, including the American Philosophical Society and Philadelphia Chemical Society (ca. 1790s), extended membership to women on an extremely limited basis in the eighteenth century, generally, local societies only became more open to admitting women as members in the 1830s and 1840s. The Academy of Natural Sciences unanimously elected Lucy Say as its first female member in 1841; Delaware County Institute of Science in Media admitted women members not long after. Women's membership in local scientific societies, though often fraught with sexism, expanded throughout the nineteenth century.

Philadelphia birthed a number of national organizations that went on to further professionalize the sciences. The most important was the American Association for the Advancement of Science (AAAS) In 1848. By the end of the nineteenth century the society, which had moved to New York and then Washington, D.C., had become the most prominent advocate for the promotion of scientific knowledge and cooperation, regardless of discipline. Smaller, specialist organizations also had roots in the city. 1859 saw the founding of the Entomological Society of Philadelphia, the precursor to the American Entomological Society, and the Zoological Society of Philadelphia, which established the Philadelphia Zoological Gardens, the first zoo in the United States, in 1874. These societies adopted the strategies of larger, earlier societies—establishing prizes, founding journals, communicating abroad—but became increasingly interested in engaging local citizens through educational outreach.

In the twentieth and twenty-first centuries, Philadelphia's old guard of scientific societies, the American Philosophical Society, Academy of Natural Sciences, and Franklin Institute, acted as public museums and scholarly libraries in addition to maintaining several of their traditional roles. The Franklin Institute began its shift toward functioning primarily as a museum during the Depression; the Academy of Natural Sciences, which had maintained a museum for much of the nineteenth century, was acquired by Drexel University in 2011, becoming involved with its teaching mission. The American Philosophical Society maintained an impressive scholarly library for the study of early American history, Native American cultures and languages, and the history of science, offering in addition to many of its longstanding prizes and premiums, research fellowships for scholars.

As degree-granting institutions and national organizations became the primary arbiters of scientific knowledge by the late nineteenth century, a number of Philadelphia's smaller societies faded away, or became more club-like over time, abandoning many of their professionalizing aims to prioritize maintaining public interest in their discipline. In the twenty-first century, the region's scientific societies, which were premier professional bodies in the eighteenth and nineteenth centuries, remained dedicated to the dissemination of scientific knowledge.

## Colleges and Universities

**Andrew Heath**

Higher education in the Philadelphia region, which dates to the colonial era, has carried the imprint of international influences through its providers' missions and curricula, the origins of its students and faculty, and its entanglements with decolonization, superpower struggles, and globalization. Major Delaware Valley institutions, such as the University of Pennsylvania, transitioned from their eighteenth- and nineteenth-century roles as importers of Scottish and German models to become exporters of research and sought-after destinations for students from around the world. Much like Philadelphia's scientific societies, which they supplanted as sites for the production of knowledge, universities have served as nodes for the global transmission of ideas.

### ATLANTIC PRECEDENTS

College education in the Delaware Valley built on long-established precedent from the other side of the Atlantic. Medieval universities in Europe, led by scholar-clerics, taught grammar, rhetoric, and logic alongside Aristotelian philosophy. During the Renaissance, curricula broadened to include works of Greek and Latin literature, and a college education became the hallmark of a gentleman rather than just preparation for a career in the church or government. Amid the upheavals of the Reformation, meanwhile, some institutions of higher learning became incubators of Protestant dissent. John Harvard, who endowed British North America's first college after its founding in Massachusetts in 1636, had studied at Emmanuel, Cambridge, which served as a training ground for Puritan ministers. A century later in Philadelphia Benjamin Franklin sought to break the mold by calling for a place of practical learning in the mid-eighteenth-century city. To secure support for his scheme, though, he joined forces with other Philadelphians who had more traditional models in mind. The result was a compromise. Together, they secured a charter for the Academy and College of Philadelphia, initially based at Fourth and Arch Streets, which ran on different principles than other colonial colleges. Princeton, founded in 1746 as the College of New Jersey, prepared New Light Presbyterians for service in the church. Rutgers, which obtained a charter in 1766 under the name Queen's College, did likewise for the Dutch Reformed Church. Franklin and his allies' institution, in contrast, admitted students regardless of denomination. Nevertheless, the curriculum remained wedded to the classics rather than English and science as Franklin envisaged. By 1760, just five years after its founding, it boasted around a hundred students.

The College of Philadelphia mirrored intellectual developments in eighteenth-century Scotland. The brilliant Irish-born and Glasgow-educated Presbyterian Francis Alison served as an early vice provost. Presbyterian Synod of Philadelphia had already employed Alison in an earlier effort to create a free school for training ministers. Situated outside the city in New London, Chester County, the school moved in 1765 to Newark, Delaware, where it later became the cornerstone of the University of Delaware. Alison, having relocated himself to Philadelphia's new nonsectarian college, continued to popularize the work of his former tutor at Glasgow, Francis Hutchinson, one of the first practitioners of a "common sense" philosophy that sought to find a middle ground between reason and religion. During his stint as vice provost, Alison, who like other Enlightenment thinkers opposed the concentration of power in church and state, taught several future signers of the Declaration of Independence.

### UNIVERSITY OF PENNSYLVANIA CHARTERED

While in Philadelphia, however, Alison ran into the staunchly Anglican provost, William Smith. Another protégé of the Scottish Enlightenment, Smith wrote one of the first blueprints for higher education in North America, *A General Idea of the College of Mirania* (1753). His fictional college's curriculum—which reflected reforms at his alma mater, the ancient university of Aberdeen—imagined giving young men the knowledge and skills they needed for professional and political life, while leaving another route open for the kind of practical, mechanics' education favored by Franklin. In Philadelphia, where the college enrolled teenage boys who rarely lingered long enough to graduate, Smith put elements of his plan in place, but after falling out with Franklin and Alison he ran into further trouble during the Revolutionary War. Although the provost sympathized with the colonists' cause, he struggled to reconcile himself to independence, and in 1779 the Patriot commonwealth assembly got revenge on the suspected Loyalist by chartering the University of Pennsylvania (Penn). The state-approved institution absorbed the Tory-tainted college in 1791.

Scottish influence also permeated the College of Philadelphia's School of Medicine from its founding in 1765. Over the first half of the eighteenth century the University of Edinburgh established a reputation as a leading center of medical education. It drew American students, and two Philadelphians who crossed the Atlantic to study there, John Morgan and William Shippen Jr., returned to their home city determined to create a similar site of learning in the colonies. With the support of Franklin and Thomas Penn, the Edinburgh alumni started the first medical school in British North America by offering lectures in anatomy complemented by practical learning at the Pennsylvania Hospital. Among the eminent medics to teach at the institution was the future founding father and surgeon general of the Continental army, Benjamin Rush. The institution's high reputation drew students from across the Americas in the nineteenth century; the first Latino graduate, a Cuban, completed his studies in 1829, and many more followed.

Between the Revolution and Reconstruction, though, the region's reputation as a leading center of medical education was not matched in other academic fields. While the University of Pennsylvania offered an education to scions of the city's leading families, a series of small colleges catering to the Delaware Valley's faith communities sprang up. Haverford College (founded 1833) and Swarthmore College (1864) came out of the Society of Friends, though neither maintained religious bars on entry for long. With Irish immigration on the rise Catholics established what would become Villanova University (1842), St. Joseph's University (1851), and LaSalle University (1863). Meanwhile abolitionists in the 1850s helped to found what became Lincoln University in 1866, an institution that provided a crucial training ground for aspiring African American professionals and which became one of the region's two major HBCUs (Historically Black Colleges and Universities) alongside Cheyney University. While provision for higher education in the region widened, however, the curriculum at Penn remained rooted in the classics, and students graduated more as gentleman ready for the social world of the region's upper class than scholars. New knowledge still came from wealthy amateurs and learned societies rather than the region's institutions of higher learning. The publisher Henry Charles Lea provides an example. He shared his early work on conchology (the study of mollusk shells) at the Academy of Natural Sciences. After his interests shifted to the history of the medieval church, his immense wealth allowed him to draw on archival collections in Europe and the Americas. Although he left his immense collection of books and codices to Penn, he neither attended college nor held any university post.

## EXPANSION AND GERMAN INFLUENCE

The winds of change shook higher education in the region during and after the Civil War. The Morrill Act of 1862 allowed states to put revenue from federal land sales toward colleges for the teaching of agriculture and industry alongside traditional liberal arts subjects. Rutgers College in New Brunswick and Delaware College (renamed the University of Delaware in 1921) in Newark benefited from the legislation. Industrialization, urbanization, and armed conflict meanwhile spurred interest in new fields of inquiry like social science. An increasingly complex society, some Americans reasoned, needed credentialed experts to direct its development. Many of those aspiring experts went to study in Germany, where in the early nineteenth century the Prussian reformer Wilhelm von Humboldt had reimagined universities as centers of research as well as teaching. In the Humboldtian tradition, American institutions like Johns Hopkins in Baltimore began to offer doctoral training. Penn, in its somewhat laggardly fashion, created its own Graduate School of Arts and Sciences in 1882, which opened on a new campus in West Philadelphia, just a year after the founding of its Wharton School to train a new business elite. Over the following eighty years additional research universities on the German model appeared in the region. Temple University, first established as a Baptist college in 1884 but primarily intended to provide a practical education for Philadelphia's working people regardless of denomination, became a university in 1907, quickly expanding its professional programs thereafter. Rutgers College, which began to award doctoral degrees in the 1880s, took the university name in 1924. Princeton University, under the presidency of Woodrow Wilson from 1902–10, remained wedded to the liberal arts ideal, though resistance to the idea of the research university there faded over the early decades of the twentieth century. When Princeton created the Institute for Advanced Study in 1930, it drew a wave of Jewish refugees from Europe, among them Albert Einstein. Though universities continued to collaborate with learned societies, they moved more toward the forefront of knowledge production in the region.

Like their German predecessors, the new American research universities attracted overseas students, as did other local colleges. Penn's international contingent had largely been confined to its medical school until the late nineteenth century, but its growing academic reputation brought students from around the world to its campus. The earliest documented Japanese student in the United States, Tosui Imadate, graduated in 1879, the same year African Americans matriculated for the first time. By 1910, three years after the first Puerto Rican student received his degree from nearby Haverford College, Penn was circulating a Spanish prospectus in Latin America. Chinese students, exempted from the tight restrictions of the Chinese Exclusion Act of 1882, arrived in significant numbers during an era in which late imperial and early republican reformers encouraged study in Europe and the United States. Over the first two decades of the early twentieth century Chinese clubs formed on Penn's campus and by 1915 an alumni club, headed by Wu Tingfang, the ex-Chinese ambassador to the United States and recipient of an honorary doctor of laws from Penn, was up and running in Shanghai.

The cosmopolitan character of Penn's early twentieth-century campus spurred efforts to make overseas students feel at home in Philadelphia, too. In 1908, the Reverend A. Waldo Stevenson began to hold Friday evening gatherings for Chinese students, and ten years later, with the help of the Christian Association, he became the first director of an International House at 3905 Spruce Street. During the 1920s the International House advertised events for Filipino, German, and Japanese students.

Such endeavors did not cut off international students from the struggles going on in their homelands. Imperial conflicts and world wars shaped those students' experiences in the Delaware Valley. For a select few, the United States' colonial conquests created pathways for study. Honoria Acosta-Sison, who attended the Woman's Medical College of Pennsylvania, moved to the city on a scholarship after her native Philippines came under Washington's control following the Spanish-American War of 1898. After founding a magazine to advance the interests of U.S.-based Filipinos, she graduated in 1909 as the first credentialed female doctor of her nationality, then went on to a career as a prominent obstetrician in Manila. Acosta-Sison steered clear of anticolonial politics during her sojourn in Philadelphia, but during an age in which the United States paid lip service to the cause of national self-determination, education in the region provided one route to fighting imperialism. Many early graduates from China studied economics at the solidly protectionist Wharton School, and while the transmission of ideas is difficult to trace with certainty, the Wharton curriculum likely buttressed support among Chinese nationalists for a high tariff regime designed to build up home industry and weaken the stranglehold of Japan and Western powers in East Asia.

## PAN-AFRICANISM

In Chester County, Pennsylvania, Lincoln University became a stronghold of Pan-African politics. Rejecting the industrial education offered at other HBCUs, the institution remained committed to the liberal arts, which held more appeal to colonized Black Africans than the prospect of preparing for a life of manual labor in the segregated South. Those who crossed the Atlantic to study at Lincoln entered a radical milieu shaped by the NAACP, Marcus Garvey's United Negro Improvement Association, and various socialist factions. Lincoln's Black students grappled with what the former Penn instructor in sociology W. E. B. Du Bois had called the global "problem of the color line." James M. Thaele, an early leader of the African National Congress, matriculated at Lincoln in 1909 and absorbed Garveyite ideas, which he worked to popularize in South Africa. Following in his footsteps came Nnamdi Azikiwe, who studied at Lincoln (where he introduced an African history course) and Penn before returning to his native Nigeria, where he eventually became its first postindependence president.

While working as a journalist back in Nigeria, Azikiwe met the Ghanian Kwame Nkrumah, then a student at Ghana's Achimota College. Nkrumah, who had read works by Du Bois, had just been rejected for entry at the University of London, so Azikiwe advised him to try Lincoln instead. With the help of relatives, he gathered the money he needed to travel to Philadelphia, where he secured a scholarship at Azikiwe's alma mater. Nkrumah still struggled to fund his studies, working at one point as a longshoreman on the Chester docks to make ends meet, but he found time to immerse himself in the region's Black culture. He joined Father Divine's radically egalitarian International Peace Mission movement, became involved in Trotskyist and Pan-African politics, and contributed to the establishment of the African Students' Organization of the United States and Canada. Like Azikiwe, he also taught at Lincoln and studied at Penn before returning to Ghana after World War II. There he became its first postindependence leader and one of the foremost advocates of African unity. After one of his intellectual heroes, Du Bois, faced persecution in the anti-communist McCarthy era, in 1961 Nkrumah invited him to Accra, where the pioneering sociologist and civil rights leader died two years later.

By the 1950s Greater Philadelphia's universities had become critical nodes in the superpower struggle with the Soviet Union. New and enlarged institutions provided an education to the postwar baby boom

**FIGURE 51.** Prime Minister Kwame Nkrumah of Ghana meeting President Dwight D. Eisenhower, 1958. Nkrumah, the first leader of postindependence Ghana and a committed Pan-Africanist, studied at Lincoln University and the University of Pennsylvania. PHOTOGRAPH BY WARREN K. LEFFLER, U.S. NEWS & WORLD REPORT MAGAZINE COLLECTION, LIBRARY OF CONGRESS.

generation. Penn, Temple University, and Drexel University (founded in 1891 by a local banking dynasty but not operating as a research university until the 1960s) drove military and economic expansion. The Moore School of Electrical Engineering at Penn, for example, built the Electronic Numerical Integrator and Computer (ENIAC), a landmark general-purpose computer, in 1946. Curricula, too, reflected geopolitical priorities. Penn, which had taught East Asian languages and culture from the 1920s, began to offer classes in African languages during World War II. As Cold War divisions hardened it joined the trend toward teaching and research in interdisciplinary "area studies." With funding from the Ford Foundation and similar organizations, area studies experts used social scientific methods to enhance understanding of regions of the globe in which the United States had a strategic interest.

## COLLEGES AND UNIVERSITIES IN THE COLD WAR

But as the United States vied for hearts and minds around the globe the "soft power" of the region's higher education providers proved an asset in cementing Cold War alliances, too. The Fulbright Program, created by Congress after 1945, promoted international exchanges, while at Penn the Thouron Award—endowed by a member of the Du Pont family and her husband—promoted the "special relationship" between Britain and the United States. Temple took a different route to extending its international influence by expanding overseas. It opened a French language center in Paris in 1950, a Rome campus in 1966, and an outpost in Tokyo in 1982. Between 1980 and 1984 it also sent education faculty to Bendel State in Nigeria to run a teacher training program. Other colleges and universities developed study abroad programs for students. Beaver College (renamed Arcadia University in 2000) in Glenside, Pennsylvania, proved one of the most innovative. After a Beaver professor took a handful of students on a postwar tour of Europe, the college developed its international offerings, creating a Center for Education Abroad in 1965. By 1983 it boasted of enrolling more of its students abroad than any other college in the United States.

As American higher education grew in resources and reputation during the Cold War, its international appeal increased. The number of international faculty and students in the region grew markedly. On the eve of World War II an estimated five hundred studied in the Philadelphia vicinity, but this had more than doubled by 1954. International House soon outgrew its West Philadelphia villa and moved to Fifteenth and Cherry Streets in 1959, then returned across the Schuylkill to a modernist housing block at Thirty-Seventh and Chestnut Streets in 1970. Geopolitics shaped which students arrived—the Chinese contingent that had been so visible in the first half of the twentieth century diminished after the Communist Party seized power in 1949—but every inhabited continent was represented. Numbers grew in the 1960s and 1970s as Cold War allies in "tiger economies" such as Taiwan and South Korea sent more students overseas and U.S. immigration policy liberalized. Many graduates stayed in the region in academic and nonacademic roles.

While the Cold War left its mark on the region's universities, student protest provided a very different impetus in the reshaping of curricula and institutions. Inspired by Black Power and the anti–Vietnam War movements, students demanded greater study of Africa and Asia, and more spaces and representation for students and scholars of color. Penn, for example, established what would become W. E. B. Du Bois College House in 1972 to support students from the African diaspora. Temple University had created its Afro-Asian Institute the preceding year, which soon became the Pan-African Studies Department. After years of under-resourcing the department, Temple hired Molefi Kete Asante in 1984, and under his direction the Department for Africology and African American Studies built an international reputation. The prominent historian and antiracist writer Ibram X. Kendi received his doctorate from the program in 2010. Similar changes took place at other colleges and universities in the region as Africana studies extended beyond its earlier home in HBCUs like Lincoln.

### POST–COLD WAR ALLIANCES

As the Cold War wound down and socialist regimes lost power or opened up, another wave of international engagement commenced. Penn concluded an agreement to cooperate with Shanghai's Jiao Tong University in 1980 and a year later Wharton faculty assisted in developing a business program there. Over the following decades Chinese student numbers grew significantly, while the region's colleges and universities carefully cultivated a global brand with agents and recruiters across the world. By the 2020s, Temple drew students from 130 countries. Bryn Mawr College, founded in the late nineteenth century as a Quaker college for women, boasted 20 percent of its admissions were non–U.S. citizens. Rutgers University–Camden, a campus of New Jersey's main state university, attracted 120 Chinese nationals. At the start of the decade about one in twelve students in the region came from overseas. Meanwhile, the work undertaken in the region's research universities had global impact. Katalin Karikó, a Hungarian-trained biochemist, came to Temple as a postdoctoral fellow in 1985 before moving in 1989 to Penn Medicine, where she mostly worked on insecure contracts. Her collaboration with Drew Weissmann led to a breakthrough in mRNA technology that paved the way for the mass production of COVID-19 vaccines during the 2020 pandemic, saving millions of lives around the world.

From the Scottish roots of the colonial College of Philadelphia to the globalized universities of the twenty-first century, centers of higher education in the Delaware Valley have often been nodes in global networks. Initially importers of European models, they transformed over the course of the nineteenth and twentieth centuries into international behemoths, drawing students and staff from across the globe, influencing anticolonial struggles and superpower rivalries, and producing world-changing research.

## Bartram's Garden

**Sarah Chesney**

Located on the west bank of the Schuylkill River, Bartram's Garden, considered the oldest surviving botanical garden in North America, has served as a monument to the storied history of Philadelphia's botanical endeavors and to the genius of John Bartram and his descendants. Established as a family farm and garden by John Bartram in the early eighteenth century, the garden has functioned as a commercial and public botanical garden, a private retreat, a native plant repository, and a botanical education center of national and international importance.

Originally part of a 1,000-acre tract of land in Kingsessing Township first settled by the Swedish in the mid-seventeenth century, Bartram's Garden began in 1728 when John Bartram purchased a 102-acre tract for his family farm. Bartram was a self-taught naturalist who sought out the company of other like-minded individuals, both at home and abroad. Bartram's friendships with Benjamin Franklin and James Logan led to his introduction to London and Royal Society fellow Peter Collinson, with whom he began a correspondence in 1731. Bartram and Collinson soon began to exchange plants along with botanical notes on experiments and other discoveries. By 1750, Bartram was sending regular shipments of North American seeds to a wide variety of European collectors, including Sir Hans Sloane and Carl Linnaeus, and advertising his seeds for sale in London periodicals. Bartram expanded his garden to keep up with his growing plant trade business and performed experiments on the *lychnis dioica* that corroborated Logan's experiments on Indian corn. As Bartram's fame grew, so did his garden. He traveled farther and farther afield to collect new plants and seeds, and he recreated their environments at home by constructing ponds and swamps for aquatic plants, areas of forest and grassland, as well as sections for nursery seeds and greenhouses for more tropical specimens. By the turn of the century, Bartram's Garden boasted the most varied collection of North American plants in the world.

When John Bartram died in 1777, his sons, John Bartram Jr. and William Bartram, continued the business. They expanded the grounds as well as the garden's reputation in national and international circles through their commercial and educational activities. William Bartram's growing renown as a botanical illustrator and plant collector attracted botanical enthusiasts from near and far who came to exchange both plants and knowledge. French botanist André Michaux visited Bartram's Garden during his North American sojourn, for example.

Both George Washington and Thomas Jefferson visited and purchased plants from Bartram's Garden for their own estates in Virginia, and near neighbor William Hamilton exchanged many plants with the Bartrams, even sending William Bartram one of the three ginkgo trees he introduced to America from England in 1785. Bartram's Garden's reputation as a destination grew, especially among the delegates to the Continental Congress in Philadelphia. In 1784, the congress ended a session early to allow several delegates to indulge their curiosity about Bartram's Garden and venture across the Schuylkill River for an afternoon visit with the family.

In the early decades of the nineteenth century, Bartram's Garden expanded again under the third generation of Bartrams. Ann Bartram Carr and her husband, Colonel Robert Carr, took over the business from Ann's father, John Bartram Jr., and expanded both the commercial business and the garden itself. At its largest, Bartram's Garden comprised twelve acres of gardens and ten greenhouses filled with over 1,400 native plant species and as many as 1,000 varieties of more far-flung exotics. In 1844 and 1845, the Carrs added another dimension to Bartram's Garden when they opened the grounds as a summer pleasure garden, selling ice cream and other refreshments to visitors and offering steamboat trips three days a week from the Delaware River wharves.

By midcentury, however, increasing financial difficulties forced the Carrs to sell Bartram's Garden. Railroad magnate and industrialist Andrew Eastwick purchased the house and grounds in 1850. Eastwick planned to construct a villa near the original Bartram house. Recognizing the historic significance and aesthetic appeal of the site, he preserved the original house and grounds as part of his private estate.

After Eastwick's death, Bartram's Garden fell into neglect until Eastwick's former gardener, the common councilman Thomas Meehan, aided by Boston botanist and head of the Arnold Arboretum Charles S. Sargent,

**FIGURE 52.** Illustration from the botanist William Bartram's *Travels*, 1794.

conceived a plan to purchase the estate for the city as part of Meehan's campaign to create parks in Philadelphia. After a prolonged campaign by Meehan, Bartram's Garden finally came under the control of the City of Philadelphia in 1891. In 1923, the Fairmount Park Commission assumed control of the property and worked to preserve and restore the gardens and buildings while continuing to operate the garden as a city park.

In October 1960, the secretary of the interior designated Bartram's Garden a National Historic Landmark in acknowledgement of the importance of the garden to John Bartram's career as a botanist and to the history of American botany. Through restoration and interpretation of the site, the John Bartram Association continued to preserve the historical and contemporary gardens for visitors into the twenty-first century, including the original ginkgo tree (1785), a yellowwood tree sent by Michaux (1784), the *Franklinia alatamaha* from which all current examples descend, and the Bartram oak. Since the third decade of the eighteenth century, Bartram's Garden served as a repository of North American plants of national and international importance, bringing together the commercial, public, and educational aspects of Philadelphia's botanical legacy.

## Coffeehouses

**Michelle Craig McDonald**

Philadelphia's first coffeehouse opened in 1703, and by midcentury half a dozen operated within the city limits. Their purpose, however, changed in important ways as the eighteenth century progressed. Early coffeehouses primarily served the needs of traders and mariners, acting as crucial centers of commerce. In the decades following the American Revolution, however, some coffeehouse functions—such as banking and maritime insurance—had developed into separate industries. As a result, proprietors reached out to new clientele, competing with taverns, inns, and hotels by offering elaborate menus as well as social and intellectual entertainments. Philadelphia's coffeehouse scene transformed yet again in the twentieth century with the arrival of regional and national franchises. At the beginning of the twenty-first century, coffeehouses remained an integral part of the social fabric, with hundreds operating in the city's center and scores more in surrounding neighborhoods and suburbs.

The first coffeehouses sprung up in the Ottoman Empire in the fifteenth century and spread to Europe over the following two hundred years. By 1663 the City of London boasted over eighty establishments, which often became hubs of economic and political life. They soon crossed the Atlantic, though early American coffeehouses were often modest ventures. A land deed for Philadelphia's first coffeehouse, opened by Samuel Carpenter in 1703 on Front Street just north of Walnut Street, described a "tenement" measuring just twenty-four feet wide by thirty feet deep. Later coffeehouses grew in size and often set aside rooms for special groups or functions. The coffeehouse opened in 1720 by a Captain Roberts, also on Front Street, had enough space to host board meetings of the Library Company, North America's first circulating library. His wife, the "Widow Roberts," continued to manage the business after his death until 1754. She was one of three women known to operate coffeehouses in Philadelphia by the 1750s.

In some ways colonial coffeehouses functioned like taverns or inns. They offered food and drink, and both served coffee and alcohol. But there were also important differences. Coffeehouses were centers of commercial activity, particularly during exchange hours, when traders compared currency prices and bought or sold bills and coins. Period prints and paintings usually depict these first-floor spaces as large public halls, with communal tables dominating their centers and booths arrayed along the walls where more private business could be conducted. Even the front porches and walls of coffeehouses were put to commercial use. The space in front of the Old London Coffee House at Front and Market Streets was one of Philadelphia's most popular auction blocks and was used to sell everything from imported bags of coffee and barrels of rum to indentured servants and enslaved Africans.

Because of their business orientation, eighteenth-century coffeehouses subscribed to a variety of newspapers. In 1796, the Merchants' Coffee House and Exchange boasted both local Philadelphia newspapers

**FIGURE 53.** Lithograph of the London Coffee House showing a colonial-era auction of enslaved people, 1830. One of several coffeehouses in Philadelphia, the London—established in 1754 at the corner of Front and Market Streets—provided a place for merchants to share gossip, strike deals, and participate in the trade in enslaved people. LIBRARY COMPANY OF PHILADELPHIA.

as well as periodicals from New York, Boston, Baltimore, and Europe, a subscription series costing a hefty £500 or more annually. Such publications were invaluable to savvy traders who needed to be kept abreast of the latest news.

By the 1760s, the Old London was Philadelphia's leading coffeehouse, owned by printer William Bradford. Centrally located in the business district and adjacent to the waterfront, it was a well-known landmark. It was thus the ideal meeting place for merchants and storekeepers when they began formulating their responses to new, and largely unwanted, British commercial legislation and voicing their discontent. When several Philadelphia merchants and store owners assembled at the Old London to discuss their response to the Stamp Act in September 1765, political discourse quickly escalated into threats against John Hughes, Philadelphia's tax collector, that left him so terrified he would later recall how he had fortified himself "with Fire-Arms" and resolved "to stand a Siege" while several of his friends patrolled the neighborhood "between my house and the Coffee House."

Hughes's fears were well founded. During the American Revolution, local leaders used Philadelphia's coffeehouses to stage ritual destruction of hated pieces of legislation, as well as to post the nonimportation agreements that they circulated and signed. Coffeehouses also hosted meetings of the city's Committee of Correspondence, which sought to strengthen communication about protest between colonies, and the Committee of Compliance, which enforced the embargos designed to compel Parliament to reconsider its approach to governing trade. The "deliberations of Congress are impenetrable secrets," John Adams mused from Philadelphia in 1775, "but the conversations of the city, and the chat of the coffee house, are free, and open."

By the 1790s and early 1800s, many of the commercial functions formally associated with coffeehouses had become professional industries in their own right, such as banks, insurance companies, post offices, and auction houses. As a result, coffeehouses had to remake themselves. Some relocated to the outskirts of town, such as Manayunk and Passyunk, or near suburban parks. Abraham Streaper, for example, opened his coffeehouse on the banks of "that beautiful and airy situation on the west of the Schuylkill River" two miles from the city where he advertised a relaxing atmosphere, fresh fish in season, and the best liquors. With such amenities as gardens, summer houses, and country air for the genteel, they bore little resemblance to the mercantile coffeehouses of a generation before.

Other coffeehouses expanded their services in the city. Some offered menus that changed by time of day and season of the year, competing with taverns and restaurants. Some entrepreneurs featured special shows, including lecturers on topics from philosophy to politics, scientific experiments, and traveling music or theater productions. Concert tickets for a chamber music performance were sold by the Merchants' Coffee House and Exchange in 1783, and the following year Bradford's coffeehouse featured the work of an itinerant scientist presenting "A Lecture on Heads." The American Coffee House, which operated between 1831 and 1834 on the second block of Chestnut Street, was really more of a creative restaurant, replete with pools filled with turtles, fish, and crabs cooked to order, and roaming black bear cubs, until the animals outgrew the venue.

These trends continued during the nineteenth century, as coffeehouses became less associated with the world of business and more with entertainment, culture, and the culinary arts. By the turn of the century, patrons of the region's coffeehouses saw them as places to chat about the shows they had just attended, or as purveyors of artisanal breads and pies. In these respects, the coffeehouses of the late nineteenth century were much more like what would emerge in the years to come than the busy, noisy haunts of the eighteenth-century merchant.

At the beginning of the twentieth century, the number of coffeehouses had declined in most urban settings. Too many kinds of businesses competed for the same diners, and the functions that had differentiated coffeehouses in earlier years had waned. In the 1920s, however, coffee shops slowly made a comeback. Like the first American coffeehouses, modeled after English antecedents, this latest iteration was a European import, although this time the inspiration came from Italy. A small coffeehouse in New York's Greenwich Village, which installed an Italian espresso machine in 1927, claims to be the first cappuccino bar, but Philadelphia was not far behind. Several coffee shops clustered around Ninth and Christian Streets, in what became known as the Italian market.

Most of these venues initially served a very local clientele, recreating experiences that migrants had left behind. But the association of coffeehouses with alternative authors and songwriters, particularly the Beat Generation of the 1950s, revitalized the institution. The Gilded Cage, a coffeehouse opened by Esther and Edward Halpern at Twenty-First Street and Rittenhouse Square in 1956 exemplified this era. It became a popular venue for folk musicians, including Peter, Paul, and Mary, Pete Seeger, Arlo Guthrie, and Simon and Garfunkel, until closing its doors in 1969.

The 1990s witnessed a new iteration of the coffeehouse, as what became known as the Starbucks generation emerged. The first Starbucks opened in Seattle in 1971, and the company went public in 1992. By 1995, Starbucks had come to Philadelphia. By 2015, almost two dozen Starbucks coffee shops operated in the city, alongside other franchises such as Dunkin' Donuts, regional chains such as Philadelphia-based La Colombe, and scores of independent operators, which often sprang up in gentrifying neighborhoods like Northern Liberties as alternatives to the chains. The end result was a profusion of choices for the modern coffee drinker, catering to a wide range of different tastes and price points, but all reinforcing the centrality of coffee in modern American life.

## Prisons and Jails

Annie Anderson

In the late 1700s, on the heels of the American Revolution, Philadelphia emerged as a national and international leader in prison reform and the transformation of criminal justice practices. More than any other community in early America, Philadelphia invested heavily in the intellectual and physical reconstruction of penal philosophies, and the region's jails and prisons reflected these evolving principles. Throughout the 1800s, global and local observers looked to Philadelphia—particularly the Pennsylvania system of solitary confinement pioneered at Eastern State Penitentiary—as they modeled penal practices in their communities. By the late twentieth century, however, Philadelphia led the nation not in reform, but in rates of incarceration.

Philadelphia erected its first jail—essentially a well-fortified box-like room, seven feet by five feet—in late 1682 or early 1683 at the corner of Second and High (Market) Streets. Other small jails soon followed across the city and region. Still, incarceration was used sparingly in colonial America and was typically reserved for those awaiting trial or sentencing. Overcrowding, corruption, violence, and bribery ran rampant in Philadelphia's early jails. The city's first stone prison earned the nicknames "school for crime" and "seminary of vice." Administrative control of the jail rested with the local sheriff, who extorted money from prisoners, sold liquor from a well-stocked bar, and withheld food and other necessary goods. Individuals—regardless of sex, age, or crime committed—mingled indiscriminately. A new building on Walnut Street, completed in 1776, failed to improve matters. A 1787 grand jury reported that the jail permitted the "general intercourse between the criminals of the different sexes" without "even the appearance of decency."

Prompted by the scandals of vice-ridden jails and the inhumanities of public punishment and spurred on by post-Enlightenment thinkers such as British prison reformer John Howard, a group of prominent citizens formed the Philadelphia Society for Alleviating the Miseries of Public Prisons (later renamed the Pennsylvania Prison Society) in 1787. The group, including physician Benjamin Rush, politician Tench Coxe, statesman Benjamin Franklin, and Episcopal bishop William White, advocated for prisoners' rights, as well as the restructuring of correctional spaces. The Prison Society shunned a corrupt criminal legal system and grotesque public punishments in favor of a rational, humanistic—and newly private—correction of the spirit. The group drew on Howard's ideas that safe and decent jail spaces—and thus, true rehabilitation—could only be ensured by segregation of individuals by class of offense. In April 1790, the society's lobbying paid off: a new law mandated solitary confinement at the Walnut Street Jail and called for the erection of a new "penitentiary house" at the jail for "the purpose of confining therein the more hardened and atrocious offenders."

With this new law, the Walnut Street Jail became the Walnut Street Prison—the country's first state prison. Jails now came to house individuals awaiting trial or sentencing, along with those convicted of minor offenses, while prisons housed individuals convicted of felonies, more serious crimes that demand longer sentences. The Walnut Street Prison incarcerated convicted offenders from every part of Pennsylvania—a practice never before attempted in the fledgling United States. New Jersey soon followed suit. It began construction on its first state prison, in Trenton, in 1797 and opened it in 1799. The inscription over its front door read, in part: LABOR, SILENCE, PENITENCE, THIS PENITENTIARY HOUSE . . . THAT THOSE WHO ARE FEARED FOR THEIR CRIMES MAY LEARN TO FEAR THE LAWS AND BE USEFUL. Delaware did not establish a state penal facility until well into the twentieth century, opting instead to send adult offenders to county facilities.

Untidy and experimental at first, Philadelphia's prisons nearly perfected the separation of individuals in jails and prisons based on sex, age, and type of offense by the 1820s. The early experiment of solitary confinement at Walnut Street Jail inspired them to push for a prison where this penal practice could be implemented on a large scale. The first such prison, Eastern State Penitentiary admitted its first inmate, Charles Williams, in October 1829. Eastern State's founders believed that in isolation, prisoners would reflect on their crimes and grow penitent, access their inner goodness and shun future criminal activity, and

**FIGURE 54.** Eastern State Penitentiary, Twentieth Street and Fairmount Avenue, Philadelphia, by John Caspar Wild, 1838. LIBRARY COMPANY OF PHILADELPHIA.

cease to corrupt or be corrupted by criminal associations in overcrowded jails. Prisoners spent twenty-three hours a day alone in their cells; they had two half-hour breaks for outdoor exercise in small yards attached to each cell. Prisoners ate, slept, and labored in their cells.

Though internationally admired for its novel design and methodology—its early visitors included the French political scientist Alexis de Tocqueville, sent by his government to report on U.S. penitentiaries—Eastern State's use of solitary confinement drew criticism almost immediately after the prison opened. The British author Charles Dickens, who visited Eastern State in 1842, claimed that prolonged isolation would inspire troubling mental health consequences. Despite ample evidence confirming Dickens's fears, Eastern State's architect, John Haviland, and the prison's Quaker exponents wielded wide regional influence. Haviland was drafted to design New Jersey's second state prison in Trenton, which opened in 1836. Built on a radial plan, it also imposed the Pennsylvania system of solitary confinement. Eastern State itself did not officially abandon the philosophy of solitary confinement until 1913—more a veneer at that point—when inmates were allowed to congregate for worship, sports, and other activities. Outdated and expensive, it closed in 1970.

Over the following decade, the national prison population grew steadily due to a series of policy decisions: longer prison sentences and mandatory minimums, new laws and enforcement techniques, and increased reliance on prisons as a punishment for all crimes. Because of growing incarceration rates, the number of state prisons in Pennsylvania grew from seven in 1970 to twenty-four in 2017. By the early twenty-first century, the state was also home to dozens of additional local jails, federal prisons, and immigrant detention facilities. Many Pennsylvania prisons and jails operated over their capacity. To ease overcrowded conditions, advocates lobbied for a range of reforms: more lenient sentences, the end of cash bail, and modernized facilities. Once a trailblazer in prison reform, a pioneer in both prison architecture and philosophy, by 2017 Philadelphia had the highest incarceration rate of any large jurisdiction in the country, with about 810 per 100,000 people in jail—making it one of the most incarcerated places in the world.

## Lewis and Clark Expedition

**Luke Willert**

On a November day during the severe winter of 1805, a parcel containing over sixty plants, rocks, and fossils arrived at the American Philosophical Society in Philadelphia. Collected by Meriwether Lewis, these

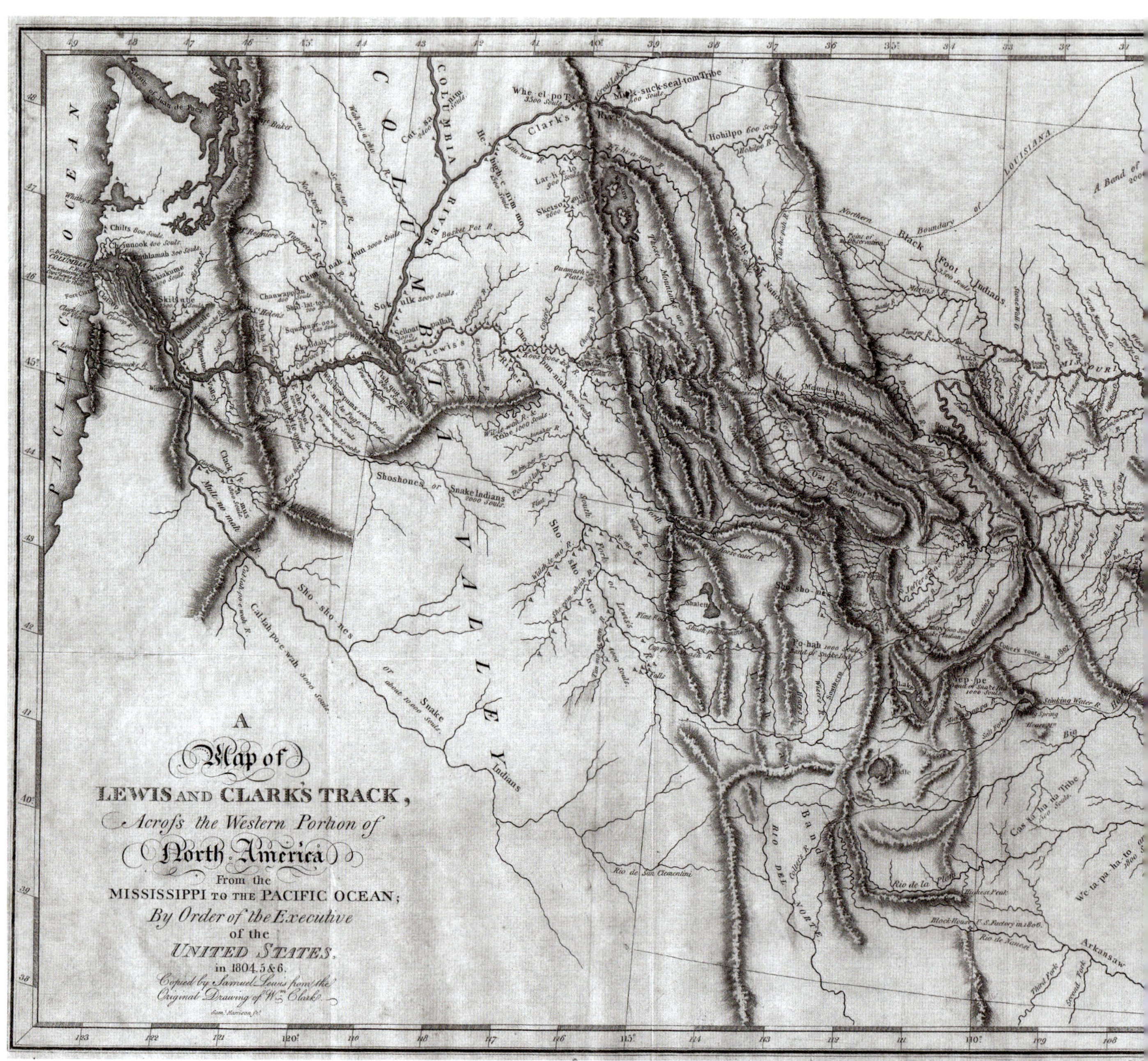


**FIGURE 55.** Map of the 1804–6 Lewis and Clark expedition, 1814. WIKIMEDIA COMMONS.

were specimens from the Corps of Discovery Expedition (1803–6), the western journey of Lewis and William Clark. While the explorers became renowned for crossing the Rocky Mountains and canoeing over the Columbia River, the inspiration and education for their travels came from Philadelphia's libraries and scientific societies.

For several decades, Thomas Jefferson had planned a national expedition into the West. After winning the presidential election of 1800, he put the idea into motion. Exploration became particularly important after the Louisiana Purchase of 1803, which added to the nation extensive and unmapped lands west of the Mississippi River. Jefferson's fundamental vision for the continent's future—an American "empire for liberty"—rested upon the gradual settlement of this enormous space by the nation's farmers and their growing families. The

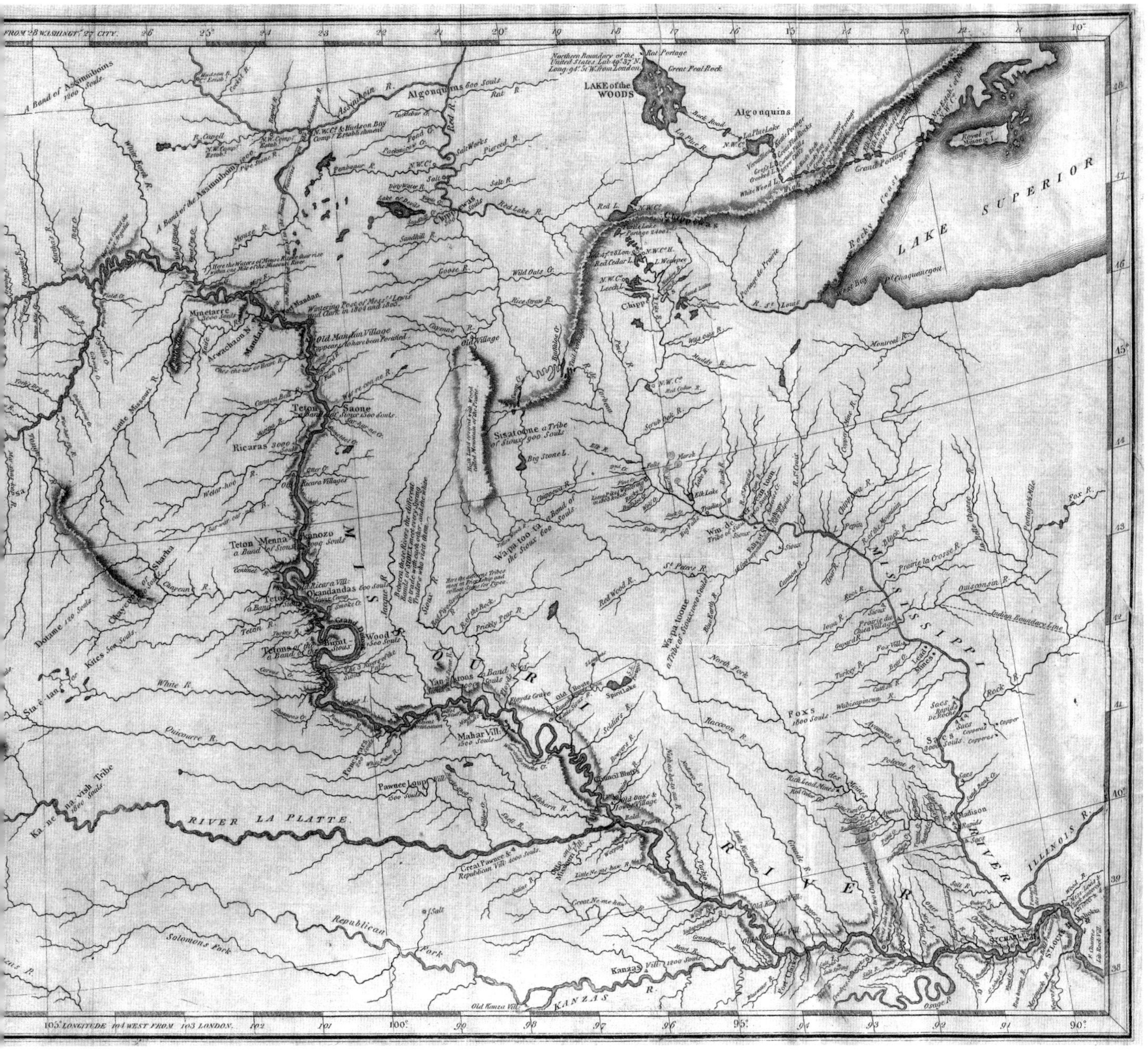

nation must expand its borders outwardly, he and other leaders believed, if successive generations were to remain as independent as the Revolutionary founders. More and more western land was the only antidote against the corruption fostered by the overcrowded cities and plantations of the East. One primary function of early American science, then, was to aid this national growth by cataloguing the strange, often dangerous natural world of the West so that it might quickly be subdued and transformed. In the same way, U.S. ethnologists learned about Indians as a step toward the nation taking their land. Nineteenth-century explorers traveled, collected, and wrote with an eye toward ordinary American citizens eventually following them and staying put as settlers. Because Philadelphia was the original scientific capital of the United States and the intellectual base of its earliest expeditions, the city played an important role in the nation's colonization of the West.

Jefferson chose as leader of the expedition his private secretary Meriwether Lewis, who was experienced in both the study of natural history and the grit of rustic survival. For his partner, Lewis selected William Clark, a friend from Kentucky who had served in several military campaigns against American Indians. The president's specific goals for their journey included identifying a route to the Pacific Ocean, making diplomatic contact with western Natives, and gaining geographic knowledge of the vast and mysterious expanse.

Before they went west, Lewis and Clark turned to scientists in Philadelphia to help shape their mission. During the Revolutionary era and early republic, Philadelphia was the place where the nation's best naturalists named new specimens and published their books. Then, during and after the journey, Philadelphia scientists received, organized, and disseminated the explorers' western findings. Lewis, who came to Philadelphia in May 1803, purchased most of the supplies locally: camping gear, clothing, books, trading goods, food, containers, guns and ammunition, scientific instruments. He learned from the city's naturalists how to locate new specimens and preserve them. At the University of Pennsylvania, Benjamin Smith Barton taught him about botanical collecting and the French presence in Louisiana. Lewis then learned about medicines and diseases from Benjamin Rush and animals and fossils from Caspar Wistar. Lewis visited the surveyor Andrew Ellicott in Lancaster for lessons in geography, and he almost certainly toured the museum of Charles Willson Peale, who had recently put the world's first excavated mastodon skeleton on display. Famously, Jefferson suggested to the explorers that they might encounter a living one in the field, the idea of extinction being then uncertain.

After completing the expedition in 1806—over seven thousand miles back and forth between the United States' western terminus St. Louis and the Pacific Ocean—Lewis returned to Philadelphia and bequeathed many of his western treasures to Peale. Peale then displayed the objects, mostly diplomatic gifts from western Indians, in a special exhibit and painted portraits of both Lewis and Clark that remain on display at Independence National Historical Park. (Many of these objects were lost over the years, while others ended up in Harvard University's Peabody Museum.) Philadelphians also published the journals of Lewis and Clark, including Lewis's posthumous official journal in 1814. Even a forged account of the expedition from 1809, created by a shady printer named Hubbard Lester, came out of Philadelphia. Whether Lewis and Clark are remembered as national heroes or imperial soldiers, their project connected the extraordinary scientific world of Philadelphia with the extraordinary American West.

## Anatomy and Anatomy Education

**Christopher Willoughby**

During the eighteenth and nineteenth centuries, dissection and study of human corpses became the primary method for medical students to gain intimate visual and tactile knowledge of the body and prepare to perform surgery on the living. As the chief medical city in the United States during this period, Philadelphia also became the leading center of anatomical education. Simultaneously, Philadelphia anatomists spearheaded the production of a new racial science based in the measurement of human skulls that reflected the disproportionate use of Black people's corpses in dissecting rooms.

Private and university-based anatomical courses in Philadelphia dated back to the 1750s. However, anatomical education expanded in 1762, when William Shippen Jr., who had studied medicine in Edinburgh, began a public course of lectures on anatomy, which included human dissections. Within four years, Shippen joined another Philadelphia physician, John Morgan, to found the Medical School of the College of Philadelphia (later the University of Pennsylvania).

Despite the first medical school emerging from Shippen's anatomical lectures, the quality of anatomical education for the rest of the eighteenth century and early nineteenth century was stymied by limited access to fresh corpses, partially the result of popular opposition to dissection. Public angst about dissection reached a boiling point in 1765 when a mob of sailors interrupted Shippen's course and marched on his home. Philadelphians had suspected since his earliest lectures that Shippen had stolen bodies for dissection from a church graveyard, but he explained that he only dissected executed convicts and occasionally a body from the potter's field, a public graveyard for the poor. Black Philadelphians even had to resort to nightly patrols of such burial sites and rescued their dead from Shippen. Resistance also came from other physicians. Benjamin Rush, a professor of chemistry at the Medical School of the College of Philadelphia from 1769 until his death in 1813, described anatomical study as just "a mass of dead matter. It is physiology which infuses life into it." The influential Rush rooted his theory that all diseases were caused by states of imbalance in the body in eighteenth-century approaches to medicine.

Following trends in Paris that emphasized pathological anatomy through postmortem dissections to understand disease, the generation of educators after Rush made anatomy the centerpiece of their educational system, which contributed to Philadelphia's status as the focal point of American medical and scientific thought in the nineteenth century. During this era, with the University of Pennsylvania, Jefferson Medical College, the short-lived Pennsylvania Medical College, and three private supplemental anatomy schools, Philadelphia developed the most robust culture of anatomical education in the United States and provided a home to several authors of major textbooks in the field. At the University of Pennsylvania Joseph Leidy even had his personal copy of his textbook bound in human skin.

During this period, medical schools began to assemble significant anatomy collections in museums featuring objects like diseased organs, human skulls, and animal skeletons, which were often used to buttress the theories of racial scientists. The University of Pennsylvania's anatomical museum (first assembled by Caspar Wistar from 1808 to 1818 and later part of the Wistar Institute) and the College of Physicians and Surgeons' Mutter Museum (founded in 1858) represented two of the largest American anatomy museums in the nineteenth century. Many professors also incorporated artifacts from these collections into their classes. Utilizing museum collections and their professors' lectures, students in Philadelphia learned about comparative anatomy between animals and humans, along with the supposed differential anatomy of the human races. At the University of Pennsylvania, Leidy even told his students that Black and white people were different species. As a result, in addition to its value as a medical subject, the study of anatomy carried social and political implications.

Because Philadelphia housed so many venues for dissection in the nineteenth century, anatomy professors competed for fresh corpses. Anatomists fashioned a secret arrangement with the city government, which gave them open access to potter's fields. This arrangement yielded approximately 450 corpses per year, but Philadelphia physicians sometimes still had to ship in bodies from New York City. In 1828, Philadelphia anatomists signed a contract to ensure that each professor received a fair portion of available anatomical material, which helped alleviate tension between anatomy teachers.

The city's most public body-snatching scandal took place in 1882, after gross anatomy had lost its central position in medical pedagogy. In 1882, Jefferson University professor of anatomy William Smith Forbes was publicly tried on charges of stealing six cadavers for his anatomy course from the historically African American Lebanon Cemetery. While Forbes was eventually acquitted, the case revealed a previously little-known illicit market in corpses that went back to the beginning of the century. In spite of scandals like the Forbes case, students continued to view dissection as a rite of passage. Into the twentieth century, they persisted in a ritual of posing for photographs with cadavers, a practice that underscored the continued influence of anatomy and dead bodies on medical students and their relationship to patients and death.

The study of anatomy and Philadelphia's role in it rose to the peak of their importance within American medicine in the antebellum era. Even after the rise of German laboratory medicine and the ascendance of germ theory in the 1870s and 1880s made gross anatomy just one subject among many in the medical curriculum, Philadelphia physicians continued to make breakthroughs in histology (microscopic anatomy).

While gross anatomy fell into the background of American medical education, professors at Philadelphia universities continued to make names for themselves in anatomy-related branches of inquiry, including neuroanatomy and neurosurgery. At the turn of the twentieth century, the University of Pennsylvania emerged as one of the country's leading centers for neuroscience. Charles Harrison Frazier led a cohort of neurosurgeons in Philadelphia who contributed to the creation of the departments of neurosurgery at the University of Pennsylvania and Temple University. Frazier and William Gibson Spiller pioneered a new surgical method for treating trigeminal neuralgia and made additional breakthroughs in treating pain in the nervous system. Through the neurosciences, Philadelphia continued to maintain a prominent position in the American medical profession, and anatomy continued to occupy a central role in the production of medical knowledge.

## Academy of Natural Sciences

**Matthew A. White**

A group of six amateur scientists with an interest in natural history gathered at a private residence at High and Second Streets in Philadelphia on January 25, 1812, and founded the Academy of Natural Sciences of Philadelphia for, according to its charter, "the encouragement and cultivation of the Sciences" and "the advancement of useful learning." These enthusiastic and mostly young men, soon joined by entomologist and conchologist Thomas Say, created what has become the oldest institution of natural history in America. The academy continued to produce important original research in biological and molecular systematics, ecology, and biodiversity as it forged important partnerships in the region and the world and eventually affiliated with Drexel University.

In the early nineteenth century, Philadelphia was already home to the American Philosophical Society, the Philadelphia Museum established by Charles Willson Peale, and a thriving medical community. But the academy founders, members of the city's growing professional class, felt excluded and poorly represented by the city's established elite institutions. For its first home, the young academy rented rooms above a milliner at 94 N. Second Street that included meeting space, a reading room, and a room to keep their growing specimen collection.

While the academy's founders considered the creation and diffusion of knowledge about the natural world important for its own sake, they also enthusiastically embraced the idea that the study of natural science built character in urban young men and was a patriotic duty that would place the sciences in the young United States on an equal level with those in the Old World. Even though membership was restricted to people nominated by two current members, the academy continued to grow in the early republic. With backing from the Scottish-born geologist and academic member William Maclure (1763–1840), it established the *Journal of the Academy of Natural Sciences*, which, along with the later *Proceedings*, became important natural science journals.

In 1812, a mere month after its founding, the academy sponsored its first "expedition" to visit the zinc mines in nearby Perkiomen, Pennsylvania. As it grew in size and prestige it organized, sponsored, and staffed more expeditions, often in collaboration with the federal government and other institutions. Army topographer Major Stephen Harriman Long led one such expedition in 1819 to the upper Mississippi Valley, which included academy members Thomas Say and Titian Peale, to study and collect the area's flora and fauna.

By the mid-nineteenth century, the academy's amateur naturalists gave way to a more professional membership, reflecting a larger trend in American science. The academy continued to collect specimens from around the world through trade, purchase, donation, and sponsorship of expeditions of exploration. In 1834, it cosponsored an expedition to the mouth of the Columbia River with the American Philosophical Society. In 1838 academy members Charles Pickering and Titian Peale, along with several corresponding members, joined the four-year Wilkes Expedition, which explored and surveyed the Pacific Ocean and adjacent land.

The academy's collection grew quickly throughout the nineteenth century, forcing it to move five times to progressively larger buildings. In 1840 the institution moved to a new, fireproof building at Broad and Sansom Streets where it became one of the most modern, best-equipped natural history museums in the United States. It boasted, among other holdings, the world's largest ornithological collection. The academy made its final move in 1876, constructing a new building at the corner of Race and Nineteenth Streets, a remote location that later became the heart of Philadelphia's cultural district. The academy's location was further enhanced by the creation of the Benjamin Franklin Parkway as the showpiece of the City Beautiful movement in 1917.

**FIGURE 56.** Samuel G. Morton, 1854. A prominent figure in Philadelphia's learned societies, Morton contended that the human race was divided into distinct species. As a leading exponent of craniology, he amassed around a thousand skulls in an effort to prove Caucasian superiority. LIBRARY OF CONGRESS.

Paleontological work preoccupied the academy during the late nineteenth century, thanks to men such as Joseph Leidy and Edward Drinker Cope. Leidy trained as a medical doctor, taught anatomy at the University of Pennsylvania and later Swarthmore College, and was a curator at the Academy of Natural Sciences from 1846 until his death. He described some of the first dinosaur fossils in America and led the field of vertebrate paleontology for most of the nineteenth century. Leidy did some collecting locally but relied largely on field naturalists such as Cope and Ferdinand Hayden to send fossils from the American West.

Following early successes by men such as Leidy and Hayden, the field of paleontology exploded and the academy was at its center, not always for the better. The most brilliant and controversial of these later scientists was Edward Drinker Cope. A student of Leidy's, Cope was talented and ambitious, and after the Civil War he embarked on several expeditions to the American West that sent huge numbers of paleontological specimens back to the academy. Unfortunately, Cope maneuvered himself into a petty, and sometimes violent, feud over access to fossil excavation sites, interpretations of specimens, and prestige with fellow paleontologist O. C. Marsh of Yale University, a feud dubbed by many historians as the "Bone Wars." This feud had important consequences for the academy and Joseph Leidy. Outlandish stories of the feud published in the popular press sullied the academy's reputation, and Leidy, disgusted by Cope's behavior, eventually abandoned paleontology in the West and turned his attention to other projects and helping local organizations, including serving as the president of the faculty and head of the museum at the Wagner Free Institute of Science of Philadelphia.

Over the middle decades of the nineteenth century, the academy also nurtured racial science. A leading member of the organization, the physician and naturalist Samuel G. Morton, seized almost a thousand skulls from the likes of Egyptian tombs and Native American burial grounds. His globe-spanning collection provided a body of evidence for claims about hierarchies of race. After Morton's death, the academy's curator James Aitken Meigs continued his work in the fields of craniology and phrenology. Their work influenced the southern proslavery propagandist Josiah Nott. Nott dedicated his *Types of Mankind* (1854) to Morton's memory.

By the turn of the century, study of natural science began to shift away from museums to university biology labs. However, the academy continued to sponsor expeditions to the Arctic, Asia, Africa, and Central America and conduct original research in several fields. Years before ecology, pollution, and conservation became topics of public debate, in 1947 the academy embarked on a research agenda to study aquatic ecosystems through its Department of Limnology, and in 1948 it established an Environmental Research Division. Throughout the twentieth century, the academy conducted important research in ecology and biodiversity on its own and in partnership with other area institutions.

In 2011 the academy became the Academy of Natural Sciences of Drexel University when it formed an official affiliation with Drexel University. The affiliation facilitated, among other projects, creation of a joint Department of Biodiversity, Earth, and Environmental Science (BEES) dedicated to research and education in the fields of environmental science, ecology and conservation, biodiversity and evolution, geoscience, and paleontology. The mission and motto of this new department, "Field Experience, Early and Often," echoed the interests and ambitions of the founders of the Academy of Natural Sciences. By remaining true to the vision of its founders, America's oldest institution of natural history remained relevant into the twenty-first century.

**FIGURE 57.** Henry Charles Carey, ca. 1870. The son of the Irish-born Philadelphia political economist Mathew Carey, Henry Charles Carey became a leading advocate of a high protective tariff during the middle decades of the nineteenth century. His work, which proved popular with Delaware Valley industrialists, also influenced the early Republican Party, which popularized Carey's claim that high taxes on foreign imports benefited U.S. workers. Carey's hostility to free trade drew notice overseas. Karl Marx, who fundamentally disagreed with Carey, nevertheless called him the only American economist of note, and Carey's vision of harmony and unity coming from a protected national market shaped economic thought elsewhere. His works appeared in French, German, Italian, Swedish, Russian, Magyar, Japanese, and Portuguese, while closer to home, he shaped the thinking of the Quaker manufacturer Joseph Wharton. When Wharton endowed a business school at the University of Pennsylvania in 1881, it initially taught Carey's "Philadelphia School" economics. Although Careyite ideas faded from prominence after the Great Depression, they saw a revival of sorts with the twenty-first-century political career of Donald Trump, a Wharton graduate. LIBRARY COMPANY OF PHILADELPHIA.

## Missionaries

**Gretchen E. Boger**

The Philadelphia region historically produced fewer missionaries than other areas of North America. Ironically, William Penn's decision to make Pennsylvania a "Holy Experiment" in religious tolerance may explain why the city and its surroundings did not experience the flowering of missions seen to its north and south, as fewer settlers were inclined toward persuading others to adopt their religious perspective. Even so, the area's rich religious heritage provided impetus for some missionary efforts.

The earliest Christian missionaries in the Americas worked among Native Americans, though efforts in British North America were muted compared to those of French Jesuits in the Great Lakes region and Spanish priests establishing missions throughout New Spain. Among the Swedes who settled Fort Christina in 1638 at present-day Wilmington, Delaware, Lutheran minister John Campanius learned the language of the area's Delaware Indians and sought converts using a translated catechism. A century later David Brainerd, a young Presbyterian from Connecticut who was influenced by the New Light theology of the Great Awakening, procured a commission as Native American missionary and in the course of three years' work with Delawares near present-day Crosswicks in central New Jersey, baptized and organized a community of over 130 converts before succumbing to tuberculosis in 1747. Although many persecuted religious groups coming to colonial Pennsylvania sought to insulate their members from the corrupt or bruising influences of wider society, the Moravians were committed to missions work, preaching to Native Americans and establishing towns on the Pennsylvania frontier that welcomed converts. The most influential Moravian missionary of the eighteenth century was David Zeisberger, a native of Saxony who migrated first to Georgia before helping found Bethlehem, Pennsylvania, in 1741. From there, he ventured out to Native peoples on the Pennsylvania and Ohio frontiers. Zeisberger learned Iroquoian and Algonquian languages and produced dictionaries and religious tracts in each and established several communities of converts. Efforts like Zeisberger's laid early groundwork for continued Christian missions to Native peoples throughout North America as European-American settlement expanded west in subsequent centuries.

In the same era Henry Muhlenberg came from Germany to minister to Lutherans in North America. Landing in Philadelphia in 1742, he traveled from his base in New Providence (later Trappe), Pennsylvania, up and down the Atlantic seaboard, preaching to European settlers in multiple languages and successfully consolidating the Lutheran denomination in North America. Anglican missionaries sent to Philadelphia by the British Society for the Propagation of the Gospel in Foreign Parts were less successful. Charged by the Church of England with countering dissidents' influence in the British colonies, they struggled to find willing converts in a colony dedicated to religious tolerance, and many were forced to close their missions during the American Revolution to avoid persecution.

After independence, most Philadelphia missions focused on domestic matters, bringing religious literature to the public and serving the spiritual and material needs of the city's so-called "heathen" poor. Among these domestic missions was the rapidly expanding African Methodist Episcopal Church, founded and headquartered in Philadelphia in 1816, which sent clergy to establish AME churches across the northern and western United States, then to Canada and the Caribbean. The church grew most rapidly during and after the Civil War, when missionaries moved into southern states to minister to newly freed people. Dedicated AME evangelists established connections that helped spur southern Black migration to Philadelphia in the early twentieth century. Meanwhile, among the first Philadelphians to serve as a missionary overseas was African American Presbyterian Betsey Stockton. Born into slavery in Princeton, New Jersey, Stockton came as a child to work in the Philadelphia home of Presbyterian minister and future Princeton University president Ashbel Green. Religiously educated in the Green household, Stockton secured her freedom and applied to serve as a missionary in the Sandwich Islands. In 1822 she became the first single woman to serve as an American missionary overseas.

American missions work grew steadily through the nineteenth century, then soared after the 1890s in conjunction with the expansion of empire, increased ease of transoceanic travel, and the growth of a class of college-educated youth seeking meaningful life work. At home, several million members of Protestant missions societies sponsored field workers, published missions journals, and ran missions study programs for church members. Middle-class women played a significant role in the American missions movement at home and abroad, as missionary service gave single women a socially approved means to travel, while married women accompanied missionary husbands and found roles ministering to women and children, work often considered culturally inappropriate for male evangelists. Among such women was Fannie Jackson Coppin, who had been a newspaper columnist and principal of the Philadelphia Institute for Colored Youth before marrying African Methodist Episcopal minister Levi Jenkins Coppin in 1881. In 1902 the Coppinses moved for a decade to South Africa, there founding a missions school they named the Bethel Institute.

Burgeoning Chinese and Indian nationalist movements after World War I prompted Asian resistance to claims that Christianity was the one true faith, critiques that influenced some missionaries to reassess their goals and relationship to local cultures. Those at home took note. In the early 1930s Baptist layman and financier John D. Rockefeller Jr. assembled a committee of well-heeled Protestants to travel to Asia as the Laymen's Foreign Missions Inquiry. Their goal was to study the state of the mission enterprise and issue a report recommending its future direction. Haverford College philosophy professor and Quaker mystic Rufus Jones was the best known of those on the commission. In 1926 Jones toured missions fields in Asia and in 1928 authored a paper for a missionary conference at Jerusalem urging Christians to embrace the best in other religious traditions. That view was echoed in the Commission of Appraisal of the Laymen's Foreign Missions Inquiry 1932 report, *Re-Thinking Missions*, which advanced a pluralist vision of religious accommodation and recommended that missionaries deemphasize Jesus and overt Christian symbolism in their appeals. Together with Harvard University philosopher William Ernest Hocking, Jones authored the report's key chapters. *Re-Thinking Missions* roiled American Protestantism, accelerating growing theological divisions. Its institutional impact was most prominent on the northern Presbyterian Board of Foreign Missions.

Writer Pearl Buck, the American daughter and wife of Presbyterian missionaries in China, publicly praised *Re-Thinking Missions* as "the only book I have ever read which seems to me literally true in its every observation and right in its every conclusion." A fierce intellectual who was ambivalent about the role of Christian missionaries in her beloved China, Buck was growing in fame as a novelist (she won the Pulitzer Prize in 1932 for *The Good Earth*), and her endorsement of the report garnered international attention. It outraged fundamentalist Presbyterian professor J. Gresham Machen, who in 1929 had left Princeton Theological Seminary to found the conservative Westminster Theological Seminary in Montgomery County, Pennsylvania. Machen called on the Presbyterian Board of Foreign Missions to censure Buck and withdraw financial support for her and her husband. Instead, Buck resigned as a missionary, but Machen was sufficiently troubled by the board's failure to censure her that he founded the Independent Board for Presbyterian Foreign Missions at Plymouth Meeting in 1933. Suspended by his presbytery in 1935 for his separatist actions, Machen and fellow fundamentalists next established what would become the Orthodox Presbyterian Church, headquartered in Willow Grove, to counter the liberalizing tendencies of the Presbyterian Church USA.

**FIGURE 58.** Statue of Pearl S. Buck, Nanjing, China, 2018. Born to Presbyterian missionary parents, Buck spent most of her first four decades in China, before moving to Bucks County in the mid-1930s. She became the first female American winner of the Nobel Prize for literature in 1938, but World War II and the Communist seizure of power in 1949 prevented her from ever returning to the land of her childhood. From her Bucks County homestead, Buck supported a range of causes, including Black rights and disability rights, while establishing an adoption agency for interracial children. In 2012, Nanjing University opened her former residence to visitors. WIKIMEDIA COMMONS.

Philadelphia remained home to several missions initiatives, the largest of which was the American Baptist's International Ministries housed at American Baptist national headquarters at Valley Forge from 1962. The relatively small Independent Board for Presbyterian

Foreign Missions remained in Plymouth Meeting, while the newer Center for Student Missions in Germantown placed students on short-term urban service missions around the United States. The Church of Jesus Christ of Latter-Day Saints (Mormons), arguably the most prominent missional church in the United States, with active missions around the globe, in summer 2016 completed construction of a temple and education center near Logan Circle in Center City. The first Mormon temple in Pennsylvania, it was planned as the center for LDS worship and activity in the region.

Since the early twentieth century, missions activity in many Christian churches has emphasized medical, educational, and economic development assistance to others in Christ's name in place of, or in addition to, explicit evangelism with the goal of conversion. In keeping with that trend, churches throughout the Philadelphia region have sponsored local, national, and international missions initiatives, working with community institutions that aid the poor in Philadelphia, Chester, Camden, and elsewhere in the region and sending members to provide disaster relief, build infrastructure, teach Vacation Bible School, and form relationships with Christians worldwide.

## Scientific Management

**Daniel Sidorick**

The "Scientific Management" movement was born in early twentieth-century Philadelphia factories but spread rapidly, transforming not only management techniques but also popular conceptions of industrialized society itself. According to its founders, the system simply sought the "one best way" to perform any task. But its time-study engineers, along with the assembly line, came to symbolize the bleak and mechanical organization of workers' lives by industrial engineers. Its advocates, on the other hand, hailed scientific management as the basis for the transformative increases in productivity that, they argued, improved the lives of working people.

Although many early management consultants contributed to the development of the system, Philadelphia's Frederick Winslow Taylor is acknowledged as the "Father of Scientific Management"; in fact, the system is also known as "Taylorism." His concepts and practices were embraced by industrialists and municipal reformers, attracted devoted followers and harsh critics, and inspired, if indirectly, numerous movements seeking to reorganize society by making it more efficient. The first incubators of Taylor's experiments were Philadelphia factories, and by the mid-twentieth century his associates and imitators had installed "scientific" systems of management in all kinds of establishments throughout the region and, from there, the world. By the twenty-first century, timed-to-the-second fast-food and help-desk workers were so commonplace that most Americans did not realize how Taylorized their workplaces had become.

According to its proponents, scientific management sought the "one best way" to perform any task. Applied to manufacturing, and later to other fields, it meant that "waste" of any kind, especially waste of time, must be eliminated, resulting in vastly improved productivity. Whereas earlier manufacturing relied on the expert knowledge and decision-making of craftsmen, the new approach attempted to transfer all knowledge of the manufacturing process to management—and in particular to new planning departments—which would then instruct workmen on the precise methods and motions to be used to perform each job.

The system's implementation, in companies as varied as the Link-Belt Engineering Company at Hunting Park Avenue and Twenty-First Street in Nicetown, Cramp Shipbuilding Company in Port Richmond, and Bethlehem Steel in South Bethlehem, Pennsylvania, was often beset with problems and sometimes ultimately rejected. Yet the "efficiency craze" that Taylor launched spawned numerous management consulting firms as well as do-it-yourself efforts at many companies. His arguments also convinced corporate management that it must control all aspects of how work is done if it was to survive in the cutthroat competitive world of twentieth-century capitalism. Not unexpectedly, unions like the International Association of Machinists fought these new management schemes in order to defend their members' prerogatives and union work rules, and in other cases to oppose "speedup" or at least gain a larger share of the increased proceeds from greater productivity.

Despite the global spread of scientific management, its origins and first several decades were a thoroughly Philadelphia story. Frederick Winslow Taylor was born in 1856 in Germantown to an old Quaker family. He spent his youth attending Germantown Academy, touring Europe, and engaging in cricket with friends from similarly wealthy families, though he never matriculated at Harvard as expected. He then used family connections to begin an apprenticeship as a patternmaker and machinist at the Enterprise Hydraulic Works, a pump manufacturer at Twenty-Second and Race Streets. With Philadelphia becoming the "Workshop of the World" it was not unusual for some young men from wealthy families to use apprenticeships to advance in industry.

After he completed his apprenticeship at Enterprise, Taylor began working at Midvale Steel in Nicetown. He started at the bottom, working as a laborer for a few weeks to learn how jobs were done and to attempt to understand the motivations of workers. Taylor moved up quickly, eventually becoming chief engineer of the works, and it was in the course of his employment there that he developed the prototypes for the innovations for which he would become famous.

Although Taylor is most remembered for his management and organizational ideas, he also made contributions to mechanical processes and machinery, designing a giant steam hammer at Midvale, developing "high-speed steel" at Bethlehem Steel, and earning forty-two patents. In fact, he first used a stopwatch to gauge the performance of machine tools, but he soon applied the same techniques to measure the motions of human workers. As Taylor formulated and refined his approach to scientific management at a succession of companies in the Philadelphia region from the late 1870s to the early 1900s, he increasingly regarded workers as elements of the production process. In his view, their actions could be precisely molded, with the right incentive schemes, by a new type of management that left no leeway for personal discretion.

In Taylor's most well-known, if partially fabricated, description of his techniques, he claimed to have turned an average laborer at Bethlehem Steel he called "Schmidt" (actually named Henry Noll) into a superhuman loader of pig iron (although he "firmly believe[d] that it would be possible to train an intelligent gorilla so as to become a more efficient pig-iron handler than any man can be"). Revealing his own class attitudes toward laborers, Taylor related, in his lectures and writings, what he thought of Schmidt, a "man so stupid that he was unfitted to do most kinds of laboring work," though he built his own house, was married, and had a grade-school education.

Although Schmidt was purportedly happy with the deal, other workers at Bethlehem and elsewhere were not. Taylor claimed that he did not oppose unions, but he believed they would be an unnecessary encumbrance in a scientifically managed company, where increased wages for greater output would make everyone richer—and happier. Consequently, he urged companies like Link-Belt to keep unions out and was disappointed when they ignored his advice. The experience of scientifically managed companies in regard to organized labor was checkered. Taylor proudly noted that workers at companies for which he consulted, such as Link-Belt and Tabor Manufacturing, did not participate in Philadelphia's massive general strike in 1910. But he did not mention the long and bitter strike that same year that targeted the bonus system at Bethlehem Steel, one of the remnants of Taylor's earlier efforts there. The resentment expressed by one employee of a Philadelphia manufacturer for the "silk-shirted bespectacled slide rule and stopwatch expert" who watched and timed his actions was not uncommon. Labor opposition to "speedup" systems grew rapidly, and Bethlehem workers even gave the system's founder a new moniker: "Speedy Taylor."

Unionists were not the only opponents of scientific management, however. Philadelphia companies like Baldwin Locomotive relied heavily on the expert skill and knowledge of their craftsmen and had no interest in Taylor's ideas. Others, like Cramp Shipbuilding and Bethlehem Steel, experimented extensively with the new approach but eventually rejected it, claiming it was expensive and highly disruptive. Yet even those companies kept some parts of the system in place: Bethlehem simply renamed Taylor's "instruction cards" to "speed cards."

Workers and socialists attacked Taylor's version of scientific management for turning workers into automatons, deskilling craftsmen, and firing those who could not or would not perform as "first-class men." Yet, if managers strictly followed Taylor's prescriptions, the workers who remained did at least see pay increases, and piece rates were not reduced (at least initially).

But after Taylor withdrew from active consulting in 1901, his disciples and followers, and soon other "consultants" who saw an opportunity to cash in on the latest management fad, were often less scrupulous about how the returns from increased productivity should be shared.

Several of the consultants who installed Taylor's system in Philadelphia became important in their own right and were responsible for the spread of "Taylorized" management systems far beyond the relative handful of companies that the founder implemented himself. His assistants worked on the two installations that became Taylor's showpieces of scientific management for visitors to Philadelphia, Link-Belt and the Tabor Manufacturing Company, and implemented some elements of the system at Philadelphia's Frankford Arsenal and the Navy Yard. The Link-Belt Engineering Company also led to the longest lasting direct Philadelphia descendant of Taylor's original group, the Day & Zimmermann management consulting firm, which was started as Dodge & Day by Link-Belt founder's son Kern Dodge and his friend Charles Day.

Another close confidante of Taylor's, Morris L. Cooke, broadened the reach of the system to Philadelphia's city government and marked the further integration of scientific management with the Progressive movement when he became the city's director of public works in 1911 and introduced several efficiency measures. Taylor's principles in city work, Cooke wrote, "opens up a field of endeavor which staggers the imagination." He followed up by firing a thousand city employees for inefficiency, brought in two hundred "expert" engineers to direct highway workers, and claimed to have saved the city some $5 million.

The "efficiency craze" spread across the country and the world after future Supreme Court justice Louis Brandeis coined the term "scientific management" during the famous Eastern Rate Case in 1910 and Taylor published his *Principles of Scientific Management* the next year. But paradoxically, the founder's original strict interpretation of the system was diluted as more "efficiency experts" rushed to take advantage of the new opportunities. In 1911 Taylor complained that Harrington Emerson, a former close adherent of the Taylor method, had told Navy Yard officers that he could install all the "important" parts of Taylor's system in a few short months. Emerson later introduced his quicker and cheaper alternative in many other plants, including Lukens Steel in Coatesville, Pennsylvania.

Other companies like DuPont decided to try converting to "scientific" management methods on their own. Unfortunately, DuPont began its experiment in its High Explosives Operating Department plant near Gibbstown, New Jersey, in 1913. Although some employees complained that foremen were "rushing the men," the project continued until a massive explosion killed four workers. The experiment was moved to another building. It, too, suffered an explosion soon after, killing several more men. Interest in putting an efficiency scheme into practice did not resume until the Great Depression induced the company to find new ways to reduce costs.

When DuPont did again embark on systematizing its operations, it did so with the consulting company of the colorful and controversial Charles Bedaux. His simple and relatively inexpensive program promised a quick return on investment without the lengthy and painstaking selection of workers, plant redesign, and job study required in Taylor's approach. In addition to DuPont, Lukens Steel also switched to the Bedaux plan, as did numerous other Delaware Valley companies. At Campbell Soup's flagship plant in Camden the system became the flashpoint for innumerable conflicts between workers and management for several decades starting in the early 1930s. Yet the efficiency program was a central element of Campbell's successful drive to keep costs down and profits high. Workers at Keasbey & Mattison, an asbestos shingle manufacturer and the largest employer in Ambler, Pennsylvania, however, were more successful in ending the Bedaux system there; the company threw the system out in 1937 due to "labor unrest."

By World War II, time-and-motion study and job standards were no longer a novelty. Young women working in the secretarial pool at the Army Ordnance Department offices on S. Broad Street and machine tenders in steel fabrication plants had become accustomed to "efficiency experts" timing and monitoring their work. Later management trends claimed to replace Taylorism with newer approaches to work and workers, but most of them were deeply indebted to the Germantown native. The central concepts of "lean production," for example, were the elimination of waste—especially waste of time—and continuous improvement, all with the goal of increasing productivity.

The central argument for the beneficial effects of Taylorism for employees rested on the premise that the proceeds from increased productivity would be shared equitably between management and labor by the mechanism of the system's bonus incentive plan. It has even been credited with raising the standard of living for Philadelphia's working class generally. The first objection to this argument concerned all those left out of it. Taylor himself said there were very few "first-class men" for any job, and those who could not make the grade, whether at Bethlehem Steel or Campbell Soup, were dismissed. Those who survived the cut worked much harder than before and lost any discretion they previously had in determining how they performed their jobs, but they did see increased wages—in companies that strictly followed Taylor's rules. The cardinal principle here was that management would not raise the amount of work needed to reach the bonus level once a job had been "scientifically" studied and rated. Very few companies kept to this precept for very long, however.

At its core, Taylorism was a class philosophy in which strict but benevolent masters would provide well for their subordinates as long as they did exactly as they were told. Far more responsible for raising Philadelphia's workers' standard of living were the efforts they expended themselves. In the defensive strikes of unionized craftsmen early in the twentieth century and the mass unionization drives by industrial workers during the Great Depression and World War II, workers fought for and often won a greater share of the increased productivity resulting from Taylorism and other efficiency schemes.

## University of Pennsylvania Museum of Archaeology and Anthropology

**Mabel Rosenheck**

The Penn Museum—officially the University of Pennsylvania Museum of Archaeology and Anthropology—originated in 1887 through the combined efforts of university scholars, administrators, and Philadelphia philanthropists. Created as part of a broader movement to expand, modernize, and professionalize the university, the museum also performed a public role of bringing ancient and faraway cultures to Philadelphia for both academic research and spectacular display. Although always an independent entity, the museum also served the mission of the affiliated university. In the twenty-first century, as museums and the disciplines of archaeology and anthropology became more critical about the ways they represented nonwhite and non-Western cultures, the Penn Museum reconsidered the form and content of its dual academic and public roles.

The idea for the museum originated in 1887, when John Punnett Peters, a professor of Hebrew at the University of Pennsylvania, persuaded university provost William Pepper to fund an expedition to the Sumerian city of Nippur in modern-day Iraq. In agreeing to do so, Pepper stipulated that anything Peters collected would be held at the university in a new museum. The museum, the expedition, and the scholarship that resulted combined anthropology—the study of man, his origins, and the evolution of human culture—with archaeology, a field rooted in the search for evidence to verify Greek mythology, the Bible, and other founding myths of Western, Christian civilization.

The museum created to house the fruits of the Sumerian expedition and other collections had its first home in the Furness Library on the university's new West Philadelphia campus from 1890 until 1899. It then moved to its permanent home in a stylishly eclectic building designed by a team led by Wilson Eyre. Although the university faculty members often led expeditions, funding came primarily from independent groups like the Babylonian Exploration Fund, the Egypt Exploration Society, and the University Archaeological Association. These organizations were usually headed by prominent, wealthy Philadelphia philanthropists who continued to be a key source of income throughout the museum's history.

The institution's original name, the Free Museum of Science and Art, reflected its interdisciplinarity and dual purposes. For researchers, the museum housed and displayed artifacts of human culture as scientific resources. At the time, anthropology and archaeology were not the interpretive, liberal arts fields that they later became, but were disciplines dedicated to systematic classification and scientific observation. However, while scholars and researchers used the collections for science, public displays also enriched the museum experience for visitors and allowed those who felt welcome to demonstrate their elite aesthetic taste. As was typical of endeavors in anthropology and archaeology, the museum sought to demonstrate both similarities and differences among diverse communities. Many cultures were collected under one roof, but their arrangement reinforced ideological hierarchies by presenting an inevitable march of human progress and creating contrasts between supposedly primitive crafts and civilized tastes. In Philadelphia, this was reflected in curatorial and architectural choices that saw ethnological artifacts collected from Indigenous people arranged on the lowest floor and archaeological collections of Greek, Roman, and Babylonian civilizations on the floors above. It tied a literal, physical march from bottom to top to an intellectual and ideological one.

In 1913, the museum officially changed its name to the University Museum, reflecting the growing role of the University of Pennsylvania in its governance, which by 1930 exclusively appointed the institution's Board of Overseers. During the first half of the twentieth century, as the museum and the fields of anthropology, ethnology, and archaeology grew, so did the museum. Ethnographic expeditions, excavations of ancient artifacts, and acquisitions through purchase grew the collections and programs of research and display. While the research had academic value, these objects also came from areas of the world that were colonized by Western empires—and thus were embedded in problematic politics recognized only later by most American curators and scholars.

In the 1920s and 1930s, one of the most important curators at the museum—although never a professor at the university—was Louis Shotridge, a Tlingit Indian from the Pacific Northwest. Conducting salvage ethnographies, Shotridge collected and documented languages and traditions at risk of being destroyed by settler colonialism and government policies that criminalized Indigenous culture and decimated Native populations. On the one hand, Shotridge assured that some part of Indigenous culture—in some cases his own culture—would survive. On the other hand, he knew the institution where he worked took sacred objects and sterilized them, that it interpreted Indigenous people as primitive savages, and that it expected nonwhite scholars like himself to assimilate themselves and their scholarship into the authoritative voice of academic institutions.

After World War II, old tensions between white, Western scholars and postcolonial or third-world nations arose, but they were sometimes addressed in new ways. Research continued to be largely generated and validated by elite European and American institutions with systems of knowledge and hierarchical classification that changed little from the nineteenth century, but museums also became more dedicated to leaving artifacts in their places of origin so they might be interpreted and appreciated by the communities from which they came as well as used in scholarship.

At the same time, the black market for antiquities, fostered by the poverty of so-called third-world nations and by the exploding value of artifacts in commercial markets, also challenged museums in the post–World War II era. In 1970, the University Museum under director Froelich Rainey influenced acquisitions policies throughout the museum field by issuing the Pennsylvania Declaration, which pledged to end the purchase of artifacts without "a pedigree—that is information about the different owners of the objects, place of origin, legality of export, and other data useful in each individual case." The statement called attention to the complex question of ownership: Was the object obtained "legally" or was there proof that it had been looted? Ultimately, in addition to restricting new acquisitions, the museum returned objects to countries including Italy, Turkey, and Peru. In 2008, the museum created the Penn Cultural Heritage Center to address related issues. An exhibition a decade later in the Africa galleries documented the colonial violence that led to the acquisition of artifacts from the Kingdom of Benin, and in the early 2020s, the museum announced its intention to return the objects to Nigeria.

The museum's considerable collection of human remains proved especially controversial. The U.S. Native American Graves Protection and Repatriation Act (NAGPRA) enacted in 1990 provided the most effective and widely enforced mechanism to address the concerns of Indigenous people in the United States with regard to cultural heritage. For the University Museum, between 1990 and 2016, this federal law led to twenty-five tribes successfully filing claims to have human remains and other religious objects returned to them from the museum's collections. Then in 2021, the museum apologized for its possession of skulls—including those of Black Philadelphians—acquired by the nineteenth-century racial scientist Samuel Morton. It promised to repatriate the remains to communities around the world. Facing fierce criticism from local community leaders, it also apologized for its ownership of human remains of West Philadelphians killed in the Philadelphia Police Department's bombing of the MOVE house in 1985.

The University Museum—which by 1996 was rebranded as the Penn Museum to make its institutional affiliation clearer—also confronted the complex issues of who should tell the stories of objects on display. Historically, Western museums presented narratives of hierarchical evolution and inevitable progress that either demonstrated continuities between ancient and modern societies or juxtaposed "primitive" and "civilized" cultures in ways that justified colonialism and racism. By the twenty-first century, however, museums like Penn's sought to generate more understanding and appreciation of diversity and inclusion even though white, Western academic standards of science and objectivity tended to remain the arbiters of knowledge and worth.

In 2014, a reimagining of the Penn Museum's North American gallery caught up with trends toward sharing authority for exhibit development with Indigenous people. *Native American Voices* challenged old, racist narratives by representing Native people as alive and thriving while also acknowledging how American and European colonialism decimated these communities and their cultures. For this exhibit, museum curators consulted with Indigenous leaders, which resulted in a richer, more multivocal, and inclusive exhibit. Nevertheless, the museum clearly retained authority.

Other exhibit strategies focused on bringing more diverse voices and more relevant themes into the museum's interpretation of its archaeological collections. Reinstalled Middle East galleries opened in 2018 with a focus on urbanization, and plans called for future renovations, restorations, and reinstallations of the Africa and Mesoamerica galleries, the Harrison Auditorium, and the Egyptian wing. A Global Guides program, initiated in 2018, incorporated the varied perspectives of contemporary Philadelphians who grew up in the areas of ancient cities excavated by the museum.

In the twenty-first century, the Penn Museum faced the challenge of how to use old collections, many of which were collected in exploitative, colonial contexts, to tell new stories that incorporated communities and perspectives that the museum historically marginalized. Although hindered by its own history and the colonial history of its disciplines, new strategies were making this museum more engaged, and visitorship, especially for special events that showcased diverse cultural traditions, reflected that. William Pepper's idea to create a museum that served both the university and the people of Philadelphia was being realized in new ways for a new era. Indeed, the institution whose mission was to explore "the human story: who we are and where we come from" was gradually and powerfully beginning to reassess who we are, who gets to speak for us, and where we get to do so.

## Commercial Museum

**Grace Schultz**

Opened to the public in 1897, the Commercial Museum was the foremost source of international trade knowledge for American manufacturers at the turn of the twentieth century. Located on the western bank of the Schuylkill River in Philadelphia, the museum served as a reference library for merchants, facilitated connections between American export traders and foreign markets, and housed exhibits featuring hundreds of thousands of raw materials and goods from around the world. The rise and fall of the Commercial Museum paralleled Philadelphia's transition over the twentieth century from a hub of industry and trade to a city with a postindustrial economy.

Central to the mission of the Commercial Museum was the notion that commerce was the unifying principle of mankind: past, present, and future. The 1890s marked a period of global transformation, during which the industrial economy of the United States continued to expand. In response to the manufacturing

**FIGURE 59.** The Bureau of Information at the Philadelphia Commercial Museum, n.d. INDEPENDENCE SEAPORT MUSEUM.

boom, American manufacturers began to seek foreign markets to sell their products. They also exhibited their wares at the world's fairs that characterized the latter half of the nineteenth century. One of those fairs, the 1893 World's Columbian Exposition in Chicago, had a role in the creation of Philadelphia's Commercial Museum. Among the many American traders and manufacturers enticed and inspired by the Chicago fair was a former botanist and University of Pennsylvania professor, William P. Wilson. After visiting the Columbian Exposition, Wilson officially founded the Commercial Museum the same year, housing the collections in a variety of temporary locations until the building was officially completed in 1897. Borrowing the neoclassical style of the Columbian Exposition, the Commercial Museum also acquired many items from the Chicago fair, and eventually became the official repository for artifacts from many of the world's fairs of the era.

The Commercial Museum aimed to educate everyone about the merits of international trade. Schoolchildren from across the region came to learn about the pivotal role of commerce throughout history and to explore strange artifacts from faraway lands. Merchants came from around the globe to educate themselves about foreign markets and production methods by examining raw and manufactured goods held in the collections. The Commercial Museum also administered a Bureau of Information, which compiled and published international trade and market reports to aid American entrepreneurs as they expanded their enterprises at home and abroad. Inspired by the idea of a commercial museum, American and foreign business leaders in California, France, Berlin, China, and more developed similar museums and hosted world's fair–style expositions in order to develop transnational trade relations. The museum reigned as the foremost authority on information regarding manufacturing and international commerce in the United States for a quarter century.

The Commercial Museum's prominence as a beacon of commercial knowledge and exhibits began to wane by the 1920s. A variety of social, political, and economic factors rendered it increasingly irrelevant, the most significant of which was the rise of the International Trade Commission. Developed by the United States Department of Commerce in 1916, the International Trade Commission was closely modeled after the Commercial Museum's Bureau of Information. Until then the museum acted as the unchallenged provider of international trade intelligence, market reports, and commercial knowledge. The Trade Commission, among other newly formed transnational trade institutions, began to assume this role by publishing international trade and market reports.

By the 1950s the museum had become obsolete. After decades of decreased public interest and visitation, in 1952 the City of Philadelphia restored and attempted to revitalize the Commercial Museum and neighboring Convention Hall. The museum was rebranded as a part of the Philadelphia Civic Center, but its staff was drastically reduced. Thereafter known as the Civic Center Museum, it continued to provide educational programming and display exhibits until 1994, when it closed permanently.

In 2001 the City of Philadelphia, through the Orphans' Court, dispersed the majority of the Commercial Museum's holdings to universities, museums, and archives around the city. Among these, Temple University's Anthropology Lab, the University of Pennsylvania Museum of Archaeology and Anthropology, the Independence Seaport Museum, and the Philadelphia History Museum gained significant collections. The Civic Center and museum building complex were razed in 2005 and became the site for the University of Pennsylvania's Ruth and Raymond Perelman Center for Advanced Medicine. The Philadelphia Convention Center, located at Eleventh and Arch Streets, became Philadelphia's center for commerce and trade, acting as a venue for international trade shows and other events.

## American Friends Service Committee

**Guy Aiken**

The American Friends Service Committee (AFSC), corecipient of the Nobel Peace Prize and coiner of the phrase "speak truth to power," was founded in Philadelphia by members of the Religious Society of Friends (Quakers) in spring 1917, shortly after the United States declared war on Germany on April 6. Over the following century, AFSC embodied the pacifist convictions and social-reform impulses of Philadelphia's Quaker elite.

At the outset of U.S. involvement in the First World War, the major branches of U.S. Quakerism created AFSC to coordinate alternative service for young Quaker men who conscientiously refused to serve in the military after being drafted under the Selective Service Act. The alternative consisted mostly of over six hundred Quaker and other pacifist volunteers reconstructing modular housing for displaced persons along the Western Front in France under the auspices of the American Red Cross. It was a version of what William James had called the "moral equivalent of war," and AFSC saw it as a chance for Quakers and other pacifists to make a positive contribution to peace instead of taking a merely negative stance against war. After the war, between 1920 and 1924, AFSC organized and directed the feeding of over five million children in Germany.

During the organization's early years, Philadelphia's solidly middle- and upper-middle-class Quaker elite largely constituted the executive board and administrative leadership and so largely determined its mission and programs. A large contingent of early AFSC workers attended Germantown Friends Meeting. This concentration positioned AFSC on one side of theological differences between the more liberal Quakers of Philadelphia, New England, and the Middle Atlantic and the more conservative Friends of the South, Midwest, and West. As early as the mid-1920s more conservative Friends were disowning AFSC as in any way representative of American Quakerism as a whole. Generally subscribing to the middle-class Social Gospel, a liberal movement for political and economic reform whose influence on Protestantism at large had just passed its peak, AFSC members often worked with the Federal Council of Churches (FCC) on domestic projects in the interwar years, most notably among coal-mining families in southern Appalachia.

During World War II, AFSC (somewhat controversially) worked with representatives of the other historic peace churches, the Mennonites and Brethren, to administer the federally established Civilian Public Service (CPS) system of work camps for conscientious objectors. AFSC helped resettle European refugees in the United States, and by establishing a regional office (one of the first of several) in San Francisco, also protested Japanese American internment and helped relocate over four thousand Japanese American college students from the internment camps. In 1947, after another round of postwar feeding and service in Germany and on the strength also of its administration of prewar relief programs in Russia and Spain during those countries' respective civil wars, AFSC (together with its British counterpart, the Friends Service Council) was awarded the Nobel Peace Prize on behalf of Quakers worldwide.

After World War II, AFSC resolved a long-standing internal debate over what it should prioritize in its hiring: Quakerism or practical expertise. It became increasingly professionalized and soon employed a majority non-Quaker staff, moving the debate over AFSC's Quaker identity outside the organization to liberal Quaker circles, where it raged into the twenty-first century. Also, AFSC began to focus less and less on material aid and more and more on ending military conflict and poverty in the Global South and on improving race relations and civil rights at home. AFSC started delivering aid to refugees in Gaza in 1948 at the request of the United Nations and became one of the first organizations in the United States to call for Palestinian rights. Over the 1950s and 1960s its humanitarian

**FIGURE 60.** Members of the American Friends Service Committee in Europe at the end of World War II, 1945. SPECIAL COLLECTIONS RESEARCH CENTER, TEMPLE UNIVERSITY LIBRARIES.

work extended to the likes of China, India, Algeria, and Vietnam, where it aided civilians on both sides of the conflict. It also provided draft counseling for thousands of young men in the United States.

AFSC became perhaps most famous for coining the phrase "speak truth to power," the title of a pamphlet it issued in 1955 advocating nonviolent resolution of international conflicts. Although the lead authors of *Speak Truth to Power* attributed the phrase to an eighteenth-century Friend, it originated with Bayard Rustin, one of the pamphlet's coauthors. Rustin was an African American Quaker civil rights leader from West Chester, Pennsylvania, and the chief organizer of the August 1963 March on Washington for Jobs and Freedom. AFSC itself sponsored Martin Luther King Jr. and Coretta Scott King on a visit to India in 1959 to help strengthen the nonviolent African American civil rights movement's ties to its Gandhian roots. AFSC also first published Martin Luther King Jr.'s "Letter from Birmingham Jail" as a stand-alone pamphlet.

In the 1970s and 1980s, AFSC protested apartheid in South Africa as well as the proliferation of nuclear weapons. In the 1990s, AFSC established a major health clinic in Haiti and, in the midst of a famine in North Korea, advised farmers in that country on how to increase food production sustainably. In 2004, AFSC continued its practice of protesting U.S. wars by curating a traveling exhibit, *Eyes Wide Open*, which displayed a pair of boots for every American soldier killed in Iraq along with shoes representing civilian deaths. In the 2010s, AFSC focused on criminal-justice and immigration reform, opposing solitary confinement (in particular) and providing legal services for immigrants.

While AFSC became a majority non-Quaker organization with offices around the United States and on four continents, Philadelphia remained the organization's headquarters. In the twenty-first century, the Quaker values of peace, integrity, and equality continued to animate AFSC programs.

## International Peace Mission Movement and Father Divine

**Leonard Norman Primiano**

The International Peace Mission Movement, an American communitarian religion founded in the early decades of the twentieth century, established a significant presence in Philadelphia under the leadership of its African American minister, the Reverend Major Jealous Divine, better known as Father Divine. As an American sectarian religious innovator, Father Divine reached the height of his national renown during and following the Great Depression. Believed by his followers to be an incarnation of the creator God of the Christian Trinity, Father Divine has been both appreciated as an early leader in the movement for African American civil rights and social justice and criticized as a self-promoter and instigator of a "cultic" religion.

Father Divine was the guiding theological, liturgical, scriptural, and administrative force behind the indigenous American religion he founded. While his adherents never associated him with a legal birth name, he has been identified by researchers as George Baker, a native of Rockville, Maryland. Influenced as a youth by the multitude of religions around him, from Methodist and Catholic to storefront African American churches and the New Thought movement, he traveled the country as a young itinerant preacher. Gradually, he formulated his own unique system of belief: a celibate, perfectionist, communitarian, racially integrated, and economically self-sufficient American religion known as the International Peace Mission Movement.

Under Father Divine's charismatic leadership, the Peace Mission grew nationally and internationally, located by 1914 in Brooklyn, New York, then moving on in 1919 to Sayville, Long Island, and in 1932 establishing a headquarters in Harlem. Through dynamic preaching, Father Divine taught that a positive consciousness in unity with his own "Divine Mind" was the only reality that would lead to good health, prosperity, and true happiness. Because he taught that this present earthly reality was heaven, his followers had no expectation of rewards in an afterlife. They would have a blessing of earthly and spiritual benefits by living up to his teachings and standards, which included positive work, good food, and a clean, safe place to reside. The Peace Mission was particularly known for its spotlessly clean cafeterias and restaurants, which served plentiful food at remarkably reasonable prices to the general public and the followers.

On September 3, 1939, Father Divine made a grand entrance into Philadelphia. Citing an invitation from municipal leaders, he traveled from Manhattan on the "Divine Special," a sixteen-coach train that also carried his staff and followers. Leading a large parade from Broad Street Station through the streets, he invited guests and the curious to enjoy a bountiful "Holy Communion Banquet Service" at Musical Fund Hall, Eighth and Locust Streets. Over the next three days, he preached and served banquets at Shibe Park, then the home of the Phillies baseball team, and the Baker Bowl, the Phillies' former ballpark. Father Divine's personal relationship with the City of Brotherly Love had begun.

By the time Father Divine came to Philadelphia, Peace Missions existed in many American cities and in Canada, Australia, New Zealand, England, France, Germany, Austria, and Panama. While most communities in the northeastern United States were African American, the great majority in the Midwest and the West were white. Father Divine and his followers were "radical" (to use their own words) critics of the way Americans permitted rampant race hatred and discrimination. Such teachings were outlined in his 1936 Righteous Government Platform. Father Divine and his faithful were "fanatical" (their words) in their adherence to Father Divine's standards of living, known as his "International Modest Code," which included celibacy, no smoking, no drinking, no undue mixing of the sexes, no profanity, no vulgarity, and no obscenity in everyday speech.

Father Divine's theology of positive consciousness also informed his economic principles. He taught that God wanted his community to work hard and make money and that there was tremendous social power in accumulated community wealth. He guided his followers to pool their financial resources to obtain, preserve, beautify, restore, and secure land and properties. They learned how to repair, construct, or restore buildings bought at low cost, as well as do their own landscaping, gardening, plumbing, and heating work. The minister's "Divine Cooperative Plan" called on the membership to be honest, never accept government monies or welfare, never make purchases on credit, and pool personal finances to make group investments. Followers never insured homes, businesses, automobiles, or their own lives because the only insurance needed was the assurance to be blessed by God, Father Divine. The Peace Mission also created employment opportunities for followers—many of whom were female and uneducated—by establishing well-regarded domestic work agencies.

In 1939, the Peace Mission purchased buildings at S. Broad and Catharine Streets in Philadelphia, formerly the Hotel Dale, and christened them the Circle Mission Church, Home and Training School of Pennsylvania. Father Divine moved to Philadelphia in July 1942 and established the Circle Mission Church as his international headquarters.

In need of housing in Philadelphia for migrating believers from New York and new adherents, Father Divine directed church members to purchase structures throughout Center City, West Philadelphia, and North Philadelphia. Referring to their residences as "heavens," male and female followers lived separately. In 1949, the Tracy Hotel adjacent to the University of Pennsylvania at Thirty-Sixth Street near Chestnut Street came under Peace Mission control and was soon operating as the Divine Tracy, an interracial residential and transient hotel. The purchase of the smaller 150-room Divine Tracy followed the 1948 acquisition of the building that became most emblematic of Father Divine's presence in Philadelphia: the 246-room Lorraine Hotel at N. Broad Street and Ridge Avenue between city hall and Temple University. The hotels required even married couples to rent single rooms on separate same-sex floors. Both hotels were closed by the first decade of the twenty-first century, the Divine Lorraine in 1999 and the Divine Tracy in 2006.

After the mission became established locally, Father Divine theologically defined Philadelphia as a new city of God and "the International Country Seat of the World." Philadelphia remained a blessed space and place to his followers even after Father Divine's death in 1965. He had two celibate spiritual marriages: one to a "dark complected" woman—references to race are avoided in Peace Mission discourse—named Peninnah or "Sister Penny," who died in the early 1940s. In 1946, he took a second wife, the "light complected" Canadian follower Edna Rose Ritchings, also referred to as Mother Divine. This second wife, who was twenty-one at the time of their marriage, maintained his religious movement with Father Divine's aesthetic style of positive thinking and a gospel of wealth remaining richly in evidence at

**FIGURE 61.** Mother Divine (born Edna Rose Ritchings) next to a portrait of her late husband, Father Divine, 1965. SPECIAL COLLECTIONS RESEARCH CENTER, TEMPLE UNIVERSITY LIBRARIES.

Woodmont, the church's seventy-two-acre suburban estate in Gladwyne, Montgomery County. Down to a few dozen celibate followers by the time of Mother Divine's death, the Peace Mission's members assumed responsibility for administering the property and the library and museum at Woodmont in order to preserve Father Divine's legacy and his teachings about how to sustain a life harmonious with God's consciousness.

## United Nations World Capital

**Charlene Mires**

In 1945 and 1946, Philadelphians campaigned aggressively to persuade the United Nations to place its new permanent headquarters in Philadelphia. As they chased the honor of becoming the "capital of the world," however, they discovered that the city's historic associations with the American Revolution did not impress the world's diplomats at the end of World War II. The campaign succeeded in making Philadelphia one of three finalists for the headquarters site, but it ultimately failed in the face of John D. Rockefeller Jr.'s offer to spend $8.5 million for a Midtown Manhattan location.

The campaign to attract the United Nations to Philadelphia began in March 1945 with J. David Stern, publisher of the *Philadelphia Record* newspaper. Stern, a Philadelphia native then living in Haddonfield, New Jersey, published a front page editorial headlined "Philadelphia—Home of the United Nations" next to a photograph of Independence Hall. In the editorial and in a letter to President Franklin D. Roosevelt, Stern argued for placing buildings for the United Nations around Independence Hall to inspire diplomats with the American example of political liberty and democracy.

The United Nations had not yet formally organized when Stern advanced his idea for bringing the world organization to Philadelphia. That occurred later, during a conference in San Francisco in May 1945 and a UN Preparatory Commission meeting that autumn in London. But Philadelphia government and business leaders leaped energetically to pursue the prize, encouraged by daily coverage in Stern's newspaper. Without invitation, determined to win the honor, they sent emissaries to San Francisco and London and produced an elaborate booklet with the Liberty Bell on the cover and photographs of historic and scenic Philadelphia. They sold themselves as the best possible setting despite Philadelphia's lack of international commercial air service at that time. To get to London, the city's promoters had to first take a train to New York.

Philadelphia's promoters quickly discovered that the idea of becoming the "capital of the world" had ignited the imaginations of boosters from other American cities and towns. A competition began among a few early contenders and escalated to at least eighty before the UN's diplomats even began to consider the question of a headquarters site. The hopefuls included other major cities such as Boston, New York, Chicago, and San Francisco, as well as seemingly remote places like Claremore, Oklahoma; Sault Ste. Marie, Michigan; and the Black Hills of South Dakota. Ultimately, more than one hundred American cities and towns (but few from other countries) angled for the diplomats' attention. Philadelphia's interest did not stop competition from the nearby region, including Valley Forge, Easton, the Poconos, and Atlantic City. At the end of World War II, which had connected every local community with global conflict, and at the dawn of widespread commercial aviation, any spot in the United States could imagine itself as the center of the world.

Philadelphia and other American communities extolled local and national attributes, but the UN diplomats who set criteria for a headquarters site at the end of 1945 had other needs in mind: good worldwide communications and favorable public opinion toward the new world organization. The UN needed a hall to accommodate six hundred delegates, plus committee rooms and accommodations for the press and support staff. Imagining a headquarters compound with its own identity, the diplomats initially ruled out cities and looked for sites of forty-two acres or more in suburban areas surrounding New York or Boston. The specified radius around New York excluded Philadelphia but still incorporated Atlantic City, which for a time became an option as a temporary meeting place because of its hotels and convention facilities.

**FIGURE 62.** Map showing the proposed site in Fairmount Park for the United Nations headquarters, 1945. HISTORICAL SOCIETY OF PENNSYLVANIA.

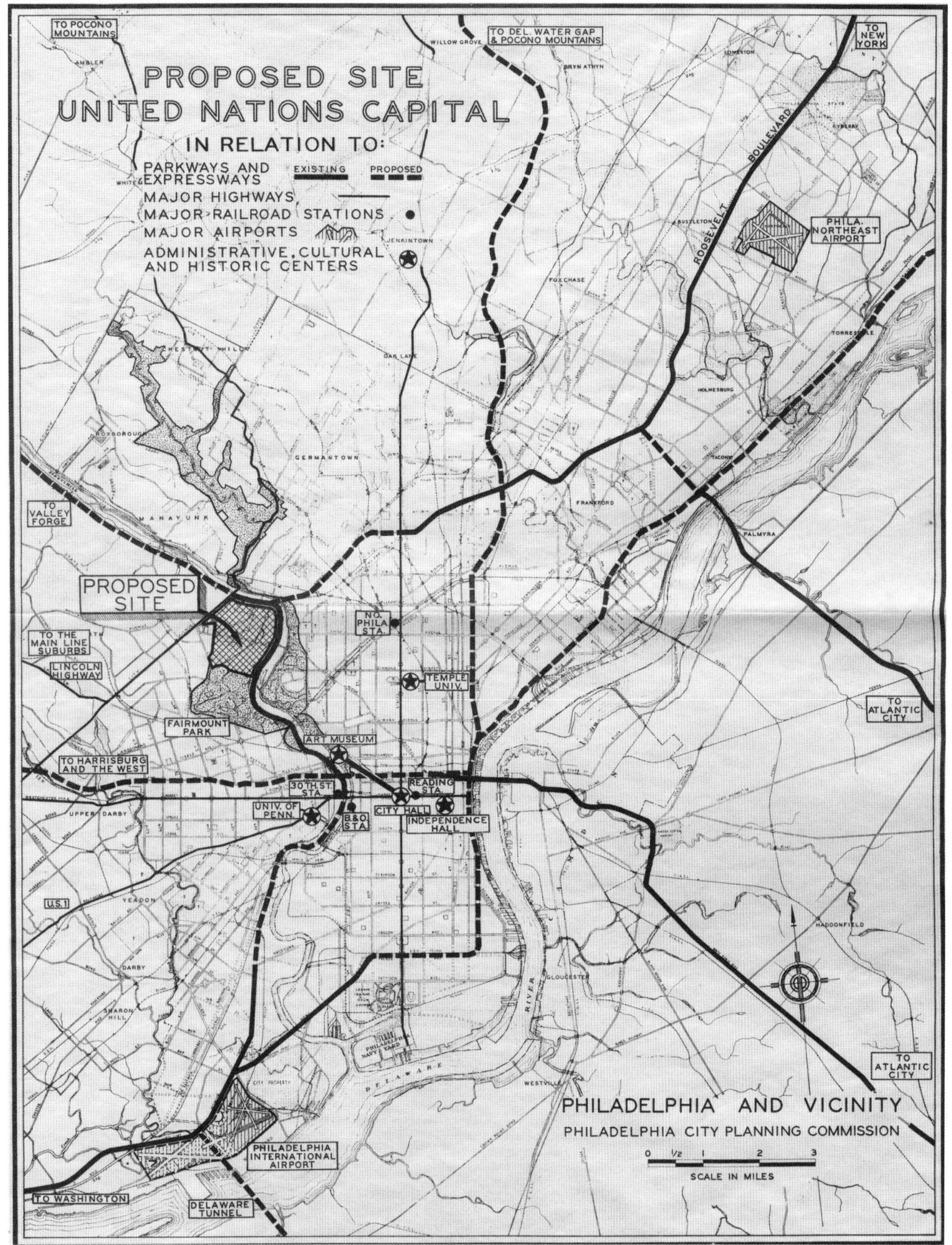
PROPOSED SITE
UNITED NATIONS CAPITAL
IN RELATION TO:
PARKWAYS AND EXPRESSWAYS
EXISTING
PROPOSED
MAJOR HIGHWAYS
MAJOR RAILROAD STATIONS
MAJOR AIRPORTS
ADMINISTRATIVE, CULTURAL AND HISTORIC CENTERS
TO POCONO MOUNTAINS
TO DEL. WATER GAP & POCONO MOUNTAINS
TO NEW YORK
ROOSEVELT BOULEVARD
PHILA. NORTHEAST AIRPORT
TO VALLEY FORGE
PROPOSED SITE
TO THE MAIN LINE SUBURBS
LINCOLN HIGHWAY
NO. PHILA STA.
TEMPLE UNIV.
FAIRMOUNT PARK
ART MUSEUM
TO HARRISBURG AND THE WEST
30TH ST. STA.
READING STA.
UNIV. OF PENN.
B.&O. STA.
CITY HALL
INDEPENDENCE HALL
TO ATLANTIC CITY
U.S.1
TO ATLANTIC CITY
PHILADELPHIA INTERNATIONAL AIRPORT
TO WASHINGTON
DELAWARE TUNNEL
PHILADELPHIA AND VICINITY
PHILADELPHIA CITY PLANNING COMMISSION
0 1/2 1 2 3
SCALE IN MILES

Stung by their exclusion, Philadelphians pivoted to a new strategy that emphasized the modern facilities sought by the UN or, if they did not exist, the capacity to create them. Setting aside the earlier vision of a UN complex around Independence Hall, they offered Belmont Plateau in Fairmount Park as a suitably pastoral setting with potential housing sites for staff in Roxborough and Chestnut Hill. They lobbied persistently in 1946 as the United Nations gathered for its first official sessions in temporary quarters at the site of the World's Fair of 1939 in Flushing Meadows, New York.

Philadelphia's hopes to become the United Nations world capital sprang anew when the diplomats encountered resistance from residents near the suburban site they most favored, north of New York City near Greenwich, Connecticut. A new round of consideration opened, and this time Philadelphia merited a site visit in a narrowed competition with San Francisco and New York. In the end, however, the fortunes of the Rockefeller family settled the matter. John D. Rockefeller Jr. provided the funds, and his son Nelson brokered the deal to place the UN on a site that New Yorker boosters favored, in Midtown Manhattan facing the East River. Despite all previous plans and aspirations, the United Nations would occupy an office complex, not a freestanding capital of the world.

In the publicity campaign they constructed to attract the United Nations, Philadelphians at the end of World War II revealed how they perceived their city and its place in the world. Their campaign initially celebrated the symbolic significance of Independence Hall and the Liberty Bell, which they assumed to be indisputable inspirations for the world. Philadelphia's promoters learned that in the postwar era, the symbols they treasured were less important than the modern communications and transportation systems necessary to be competitive on a global scale.

## Sullivan Principles

**Molly Roth**

The Global Sullivan Principles, launched in 1977 by Philadelphia civil rights leader Leon H. Sullivan, represent one of the twentieth century's most powerful attempts to effect social justice through economic leverage. More a sustained movement than a static document, the principles sought to bring the power of American investment in South Africa to bear on the cruel injustice of the apartheid state by establishing baseline commitments to fairness and empowerment as conditions for operating in the country.

Sullivan, a native of West Virginia coal-mining country, came to Philadelphia in 1950 to pastor Zion Baptist Church on N. Broad Street by way of a stop in Harlem, New York, where he served as assistant minister to Adam Clayton Powell Jr. at the Abyssinian Baptist Church. Sullivan believed that Christian ministry needed to be geared to action and described himself as preaching a "pragmatic gospel."

Sullivan had honed his economic activism through what he called the "selective patronage" campaign, begun in 1958. Dissatisfied with the economic opportunities open to minorities and women, he helped to organize a coalition of four hundred Black ministers across Philadelphia to address discrimination in employment. If companies declined appeals from the coalition to hire Blacks into professional and managerial positions, the ministers would urge their congregants to withhold their patronage. "Don't buy where you can't work," they advised. This flexing of consumer muscle by Philadelphia's Black population yielded impressive results in terms of access to employment.

The campaign's success also won Sullivan national attention. *Life* magazine included him in its list of the country's one hundred leading citizens in 1963, and the Reverend Dr. Martin Luther King Jr. called on him to help develop "Operation Breadbasket," later headed by the Reverend Jesse L. Jackson. This exposure also contributed to Sullivan's appointment in 1971 to the board of General Motors as the first Black director of a major U.S. corporation.

Sullivan voiced his opposition to General Motors' involvement in South Africa beginning with his first shareholder meeting, taking the highly unusual step of speaking in opposition to a majority position of the board. "To a great measure, the system of apartheid is being underwritten by American industry, interests, and investments," Sullivan said. His commitment to the anti-apartheid cause intensified during a 1975 trip to South Africa, where he saw some of apartheid's evil effects up close. He wrote that the inspiration for the principles was born out of suggestions by African leaders he met with on that trip.

"Why doesn't someone do something about apartheid?" Sullivan described himself as asking. "I prayed to God. God spoke back to me and said, 'You do something about it.'"

On April 1, 1977, the Principles of Equal Rights, which became known around the world as the Sullivan Principles, were publicly announced with twelve signatories that included Ford, General Motors, and IBM. Companies that signed up committed themselves to fair employment practices such as equal pay for equal work, greater Black representation in managerial and supervisory positions, and support for social programs that addressed inequality. By 1987, 125 companies from around the world had subscribed. The Sullivan Principles were enshrined in the Anti-Apartheid Act of 1986, legislation introduced by Philadelphia congressman William H. Gray and passed with a congressional override of a veto by President Ronald Reagan. The measure prohibited U.S. companies from engaging in segregationist practices anywhere in the world.

In his book *Moving Mountains*, Sullivan described his struggles with the proper formulation of his principles, because he believed that the correct course was to compromise at some moments to win acceptance and support. "Each year . . . the principles became more ambitious and thus more difficult to implement," he wrote. In their original form, the principles lacked the demand that foreign companies recognize Black labor unions; this was added in 1984.

After a decade, Sullivan came to believe that the principles were no longer exerting sufficient pressure on South Africa's government to end apartheid, and so he moved from the original principles' call for constructive engagement to worldwide boycott. Sustained international opposition eventually brought about multiracial democratic elections and the election of Nelson Mandela as the first Black president of South Africa in 1994.

Continuing the principles' evolution, in 1999 Sullivan and then-United Nations secretary general Kofi Annan unveiled the Global Sullivan Principles of Social Responsibility, an expanded formulation of the principles of corporate citizenship. Into the twenty-first century, the legacy of the Global Sullivan Principles continued to be invoked in strategies to use buying and investing power to promote social change.

## EXPLORE MORE

The institutions that underpinned ambitions to make Philadelphia the "Athens of America" endure today. In Old City, the American Philosophical Society still uses Philosophical Hall at 104 S. Fifth Street for its museum; its library is opposite. The organization now meets at Benjamin Franklin Hall at 427 Chestnut Street. Other scientific societies relocated to the Benjamin Franklin Parkway. The Academy of Natural Sciences and the Franklin Institute occupy two sides of Logan Square. From the parkway it is only a few blocks to the imposing façade of Eastern State Penitentiary at 2027 Fairmount Avenue, which runs tours of a prison that drew intense international interest in its early years and is now part of the International Coalition of Sites of Conscience. Back in Old City, the Benjamin Franklin Museum, located in Franklin Court, provides an introduction to eighteenth-century Philadelphia's greatest transatlantic celebrity.

Across the Schuylkill River in West Philadelphia, the Penn Museum at 3260 South Street has archaeological and anthropological artifacts from around the world and sits on the edge of the University of Pennsylvania's campus. Kwame Nkrumah, the Pan-Africanist and postindependence leader of Ghana, lived on the 600 block of N. Thirty-Ninth Street in what is now a private residence. Bartram's Garden, which dates back to 1728, lies a little farther out at 5400 Lindbergh Boulevard.

Philadelphia's links to peace networks and social and religious uplift can be seen in the American Friends Service Committee, which has its headquarters at the Friends Center at 1501 Arch Street. The International Peace Mission's imposing Divine Lorraine Hotel is no longer in the hands of Father Divine's movement but still looms over N. Broad Street as converted apartments. The movement's other main Philadelphia location, the Divine Tracy Hotel, is at 20 S. Thirty-Sixth Street. It too is now privately owned. Swarthmore College's Peace Collection in Delaware County is one of the world's leading archives for the study of peace movements across the globe. Out of the city, the Pearl S. Buck House in Perkasie, Bucks County, documents the life of the Nobel Prize–winning writer and daughter of missionaries in China. Her career is considered in Peter Conn, *Pearl S. Buck: A Cultural Biography* (Cambridge University Press, 1996).

On Philadelphia's internationally connected early institutions, see Edward C. Carter II, *"One Grand Pursuit": A Brief History of the American Philosophical Society's First 250 Years, 1743–1993* (American Philosophical Society, 1993) and Robert McCracken Peck and Patricia Tyson Stroud, *A Glorious Enterprise: The Academy of Natural Sciences of Philadelphia and the Making of American Science* (University of Pennsylvania Press, 2012). The wider scientific culture of the city is considered in Amy R. W. Myers, ed., *Knowing Nature: Art and Science in Philadelphia, 1740–1840* (Yale University Press, 2012). Franklin's time abroad is chronicled in George Goodwin, *Benjamin Franklin in London: The British Life of America's Founding Father* (Yale University Press, 2016) and Stacy Schiff, *A Great Improvisation: Franklin, France, and the Birth of America* (Henry Holt and Company, 2005). The legacy of 1776 outside the United States is explored in David Armitage, *The Declaration of Independence: A Global History* (Harvard University Press, 2007). Philadelphia's bid to leverage its Revolutionary reputation after 1945 is told in Charlene Mires, *Capital of the World: The Race to Host the United Nations* (New York University Press, 2013).

The region's colleges and universities often have good institutional histories, although these pay only intermittent focus to global links. Edward Potts Cheyney, *History of the University of Pennsylvania, 1740–1940* (University of Pennsylvania Press, 1940) offers insights into Penn's early entanglement with the Scottish Enlightenment. On Quaker education see John W. Oliver Jr., Caroline L. Cherry, and Charles L. Cherry, *Founded by Friends: The Quaker Heritage of Fifteen American Colleges and Universities* (Scarecrow Press, 2007). Richard Joslyn and Bruce Stronach, *The History of Temple University Japan: An Experiment in International Education* (Temple University Press, 2023) offers an unusual global perspective on a regional university.

Museums, which provided a window onto the world in the nineteenth-century city, are explored in Steven Conn, *Museums and American Intellectual Life, 1876–1926* (University of Chicago Press, 1998); Ann Fabian, *The*

*Skull Collectors: Race, Science, and America's Unburied Dead* (University of Chicago Press, 2010); and Josef Wegner and Jennifer Houser Wegner, *The Sphinx That Traveled to Philadelphia: The Story of the Colossal Sphinx in the Penn Museum* (University of Pennsylvania Press, 2015). Philadelphia's renown as a center for botany, meanwhile, is covered in Andrea Wulf, *The Brother Gardeners: Botany, Empire, and the Birth of an Obsession* (Windmill Books, 2009) and Judith Mcgee, *The Art and Science of William Bartram* (Pennsylvania State University Press, 2007).

Ideas and institutions that developed in the Delaware Valley before spreading elsewhere are covered in Paul Kahan, *Eastern State Penitentiary: A History* (History Press, 2008); Frederick Winslow Taylor, *The Principles of Scientific Management* (Harper & Brothers, 1911); Charles D. Wrege and Ronald G. Greenwood, *Frederick W. Taylor, the Father of Scientific Management: Myth and Reality* (Business One Irwin, 1991); John T. Campbell, *Songs of Zion: The African Methodist Episcopal Church in the United States and South Africa* (University of North Carolina Press, 1998); Allan W. Austin, *Quaker Brotherhood: Interracial Activism and the American Friends Service Committee, 1917–1950* (University of Illinois Press, 2012); and Leon H. Sullivan, *Moving Mountains: The Principles and Purposes of Leon Sullivan* (Judson Press, 1998). The International Peace Mission Movement, which began in Harlem but relocated to Philadelphia, is explored in Robert Weisbrot, *Father Divine and the Struggle for Racial Equality* (University of Illinois Press, 1983) and Mother Divine, *The Peace Mission Movement: Founded by Reverend M. J. Divine, Better Known as Father Divine* (Imperial Press, 1982). These works offer insights into how Philadelphians have adapted ideas from abroad and shaped the world themselves.

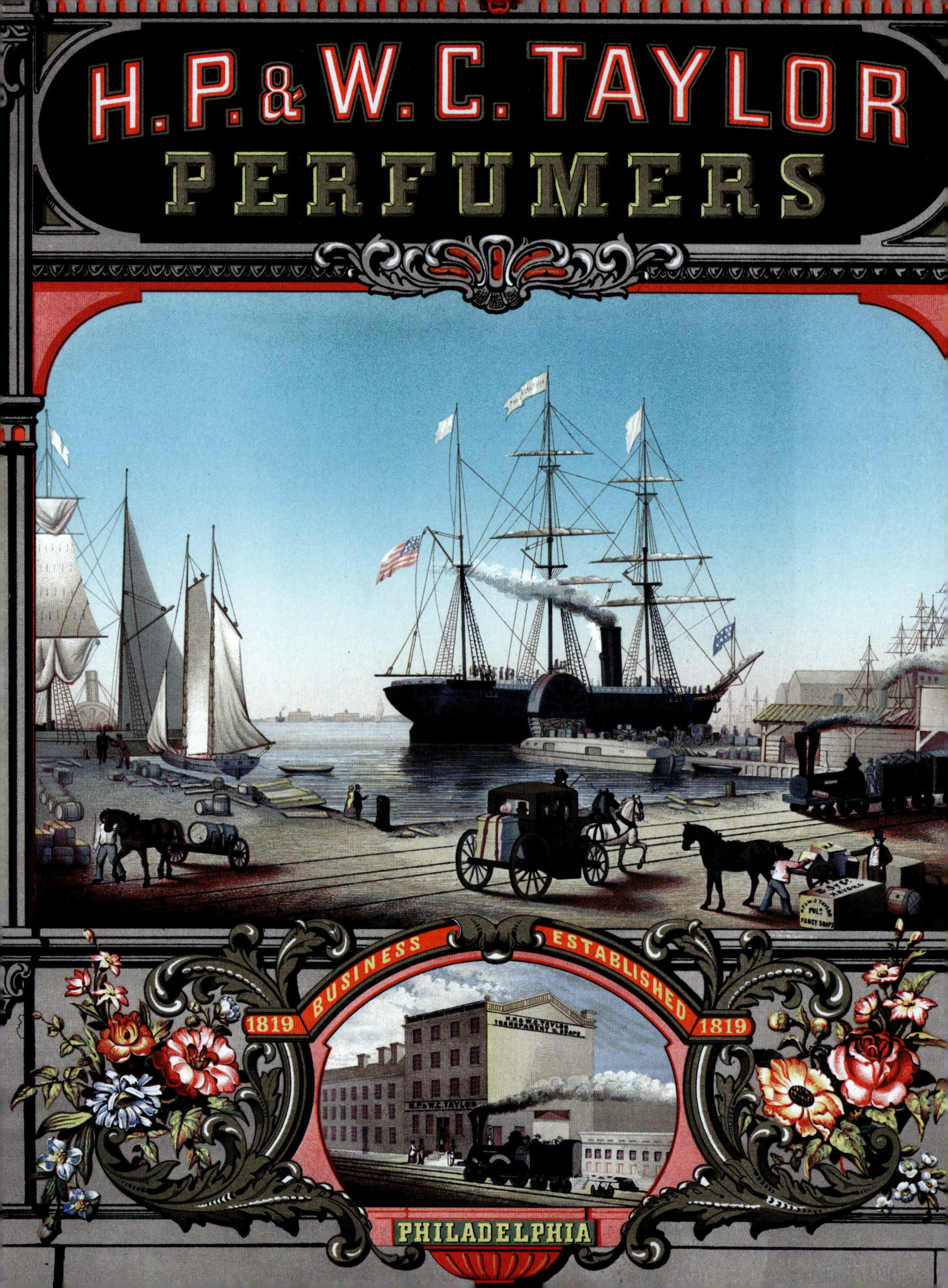

H. P. & W. C. TAYLOR
PERFUMERS

1819 BUSINESS ESTABLISHED 1819
PHILADELPHIA

# Chapter 9

# Commerce, Industry, and Labor

## Introduction

The Philadelphia region, once known as the "Workshop of the World," boasts a long history of economic innovation and adaptation. From the artisanal production of Benjamin Franklin's era to the large-scale industrial enterprises of the twentieth century, like the Campbell Soup factory in Camden, the region attracted workers from around the globe and supplied finished products for local, national, and international markets. Philadelphia became a site of economic experimentation as its population grappled with the challenge of reconciling American republicanism to an increasingly urban and industrial society. In the vanguard of both industrialization and deindustrialization, the Delaware Valley spurred global innovations in labor organizing, economic theory, and managerial practices.

Though founded as a haven for religious refugees, Philadelphia quickly transformed into an economic hub. Commerce provided its initial lifeblood, with wharves along the Delaware River receiving ships from Europe and the Caribbean. The city flourished as a key North American outpost in British imperial trade, but it also forged connections with other colonial centers in the hemisphere, like French Saint-Domingue (later Haiti) and Spanish Cuba. Philadelphia's hinterland, blessed with bountiful agricultural resources, provided a source of exports. By the conclusion of the American Revolution, the city had become the infant republic's premier port and its financial hub.

The nineteenth century saw a shift in the region from commerce to industry. By the Civil War, New York had superseded Philadelphia in trade and finance. International banking networks and shipping routes converged on Manhattan rather than the Delaware Valley. Philadelphia's prosperity came to rest instead on a wide variety of industries. The city and its surroundings, unlike twentieth-century Detroit, did not depend on a single industry. Instead, the region produced an enormous variety of goods. Iconic American products like the Stetson hat that graced many a Hollywood Western and the Campbell's soup can, turned into pop art by Andy Warhol, came from the Delaware Valley. Moreover, even some of the city's most renowned employers, like the Baldwin Locomotive Works, maintained aspects of craft production long into the industrial age, avoiding the large-scale, standardized approach found elsewhere. The diversity of industry and reliance on skilled labor offered a measure of protection against economic downturns, as a slump in one trade would not necessarily impact others, and kept wages higher, too. Philadelphia, with its characteristic row houses often located near workplaces, earned the enviable reputation as a "city of homes." In New York, immigrants crowded into tenements; in Philadelphia, property ownership seemed within their grasp.

Those homes also owed much to the strength of the region's organized labor. Industrialization around the world met resistance from workers and the Philadelphia region proved no exception. Workers, laboring in one of the first and most industrialized regions of the Americas, led the way in organizing. The city nurtured the first citywide trade union federation in the United States in 1835, the General Trades' Union. After the Civil War, its textile workers—led by Uriah Stephens, a native of Cape May, New Jersey—founded the Knights of Labor, which spread across the nation and extended overseas as far as New Zealand. The early 1900s witnessed the rise of the radical Industrial Workers of the World (IWW) on the Delaware waterfront, and though organized labor struggled in the hostile climate that followed World War I and the Russian Revolution, a new wave of militancy in the Great Depression brought lasting gains. In the mid-1930s, workers struck against major employers, such as Campbell Soup, New York Shipbuilding, and the Radio Corporation of America (RCA) in Camden alone. With Roosevelt's New Deal turning the region's manufacturing districts into Democratic Party strongholds, unions gained significant political influence, and their leaders became kingmakers in mayoral and gubernatorial elections. Over this period influences from overseas shaped strategy. Experiments with producer and consumer cooperatives in the mid-nineteenth century, for instance, borrowed from developments in Britain and France.

Greater Philadelphia's working people, however, have rarely been united. While the city's immigrant communities carved out niches in various industries—the Irish in weaving, the Germans in brewing, Cubans in cigar making, for example—they often encountered discrimination from native-born workers. When demand spiked, larger employers sought new sources of labor, as the Campbell Soup Company did in collaboration with the federal government during World War II when it recruited Puerto Rican workers. Additionally, some unions, aiming in part to protect wages, tried to exclude newcomers. Prior to the mid-twentieth century, Black Philadelphians in particular faced barriers, excluded from all but the most radical unions and prohibited from certain jobs. Notably, the IWW embraced interracial unionism on the waterfront, and Frederick Winslow Taylor, the pioneer of scientific management, encouraged hiring Black workers at Midvale Steel in Nicetown. But overall, opportunities for Black workers came only through persistent pressure.

Just as Philadelphia had championed political independence, so too did its political economists advocate for economic independence. As the region became a leading industrial center, its goods attracted buyers worldwide, often in nearby markets like Latin America. The locomotive industry, in particular, competed with Britain to sell engines in the Western Hemisphere, with South America's first steam train made in Philadelphia's Norris Locomotive Works. But as the U.S. population and territory increased, the prospect of selling to a vast national market appealed most to the region's manufacturers. Facing competition from cheap European goods produced with inexpensive labor, many industrialists lobbied for high tariffs, arguing that such protectionism shielded the Delaware Valley's workforce from a race to the bottom in wages. This doctrine, which drew on the ideas of Alexander Hamilton but found capable local champions in the political economist Henry C. Carey and Congressman William D. Kelley, came to be known as the Philadelphia or American School of Economics, and it found an institutional home in the University of Pennsylvania's Wharton School as well as the national Republican Party. Careyite theory, which cast protection as a guarantor of the "harmony of interests" between labor and capital, influenced U.S. economic policy between the Civil War and the New Deal. Despite ample evidence of labor strife in the region, the defenders of high tariffs argued that protection to home industry could keep out of the United States the kind of class conflict that regularly rocked Europe. But the American School also garnered attention abroad from nation builders from Prussia to East Asia, who saw in its promise of self-sufficiency a blueprint for self-strengthening.

In providing a model for industrialization abroad, the region may have become a victim of its own success. Over the second half of the twentieth century, competition from developing countries undermined many of the city's traditional industries. Some locally owned businesses survived through sale to national and international competitors and conglomerates. But companies that could not bring cheap labor to Greater Philadelphia increasingly outsourced jobs, with RCA, for instance, moving work from Camden to the Midwest, South, and then Mexico. For communities that had grown up around the Delaware Valley's workshops and factories, the consequences proved devastating. Yet even amid the massive job losses of the post-1970s, some sectors prospered. Philadelphia remained a leading center for the likes of biotech, financial services, and telecommunications, while its oldest economic lifeline—the Delaware River—continued to bring freight into and out of the United States. No longer the world's workshop, the twenty-first-century region found ways to adapt.

## Delaware River Ports

Peter Seibert

Over the course of its history the Delaware River has provided a critical conduit for the movement of goods and people into, out of, and through the region. The river sits at the center of the history and development of Philadelphia and the surrounding communities including the cities of Camden, New Jersey, and Wilmington, Delaware. Beginning in the Catskill Mountains of New York and ending 326 miles south at the mouth of Delaware Bay and the Atlantic Ocean, the Delaware is navigable only to Trenton by deeper draft vessels. Yet its ports have linked the inhabitants of the region to the interior of the North American continent to the north and west and the world beyond to the east.

### EARLY HISTORY

Native Americans used the river for trade. Henry Hudson documented a settlement by the Lenni Lenape (Delaware) Indians during his exploration of the river in 1609 as he sought the Northwest Passage. In the early eighteenth century, William Penn's land commissioners, appointed to define the boundaries of proposed English settlements, identified three large Native American villages along the river at Philadelphia. Archaeologists found evidence of intertribal as well as European trade in the remains of Lenni Lenape settlement sites along Philadelphia's riverfront, while excavations around Front and Dock Streets revealed evidence of a large campsite, dated between 2000 BCE and 1600 BCE, associated with food production.

During the seventeenth century, Swedish, Dutch, and English traders established a network of trading posts that fanned out from the Delaware into the backcountry. Lenape Indians traded in the likes of fur and corn with Europeans but resisted efforts to colonize the region. By the early eighteenth century, however, the English had gained both political and economic hegemony, and the Delaware became a vital node connecting Pennsylvania to British ports.

Over the course of the 1700s, British colonists settled riverbank areas along the Delaware and built a riverbank infrastructure that linked local communities and connected the region to the Caribbean, Europe, and Asia. Cross-river transportation spurred urban development. In 1688, the Gloucester (New Jersey) Court ordered the construction of ferries to traverse the Delaware, and the Cooper family had established a service by 1695. Their operation on the New Jersey side of the river opposite Philadelphia became a prosperous community, incorporated in 1838 as the town of Camden. In early Philadelphia and Wilmington, meanwhile, wharves facilitated long-distance trade and shipbuilding began to flourish. Sailing vessels routinely arrived with a wide range of domestic goods and in turn returned to Europe carrying raw commodities such as flaxseed, wood, iron, wheat, and leather. By 1772 Philadelphia exceeded all other Atlantic ports in the volume of goods passing into the region. Its crowded waterfront, with taverns and coffeehouses brimming with merchants, sailors, and stevedores, stretched about a mile and a half from Southwark to Northern Liberties.

While the shipment of goods proved important to the economic prosperity of the ports, the passage of people was arguably even more significant. Philadelphia rapidly became a center for immigrants arriving from Britain and continental Europe. In 1749 alone, for example, more than seventy thousand German settlers passed through the port of Philadelphia before heading westward to the fertile lands of south-central Pennsylvania. To do so they often had to spend time in quarantine stations, with the first built in 1743 at the confluence of the Schuylkill and Delaware, and the second, the Philadelphia Lazaretto, completed in 1799 eight miles downstream of the city in Essington. The influx of new arrivals and sailors on shore leave gave a cosmopolitan air to the banks of the Delaware, where the German language was common in print, heard in the streets, and preached from the pulpit. Lutheran

**FIGURE 63.** Tall-ship mural, Second and Federal Streets, Philadelphia, 2019. Robert Bullock's mural, completed in 2000, stands a couple of blocks away from the site of the Washington Avenue Immigration Station, where, from 1873–1915, immigrants entered the United States after crossing the Atlantic. CAROL M. HIGHSMITH ARCHIVE, LIBRARY OF CONGRESS.

and Reformed churches and Mennonite meetinghouses flourished next to Anglican and Presbyterian places of worship.

By no means did all of those who arrived on the banks of the Delaware do so voluntarily. The Dutch brought the first enslaved people into the region in the 1630s, and in 1684 the first recorded slave ship arrived in Philadelphia. Delaware merchants equipped vessels that plied the Atlantic trade in human beings although most enslaved arrivals were trafficked from the Caribbean. In 1773, a prohibitively high duty all but ended the trade, though enslavement persisted in the region after the American Revolution, and local ports continued to trade in sugar and other produce grown by enslaved labor.

## COMMERCE AND SHIPBUILDING

At the dawn of the nineteenth century, such overseas trade remained key not only to the economic prosperity of the region, but also to the finances of the new republic. With tariffs a major source of government revenue, the role of collector of the Port of Philadelphia became a plum patronage job, and President George Washington appointed the Irish-born Patriot Colonel Sharp Delany as the first incumbent following the establishment of the U.S. Customs Service in 1789. In 1819 the Philadelphia Custom House secured a purpose-built home near Second and Dock Streets, before moving to the Greek Revival splendor of the former second Bank of the United States in 1845. The port of

Wilmington built a similar neoclassical customs house in 1855.

By then, however, commercial patterns had shifted amid the upheavals of an age of Atlantic revolution. In the first decades following American independence, the Delaware ports provided a point of convergence for raw materials from the backcountry of Pennsylvania and domestic goods from Europe. But the undeclared war with France in the 1790s and the War of 1812 heavily impacted Atlantic commerce. Philadelphia businessmen responded by shifting their business to the lucrative China trade. In 1785, the Philadelphia-built Canton began making regular trips to East Asia, returning with a wide range of domestic goods. The city's elite decorated their homes with Chinese porcelains, furnishings, and textiles. By 1800, estimates suggest more than forty ships made regular trips to China and other Asian ports. Merchant Stephen Girard built his commercial empire primarily upon this trade, becoming one of the republic's first millionaires in the process. His success, along with that of other merchants, prompted Philadelphians to ponder Baltic and Russian trading alliances, although these did not prove to be as lucrative as the Asian markets.

The development of a large regional shipbuilding industry connected Philadelphia to the wider world while helping to establish the United States as a global maritime power. Rich natural resources in the hinterland enabled the industry's growth. Log rafts floated down the Delaware carried potential masts to shipbuilders. Furnaces from inland Pennsylvania shipped bar iron by wagon to the ports for conversion into spikes, nails, and anchors. In 1700, there were four shipyards in what is now Philadelphia, and by 1830, this number had more than tripled to thirteen. The industry extended downstream, too, when Irish-born John Roach, in 1871, established works at Chester, Pennsylvania, continuing a longer tradition of shipbuilding in the vicinity of Wilmington. The U.S. Navy, founded in Philadelphia in October 1775, proved a regular customer for such enterprises. Government contracts awarded to the city's Navy Yard (established in Southwark in 1801 before moving to a larger site at League Island in 1871) also supported the local economy. The construction of military vessels reached its peak during the nineteenth and early twentieth centuries. In 1837, for instance, the 120-gun USS *Pennsylvania*—the largest sailing vessel ever constructed for the U.S. Navy at that point—launched in the city.

By the middle decades of the nineteenth century, however, Philadelphia had lost its position as the premier port for foreign trade to New York. Despite periodic efforts to rejuvenate overseas commerce, the port never regained ascendance. Domestic traffic on the other hand flourished. From the eighteenth century onward, trade and travel on coastwise short-line ships boomed.

Steam power also reshaped the port economy. In the age of sail the vagary of wind along the Delaware could leave ships stranded or forced to oar or pole along. As a result, efforts began in the 1780s to construct steamboats to provide fast and reliable access along the length of the river. John Fitch operated the steamboat *Perseverance* between Philadelphia and Trenton. River steamboats provided service throughout the nineteenth century and were particularly important in transporting casualties from Washington, D.C., to Philadelphia hospitals during the Civil War.

By the eve of that conflict the pace of technological change had accelerated, and new developments left their marks on the ports. Steam boiler-powered vessels ensured a more consistent delivery of goods. The new vessels required fuel, and the coalfields of Pennsylvania offered both a seemingly inexhaustible source of energy and an additional commodity to trade. Warehouses and wharves extended the length of the city and spilled over into Delaware County. On the New Jersey side, they ran southward from Camden to Gloucester City, which later became a major shipbuilding center in World War I. A widespread network of inland manmade canals and natural waterways connected all parts of Pennsylvania to the lucrative shipping ports along the Delaware River. Specially built boats known as arks transported anthracite coal from the Lehigh Valley south along the Delaware. Canal boats brought agricultural products, timber, and iron from central Pennsylvania to the ports as well. With rail lines spoking outward from the river, freight trains did likewise, and the Reading Railroad's depot at Richmond became a center of the coal trade. In the post–Civil War years, visitors to the waterfront would have seen a mixture of large oceangoing vessels along with smaller coastal and river craft. Steamships transported domestic goods and people, while sail, as a cheaper source of power, proved better suited to heavy cargo. The tides that carried Philadelphia's wealth nourished a diverse regional economy.

As the ports grew, efforts increased to overcome the obstacles the Delaware presented to trade. The silting of docks and moving sandbars made the river difficult to navigate. These issues had impacted shipping since the colonial period. In 1766, the City of Philadelphia established the Port Wardens of the Port of Philadelphia to deal with a host of issues including breaking up the winter icepack, positioning navigation buoys, managing river pilots, and addressing the complex issue of river dredging. Early solutions gave individual pier owners the duty of dredging around their own piers. This strategy met with mixed results. Therefore, in 1885, the U.S. Army Corps of Engineers assumed responsibility for river dredging. Under its efforts, the channel grew in depth as deeper draft vessels moved along the Delaware.

Other improvements sought to stabilize and significantly expand the shoreline to allow for warehouses, shipping facilities, and new and larger piers. During the nineteenth century, these changes included removing many of the river islands. The fill from the islands stabilized the shoreline and created a new riverbank several hundred yards into the river. In Philadelphia, that riverbank expanded from Front Street to a new high tide mark a quarter mile to the east. Such a shift required the construction of new warehouses and docks. The reshaping of the landscape provided much-needed room for railroad car access, particularly along the northern and southern parts of the waterfront. Meanwhile, in Camden, firms like the Campbell Soup Company expanded their business into the waterfront.

## THE PORTS AFTER 1900

By the early twentieth century, the regional economic production tied to the ports neared its peak. Major shipbuilding endeavors such as Cramp Shipbuilding in Philadelphia and New York Shipbuilding in Camden produced military warships. The consolidation of many smaller rail lines by the Pennsylvania Railroad Company led to a constant stream of rail cars bringing coal, lumber, and other commodities to the ports. The waterfront was a vibrant mix of warehouses, commercial docks, ferries, and market houses. Immigration into the region also continued to flow through the port communities. Over one million immigrants disembarked at the Port of Philadelphia from 1873 to 1915 at the Washington Avenue Immigration Station. Processing then shifted to a new entry station in Gloucester City, New Jersey, which at its busiest was second only to Ellis Island in the number of new arrivals.

Many newcomers to the Philadelphia region sought work on the waterfront and increasingly sought to organize. The Industrial Workers of the World (IWW) became an important voice for labor along the river. Local 8, made up of a racially diverse group of longshoremen between 1913 and 1922, had long-term impacts for the port. In May 1913, an estimated four thousand longshoremen went out on a twenty-eight-day strike to protest labor conditions along the river. Regarded as one of the first interracial strikes, it resulted in changes to working conditions and better pay.

The Great Depression heralded changes for the ports that continued through much of the twentieth century. With oil replacing coal as the dominant fuel, massive tank storage facilities were constructed south of Philadelphia down to Wilmington, Delaware, which had expanded its port facilities in the early 1920s. The collapse of the mighty Pennsylvania Railroad Company in the 1970s and the rise of the trucking industry led to a new model for the movement of maritime goods. Regional industrial parks, usually located close to highways, shifted business away from the river. Interstate highways also isolated the riverfronts from their cities. In particular, this occurred in Philadelphia where the construction between 1959 and 1985 of the north-south highway Interstate 95 cut off access to the river for local communities. Bridge building, meanwhile, made the river easy to traverse for anyone with access to an automobile and the requisite toll. By the early twenty-first century, the Benjamin Franklin (1926), Tacony-Palmyra (1929), Burlington-Bristol (1931), Delaware Memorial (1951), Delaware River–Turnpike Toll Bridge (1956), Walt Whitman (1957), Commodore Barry (1974), and Betsy Ross (1976) bridges crossed the river downstream of Trenton.

The operation of four of those bridges came under the auspices of the Delaware River Port Authority, founded in 1951, one of several regional bodies with responsibility for the river. Regulating the ports, which had traditionally been a matter for municipal authorities, increasingly fell into the hands of state-created corporations in the twentieth and twenty-first centuries. The South Jersey Port Corporation, a quasi-state organization with oversight of port facilities in Burlington, Camden, Gloucester, Salem, Cumberland, Mercer, and Cape May Counties, that came into operation in 1968. PhilaPort, previously the Philadelphia Regional Port Authority, switched from city to state hands in 1989, while Wilmington's port did likewise in 1995 when the state created the Diamond State Port Corporation. State ownership provided more financial resources to help the ports adjust to ever-larger container ships.

Federal intervention left its mark on the Delaware, too. From 1866, the U.S. Army Corps of Engineers Philadelphia District took responsibility for aspects of the river's governance, which extended by the twentieth century to enforcing federal regulations on inland waterways and managing flood risk. Congress's Clean Water Act in 1972 marked a bellwether moment for the ports. Efforts to clean the water resulted in some polluting industries leaving the waterfront. While beneficial to the river's health, the measure led to concentrations of toxic waste at sites in Philadelphia, Camden, and elsewhere instead, and the dredging of the river for channels now had the added complication of treating highly contaminated sand and silt for reuse.

Organized labor by the early 2000s felt the winds of global change and dockworkers' political and economic power waned. In 2010, Camden longshoremen staged a symbolic re-creation of the Boston Tea party by dumping pineapples in the river to protest the Del Monte fruit company's plans to move to a lower-wage facility at Gloucester. While garnering national attention, the effort did not result in significant gains for the union.

In 2021, the Delaware River cargo terminals moved 55.8 million tons of cargo through their facilities in Pennsylvania, New Jersey, and Delaware. Commodities such as fruit, gasoline, and automobiles landed in the region's ports. This cargo, moving through public and private terminals, supported 17,949 jobs and generated $3.1 billion in revenue. The history of the Delaware River valley continued to be tied to the economic capacity of its ports. From beaver pelts in the seventeenth century to bananas in the twenty-first century, the Delaware River has been the vehicle for moving goods, people, and ideas in and out of the region.

**TABLE 3. TOP TEN AGRICULTURAL IMPORTS AT PORT OF PHILADELPHIA, 2011**

| COMMODITIES | METRIC TONS | SHARE OF OVERALL U.S. IMPORTS |
|---|---|---|
| Bananas | 497,976 | 10% |
| Other fruit | 495,999 | 21% |
| Meat | 255,330 | 41% |
| Pineapple | 180,619 | 20% |
| Raw cotton | 86,049 | 69% |
| Cocoa | 85,513 | 28% |
| Beverages | 77,971 | 3% |
| Wine | 75,331 | 4% |
| Honey | 59,335 | 45% |
| Mandarin oranges | 56,068 | 24% |
| Other | 444,914 | 19% |
| Total | 2,315,106 | 6% |

SOURCE: Port Import Export Reporting Service, United States Department of Agriculture.

## Airports

**Demian Larry**

Commercial aviation grew dramatically in the United States in the twentieth century, and a number of airports in the Philadelphia area grew to become regional centers of the industry. There was nothing assured or inevitable about this growth, however. It depended on the efforts of local political leaders, investments by the aviation companies, and state and federal aid.

Parks and racetracks served as the first landing areas for airplanes in Philadelphia, but by the late 1920s designated airfields dotted the city and surrounding region. An early design for Thirtieth Street Station even envisaged a landing strip on the roof. While most airfields were privately owned, the federal government established a flying field at the Philadelphia Navy Yard and a seaplane base on the Delaware River in Essington, Pennsylvania. Just upstream from Essington in the Eastwick section of Southwest Philadelphia, the city built its first municipal airport in 1926 to serve as a site of operations for a Pennsylvania National Guard squadron, a commercial flying service called the Ludington Exhibition Company, and the U.S Post Office's new airmail flights between Washington, D.C., and New York City.

While the Eastwick field was soon deemed inadequate for Philadelphia's needs, constructing a larger city-owned and operated airport proved difficult. Work began in 1931 on an expanded tract, which included the Eastwick property and land on adjacent Hog Island purchased from the federal government, but this project ground to a halt the next year, a victim of the Depression and a fiscally conservative mayor, J. Hampton Moore, who cut the city's public works budget. Most flying activity, including the airmail service, had already shifted across the Delaware River to the less flood prone Central Airport on Crescent Boulevard in Pennsauken, New Jersey, and construction languished until 1936 when a new mayor, S. Davis Wilson, restarted the work with funds made available under the New Deal. Although a laborer strike and a dispute between the city and the federal government over the location of a runway delayed completion, the new Philadelphia Municipal Airport officially opened in 1940.

When the United States entered World War II, military operations at area airports increased. Philadelphia Municipal Airport and the New Castle County Airport in Delaware, served as U.S. Army Air Corps bases, and Skillman Airport near Trenton functioned as a test site for navy planes built at a nearby plant. The government also purchased a few privately owned airfields across the region during the war.

With the war's end, commercial aviation in the United States boomed, and the City of Philadelphia worked to make its municipal airport a part of the growing industry. It renamed the facility Philadelphia International Airport and turned to the federal government for money to help build longer runways and a larger terminal. Before 1946, the U.S. government funded municipal airport development on an ad hoc basis, via New Deal work relief programs and wartime national defense projects. In 1946, though, Congress established a grant program to subsidize construction and renovation and thereby promote a national network of airports. Federal grants became a continuous source of funding for airport construction from the late 1940s into the twenty-first century and helped fund a new international airport on Hog Island that opened in December 1953. Over the following years Philadelphia International gained more flights to other cities in the United States and abroad.

By the mid-1960s, traffic at Philadelphia International had reached record levels, and officials decided it would have to be expanded to accommodate future growth. With financial support from the state and federal governments, the city began construction of new runways, terminals, parking lots, and a SEPTA regional rail line connecting the airport to Center City. While the investments were welcome, their management drew heavy criticism in the 1970s because of delays, cost overruns, and revelations that city and political party officials had accepted bribes from construction firms. Some critics called on Philadelphia to cede its control of the airport to an independent authority that they said would manage it impartially and in the best interests of the whole metropolitan region, but city leaders successfully resisted the idea.

When Congress voted in 1978 to deregulate the airline industry by abolishing the Civil Aeronautics Board (CAB), the airline business and the business of airport management both changed. For forty years, the CAB had dictated who could start an airline, what cities it could serve, and what fares it could charge. After 1978, market competition answered these questions and cities assumed more direct responsibility for attracting airlines to their airports. Greater competition encouraged airlines to establish hubs—specific airports where they concentrated their operations—and cities competed for hub status to gain more flights, jobs, and revenues. Deregulation also allowed low-cost carriers to proliferate.

While the 1980s and 1990s were a volatile time for the industry as airlines grappled with the realities of deregulation and many new and long-established carriers went out of business, traffic at Philadelphia International generally increased. The airport became a hub for US Airways and United Parcel Service, attracted service from a number of low-cost carriers, and saw new facilities develop to handle growing airplane, passenger, and automobile traffic. This expansion sparked conflicts with neighboring communities such as Delaware County's Tinicum Township, where much of the airport was located, over property tax payments and plane noise.

In the early twenty-first century, discount airlines began flying from some of Greater Philadelphia's smaller regional airports. With reduced operating costs and less tenant demand, the fields charged airlines lower rents and landing fees, making them compatible with the budget airline business model, and the airports' locations along limited-access freeways made them accessible to area travelers. The Atlantic City, Skillman (now Trenton-Mercer), and New Castle County (now Wilmington-Philadelphia) airports all gained new service from discount airlines in this period.

By the early twenty-first century, many of Greater Philadelphia's airports were regional centers of the world's commercial aviation industries. While globalization led to the loss of traditional industrial jobs in the area, it fostered new employment, including manufacturing and mechanical jobs, at the airports. The growth of the local aviation economy was not an inevitable consequence of globalization, however. Intentional policies of development and investment, both public and private, made it possible.

**TABLE 4. TOTAL PASSENGERS, PHILADELPHIA INTERNATIONAL AIRPORT**

| | |
|---|---|
| 1977 | 8.6 million |
| 1980 | 9.6 million |
| 1985 | 11.4 million |
| 1988 | 15.6 million |
| 1995 | 18.5 million |
| 2000 | 24.9 million |
| 2010 | 30.8 million |
| 2015 | 31.4 million |
| 2022 | 25.2 million |

SOURCE: Airlines.org, Department of Transportation, Philadelphia International Airport.

## China Trade

Dael A. Norwood

First pursued by the city's merchants after the American Revolution, the China trade linked Philadelphians to the rest of the world through commerce. Alongside merchants in New York, Boston, and Salem, Philadelphians were pioneers in the trade, risking their ships and capital in new long-distance sailing routes that crisscrossed the globe to generate the silver coin and exotic commodities needed to make purchases in China. In exchange, the China trade provided Philadelphia and its hinterlands with teas, porcelains, silks, and spices, filling cupboards while boosting activity in shipbuilding, insurance, and banking. The global contacts the China trade provided defined Philadelphia as a cosmopolitan commercial center in the early American republic.

The China trade was a complex system of commercial circuits linking economies in the Atlantic world to those of what early Americans called the East Indies—the wide zone between the Cape of Good Hope and Cape Horn, encompassing China, India, Southeast Asia, and the Pacific islands. The traffic centered on Canton (Guangzhou), the biggest city of the Pearl River Delta and the only Chinese-controlled port open to Western traders. Beginning in the seventeenth century, Canton became the most important market for teas and Chinese manufactured goods. Lacking commodities in demand in Asia, westerners paid for their purchases in silver—usually Spanish dollars minted from New World silver mines—and accepted stringent regulations, including limiting their trading partners to a special guild of merchants, the *Co-hong*, setting a specific season for all business, and confining them to rented factories (buildings that combined warehouses, offices, and living quarters) beyond the city's walls.

Colonial Philadelphians, like other British subjects, developed a taste for Asian goods. However, access was mediated by the British East India Company, which held a monopoly on East Indies trade. In 1773, Parliament's preferential treatment of the East India Company's tea business helped spark widespread protests—most famously in Boston, but also in Philadelphia.

Philadelphia's relationship to the China trade changed with the American Revolution. While the war gained Americans political independence, it cost them the markets of the British Empire, including the West Indian ports that Philadelphians depended upon as outlets for the region's agricultural products. Faced with a dire economic situation, Philadelphians gambled on new trades—including with China. The first American ship to reach Canton, the *Empress to China*, departed New York harbor on February 22, 1784. It was a joint venture of Philadelphians and New Yorkers, organized by the Philadelphia financier Robert Morris and captained by Philadelphian John Green. A financial success, the *Empress*'s voyage inspired imitators, which helped establish Philadelphia as a major center for U.S. trade with China.

The founding generation of Americans saw their new trade with Asia as a matter of national pride as well as a source of prosperity. Philadelphia politicians used the establishment of a new federal government in 1789 to aid the trade, passing legislation that gave special protections to American merchants shipping East Indies goods. Still, bereft of cheap silver at home, and without all the monopoly protections of their European rivals, Philadelphia merchants like Stephen Girard had to adapt to compete. They used smaller ships and crews to save on operating costs and more nimbly respond to markets. They also persistently sought new sources of Spanish dollars as well as new commodities that might sell well at Canton, including ginseng, sea otter pelts, sandalwood, and bêche-de-mer (sea slugs).

These innovations, along with good timing and a relaxed approach to commercial legality, were crucial to the trade's early success. The Napoleonic Wars provided neutral American shippers with an advantage as suppliers of tea to Europe, but also risked British interference. Philadelphia merchant Benjamin Chew Wilcocks helped inaugurate an American opium smuggling trade in 1805, shipping the drug to China from Smyrna (Izmir), Turkey, and later from British India. Well-known as a painkiller, opium had become increasingly valuable in Asia as the practice of recreational smoking spread. Seeking to curb this addictive habit, Chinese authorities had long banned opium importation, though with little effect on smugglers' business (the drug was legal in the United States). While not every Philadelphia merchant was an opium trader—a few, like Quaker Nathan Dunn, refused it on religious grounds—the illicit market for the drug was robust, and by the late 1820s, opium outpaced silver as the main payment for goods in China.

Opium smuggling's profits proved to be the undoing of the *old* China trade. The elaborate networks that British and American merchants created to facilitate opium trafficking caused friction with Chinese officials, culminating in Britain's invasion in 1840 (the First Opium War). Though not belligerents, Americans benefited from Britain's 1842 victory, as the treaties the Qing Empire made in its aftermath eliminated trading restrictions and opened new ports. Conflict over opium also accelerated consolidation among American China firms, which increasingly shifted their operations to New York. Philadelphia's participation in overseas trade decreased, as its merchants invested in manufacturing, transportation, and domestic commerce instead.

The China trade had a lasting impact on Philadelphia's culture and society. Chinese goods were for decades markers of high status and fashion. China merchants were leaders in the commercial community, serving as bank and insurance company directors as well as members of the Philadelphia Chamber of Commerce. Some of them, like Nathan Dunn and Andreas Everardus van Braam Houckgeest, built country estates in the Chinese style, filled with chinoiserie, and occasionally staffed by Chinese servants. Their fortunes also helped fund major charitable and educational institutions, including the American Philosophical Society, the Pennsylvania Hospital, and Girard College. The trade also influenced popular perceptions of China and its people among Philadelphians, long before any significant immigration from Asia. Grocers' advertising for teas commonly featured Chinese people and landscapes, and beginning in 1839, Nathan Dunn's Chinese Museum gave thousands of visitors an experience of "China in miniature" through dioramas of daily life in the Middle Kingdom. Through the China trade, Philadelphia came to know the world—and it, Philadelphia.

## General Trades' Union Strike

Patrick Grubbs

The first general strike in the United States occurred in Philadelphia in 1835 when the short-lived General Trades' Union (GTU) of the City and County of Philadelphia led a citywide strike to demand a ten-hour workday. The successful action set a precedent followed by other labor organizations in the nation later in the nineteenth century.

The GTU strike occurred after several failed attempts to organize working people through the creation of a Mechanics' Union of Trade Associations and a Working Men's Party. In 1833 Philadelphia labor leaders met in hopes of reigniting the city's nascent labor movement, and they created the GTU the following spring. The GTU, which broke barriers as one of the first labor organizations to accept unskilled workers, became the most remarkable citywide union of its time.

The strike began as an impromptu affair in late May 1835 when coal heavers of the Schuylkill docks went on strike for a ten-hour day. As they paraded down the streets of the city on June 3, cordwainers, carpenters, and other tradesmen followed with shouts of "We are all day laborers!" Throughout the week leaders of the GTU used labor presses, posters, and parades complete with drum and fife corps demanding a ten-hour day, to rally Philadelphia workers to join their brethren in the fight. By June 10 over forty trades and nearly twenty thousand workers, including city employees, joined the strike. Shortly after city workers struck, the common council announced that workers employed under the authority of the city corporation would be granted a ten-hour day. By the end of June, most laborers received the concessions they asked for, and membership in the GTU soared.

With this initial success, worker solidarity expanded to include unskilled workers, traditionally omitted from unionizing efforts. In the spring of 1836 Schuylkill dockers clashed with coal merchants when they sought a wage advance from their employers. When dockers struck, merchants won the assistance of Mayor John Swift, who had eight day laborers arrested and set their bail at an exceedingly high rate of $2,500 in hopes of breaking the strike. Swift's plan backfired, however, as the high bail made martyrs of those arrested. The GTU came to their aid, admitted the dockers into the organization, and helped fund their defense, which proved successful when they were acquitted of both breaching the peace and of charges of conspiracy.

GTU power helped to organize the city's labor and gained the workers of Philadelphia the ten-hour day. Every strike funded and supported by the GTU in the seven months following the general strike ended in victory for the workers, including that of the unskilled dockers. But the organization met a sad end. Many who joined the union left once concessions were made. Workers also faced a backlash from employers who formed masters' associations to defeat striking workers. By 1837 only thirty unions remained, down from fifty-one in 1836. That year the first effects of the Panic of 1837 were felt by city workers, and within a year the organization was dead. Over the following decades workers who had come together in the strike often divided into Protestant and Catholic camps, making citywide organization harder.

While the GTU of Philadelphia proved short-lived, its significance to organized labor movements reached into the next century. The General Strike of 1835, the nation's first general strike, proved successful and its techniques were employed by other American labor movements in the postbellum years, most notably in St. Louis in 1877 and throughout the nation in 1919. By admitting unskilled dockers into their union, the GTU of Philadelphia set a precedent not replicated until after the Civil War when it became a primary objective of the Knights of Labor. Together, the general strike and the inclusion of unskilled laborers in unions ultimately proved effective for organized labor during another dire period for American workers: the Great Depression.

## Knights of Labor

Patrick Grubbs

The Knights of Labor, the first national industrial union in the United States, was founded in Philadelphia on December 9, 1869, by Uriah Stephens and eight other Philadelphia garment cutters. Intended to overcome the limitations of craft unions, the organization was designed to include all those who toiled with their hands. By mid-1886 nearly one million laborers called

**FIGURE 64.** Detail of Uriah S. Stephens, founder of the Knights of Labor, 1886. Established by Philadelphia textile workers in 1869, the Knights spread to Canada, Europe, Australia, and New Zealand over the following decades. LIBRARY OF CONGRESS.

themselves Knights, making the organization the largest and most influential labor union in nineteenth-century America. Originally called the Noble and Holy Order of the Knights of Labor, the Knights began as a replacement for the failed Garment Cutters' Association of Philadelphia. To sustain the organization, Stephens insisted on a high level of secrecy and fraternalism. Not referred to by name until 1879, the organization chalked symbols on sidewalks and buildings to call meetings. For example, the symbol $8={}^{415}/_{1}$ meant Local Assembly (LA) No. 1 would meet on April 15, at 8 o'clock.

Stephens aspired to unite all wage earners into a single organization regardless of skill, race, or sex. The organization excluded liquor dealers, lawyers, bankers, and professional gamblers. Stephens stressed the importance of solidarity within the ranks of labor in order to meet the power of capital. He did not limit the organization's goals to increased wages and lower hours but believed that workers should strive to build cooperatives to gradually replace the prevailing capitalistic system. Because of this outlook the slogan for the organization became "an injury to one is the concern of all." Despite this lofty goal early membership in the Knights consisted primarily of skilled, male workers. Even LA 1, Stephens's garment cutters' assembly, admitted only garment cutters and no women. Women were not initiated into the Knights until 1882.

Between December 1869 and April 1875 the Knights made few gains outside of the city. During that time eighty-five local assemblies were established, seventy within the Philadelphia region. After the Great Railroad Strike of 1877 membership expanded and the first national officers were initiated after a convention in Reading, Pennsylvania, in 1878. In 1879 Terence V. Powderly, a native of Carbondale, Pennsylvania, became grand master workman after Stephens resigned the position. Powderly, who also served as the socialist mayor of Scranton from 1878 to 1884, led the Knights until 1893.

Powderly eliminated the secrecy of the Knights and membership grew to more than 750,000 by the summer of 1886. From 1879 to 1886 the Philadelphia region maintained a high percentage of the Knights' national membership and established a meetinghouse across the street from Independence Hall at 505 Chestnut Street. The Knights in the city also participated in numerous actions on behalf of labor, such as organizing a successful shoemakers strike, striking in sympathy with female carpet makers in 1884, and formulating a local assembly of Italian barbers in 1886.

The Knights declined after 1886, due in part to internal discord in the aftermath of the disastrous violence that erupted during a labor protest in Haymarket Square in Chicago, strong opposition from capital, and competition from the trade unions of the American Federation of Labor. In 1893 the Knights removed Powderly as its national leader and staggered into the twentieth century after Daniel DeLeon's failed attempt to make the Knights a Marxist organization. When DeLeon and his followers left the organization in 1895, Knights membership declined and the organization went back into secrecy. Despite its decline, the influence of the Knights continued into the twentieth century. In 1903 labor organizer Mary "Mother" Jones, who was inspired to fight for labor while attending Knights meetings in Chicago in the 1870s, came to Philadelphia to encourage striking textile workers in the Kensington district.

## Industrial Workers of the World (IWW)

**Peter Cole**

In the early 1900s thousands of workers in Greater Philadelphia belonged to the Industrial Workers of the World (IWW)—a militant, leftist labor union. Local 8, which organized the city's longshoremen, was the largest and most powerful IWW branch in the mid-Atlantic region and the IWW's most racially inclusive branch. Indeed, there might not have been a more egalitarian union or even institution anywhere in the nation in the early twentieth century. Nicknamed Wobblies, these union activists also organized Philadelphians in other industries, especially textiles and metal making.

Founded in 1905, the IWW believed that capitalism was inherently unjust, resulting in the oppression of the great majority (workers) by a tiny, wealthy elite (employers). According to the IWW preamble, these groups "shared nothing in common." Hence, the Wobblies called for revolutionary changes to create a more just world where everyone could enjoy the fruits of industrialization.

Shortly after its founding, workers in Philadelphia's largest industry, textiles, started joining the IWW, as did those in textile centers across southeastern Pennsylvania and New Jersey, especially Paterson. Similarly, Philadelphia Wobblies maintained ties to Chester, Camden, and Wilmington. Many renowned Wobblies spoke in Philadelphia, including Elizabeth Gurley Flynn, "Big Bill" Haywood, John Reed, Arturo Giovannitti, and Carlo Tresca. However, the most important leader and greatest speaker was the locally born African American dockworker Ben Fletcher.

As one of America's busiest ports, thousands of longshoremen toiled on both sides of the Delaware and Schuylkill Rivers, loading everything from Baldwin locomotives to Stetson hats and unloading unrefined sugar from Cuba and coal from nearby mines. Reflecting the city's diversity, the city's roughly five thousand longshoremen in 1913 were about one-third African Americans, a third Irish and Irish Americans, and a third other Europeans, especially Lithuanians and Poles. Employers counted on racism and xenophobia to keep workers from unionizing. However, thousands struck that year and quickly joined Local 8 because it practiced equality by ensuring, for example, that every major ethnic group was represented on the negotiating committee.

The IWW's militant tactics worked. Over the next decade, Local 8 dominated area labor relations because its members proved willing to fight together for better conditions. Predictably, the empowered longshoremen experienced intense opposition from employers and the government (including the wartime arrests of Fletcher and other leaders on bogus charges of "espionage

**FIGURE 65.** Detail of longshoreman and "Wobbly" leader Benjamin Fletcher, 1918. In 1913, Fletcher helped to found Local 8 of the Industrial Workers of the World, a radical interracial union which organized Black Philadelphians alongside the likes of Irish, Lithuanian, and Polish workers. NATIONAL ARCHIVES.

and sedition"). Beyond winning raises and improving work conditions, Local 8 also integrated work gangs, gatherings, and leadership posts—all unprecedented.

In 1922 employers taking advantage of postwar America's worsening labor and race relations "locked out" Local 8 members and broke their hold. This pushback was part of the first, national "Red Scare," also signaling a backlash against the growing number of African Americans in the area. Locally and nationally, the IWW went into decline, but its ideals persisted. When the more conservative International Longshoremen's Association returned unionism along the Delaware River, it had to acknowledge the power of African Americans. Further, the Wobbly commitment to ethnic, gender, and racial inclusion regardless of craft or skill was championed in the 1930s by the Congress of Industrial Organizations.

Although the IWW never was as strong or large in Philadelphia, or elsewhere, after the 1920s, the organization and its ideals lived on, revived by activists across the country in the 1960s and, in Philadelphia, in the 1980s. Indeed, this new generation of Wobblies continued to demonstrate impressive passion with their still-radical commitment to equality across all lines, use of direct-action tactics (on the job and in the streets), and brilliant use of language to skewer the status quo in song and posters and later on the Internet.

In the 1980s, a small but impressively organized community of Wobblies, anarchists, and other leftist radicals established beachheads in West Philadelphia, including by squatting in abandoned row houses, later taking ownership of some and turning them into collectively owned properties. Local Wobblies also set up a bookstore in West Philadelphia and were active in the Occupy Philadelphia encampment at city hall in 2011. By the early 2020s, the Philadelphia General Membership Branch had more members than at any time since the 1940s, with its logo incorporating Local 8 to honor its history. As in numerous other cities in the United States and worldwide, Philadelphia's IWW persisted, still deeply committed to charting a path to a postcapitalist, postracist world.

## March of the Mill Children

**Gail Friedman**

The March of the Mill Children, the three-week trek from Philadelphia to New York by striking child and adult textile workers, launched on July 7, 1903, by Mary Harris "Mother" Jones, trained public attention on the scourge of child labor and energized efforts to end it by law. Jones, the storied Irish-born labor organizer who had emigrated to North America as a result of the 1840s famine, came to the Kensington section of northern Philadelphia in mid-June 1903 to rally support for some forty-six thousand textile workers, including many youths, who were staging the largest strike in city history to demand a reduced work week of fifty-five hours and a ban on night work by women and children. Told that newspapers were ignoring child labor because mill owners were stockholders, she retorted, "I've got stock in these little children, and I'll arrange a little publicity."

A fierce opponent of child labor and a masterly tactician, Jones seized on a march of young workers as a way of publicizing the strike while also exposing the evils of child labor and the excesses of industrial capitalism. Children were sent to work in coal mines and mills to supplement meager family incomes and as a result suffered stunted growth and maiming injuries. The 1900 census reported that one-sixth of American children under age sixteen were employed, likely a gross undercount. More children worked in textile manufacturing than in any other trade. By 1900 textile factories and allied trades dominated Kensington, an early manufacturing center.

At a rally in Kensington's Labor Lyceum Hall (2914 N. Second Street), Jones revealed plans to lead an "industrial army" of hundreds of child strikers and their parents on a march of nearly one hundred miles to New York City to dramatize their cause. She later expanded the itinerary to include a pilgrimage to President Theodore Roosevelt's Long Island summer home to plead for child labor laws.

The marchers left Kensington to the sound of fifes and drums, heading to Bristol and Morrisville in Pennsylvania. From there, dwindling in numbers, fed and sheltered by unionists, farmers, socialists, and

**FIGURE 66.** Mother Jones with child textile workers and their parents, 1903. LIBRARY OF CONGRESS.

other allies, the ragtag crusaders slogged through heat and rain into the manufacturing belt of New Jersey, soliciting donations and staging rallies often attended by thousands. Their route extended from Trenton, Princeton, and New Brunswick north toward Jersey City.

Reaching New York City on July 23, sixty marchers paraded up Second Avenue by torchlight. On Coney Island three days later, Jones put children in animal cages to dramatize what she labeled bosses' attitudes toward workers. She and a delegation of five arrived July 29 at Roosevelt's Sagamore Hill summer home, where they were rebuffed by his secretary. In the meantime, even before the crusade's end, strikers thwarted by the manufacturers' strategies and their own factional divisions had begun returning to the mills.

Nevertheless, the march advanced efforts to abolish child labor. In 1904, the National Child Labor Committee formed for advocacy and action. A year later Pennsylvania toughened its child labor laws, though it took another thirty-three years, until the New Deal presidency of Franklin D. Roosevelt, for nationwide legislation protecting young workers, the Fair Labor Standards Act of 1938, to replace a patchwork of state laws.

## Shirtwaist Strike, 1909–10

**Julianne Kornacki**

On December 20, 1909, more than seven thousand of Philadelphia's twelve thousand shirtwaist workers walked out on their jobs, one month after the "uprising of 20,000" commenced in New York City's shirtwaist industry. The strike lasted until February 6, 1910, when manufacturers agreed to comply with workers' demands (though ultimately refused union recognition). Occurring in an era of increased unemployment, labor market instability, and worker militancy, the shirtwaist strike revealed tensions between Philadelphia's Republican machine government and organized labor, as well as among elite members of the Jewish community, clubwomen, and the young shirtwaist workers.

About 85 percent of the shirtwaist strikers were Jewish women and girls from Russia, demonstrating the ethnic and gender segregation of Philadelphia's labor market. Overall, 40 percent of workers in Philadelphia's garment trades were Jewish, and young women and girls from Russia had high rates of employment. Most Jewish workers worked for Jewish employers, who often paid low wages and were generally first- or second-generation Jewish elites from western Europe who had settled in Philadelphia decades earlier. Members of this elite welcomed new immigrants hesitantly, devoting considerable resources to forge a pliant, assimilated working class. However, many newly arrived immigrant workers agitated for better working conditions against the call for "unity and harmony" among the community's intellectual and business leaders.

The shirtwaist industry operated under a subcontracting system, wherein manufacturers distributed work to contractors who, in turn, hired operators to make the garments. The manufacturers were not liable for any injury or illness workers suffered on the job, and workers were often responsible for purchasing their own equipment and supplies. To alleviate these conditions, strikers demanded a 10 percent increase in wages on all piece and contract work, regular and consistent payment, an end to punitive firings, a cap of fifty hours work per week, sanitary working conditions, union recognition, and a free supply of work materials (thread, for example).

In response to the strike, the city government pledged "sufficient protection" for shirtwaist manufacturers and began rounding up hundreds of picketing strikers per day. Workers and their allies were arrested for allegedly committing crimes that included intimidating, insulting, or "annoying" workers who were not on strike, assault and battery of police officers and strikebreakers, inciting to riot, disorderly conduct, and conspiracy. To maintain the strike, leadership from the International Ladies' Garment Workers' Union (ILGWU) and the Women's Trade Union League solicited the aid of society women, who supplied the material support necessary for the workers to hold out. More than one hundred local unions also pledged solidarity, linking the strike to broader organizing efforts in the city, as well as to concurrent shirtwaist strikes in other United States and Canadian cities.

The strikers faced tremendous opposition from the city's business community, the Republican administration of Mayor John E. Reyburn, the police department, mainstream press, and Jewish elites. However, with the support of clubwomen (including Helen Taft, the daughter of President William Howard Taft), labor organizations, and rank-and-file workers, the shirtwaist strikers were able to stay on the picket lines long enough to secure substantive gains—including a system for negotiating piece-work prices, reduced work hours, and the elimination of charges for materials. More broadly, the political corruption of the Reyburn administration had alienated both reform groups and members of the Republican Party. At a moment when growing numbers of elite women were organizing for universal suffrage, enough saw the plight of shirtwaist workers as a symbol of political oppression against women more broadly. While clubwomen were most comfortable participating from a distance and on their own terms, their arrests from the picket lines populated front-page headlines.

Overall, the strike revealed tensions that had already existed in Philadelphia, as well as the growing political involvement of elite women and the entrenchment of the city's police force. Further, the strike showcased the power of organized labor, which would be witnessed in full force during the 1910 General Strike, which involved between sixty thousand and seventy thousand Philadelphians striking in solidarity with streetcar workers.

## AFL-CIO

**Francis Ryan**

As the largest coalition of trade unions in the nation, the American Federation of Labor–Congress of Industrial Organizations (AFL-CIO) has, since its formation in 1955, served as the central body directing the U.S. labor movement. Philadelphia's AFL-CIO council, which at its peak in the early 1970s claimed more than two hundred thousand members across the metropolitan region, has been one of the most active sections of this national movement. Building on the long history of labor struggles in one of the world's earliest industrial heartlands, Greater Philadelphia's unions have organized workers, engaged in political campaigns, and established economic standards that have been a benchmark across the country. At the same time they have often reflected, contributed to, and challenged divisions over race, immigration, and culture.

The roots of Philadelphia's trade union movement trace back to the early republic and the region's early industrialization. Among the first worker-run organizations was the Federal Society of Journeymen Cordwainers of Philadelphia, which formed in the 1790s to address industry wage scales. When journeymen called a work stoppage in 1805, master shoemakers brought legal charges, and a trial the following year ruled such workplace actions illegal. Workers turned to political mobilization as a primary tactic instead. In 1827, they formed the Mechanics' Union of Trade Associations, the first citywide labor council in the United States. Early workingmen's parties also existed in Philadelphia, often advancing measures such as an eight-hour workday in labor newspapers and educational forums and supporting producer and consumer cooperatives that built on blueprints and precedents from Britain and France. Few survived for long, and the greatest success for organized labor in the early nineteenth century came in 1835 in the form of the citywide General Trades' Union (GTU), which united skilled and unskilled workers in the republic's first general strike. While the GTU fragmented in hard economic times, the Philadelphia iron molder William H. Sylvis, who led his trade's fledgling union during the Civil War, tried to build on its success. He helped to form the federative National Labor Union in 1866, which pursued many of the goals of the so-called "workie" parties while supporting workplace militancy. The same year Sylvis died, Philadelphia garment cutters formed the Noble and Holy Order of the Knights of Labor, which continued these earlier traditions and also admitted female loom weavers and Black workers as members, advancing the causes of women's suffrage and equal pay. Its founder, Uriah Stephens, envisaged the organization spanning the globe, and over the following decades the Knights extended as far afield as Britain, continental Europe, South Africa, and New Zealand.

Although the Knights proved a powerful force in Philadelphia, their demise in the 1880s coincided with the rise of a new coalition of trade unions, the American Federation of Labor (AFL), which came to be led by the British-born, Jewish cigar maker Samuel Gompers. The AFL had a strong base in the city's building trades and skilled crafts such as butchers, brewers, and carpet weavers, and often succeeded in advancing wage scales and working conditions. Through these early years, Philadelphia's AFL reflected the range of ethnic-based economies in the city. Groups such as the German Federated Trades Council represented the likes of German brewers, bookbinders, shoemakers. The Jewish Trades Union did likewise for skilled workers of that faith. Nevertheless, AFL unions disproportionately represented native-born white men.

As labor conflict escalated in industrializing nations, Philadelphia trade unions sometimes resorted to militant strategies themselves. In the first years of the twentieth century, workers joined several general strikes in the city's Kensington section. Stoppages in individual trades, meanwhile, occurred in such places as Camden, Wilmington, and Atlantic City. Over the years that followed, the region's industrial barons weakened these unions, and by the 1920s the labor movement in the Delaware Valley withered. Conditions changed in the early 1930s when a global depression led thousands across the region to organize into industrial trade unions. Hosiery workers, street cleaners, waitresses, insurance agents, newspaper distributors, boot blacks, and steelworkers, among others, joined unions in unprecedented numbers. Philadelphia's manufacturing unions mostly aligned with the newly created Congress of Industrial Organizations (CIO), a rival to the more conservative and exclusive AFL, which aggressively advanced the principles of industrial unionism and inclusion. By 1937, the city had CIO affiliates such as the United Auto Workers (UAW), which represented several thousand assembly-line workers at the Edward G. Budd Manufacturing Company auto body plant, as well as employees at Disston Saw Works who joined the United Steelworkers (USW). Collective bargaining agreements negotiated by AFL and CIO unions established progressive wage scales and seniority along with a range of benefits including expanded health coverage and vacation time. Organized labor also united behind

President Franklin D. Roosevelt and were the staunchest supporters of the city's Democratic Party, coordinating efforts through the CIO's Labor's Non-Partisan League and the AFL- sponsored Labor's League for Political Education.

Philadelphia's labor movement also demonstrated the paradoxical nature of race in the workplace. Since the late 1800s, many AFL unions enforced a rigid color line. Entire sections of the region's economy, including the vast textile production centers and most building trades were closed to Black workers and, to a lesser extent, women. In response, they often formed their own associations including the Hotel Brotherhood, an organization of waiters that took shape in the 1880s. Some AFL unions were biracial, placing racial and sometimes ethnic groups into separate locals. One bastion of interracial activity was the International Brotherhood of Teamsters, which through the early twentieth century united members of different races into one unit, sometimes with Black officers. Longshoremen established strong interracial unions such as the Industrial Workers of the World, which for several years in the 1920s controlled operations at what was, then, a bustling port, and whose wider reach extended into Mexico and Canada. In the 1930s, the CIO continued these commitments, with unions such as the United Cannery, Agricultural, Packing and Allied Workers of America, which represented Campbell Soup workers in Camden, New Jersey. When a section of white transit workers walked off the job to protest the promotion of Black employees to conductor positions in 1944, President Roosevelt broke the hate strike by ordering troops to oversee the city's mass transit. Shortly after, a new union replaced the former racist group. Transport Workers Union Local 234, a CIO affiliate, committed to maintaining interracial unity and promoting Black advancement in all sections of transit service.

During the New Deal and after, the AFL represented higher numbers of union members across the region and gained more political leverage, uniting its council with the CIO in 1960. Organized labor formed the most significant base for the city's Democratic Party, which would come to dominate Philadelphia over the postwar decades. Unions allied with Democrats elsewhere in the region, too, as workers set out to build on the gains they had made under Roosevelt. The Committee on Political Education (COPE) formed to educate members on political concerns and to direct Election Day mobilization. Plasterers' union representative Edward F. Toohey, as COPE director, coordinated a major registration drive that helped shift the city's voters toward a majority Democratic affiliation. COPE also played a critical role in mobilizing support for the 1960 presidential campaign of John F. Kennedy, who took Philadelphia by more than 320,000 votes.

With Kennedy in the White House, expenditures for urban infrastructure increased. Disputes over the city's construction hiring practices soon placed the Philadelphia AFL-CIO in national headlines over "affirmative action." In 1963, the local National Association for the Advancement of Colored People leader and World War II veteran Cecil B. Moore led protests demanding an end to racial hiring bars in the city's construction industry. Moore's backers included James H. "Jimmy" Jones, a regional United Steelworkers representative who formed the Negro Trade Union Leadership Conference (NTULC) in 1960 to advance Black leadership in unions. The Philadelphia Building and Construction Trades Council resisted efforts to desegregate its union and open its apprenticeship program to African Americans but succumbed when a presidential order mandated equal job access on all federal construction projects. This program, known as the Philadelphia Plan, become a model for national affirmative action programs in the coming decade, though the Supreme Court's *Bakke* decision in 1978 signaled an early end to any commitment to repair a century of Jim Crow. The NTULC also continued to push for Black leadership across unions. In 1964, a slate of African American unionists usurped the white leadership of the city's sanitation local and moved the city's American Federation of State, County, and Municipal Employees (AFSCME) District Council 33 toward more militant actions, at times initiating service disruptions that helped gain modest wage boosts by the end of the decade.

In 1967, Philadelphia labor leaders supported the reelection of Democratic mayor James H. J. Tate. With their backing, Tate won a contested primary and narrowly defeated Republican Arlen Specter later that year. His victory proved the high point of labor's influence in Philadelphia. A staunch union advocate, he recognized the Philadelphia Federation of Teachers, Local 3, which negotiated a strong contract for public school teachers. Women emerged as key activists in the union across these years, including Sonny Richman, Pat Halpin, Rita Schwartz, and labor educator Alice Hoffman. Other organizing drives extended union representation into new sectors of the region's economy. In 1970, municipal social workers and professionals established AFSCME District Council 47, which under the leadership of Thomas Paine Cronin became one of the most progressive unions in the city. Philadelphia's low-paid and mostly Black and Puerto Rican hospital workers also won collective bargaining rights. Over a five-year period, Henry Nicholas, who hailed from a sharecropping family in Mississippi, signed up ten thousand into the National Union of Hospital and Health Care Employees 1199c. Under his direction, 1199c proved a major force in establishing better work conditions for health-care workers across the region.

Divisions over the Vietnam War, the civil rights movement, and other cultural shifts also impacted the city's labor movement. Toohey, who backed the foreign policy of Lyndon B. Johnson, called Philadelphian antiwar protesters in 1965 a "national disgrace" and blamed communist infiltrators. By the early 1970s, the AFL-CIO had a liberal wing—led by Nicholas, Norman Laudenslager of the International Association of Machinists, and Retail Clerks International Union chief Wendell W. Young III—that often opposed a more conservative block led by Toohey and based in the city's building trades and trucking unions. Mayor Frank L. Rizzo, with his hostility to Black civil rights, proved a lightning rod. Conservatives enthusiastically supported Rizzo's election bids in 1971 and 1975, but labor's liberal wing joined efforts to recall the mayor in 1976 and later successfully campaigned against Rizzo's bid to revise the city charter to allow him to run for a third term.

By the end of the 1970s, as deindustrialization gathered pace across the region, the strength of Philadelphia's AFL-CIO diminished. The city lost more than one hundred thousand industrial jobs in a ten-year period, a trend paralleled in nearby industrial centers like Camden, resulting in huge membership drops. In response to this economic rollback, Philadelphia unions put forward tangible proposals. An AFL-CIO plan in 1982 specifying that companies with more than fifty employees provide a sixty-day period of notice before shutting down passed Philadelphia City Council, the first municipal measure of its kind in the nation. This provision became the foundation of the federal Worker Adjustment and Retraining Notification Act, which passed Congress in 1988. But traditional forms of action continued too, especially in sectors where jobs could not be outsourced. Teachers waged several major strikes, including a thirty-eight-day walkout in 1973 and another in 1981 that lasted fifty. In the late 1980s, however, increasing numbers of union members saw the septuagenarian Toohey as an ineffective voice for the movement. In 1992, Joseph Rauscher, president of the Bakery, Confectionery, and Tobacco Workers Local 6, replaced him as Philadelphia Council AFL-CIO president. After a brief period, Patrick J. Eiding of the Asbestos Workers Local 14 then assumed the title, which he would retain until his retirement in 2022. Into the new century, the AFL-CIO flexed its political muscle, its endorsements often determining who gained access to local political office.

Leaders from the Philadelphia region often played a significant role in the national labor movement. Gerald W. McEntee, elected president of AFSCME in 1981, pushed the national AFL-CIO to organize the service sector, a segment of the economy with a high proportion of Black and immigrant workers. McEntee's efforts paved the way for the election of John Sweeney of the Service Employees International Union (SEIU) as president of the confederation in 1995. Andy Stern, hailing from West Orange, New Jersey, won election as SEIU president in 1996. In 2005, he broke with the AFL-CIO to establish a new national union coalition, Change to Win Federation, which united nearly six million members from seven major unions.

Elements of the AFL-CIO, meanwhile, took a stand in international struggles. Henry Nicholas and Thomas Paine Cronin campaigned against apartheid, with the latter arrested for his protests outside the South African embassy in Washington, D.C., in 1985. Some Philadelphia trade unionists protested U.S. intervention in Central America during the administration of President Ronald Reagan. And as the Eastern bloc teetered on the brink of collapse in 1989, the anti-communist Toohey welcomed the Polish trade unionist and Solidarity leader Lech Walesa to the union hall at Fourth and Market Streets, where he made him an honorary delegate of the Philadelphia Council AFL-CIO. Veteran labor organizers also allied with new movements like United Students Against Sweatshops to fight for better working conditions in parts of the developing world that were now making the garments once sewn in Philadelphia.

In 2020, Ryan Boyer secured the presidency of the Philadelphia Building and Construction Trades Council, the first African American to hold that post. Boyer committed a new generation of labor officials to supporting proposed federal green infrastructure programs and opening apprenticeships that encouraged greater access to non-whites and women in the building trades. In 2022, Danny Bauder took over as Philadelphia Council AFL-CIO president as a series of organizing drives brought previously nonunionized coffeehouse baristas, employees in cultural institutions such as the Philadelphia Museum of Art, and physician interns at the University of Pennsylvania Hospital system into the union fold. And a year later employees at Rutgers–Camden joined the first strike in the history of Rutgers, which concluded after five days with significant gains for insecure faculty. These developments reflected the continuing cycles of advancement and setbacks that have characterized the U.S. labor movement and its Philadelphia chapters for over two hundred years.

## Aeronautics and Aerospace Industry

**Hillary S. Kativa**

From the aeronauts of the early republic to the jets, missiles, and rockets of the Cold War era, the growth and development of the aeronautical and aerospace industry in the Philadelphia region has exemplified a gradual shift from amateur pursuits to a more formalized industry and infrastructure. Across several centuries, the city and surrounding suburbs emerged as a hub of experimentation and innovation driven by the interests of prominent Philadelphians, by a favorable geographic locale, and by increasing interaction between industry and government, particularly in the latter half of the twentieth century.

Beginning in the eighteenth century, early explorations in flight primarily followed two distinct avenues: hot-air balloons developed by brothers Joseph-Michel and Jacques-Étienne Montgolfier in Paris and hydrogen-inflated balloons tested by the Montgolfiers' contemporary and fellow Frenchman Jacques Alexander Caesar Charles. Serving as ambassador to France from 1778 to 1785, Benjamin Franklin witnessed and reported on such experiments to associates and friends in Philadelphia, stoking American interest in aeronautical flight.

As Philadelphia, then serving as the national capital, emerged as a focal point for ballooning in the new republic, early aeronautical endeavors in the city had mixed success. On May 10, 1784, Dr. John Foulke successfully recorded the first balloon flight in America, a small, unmanned paper test balloon released from the courtyard of the Dutch minister's residence. Following Foulke's demonstration, Maryland innkeeper and lawyer Peter Carnes's ascension in a tethered hot-air balloon at the city prison yard on July 17, 1784, failed spectacularly when a gust of wind knocked Carnes from the balloon before it caught fire and fell to earth. Nine years later, citizens paid two to five dollars per ticket to witness the European balloonist Jean-Pierre Blanchard's ascent from the Walnut Street Prison yard at Sixth and Walnut Streets, a spectacle sponsored and attended by President George Washington.

While public enthusiasm for ballooning waxed and waned throughout the nineteenth century, early aeronautics nonetheless fostered a public receptiveness to flying that increased as inventors turned their attentions to the problem of heavier-than-air flight. At the dawn of the twentieth century, interest in fixed-wing aircraft and other flying machines drew together a mix of scientists, engineers, part-time researchers, and enthusiasts to form a growing aeronautical community in the Philadelphia region. Notable among these individuals was George A. Spratt, a medical student from Coatesville, Chester County, Pennsylvania, who channeled his scientific training into the study of aerodynamics and participated in the Wright brothers' gliding experiments at Kitty Hawk, North Carolina, in the summer of 1901. Following the Wright brothers' success in 1903, airplanes, like balloons a century earlier, gripped the public imagination and developed initially as a form of entertainment. Between 1908 and 1915, the Point Breeze racetrack and the Philadelphia Navy Yard at League Island became popular destinations for exhibition flights and air meets sponsored by the Aero Club of Pennsylvania, which formed in December 1909 from the merger of the Aero Club of Philadelphia and the Philadelphia Aviation Society. In addition to exhibition flights, races between airplanes were also a popular attraction; locally, department store chain Gimbel Brothers (Gimbels) sponsored a 1911 contest from New York to Philadelphia that concluded at Belmont Plateau in Fairmount Park.

While the Aero Club of Pennsylvania, as well as aero clubs at local colleges and universities including the University of Pennsylvania, Haverford, and Swarthmore, brought a degree of organization to amateur aviation, American involvement in World War I served as a catalyst for the emergence of a true aeronautical industry in Philadelphia and the nation. New government-owned and operated facilities like the Naval Air Station Lakehurst (New Jersey) and the Naval Aircraft Factory at the Philadelphia Navy Yard built planes and engines. Established in 1917, the Naval Aircraft Factory quickly became a critical hub for the manufacture of flying boats, seaplanes, motors, and other accessories; by war's end, the facility employed more than 3,600 workers. The region's contributions to the war effort also included the manufacture of component parts by Philadelphia-based firms like G.E.M. Manufacturing, which specialized in aerial cameras, and the J.G. Brill Company, which produced rough cylinder motor liners at its trolley and rail car plant at Sixty-Second and Woodland Avenue, as well as the training of aviators and support personnel at the Essington aviation station located on the former site of the Lazaretto quarantine station.

Following the war, the symbiotic relationship between government and the nascent aviation industry remained critical, as military needs continued to influence industrial production and priorities, particularly in Philadelphia. Most significantly, the Naval Aircraft Factory scaled back its workforce to approximately 1,200 workers and, throughout the 1920s, shifted focus from the production of aircraft to research and development of experimental designs. Initially, private industry followed suit and increasingly focused on the engineering and testing of materials and component parts until federal legislation expanding airmail service contracts for private carriers spurred demand for new and more efficient aircraft. Among others, aviation enthusiast Harold F. Pitcairn capitalized on the 1925 Kelly Air Mail Act to establish a manufacturing facility for light utility aircraft at his Bryn Athyn airfield under the auspices of Pitcairn Aviation, the passenger service and flying school based in Willow Grove. Renewed demand for military and civil aircraft similarly spurred companies like the Huff-Daland Aero Corporation of Ogdensburg, New York, to establish a new headquarters and production plant along the Delaware River in Bristol, Bucks County.

Aircraft manufacturing and airfield construction contracted sharply during the Great Depression, as companies once again redirected their focus from aircraft manufacturing to component parts. Amid this shift, the Edward G. Budd Manufacturing Company of Philadelphia distinguished itself for its innovative use of stainless steel and a pioneering shot-welding fabrication process used to produce aircraft materials that were stronger and more resistant to corrosion. Similarly, the production of engines, rotary wings, and propellers by companies like Fleetwings Inc. of Bristol and Jacobs Aircraft Engine Company of Pottstown helped to sustain the local aviation industry until demand for new aircraft rebounded in the lead-up to World War II. As the nation mobilized for war, the Naval Aircraft Factory once again stepped up production to meet rising demand and expanded into a wealth of experimental, highly classified projects on pilotless aircraft and guided weapons systems. The shift toward research and development continued in 1943, when the Naval Aircraft Factory was renamed the Naval Air Material Center and the facility's primary duties divided into two units: the Naval Aircraft Modification Unit, which focused on the conversion of service aircraft and special weapons work, and the Naval Air Experimental Station, which conducted laboratory and materials testing. Technological research and innovation similarly dominated wartime work at the Philadelphia-based Steam Division of the Westinghouse Electric Corporation, which engineered and produced the first operational American turbojet for the U.S. Navy in March 1943.

Across the state of Pennsylvania, employment in the aircraft, engines, and parts industries peaked at approximately forty-five thousand workers in July 1944; from there, employment and production statistics steadily declined into the postwar period, as industries struggled with the effects of demobilization and a market oversaturated with readily available used aircraft. In response, the Naval Air Material Center doubled down on the research and development of specialty parts and materials, including advanced catapult systems, rocket-powered ejection seats, and improved arresting gear. Similarly, in 1947, the navy's aircraft plant in Johnsville (Warminster), Bucks County, was converted into the Naval Air Development Station and embarked upon research in aviation electronics, medicine, and unmanned aircraft. Over the next decade, the two facilities evolved further, increasingly focusing on missile and spacecraft technologies.

Throughout the 1950s and 1960s, a number of private corporations across the region joined in these endeavors, including the Boeing Vertol facility in Ridley Park, which specialized in helicopter and rotary-wing aircraft; the Radio Corporation of America (RCA) facility in Camden, New Jersey, which developed guided missile and checkout equipment; and General Electric's Missile and Space Vehicle Department based in Philadelphia, which in 1957 received the company's first air force contract to develop a reentry vehicle for intermediate-range ballistic missiles. In April 1960, General Electric broke ground on a new Space Technology Center in Valley Forge, which became the hub for the company's Space Division and its work on a range of missile and satellite projects for the remainder of the 1960s and into the 1970s. Despite the growth of private industry in the postwar period, the aerospace industry in Philadelphia arguably reached its apex in Johnsville, which in 1959 became headquarters of the Naval Air Research and Development Activities Command. In this capacity, the facility oversaw the Naval Air Engineering Center's work on pressure suits used by Project Mercury astronauts, as well as jet and rocket engine research and centrifuge testing to measure the effects of G-force on humans. Several Gemini and Apollo program personnel and astronauts, including John Glenn and Neil Armstrong, trained at the facility, as well as a number of X-15 space plane pilots.

True to the aerospace industry's increasing dependence on government contracts and projects, cuts in military spending and the consolidation of facilities toward the end of the Cold War hastened the industry's decline in the Philadelphia region in the 1980s and 1990s. In 1986, General Electric acquired the RCA Corporation and subsequently sold its entire aerospace division, including the Camden facility, to the Maryland-based Martin Marietta Corporation (later renamed Lockheed Martin) in April 1993. Similarly, the Naval Air Research and Development Activities Command in Johnsville closed in 1996 and many of its buildings were subsequently demolished in 2001, a symbolic end to the long history of the aeronautical and aerospace industry in the Philadelphia region.

## Carpet Weaving and Rug Making

**Philip Scranton**

In its early twentieth-century heyday, Philadelphia's carpet and rug industry represented this nation's greatest concentration of factories making household and commercial floor coverings. The *Public Ledger* boasted that "two wards, in the northern section of the city, produce more carpets than the whole of Great Britain and Ireland." Indeed, as early as 1882, those Kensington wards (the Nineteenth and the Thirty-First) held 141 carpet firms, valued at $12 million and employing over six thousand workers. Lorin Blodget, the nineteenth-century industrial statistician, estimated that around ninety additional carpet and rug works operated elsewhere in the region. Altogether, the sector's workforce ran more than 4,000 hand looms and 1,200 power looms in 1880, using an estimated thirty million pounds of raw wool to create some thirty-three million yards of output yearly, selling for just over $21 million.

A century earlier, at the time of the Revolution, Philadelphia already was producing virtually all the carpets and floor cloths made in Pennsylvania. The carpets were mostly narrow, woven hall runners, whereas large floor cloths were created by oiling or waxing heavy canvas (like sailcloth, also a local textile), then painting bright, geometric designs on the smooth surface. Both were handmade. A third variety, chain braided rugs, were the result of recycling rags, which women workers cut into strips and sewed into long, multicolor ropes, the foundation for rectangular, oval, and circular rag rugs. All three varieties persisted as main elements in Philadelphia industries. Floor cloths became linoleum flooring, following a British invention of the 1850s. Narrow runners became "broadloom" carpeting, woven from tough wools on looms six and nine feet wide, and rag rugs held sway at the bottom edge of the market, without technological innovations, well into the 1920s.

When Edwin Freedley surveyed Philadelphia manufacturing in 1857, he reported some two thousand carpet looms in operation (five hundred on rag rugs), almost all for hand weaving. Only Andrew McCallum and Company's Glen Echo Mills in Germantown operated power looms. The area's two thousand hand weavers each earned an estimated $300 per year in the late 1850s. Small wonder that one textile industry observer dubbed Philadelphia "the paradise of the skilled workman."

Troubles visited paradise, however, not least during economic downturns. As household goods, carpets and rugs were far from being necessity purchases when budgets tightened. Thus sales collapsed when the national economy crashed, as it did in and after the Panic of 1873. Kensington carpet mills allied to announce rate cuts, but workers struck in response, setting off a decade of conflict and a decided effort by the larger firms to install power looms and hire "more docile" women weavers.

Handlooms remained effective in fine carpet weaving through the 1880s partly due to the difficulty of speedily producing complex designs, especially those generated through use of a Jacquard mechanism. The "Jacquard chain" was a sequence of punched cards, each of which represented one line's setting for weaving an elaborate pattern. Moving the chain rapidly, as a power loom would, risked weaving errors, so the hand weaver's close attention to the process long remained essential. Reportedly, Charles Babbage transferred the punched-card idea from weaving to computing in 1839, having marveled at a silk portrait of Jacquard, produced by a twenty-four thousand–card set.

The 1880s' erratic markets and owner-worker battles proved disastrous for small firms, especially hand-weaving ones, in carpets and rugs. Though roughly the same workforce occupied mill places in 1893 as in 1880 (about 11,000 regionwide), the number of firms dropped by two-thirds, from about three hundred to ninety-nine. Whereas nearly 14,000 textile jobs could be found in Philadelphia's suburban counties, about 1893 fewer than 5 percent of these (690) lay in the carpet trades. Then and thereafter, carpet weaving was a city business.

The most important carpet mills outside Kensington were those of James and John Dobson, English immigrant brothers whose massive factory complex at the Falls of Schuylkill employed thousands in a set of "integrated" mills. Unusual for Philadelphia, the Dobsons spun and dyed their own yarns, then used them to weave blankets, worsted woolens, mohair plushes (for upholstery), and a broad array of carpetings. When the factory complex burned spectacularly in January 1892, some 4,800 workers faced instant unemployment. Eight mills were lost, but the plush factory remained, anchoring a thousand jobs. Still over half the Dobson workers, chiefly women, had to seek temporary positions in Germantown or Manayunk until the mills reopened, one by one, during the summer. Six years later, as the effects of the mid-1890s depression wore off, Pennsylvania's factory inspector counted over 4,500 workers in the Dobsons' four "departments," half of them (2,245) running carpets. This force included 1,110 adult men, 720 adult women, and 425 workers under twenty-one, of whom 135 were sixteen or younger. Unlike largely feminized cotton weaving, carpets relied on thousands of skilled male workers, even in the power-loom era.

Such men readily (and repeatedly) organized trade unions to advance their wage scales (different piece rates for varied types of carpets) and in hard times defend them. Owners, allied in the carpet "sections" of the Textile Manufacturers Association, worked relentlessly to protect their profits and privileges in the early twentieth century. But a more potent threat than walkouts gathered by the World War I era: carpet mill mergers and brand name promotions that gradually turned the market tide against Philadelphia's high-end, but largely unbranded goods. With New England's Bigelow-Hartford Carpet Mills and New York's Alexander Smith Carpet Mills leading emergent price wars in the 1920s, Philadelphia mills ran full only in busy markets and were the first to feel the slack of downturns. When Bigelow hatched another carpet merger in 1929, not one Philadelphia-area company was invited to join the new enterprise. Indeed, as branding became central to selling, only Hardwick and Magee, among the city's leading companies, was able to establish national visibility.

The Great Depression greased the downward slope. Of 9,500 carpet workers active in 1925, just 4,000 remained at work in 1934. During World War II, carpets were anything but necessities. Mills either closed or turned to making blankets, tarpaulins, and other military fabrics. The postwar advance of a new technology, weft-inserted tufted carpeting, usually inexpensive in solid colors, expressed a 1950s modernism in home decoration that devalued the elaborate designs, the complex machinery, and the skilled workforce that long made Philadelphia the apex of the American carpet manufacture. The last survivor, Kensington's Pennsylvania Woven Carpets, continued to produce woolen specialties well past the turn of the twenty-first century, a fading echo of a memorable era.

## Chemical Industry

**John Kenly Smith Jr.**

Since the eighteenth century, chemical or chemical processing industries have been an important part of the economy of Philadelphia and the Delaware Valley region and have reflected larger trends in the industry. The earliest chemical companies manufactured products such as sulfuric acid and white lead pigments for local consumption, while other manufacturers, such as tanners, brewers, and soap makers, also employed chemicals and chemical processing. During the nineteenth century, new industries, such as textiles, required many different types of chemicals, including dyes, soaps, and bleaches. Pharmaceutical production also became important. World War I led to the rapid expansion of local chemical production. Following the war, the American chemical industry thrived by developing many new products, especially synthetic materials. After 1980, however, industry innovation declined, growth rates slowed, and competition increased, leading the region's largest chemical manufacturers to be consolidated on a national level.

In Philadelphia, John Harrison built the first chemical plant in the United States in 1793. His plant on Green Street, west of Third, produced sulfuric acid using a lead-chamber process, originally developed in Europe. Sulphuric acid was the first chemical produced on an industrial scale, leading to its widespread use. In 1802, the French immigrant family led by Éleuthère Irénée Du Pont founded the DuPont Company, which manufactured gunpowder, a mixture of charcoal, sulfur, and saltpeter, on the Brandywine River a few miles northwest of Wilmington, Delaware.

The regional chemical industry grew along with the local economy. By the start of the War of 1812, Philadelphia had twenty-eight soap and candle works, eighteen distilleries, fourteen glue factories, ten sugar refineries, seven paper mills, and six drug-making concerns. By 1830 Charles Lennig operated the largest sulfuric acid plant in America, located in Bridesburg. He diversified into other chemicals, and by 1859 his plant was one of the most important chemical operations in the United States. During the Civil War, the DuPont Company prospered by selling gunpowder to the Union. Later, the company diversified into dynamite and military smokeless powder. DuPont was one of 105 local chemical manufacturers to mount exhibits at the 1876 Centennial Exhibition in Philadelphia.

In the twentieth century, the DuPont Company and Rohm and Haas emerged as the two most important chemical enterprises in the Philadelphia area. Rohm and Haas became a Philadelphia company in 1909 when Dr. Otto Haas arrived to sell a leather-tanning chemical, Oropon, which had been developed by his partner Otto Rohm in Germany. After World War I, Rohm and Haas began making chemicals for Philadelphia's leather and textile industries. In 1920, it acquired the Charles Lennig & Company. In the 1930s, company researchers developed a lightweight clear acrylic polymer that was trademarked Plexiglas. Plexiglas was widely used for windows in airplanes during World War II. After the war the company continued to develop important products from acrylic polymers, such as water-based paints. In the postwar decades, Rohm and Haas became a large and profitable manufacturer of specialty chemicals.

By 1912, DuPont had grown so large that the U.S. government had filed an antitrust suit, which forced the company to spin off parts of its explosives business. DuPont's assets nevertheless grew tremendously during World War I, when the company supplied the Allies and the United States with explosives. DuPont used its newfound wealth to diversify into chemical manufacture, principally by buying other firms, such as the venerable

**FIGURE 67.** Advertisement for H.P. and W.C. Taylor, 1851. The international ambitions of the Philadelphia perfumers are evident in the steamship on the Delaware and the boast of recognition at that year's world's fair, the Great Exhibition in London. LIBRARY OF CONGRESS.

the war, DuPont began a major research initiative to manufacture the dyes that the Germans had supplied before the war. To make dyes, the company built a large plant on the Delaware River at Deepwater Point, New Jersey (just north of the Delaware Memorial Bridge).

After the war DuPont continued to diversify into rayon fibers, cellophane films, and plastics. Having been one of the first American companies to establish research laboratories (early in the twentieth century), DuPont called upon its chemists to improve these 1930s researchers began a decades-long investigation of polymers (long-chain) molecules that produced, among many iconic products, neoprene synthetic rubber, nylon, Teflon polymers, Lycra spandex, Tyvek spun-bonded fabric, and Kevlar fibers. A prospering DuPont employed tens of thousands of Delaware Valley residents in several local plants.

Beginning in the 1980s, the chemical industry generally began to experience a decline in innovation, slowing growth, and shrinking profits. Rohm and

Haas's performance, following these trends, deteriorated significantly, and it was acquired in 2008 by the Michigan-based Dow Chemical Company. DuPont survived by shifting its focus to pesticides and seeds. However, competition in this field led the company to merge with Dow Chemical, its longtime competitor, in 2015. By the early decades of the twenty-first century, the chemical industry had been radically reorganized through numerous mergers and acquisitions.

Chemical production began in Philadelphia in the late eighteenth century to serve nearby manufacturers in what soon would become one of America's major industrial cities. By the middle of the nineteenth century, Delaware Valley companies, notably DuPont, were taking advantage of railroad transportation to serve larger markets. In the twentieth century, the regional chemical industry served national and international markets, expanding to become a significant contributor to the local economy. Since 1990, however, the chemical industry globally matured, leading to a decline of its importance locally.

## Food Processing

**Daniel Sidorick**

The food industry has always held a special place in Greater Philadelphia, though the region never became a center of a massive industry like meatpacking in Chicago. Still, the methods of processing food at different periods and the people who did the work tell much about the state of Philadelphia's economy and its residents. From colonial times, when most Americans processed their own foods, through the rapid changes in food manufacture introduced by the Industrial Revolution, to the consolidation and globalization of the food industry in the late twentieth century, the ways agricultural produce has been transformed into food and consumed at Philadelphians' dinner tables has defined both the changing economic structure of the region and its level of integration within the larger world.

The Indigenous and early colonial residents of the Delaware Valley were largely self-sufficient. The minimal processing needed to make bread or to preserve meat was done mostly at home or on the farm. Yet the inklings of the future food industry were visible in the trades marching in the Philadelphia Grand Federal Procession in 1788 celebrating the new Constitution: bakers, butchers, sugar refiners, and brewers joined their fellow predecessors of the coming Industrial Revolution in the line of march. And even in this early period, food processing brought the region into the global economy. Hogs driven to Philadelphia for slaughter and grain transported to the city for milling ended up not only in market stalls on High Street (later Market Street) but also as provisions traded for Caribbean sugar destined for the city's refiners.

Philadelphia's propitious location amid the rich agricultural lands of southeastern Pennsylvania and southern New Jersey made it the natural location for the artisans and merchants who would establish a wide array of food-processing businesses. Yet until the mid-nineteenth century only flour milling, brewing, and sugar refining had established enterprises beyond the size of small artisanal shops. Philadelphia, in fact, became the center of the new country's largest food industry, dominating flour milling in the late eighteenth century through the first third of the following century and exporting some four hundred thousand barrels of flour (and a smaller quantity of cornmeal) per year. The city also housed many sugar refineries from the late eighteenth to the late twentieth century.

Although leadership in flour milling fell first to Baltimore and then the Midwest, Philadelphia, Camden, and nearby towns soon saw phenomenal growth in an amazing range of food-related industries: canning; the baking of bread, biscuits, and soft pretzels; candy making; meat processing; the production of ice cream, mustard, and vinegar; and much more. Most new companies were of the type Philadelphia was best known for, small to medium sized and family owned, often operating in the production of specialty items. But some of them grew to become national or world leaders in the mass production of food products and obtained financing from sources of capital beyond the wealth of their founding families.

Spurred by the demands of war and growing urban populations, food industry expansion nationally outpaced manufacturing as a whole in the late nineteenth century, and, in Philadelphia, food processing became the city's second-largest industry (after textiles) by 1910. Urbanization separated more and more people from the farms that produced their food, and the new advertising industry, as well as the promise of lightened housework, helped convince Philadelphia housewives (and others) that they needed factory-made canned soup and mass-produced sliced bread. Fears of contamination that led to governmental regulation also provided advertisers with arguments for why consumers should buy brand-name (and government-inspected) ice cream and cellophane-wrapped chocolates. Philadelphia's many ethnic groups expanded the range of food-processing methods and markets even further. Meat processing, for example, took the form of a first-floor kosher butcher shop in West Philadelphia, an Italian basement butchery in South Philadelphia, and a Polish smokehouse in Port Richmond.

Canning, more than any other food-processing sector, brought the Industrial Revolution to the cities, towns, and hamlets of the Delaware Valley in the second half of the nineteenth century. In virtually every town in the lush agricultural region surrounding Philadelphia, tinsmiths built canneries, partnered with farmers and merchants, and sold their products along the trade

**FIGURE 68.** Campbell's soup cans, 1980. As new immigration and travel broadened American tastes, Camden's Campbell Soup Company launched a range of Asian-influenced products. SPECIAL COLLECTIONS RESEARCH CENTER, TEMPLE UNIVERSITY LIBRARIES.

**FIGURE 69.** Antique Tastykake truck, 1979. Founded in 1914, the Tasty Baking Company soon became a popular bakery in the Philadelphia region. In 1959, Black civil rights campaigners, led by the Rev. Leon Sullivan, launched a consumer boycott of the company's products. Their "selective patronage" pushed Tasty Baking to open better paid roles to Black workers. SPECIAL COLLECTIONS RESEARCH CENTER, TEMPLE UNIVERSITY LIBRARIES.

routes stretching west along the railways. When the steamboat *Bertrand* sank in the Missouri River in 1865, it carried to the bottom peaches and cranberry sauce from canneries in Philadelphia and southern New Jersey (as well as rival Baltimore).

Most canneries remained fairly small, but several grew into sizable establishments, employing hundreds or even thousands of workers, typically doubling in size during harvest season. Philip J. Ritter first tried his hand at confectionery but had more success when he began selling his wife's preserves in 1854. When operations outgrew the family's Kensington home twenty years later, he opened a factory on Dauphin Street. By 1894 his cannery employed 150 workers year-round and 300 at peak season. To get even closer to its raw materials, especially tomatoes for its award-winning Ritter Catsup, the company opened a plant across the river in Bridgeton, New Jersey. An even more famous product, Campbell Soup, rolled off the lines of that company's mammoth plant in Camden.

Eating new items like canned soup was something Philadelphians were learning to do, but bread and other baked goods had been part of their diet from colonial days. Yet even with the onset of the Industrial Revolution, most people in the city and surrounding towns continued baking bread at home or purchasing it from the hundreds of small neighborhood bakeries. The first attempt at building a large, mechanized bread bakery at Broad and Vine Streets in 1857 ended in failure three years later. But by the end of the nineteenth century a number of local bakeries and branches of national bread makers had implemented modern production and distribution methods, and brands like Freihofer's and Stroehmann became household names.

One of the main obstacles to commercial production of bread was overcome by Charles Fleishmann's invention of consistent packaged yeast in 1868 in Cincinnati. His "Vienna Model Bakery" became one of the highlights of the Philadelphia Centennial Exposition in 1876. Other bakers quickly adopted the use of commercial yeast, and store-bought brand-name bread spread rapidly. Philadelphia baker Charles Freihofer continued the Vienna theme when he teamed with his brother to open the Freihofer Vienna Baking Company in Camden in 1899 and a similarly named company at Twenty-Fourth and Master Streets in North Philadelphia a year later. Rapid growth in the business led to a move to Twentieth and Indiana Streets in 1913 and expansion to several other cities. Freihofer's and competitors' home-delivery vans, originally horse drawn, became a fixture in Philadelphia's neighborhoods as many smaller bakeries closed their doors.

Entrepreneurs Philip Bauer and Herbert Morris conceived the idea of mass producing and marketing small "sanitary wrapped" cakes and opened a plant on Sedgley Avenue in 1914. Their Tasty Baking Company was so successful that "Tasty Kakes" became a Philadelphia icon. By 1922 they moved to a much larger facility on Hunting Park Avenue. Other Philadelphia traditions remained the province of smaller establishments. Small soft pretzel bakeries were found in almost every neighborhood, though some, such as Federal Pretzel Baking Company in South Philadelphia, introduced limited mass-production techniques to increase their output. Similarly, the rolls used for Philadelphia's cheesesteak sandwiches and hoagies came from a variety of bakers. But the Amoroso family enterprise, originally just another small bakery in Camden in 1904, repeatedly outgrew its facilities until it was able to produce enough rolls to meet regionwide demand in a large plant on S. Fifty-Fifth Street in Southwest Philadelphia.

Although large-scale production of breads and cakes got off to a slow start in Philadelphia, the manufacture of biscuits and crackers was well established by the Civil War, when "hardtack," a hard, usually saltless biscuit, was widely used for military rations. Godfrey Keebler had worked in a number of bakeries by the onset of the war and in 1862 opened a bakery in South Philadelphia. His success from supplying the Union army as well as the Philadelphia market led to expansion to a mechanized facility at 258–264 N. Twenty-Second Street and later, after a merger that formed the Keebler-Weyl Baking Company, to a large plant at G Street and E. Hunting Park Avenue. The National Biscuit Company conglomerate (formed in 1898) also opened operations in Philadelphia at Broad Street and Glenwood Avenue and later near the Roosevelt Boulevard in the Far Northeast section of the city.

Philadelphia has also long been a leader in the confectionery industry. Stephen F. Whitman opened a confectionery shop on the waterfront in 1842 and introduced prepackaged candy in 1854. His company pioneered the use of cellophane in its famous Whitman's Sampler (1912) and moved several times, eventually to Fourth and Race Streets. It relocated once again, in 1960, to a new industrial park in the Far Northeast, where it employed 1,650 workers. (Another Philadelphia candy shop, opened in 1873 by the young Milton Hershey, failed after a few years; he moved about a hundred miles west where he founded the Hershey Chocolate Company in 1894.) Among other well-known Philadelphia candy makers were Richardson Mints (1893), Asher's Candy (1892, moved to Germantown in 1899), and David Goldenberg (who started his candy store on Kensington Avenue in 1890 and created Goldenberg's Peanut Chews as a World War I ration in 1917).

Meat, poultry, and seafood processing have been small but continual parts of Philadelphia's food industry from the beginning. Excellent transportation to the West enabled meat processors to supply the needs of the large regional market. A few small- to medium-sized slaughterhouses were found in the area, such as Cross Brothers in Kensington and Triolo's in Burlington County, New Jersey. Dietz & Watson started making delicatessen meats in 1939 and expanded to other cities while maintaining a large plant in the Tacony section of the city. The nineteenth-century shad fisheries and markets of Shackamaxon even resulted in the change of that neighborhood's name to Fishtown.

Philadelphians were not only consumers of the products of the companies founded by the area's food-industry entrepreneurs; residents of working-class neighborhoods throughout the region were also the ones who did the work that turned agricultural raw or semiprocessed materials into finished products. And that work was often long, hard, and low paying, especially before employees joined together in unions to press for better pay and working conditions. Among the first recorded activities of united Philadelphia food workers was a strike for higher wages by the journeymen bakers in 1835. Some crafts in the industry were unionized over the next century, but it was only after the organizing drives of the Congress of Industrial Organizations in the 1930s that most of the area's food workers became union members—even the 1,500 confectionary workers who organized Candy Workers Local 350. Union contracts improved the lives of food workers but often only after strikes and other industrial actions. One example among many was the strike of 1,900 bakers in 1946 against eight major bakery firms including Freihofer's and Fleischmann in Philadelphia and Stroehmann Brothers in Norristown. Working-class support for unions and picket lines was impressive.

Several of the most intense clashes between workers and management in the food-processing industry occurred in South Jersey, especially at Campbell Soup in Camden and Seabrook Farms in Cumberland County. The workers at Seabrook, mostly African Americans and Italian immigrants, who were paid twelve to fifteen cents per hour, initially won a big increase in their wages when they struck in 1934, but their union was destroyed a few months later after concerted attacks by the company, police, and vigilantes.

By the early twenty-first century much of Philadelphia's food-processing industry had disappeared or been absorbed into global food megacorporations, though, just as in earlier centuries, small establishments continued to compete in various niches. There were many reasons for the decline. The rich agricultural hinterlands of the city that had supplied canneries and other food processors were no longer the source of raw materials. Although local farms still produced a smaller amount of food for the fresh market, food processors preferred cheaper mass-produced intermediate inputs like tomato paste from California and China. Beyond reasons specific to the food industry, Philadelphia's food workers suffered along with others from the increasingly aggressive cost-cutting strategies of global capitalism that ramped up in the 1970s. The lure of highly automated factories with fewer workers, remaining workers who would accept lower pay and not join unions, states and counties offering corporate tax breaks and little regulation, and repeated bouts of merger-and-acquisition mania all took their toll on Philadelphia's industries, including its food processors.

Freihofer's and Stroehmann breads (along with Arnold, Entenmann's, and others) had been absorbed into the largest bakery corporation in the United States, Bimbo Bakeries, a unit of Mexico's Grupo Bimbo. Area residents might have taken some comfort from the fact that Bimbo's American headquarters remained in Horsham in Montgomery County. Tasty Baking Company closed its Nicetown plant and moved to a new taxpayer-subsidized facility at the former Navy Yard in 2010. Because the new plant was highly automated, hundreds of employees were laid off. Yet the company avoided bankruptcy only by becoming part of Georgia-based Flowers Foods (a Bimbo competitor). After Whitman's Chocolates' much-heralded move to the new Philadelphia Industrial Park in 1960, it was sold to Pet Inc. When Pet later sold the brand to Russell Stover Candies in 1993, it closed the Philadelphia plant. One of the city's oldest industries—sugar refining—ended with the closing of the National Sugar refinery (Jack Frost sugar) in Fishtown in 1981 and the Amstar (formerly Franklin) refinery (Domino sugar) in South Philadelphia a year later.

Still, food-processing companies large and small remained in the area in the twenty-first century. Cross Brothers was gone, but four hundred workers at Dietz & Watson continued curing meat in Tacony, and the Czerw family still smoked kielbasa in its Port Richmond smokehouse. Keebler's factory in Juniata was closed long ago (and the company itself had been absorbed into Kellogg's), but seven hundred workers still made cookies and crackers at the Nabisco plant in Northeast Philadelphia, though it had changed ownership by then to Kraft Foods. Federal Pretzel Baking Company was sold to snack food giant J&J Snack Foods Corporation across the river in Pennsauken in 2000, but Philadelphia Soft Pretzels continued hand-twisting pretzels at its Feltonville bakery, though by then it was competing with dozens of new franchised pretzel makers; it eventually fell victim to the COVID-19 pandemic in 2022.

The Philadelphia food-processing industry had fallen far from its important position of the early twentieth century. Most large mass-production facilities had taken the same route as the region's other large manufacturers and moved to newer and cheaper locations in the globalized food economy. Some foods that had short shelf life or were difficult to transport were still made in plants in or near large cities, including Philadelphia. A few independent companies with strong local ties still employed hundreds in the area, and the growing ranks of "foodies" and newer immigrant groups provided opportunities for numerous niche producers of specialty and ethnic foods. These, along with a handful of national and global corporate headquarters of food companies like Campbell and Bimbo, marked the latest stage in the history of food processing in Philadelphia.

## Garment Industry

**Christina Larocco**

Garment work was once one of Philadelphia's largest industries. Clothing and textiles (a category including hosiery, a Philadelphia specialty) employed more than 40 percent of the city's paid workforce by 1880. Starting in the first third of the nineteenth century, the garment industry became a center of labor activism, experiencing periodic strikes and union organizing drives until it began to decline in the mid-twentieth century. Although the structure of Philadelphia's garment industry, which consisted mostly of small shops financed largely by cash on hand, provided flexibility, a reluctance to use credit also meant that deindustrialization hit the city's garment industry harder than the same sector elsewhere in the nation.

Before the Civil War, women working for their families or as seamstresses and journeymen tailors working under master artisans made Philadelphia's clothing. Though work as a journeyman could be a route to self-employment, master artisans' reluctance to increase wages or heed labor agreements often led to conflict. In 1806, a group of journeymen tailors formed a protective association, the Tailors' Benevolent Society, and convinced their employers to agree to standardized prices and a closed shop.

Despite this agreement, five journeymen at Robb and Winebrener (Third and Chestnut Streets) discovered later that year that they had been paid less than the agreed-upon prices for women's riding outfits. When they argued with their employer, they were fired. Over the course of the next week, fourteen other journeymen in the shop walked out over the firings. Strikers surrounded the shop, discouraging potential replacement employees from breaking the strike. The Commonwealth of Pennsylvania took the men to court on the owners' behalf, accusing them of conspiring to get unfairly high wages and of attacking strikebreakers. The court, however, largely sided with the journeymen. Members of the Tailors' Benevolent Society won wage increases from their employers again in 1844 and 1847.

Journeymen tailors' skills gave them leverage in labor disputes. By the mid-nineteenth century, however, factory work existed alongside the artisan shop and outwork. Three factors lay behind this transition: new technology—including the foot-powered sewing machine (1846); mechanical cutting knife (1876); and steam power, adopted by most factories by the 1890s as it grew less expensive over the previous several decades—increased speed and efficiency; improvements in transportation meant more consumers had access to manufactured goods; and new waves of immigrants—first from northern and western European nations including Germany and Ireland, later from Russia and other southern and eastern European nations—many skilled in garment making, provided a ready supply of workers. In 1850, Philadelphia was home to over twenty thousand workers in clothing and textiles; by 1880, that number increased to over seventy thousand.

Such developments did not take place evenly across the nation, and the garment industry in Philadelphia developed differently from the large textile mills in Lowell, Massachusetts, or Newark or Paterson, New Jersey. Most strikingly, garment shops in Philadelphia remained small. Manufacturers were loath to take on debt to expand their operations, preferring to pay with cash on hand. The result was a decentralized industry scattered across small shops, tenement-based production, and outwork (contractors, often women and children, paid by the piece for work completed in their own homes). In both 1850 and 1900, shops tended to employ no more than twenty-five people.

The decentralized nature of Philadelphia's garment industry posed challenges. Labor organizers found it difficult to organize a scattered workforce. Employment

**FIGURE 70.** The Egyptian Hall, Wanamaker's department store, ca. 1910. Philadelphians purchased clothes produced in the region in palaces of consumption such as Strawbridge & Clothier and Wanamaker's. The latter, a lavishly decorated store at Thirteenth and Market Streets, evoked the luxury and grandeur of ancient civilizations like Rome and Egypt. LIBRARY COMPANY OF PHILADELPHIA.

could also be cyclical. Large manufacturers such as Morris Haber outsourced excess orders to smaller firms that kept workers on only when they had orders to fulfill and let them go during slack periods. Such periodic unemployment could be particularly devastating for outworkers and other contractors. This arrangement also had benefits, however: Philadelphia garment shops were more nimble and could change direction more quickly than mass-production shops elsewhere, which often kept large amounts of stock on hand. With the onset of the Civil War, for example, the government urgently needed uniforms, and Philadelphia firms were well-positioned to secure lucrative contracts to produce them.

After the Civil War, firms that had mobilized to produce uniforms found ready buyers in the new ready-to-wear market. Justus Clayton Strawbridge and Isaac Hallowell Clothier founded Strawbridge & Clothier, and John Wanamaker opened his own department store. Firms that had built up capacity during the war and grown accustomed to high levels of production were prepared to fill these retailers' bulk clothing orders. Changing fashions meant that retailers regularly placed new orders, a boon for the garment industry. In 1882, Old City alone hosted almost 1,700 clothier employees (many in outwork).

Though large corporations did not dominate the economic landscape of Gilded Age Philadelphia to the same extent as they did elsewhere, the city was not exempt from the labor strife experienced across the nation. As tensions grew among skilled workers, unskilled workers, and owners, new organizations formed to represent the interests of each. The most skilled of factory clothing workers were the garment cutters, and in 1869, Philadelphia garment cutter Uriah Stephens formed the Knights of Labor, an organization to represent the interests of all working people. After the Knights became associated with radicalism following Chicago's deadly Haymarket bombing in 1886, the United Garment Workers of America received an American Federation of Labor charter in 1891, though the union only included skilled workers. The two most important organizations representing the interests of less-skilled workers, the International Ladies' Garment Workers' Union (ILGWU) and the Amalgamated Clothing Workers of America, organized in 1900 and 1914, respectively.

Though New York City was the center of garment-worker activism, developments there could not help but affect Philadelphia workers. In late 1909, thousands of New York City garment workers—many of them young, Jewish, immigrant women from southern and eastern Europe—walked out of their jobs. The strike spread to Philadelphia after the ILGWU learned that many New York City firms were sending their work there. Strikers in both cities eventually won many of their demands. In Philadelphia these included a fifty-four-hour week, higher wages, and an end to the practice of charging for work materials. They did not, however, win a closed shop, in which employers recognize the union as sole bargaining agent for all employees.

Philadelphia garment workers demographically resembled their New York City counterparts. Jewish Philadelphians predominated in the early twentieth-century garment industry, both as factory owners and employees. Factory owners tended to be German Jewish, while their employees were largely Russian Jewish. Concentrated in South Philadelphia, garment workers often lived close to their workplaces. In 1909, 85 percent of Philadelphia shirtwaist (a woman's garment resembling a man's shirt) makers were female, and 85 percent were Jewish. A handful of Italians also worked in the garment industry. As in other industries, however, African Americans first gained access to the garment industry, including in 1909–10 and again in 1921, as strikebreakers. For this group, the expanded production of World Wars I and II brought about longer-term, though not permanent, opportunities.

In the interwar era, anti-union firms such as Philadelphia's A.B. Kirschbaum Co. tried to lure workers away from unions with corporate welfare—employer-dominated company unions and other benefits meant to encourage loyalty to the company and discourage independent organizing. Union strength continued to grow, however, and a 1933 general dress-industry strike forced Philadelphia employers to recognize the ILGWU. The labor-friendly legislation of the New Deal helped consolidate these gains, though not consistently. A 1934 Pennsylvania Department of Labor and Industry survey of garment workers in Allentown, Doylestown, Philadelphia, and Shamokin found National Recovery Act regulations laxly and sporadically enforced.

Deindustrialization affected the Philadelphia garment industry as early as the 1920s. In search of cheaper labor, employers increasingly turned to "runaway shops"—firms that relocated to areas where unions were weaker—setting up factories in parts of New Jersey, Pennsylvania (including its anthracite region), and the South. Post–World War II, the cost of adapting to synthetic production, labor militancy, and international competition hit the industry. Nationally, imports made up only 3 percent of the garment industry in 1955, but this had increased to 88 percent in 2000. Between 1947 and 1986 in Philadelphia, the garment industry alone lost ninety-one thousand jobs, 79 percent of the city's total manufacturing job losses in those years.

Philadelphia garment work bore many similarities to the industry elsewhere, especially New York City. In both places, the industry grew to employ large numbers of young, immigrant women who worked for low pay and long hours under sometimes dangerous conditions. The Philadelphia garment industry was not simply a smaller version of New York's, however. The city had its own demographic, economic, and geographic factors that influenced the shape and development of this sector. Employers were more likely to be risk averse, and employment was scattered across factories, shops, and homes. The decentralized nature of the industry gave employers flexibility but could mean insecurity for employees. Unions also had difficulty organizing such a diffuse workforce. Ultimately, however, both the large factories of other cities and Philadelphia's smaller shops and factories faced the same fate. They could not compete with overseas manufacturing, and the industry declined.

## Locomotive Manufacturing

John Hepp

For over 120 years, railway locomotives were built in greater Philadelphia. From the pioneering manufacturers of steam locomotives in the Spring Garden section of the city in the 1830s to the sprawling plant of the Baldwin Locomotive Works in Delaware County in the twentieth century, the products, the companies, and the buildings were archetypes of Philadelphia's industrial might at its manufacturing peak. Baldwin Locomotive became the largest producer of steam railway locomotives in the United States. By the mid-twentieth century, however, even Baldwin could no longer compete in the world market, which had shifted to diesel and electric locomotives.

The rise, dominance, and decline of locomotive manufacturing in the region had two complementary contexts, one local, the other transnational. In the late 1820s American railroads imported steam locomotives from Britain and, because the locomotives had to be partially disassembled for shipping, employed local artisans to put them back together. Because these imported locomotives were expensive and often too heavy and rigid for the poorly constructed track used in the United States, engineering firms on the East Coast quickly began to build local alternatives. In Philadelphia, entrepreneurs drew on the city's broad engineering base and its skilled workforce to adapt the British technology.

This first phase of locomotive building in Philadelphia lasted from the 1830s to the American Civil War and consisted of a variety of small-scale enterprises that tended to have difficulty surviving economic downturns, such as the Panic of 1837. In 1830, the American Steam Carriage Company was founded in Philadelphia and manufactured its first locomotive the next year. It failed. In 1831, Matthias W. Baldwin, a Philadelphia jeweler and machine maker, built a working scale model of one of these British imports for Peale's Philadelphia Museum. That same year, he reassembled the English locomotives constructed for the New-Castle and Frenchtown Turnpike and Railroad, Delaware's first railway, and learned still more about the new technology. In 1832, Long & Norris, a successor to American Steam Carriage, and Baldwin built successful locomotives for the Philadelphia, Germantown & Norristown Railroad, the first line to open in the city.

During this period the most successful builder in the city was the Norris Locomotive Works (the successor to Long & Norris). Norris produced nearly one thousand locomotives between 1834 and its closure in 1866 or 1867. The firm achieved success through engineering innovations (it substituted a movable truck or bogie for the standard fixed front axle on English locomotives, which worked better on the poor American track) and by generating publicity (on July 10, 1836, it operated

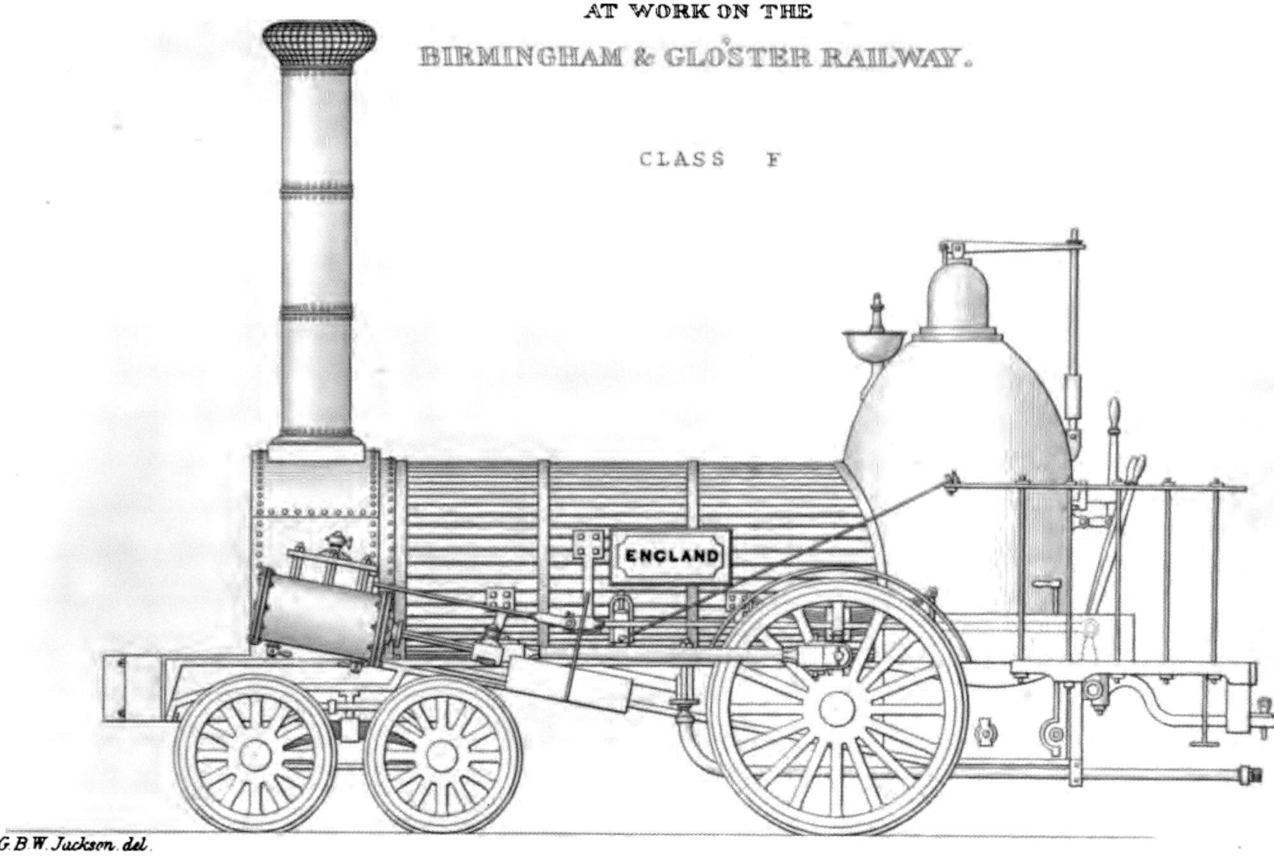


**FIGURE 71.** A Philadelphia locomotive used on the Birmingham and Gloucester railway in the United Kingdom, 1840. The Norris Locomotive Works exported to Europe and the Americas before the Civil War. From Berlin, a satisfied customer reported that its locomotives deserved "the confidence of every Rail Road company." UNIVERSITY OF MICHIGAN VIA INTERNET ARCHIVE.

a steam locomotive up the steep rope-worked inclined plane in West Philadelphia on the Philadelphia and Columbia Railroad). Its designs became so popular that it became the first American exporter of locomotives. By 1840, 30 percent of the firm's production went to foreign markets. Norris locomotives operated in England, France, Prussia, Austria, Saxony, Belgium, Italy, Canada, Cuba, and Colombia. By the 1850s, Norris was the largest locomotive builder in the United States, but it closed shortly after the Civil War during a downturn in demand for steam locomotives.

The second phase of railway locomotive production lasted from the end of the Civil War to the 1930s, a period when Philadelphia's Baldwin Locomotive Works dominated the industry nationwide. With a plant located near the Norris Locomotive Works in the city's Spring Garden section, in the 1830s, 1840s, and 1850s, Baldwin, although less innovative than Norris, produced higher-quality products. This, combined with innovations in financing, allowed Baldwin to thrive in the second half of the nineteenth century. By 1870 (four years after the death of its founder), the Baldwin Locomotive Works was by far the largest producer of steam locomotives in the United States and one of the largest manufacturers in the world. It, like Norris earlier, also exported its products worldwide. The peak of Baldwin's production in Philadelphia came between 1898 and 1906. In 1906 alone, Baldwin produced 2,666 steam locomotives and employed more than eighteen thousand workers. Although the locomotive manufacturers did not know it at the time, increased regulation, two world wars, a Great Depression, and technological change would mean that demand for steam locomotives would never again reach this high point.

In the early twentieth century, as part of the City Beautiful movement, Philadelphia and other American cities sought to relocate large-scale manufacturers like Baldwin away from central business districts and their peripheries. At the same time, Baldwin's management desired a new and enlarged plant. The company acquired a large tract of land in suburban Eddystone, Delaware County, and slowly transferred all production there, completing the move by 1928. Constructed on a grand scale, the facility at Eddystone never operated at more than one-third of its capacity.

From the 1930s through 1956, Baldwin survived as not only the sole locomotive builder in Philadelphia but also as just one of a handful nationwide. Two technological changes in the first half of the twentieth century in the American railroad industry combined to decrease the demand for steam locomotives from Baldwin and its competitors. First came the electrification of commuter lines in New York and Philadelphia in the first three decades of the century. This eventually encouraged one of the railroads—the Pennsylvania—to electrify its busy main lines. Then, although railroad electrification slowed, the development of diesel locomotives accelerated. By the 1940s they were replacing steam locomotives in general service on most American railroads. Yet as late as 1937, Baldwin's management thought its future depended on the production of steam locomotives. The next year, when Baldwin emerged from a bankruptcy in 1935 with new management, it finally began to develop the newer diesel locomotives on a much larger scale. During the Second World War, Baldwin continued to produce steam locomotives for both the United States and abroad and built tanks for the military at its massive Eddystone works. However, the War Production Board authorized Baldwin's main national competitors—the Electro-Motive Division of General Motors and the American Locomotive Company (Alco)—to build diesels. This meant that Baldwin entered the postwar market in a weaker position.

After 1945 Baldwin entered a period of decline. It did introduce a full line of diesel locomotives and merged with a smaller locomotive builder to form Baldwin-Lima-Hamilton in 1950. But despite continual improvements in the products, the company's sales remained well behind General Motors and Alco. In 1956, when the usually dependable Pennsylvania Railroad decided to place a large order with General Motors instead of Baldwin, the company ended the production of locomotives, although it continued to make construction equipment until around 1970. Baldwin had constructed over seventy thousand steam, electric, and diesel locomotives since 1832. With the closure of the once-massive Eddystone plant, locomotive production ceased in the greater Philadelphia area after 125 years.

Baldwin's fate was not unique. On a global scale none of the major steam locomotive builders that dominated the world market in the early twentieth century successfully made the transition to the construction of diesel and electric locomotives in the twenty-first. The new era simply required technology and skills that differed from steam locomotives. Baldwin, and with it the Philadelphia region's role in locomotive manufacturing, became a casualty of massive industrial change in the second half of the twentieth century.

## Machining and Machinists

**Robert F. Smith**

Hundreds of machine shops, large and small, built and maintained Philadelphia's position as the "Workshop of the World" through the nineteenth and twentieth centuries. In the city and beyond, especially in Conshohocken, Pottstown, Phoenixville, Chester, and Camden, machining made the Delaware Valley a hub of foundries, craft shops, mills, workshops, and manufactories. During the latter half of the twentieth century, however, rising labor costs and international competition led to the decline of this segment of the region's economy.

Machining activities in Philadelphia began in the colonial period when craftsmen used hand tools to produce individual items to customer specifications. Furnacemen cast iron, brass, tin, and pewter items that finishers like blacksmiths, tinsmiths, and carpenters turned into consumer goods. One of the first metalworking operations in the city was Binny & Ronaldson (later Johnson Type Foundry), which opened at Seventh and Sansom Streets to provide type settings to printers. It operated until 1897, when it became part of the American Type Founders Company, which ceased operations in 1993.

During the American Revolution a continental arsenal employing over one hundred men and women initiated large-scale forging and finishing in the city. Private craftsmen and forges also supplied finished metal products to the army. Numerous regional forges and furnaces produced metal products for colonial and Revolutionary Philadelphia including Pennsylvania locations in Colebrookdale and Hopewell near Pottstown, and Durham near Easton.

Metalworking and manufacturing in the city grew after the war so that by 1800, 42 percent of Philadelphia's sixty-eight thousand people worked in industrial activities. Similar growth occurred across the region. In Coatesville, the Federal Slitting Mill, for example, laid the foundations in 1793 for what would become Lukens Steel.

The national government played a key role in Philadelphia machining after the Revolution. The U.S. Mint opened in 1792 on E. Seventh Street above Market (later moving to Juniper and Chestnut Streets in 1833, to 1700 Spring Garden Street in 1901, and finally to Fifth and Arch Streets in 1969). The later versions of the mint grew to be the largest such operations in the world and turned out 501 million coins annually. The Philadelphia Naval Shipyard, which grew to include numerous machining shops, began operations in 1801 at Delaware Avenue and Federal Street. In 1816, the federal government opened Frankford Arsenal, which forged and machined mostly small-arms ammunition until its closure in 1977.

In the nineteenth century the development of machine lathes, milling machines, drill presses, and cutting tools allowed laborers to turn, bore, drill, mill, ream, and shape items faster with more precision. The result in Philadelphia was the rapid expansion of machining operations to match the rise of large manufacturing sites, building construction, and commercialism. Operations like the Baldwin Locomotive Works, the William D. Rogers & Co. carriage factory, and the Cramp & Sons' shipyard required support from small item forgers and finishers. For commercial buildings and private housing, machining provided items like pipes, lumber, nails, and other castings. The growing population of the city purchased all types of machined products like irons, kitchen utensils, stove plates, and sewing needles.

Machining firms that answered the growing Philadelphia economy varied in size and product. The Point Pleasant Foundry, founded in 1809, and the Cresswell Iron Works, opened in 1835, supplied custom castings for buildings, bridges, plumbing, and transport. Henry Troemner & Company, founded in 1840, manufactured weights, measures, and scales for doctors, pharmacists, and banks. In 1844, Samuel White began what became S.S. White Dental Company, making false teeth and other oral health products. In Camden, Richard Esterbrook's steel pen factory and the Camden Iron Works became suppliers of various consumables.

By the time of the Civil War, manufacturing employed nearly half of Philadelphia's population (roughly 210,000 people in a city of about 500,000). Frankford Arsenal was critical to the war effort, as were firms like Sharp and Rankin, which machined breech-loading rifles, and Cramp & Sons, which built the USS *New Ironsides*. During this period machining operations began in Norristown and Bridgeport and worked metal supplied from Pottstown and Phoenixville. Phoenix Iron Company cast and worked artillery for the Union and in the process developed the Phoenix cylinder, which revolutionized metal construction.

The Delaware Valley machining industry continued to grow in the decades following the Civil War. In Philadelphia, new foundries included Yale & Towne, American Machine Works, the Eagle Bolt Works, and Fox Foundry. Tacony Iron Works, founded in 1881, cast the William Penn statue that was placed atop Philadelphia City Hall. Penn Steel Casting and Standard Steel Casting opened in Chester during the period, while in Camden Joseph Campbell opened a canning factory and several railroads built repair yards.

Machining, like Philadelphia manufacturing generally, remained close to its crafts roots throughout the nineteenth century. Of the city's 9,100 manufacturing firms, 62 percent employed between one

**FIGURE 72.** View of Centennial Hall at the Centennial Exhibition, 1876. The Fairmount Park event gave Philadelphians the opportunity to show visitors from around the world their region's manufacturing might. LIBRARY COMPANY OF PHILADELPHIA.

and five people. Skills passed from one generation to another within families, or companies trained workers recommended by employees. Guilds of skilled workers protected their rights to manage apprenticeships and training that limited access to machining. Outwork continued to be done at home, and street peddlers were widespread, offering custom products and finishing.

The small size, specialization, and plethora of machine shops had several implications. Machine workers retained craft skills lost by workers in industries adopting factory production. Workers had little power to organize themselves, either by specialty or business. And the number of African Americans, immigrants, and women in machining remained low. By 1900, 55 percent of the machining workforce were still white, native-born men.

Diversity within the ranks of machining workers was driven by the Philadelphia School District and private schools looking to increase access to skilled jobs for their students. In 1880, the district founded the Industrial Arts School to provide public education in trades. Five years later the Philadelphia Manual Training School was founded, and by the 1890s the city had a dozen manual arts schools. By the 1910s most high schools offered vocational training. Girard College created an industrial school to offer higher levels of training, and Drexel Institute was founded in 1891 for the same reason. Educational opportunities competed with guild and corporate training, allowing women, immigrants, and African Americans at last to enter the skilled labor force.

The city's skilled workforce drove expansion among local firms and investment by regional firms. Edward G. Budd Manufacturing Company started in 1912 to manufacture auto bodies and railroad components. Its most famous product was the original Metroliner car that became the backbone of Amtrak's passenger train operation. Arthur Atwater Kent began building telephone components and voltmeters in Massachusetts but moved into manufacturing radios in Philadelphia in 1923; until 1936 his company machined tubes, receivers, and other radio components.

Local markets like Camden, Chester, and Pottstown also saw development in this period. In 1901, Eldridge R. Johnson, a machinist working with the Berliner Gramophone Company in Philadelphia, started his own sound-recording company in Camden, the Victor Talking Machine Company. RCA (Radio Corporation of America) acquired Victor in 1929. Ford Motor Company built an integrated steel mill and machining plant along the Delaware River in Chester in 1927. Bethlehem Steel entered the regional market by taking over sites in Pottstown and expanding them to supply Philadelphia machinists.

Philadelphia machining reached its pinnacle during the two world wars. Most firms refitted their works to manufacture military goods like tanks, tank guns, artillery, and weapon parts. Cramp Shipbuilding built several cruisers and destroyers, while Philadelphia Naval Shipyard built the battleships *West Virginia*, *New Jersey*, and *Wisconsin*. Another innovation from the period came from Dodge Steel, which replaced Tacony Iron Works. Foreman John Williams developed a casting process using an apparatus that maintained the pressure of molten metals during a cast. The level of production necessary to support the war effort required the hiring and training of unskilled labor. As a result, women, immigrants, and African Americans became a significant part of the machining workforce.

The rise of larger firms, increasing diversity, and economic collapse during the Depression led to greater organization among machine workers. Skilled workers demonstrated and struck in 1893 and 1903 for better pay and against child labor, but generally, the familial nature of craftwork made unionizing difficult. By the 1910s local guilds became more formalized in organizations like the Iron Molders' Union of North America, Amalgamated Sheet Metal Workers, and Philadelphia Engravers Union, but they did not have much political influence. The Great Depression, however, challenged the labor status quo and took advantage of changing worker demographics brought on by education. Closures and consolidations cut the number of firms in Philadelphia to 5,760, each with an average of fifty-three workers. This fostered organization and activism among workers. The Congress of Industrial Organizations (CIO) and American Federation of Labor (AFL) molded local groups into larger unions such as United Electrical, Radio and Machine Workers of America with the power to press for better conditions and pay. They succeeded, securing wage increases totaling 500 percent between 1950 and 1980.

The city's casting, machining, and finishing workforce of nine hundred thousand in 1950 dropped precipitously by century's end. Rising wages and foreign competition undermined machining in Philadelphia following World War II. As Europe and Japan recovered from the war, they became producers of custom-made consumer goods, and inexpensive machined products. Lower Asian labor rates and access to inexpensive resources led large domestic manufacturers in shipbuilding, electronics, and automobiles to relocate overseas, laying off mostly skilled workers in the process. By 2007 the total number of manufacturing jobs left in Philadelphia was just over twenty-eight thousand. The majority of the remaining jobs were in small-shop machine production and finishing for local construction and fabrication firms.

The Philadelphia region was home to numerous machining and custom manufacturing and finishing operations that contributed greatly to the development of the United States and shaped the region as a home for high-quality goods. Factors including high wage costs, consolidation, and foreign competition undermined urban operations and the number of regional machining employees. However, machining continued to be an element of the regional economy in suburban locales into the twenty-first century.

**TABLE 5. PHILADELPHIA'S NATIONAL RANK IN LEADING INDUSTRIES, 1880**

| INDUSTRY | NATIONAL RANK (GROSS MANUFACTURING PRODUCT) |
|---|---|
| Agricultural implements | 7 |
| Blacksmithing | 2 |
| Boots and shoes | 2 |
| Bread and baking | 2 |
| Carpentering | 2 |
| Carriages and wagons | 3 |
| Clothing | 2 |
| Cooperage | 6 |
| Cotton goods | 3 |
| Drugs and chemicals | 1 |
| Dyeing and finishing textiles | 1 |
| Foundry and machine shop products | 2 |
| Furniture | 3 |
| Malt liquors | 2 |
| Marble and stonework | 2 |
| Mixed textiles | 1 |
| Paper | 2 |
| Printing and publishing | 2 |
| Sash doors and blinds | 5 |
| Shipbuilding | 1 |
| Silk goods | 3 |
| Sugar and molasses | 2 |
| Tinware, copperware, and sheet iron | 3 |
| Tobacco, cigars, and cigarettes | 4 |
| Woolens | 1 |

SOURCE: Manufactures of the United States at the Tenth Census (Washington, D.C.: Government Printing Office, 1880).

## Paints and Varnishes

**Augustin Cerveaux**

From colonial times to the nationwide deindustrialization trend starting in the 1950s, Philadelphia played a leading role in providing American and overseas markets with quality paints and varnishes. "Oil and Colours" merchants of the colonial period turned, during the early nineteenth century, into family-owned and managed manufacturing companies, as they opened paint and varnish factories in Center City and later in the industrial suburbs of Kensington, Camden, and South Philadelphia.

Even before rising to industrial supremacy in the early nineteenth century, Philadelphia imported, prepared, consumed, and exported coating materials in a comparatively large scale. Shipyards and carriage-making workshops often included a paint shop where professional painters ground and mixed pigments with boiled oils and resins to prepare a coating intended for a specific use. Painters or merchants engaged in the commerce of drugs, glass, oils, and "colours" (pigments) imported most of their raw materials for paint preparations from Europe, particularly England. Philadelphia was the point of entry to the New World for expensive pigments, including chrome yellow, vermilion (red mercuric sulfide), verdigris (green copper acetate), and Prussian blue (ferrocyanide acid). Some prominent merchants, such as the Elliott family established on Front Street by the mid-eighteenth century, also were apothecaries and compounded small quantities of bright pigments. Linseed oil, the most widespread binder for paints and drying oil for varnishes, came entirely from transatlantic imports until domestic production started in the late eighteenth century. Later, mills erected on the Pennypack Creek watershed in 1842 supplied Philadelphia with large quantities of linseed oil, extracted from flaxseed.

Dependence on foreign imports was particularly acute for lead-based pigments, which were pervasive prior to a federal ban on lead paint in 1978. White lead, red lead, and litharge (lead oxides) were key ingredients in nearly all paints and varnishes. Thus, when prominent pigment merchants or apothecaries of Philadelphia turned to large-scale manufacturing at the turn of the nineteenth century, they first concentrated on lead-based pigments; establishing a domestic paint and varnish industry depended on their success in competing with English manufacturers.

Philadelphians initiated in the United States the transition from imports and small-scale preparation to large-scale manufacturing of paint materials. Samuel Wetherill, a former textile manufacturer once in business near Market and Fifth Streets, ventured into drug, dye, and pigment compounding during the 1760s after the Crown suddenly increased taxes on these commodities. He was an ardent Revolutionary and early advocate of domestic manufacturing. His son, Samuel Wetherill Jr., erected a factory in 1809 at Broad and Chestnut Streets to produce lead pigments. His business prospered, and by 1845 the family company Wetherill & Brothers had a network of sales agents and retail stores in Baltimore, Norfolk, Boston, Providence, Richmond, and New Orleans. The company expanded production in 1847 with a new paint factory on S. Thirtieth Street, on the bank of the Schuylkill. John Harrison, a trained chemist, druggist, and manufacturer of "oil of vitriol" (sulfuric acid) at Third and Green Streets, also successfully engaged in large-scale manufacturing of white lead during the 1810s, when he erected a plant in Kensington. The family company, Harrison Brothers, then opened permanent offices in New York City, and later in Cincinnati after erecting a new factory on Grays Ferry Avenue between Thirty-Fifth and Thirty-Sixth Streets in 1863.

By 1870, twenty-nine establishments manufactured paints and varnishes in Philadelphia and Camden Counties, including sixteen manufacturers of lead pigments, for a total product value of $2.5 million, about 11 percent of the national production of paints and varnishes. But the early lead pigment factories of Philadelphia had by that time lost the lead in white-lead production, as competitors from Missouri, Ohio, and Illinois achieved much larger scale than the Wetherill and Harrison companies. Following an industrial trajectory taken by other prominent Philadelphia manufacturers, paint manufacturers did not compete head-on against distant mass producers of white lead, but instead maintained a stronghold on specialty paints while selling a diversity of products. They continued manufacturing, importing, and marketing expensive pigments, varnishes as well as other chemicals, and even spices in the case of Wetherill & Brothers. C. Schrack and Co., 80 N. Fourth Street in Philadelphia and Fifteenth and Mickle Streets in Camden, was famous for its fine varnishes and dry color pigments. Founded in 1816 by Christian Schrack, a former carriage maker, the company supplied specialty paints and varnishes to numerous local and remote coating-consuming companies, including Delaware shipbuilders, the Baldwin Locomotive Works, and the Pennsylvania Iron Works, as well as French carriage makers. Numerous varnish formulas secretly kept by Schrack and Co. have survived and hint at the diversity of materials, processes, and tricks that together constituted the material basis of the trade.

From a consumer point of view, the advent of "ready-mixed" paints, sold in cans ready to stir and apply, was probably the most important contribution of a nineteenth century industrialization trend to the paint trade. The driving force was less economic patriotism, as in the industry's early development, and more the prospect of access to a mass market. Ready-mixed paints transformed the regime of on-site paint preparation and condensed the diverse materials and techniques once required into a single, packaged product controlled by manufacturers. Although Philadelphia did not initiate this revolution—ready-mixed paints were first patented in 1867 by a Cleveland company—its paint companies wasted no time in manufacturing the new "liquid paint." John Lucas & Co., established in 1848 at 33 N. Front Street with a plant in Gibbsboro, Camden County, marketed "Lucas Liquid Paint," and George D. Wetherill, heir of Wetherill & Brothers, "Atlas Ready-Mixed Paints." Harrison Brothers became popular for its "Town and Country" brand, first introduced at the 1876 Centennial Exhibition in Fairmount Park. Clearly targeting the house-painting market, the company teamed with Philadelphia-based architects Hazlehurst & Huckel to design appealing advertisements featuring beautiful houses. Revivals of this colorful architectural period, known as Victorian, later permeated neighborhoods in West Philadelphia.

Competition and concentration dominated the post–First World War paint industry. Harrison Brothers was acquired by DuPont in 1917. Technical and marketing skills flowed from Harrison to DuPont, and the Grays Ferry Avenue plant manufactured some of DuPont's paint products. Later, during the 1950s, DuPont transferred its production capacities to other sites and turned the plant into a research and development center on coatings. The Grays Ferry Avenue site shut down in 2009. John Lucas & Co. was acquired by Sherwin-Williams in 1930, and its Gibbsboro plant closed in 1978.

Harrison's and John Lucas's company trajectories encapsulated the trends of Philadelphia's paint industry during the second half of the twentieth century. In a period of citywide and nationwide deindustrialization, Philadelphia's paint industry declined. From 1939 to 2010 the proportion of the nation's paints and varnishes enterprises in Philadelphia fell from 5.8 percent to 1.8 percent, while the associated proportion of employees shrank from 6.8 percent to 2.3 percent. By the twenty-first century, few remnants remained of the companies that provided color and protection for homes and industries in the Philadelphia region, the nation, and the world.

## Pharmaceutical Industry

**Jack McCarthy**

Philadelphia played a key role in the birth of the American pharmaceutical industry in the early nineteenth century, and the region remained a major pharmaceutical center into the early twenty-first century. Home since the colonial period to many of America's leading scientific, educational, and medical institutions, Philadelphia stood well positioned to support the emergence of a pharmaceutical industry. The nation's first drug mill was established in Philadelphia in the 1810s, and the city hosted a significant concentration of pharmaceutical companies over the years, as well as related industries such as chemical manufacturing and supporting institutions such as research universities and hospitals.

In the eighteenth and early nineteenth centuries, doctors and pharmacists generally made their own medicines, grinding and mixing materials into powders and extracts themselves. Most medicines were imported from England, however, until the War of 1812 interrupted the supply and spurred domestic drug manufacturing. It was at this point that the American pharmaceutical industry began in earnest. Several Philadelphia pharmacists and chemists branched into small-scale drug manufacturing, and some of these evolved into wholesalers or larger manufacturers.

Philadelphia's first large-scale drug manufacturer was not a pharmacist or chemist, but mill owner Charles Hagner, who in 1812 used waterpower in East Falls to grind several tons of cream of tartar into powder for a local druggist. Hagner's milling process accomplished in one day what would have taken months by the traditional mortar and pestle method, a feat that generated great interest in the nation's emerging drug industry. Hagner thereafter focused on grinding materials for medicines, establishing America's first drug mill at his East Falls location. In 1820 he moved his business to Manayunk, and in 1839 he built a large steam-powered plant in Northern Liberties.

The antebellum period saw the establishment of dozens of pharmaceutical and chemical manufacturers in Philadelphia, fostered by the city's strong medical, scientific, and educational communities. Powers & Weightman, founded in 1818 by English immigrants, and Rosengarten & Sons, founded in 1822 by a German immigrant, became two of the world's largest manufacturers of quinine in the nineteenth century. Advertising themselves as "manufacturing chemists," the two companies made a wide variety of chemicals and medicines before merging in the early twentieth century. John K. Smith & Company, founded first as Smith & Gilbert in 1830 by John Smith and John Gilbert, and John Wyeth & Brother, founded in 1860 by brothers John and Frank Wyeth, were two other drug companies established by pharmacists in antebellum Philadelphia. Both began as small-scale operations and grew into pharmaceutical giants. Following various mergers and acquisitions over the years, both remained active in the Philadelphia area in the early twenty-first century.

Robert Shoemaker was yet another early nineteenth-century Philadelphia pharmacist turned drug maker. Shoemaker took over a local pharmacy in 1837 and shortly thereafter began developing glycerin. In 1846 he became the nation's first commercial manufacturer of the drug. In 1856 William Warner opened a drugstore in Philadelphia, where he developed a process for coating medicine tablets with sugar to improve their taste. Warner later gave up his retail business to focus on manufacturing medicines. His company

**FIGURE 73.** Powers-Weightman-Rosengarten Co., East Schuylkill Falls, Philadelphia, ca. 1905. With a history tracing back to 1818, the company manufactured medicine and other chemical goods. Drawing on the insights of French chemists, the Rosengarten branch of the conglomerate introduced quinine to the U.S. market before the Civil War. FREE LIBRARY OF PHILADELPHIA, PRINT AND PICTURE COLLECTION.

eventually became Warner-Lambert, a major national pharmaceutical firm.

Philadelphia's status as America's preeminent early drug manufacturing center was further enhanced by the founding in 1821 of the nation's first pharmacy college, the Philadelphia College of Pharmacy (PCP), later renamed the University of the Sciences, which merged with St. Joseph's University in 2022. Many of the nation's leading pharmaceutical executives of the nineteenth and twentieth centuries graduated from PCP, which also served as a center for research.

Philadelphia dominated the American pharmaceutical industry throughout the antebellum period. Forty Philadelphia firms accounted for approximately 30 percent of the total value of the medicines, drugs, and extracts produced in the United States in 1860. Many of these companies benefited significantly from supplying medicines for the Civil War effort and saw considerable growth in the postwar period. In 1872 Wyeth employee Henry Bower developed a rotary tablet machine that allowed for mass production of medicines with precise dosages. The machine won awards at the 1876 Centennial Exhibition in Philadelphia.

Local pharmacists continued to branch into drug manufacturing in the late nineteenth and early twentieth centuries. In 1879 Robert McNeil, a PCP graduate, became proprietor of a drugstore in Kensington, from which his son established McNeil Laboratories. The company grew to be one of the region's major drug makers. Pharmacist Henry Kendall Mulford, also a PCP grad, founded the H. K. Mulford Company in the 1880s from his drugstore in downtown Philadelphia. Mulford later focused on making vaccines and in 1895 offered the first commercially available diphtheria antitoxin produced in America. The company built a large plant in Glenolden, Delaware County, which produced several types of vaccines.

Young chemist Albert Barnes took a job at H. K. Mulford in 1898 but left the following year to form a partnership with another chemist to make a new antiseptic they developed. After the partnership dissolved in 1908, Barnes created the A.C. Barnes Company to manufacture the product. The company was very successful, and Barnes used the wealth he amassed to collect art and establish the world-renowned Barnes Collection.

Philadelphia was also a major producer of "patent medicines," commercially available over-the-counter nostrums that were sold under brand names. Although their effectiveness was often dubious, patent medicines were marketed with colorful, exaggerated claims of their therapeutic qualities and were very popular in the nineteenth and early twentieth centuries. Thomas Dyott, America's first successful patent medicine manufacturer, made and sold a variety of elixirs and ointments in Philadelphia in the early nineteenth century. In the 1810s he built a substantial glassworks in Kensington to make bottles for his products. At the turn of the twentieth century, Philadelphia was home to two major patent medicine manufacturers, Dr. D. Jayne & Son and Johnston, Holloway & Company.

By 1909, there were 174 drug makers in Philadelphia, along with numerous chemical companies and several major research universities and hospitals. The concentration of these industries and institutions made the region a key center for pharmaceutical research and development throughout the twentieth century. In the early 1940s, West Chester, Pennsylvania, chemist G. Raymond Rettew developed a method for mass producing penicillin, based on his work with mushrooms (mushroom growing was a major industry in Chester County). Sponsored by Wyeth (then operating as American Home Products), Rettew's Chester County Mushroom Laboratories in West Chester became the world's leading producer of the drug, which was put to immediate, extensive use during World War II.

Graduates of the Philadelphia College of Pharmacy continued to play leading roles in the local pharmaceutical industry, particularly in family-run companies. At McNeil Laboratories, Robert McNeil Jr., grandson of the company founder, joined the firm after graduating from PCP in 1938. In the 1950s he oversaw development of the pain reliever Tylenol, which became the company's signature product. Similarly, at William H. Rorer Inc., founded in 1910, Gerald F. Rorer, son of the founder and a 1931 PCP graduate, took over the family-run drug company, based in Fort Washington, Pennsylvania, and transformed it into a major pharmaceutical firm, largely on the strength of its popular antacid, Maalox.

Mergers and acquisitions, common in the pharmaceutical industry from its earliest years, continued over the course of the twentieth century. Powers-Weightman-Rosengarten, formed through the merger of two Philadelphia pharmaceutical giants in 1905, consolidated with Merck & Co. in 1927 and moved to northern New Jersey. John K. Smith & Company became Smith, Kline & French in 1929, and in 2001 merged with English drug maker Glaxo to form GlaxoSmithKline. French multinational firm Rhône-Poulenc acquired Rorer in 1990. Wyeth, which came under the control of American Home Products in 1932, was acquired in 2009 by Pfizer, a multinational pharmaceutical company with headquarters in New York City. Nine years earlier, Pfizer had acquired Warner-Lambert.

Increased consolidation among drug makers in the late twentieth and early twenty-first centuries gave rise to "Big Pharma," a select group of very large multinational pharmaceutical firms that dominated the industry. The Philadelphia area was home to several of these pharmaceutical giants. Some had originally been founded in the city and remained in the region; others moved to the area later in their development. Of the former, the only company still located within the city itself was GlaxoSmithKline, which in 2013 moved one of its two North American headquarters from Center City to the Navy Yard in South Philadelphia. Both Wyeth and McNeil remained in the area but moved to the suburbs, McNeil to Fort Washington in 1961 after being acquired by Johnson & Johnson in 1959, and Wyeth to various suburban locations before consolidating in Collegeville, Pennsylvania, in 2003.

At the turn of the twenty-first century, Philadelphia stood at the center of a mid-Atlantic pharmaceutical corridor stretching from Delaware to northern New Jersey that included many of the world's Big Pharma companies. In addition to GlaxoSmithKline, Wyeth, and McNeil, those in the Philadelphia region were Endo Pharmaceuticals in Malvern, Pennsylvania; AstraZeneca in Wilmington, Delaware, established in 1999 through a merger of two large English and Swedish pharmaceutical companies; and Teva, an Israeli generic drug maker that established a North American headquarters in Montgomeryville, Pennsylvania, in the early 2000s. Numerous other pharmaceutical companies, large and small, were based in the broader Philadelphia metropolitan area in the early twenty-first century as well. They ranged from traditional drug makers to biotechnology firms to research-and-development companies, all part of the expansive "Life Sciences" sector that comprised a major part of the regional economy. A 2016 report commissioned by a consortium of local business and industry organizations noted that the sector encompassed 1,200 life sciences companies across the region, employed 48,900 workers, and was responsible for $24.6 billion in output.

From its key role in the creation of the American pharmaceutical industry in the early nineteenth century to its position as home to a number of major drug companies in the early twenty-first, the greater Philadelphia region was an important pharmaceutical center for over two hundred years.

## Recording Industry

**Charles Hardy III**

The birthplace of the American "record" industry, the Philadelphia region has been home to a thriving industry of recording studios and record companies since the late 1800s. Greater Philadelphia's unique concentration of diversified industries, entrepreneurship, and musical creativity among its ethnically and racially diverse communities have produced new iterations of a unique Philadelphia "sound" that has had national and international appeal.

On May 16, 1886, Philadelphia's Franklin Institute hosted the first demonstration of the newly patented "gramophone." Inventor Emile Berliner gave the four hundred in attendance a history of recorded sound and explained how his new mechanism for "etching the human voice" on a horizontal disc improved upon the vertically inscribed "phonograph" patented by Thomas Edison in 1878. After his Philadelphia unveiling Berliner, based in Washington, D.C., worked on technical improvements to his "phonautograph" and incorporated the United States Gramophone Company. His venture floundered, however, until a group of Philadelphia investors provided a life-saving infusion of new capital and formed the Berliner Gramophone Company in 1895.

The company faced a steep challenge. The Edison Electric Light Company's higher fidelity cylinders had a longer playing time and a spring-driven motor that kept the stylus moving at a constant speed. Berliner's horizontal discs, however, could be mass-produced from a single master disc. Needing a mechanism to replace the hand-driven crank that powered the original gramophone turntable, Berliner ordered about two hundred small, inexpensive, hand-wound spring motors made by Eldridge Johnson, who ran a small machine shop just across the Delaware River in Camden, New Jersey. The Berliner Gramophone Company opened its first offices at 424 S. Tenth Street in Philadelphia, set up a makeshift factory for production of gramophones at 1026–28 Filbert Street and a recording studio, and in 1897 inaugurated a retail salesroom—the nation's first record store—at 1237 Chestnut Street.

An avid amateur musician and composer, Berliner focused from the start on "canned music" for the home entertainment market. At its Philadelphia recording studio, the Berliner Company began to record what biographer Frederic William Wile called "the whole gamut of audible phenomena," including John Philip Sousa's famous U.S. Marine Band, the most popular American musical ensemble of the era. Berliner rounded out the catalogue with recordings of band musician solos; orchestral pieces; comic, "coon songs" (popular music with Black stereotypes); German and Italian songs; "Negro shouts"; recitations, both serious and humorous; and the world's first operatic recording on disc, "La Donna e Mobile" and "Quest o Quella," sung by Philadelphia tenor Ferruccio Giannini.

By 1898 gramophone and disc sales were soaring. Patent suits and financial struggles, however, forced the Berliner Gramophone Company into receivership. In

1900, Johnson bought its patents and formed his own company. The following year he incorporated the Victor Talking Machine Company, moved his recording studio from Camden to the old Berliner offices at 420 S. Tenth Street in Philadelphia, and constructed a matrix-plating plant in the building's basement. Making shrewd use of advertising under the Berliner "His Master's Voice" logo for national branding, Victor released recordings of international celebrities from the world of classical music on its Red Label records, introduced in 1902. Victor opened its own pressing plant in Camden in 1905 and the next year introduced the "Victrola," the first consumer record player with an internal horn and record storage space.

To meet soaring consumer demand, the Camden plant exploded in size. By 1915, it included the world's largest talking-machine and record factories. In the 1920s more than thirteen thousand men and women manufactured records and Victrolas on a sprawling fifty-one-acre physical plant that included thirty-eight buildings. Victor's massive and ever-growing catalogue of recordings included country and ethnic music, jazz and dance music, spoken word, race records, show tunes, and more. The presence of the world's largest record label in Camden proved a boon for Philadelphia-area musicians and ensembles. In the 1910s Victor cemented a close relationship with the Philadelphia Orchestra. Its conductor, Leopold Stokowski, worked closely with Victor engineers to produce orchestral recordings of unparalleled clarity, recording first in the Victor Executive Building in Camden and then in Trinity Church on N. Fifth Street.

Close proximity to the Victor studios also provided Philadelphia musicians and singers opportunities for session work and other recordings. In 1923 Victor presented a young Marian Anderson singing the African American spiritual "Deep River," five years before her first Carnegie Hall recital. With a rich musical heritage and multicultural population, Philadelphians produced popular music with broad appeal. Ethel Waters's clear northern diction and refined vocal style enabled her to become one of the first stars for Black Swan in New York, the nation's first Black-owned record company. Jazz greats Charlie Gaines, Joe Venuti, and Eddie Lang, and bandleaders Howard and Sam Lanin all developed their sounds in Philadelphia.

**FIGURE 74.** Nipper the Dog listening to his master's voice, 1915. One of the original stained-glass windows at the Victor Talking Machine Company factory in Camden. CAMDEN COUNTY HISTORICAL SOCIETY.

In the 1920s the emergence of commercial radio created new challenges and opportunities for the live music and recording industries. Philadelphia quickly became a center of radio manufacturing, its Atwater Kent Company producing as many as one-third of the radios sold in 1927–28. For a while the popularity of radio drove down record sales, but radio broadcasts also carried Philadelphia-based musicians and ensembles to new audiences. It also forced Victor to innovate. After record sales plummeted in 1924, Victor secured patents from Western Electric for a new, electrical method of recording. Victor then opened a large studio in Building 15, where in 1925 it produced its first electrical orchestral recordings, with the Philadelphia Orchestra (Camille Saint-Saëns's *Danse Macabre*). Record sales soared to a new high of 104 million discs in 1927. Two years later, Radio Corporation of America (RCA) purchased the company and retooled its sprawling Camden plant for the manufacture of radios. In the decades that followed, RCA's Camden complex played important roles in the development of radio, stereophonic sound recording, and television.

Technological innovations, sustained economic prosperity, and the coming of age of American mass consumer culture drove a new transformation of the American recording industry in the decades following the end of World War II. Both analog open-reel audiotape and recorders brought from Germany at the end of the war and improving vacuum-tube technology increased fidelity, drove down the cost of sound recording, and gave rise to new, small recording studios. The introduction of the twelve-inch long-playing (LP) vinyl disk by Columbia in 1948 and the smaller and less expensive seven-inch forty-five rpm vinyl disc by RCA Victor in 1949 enabled small pressing plants to manufacture (and small labels to release) records for niche markets. In postwar Philadelphia these upstart recording studios and labels grew by recording and selling the sounds of the city's vibrant subcultures of jazz, doo wop, and rhythm and blues.

In the 1950s, Philadelphia emerged as a breakout market for records appealing to local and national teenage consumers. Close enough to New York and large enough to have some of the Big Apple's energy, newness, and ethnic and racial diversity, the city was also distant and conservative enough to be more closely attuned to the tastes and culture of American mainstream audiences. And here, in 1952, WFIL debuted *Bandstand*, which brought not just the sound, but also the dances and look of young Philadelphians, many of them high school students from the city's ethnic neighborhoods, to a regional television audience.

From 1957, when it began national broadcasts, until it moved to Los Angeles in 1963, *American Bandstand* carried the highly produced and orchestrated "Philadelphia Sound" across the nation and made stars of "teen idols" Bobby Rydell, Frankie Avalon, and Fabian. By featuring local performers, *Bandstand* drove up the record sales of new labels, the most successful of which was Cameo Parkway. Founded in 1956, by bandleader-turned-songwriter Bernie Lowe, Cameo, recording in its own studios in the Schubert Building on S. Broad Street, released a string of hits by Bobby Rydell, the Orlons, and Dee Dee Sharpe, all products of the local Philadelphia music scene. First appearing on Cameo's subsidiary Parkway label in 1960, Chubby Checker performed "The Twist," launching an international dance craze. Cameo Parkway followed this up with the Dovells' "The Bristol Stomp" and "Hully Gully." In the early 1960s Cameo Parkway was the hottest independent label in the country. At the same time, Singular, Swan (1957–65), Chancellor (1957–64), and other Philadelphia labels turned out records by the dozens that, when pushed by local DJs and played at local record, or "sock hop," dance parties, could quickly sell fifty thousand to sixty thousand copies.

The Philadelphia Sound, however, proved short-lived. In the early 1960s consumer dollars moved to the Motown sound coming out of Detroit, and then the British invasion and psychedelic rock. Simultaneously, however, a new musical scene was emerging in Philadelphia, with its own small, low-budget recording studios, start-up labels, and songwriters and producers who would help shape the next iteration of the Philadelphia Sound. To compete with Motown's extraordinary success in marketing Black soul music to national audiences, Atlantic Records in New York and other major labels sought out three young Philadelphia-based songwriter/producers, Leon Huff, Kenny Gamble, and Thom Bell, who produced soul records for them at the new state-of-the-art Sigma Sound Studio on 212 N. Twelfth Street, founded by former Parkway Cameo engineer Joe Tarsia in 1968. In 1970 Columbia Records in New York created a separate soul music division, then signed an exclusive production agreement with Gamble and Huff in 1971 to write and produce records released on their own Philadelphia International Records label. Recording at Sigma Sound, Philadelphia International Records produced a string of hits with lush string arrangements; a strong, contagious beat and thumping bass line; melodies melded from gospel, soul, and doo wop; and accessible lyrics about family and survival.

Between 1971 and the early 1980s, the company produced more than 170 gold and platinum records with artists—a number of them also from Philadelphia—that included the O'Jays, Wilson Pickett, Harold Melvin and the Blue Notes, Teddy Pendergrass, Lou Rawls, and the Jacksons. Attracted by "The Sound of Philadelphia," as it became known, artists from all over the world came to record at Sigma Sound, including Dusty Springfield, the Rolling Stones, David Bowie, and the Bee Gees. With studio time at Sigma becoming increasingly dear, Tarsia in 1974 rented space in the Gamble, Huff & Bell offices at 309 S. Broad Street, where they had moved from the Schubert Building the previous year. There he built, equipped, and operated Sigma Sound South until 1988.

While Philadelphia International was thriving, the RCA Victor label struggled. RCA had been smart enough to sign Elvis Presley in 1955, and the company continued to innovate, introducing the first stereo eight-track tape music in 1965 and the first quadraphonic eight-track tape cartridges in 1971. But as one unit in a large corporate conglomerate that focused its attention on larger, more profitable divisions, the once-mighty RCA label floundered. After buying RCA in 1986, General Electric sold its interest in the RCA/Ariola International record label to Bertelsmann, then ceased manufacturing in Camden in 1992.

By the late 1970s Philadelphia International Records was also in decline. After a plunge in record sales in the late 1970s and another shift in popular tastes, the company recorded fewer and fewer artists, then closed its doors in 2001. In the 1980s, however, the analog cassette recorder, affordable multitrack tape decks and mixers, and other emerging technologies enabled a new generation of small studios and independent producers to record and distribute their recordings. One company that thrived was Philadelphia-based Disc Makers, which began as a small recording studio and pressing plant in the 1940s, became a regional supplier of vinyl and cassettes for the recording industry in the mid-Atlantic region by the 1970s and then emerged as a leading digital optical disc manufacturer for independent artists, filmmakers, and businesses. In the early 1980s Disc Makers began to offer short-run vinyl pressing and cassette duplication to independent artists, including those in the emerging indie rock movement who were producing their own recordings, often in small home studios. After 1990, Disc Makers moved into short-run CD duplication, small-batch CD-ROM packages for businesses, and then short-run DVD replication. Having outgrown its Philadelphia location, Disc Makers in 1995 moved to Pennsauken, New Jersey, where by 2010 it had produced more than forty thousand titles.

Market segmentation also gave rise to niche recording studios that catered to specific musical subcultures and worked with local artists. Among these were Dreambox Media, a musicians' co-op launched in 1986 that focused on recordings of Philadelphia jazz; Relapse Records, founded in Upper Darby in 1990, which diversified from underground "extreme metal" music into ambient, industrial, experimental, noise, and heavy rock; MilkBoy, founded in 1994 in North Philadelphia, which initially focused on punk and hip-hop groups; and Dylanava Studios, set up in Gwynedd Valley in 1999. Close to New York City and offering high quality at comparatively low cost, Philadelphia recording studios attracted national and international artists, including native Philadelphians Will Smith, Jazzy Jeff, and Boyz II Men.

The most successful of this next wave of Philadelphia recording studios was The Studio, founded by Larry Gold, a Curtis Institute–trained classical cellist. Gold had been a member of the Philadelphia International Records in-house band of studio musicians, MFSB (Mother Father Sister Brother), whose instrumental recordings included the 1974 number-one hit "TSOP (The Sound of Philadelphia)," best known as the theme song for *Soul Train*, the long-running African American musical variety television program. After Gold launched The Studio in the mid-1990s, it quickly became one of the best-equipped and most successful recording studios in the nation. Closely identified with Neo Soul music, The Studio helped launch the careers of Jill Scott, Bilal, and other local artists and became the home recording space for the Roots, another Philadelphia ensemble. Already established as one of the nation's best studio musicians and string arrangers, Gold also worked at The Studio with Tori Amos, Erykah Badu, Mary J. Blige, R. Kelly, Jennifer Lopez, Musiq, Justin Timberlake, and Kanye West.

The Studio opened just as emerging digital technologies were beginning to drive the next revolution in sound and moving-image recording technologies, which were again transforming the recording industry. The digital revolution gave rise to unprecedented media convergence and a new wave of democratization far greater than that unleashed by analog tape, audiocassettes, CDs, and other earlier technological innovations. It also forced Sigma Sound and other large, expensive recording studios to adopt new business models. Sigma, for example, retooled as a multipurpose audio and video production complex that included a video studio and live performance space.

In the early 2000s, new studios emerged in Philadelphia and its greater metropolitan region that could produce sophisticated, multitrack, high-fidelity recordings at lower and lower cost. More and more artists recorded entire albums on their laptop computers; released their music digitally on iTunes, YouTube, and other media players; and sent media files via the Internet to multiple studios, whose physical locations were of less and less significance. Digital media raised exciting and perplexing questions about what new forms "canned music" would take and about how sounds and moving images could be captured, marketed, disseminated, and experienced.

## Refineries (Oil)

**Carola Hein**

Philadelphia emerged as a petroleum hub in the second half of the nineteenth century. As an industrialized port city with global networks and extensive unbuilt land available on the Schuylkill and Delaware Rivers, the city offered the necessary rail and water infrastructure as well as access to water for the new industry. Extensive construction of refineries, storage tanks, pipelines, and railway lines began in the 1860s. Once consolidation of the refineries on a handful of sites, notably on the Schuylkill, was complete, the oil industry presence continued to influence spatial decisions into the twenty-first century.

The American oil story began in western Pennsylvania, where Edwin Drake drilled for oil in 1859, but the slippery substance had to be transported elsewhere to be refined and ultimately consumed. As consumers discovered new uses of petroleum—in particular, it quickly replaced whale oil for lighting—new businesses rapidly expanded storage, refining, and shipping capacities. The production of oil increased from some 4,450 barrels in the first year, to 220,000 barrels in 1860 and 2,114,000 barrels in 1861, almost a five hundred–fold increase in two years. Once oil had been found, the main challenge was transportation to appropriate sites for refining; horse carts, ships, trains, and pipelines all played a role starting in the early years of the industry.

During the industry's first decade, several oil interests battled each other, among them John D. Rockefeller who based his fortune on the control of refineries and railways rather than oil sources. Companies initially built refineries close to the sites of production. Within a few years, however, they established them in transportation hubs. Building on its long history as a port city, its emergence as a rail center, and its early transportation connections to western Pennsylvania, Philadelphia became a home to a large group of oil investors. From the earliest days of the oil industry, Philadelphia developed into one of the major storage and refining sites for petroleum. The location of oil facilities within the city was determined by a range of factors, importantly access to water, both for industrial processes and shipping. In the early years of the new industry, companies built oil storage sites and refineries in multiple locations throughout the city. By 1866 the city listed seven petroleum storage facilities and six refineries. Several more appeared before 1875. Security issues only became relevant after a range of disasters. The *Philadelphia Inquirer* reported on several refinery fires, big and small, with and without insurance, in the city or beyond its borders. When fire destroyed some of these facilities, affected companies sought more isolated locations at the urban periphery.

Environmental considerations became an additional reason for relocations, as was the case with the Belmont Petroleum Refinery. Located in an area that would become Fairmount Park, the facility produced some two million gallons in 1868, but concerns mounted that its wastewater endangered the city's water supply. As it was located on the Schuylkill River upstream from the Fairmount Water Works, city officials feared for the quality of the drinking water. Together with other mills and industrial properties, the Belmont refinery ultimately closed when the state bought the land for park purposes.

Despite such state action, the Schuylkill still was not safe from petroleum waste pollution after the Belmont refinery stopped operations. Refineries simply moved further downstream and closer to the meeting point with the Delaware River, starting the growth of the industrial hub that subsequently defined the city's southern boundary. In the late nineteenth century, a refinery cluster emerged on both sides of the Schuylkill, with one facility at Girard Point and the other at Point Breeze. Dating to 1866, Point Breeze initially refined lighting oil and subsequently became the oldest continuously operating petroleum facility in the world. A second petroleum center emerged on the Delaware River at

Greenwich Point, south of the existing port on the Philadelphia side.

Many of the early refineries close to the Schuylkill and Delaware Rivers were built on agricultural land (though still within the city limits), making it easier to create industrial complexes and to run new railroads to them. By 1867, oil was so important in the city that the *Philadelphia Inquirer* asked whether petroleum had come to rival "King Cotton." The *Inquirer* recognized the Atlantic Petroleum Storage Company as one major oil player. Established as a corporation in 1866, Atlantic was active in all the parts of the petroleum industry from drilling to refining and shipping. It occupied a seventy-acre property on the Schuylkill just below the Point Breeze Gas Works.

In 1874, Standard Oil Company purchased Atlantic Petroleum as part of its attempt to consolidate the oil transporting and refining business into a single enterprise. Five years later, lightning destroyed the Atlantic oil refinery along with several ships that were moored on its wharves. Two thousand men lost their jobs. Standard Oil carried no insurance and had to pay for the reconstruction.

The interplay of oil ownership, transportation opportunities, and refining capacity made the early oil trade a complex business. Landowners and oil traders were not necessarily the same. The Pennsylvania Railroad's oil interest in the early years extended beyond transport to the purchase of large plots of land in Philadelphia, notably on the Delaware at Greenwich Point. The Greenwich facility grew rapidly to bring together several oil companies in 1875. The Pennsylvania Railroad (PRR) owned the land of the oil facilities on the Delaware, whereas independent producers controlled the oil business. Together they entered a price war over shipping rates that pitched them against Standard Oil and the Baltimore and Ohio, New York Central, and Erie Railroads. Ultimately, the PRR lost the contest and sold its own oil interests to Standard Oil. The Delaware facilities continued to work until 1911, then disappeared.

In the late nineteenth century, the area experienced a major surge in the oil industry. By 1880, the Standard Oil Company controlled the refining of 90 to 95 percent of all oil in the United States, and it expanded its Atlantic Petroleum facilities. By 1891, 50 percent of the world's illuminating fuel and 35 percent of all U.S. petroleum exports came from the 360-acre Atlantic refinery in Point Breeze that featured a navigable waterfront of 1.7 miles and 6 miles of private railroad track. The facility was burning 350,000 tons of coal each year to refine forty thousand barrels of petroleum daily, emphasizing a connection between Philadelphia as a center of coal transport and as a petroleum hub. As of 1907, petroleum products exported by Atlantic Petroleum accounted for 22 percent of the city's export trade and were valued at $23,647,194 in foreign gold (surpassing cotton, which held 2.5 percent). Meanwhile a competitor had emerged in Philadelphia after 1901, as the region witnessed a second surge in the oil industry. Joseph Pew, cofounder of Sun Oil, built a refinery in Marcus Hook just outside Philadelphia in Delaware County for refining and resale of Texan crude that his company shipped on coastal tankers to avoid Rockefeller's railroads.

The invention of gasoline-powered automobiles sparked new demand for petroleum. But as oil production and consumption increased and globalized, Philadelphia's role as a major oil refiner decreased. Pennsylvania and New York had already reached a peak in production of 33,009,000 barrels in 1891. These states had already been overtaken by Russian production in 1888. The discovery of new oilfields in the United States, notably in Texas, between 1880 and 1905, had further reduced Pennsylvania's prominence as a producer. The growing political and geopolitical importance of oil made it a major factor in colonialism, as European nations struggled to maintain their hold over the resource, and investment flowed outside the United States. As German submarines sank American oil ships during World War I, traffic along the Eastern Seaboard (including to Philadelphia) decreased, and the United States promoted the construction of pipelines within and across the country in another major blow to the port. Over the next decades both the port and the oil industry in Philadelphia declined even further.

The end of Philadelphia's role in the oil industry seemed close in 2011, as the price of imported crude oil rose and Sunoco, formerly Sun Oil, announced it would exit the refining business, threatening to close its struggling refineries on the Schuylkill River. Local and regional forces pushed to keep the plants open and

**FIGURE 75.** Oil refinery in front of the Center City skyline, ca. 1990–2006. CAROL M. HIGHSMITH ARCHIVE, LIBRARY OF CONGRESS.

maintain employment for its remaining 850 workers. The fracking boom revived the financial viability of the refineries, as shale oil started to arrive by rail from North Dakota. In 2012, Sunoco entered a joint venture with the Carlyle Group under the PES name (Philadelphia Energy Solutions) to update and expand the refineries. But a huge explosion at the Girard Point refinery in 2019 pushed PES into bankruptcy, leading to the plants' closure and the loss of a thousand jobs.

Throughout the twentieth century, oil companies and states sought to transport oil from the production sites to the refineries and, ultimately, to the consumer. Because petroleum extraction sites were located far from sites of consumption, major oil companies expanded their distribution networks, built new shipping fleets, and established ports in Indonesia, Russia, the Middle East, and South America. Over this period, as Philadelphia went from being a major oil exporter to being an importer, the city's oil facilities on the Schuylkill continued to work when production, distribution, and consumption patterns completely changed; when oil companies reinvented themselves with the emergence of the car as the main consumer of oil products; and as companies figured out how to produce a multitude of other products from oil. In the early twenty-first century, they even attracted oil business back into the city, until the 2019 explosion brought refining in Philadelphia to an end.

## Saws and Saw Making

Jack McCarthy

Philadelphia ranked as one of the nation's foremost saw manufacturing centers for much of the nineteenth and twentieth centuries. Large-scale saw making began locally in the early nineteenth century, and by midcentury a number of major saw manufacturers operated in the city, including the world's largest, Henry Disston's Keystone Saw Works. Disston created a unique company town around his saw works and joined other industrialists in making Philadelphia one of the world's premiere manufacturing cities. Saw making remained strong through the mid-twentieth century, after which it went into decline, part of a broader deindustrialization of the region.

Saw making required a particularly high level of craftsmanship. Few artisans in early America possessed the technical skills needed to produce a quality saw with the right proportions of strength, flexibility, and smoothness of surface. As a result, most saws were imported. The few saw makers in the Philadelphia region in the eighteenth century included English immigrant Isaac Harrow, who set up a plating and blade mill in Trenton, New Jersey; John Harper, who had a saw-making shop at Sixth and Cherry Streets in Philadelphia in the early 1790s and one in Trenton in 1795; and English immigrant Francis Mason, who first appeared in a 1799 Philadelphia directory as a saw maker on S. Fifth Street.

Saw production grew in the city in the nineteenth century. The nation's first large-scale saw manufacturer was William Rowland, who had premises on Market Street by 1804. By the 1820s Rowland had moved to Filbert Street between Seventh and Eighth Streets, where he employed twenty workers and made saws that the Franklin Institute recognized for their excellence. In 1845 Rowland began making his own steel, and by the mid-1850s he had fifty workers and was producing two hundred saws daily. By then Rowland was one of several saw manufacturers: An 1844 city directory listed twenty. Most had small shops, but within a decade a few had grown into large operations. They originally concentrated in the highly industrialized downtown area north of Market Street and east of Eighth Street, although most eventually moved to larger quarters elsewhere. Among the saw makers who opened small shops in this part of the city in the 1840s before expanding were Henry Disston, who in 1840 opened what would become the Keystone Saw Works; Charles Johnson and William Conaway, who in 1846 established the future Union Saw & Tool Manufactory; and Walter Cresson, who began making saws in the late 1840s. In 1850 Cresson opened a saw factory on the Schuylkill River in Conshohocken, Montgomery County, while also keeping his Old City location. One of Cresson's chief saw makers, Irish immigrant William McNiece, left Cresson's employ in 1863 and with a partner established the company that became the Excelsior Saw Works at Fifth and Cherry Streets.

Of these leading mid-nineteenth-century Philadelphia saw makers, one—Henry Disston—emerged as the most successful, building his Keystone Saw Works into a massive enterprise that became the largest saw manufacturer in the world. Born in England, Disston came to Philadelphia with his father at age thirteen. His father died three days after arriving, however, and Henry eventually apprenticed with a local saw maker. After opening his own shop in 1840, he moved a few times before settling in 1846 at Front and Laurel Streets in Northern Liberties, where his business prospered. A gifted mechanical engineer with an unwavering commitment to quality, Disston developed several new products and techniques in saw manufacturing, including introducing the first crucible steelmaking process in the nation in 1855. Disston actively recruited skilled workers from England's famed Sheffield metalworking district; many of his key employees were immigrants from this area. By the Civil War, Disston's Keystone Saw Works had become the largest saw manufacturer in the United States, employing over 150 workers in four buildings totaling twenty thousand square feet of space. He grew his business by acquiring many of the region's other saw manufacturers. To accommodate his expanding operation, he purchased a large tract of land along the Delaware River in Tacony and began moving the company there in 1872.

The Disston saw works in Tacony grew to be an enormous, sprawling complex. To provide a safe, family-centered environment for his employees, Henry and his wife, Mary, created the Disston Estate, a 158-acre tract in Tacony west of the industrial area that they designated as a residential community. Within the Estate, separated from the industrial section by railroad tracks, the Disstons provided affordable housing for company workers, offering quality homes for sale or rent at reasonable prices. Deed restrictions prohibited the sale of alcohol and the operation of factories, slaughterhouses, or other activities that would compromise the residential character of the neighborhood. (The prohibition on the sale of alcohol within the Disston Estate was upheld after a legal battle in the 1990s and remained in effect in the early twenty-first century.) Of an estimated 2,500 company towns established in the nineteenth-century United States, the only other paternalistic town of this nature within an urban area was George Pullman's community in Chicago.

By 1909 the Disston company occupied fifty-seven buildings on fifty acres. Its four thousand workers produced nine million saws annually, from traditional handsaws used by carpenters and do-it-yourselfers to huge circular and band saws employed by the lumber industry and in industrial settings. The company also made a wide range of other tools, mostly notably files, which it produced in the millions annually. It sold its products worldwide and dominated the industry.

Henry Disston died in 1878 and did not live to see the vision for his company or community come to full fruition. His widow managed the Estate, while his sons and grandsons ran the company, which they incorporated as Henry Disston & Sons in 1886. It remained a profitable family-run firm until the mid-twentieth century, when, like many of Philadelphia's heavy industries, it began to experience serious business challenges. In 1955 family members sold the firm to H.K. Porter Company , a holding company that largely broke up the enterprise. After several subsequent ownership changes, the company continued operating, at a greatly reduced scale, at the Tacony plant into the early twenty-first century. Known as Disston Precision, in the late 2010s it employed a few dozen workers who made precision saw blades, custom metal

**FIGURE 76.** The Disston Saw Works, Tacony, Philadelphia, 1876. LIBRARY OF CONGRESS.

plates, and other specialty items, using both century-old machines still in place at the plant and modern computer-driven equipment. Disston remained the only major manufacturer from Philadelphia's late nineteenth and early twentieth-century industrial heyday still in operation in the city.

## Shipbuilding and Shipyards

**Jeffery M. Dorwart**

Perhaps no business, industry, or institution illuminates the history of the Greater Philadelphia region from the seventeenth century to the present day more clearly than shipbuilding and shipyards. Despite its distance from the sea and the challenges its location posed to navigation, the city and surrounding southeastern Pennsylvania, Delaware, and New Jersey riverfront ports developed shipyards and became one of the greatest shipbuilding regions in the United States.

As early as the 1640s Swedish boatbuilders fabricated several small craft on the Delaware River in their short-lived New Sweden colony, but large-scale shipbuilding started when skilled Quaker artisans and maritime merchants settled William Penn's proprietary grant beginning in the 1680s. In fact, six years before he founded Philadelphia, Penn had helped shipwright James West develop a small shipyard in 1676 along the Delaware riverfront in what later became Vine Street in the city of Philadelphia. Meanwhile, Penn recruited Welsh, Irish, Scots, and English Quaker craftsmen who were involved in shipbuilding in Bristol, England, and more fully along the Thames River, already by 1682 a great center of ship construction and merchant houses. Indeed, the Southwark section of London's Thames riverfront soon gave rise to the Southwark shipbuilding and merchant community along the Delaware riverfront of Philadelphia. When the Philadelphia riverfront became too crowded with merchant docks and buildings for establishment of shipyards, many shipwrights moved a few miles upriver to the Kensington neighborhood, which soon rivaled Southwark as a shipbuilding center.

The first settlers of Penn's colony turned to shipbuilding as a major industry because they found an abundant supply of trees, particularly oak for masts, pine for hulls, and pine tar for caulking both across the river in the West New Jersey colony and in the nearby woodlands of interior Pennsylvania. Deposits of iron for forging anchors, nails, and other ship parts were discovered nearby. As lucrative trade in lumber, furs, and agricultural products spurred demand for merchant ships—particularly scows, sloops, brigs, and schooners—shipbuilding along the Delaware riverfront flourished. By 1720 there were at least a dozen shipyards in Philadelphia and the surrounding waterfront producing wooden sailing ships of up to three hundred tons. At midcentury, Philadelphia had replaced Boston as the major colonial shipbuilding center.

The colonial era was in some ways the golden age of Philadelphia shipbuilding, with master shipbuilders and carpenters including Joshua Humphreys, Manuel Eyre, the Wharton family, and Penrose brothers designing and building fast coastal sailing ships and Atlantic brigantines. The approach of troubles with Great Britain in the 1760s, though, connected in part to American colonial violations of British navigation laws and maritime regulations, threatened Philadelphia's shipbuilding primacy. As affairs moved toward protest and then revolt, Philadelphia became the home of the Continental Congress, which required naval defense. Benjamin Franklin's Committee for the Defense of the Delaware raised money for small gunboats for the Pennsylvania Navy to defend the river and city. Meanwhile, the Continental Congress raised money for the Continental navy. These developments stimulated Philadelphia shipbuilding that included the construction of many small row gunboats, floating batteries, and even four innovative fast frigates. These frigates, designed by naval architect and Southwark shipbuilder Joshua Humphreys, became the prototype of the U.S. Navy's first forty-four-gun frigates such as the *Constitution*.

British occupation of Philadelphia in 1777–8 set back Philadelphia shipbuilding. Frigates were burned, gunboats sunk, and tiny riverfront shipyards from Southwark to Kensington closed. But after British evacuation of the Continental capital, shipbuilders returned to construct warships for the Revolutionary government. Independence and Philadelphia's dominance of the China trade gave local shipbuilders, most notably the Grice shipyard, contracts to construct fast China traders and frigates for the U.S. Navy. Indeed, the old Joshua Humphreys and John Wharton shipyard in Southwark served between 1794 and 1797 as the site for construction of the 1,576-ton, forty-four-gun frigate *United States* for the U.S. Navy. In 1801, the Southwark yard became the location of the first Philadelphia Navy Yard.

However, after the brief revival of shipbuilding during the Federalist era, Philadelphia maritime prominence fell on hard times. Britain closed the West Indies trade to American ships. The wars of the French Revolution created problems for American neutral trade. Thomas Jefferson and the Republicans advocated a coastal defense and gunboat navy and refused to fund the deepwater navy of larger warships, while in 1807 instituting an embargo against all but coastal American shipping. Meanwhile, New York and Baltimore began to take prominence both in trade and in shipbuilding. The War of 1812 momentarily revived Philadelphia's shipbuilding as private Delaware River shipyards secured contracts for Jeffersonian gunboats and privateers, while the Samuel Humphreys and Charles Penrose shipyard, adjacent to the Southwark Navy Yard, constructed gunboats and laid the keel for the seventy-four-gun ship *Franklin*.

Philadelphia had lost its leadership in overseas trade by the time of the War of 1812, and Delaware River shipyards suffered setbacks. Many small privately owned yards simply ceased to construct boats or ships. Nevertheless, a number of early nineteenth-century industrial and economic developments revived Delaware River shipbuilding in the years before the Civil War. An abundant supply of Pennsylvania coal promoted steam-powered technology. Shipyards began to subcontract with the region's machine shops, iron, and, later, steel producers. This meant that the small craft shipyards of colonial times would eventually be replaced by larger industrial firms.

The first to adopt a larger corporate organization was the Philadelphia Navy Yard along the Southwark riverfront. With government contracts, the yard was able to build machine shops on site. It meant that the Navy Yard could experiment with the innovative screw-propeller technology of John Ericsson, building the trailblazing first propeller-driven warship, *Princeton*. The screw propeller eventually replaced all side paddle-wheeled warships that were so vulnerable to cannon fire. At the same time, the yard built two huge, covered ship houses that allowed wooden warships to be constructed year-round, with a skilled workforce protected from the weather. This led to the construction of the largest wooden warship ever built for the U.S. Navy, the 120-gun *Pennsylvania*, launched in 1837.

Meanwhile, a private shipbuilding yard was organized by the Cramp family on the Kensington waterfront that would become one of the most important shipyards in Philadelphia and American history. In the years before the Civil War, the William Cramp & Sons Ship and Engine Building Co. began assembling wooden sloops, tugs, schooners and passenger ships, many powered by steam. As the Cramps' yard expanded, it became a modern industrial plant, incorporating all the latest technology in propulsion, steam engines and hull design, and iron siding. It worked with the Philadelphia engineering firms of Merrick & Towne, Reaney, Neafie & Co. (later Neafie & Levy Ship & Engine Building Co.), and Richard Loper, the last a pioneer of contract shipbuilding and an inventor of innovative curved screw propellers for ships. In 1849 Cramp launched *Caroline*, claimed to be the fastest propeller-driven vessel in the world. This also prepared the firm to build one of first great battleships during the Civil War, *New Ironsides*, and several innovative iron turret ships (monitors) for the U.S. Navy in its battle against Confederate ironclads. The Philadelphia Navy Yard was not far behind, building monitors and experimenting during the Civil War with steel plating and steam engines. Soon, the government yard (that also housed the U.S. Marine Corps) became overcrowded in the Southwark neighborhood. Shortly after the war the U.S. Navy began to relocate its plant and lay up iron monitors in a wet basin at League Island just down river. After Philadelphia presented the site as a gift in 1868 to the federal government, the U.S. Navy moved the Navy Yard entirely by the mid-1870s to this island located at the confluence of the Delaware and Schuylkill Rivers.

Post–Civil War Philadelphia suffered a shipbuilding depression. Skilled shipyard workers were laid off and machine shops closed. But the Cramp shipyard kept Philadelphia's shipbuilding industry alive, constructing iron tugs to tow Pennsylvania coal barges, fast propeller-powered steamships, and other commercial vessels. The Kensington yard was therefore in a perfect position to join the large contracts that the government issued to construct the modernized "New Navy" to compete in the late nineteenth-century world of imperialism. But the first shipyard on the Delaware River to benefit from the U.S. drive to compete with European navies to secure overseas empire was actually John Roach's Delaware River Iron Shipbuilding and Machine Works downriver in Chester. The yard laid the keels for the "ABCD" warships of the New Navy (*Atlanta*, *Baltimore*, *Charleston*, and *Dolphin*). The Roach shipbuilding company ran into financial problems, however, and Cramp, with intimate political connections, took over contracts for future iron and steel shipbuilding. Cramp became during the late nineteenth and early twentieth centuries the most significant shipyard in the United States, constructing modern battleships, cruisers, and torpedo boat destroyers for the U.S. Navy and warships for Latin American and Russian contractors. Its corporate organization, subcontracting to dynamic Philadelphia industrial firms, and U.S. government support propelled the yard to the center of American naval development. Several U.S. presidents attended ship launchings, attesting to the Philadelphia yard's political and naval importance. At the same time the Philadelphia firm built innovative modern Atlantic commercial steamships, passenger ships, and cargo vessels.

**FIGURE 77.** Launching the cruiser *Miami* at William Cramp and Sons Shipyard on the Delaware, 1942. SPECIAL COLLECTIONS RESEARCH CENTER, TEMPLE UNIVERSITY LIBRARIES.

By the First World War (1914–18), Cramp had major competitors along the waterfront. In 1899, New York shipbuilder and Wilmington, Delaware, ship engineer Henry G. Morse located his New York Shipbuilding Corporation's shipyard in Camden, New Jersey. Soon, his innovative template construction and shipbuilding methods began to overshadow the assembly system at the Cramp industrial plant. At the same time, the Philadelphia Navy Yard built modern dry docks, machine shops, and other support facilities, making it competitive with private shipyards. With three great shipyards in the Philadelphia area during World War I it was inevitable that the region would become a major contributor to the naval war effort. Moreover, the Sun Shipbuilding and Dry Dock Company (founded in 1916) of Marcus Hook, below Philadelphia; the Pennsylvania Shipbuilding Company's and New Jersey Shipbuilding Company's yards at Gloucester City, New Jersey, just below Camden (later operating under Pusey and Jones Company); and the federal shipyard of Pennsylvania on Hog Island, below the city, constructed tankers, cargo ships, and troop transports. Entire shipyard worker communities including Yorkship and Morgan villages in Camden City and Noreg Village (later Brooklawn), Camden County, New Jersey, were founded around the shipbuilding industry. These villages provided homes for laboring families of Irish, Italian, and eastern European, mostly Polish, descent.

But if war stimulated shipbuilding, the postwar era and accompanying economic depression devastated the industry in Philadelphia. Cramp closed in 1927 in bankruptcy. Owing taxes to the City of Philadelphia, the yard decayed and the plant rotted away. Labor unrest and strikes by shipyard workers unionized under the Industrial Union of Marine and Shipbuilding Workers of America disrupted shipbuilding. Yet, the Franklin D. Roosevelt administration kept shipbuilding alive in Philadelphia. The government gave the Navy Yard contracts to build treaty cruisers allowed under the post–World War I naval disarmament agreements and to modernize old battleships mothballed in the wet basin on League Island. Philadelphia's commercial port actually prospered during the economic setbacks of the 1930s, with three hundred wharves doing business. Having supported Roosevelt's presidency, Philadelphia and Camden received funding for naval ship construction both at New York Shipbuilding in Camden and the Philadelphia Navy Yard on League Island.

World War II was arguably the most important period for Philadelphia and Delaware Valley shipbuilding as the region became a key part of the "Arsenal of Democracy." As the international situation deteriorated, Philadelphia received more huge contracts to build modern warships. Meanwhile, the government funded construction of the first of many federal defense housing projects for shipyard workers, including African Americans and women. During the conflict, the Philadelphia Navy Yard employed more than thirty thousand workers, including several thousand "Rosie the Riveters." Indeed, women made up 16 percent of the shipyard's workforce. The yard built two great battleships, *New Jersey* and *Wisconsin*, and over fifty warships including innovative torpedo (PT boats) and fast aircraft carriers. Meanwhile, New York Ship hired forty thousand workers who constructed battleships, aircraft carriers, and destroyers. Nearby, Camden Forge and RCA Victor of Camden, New Jersey, received large

**FIGURE 78.** The Pennsylvania Sugar Refinery, Delaware Avenue and Shackamaxon Street, ca. 1883–96. Between the colonial era and the late twentieth century, ships brought Caribbean-grown sugar cane for refining in Philadelphia. Trade with the Caribbean linked the city to enslavement but also spurred abolitionist activity. For example, in the 1830s antislavery Philadelphians tried to replace the sugar grown by enslaved people with beet sugar produced by free labor. By the late nineteenth century, New York had emerged as the nation's major sugar port, but Penn Sugar—founded in 1868 by the German immigrant John Hilgert—remained a major employer on the Delaware River. Acquired in 1947 by a New York firm, its refinery finally closed in 1984. HISTORICAL SOCIETY OF PENNSYLVANIA.

contracts to provide forgings and electronics for warships constructed in the Greater Philadelphia region. Sun Shipbuilding of Chester expanded to twenty shipways and employed nearly forty thousand workers at its four yards. One of Sun Ship's yards employed mostly African Americans. Cramp Shipbuilding Company revived momentarily, as well, with eighteen thousand employees that produced naval vessels.

Demobilization after 1945, however, challenged the region's shipbuilders. Cramp closed permanently after the war though New York Ship and the Philadelphia Navy Yard stayed alive for years with government contracts. New York Ship, the industry's largest postwar employer, built several modern postwar ships, including the aircraft carrier *Kitty Hawk*, and the first (and only) nuclear-powered merchant ship, *Savannah*. It also signed contracts to construct nuclear submarines. However, mismanagement, labor unrest, construction accidents on the carrier, and growing restrictions on building nuclear warships so near a great city led to the closing of the Camden shipyard in 1967. Meantime, Sun Ship was sold to the Pennsylvania Shipbuilding Corporation (Penn Ship) and operated until closure in 1989. The former Penn Ship site soon hosted a cargo terminal, casino, racetrack, and a penitentiary.

The Philadelphia Navy Yard continued to build ships for the U.S. Navy, including U.S. Marine Corps assault ships, and received Service Life Extension Program (SLEP) contracts to modernize conventionally powered (nonnuclear) aircraft carriers. But the yard could not support a nuclear navy since during World War II an accident in the uranium-enriching plant on base had illustrated the potential for a nuclear accident in the Delaware Valley. Without the ability to either build or modernize a nuclear navy, Philadelphia's Navy Yard gradually became an outdated relic and closed for shipbuilding in 1996. The City of Philadelphia assumed ownership of the old Navy Yard in 2000, and in order to provide employment for the thousands of laid-off shipyard workers in the region contracted with the Kværner shipbuilding corporation of Oslo, Norway, to use the large dry docks to construct modern tankers and container ships for Exxon and other companies. At the same time, the U.S. Navy leased the old wet basin and part of the former Navy Yard's historic center for its Naval Facilities Engineering Command Mid-Atlantic and its Naval Inactive Ship Maintenance Facility to lay up warships for scrapping or historic preservation.

Meanwhile, the city of Philadelphia started to develop a plan to transform the thousand-acre industrial plant on League Island into a multipurpose postindustrial business, shopping, and tourism park. And when Kværner encountered financial troubles that forced the Norwegian shipbuilder to merge with the Norwegian oil services company Aker, the Philadelphia and U.S. governments became partners with the private Norwegian firm to ensure the continuation of shipbuilding along the Delaware River. Soon, Aker began the construction of Aframax tanker hulls for SeaRiver Maritime Inc. in the two great dry docks at the former Navy Yard. This public-private partnership to promote the construction of ships on the Delaware River revealed once again the importance of shipbuilding to the Greater Philadelphia region.

## Textile Manufacturing

**Jack McCarthy**

Textile manufacturing began in Philadelphia soon after the city's founding in 1682 and grew to be one of its chief industries. By the turn of the twentieth century Philadelphia was one of the world's greatest textile manufacturing centers, with tens of thousands of workers making a wide range of products. The industry declined dramatically in the late twentieth century, part of a broader deindustrialization of the Philadelphia region at that time.

As early as 1690 three woolen weavers were working in Philadelphia, and in 1691 William Penn wrote of "very good German linen" being made in Germantown. By the mid-eighteenth century, Philadelphia textile workers were making a variety of products. Andrew Barnaby, an Englishman who visited the city in 1759–60, noted the high quality of thread stockings made in Germantown, that Philadelphia's Irish settlers made very good linens, and that some wool products had been fabricated in the city. While textile manufacturing increased as Philadelphia's population grew, it was carried out mostly on a small scale—spinning, weaving, and knitting done primarily by hand in homes and small shops in the colonial period.

The late eighteenth century saw the first attempts at machine-based textile production in factory settings. The April 1775 issue of the *Pennsylvania Magazine* featured a drawing of a new "Machine for spinning twenty-four threads of cotton or wool at one time." The magazine noted that the machine, built in Philadelphia by Christopher Tully, was the first one made in America. The United Company of Philadelphia for Promoting American Manufactures, established in 1775, used Tully's machine in a factory it set up at Ninth and Market Streets and also employed some four hundred local women in hand spinning and weaving. The company's initiatives were part of an effort by colonial leaders to spur domestic manufacturing in order to compete with England militarily and economically. The United Company ceased operations when the British occupied Philadelphia in September 1777 during the Revolutionary War. One of the members of the company was Samuel Wetherill, an early Philadelphia industrialist who carried on a substantial textile manufacturing business and was a major supplier to the Continental army.

After the war, Wetherill was active in another Philadelphia organization that sought to undertake large-scale textile manufacturing, the Pennsylvania Society for the Encouragement of Domestic Manufactures and the Useful Arts, established in 1787. The society's chief spokesman was Philadelphia merchant and economist Tench Cox, an influential advocate for the development of American manufacturing. The society set up a textile factory in 1788 in the same building the United Company had used, but the factory was destroyed by fire in 1790 and not rebuilt. In 1791, Philadelphia merchant William Pollard, an English immigrant, was awarded the first U.S. patent for a machine for "Spinning and Roving Cotton." His attempt to set up cotton factories in the city was thwarted by the business failures of his financial backers, however. Much of the technology for these initiatives was imported surreptitiously from England. However, unlike in New England, which boasted full integrated operations that mass-produced materials, late eighteenth-century attempts at large-scale mechanized textile manufacturing in Philadelphia were largely unsuccessful, textile mills nevertheless proliferated in the region in the early nineteenth century. Numerous European immigrants with expertise in textile production settled in the region and set up factories. The invention of the cotton gin in Georgia in 1793 made possible the processing of enormous amounts of raw southern cotton, grown by enslaved laborers, for shipment to Philadelphia mills, while the introduction of steam power and rail transportation in the 1820s and 1830s spurred further expansion of the local textile industry. Industrial communities such as Manayunk and Frankford, which had developed on the strength of their early water-powered mills, became major textile centers in the antebellum period, joining Germantown, which had long been a locus of the hand-frame knitting industry, and the emerging industrial powerhouse of Kensington.

Other textile centers developed throughout the greater Delaware Valley as Philadelphia and its surroundings became one of the most industrialized parts of the globe. In the early 1830s the Trenton Delaware Falls Company built a canal in Trenton, New Jersey, to provide waterpower for a number of that city's textile mills. In Wilmington, Delaware, in 1831, Joseph Bancroft established Bancroft Mills, which grew to be one of the nation's largest textile manufacturers. Textile mills operated throughout the region in the early nineteenth century, particularly in towns that grew up along rivers and creeks, where waterpower fueled industries until the introduction of steam engines in the 1820s and 1830s. While hand weaving and home-based textile production continued, machine-based manufacturing in mills became the foundation of Philadelphia's rapidly expanding textile industry. By the Civil War the city was one the nation's premier textile centers.

The mechanization of textile manufacture gave rise to serious labor issues. Work that had previously been done by hand in homes and shops was now centralized and automated in large mills that employed hundreds or thousands, such as those of William Logan Fisher in Germantown and Joseph Ripka in Manayunk. Both men and women comprised the workforces in these mills; women had always played a significant role in textile production. Working conditions in the mills were often miserable. Employees worked twelve- or fourteen-hour days, six days a week, doing monotonous tasks in unhealthy conditions for low pay. Strikes and

FIGURE 79. Manayunk, Philadelphia, 1838. John Caspar Wild's lithograph shows Joseph Ripka's cotton mills on the banks of the Schuylkill. LIBRARY OF CONGRESS.

other labor actions were common, as were aggressive, sometimes violent responses by mill owners. Child labor was another major issue. Children made up a considerable percentage of the textile workforce and were also subjected to terrible working conditions. There were also conflicts between factories and Philadelphia's many independent handloom operators, who viewed mechanization as a threat to their livelihood. In the 1830s a group of Kensington handloom weavers tried to burn down a Manayunk mill that had installed new labor-saving machinery.

Labor issues notwithstanding, the mid-nineteenth century saw tremendous growth in Philadelphia's textile industry. This gave rise to a number of local textile family dynasties: the Fisher family with factories in Germantown; the Campbell, Schofield, and Dobson families in East Falls and Manayunk; Ripka's extended family in Manayunk and along the Pennypack Creek in Northeast Philadelphia; the Bromleys in Kensington and Frankford; the Dolans in North Philadelphia; and others. As titans of the local textile industry, many of these families became part of Philadelphia's social elite, taking active roles in city business and political affairs. Some of them suffered significantly during the Civil War, when their connections with Southern cotton growers were severed by the conflict. While most survived, one who did not was Joseph Ripka, who closed his Manayunk cotton mills during the war and died in 1864.

In 1850, Philadelphia had approximately twelve thousand textile workers. By 1882, it had over sixty thousand, employed by nearly one thousand different firms. Many of these workers were low-skilled immigrants, particularly Irish Catholics who settled in Kensington in large numbers in the mid-nineteenth century and made up a significant percentage of that neighborhood's mill workers. Religious tensions between Kensington's Catholic and Protestant textile workers led to Philadelphia's deadly 1844 nativist riots.

While the city had its share of large mills that employed thousands of workers, the real strength of its textile industry was its many small to midsize specialty firms. Textile products made in Philadelphia often went through a multisite process in which different companies did different types of work. Textile fibers were spun in one factory, woven in another, dyed in a third, and finished in a final one. This interconnected network of smaller, specialized textile firms was a defining characteristic of Philadelphia's textile industry in the nineteenth and early twentieth centuries.

Another key aspect of Philadelphia's textile industry was the great variety of products it generated. Whereas other major American textile centers usually focused on a single product, Philadelphia's textile sector produced a wide range of materials. The 1912 book *Manufacturing in Philadelphia, 1683–1912* listed among the city's textile products carpets, cordage, jute, linen goods, nets and seines, cotton goods including small cotton wares, hosiery and knit goods, shoddy (a recycled wool product), silk fabrics, woolen and worsted products, wool pulling and wool scouring, felt goods, wool hats, and fur felt hats.

Of the many areas of the city where these products were made, the largest by far was Kensington, the sprawling industrial neighborhood to the northeast of Center City. Home to hundreds of textile mills, large and small, and a vast, primarily immigrant workforce, Kensington boasted one of the greatest concentrations of textile activity in the world. By 1910 there were four hundred textile firms employing thirty thousand workers in Kensington. *Manufacturing in Philadelphia, 1683–1912* noted that from the tower of the Bromley mill in Kensington there were more textile mills within the range of vision than in any other city worldwide.

Labor strife continued in Philadelphia's textile industry in the late nineteenth and early twentieth centuries, as mill owners periodically cut wages or work hours in response to changing economic conditions and workers responded with strikes and other actions. The Knights of Labor, which began in Philadelphia in 1869 as a secret society of city garment workers and grew into a huge nationwide labor organization, organized several strikes in Philadelphia in the late nineteenth century. There were major strikes in the early years of the twentieth century as well, including particularly large strikes in 1903 and 1910.

Despite the industrial unrest the period marked the heyday of textile manufacturing in Philadelphia. In 1909 the total value of textile products reached $153 million, greater than any city in the world and more than double that of any other American city. Longtime Philadelphia family textile dynasties such as Dobson and Bromley employed thousands of workers, while hundreds of smaller companies provided specialty services. The Great Depression of the 1930s curtailed the industry significantly and led to the decline of some of the city's major textile companies, but many survived and several important new ones were established.

While traditional textile manufacturing continued in Philadelphia, firms elsewhere in the region developed new types of materials in the early twentieth century. In 1908 immigrant English businessman Samuel Agar Salvage founded the American Viscose Corporation to make rayon, a type of artificial silk. In 1911 he built a large plant in Marcus Hook, Delaware County, to make the product. He also built a planned English-style worker community, known as Viscose Village, for his employees. In Wilmington, Delaware, the DuPont Company transformed the textile industry with the introduction of synthetic fibers in the 1930s and 1940s. DuPont-developed products such as nylon, Orlon, and later Dacron revolutionized how textiles were made and used in the mid-twentieth century. Some of these products were manufactured in DuPont plants in Delaware, but many were made in company plants in other parts of the nation.

Philadelphia's textile industry remained strong through the mid-twentieth century, but, like much of the city's industrial sector, it declined significantly in the post–World War II period. A number of economic and social factors—cheaper labor and energy costs in other parts of the nation or world, competition from producers of lower-cost products, changing urban demographics—led to most Philadelphia textile factories closing or moving out of the city in the latter part of the century. Some stayed local, however; scores of mills transferred operations to surrounding counties, especially in expanding areas of South Jersey.

By the early twenty-first century, Philadelphia's textile industry was comprised of mostly small niche firms making specialized products for well-defined markets. While overall the sector operated on a fraction of its massive early twentieth-century scale, about 150 textile manufacturers operated in the city in the mid-2010s. These included firms such as Ehmke Manufacturing Company in Juniata, which made fabric products for the defense industry; Boathouse Sports, also in Juniata, maker of specialized sports apparel; Grip-Flex Corporation in Port Richmond, which made braided cords and uniform trimmings; and Humphrys Textile Products in Kingsessing, makers of industrial tarps and canvas. These and other local companies continued Philadelphia's longstanding textile manufacturing tradition, a tradition that dated to the late seventeenth century and brought the city international recognition as one of the greatest manufacturing centers in the world.

## Deindustrialization

**David Elesh**

The Philadelphia region's long-held reputation as the "Workshop of the World," though richly deserved, did not prevent it from suffering the same loss of manufacturing firms and jobs that devastated the economies of other manufacturing centers. Local products ranged widely, from locomotives and ships to silk hosiery, wool carpets, machine tools, hand tools, lighting fixtures, steel, soup, and men's and women's apparel. With the exception of a limited number of large companies such as Baldwin Locomotive, Campbell Soup, Cramp Shipbuilding, and Midvale Steel, most regional manufacturers were small- and medium-sized firms that specialized in customizing their products to consumers' needs. Yet neither the diversity and quality of products nor the flexibility of their makers checked the region's deindustrialization. The causes and pacing varied by industry, location, and time period, but after World War II the region saw its share of jobs in manufacturing decline more rapidly than the nation's.

Using the percentage of private nonagricultural jobs in manufacturing as an indicator, deindustrialization began in the nation, city, and region about 1920; however, it proceeded at different paces in Philadelphia and its suburbs. The city reached its largest number of manufacturing jobs in 1920, although the peak did not occur in its suburbs until about 1950. In part, city firms moving to the suburbs helped sustain manufacturing jobs in the wider region. The region's deindustrialization after 1920 corresponded to the national trend that—allowing for the aberrations created by the Great Depression and World War II—followed a relatively constant downward slope. Deindustrialization thus began even before concern arose about either competition from foreign companies or outsourcing by U.S. companies.

The causes of the decline in manufacturing's share of the workforce varied by time period, geography, and industry. Throughout the twentieth century, technological improvements—often driven by the desire to lower labor costs—permitted manufacturers to increase production with the same or fewer workers. "Scientific management," honed at Midvale Steel by Frederick Winslow Taylor, sought to raise labor productivity. These efforts often merged with the growing popularity of continuous-flow assembly-line production, exemplified by Ford's Philadelphia automobile plant (opened in 1914), and developments in technology such as the spread of electric power. Costly new technologies increased the efficiency and volume of production. Yet both nationally and locally, until the Great Depression the number of production jobs in manufacturing grew even as their percentage of all jobs shrank.

### The Great Depression and World War II

The Great Depression hit small- and medium-sized manufacturing firms like most in Philadelphia with particular severity. In the city and region's core industry of textiles, for example, many Philadelphia manufacturers became increasingly fragile financially as the boom of the 1920s came to a close. Their profits had been diminishing, hurt by the growing power of chain retailers to demand goods at set wholesale prices, by the competition created as consumers turned to simpler and cheaper woven goods, and by overproduction, especially in hosiery. In 1928, Philadelphia had 850 textile firms, 350 of them in the Kensington neighborhood, and employed nearly 35,000. By 1935, a study of 82 of those firms found that 30 percent had closed or moved, with a loss of 8,700 jobs.

Meanwhile, federal programs during the Depression tended to favor economic development not in the Northeast but in southern and western states, where the New Deal of the Roosevelt administration created jobs through investments in projects such as roads, bridges, and dams for electric power. When war broke out in 1941, the rapid expansion of manufacturing on the West Coast and military bases in the West and South stimulated relocations to these areas and laid a foundation for postwar migration and further economic development. For eastern producers such as those in Philadelphia, the war helped equip new competitors with the latest technology, lowered transportation costs to many markets, and often reduced labor costs. Although southern states had sought to lure manufacturers since the 1930s with cheap labor, low taxes, subsidized construction costs, and other inducements, these efforts intensified and found greater success in the postwar period.

Furthermore, the Philadelphia region risked losing jobs because much of the diversity of its manufacturing base concentrated in the production of nondurable goods (like clothing, magazines, food, and shoe polish), which were more susceptible to competitive pressures than durable goods (like machinery, automobiles, washers, and hand tools). In 1948, 31 percent of Philadelphia's privately employed labor force worked in nondurable manufactures, compared to only 19 percent for the country as a whole. Manufacturing nondurable goods often took place in small establishments, required less capital investment, demanded less-skilled workers, and paid lower wages. Less dependent on a large investment in plant and equipment, companies manufacturing nondurable goods could be more easily relocated than more capital-intensive durable-goods manufacturers. The lower wage structure of nondurable firms also encouraged them to seek locations with cheap labor.

## CHANGING TECHNOLOGIES AND MARKETS

Philadelphia firms also faced technological and market changes that reshaped plants and whole industries in ways that further encouraged moving factories from the city to outlying areas. Existing factories became outmoded because production technologies increasingly required more open space on one floor. Baldwin Locomotive, for example, found it increasingly difficult to produce the larger and more powerful locomotives demanded by its customers in its site in the city's Spring Garden neighborhood and began building a new plant in suburban Eddystone in 1906. During the more than twenty years it took Baldwin to complete the Eddystone plant, its market matured and began to fade as diesel engines and trucks became growing competitors. The Eddystone facility ceased production in 1956.

A changing market also claimed the Stetson Hat Company. Started in nineteenth-century Philadelphia,

**FIGURE 80.** Demolition of the Stetson factory, Germantown and Columbia Avenues, Philadelphia, 1979. Famed for its iconic cowboy hats, the Stetson Company operated in Philadelphia between 1865 and 1971, employing more than five thousand workers at its peak. SPECIAL COLLECTIONS RESEARCH CENTER, TEMPLE UNIVERSITY LIBRARIES.

Stetson became one of the nation's largest makers of fashionable men's hats as well as its iconic cowboy hat during the 1920s. But after World War II, men outside the West gradually stopped wearing hats. Stetson closed its factory in the city's Kensington neighborhood in 1971, although it continued to produce cowboy hats in Texas.

For other companies, the rise of continuous-flow production technologies, the large single-floor spaces they require, and the lower costs of suburban land contributed to decisions to suburbanize wholly or partially. Westinghouse Electric, Ford Motor, and Rohm and Haas were among the firms that made that choice in the first quarter of the century. Other firms—such as Chester County's Lukens Steel and American Viscose (at one time the world's largest producer of rayon) and Montgomery County's Lee Tire & Rubber Company and Alan Wood Steel—started in those suburban areas.

Some Philadelphia industries simply lost viability over time. Prior to the Depression, the diversity of the Philadelphia area's producers delayed their decline, despite competition from the South that led to a wave of closures in New England. Although the Philadelphia region's textile firms outlasted New England's, their fortunes changed for the worse after World War II. Many of these companies produced silk or rayon hosiery that was quickly supplanted by lower-cost nylons after the war. Not only was silk a significantly more expensive raw material, nylon offered a further cost advantage because DuPont, nylon's inventor, produced both the fiber and the finished product. Most silk firms, lacking capital to convert to the new machines needed to knit nylon, and simply closed. The region's carpet industry suffered a similar fate. In 1950, the development of inexpensive nylon-tufted carpeting in Dalton, Georgia, led to the rapid collapse of wool carpeting, with Philadelphia producers struggling to adapt to a completely different technology.

## RESPONSES TO GROWING LABOR MILITANCY AND FOREIGN COMPETITION

From the late 1930s into the 1950s, Philadelphia's labor climate also significantly changed, inhibiting new investment in the local textile industry. A long and bitter strike against Philadelphia's Apex Hosiery Company in 1937 opened a decade of rising labor militancy across the regional economy. Reaching a crescendo with strikes against Baldwin Locomotive, Westinghouse, and General Electric in 1945–46, workers' militancy contributed to shifts of production and investments to the nonunionized parts of the region and country in the 1950s and 1960s.

These local strikes echoed national trends in management-labor conflict, but they had particularly significant effects on Philadelphia's postwar textile industry because the timing coincided with rapid changes in technology and products. In the late 1940s and early 1950s, the industry reached a critical transition: new products had to be produced from new materials in new ways in new plants. Factory owners confronted the question of whether to build new plants in the Philadelphia metropolitan area, close, or shift production elsewhere. When they had a choice, they typically moved elsewhere or diverted their capital to other types of investments.

Even when Philadelphia manufacturers successfully adapted to changing technologies and markets, low-cost foreign competition often took a toll. The knitwear industry, for example, had always used machines more intensively in its production than other apparel manufacturers, and it therefore withstood competition from lower-wage sites until the 1970s by producing highly styled women's wear. Eventually, however, Asian firms, using profits from the low-margin knitwear that domestic manufacturers could not profitably produce such as T-shirts, along with reductions in tariffs on imported goods, moved to compete at the high end of the market as well. Starting in the 1970s, Philadelphia's knitwear manufacturers began disappearing.

Throughout the 1950s and most of the 1960s, other apparel employment remained relatively stable in the face of rising competition from southern, western, and offshore producers. Philadelphia's concentration on the production of men's and boys' clothing, less vulnerable than the larger and more competitive market for women's clothing, may have helped protect the industry. Because of the greater standardization to men's and boys' clothing, machines could be employed more extensively in its production, making it somewhat less sensitive to labor costs. By the late 1950s, however, foreign competition in men's apparel had become a significant problem, and by the early 1960s an imported sport coat could be purchased at retail in a department store for the cost of production to a Philadelphia manufacturer. In addition, producers increasingly complained of being unable to find needed space for expansion within the city at affordable rents, and they worried about a critical shortage of skilled labor. Despite some city, state, and union efforts to aid the industry, the manufacture of clothing began a universal decline in the 1970s as production shifted offshore.

Competition facing urban manufacturing plants could also be internal, as companies expanded production by adding newer, more automated facilities in other locations. In 1990, Campbell Soup closed its antiquated Camden soup plant with a loss of 940 jobs because its three remaining newer soup plants could supply its worldwide markets at lower cost. However, Camden remained the company's world headquarters, illustrating the historical pattern of dwindling numbers of production jobs supporting relatively constant or expanding numbers of marketing and administrative positions.

Although the region's postwar presence in durable-goods manufacturing lasted longer than in nondurable goods, many of the same forces were at work. A new regional steel producer, U.S. Steel's Fairless Hills plant in Bucks County, opened in 1952 using a traditional open-hearth system just as steelmaking began to shift to newer basic oxygen processes. The newer technology reduced capital costs, improved productivity, and afforded lower pricing, but U.S. Steel and Bethlehem Steel, the nation's largest producers, did not begin to adopt it until the mid-1960s, allowing significant competitors in both the United States and abroad to emerge. Although Fairless Hills had employed as many as 10,000 by 1974, only 850 jobs remained when it largely closed in 1991. The closure of its cold rolling and tin mills in 2001 left just 250. Other steelmakers also struggled. Lukens Steel, a specialty producer in Chester County, and Alan Wood Steel, in Montgomery County, underwent ownership changes, mill closures, and job losses until their acquisition in 2006 by ArcelorMittal, the world's largest steel company, Indian-owned and headquartered in Luxembourg.

A similar pattern led to the closing of Lee Tire in suburban Montgomery County. Michelin Tire introduced the radial tire in France in 1948, and its use spread rapidly in Europe and Asia. Relative to the existing bias ply tires, radials offered at least twice the tread life, better handling, and better mileage. American manufacturers, including Lee, resisted adopting the new technology because it required new tire-making machines. Although they purchased licenses to make radial tires from Michelin, American tire companies did not succeed in making a satisfactory product until years after 1968, when Ford became the first American car manufacturer to offer radials (Michelins) as standard equipment on a car. In 1966, Lee was sold to Goodyear Tire and Rubber Company and it closed in 1980.

In the second half of the twentieth century, the cumulative effects of three developments, one in transportation, one in retailing, and one in communication, dramatically affected manufacturing in the nation and the Philadelphia region. In transportation, the shipping container, a forty-foot-long steel box into which producers pack their products, revolutionized shipping. Invented in 1956, containers reduced shipping costs by facilitating automated cargo handling and massively reducing pilferage. Easily transported on trucks, railcars, and ships, the "box" dramatically reduced the ability of domestic manufacturers to compete with foreign producers and cut the geographic advantage that had protected high-cost domestic manufacturers against lower-cost domestic competitors. Its success put additional pressure on the region's small- and medium-sized manufacturers.

In retailing, the rise of Walmart as a national company during the 1970s reshaped manufacturing and retailing. Walmart's policy of purchasing only directly from manufacturers removed the costs of dealing with wholesalers and pressured manufacturers to compete by offering the lowest prices. Walmart's consolidation of legal, accounting, banking, advertising, printing, and marketing at its Arkansas headquarters hurt both local manufacturing and service businesses. For example, Philadelphia printers (commercial printing is a type of manufacturing) who made marketing materials for local retailers lost out from both the transfer of that business elsewhere and the closure of other local retailers unable to compete with Walmart's prices. Its strategy of "everyday low pricing" pushed suppliers to constantly lower costs or lose out to a lower-priced competitor—pressure similar to what Philadelphia textile makers had faced in the 1920s. Eventually, this led manufacturers to move production to where labor costs were lower, often overseas. In communication, the rise of the Internet made Amazon and other online retailers possible. Amazon, building on the prior two developments, showed that it was possible to remove the cost of the brick-and-mortar store from consumer prices. Amazon also intensified the pressure on manufacturers to constantly reduce prices, adding to the winnowing of manufacturing.

## THE TWENTY-FIRST CENTURY

By the early twenty-first century Amazon and Walmart exemplified the global consolidation of economic enterprises seen in the region's manufacturing. An Indian company owned the region's largest remaining steel producers, and a Norwegian company in partnership with the city and U.S. government owned its remaining shipyard. The world's sixth-largest pharmaceutical and medical instrument company, GlaxoSmithKline, resulted from a merger of Philadelphia's premier pharmaceutical and medical instrument manufacturer, SmithKline Beecham, with London-based Glaxo Wellcome. Such consolidation in an industry tended to reduce competition, create barriers to entry, raise prices, diminish innovation, and inhibit wage growth of production workers. Workers in one of a company's sites could find themselves competing against workers in another, with the losers often facing plant closure.

In the twenty-first century, manufacturing in the region and nation continued to slip. In 2010, manufacturing accounted for just 6.7 percent of all jobs in the Philadelphia region. Despite political promises to rebuild the nation's manufacturing base, there was little reason to believe that manufacturing's share of jobs in either the national or regional economies would materially improve, even though the total value of U.S.-manufactured goods continued to rise. Throughout the history of manufacturing newer industries tended to employ more automation than older ones, and each cycle of investment in existing industries typically replaced more workers with machines. This occurred not only in the United States but also in the countries to which American firms exported production. Because each cycle of investment required greater skills on the part of production workers, they continued to command good wages. But manufacturing supported a diminishing share of households.

The decline of manufacturing often devastated neighborhoods and communities in areas of the Philadelphia region where it has once thrived. Kensington and the suburban city of Chester were illustrative. As plants in Kensington closed, house values plummeted, making it difficult—if not impossible—for workers who owned their own homes to sell and move to places with better job prospects after plants closed. Community shops failed, banks closed, churches and schools declined, and services deteriorated. Over time, the real estate market collapsed and houses that could not be sold became abandoned. As poverty rose, crime and other social problems increased. Outside Philadelphia, smaller municipalities experienced similar but usually more severe consequences because they rarely had the resources of larger, more diverse cities. Decline often followed the loss of one or two large employers such as Ford and Sun Shipbuilding in Chester or RCA Victor and New York Ship in Camden.

Yet the abandoned factories could also hold the potential for a renaissance. In the 2010s, several city neighborhoods once dominated by factories experienced a renaissance, perhaps fragile, through waves of small business entrepreneurship (especially in services), the in-migration of empty-nest couples, and the desire of young adults to live in the city. Thus Manayunk, Northern Liberties, and sections of Kensington and South Philadelphia became magnets for housing rehabilitation and restaurant startups. Several former regional "manufacturing suburbs" (Downingtown, Phoenixville, Glassboro) began to follow suit, but others (Bristol, Camden, Chester) found it difficult to counter deindustrialization's pervasive effects. New chapters in their stories remained to be written.

# EXPLORE MORE

The history of Greater Philadelphia's economy and working people can be seen in heritage institutions, the built environment, and abundant literature. Museums cover the region's commerce and industry. Trade and shipbuilding can be explored in the Independence Seaport Museum at 211 S. Columbus Boulevard and, across the Delaware River, at the Camden Shipyard and Maritime Museum, 1912 Broadway. In Philadelphia, the Franklin Institute on Logan Square, founded by nineteenth-century industrialists and scientists, is now a science museum. Farther afield, the Hagley Museum near Wilmington, Del., is part of the Du Pont estate and has a museum and library that chronicle industrial life. Bethlehem, Pa., is the home of the National Museum of Industrial History. Other places to visit focus on specific industries. The Mercer Museum, at 84 S. Pine Street, Doylestown, Pa., has a fine collection of preindustrial tools housed in a nineteenth-century concrete castle. The castle's builder, Henry Chapman Mercer, made his fortune at the Moravian Pottery and Tile Works, now a working history museum nearby. Millville, N.J., is home to the Museum of American Glass, while the Air Victory Museum, which tells the story of American aviation, is in Lumberton, N.J. The Winterthur Museum on Route 52 in Winterthur, Del., has artifacts from the China trade. Most community history museums also cover economic life.

Industrial ruins can be found across the region, especially in areas that bore the brunt of deindustrialization, like North Philadelphia and Camden. Redevelopment in places has built over the manufacturing footprint. The Navy Yard, which closed in the 1990s, is now home to a mixed-use development that combines residential, commercial, industrial, and recreational elements. But many sites are still visible, sometimes repurposed, sometimes providing haunts for urban explorers. A good guide to the region's industrial workplaces in their heyday is Philip Scranton and Walter Licht, *Work Sights: Industrial Philadelphia, 1890–1950* (Temple University Press, 1986). Edwin Freedley, *Philadelphia and Its Manufactures* (E. Young & Company, 1867) gives a boosterish feel for the range of nineteenth-century industry in the city and is freely available online. John R. Bowie, ed., *Workshop of the World: A Selective Guide to the Industrial Archaeology of Philadelphia* (Oliver Evans Press, 1990) is another introduction.

Connections to the rest of the world via ports, commerce, shipbuilding, and aviation are explored in Charles Lyon Chandler, Marion V. Brewington, and Edgar P. Richardson, *Philadelphia Port of History, 1609–1837* (Philadelphia Maritime Museum, 1976); Jonathan Goldstein, *Philadelphia and the China Trade, 1682–1846: Commercial, Cultural, and Attitudinal Effects* (Pennsylvania State University Press, 1978); Jeffery M. Dorwart with Jean K. Wolf, *The Philadelphia Navy Yard: From the Birth of the U.S. Navy to the Nuclear Age* (University of Pennsylvania Press, 2001); Thomas R. Heinrich, *Ships for the Seven Seas: Philadelphia Shipbuilding in the Age of Industrial Capitalism* (Johns Hopkins University Press, 1997); Frank Kingston Smith and James P. Harrington, *Aviation and Pennsylvania* (Franklin Institute Press, 1981); and William F. Trimble, *High Frontier: A History of Aeronautics in Pennsylvania* (University of Pittsburgh Press, 1982).

A small sample of work on individual industries and entrepreneurs includes Miriam Hussey, *From Merchants to "Colour Men": Five Generations of Samuel Wetherill's White Lead Business* (University of Pennsylvania Press, 1956); Philip Scranton, *Proprietary Capitalism: The Textile Manufacture at Philadelphia, 1800–1885* (Cambridge University Press, 1983); John K. Brown, *The Baldwin Locomotive Works, 1888–1915: A Study in American Industrial Practice* (Johns Hopkins University Press, 1995); Domenic Vitiello, *Engineering Philadelphia: The Sellers Family and the Industrial Metropolis* (Cornell University Press, 2013); Harry C. Silcox, *A Place to Live and Work: The Henry Disston Saw Works and the Tacony Community of Philadelphia* (Pennsylvania State University Press, 1994); Andrew Dawson, *Lives of the Philadelphia Engineers: Capital, Class, and Revolution, 1830–1890* (Ashgate, 2004); Frederick O. Barnum III, *"His Master's Voice" in America: Ninety Years of Communications Pioneering and Progress* (General Electric Company, 1991); and Daniel Sidorick, *Condensed Capitalism: Campbell Soup and the Pursuit of Cheap Production in the Twentieth Century* (Cornell University Press, 2009).

The world of work and organized labor is treated in Walter Licht, *Getting Work: Philadelphia, 1840–1950* (Harvard University Press, 1992); Bruce Laurie, *Working People of Philadelphia, 1800–1850* (Temple University Press, 1980); Peter Cole, *Wobblies on the Waterfront: Interracial Unionism in Progressive-Era Philadelphia* (University of Illinois Press, 2007); Kenneth C. Wolensky, Nicole H. Wolensky, and Robert P. Wolensky, *Fighting for the Union Label: The Women's Garment Industry and the ILGWU in Pennsylvania* (Pennsylvania State University Press, 2002); Julianne Kornacki, "Revealing Division: The Philadelphia Shirtwaist Strike, the Jewish Community, and Republican Machine Politics, 1909–1910," *Pennsylvania History* 80, no. 3 (Summer 2013): 364–400; James Wolfinger, *Running the Rails: Capital and Labor in the Philadelphia Transit Industry* (Cornell University Press, 2016); and Francis Ryan, *AFSCME's Philadelphia Story: Municipal Workers and Urban Power in the Twentieth Century* (Temple University Press, 2011).

On deindustrialization, see Jefferson Cowie, *Capital Moves: RCA's Seventy-Year Quest for Cheap Labor* (Cornell University Press, 1999); Guian A. McKee, *The Problem of Jobs: Liberalism, Race, and Deindustrialization in Philadelphia* (University of Chicago Press, 2008); and Howard Gillette Jr., *Camden After the Fall: Decline and Renewal in a Post-Industrial City* (University of Pennsylvania Press, 2005). Greater Philadelphia may have lost its claim to be the workshop of the world, but in a globalized age it remains a dynamic region, where the scars of deindustrialization stand in stark juxtaposition to gleaming skyscrapers, and where new immigrants—like those who came before them—provide the labor that keeps economic life moving.

DEC 17 1918
The YANKEE BOYS
in
ITALY
©CLE440177
PIAVE
LYRIC BY
F. A. GIANNINI
MUSIC BY
VICTOR GIANNINI
Published by THE ITALO-AMERICAN MUSIC PUB. Co.
236 S. 11TH STREET, PHILADELPHIA

## Chapter 10

# WORLD AT WAR

## Introduction

Founded by a pacifist, Philadelphia has often served as the arsenal of the republic. Great power conflict and a war for independence made the region the center of a new nation that claimed the hemisphere as its sphere of influence. The Delaware Valley's emerging industrial might provided that nation with the materiel to dominate the continent and radiate its military might overseas. By the twentieth century, the United States had become a global behemoth, thanks in part to the munitions, ships, and planes fabricated by local laborers. Even as Philadelphia helped propel the nation to superpower status, though, its reputation as the heart of a successful struggle for liberty made it a place that inspired revolutionaries abroad. People displaced by conflict and upheaval fled to the region, giving the city and its environs renown as a place of sanctuary. And while Quaker influence has long since subsided in politics, the Society of Friends' legacy endured in peace movements, which have claimed local symbols like the Liberty Bell as their own in protesting militarism.

For the most part, the sheltered Delaware Valley has experienced the republic's foreign wars from a distance, but such remoteness does not mean the impact of such conflicts has not been felt locally. The region's economic fortunes provide perhaps the best example. "War is the health of the state," wrote the New Jersey progressive Randolph Silliman Bourne in the early twentieth century. It has, in the realm of industry at least, been the health of the city too. Greater Philadelphia, for all its historical associations with peace-loving Quakers, has tended to prosper in times of conflict. When war clouds have gathered, the workshops and factories of one of North America's industrial heartlands have ramped up production to meet military needs. Mobilization in wartime increased demand for labor, giving workers a prime position to demand better pay and conditions while opening new opportunities for groups previously excluded from better-paid employment. The conjoining of war to the Delaware Valley's economic fortunes is exemplified in the history of shipbuilding. Philadelphia's federal Navy Yard, established soon after the Revolution, furnished the nation with warships for over two centuries. Employment at its dry docks rose in periods of heightened tension and fell when the international situation calmed. The prosperity of the surrounding neighborhood hinged in part on the nation's willingness to commit to foreign wars.

With war, though, has come sacrifice as well as work. The Philadelphia region has not furnished warriors for the republic in the same proportion as parts of the South and West, but it has sent plenty of its sons and daughters for service. Mostly they have joined as volunteers, though during the world wars of the twentieth century and the war in Vietnam they served as conscripts too. Military installations from the frontier forts of the Seven Years' War in the mid-eighteenth century to Burlington County's sprawling Joint Base McGuire-Dix-Lakehurst in the early 2000s have provided service personnel with homes as well as workplaces. And service in uniform has provided immigrants to the region an opportunity to prove their patriotism on the battlefield. Two years after they saw their churches burned in the Bible Riots of 1844, Irish Philadelphians took up arms against Catholic Mexico in 1846; Italians and eastern Europeans, often derided as "unassimilable" in the early twentieth century, showed their mettle in the trenches of World War I. Like the Black Philadelphians who fought for the nation in multiple wars, military service to the republic gave veterans who returned the high ground to demand recognition as Americans.

The valorization of service has stood alongside a persistent peace tradition. Philadelphians who have questioned militarism have drawn inspiration from Quaker beliefs and Revolutionary idealism. Pennsylvania's early reputation as a "peaceable kingdom" for its less hostile dealings with Indians than other British colonies may not have survived the murderous settler violence of the Seven Years' War, but even as pacific Friends found themselves cast to the margins of the region's politics by more aggressive advocates of expansion, their ethos lived on. Antiwar sentiment, for sure, had myriad motives. Party politics and commercial interests influenced opposition to the War of 1812 for instance. But principle, too, played a part. The region's abolitionists who protested the war with Mexico in 1846 refused to back a conflict for the expansion of enslavement. The coalition of protesters who organized against twenty-first-century wars in Afghanistan and Iraq marched against military interventions they saw as driven by imperial greed. At various points critics of war have drawn on Philadelphia's Revolutionary heritage to highlight the discrepancy between the republic's founding principles and its subsequent actions. Such protests have in turn generated counterprotests, a tradition stretching all the way back to the political isolation of Quakers who opposed military action against Britian's French and Indian opponents in the 1750s and 1760s. Yet to plot Philadelphia's history as one that pits peaceniks against flag wavers is too simplistic. Those who have, over the centuries, supported the troops have often done so conditionally, not least out of ties to the men and women of the region who have given the full measure of devotion to their country. And those who have resisted have often done so in response to the specific issues of each conflict. The Philadelphia abolitionists who opposed the Mexican War, for example, mostly supported a righteous (and much bloodier) struggle against slavery just a decade and a half later.

The displacement caused by conflict has also left its mark on Greater Philadelphia. William Penn envisaged his province of Pennsylvania as a place of sanctuary, and at different points in its history it has offered a home to war's refugees. Upheavals abroad have even brought celebrities to the region. After his brother's defeat at Waterloo, Joseph Bonaparte—the sometime-king of Spain—fled to the Delaware Valley, where he held court in a Center City row house before moving out to an estate in New Jersey. Others, especially from Spanish America in the early nineteenth century, came as revolutionary leaders hoping to find in Philadelphia a dose of the revolutionary spirit they wanted to prescribe in their own homelands. More often, though, war and revolution have uprooted ordinary people who have remade shattered lives in the region. From the Catholic Acadians of French Canada forced to resettle in Philadelphia during the Seven Years' War to exiles from post-1945 conflicts in Vietnam, the Middle East, and other parts of the globe, the region has provided a refuge. Like other immigrants, displaced newcomers have often encountered hostility from more established residents, but they have succeeded in crafting new lives far from their homelands. War in this way has played its part in weaving the region's rich demographic tapestry, creating under the most painful circumstances enduring communities. In this way, and so many others, the City of Brotherly Love has been forged in the furnace of unfraternal conflict.

## Seven Years' War

**James R. McIntyre**

Philadelphia and the surrounding area played a significant role in the Seven Years' War (1756–63), also known as the French and Indian War and the Great War for Empire. Beginning in North America and spreading to Europe, India, and the West Indies, the war was a struggle for colonial dominance between France and Great Britain that grew to include all the major and many of the lesser powers in Europe. As the most significant port in British America, Philadelphia and the surrounding region, including New Jersey, were drawn into the conflict. The war accelerated the region's transition from a town and hinterland into a major urban area as Philadelphia became a haven for refugees and a staging area for troops and supplies. The war also transformed the region's economy and politics as Quaker power diminished and the electoral base broadened with the addition of many who benefited from the wartime economy and qualified for the franchise.

In 1754, Pennsylvania possessed no standard organization for colonial defense. While independent military organizations, known as the Associators, had existed since King George's War (1744–48), a more uniform institution would be required to meet the needs of the growing conflict. Awareness of these needs helped Pennsylvania assemblyman Benjamin Franklin garner support for passage of the first militia law in Pennsylvania in 1755. Following a pattern in the New England colonies, the law permitted volunteers the right to choose their own officers. Such a democratic approach was opposed by Governor Robert Hunter Morris, who stood in league with the Penn-aligned Proprietary interest of the colony. Morris's opposition prompted passage of a second version of the law. As a result, two competing militia organizations existed in the colony for a brief time. The Associators remained the principal defensive force of the city, while the militia served as the first line of frontier defense. New Jersey raised troops for colonial defense as well. Since the colony's borders were not threatened with invasion, its troops were sent to the New York frontier to aid in the defense of that colony. Much of the New Jersey regiment was taken prisoner at the siege of Oswego in 1756.

From the outset of the war, Pennsylvania Quakers were divided on whether they should take any role in the defense of the colony. Some Quaker leaders objected that doing so would violate their commitment to pacifism. Others who viewed support for defense as within the Quaker mission of spreading peace may have been influenced by calls for aid from frontier communities facing Indian raids. Most Quakers serving in the Pennsylvania Provincial Assembly supported appropriating money for defense purposes between the fall of 1755 and summer of 1756. As it became clear that the conflict would last longer than initially anticipated, some grew more reticent to vote money for military measures. Six Quakers resigned from the assembly, an action that provided opposition groups an opportunity to dislodge the Quaker majority in the fall 1756 elections.

In addition to raising troops, Philadelphia served as a military staging area. In late 1756, the British commander, Lord Loudon, dispatched the Sixtieth, or Royal American, Regiment to the city. At the time, Philadelphia did not possess any barracks to house them, which touched off a major controversy. Numerous inn and tavern keepers refused to take the British soldiers at the rates then being offered by the Crown. The commander of the Royal Americans, Lieutenant Colonel Henry Bouquet, failed to make an arrangement with the mayor. On receiving word of the situation, the commander of British forces in North America, Lord Loudon, threatened to use force to acquire shelter for these troops, who were suffering from the effects of exposure to the weather and an outbreak of smallpox. At this point, a committee led by Benjamin Franklin succeeded in getting the tavern owners and innkeepers to accept the prescribed rates. Philadelphia also served as the staging area for the successful campaign led by Brigadier General John Forbes against Fort Duquesne in 1758. On his return, Forbes died in the city and was interred in the cemetery at Christ Church.

The industries and port of Philadelphia, the major trading and ship-building center in North America, helped supply the needs of the British forces in North America. The city supplied British troops with everything from candles to fresh provisions. But the war interfered with commerce as well. Before the outbreak of hostilities, ships from the Philadelphia area traded up and down the eastern seaboard as well as internationally. Part of this trade had always been illegal, and during the conflict, the Pennsylvania colonial authorities made greater efforts to suppress the illicit trade with the French through the neutral ports of the West Indies.

The conflict significantly altered the social and political make-up of Philadelphia. Refugees poured into the city from western Pennsylvania because they feared Indian attacks. In addition, roughly 450 Acadians who were forced out of their homes in Nova Scotia because the English feared they would be loyal to the French settled in Philadelphia in a row of one-story wooden structures on Pine Street. Both groups became dependent on the protection and philanthropic support of the city's Quaker population. As the transformation of Philadelphia and the surrounding area from a colonial town into a city accelerated during the Seven Years' War, the conflict changed the city's politics. The power of the Proprietary Party continued to diminish, and the working classes began to feel their political power as they had been mobilized in groups such as the Philadelphia Associators. The Seven Years' War also touched off the subsequent Pontiac's War (1763–66), which caused additional upheaval on the western Pennsylvania frontier, sparked the massacre of Conestoga Indians in Lancaster County, and further eroded the political influence of the Quakers, who became increasingly associated with strict pacifism. The controversy led some rising political figures such as Benjamin Franklin to call for Pennsylvania to dispose of the proprietors and become a royal colony. The resulting political awareness among groups outside of the Quaker-dominated Proprietary Party would become a power force in the protests against British tax policy leading to the American Revolution.

## Pontiac's War and the Paxton Boys

**Michael Goode**

Pontiac's War (1763–66), a conflict between Native Americans and the British Empire, began in the Great Lakes and Ohio Valley regions but had important ramifications for Philadelphians as panic in the Pennsylvania backcountry sent refugees to the city. The arrival of the "Paxton Boys," who were determined to seek revenge against Indians, sparked a political crisis with lasting consequences.

The immediate catalyst for the war was the French surrender of its North American territories at the end of the Seven Years' War in 1763, which left Native peoples bereft of an important ally with which to check British imperial claims on their lands. Historians in the past referred to the war as an "uprising," but the term is misleading. An uprising implies rebellion against an established authority; most Indians involved in the conflict were far beyond British imperial control. Pontiac, the Ottawa warrior whom the war is named after, was only one among many Indian leaders coordinating attacks on British forts and settlers. Pontiac's treaty with the British at Fort Ontario in 1766 ended his part in the war, but Indians east of the Mississippi continued to fight British, then American expansionism in the decades that followed.

Initially, the war appeared to be far removed from eastern Pennsylvania. The conflict began in the spring of 1763 when Pontiac assaulted Fort Detroit with Ottawa, Huron, Pottawatomi, and Ojibwa warriors. Pontiac failed to take the fort, but his siege cut Detroit off from vital British supply and communication lines. Within a few months, Native groups succeeded in overtaking at least eight other British outposts in the Great Lakes region and Ohio Country.

The nineteenth-century historian Francis Parkman believed Pontiac was the mastermind behind the war who united disparate Indian groups, but in reality his influence was limited. Native groups coordinated their attacks, but each Indian community fought to preserve its own autonomy. Besides a common enemy, Indian combatants were also linked together by a network of Native religious revivalism that rejected dependence on European trade goods—especially alcohol—in an effort to keep Indian and white colonists separate. For Indian participants, Pontiac's War had religious as well as political dimensions.

Indian raids threw backcountry Pennsylvania settlers into sheer panic. Lenape and Shawnee warriors in small raiding parties of a dozen or more attacked frontier farms and settlements as far east as the Susquehanna River valley. There are no firm casualty figures, but in addition to the perhaps hundreds of colonists killed or captured, thousands of frontier settlers fled to Philadelphia and to more secure towns and fortifications in the Delaware Valley. Hastily organized militia companies could not prevent the raids, and Lieutenant Governor James Hamilton's scalp bounty of twenty-five-pounds per head accomplished nothing except to encourage armed colonists to bully or kill a few neighboring Indians who had nothing to do with the conflict.

In November 1763, the threat of settler violence motivated hundreds of Moravian Indian converts from Bethlehem to relocate to Philadelphia seeking the provincial government's protection. They were soon

**FIGURE 81.** Franklin and the Quakers, 1764. The satirical print, published soon after the Paxton Boys had massacred twenty Indians at Conestoga, attacked Quakers for their relations with Native Americans. LIBRARY COMPANY OF PHILADELPHIA.

joined by other Indians from Wyalusing, a mixed-Native settlement in the upper Susquehanna. The government housed the Indians in a city-owned infirmary on Province Island (in the Delaware River south of Philadelphia).

While on Province Island, the refugees suffered from disease and neglect, but a far worse fate awaited the small community at Conestoga, an Indian reserve near Lancaster that was supposed to be under the protection of the Penn family. In December, approximately fifty Scots Irish Presbyterian settlers from Paxton Township rode into Conestoga and massacred six inhabitants, mutilating and scalping their bodies. The "Paxton Boys," as the vigilantes came to be known, claimed the unarmed Conestogas were harboring enemy spies and providing material support to the Indian war effort. The charge was a fabrication that masqueraded as a justification for the killings. In reality, the Paxton Boys were eager to rid the Susquehanna Valley of all Indians, friendly or combatant. The remaining members of Conestoga sought protection inside a Lancaster workhouse, but the Paxton vigilantes arrived a week later and forced their way in, massacring another fourteen. A company of Royal Highlanders stationed nearby did nothing to prevent the atrocity, and the attackers were never brought to justice.

In January 1764, as many as two hundred settlers from Paxton marched to Philadelphia, making it as far as Germantown, where they decided to halt after hearing that the city's militia had mobilized. The marchers claimed they were merely protesting the government's failure to protect them. It is doubtful whether anyone believed their second stated intention to "conduct" the Indian refugees at Province Island out of the colony without harming them. Benjamin Franklin negotiated a compromise: The marchers agreed to disperse, and one of the leaders, Matthew Smith, was allowed into the city to publish their grievances.

The crisis marked a major turning point in Philadelphia's history. It ignited a tract war that pitted Benjamin Franklin and the "Quaker Party" in the assembly against backcountry settlers and their supporters in Philadelphia. The latter group depicted the city's Quaker elite as hypocrites who cared more for the welfare of Indians than for frontier settlers. One political cartoon depicted Quakers and Indians riding on the backs of Irish and German colonists; another showed the prominent Quaker leader Israel Pemberton dancing with a topless female "squaw." Franklin tried to reframe the debate by blaming the colony's problems on the newly arrived proprietor John Penn, but he badly miscalculated by advocating that Pennsylvania be turned into a royal colony—a proposition that, not surprisingly, went nowhere on the eve of the Stamp Act crisis. The elections held later that year, which saw the highest voter turnout up to that time in Pennsylvania's history, swept Franklin and members of the Quaker Party out of the assembly and inaugurated a new era of popular politics. The anti-Indian racism epitomized by the Paxton Boys also endured well beyond the American Revolution.

## French Revolution

**David Reader**

The French Revolution of 1789 created political, social, and financial instability throughout Europe, prompting many terrified French aristocrats, businessmen, and intellectuals to flee to the United States. Philadelphia, with its cosmopolitan atmosphere, accessible port, and thriving commerce, attracted many of the French émigrés. Most settled along the Delaware River in the Mulberry district of Philadelphia (an area between modern-day Market Street, Arch Street, Second Street, and Columbus Boulevard). Others spread over the region, across the Delaware into New Jersey, and across the Brandywine into Delaware.

The French Revolution's declared ideals of liberty, equality, and fraternity immediately appealed to Philadelphians in view of their own Revolution. During the 1790s, as Philadelphia served as the nation's capital, parades and celebrations welcomed French naval vessels and dignitaries, and many Philadelphians showed their support by singing "La Marseillaise," wearing liberty caps, and commemorating Bastille Day. The emerging salon culture of Philadelphia gained greater legitimacy with the arrival of Charles Maurice de Talleyrand-Périgord in 1794. His reputation as a statesman and thinker contributed to the increasing intellectual influence of French émigrés on Philadelphia's publishing houses, newspapers, schools, and academic societies.

French émigrés established political societies and charitable organizations of their own. The Société française de bienfaisance de Philadelphie helped newly arriving French émigrés adjust to life in the city. During the yellow fever epidemic of 1793, émigré physicians with the help of Stephen Girard, a wealthy French émigré who arrived in 1776, remained in Philadelphia at Bush Hill hospital to administer to the sick. Their dedication and contributions to medicine challenged the prevailing understanding of fighting disease in Philadelphia. Nevertheless, the highly selective American Philosophical Society in Philadelphia admitted few French émigrés for their contributions in science, philosophy, and other academic fields.

The Francophile atmosphere of Philadelphia delighted Secretary of State Thomas Jefferson, who shared the positive outlook on the new republicanism of France. But President George Washington and Secretary of the Treasury Alexander Hamilton were hesitant to support the French Revolution. Jefferson and Hamilton were at constant loggerheads over domestic and foreign policy issues. Philadelphia's thriving newspaper industry exploited the division within the Washington administration. Philip Freneau's *National Gazette* and Benjamin Franklin Bache's *Aurora* supported French republicanism while John Fenno's *Gazette of the United States* reinforced the views of the Federalists.

In 1793, Philadelphia welcomed French minister Edmond-Charles Genêt with residents and émigrés lining the streets from Gray's Ferry to the City Tavern. Citizen Genêt's mission was to rally support for the war developing between Great Britain and France. The conflict had weakened trade and threatened to pull the United States into a European war. President Washington had issued a proclamation to maintain a policy of neutrality, placing a priority on avoiding entanglement in the European war despite U.S. treaty obligations to France that were negotiated during the American Revolution. (Citizen Genêt's controversial decisions and the changing political landscape in France led to his removal in 1794, but divisions over U.S. relations with France continued.)

The Reign of Terror, a period of radical republicanism in France from 1793 to 1794, alienated Philadelphians who were repulsed by the executions of King Louis XVI and his wife, Marie Antoinette. They feared that the excesses of the French Revolution were infecting Americans in their chants for democracy and distrust of Federalists. Nevertheless, many Philadelphians flocked to guillotine demonstrations, dressed in the French fashion of the sansculottes, and attended celebrations dedicated to reason. In Paris, meanwhile, the British-born Philadelphian political theorist Tom Paine, whose polemic *Common Sense* had electrified American readers in 1776, won election to the French National Convention. His *Rights of Man* (1791–2), which defended the revolution against the charges of the conservative Anglo-Irish writer Edmund Burke, had made him popular in France. Despite his staunch republicanism, Paine opposed the killing of the king, and after falling out of favor with leading Jacobins like Maximilien Robespierre, he was imprisoned and narrowly avoided the guillotine himself.

When the execution of Robespierre and his faction brought the Reign of Terror to an end in July 1794, many of the French émigrés returned home. One of the last refugees from the revolutionary upheaval that convulsed Europe, the deposed king of Naples and Spain, Joseph Bonaparte, escaped to Philadelphia after his brother Napoleon's defeat in 1815. Joseph lived first on Ninth Street and later on a grand estate along the Delaware in Bordentown, New Jersey. But long before his arrival the political influence of the French émigré community in Philadelphia had begun to decline

**FIGURE 82.** Joseph Bonaparte's Point Breeze estate, Bordentown, New Jersey, 1817. Napoleon's elder brother, who had reigned as King of Spain and Naples, sought refuge in the Philadelphia region after the French defeat at Waterloo. After a short stay in the city, he retired to this country estate on the Delaware River. ART INSTITUTE OF CHICAGO. THROUGH PRIOR ACQUISITION OF THE FRIENDS OF AMERICAN ART COLLECTION.

with the election of John Adams to the presidency in 1796 and the break in Franco-American relations that came with the wars of the French Revolution during the late 1790s. Still, the cultural legacy of the French remained in the arts and sciences. At the same time, a residual, but profound, effect of the French Revolution was its part in stirring rebellion in the French colony of Saint-Domingue (later Haiti), which led to a revolt by enslaved people that overturned French power there, caused the flight of Francophone enslavers and others to Philadelphia and other American seaport cities, and invigorated local Afro-Caribbean culture in the region.

## Haitian Revolution

**Paul Campbell**

The Haitian Revolution of 1791–1804, the most successful revolt by enslaved people in the history of the modern world, led to the establishment of the first Black-led nation in the Western Hemisphere. An army of enslaved and free people of color on France's Caribbean colony of Saint-Domingue, commanded by Toussaint L'Ouverture, wrested control of the colony from its white rulers and eventually secured independence from France. Large numbers of white people fled the colony, with many relocating to the United States. Philadelphia—which had long-standing ties to Saint-Domingue through the sugar trade—received more than a thousand of these refugees, many of them enslavers who arrived with Africans they claimed as their property. As Philadelphia served as the nation's capital for much of the period, the Haitian Revolution affected the city on both the local and national level.

Refugees arriving from Saint-Domingue had a marked influence on the culture of the city. The Haitian immigrants of African descent augmented Philadelphia's Black community, which grew by an estimated 25 percent with the arrivals. It became common to find people of color with French names, and the French language could be frequently heard on the street. The congregations of the city's Catholic churches, particularly St. Joseph's, became instantaneously biracial.

The experience of exile varied by race and status. Thomas Jefferson, who identified with Saint-Domingue's white "aristocrats," hoped the exiles would find "pity and charity" in the United States. Other white residents, feeling sympathy for the enslavers who had lost land and possessions, raised nearly $14,000 in aid. The city's Black exiles—the vast majority of whom arrived in captivity—were not exempt from the terms of the Pennsylvania Gradual Abolition Act of 1780. The act stipulated that enslaved individuals had a right to claim their freedom after six months of residing in the state. As a result, the French-born Philadelphia merchant Stephen Girard, whose brother had run a Saint-Domingue sugar plantation with enslaved labor, tried to reassure his trading partner on the island that he would have an "absolute right" to dispose of his human property in Pennsylvania inside that window. Despite the threat of early sale, from 1793 to 1796 there were 456 manumissions of enslaved West Indians in Philadelphia, and dozens of captive Haitians in the city sought to free themselves by absconding. Most, however, especially if they were young, became indentured servants for varying periods of time.

Negotiations in Philadelphia led to a change of course in U.S. policy regarding the Haitian Revolution. George Washington, president until 1797, did not support the rebellion, but his successor, John Adams, took a different position following a visit by Joseph Bunel, Toussaint L'Ouverture's diplomatic representative. Bunel arrived in Philadelphia in 1798 accompanied by his wife, Marie, to meet with U.S. government officials. Bunel met with Adams, and trade subsequently reopened between Saint-Domingue and the United States. Adams probably saw this move as an opportunity to lend support to those fighting a common enemy, as the United States was then engaged in the Quasi-War with France. It was also a chance to help American merchants by gaining a valuable trading partner in the West Indies. However, the good will did not last for long. Relations between the two republics soured after Adams left office in 1800, and the United States did not officially recognize Haiti until 1862. Marie Bunel, a free Black creole and independent merchant, chose to stay and work in Philadelphia even after the Haitian Revolution concluded.

If American diplomats tried to ignore Haiti, Philadelphia's Black community did not. The Haitian Revolution and the republic it created remained important to African American politics in the nineteenth century. Black abolitionists followed events on the island closely, Black emigrationists saw Haiti as a potential refuge from white supremacy, and as late as 1854 an African American writer told a Philadelphia audience that the "history of Toussaint" paralleled that of Napoleon. Unlike the French emperor, who "fought for himself," however, the Haitian leader "fought for liberty." A revolt that appalled many white Philadelphians became in African American memory the most emancipatory of the Atlantic World revolutions.

## Spanish American Revolutions

**Monica Henry**

As a port with longstanding commercial, cultural, and political connections with Spanish America, Philadelphia played a significant role in the era of Spanish American revolutions in the late eighteenth and early nineteenth century. The City of Brotherly Love welcomed individuals escaping Spanish domination and helped to support their ideas about liberty, equality, and independence. Philadelphia's ties with Spanish America can be traced to the eighteenth century, when merchants traded flour, rum, furniture, and general merchandise for sugar, molasses, coffee, tallow, and hides from the Spanish colonies. In 1787 alone $500,000 worth of specie from the Spanish colonies entered the city. Philadelphia became the major center of Hispanic studies as the American Philosophical Society amassed the largest collection on Spanish America and became the first scientific institution to appoint Spanish Americans as corresponding members.

At the close of the century, as discontent and unrest spread throughout the Spanish Empire, Philadelphia publishers printed revolutionary pamphlets and books. In *El desengaño del hombre* (1794), the first book ever to be published in Spanish in the United States, Santiago Puglia—an exile from Spain in Philadelphia since 1790—condemned monarchism as he drew an idealized picture of U.S. democracy for his Spanish American readership. Other aspiring revolutionaries also admired the new republic. The Venezuelan leader Francisco de Miranda had been favorably impressed with Philadelphia during his visit in 1783–84 and regarded the city as the cradle of liberty. Likewise, the *Libertador* General Simón Bolívar of Venezuela, whose army was to free northern South America in the late 1810s and 1820s, visited the United States on his way back home from Europe in 1806. As he sailed from Philadelphia to La Guaira, near Caracas, he was convinced he had seen "rational liberty for the first time." Five years later, in 1811, a Philadelphia publisher issued a Spanish compendium of extracts from the revolutionary polemics of Tom Paine. The Venezuelan Manuel García de Sena's, who had resided in the city since 1803, undertook the translation.

Spanish American exiles like Puglia and García de Sena often resided in Philadelphia. Manuel de Trujillo y Torres, who fled the viceroyalty of New Granada (later Colombia) after actively opposing the Spanish authorities, was the most prominent. Upon his arrival in 1796, Torres made contacts with influential political leaders and merchants, wrote informative articles on Spanish America for the newspaper *Aurora* edited by his friend William Duane, published pamphlets and books on U.S.-Spanish American trade, and helped revolutionary envoys purchase arms and munitions for their governments. Torres's house, first on Spruce Street and later at 193 S. Tenth Street, was the meeting place for other exiles from New Granada such as Joaquín Sorondo, Francisco Zinza, and Manuel Palacio Fajardo.

When the James Monroe administration recognized the independence of the new Spanish American republics in 1822, the ailing Torres became the first official minister of the Republic of Colombia (today Venezuela, Colombia, Ecuador, and Panama) in the United States. He died the same year and was buried in the cemetery of old St. Mary's Church of his adopted city. Torres and the other Spanish Americans' work was pursued by the Cuban-born priest Félix Varela. In 1823 he was forced into exile and settled in Philadelphia. There he published *El habanero*, Cuba's first pro-independence newspaper, and translated English works into Spanish, including Thomas Jefferson's *A Manual of Parliamentary Practice*.

While merchants such as Stephen Girard continued commercial activities in Central and South American ports during the 1810s and 1820s, a Philadelphian represented U.S. political interests in the Western Hemisphere as well. In 1825 President John Quincy

Adams appointed John Sergeant, a lawyer and leader of the Philadelphia bar, delegate to the first meeting of American nations to take place at the Panama isthmus in 1826. From the 1830s, however, as Spanish Americans became more concentrated on building their nations, Philadelphians gradually lost interest in their southern neighbors while focusing increasingly on local and national issues and politics.

## Quasi-War

**Nathaniel Conley**

Philadelphia, as capital of the United States during the 1790s, played a central role in the conflict called the Quasi-War, an undeclared war, between the United States and France during the years 1798 to 1800. Philadelphia became a hotbed of public displays for and against the Federalists' response to this conflict and served as a base for naval operations against French forces in the West Indies.

After war began between Great Britain and France in 1793, relations between France and the United States became tense, particularly when the French revolutionary government known as the Directory came to power and U.S.-British relations stabilized with the Jay Treaty in 1795. The United States attempted neutrality in the war, formalized in the Proclamation of Neutrality (1793) of President George Washington. After the Jay Treaty, which settled outstanding issues between Great Britain and the United States and seemingly abrogated America's Revolutionary era treaty obligations with France regarding mutual defense, the French Directory authorized seizure of U.S. shipping, which soured relations by March 1797 when President John Adams took office. The conflict with France was especially serious for Philadelphia, a primary commercial port in the United States, as its merchants and ship owners were hard hit. Adams sent a mission to France to seek an agreement that would prevent war, stop confiscation of American shipping, and obtain compensation for seizures of American ships. French agents (named X, Y, and Z in dispatches) relayed the French Directory's demand, before negotiations could begin, for a bribe, a loan, and an apology for a speech critical of France that Adams had made to Congress. News of the XYZ Affair, as it was later known, created a storm of anti-French feeling in the United States.

**FIGURE 83.** Building the frigate *Philadelphia*, Southwark, 1800. LIBRARY OF CONGRESS.

Philadelphia experienced a tumult of both anti-French and anti-Federalist sentiment. Protests broke out demanding war with France in a city that was bitterly divided after almost a decade of partisanship over the French Revolution. The Federalists especially used the war with France to stoke fears of the French Revolution spreading to America and of a French invasion to follow. Arguing for increased national security, the Federalist-controlled Congress beefed up the military and passed the Alien and Sedition Acts, which targeted foreign nationals and made it a criminal offense to criticize the government. Their purpose was to quash Jeffersonian (Democratic-Republican) criticism of Federalist policies and silence the opposition press. The political divide was especially evident in the Philadelphia press, as newspapers sided with the Federalists or Democratic-Republicans. Particularly vociferous was Benjamin Franklin Bache, who was jailed for his anti-administration attacks under the Sedition Act. Federalist judges in the mid-Atlantic region were especially aggressive in seeking prosecutions under the act, which actions later led to efforts to impeach one Supreme Court justice and to restrict the authority of the judiciary because of its partisanship and supposed abuse of power.

The United States had a relatively small navy at the beginning of the Quasi-War. In 1794, Congress passed the Naval Act, choosing Philadelphian Joshua Humphreys to design six frigates. Philadelphia shipbuilders constructed several ships, including the USS *United States* (1797) and the USS *Philadelphia* (1799), the latter built and outfitted with subscriptions by the citizens of Philadelphia. These ships came under the control of the Navy Department, a special department created by Congress in 1798 as part of the broader program to increase military strength. Privateers also operated out of Philadelphia, preying on French shipping, the most famous of which was the ship *Louisa*. Carrying a letter of marque, *Louisa* operated as a well-armed privateer in the Atlantic and Mediterranean, where its crew successfully defended against attack by French privateers and took refuge in Gibraltar.

The Quasi-War officially ended with the Convention of 1800, or Treaty of Mortefontaine, which formally ended the alliance of 1778 between the United States and France but made provisions to reestablish trade and avoid further conflict. Depredations on American shipping continued, however, until the end of the Napoleonic Wars in 1815. The Federalist Party also suffered because of the war when it became evident that it had exaggerated fears of French invasion and used the war to threaten the press and repress political opposition. The hotly contested elections of 1800 led to Federalist losses in the state and nation and redrew the political map thereafter in favor of the Democratic-Republicans.

## War of 1812

**Paul Campbell**

Philadelphia was pivotal in supporting America's war effort during the War of 1812, the final war in which the United States and Britain fought on opposing sides. The city functioned as a major supply center for the army, and its revitalized port outfitted vessels for the navy. People from the Philadelphia area operated war-related businesses, helped build fortifications, and traveled far from home to fight on land and sea. In the aftermath of the conflict, as the country was embroiled in a severe economic downturn, Philadelphia evolved as a focal point for attempting a national economic resurgence as it became the base of operations for the second Bank of the United States.

The War of 1812 had roots in Philadelphia. On June 3, 1811, William Henry Harrison began his regiment's march to the Indiana Territory from the city. Several months later, on November 7, 1811, the unit fought the Shawnee at Tippecanoe. Some historians consider this the first battle of the War of 1812, as it made the Native peoples realize that an alliance with Britain offered their best hope of maintaining self-determination.

Pennsylvania provided substantial support for the war, though enthusiasm for the conflict varied across the region. The state provided the largest vote in Congress for the war's declaration and later played a key role in reelecting the bellicose incumbent, James Madison, in the 1812 presidential race against DeWitt Clinton. In contrast with Pennsylvania, most congressmen from neighboring Delaware and New Jersey voted against declaring war. Delaware Federalist James A. Bayard served as the minority leader in the Senate, and Federalists united in opposition to the conflict. Bayard later became one of five Americans to sign the 1814 Treaty of Ghent, establishing peace terms between the United States and Britain. All of New Jersey's delegates were Democratic-Republicans like President Madison, yet they, along with other anti-war congressmen, believed the nation stood unprepared militarily and that overseas commerce would suffer. Nevertheless, both Delaware and New Jersey acquiesced in raising troops.

Philadelphia-area residents from all economic and social backgrounds participated in the war effort. Those who joined militias fought in the western territories, Niagara theater, and Chesapeake region. Many recruits were Irish immigrants who recently arrived in East Coast cities like Philadelphia and were eager both to oppose the British and lift themselves out of poverty. On the home front, the yard of the Pennsylvania State House (Independence Hall) became an active place for drilling troops and gathering civilians for war-related labor. In 1814, when a British invasion of Philadelphia became a distinct possibility, African American businessmen James Forten and Russell Parrott used the yard for organizing more than two thousand free Black people to help strengthen fortifications at Gray's Ferry on the Schuylkill River.

The war saw Philadelphia reclaim its position as an essential port for the United States Navy. Shipyards on the Delaware River busily engaged in shipbuilding and repair. However, not all the region's maritime industries thrived. The British navy's frequent presence on the Delaware Bay adversely affected fishermen and traders. While the British never sailed upriver as far as Philadelphia, the town of Lewes, Delaware, was not so fortunate. On April 5 and 6, 1813, after refusing to provision a British flotilla, Lewes faced bombardment for twenty-two hours. Delaware militia defending the town managed to keep British troops from landing on shore, and the attackers eventually withdrew.

As the United States continued waging a war that it did not have the financial resources to afford, it plunged ever deeper into economic chaos. Uniquely, Pennsylvania—at least for a while—experienced wartime prosperity, thanks largely to the army's purchase of vast quantities of supplies within the state, and to the fact that one of the most important supply routes ran between Philadelphia and Pittsburgh. Much of the money generated by these ventures ended up in Pennsylvania banks, and Philadelphia found itself with enough money to engage in large-scale building projects. However, business failures in New York in 1814 created a ripple effect that reached Philadelphia and brought Pennsylvania's financial surge to a halt.

**FIGURE 84.** Camp Dupont, near Wilmington, Delaware, ca. 1830. In 1814, the threat British troops posed to the Dupont powder mills led to the camp's establishment on the banks of the Brandywine River. The Philadelphia militiamen encamped there proved a sufficient deterrent, and unlike Baltimore and Washington, the region did not face an invasion. HISTORICAL SOCIETY OF PENNSYLVANIA.

Philadelphians took advantage of wartime opportunities to increase their production, profits, and political standing. Philadelphia seamstress Elizabeth Claypoole, popularly known as Betsy Ross, made garrison flags for the U.S. arsenal on the Schuylkill River. In Delaware, French immigrant industrialist Eleuthère Irénée Du Pont oversaw the manufacture of gunpowder at his mills near Wilmington. His business became crucial after the British naval blockade hindered the importation of gunpowder from Europe. Militia troops were stationed at Camp Dupont to guard the mills. Other parts of the United States proved more vulnerable. On August 24, 1814, the British army marched through Washington, D.C., burning both the President's House (the White House) and the Capitol. The torching of the federal buildings opened the possibility of temporarily returning the capital to Philadelphia, but the House of Representatives defeated a bill including this provision by nine votes. The United States stumbled out of the war in the throes of one of the worst inflationary crises in its history. The expense of the conflict and damage to commerce had dealt the economy a crippling blow from which it would take years to recover. In 1816, in an effort to solve the dilemma, the government rechartered the national bank, which had ceased to exist in 1811, once again choosing Philadelphia as its residence. Later that year, the second Bank of the United States began operating in Carpenters Hall on Chestnut Street. In 1824, it moved into another Chestnut Street home, an impressive new Greek Revival structure designed by architect William Strickland. Philadelphia retained its position as the nation's financial capital until the early 1830s, when President Andrew Jackson vetoed renewal of the Second Bank's charter. While Philadelphia's preeminence in finance rapidly diminished thereafter, the expansion of manufacturing the war had stimulated proved more enduring, and the region played a critical role in supplying the nation in subsequent conflicts.

## Mexican-American War

**William V. Bartleson**

Despite taking place in the American Southwest and Central America, the Mexican-American War (1846–48) had significant ties to the Philadelphia area. As one of the most populous urban centers in the country, the Delaware Valley became a hotbed of activity for one of the most controversial wars in American history.

War between the United States and Mexico followed the admission of Texas as the twenty-eighth state of the United States in December 1845. This exacerbated preexisting tension with the Mexican government, which never recognized Texas independence, American annexation of Texas, or the proposed border of the new state at the Rio Grande. After an armed clash between U.S. forces led by General Zachary Taylor and Mexican troops in the disputed area between the Nueces River and the Rio Grande, Congress declared war on Mexico on May 13, 1846, and authorized President James K. Polk to call up fifty thousand volunteers to join the existing U.S. Army.

In Philadelphia and elsewhere, the controversy surrounding the coming and course of the Mexican-American War illustrated the widening divide in American society over the issues of territorial conquest and the expansion of slavery. Initially, support for the war was strong in the mid-Atlantic states, and Philadelphia's historic ties to the American Revolution made it a centerpiece for pro-war patriotism by politicians and cultural figures who viewed Manifest Destiny as the legacy of American independence. The *Philadelphia North American*, a newspaper owned by George R. Graham, reported news from Mexico and initially supported "Mr. Polk's War" in editorials. However, Philadelphia's active abolitionist community opposed the war as a vehicle for expanding slavery into new territory.

The war was equally controversial in New Jersey and Delaware. In New Jersey, a strong Whig Party presence in state politics made unified action difficult. In September 1847, a convention of New Jersey Whigs condemned the Polk administration's drive for territorial annexation. Their resolutions "strongly denounced the present national administration for . . . having made war without consulting the people or their representatives, and that too, for party purposes." This sentiment was common across New Jersey. When New Jersey governor Charles C. Stratton responded to President Polk's call to organize volunteers for service, the turnout was so meager that only a battalion of volunteers could be formed, not a regiment. In Delaware, opposition to the war ran so strong that only a dozen residents volunteered to serve.

Following the declaration of war, Pennsylvania governor Francis R. Shunk called for forming six regiments to serve in the U.S. Army. In contrast to the tepid response in New Jersey and Delaware, patriotic enthusiasm quickly satisfied the quotas, and several full companies had to be turned away. Recruits from the Keystone State were organized into the First and Second Pennsylvania Volunteer Regiments. Of the ten companies constituting the First Regiment, six hailed from Philadelphia, including the City Guards of Philadelphia, the Philadelphia Light Guards, and the Cadwalader Grays. The Second Regiment became home to Company F, known as the Philadelphia Rangers.

Along with the patriotism that motivated Philadelphia men to serve, the disorder and violence that had been hallmarks of Philadelphia during the 1830s and 1840s also traveled west with the volunteers who mustered in Harrisburg and then proceeded to Pittsburgh en route to Mexico. In Pittsburgh, soldiers from Company D (the City Guard) invaded a local theater in an incident that ended in a violent clash with police. This riotous behavior continued later in New Orleans, where a soldier claiming membership in the notorious Philadelphia "Killers" gang attacked citizens and destroyed property across the city. Later, a faction of the Killers intimidated Company D's commanding officer, Captain Joseph Hill. Another veteran of Philadelphia street violence, Major General Robert Patterson, led the Pennsylvania volunteer regiments after their transport down the Mississippi River and across the Gulf to Lobos, Mexico, where they landed in February 1846. Patterson, a former Pennsylvania militia commander, had led troops against rioters in Philadelphia over the preceding years. In Mexico, he commanded the Second Division of a brigade led by Brigadier General Gideon J. Pillow, which took in the Pennsylvania volunteers.

TERRITORIO OREGON
ALTA
CALIFORNIA
GREAT BASIN
MAR PACIFICO
APACHERIA
NUEVO MEJICO
SONORA
CHIHUAHUA
DURANGO
NUEVO LEON
JALISCO
TEJAS
INDIAN TERRITORY
TABLA DE DISTANCIAS.
TABLA ESTADISTICA.
CARTA DE LOS CAMINOS &c. DESDE VERA CRUZ Y ALVARADO A MÉJICO.

**FIGURE 85.** Mexico during the Mexican-American War, 1847. Library of Congress. The conflict divided Philadelphians. For supporters (like the popular novelist George Lippard), a freedom-loving American people made up of exiles from the lands of Northern Europe were driving the remnants of monarchy from the hemisphere. For critics, the assault on a sister republic amounted to a crusade for slavery. LIBRARY OF CONGRESS.

The fighting men from Philadelphia saw their first significant combat at the Siege of Veracruz in March 1847. In the thunderous twenty-day siege, the Pennsylvania regiments lost the service of fifteen soldiers to enemy cannon fire, including three who were killed. After the fall of Veracruz, the regiments moved into the Mexican interior and saw action again in April at the Battle of Cerro Gordo as part of an assault on Mexican artillery. Despite the ferocity of the engagement, the regiments suffered few casualties. For the next two months, they continued inland toward Mexico City, fighting guerillas, the elements, and disease.

In September 1847, the Pennsylvania regiments were split by General Winfield Scott to prepare for the assault on Mexico City. While three of the Philadelphia companies were reassigned to garrison duty at Puebla, the Reading Artillery of Company A and the Philadelphia Rangers of the Second Regiment proceeded with the main army toward Mexico City. Both companies saw heavy fighting at close range with the Mexican defenders. In two days of combat, the Second Regiment suffered its worst losses of the conflict with eight men killed and eighty-nine wounded.

Mexican troops flushed out of Mexico City and led by General Antonio López de Santa Anna next attacked Puebla, where the Philadelphian remnant of the First Regiment had been stationed. A nearly month-long siege began on September 14, 1847. Forces under Lieutenant Colonel Samuel W. Black, a Pittsburgh native and future territorial governor of Nebraska, faced repeated assaults and dwindling supplies until Santa Anna withdrew his troops on October 12. The Siege of Puebla was not only the Pennsylvanians' finest performance, it was also its most costly. The First Regiment suffered fifty-five casualties with twenty-one men killed in action. In December 1847, the survivors marched to Mexico City, where they reunited with the Second Regiment to much fanfare and celebration.

Philadelphia-area soldiers also served in areas of the war other than Mexico. A veteran of the War of 1812, Rear Admiral William Mervine, commanded the USS *Savannah* in the Pacific, and his Marine Corps detachment captured the city of Monterey in July 1846. Samuel Francis Du Pont of the famed Du Pont family of Delaware commanded the blockade of California and achieved the rank of rear admiral. Future U.S. senator from New Jersey Commodore Robert Stockton was instrumental in the capture of Monterey and Pueblo de Los Ángeles in California. Between July 1846 and January 1847, Stockton served as military governor of California.

In Mexico, Philadelphia native and Brigadier General Persifor Frazer Smith served as military governor during the occupation of Mexico City, when duty for the Pennsylvania volunteer regiments consisted of a mixture of drill, boredom, and sporadic chaos as Mexican guerilla units harassed U.S. forces. When U.S. troops withdrew on March 6, 1848, the regiments' long journey home took them from Mexico back to New Orleans, then up the Mississippi River and Ohio River to Pittsburgh, where they arrived in July 1848. The Pittsburgh units mustered out of service quickly, but the Philadelphia companies resolved to end their service at home. Between July 27 and August 5, parades, speeches, banquets, and community events across the Delaware Valley marked their return. Of the 2,415 men who served in the Pennsylvania volunteer regiments, 477 died in Mexico or in transport. Fifty-two were killed in combat. New Jersey's volunteers saw little combat in Mexico and most casualties were the result of disease.

The Treaty of Guadalupe Hidalgo ended the Mexican-American War on February 2, 1848, and expanded the territory of the United States by 525,000 square miles. However, the costly victory, earned after two years of ferocious combat, exacerbated the simmering tensions throughout the country. Volunteers from Philadelphia and the surrounding region participated in the military actions while local citizens debated the war's political and moral ramifications, making Philadelphia and the Delaware Valley a microcosm of the conflict.

## Spanish-American War

**Paul A. Kopacz**

Although often regarded as a minor conflict, the Spanish-American War (1898) made a major impact on Greater Philadelphia. As a populous urban center, Philadelphia and its immediate environs contributed a substantial number of troops to the United States' volunteer army and provided an outlet for those

**FIGURE 86.** Spanish-American War in the Caribbean, 1899. The war with Spain saw fighting over Caribbean islands that had longstanding ties to Philadelphia. LIBRARY OF CONGRESS.

dissenters who decried warfare. In addition, the war boosted war-production manufacturing while also creating shortages that affected local industries and consumers. After the successful conclusion of hostilities, Philadelphia hosted a three-day victory festival that drew national attention, but debate continued over the United States' acquisition of former Spanish territory.

The Spanish-American War propelled the victorious United States into the forefront of world affairs, allowed America to take a seat among leading military powers, and established the young nation as a fledgling empire. A unique combination of social, economic, and political pressures helped push the United States into open warfare against Spain, but officially, President William McKinley asked Congress for the authority to commit American troops in order to liberate Cuba, and its people, from oppressive Spanish rule. Once war had been declared on April 25, 1898, the U.S. government began recruiting state National Guard regiments to create the foundation of a national army. Aroused by months of inflammatory newspaper articles that vividly depicted Spanish atrocities and Cuban suffering, and stimulated to patriotic heights by the sinking of the USS *Maine* in Havana harbor, Philadelphia-area residents did not hesitate to enlist. Philadelphia contributed four regiments of volunteer infantry (the First, Second, Third, and Sixth), one battery of artillery (Light Battery A), and one troop of cavalry (First Troop Philadelphia City Cavalry) for a total of 4,849 soldiers. Wilmington and northern Delaware sent almost three hundred men (Companies A, C, F, H, and K) into the army. In New Jersey, Camden County opened a recruiting office to fill a proposed Sixth Regiment, but the war ended before the Sixth could be mustered into service. Of all these volunteers only Light Battery A and the First Troop City Cavalry deployed for service overseas, although an armistice was declared before they saw action. Sailors from the area, however, served aboard warships that engaged in combat in both Cuba and the Philippines.

Although local support for the war was pervasive, it was not unanimous. The Universal Peace Union, based in Philadelphia and led by Alfred H. Love, condemned armed conflict with Spain before and after hostilities began. Love went so far as to send a peace initiative to the Spanish queen regent, by a European courier, after the United States declared war. When this came to light, the *Philadelphia Bulletin* openly questioned his loyalty, inciting angry mobs to march on his home and burn his bullet-ridden effigy in Chester. Denounced as a traitor, he was even turned away by the prisoners of Eastern State Penitentiary, where he had counseled inmates every Sunday for the previous forty-two years. Meanwhile, the city council, under political pressure, evicted the Universal Peace Union from its office on Independence Square.

The war economy bestowed benefits but also imposed hardships. On the upside, military manufacturing provided employment for men, women, and even children still suffering from the Panic of 1893. E.I. du Pont de Nemours & Company, attempting to supply the government's insatiable need for gunpowder, aggressively expanded operations and hiring at its brown powder mill north of Wilmington and its smokeless powder plant in South Jersey. Camden shipbuilder John H. Dialogue & Son employed workers to build U.S. naval vessels. In Philadelphia extensive shipyards such as William Cramp & Sons Ship and Engine Building Co. and the League Island Navy Yard, in addition to building large warships, added extra shifts to provide gunboats to patrol and protect coastal waterways. Workers at Midvale Steel and the Frankford Arsenal worked around the clock to produce naval artillery and small arms ammunition, while smaller companies and seamstresses working at home labored to provide American fighting men with apparel and accoutrements. Everything from uniforms and tents to buttons, blankets, caps, and summer drawers were stored or produced in the Schuylkill Arsenal.

While the war with Spain benefited some industries, the conflict in Cuba threatened to disrupt others. During the early months of 1898, as tensions increased between the United States and Spain, local cigar manufacturers, anticipating hostilities, imported as much tobacco from Cuba as they could. By the time war began, farsighted Philadelphia-area cigar makers had stockpiled enough Cuban tobacco to keep their workers rolling and their customers smoking for at least another year. Philadelphia sugar manufacturers faced a different dilemma. An ongoing two-year struggle between revolutionaries and Spanish authorities had already impeded Cuban sugar exports and forced desperate refinery owners to search the world for other sources of supply. When war between the United States and Spain began, raw sugar from such distant places as Java, the Philippines, Egypt, and Mauritius in the Indian Ocean made its way into Philadelphia ports, as did beet sugar from Germany. These auxiliary supply strategies kept the cigar and sugar industries running but increased costs for consumers. Throughout the region, shortages caused by the war resulted in higher prices for food staples. Flour became exceptionally expensive and the price of bread skyrocketed.

After suffering two crushing naval losses and with its armies on the brink of defeat, Spain negotiated an armistice that began on August 12, 1898; a formal peace treaty followed four months later. Once hostilities concluded, the city of Philadelphia planned a Peace Jubilee to celebrate the nation's victory over Spain. The focal point of the Philadelphia Peace Jubilee was the construction of a towering, electrically illuminated, Athenian arch that spanned Broad Street near Sansom, bisecting a Court of Honor of ornate columns lining Broad Street from city hall to Walnut Street. The celebration commenced on October 25, 1898, with a grand naval pageant of boats on the Delaware River. Two days later twenty-five thousand soldiers, many from Philadelphia, marched down the Court of Honor under the respectful gaze of President William McKinley. The festivities concluded October 28 with a vast civic parade representing many of the city's diverse ethnic, social, business, civil, and educational organizations. Spectators traveled from all over the United States to attend.

As in the rest of the United States, the aftermath of the Spanish-American War led some Philadelphia-area

**FIGURE 87.** Triumphal Arch and Court of Honor for the Peace Jubilee to mark the end of the Spanish-American War, Broad Street, Philadelphia, 1898. LIBRARY COMPANY OF PHILADELPHIA.

inhabitants to openly question their nation's new role as an imperial power. After the war, American soldiers remained overseas to occupy Cuba and America's new possessions: Puerto Rico, Guam, and the Philippines. Generally, these occupations were temporary and peaceful, but in the Philippines, U.S. troops combatted a fierce native insurgency for years. Staunch Filipino resistance compelled the Philadelphia American League (1899) to condemn imperialism as a violation of the republican principle of government by consent of the governed. Philadelphia African Americans also spoke out against American colonialism. Black newspapers such as the *Philadelphia Defender* sympathized with the plight of the Filipinos but remonstrated that the United States government should worry less about foreign entanglements and, instead, redress the lack of equality endured at home by its own citizens of color.

The Spanish-American War lasted little more than three and a half months, but its legacy lived on in the Philadelphia region for years. In many ways, the conflict with Spain served as a rudimentary rehearsal for America's next war, World War I. The martial spirit and patriotism displayed in 1898 revived and grew in 1917 as tens of thousands of local men answered the call to join the army and navy. The ethos of military production that powered the region's economy during the Spanish-American War intensified during the Great War, and area civilians endured even more severe privations. The Spanish-American War had prepared the region to proceed and persevere through the First World War.

## World War I

**Jacob Downs**

Although the United States' involvement in the First World War lasted just over a year, the conflict in Europe had a lasting impact on the Philadelphia region. The war created new opportunities for industries in Philadelphia, Chester, and Camden, and as men and women enlisted for military service, the region developed a sense of a patriotic community through food drives and bond campaigns. World War I, known at the time as the Great War, also reshaped the region's social landscape. African Americans migrated from the South in large numbers to fill industrial jobs, and women found new opportunities outside the home. However, the war also caused a serious backlash toward the region's large German American population.

As Europe became engulfed in a bitter war in 1914, most Philadelphians supported the position of neutrality proclaimed by President Woodrow Wilson. While the United States did not deploy combat troops in the early stages of the war, it did send munitions, weapons, textiles, and other goods to England and France. Philadelphia played a vital role in that supply. In the region, the war in Europe sparked meetings, discussions, and public gatherings, and major events had local impact. After local newspapers reported that German armies committed atrocities in Belgium in 1914, residents of Philadelphia and the surrounding area raised money for Belgian relief. In May 1915, twenty-seven Philadelphians died when a German U-boat torpedoed and sank the British ocean liner *Lusitania*. Eight of them were members of the family of Paul Crompton, vice president of the Surpass Leather Company in Northwest Philadelphia. He was en route to England with his family and a large shipment of sheepskin accoutrements that had been purchased by the British army.

While most in the Philadelphia region supported U.S. neutrality, hostility to the Central Powers

(Germany and Austria-Hungary) led to discrimination against residents of German ancestry. Federal agents raided the offices of the *Tageblatt*, a German newspaper in Philadelphia, and arrested staff members for treason. Philadelphians pressured the school board to halt the teaching of the German language, and vandals defaced statues of Johann Wolfgang von Goethe, Friedrich Schiller, and Otto von Bismarck. As in other American communities, sauerkraut was renamed "Liberty Cabbage," and Christmas legends such as Kris Kringle and Santa Claus were banned from public mention. German Americans throughout the region, especially in Philadelphia, protested the rhetoric directed against them as well as U.S. involvement in the war. They asked Philadelphia officials to help develop a better understanding of Germany and its people and to denounce anti-German demonstrations. Many of Philadelphia's German Americans also called upon the United States to cease shipping goods to the Allies. Their actions only served to deepen suspicions.

War created a significant boost to the region's industries, which produced clothing, ammunition, weapons, and war machines for the U.S. military and the Allies. Even before U.S. entry into the conflict on April 6, 1917, the war helped to reinvigorate the region's struggling textile industry. For example, the Dobson's Mills, located in Kensington, Manayunk, and Germantown, filled an order for one hundred thousand blankets to the French army in the first year of the war. Area shipyards expanded, producing 328 ships during the war years. The New York Shipbuilding Corporation in South Camden and the Pusey and Jones shipbuilding companay in Gloucester City became major contributors to the war effort. The war also vastly expanded the Camden Forge, a major supplier for the shipyards. The Baldwin Locomotive Works manufactured artillery shells and other munitions. Seventy-five percent of the military's boots and shoes came from Philadelphia tanners.

In Delaware, the gunpowder manufacturer E.I. du Pont de Nemours & Company vastly expanded its munitions production, from $25 million in sales 1914 to $319 million in 1918. Providing 40 percent of the munitions used by the Allied Forces during World War I, DuPont became one of the wealthiest companies in history. Its profits during World War I later drew scrutiny from the U.S. Senate, which held a series of committee hearings in the 1930s to investigate the role of industry in the U.S. decision to enter the war.

Home-front civilians contributed to the war in a number of ways. They donated extensively to the three major "Liberty Loan" campaigns, which allowed Americans to contribute savings to the war effort. Philadelphia's Liberty Bell served as the campaign's official symbol. The City of Philadelphia urged residents to use less fuel and food, even going as far as to implement "heatless Mondays" and "wheatless Wednesdays." Contributions to the war effort caused dramatic shortages in food, fuel, and other necessities. During the late years of the war, some Philadelphia businesses and other commercial buildings closed due to a lack of coal and food.

While the war created difficult conditions for many, it also opened doors to new opportunities. Advocates of Prohibition, for example, used the war to their advantage by arguing that beer drinkers were anti-American and pro-German. Many women filled the jobs of men who were drafted or serving in the military. They organized Liberty Bond drives and other fundraisers. Women joined the Red Cross in great numbers and served as nurses overseas, and some women—nearly two thousand from the city of Philadelphia alone—enlisted in the military. While they did not serve in combat, they worked in offices and other clerical positions.

Wartime growth of industry and labor shortages in the North also drew Black southerners to northern industrial cities in a movement that became known as the Great Migration. African Americans who wanted to escape economic hardship, threats of violence, and discriminatory Jim Crow laws in the South hoped to find better opportunities in the North. In Philadelphia, Camden, Chester, and other cities, African Americans sought employment in industries including Baldwin Locomotive, the Pennsylvania Railroad, the Reading Railroad, and Midvale Steel. While African Americans were poorly paid and forced to perform the least-desirable jobs, their chances for economic independence and advancement proved better in the Philadelphia region than in the South.

White Philadelphians, especially recent immigrants, saw African Americans as competitors for jobs and housing and resisted their arrival. In July 1918, after an

African American woman moved into a house at 2936 Ellsworth Street in Philadelphia, a white neighborhood, angry white residents stoned the house and attacked nearby Black residents. The event triggered a riot that lasted two days and resulted in the deaths of one African American and two whites. The threat of violence became so intense that the Colored Protective Association formed to assert the rights of Black citizens.

While many of the area's residents contributed to the war effort at home, thousands crossed the Atlantic to fight for the Allies in Europe. Nearly sixty thousand men were called to arms from Philadelphia and surrounding neighborhoods. Philadelphians often served alongside one another in the same divisions. About seven thousand from the region, for example, served in the army's Twenty-Eighth Infantry Division, which saw constant combat at the front in Marne and Argonne, France, throughout 1918. The Seventy-Ninth Infantry Division also drafted a large portion of its men from Philadelphia.

The success of the Allies in Europe came at a price. As the war came to a close, the Delaware Valley faced two major challenges. First, the industrial boom came to an abrupt end. No longer supported by the high demand for war matériel, many of the factories and mills in Philadelphia, Camden, and the surrounding area closed in the early 1920s. Dobson's textile mills, which had grossed $20 million in the last year of the war, began closing mills in the early 1920s. By 1928 the last of the Dobson's mills had closed. In Camden, New York Shipbuilding as well as other industrial firms had to lay off many of their employees. Massive job cuts exacerbated growing social unrest spurred on by the red scare. The second challenge came in the form of an influenza pandemic. The epidemic struck densely populated Philadelphia, Camden, and other cities particularly hard. In just four weeks between October and November of 1919, the influenza pandemic claimed the lives of many more Philadelphians than had been killed during the entire course of the war.

World War I provided the "Workshop of the World" and the surrounding area the opportunity to flex its industrial prowess. Philadelphia produced massive quantities of goods for the war effort, and the war gave women and African Americans the opportunity to become more active in public and in the workforce. However, the conflict also brought with it discrimination against German American citizens, food and fuel shortages, and the death of nearly 1,400 Philadelphia men. The economic downturn that came with peace, meanwhile, created new challenges for the years ahead.

## World War II

**Herbert Ershkowitz**

World War II, which changed industries, populations, and politics in many urban areas in the United States, had a transforming effect on the Philadelphia region. Already industrialized, the region gained new impetus from government orders for supplies, armaments, transportation, and more. Philadelphia-area industries expanded, making the region a major "arsenal for democracy" during the war. With its federal Navy Yard, arsenal, and universities, Philadelphia also developed and produced new materials, instruments of communication, electronic tracking, and weaponry. The availability of defense work in cities such as Philadelphia, Camden, and Chester opened opportunities for women and African Americans, including new migrants from the countryside and the South. Much of the demographic movement was temporary, and it was sometimes convulsive, but it helped to redraw the social landscape of the city and region.

The war, which the United States joined in December 1941 following the Japanese attack on Pearl Harbor, had sometimes contradictory effects. For example, defense needs created more unity in the region than had existed since the early twentieth century. People mobilizing for a war against Nazism in Europe and against Japanese expansion in Asia shared a common purpose, and they were further united by the effects of federal regulations governing work, consumption, and even entertainment. But the war also created social upheavals and it reduced local autonomy. Philadelphia's Republican government, which had resisted President Franklin Roosevelt's New Deal, now found that Washington controlled almost all aspects of city and regional affairs. For example, the federal government treated the area as a single entity for air patrols and air-raid drills. Because of a labor shortage, the War Manpower Commission controlled the allotment of workers to industries in the

**FIGURE 88.** *The Yankee Boys in Italy*, 1918. The marching song, published by the Italo-American Music Company in Philadelphia, celebrated the cooperation between American and Italian troops against Germany, Austro-Hungary, and the other Central Powers. Ferrucio Giannini, the lyricist, had emigrated from Italy to Philadelphia, where he ran the Verdi Hall opera house at Seventh and Christian Streets. LIBRARY OF CONGRESS.

whole metropolitan area. Other federal agencies with headquarters in Philadelphia managed many aspects of economic and social life in the region. The Office of Price Administration determined retail prices for most consumer products and allotted gasoline and heating oil for individual use.

By the time the Japanese attacked Pearl Harbor on December 7, 1941, Philadelphia industry had revived enough to mask a long-term trend of industrial decline. When the war broke out in Europe in September 1939, Philadelphia, like the rest of the United States, had high unemployment caused by the Great Depression. After France fell to German armies in June 1940, the Roosevelt administration began a rearmament program that immediately boosted the city's economy. The ships built on the Delaware River were the area's most important contribution to the war effort. Most immediately, the Philadelphia Naval Shipyard, which had been in existence since 1801, benefited from the president's commitment to building up the navy. In 1940 and 1941 the Navy Yard also engaged in a clandestine reconstruction of British and other Allied ships damaged by enemy attacks in the Atlantic. The shipyard grew from a few thousand workers in 1939 to fifty-eight thousand workers at its peak. A number of shipyards on the Delaware River including the Cramp yard in Kensington, the New York Shipbuilding yard in Camden, and the Sun Shipbuilding yard in Chester also prospered. In 1944, these shipyards employed more than 150,000 workers and were the largest employers in the metropolitan area.

Because Philadelphia and its suburbs had played such a prominent role supplying munitions in World War I, Washington turned to many of the same facilities for the new conflict. The Frankford Arsenal, which dated from the early 1800s, hired twenty thousand workers to manufacture small arms, ammunition, and optical devices. It also engaged in munitions research. Local clothing manufacturers met the needs of the army supply depot, and the government turned to other Philadelphia industries to produce tanks, railroad equipment, and heavy weapons. The Baldwin Locomotive Works produced railroad equipment for the Allies and retooled some of its plants to make tanks. The Budd Company in Northeast Philadelphia, which in peacetime produced bodies for automobiles, turned out armored cars, tanks, and other equipment. Midvale Steel in Nicetown made armor for the Navy Yard. The Radio Corporation of America in Camden, one of the area's most important electronic companies, produced radios, radar, and other electronic and communications equipment needed by the military. Roughly 350,000 Philadelphians engaged in defense work, and many thousands more worked in other parts of the region. Camden in New Jersey and Chester, Montgomery, and Bucks Counties in Pennsylvania had large defense contractors. Almost every able-bodied adult who wanted to work found a job, but racial, gender, and ethnic divisions affected when and where individuals found employment and their pay levels.

African Americans found opportunities, especially after President Roosevelt issued an executive order prohibiting discrimination in defense hiring. The reluctance of employers to hire African Americans was reinforced by the opposition of labor unions. By the middle of 1943 the actions of the local office of the Fair Employment Practices Commission (FEPC) forced some of the largest defense contractors to reverse their policies. Since the jurisdiction of the FEPC extended over all of Pennsylvania and southern New Jersey, the largest defense contractors in the suburbs began hiring Black employees. American Telephone and Telegraph, the Pennsylvania Railroad, and the Radio Corporation of America revised their hiring practices. Discrimination remained entrenched at the Philadelphia Transit Company (PTC), which ran the buses, trolleys, and subways. Despite repeated pressures from the federal government and local civil rights groups, the company and its union refused to allow Black people to work as drivers. In August 1944, when PTC finally hired seven African American drivers, the union called a strike that tied up the city for a week. President Roosevelt sent in the military to run the transportation services so workers could get to defense jobs, and the government threatened to revoke union members' draft exemption unless they ended the strike, which led to them returning to their jobs. Before the strike's conclusion, many Philadelphians feared a race riot similar to the violence that had

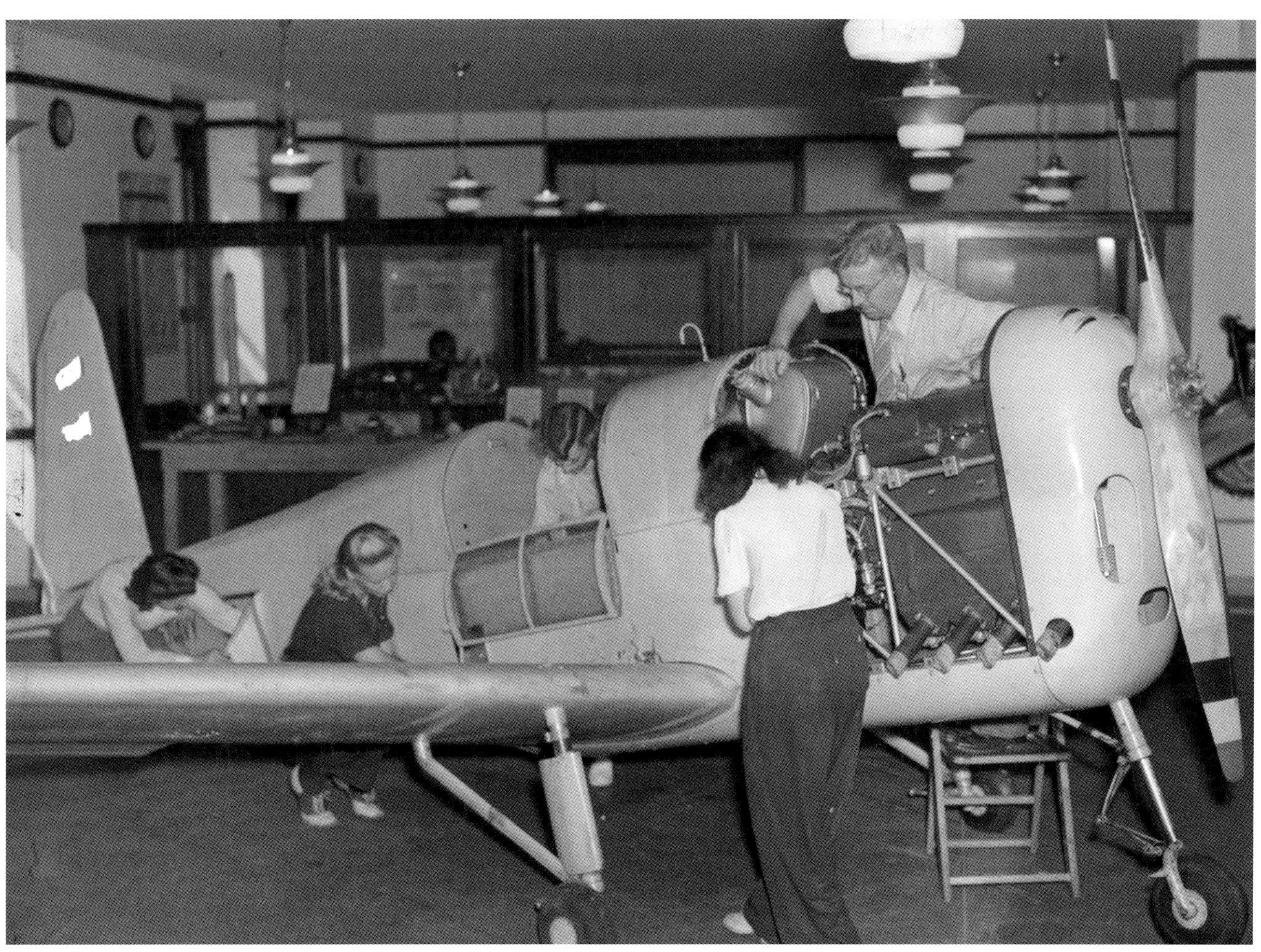

**FIGURE 89.** Wartime production at the Naval Aircraft Factory, 1942. Built adjacent to the Naval Yard in South Philadelphia after U.S. entry into World War I, the complex employed more than ten thousand workers—many of them women—during World War II. SPECIAL COLLECTIONS RESEARCH CENTER, TEMPLE UNIVERSITY LIBRARIES.

**FIGURE 90.** Cecil B. Moore, 1963. A leader of the Philadelphia National Association for the Advancement of Colored People (NAACP), Moore served in the segregated Marine Corps during World War II, joining 20,000 other Black Americans. In June 1944, Moore assaulted Japanese positions on the island of Saipan. In combat, he remembered, "all those damn color lines broke down anyway." SPECIAL COLLECTIONS RESEARCH CENTER, TEMPLE UNIVERSITY LIBRARIES.

occurred in Detroit the previous year. But quick action by the National Association for the Advancement of Colored People (NAACP) and white civil rights groups, with the cooperation of the newspapers, prevented such an action. Black organizations worked with white civil rights groups to stage street marches and a newspaper campaign fostering the "Double V," victory over the Axis abroad and victory over racism at home. Black Philadelphians who enlisted in the military proved well-placed to continue the struggle. Marine Corps veteran Cecil B. Moore, for example, went on to lead the city's postwar NAACP chapter.

Throughout the war, as more women entered the workplace, controversy also raged over the "proper" place for women and the war's effects on gender roles. For cultural, ethnic, and social reasons, many Philadelphians worried that letting women work in war plants would threaten the social structure. Several religious organizations charged that working mothers endangered their children. The conservative Republican city government echoed such concerns by refusing to create public day-care centers until near the end of the conflict. But the shortage of workers ultimately led the War Manpower Commission to recruit women for factories. By 1945, 35 percent of Philadelphia's women worked outside of the home. Most continued to fill jobs traditionally held by women, but many worked as welders, mechanics, and chemists in shipyards, in the Frankford Arsenal, and at the Pennsylvania Railroad. Before the PTC agreed to hire African Americans as drivers, the company had employed a number of women in that position.

Following a more familiar path into wartime philanthropy, women volunteered to keep Philadelphia's charities going. The United Service Organizations (USO), which entertained military men in Philadelphia in such centers as the Stage Door Canteen in the basement of the Academy of Music and an open dance floor near city hall, employed thousands of young women. The USO reached out as well to numerous regional military bases and hospitals, including Fort Dix and the McGuire Air Force Base in New Jersey and military hospitals in suburban Philadelphia. Women joined bond drives and raised money for social organizations through the United War Fund. In so many ways, women's involvement in the war gave them their own money to spend, new responsibilities, and new confidence—all of which broadened their social, economic, and political expectations. At war's end, most women lost or gave up their jobs to returning servicemen and many women settled into family life, sometimes with the benefits of the GI Bill and other federal programs that opened up developing suburbs. Despite a loss of influence, their wartime experience laid the grounds for their demands for equal rights in subsequent years.

Although federal propaganda agencies emphasized unity as a necessity for victory, that unity proved elusive in Philadelphia. Besides African Americans, other groups experienced discrimination during the war. During the Depression era, the region's Jewish population—which had protested the rise of Nazism from the early 1930s and included many refugees from the Third Reich—often suffered job discrimination and even physical attacks. These attacks increased from 1939 until 1941 during the debate in Philadelphia over

U.S. aid to nations fighting Nazi Germany. Opponents of aid accused Jews of trying to get the United States involved in another European war. As the debate intensified, vandals took aim at Jewish stores and attacked Jewish children coming home from school. Arsonists also targeted the home of a West Philadelphia rabbi. Even after Pearl Harbor, Jews continued to face discrimination from some employers and groups spreading anti-Semitic literature. Despite service to the war effort on many fronts, Jews continued to face discrimination for years afterward.

Although no massive relocation occurred on the East Coast to match the forced removal of Japanese from California, Congress classified recent immigrants from Germany and Italy who had not taken out citizenship papers as enemy aliens. The FBI searched their homes and confiscated radios, telescopes, and other instruments regarded as potentially dangerous. Several hundred enemy aliens were held for a time in a facility in southern New Jersey. Enemy aliens were not allowed to work in defense facilities. Despite such restrictions, labor shortages resulted in an unusual occurrence in Cumberland County, New Jersey, as 2,500 Japanese Americans from internment camps in the West were moved in 1944 to work on the Seabrook Farms and frozen foods factory. Some of them stayed after the war and formed a nucleus of Japanese presence in the region.

Labor strife proved to be another area in which federal efforts to maintain unity often failed. Although nationally unions had agreed to a no-strike agreement, Philadelphia gained a reputation for work stoppages. During the Depression strikes in textiles and metal manufacturing were common and usually violent. This pattern continued through the war and affected private shipyards, steel mills, and aircraft factories. City workers also went on strike for higher wages. With the support of the War Labor Board, arbitration settled most disputes. Attempting to prevent inflation, the War Manpower Commission instituted a wage stabilization program capping wages at 1942 levels. Nevertheless, with full employment and with the average laborer working forty-eight hours or more a week, Philadelphia workers enjoyed a prosperity that was in sharp contrast to the Depression. To circumvent government wage guidelines, unions often secured fringe benefits such as paid vacations and health benefits that lasted after the war.

With all kinds of government controls and interference in Philadelphia's affairs, the autonomy so valued by Mayor Bernard Samuel and the city's Republican leadership largely disappeared. Decisions made by military commanders stationed in the city largely overturned local authorities. Because of the housing shortage and the refusal of the city government to build public housing, the commandant of the Philadelphia Naval Shipyard ordered the construction of the Tasker Homes in South Philadelphia near the base. By the end of the war, the city reluctantly agreed to build several public housing projects. The same disagreements occurred over civil defense. At first the city government was reluctant to play a role in civil defense, but right before the Japanese attack on Pearl Harbor it established a Defense Council headed by Mayor Samuel. Particularly in the first two years of the war, the city

**FIGURE 91.** Securities and Exchange Commission Fifth War Loan Drive, 1944. During the Civil War, the Philadelphia banker Jay Cooke had pioneered the selling of federal government war loans to ordinary Americans. In later conflicts, including World War II, residents of the Delaware Valley were once more urged to invest their savings in a patriotic cause. SPECIAL COLLECTIONS RESEARCH CENTER, TEMPLE UNIVERSITY LIBRARIES.

was on high alert in expectation of an attack from the air. Periodically air raid drills tied up the city as air raid wardens cleared cars and pedestrians from the streets. A general blackout kept homes, stores, and businesses from displaying lights at night.

By early 1945 some of the industries with the highest employment began to lay off workers as the federal government prepared for the end of the war. The shipyards faced retrenchment first. The Philadelphia Naval Shipyard reduced its workforce to almost prewar levels. Sun Shipbuilding closed much of its facility and threw thousands of African Americans out of work. When the war ended in August 1945, almost every defense contractor laid off workers. The city never recovered. As a result, although World War II caused many dislocations and cost the lives of 3,500 servicemen from the city and 1,500 dead from the Pennsylvania counties adjoining Philadelphia, many people looked back on the era as a "golden age." They remembered the city's prosperity, the high wages, and the opportunities the war provided. They remembered wartime unity, however illusory, as a marked contrast to the racial and labor conflicts that followed.

## Cold War

**Robert J. Kodosky**

The period of international political and military tension known as the Cold War (1947–91) had military, political, and cultural implications for Greater Philadelphia. The region served as a first line of defense for a conflict that depended more on missiles than forts, and it provided the nation with an arsenal, a shipyard, and a source of manpower. While a direct military confrontation between the Soviet Union and the United States, the Cold War's principal adversaries, failed to materialize, the conflict made its mark on the region in other ways, including anti-communist suspicion, civil defense, and the 1967 summit between President Lyndon B. Johnson and Soviet Premier Alexei Kosygin in Glassboro, New Jersey.

The Cold War began after World War II when the United States and the Soviet Union—wartime allies against Nazi Germany, Imperial Japan, and Fascist Italy—reverted to their prewar ideological rivalry. As early as 1946, British prime minister Winston Churchill described the postwar divide in Europe as an Iron Curtain. In 1961 the East German government constructed the Berlin Wall, physically dividing the city. While the Soviet Union and the United States avoided direct military conflict, each became involved in proxy wars around the world, most notably in Korea (1950–53), Vietnam (1950–75), and Afghanistan (1979–89). Each nation worked to expand its international influence in a conflict carried out through propaganda, espionage, domestic surveillance, soft power, the space race, and the threat of atomic annihilation.

The end of World War II had an uneven impact on the Philadelphia region. Optimism ran high amid military demobilization and the lapsing of wartime rationing and restrictions. A building boom took place, and rows of small houses and garden apartments appeared in the city's sections of East Germantown, West Oak Lane, and the Northeast, in part due to the availability of Federal Housing Administration (FDA) loans and the GI Bill. In addition, Philadelphia's colleges and universities grew markedly in enrollment due to the educational opportunities made possible for veterans under the GI Bill. At the same time, however, apprehension grew over the detrimental impact of demobilization on local defense operations and industry. The Philadelphia Navy Yard, Frankford Arsenal, Marine Corps Supply Depot, Naval Home, Quartermaster General Depot, and Signal Corps Stock Control Office all saw significant job losses between 1945 and 1949.

In addition to the military cutbacks, the specter of communism provoked anxiety as political leaders, the media, and others warned of domestic threats. The Communist Party already had a strong presence in the region. Its membership of nearly one hundred thousand individuals by the late 1940s owed to both the economic toll of the Great Depression and the U.S.-Soviet alliance during World War II. During the postwar period, Communists recruited African Americans, who were drawn to the party's promise of racial egalitarianism. The party's newspaper, the *Daily Worker*, regularly reported instances of police brutality and frame-ups directed against African Americans in Philadelphia. Thomas Nabried, the party's city chair and then district chair for eastern Pennsylvania and Delaware, worked to organize fellow African Americans in the city and throughout Bucks County. By the 1950s, African Americans came to constitute more than one-sixth of the party's membership. The party's strength, however, proved short-lived, as it failed to withstand the anti-communist mood of the 1950s and ceased to operate as an effective political force.

Veterans' organizations emerged early as forceful proponents of anti-communism. The Catholic War Veterans, for example, organized mass demonstrations in Philadelphia in December 1946 to protest the repression of the Catholic Church in communist Eastern Europe. The Pennsylvania American Legion expressed support for the House Un-American Activities Committee (HUAC) and the McCarran Internal Security Act, a 1950 federal law that called for the registration of "subversives."

Patriotic activities to celebrate the United States, including the role Philadelphia played in its founding, accompanied anti-communist initiatives throughout the Cold War. Religious leaders played an important role. Vito Mazzone, pastor of St. Mary Magdalene de Pazzi in South Philadelphia, encouraged active patriotism among his parishioners. "Christian patriotism" was the message of evangelist Billy Graham, who attracted a crowd of nearly seven hundred thousand to his Philadelphia crusade in 1961. Philadelphia served as the point of departure for the Freedom Train, which carried an exhibit of the nation's founding documents around the country between 1947 and 1949. The era's heightened patriotism also brought increasing numbers of tourists to see Independence Hall and the Liberty Bell, which became the centerpieces of Independence National Historical Park, authorized by Congress in 1948.

The Cold War turned hot in June 1950, when North Korea invaded South Korea. This followed the Soviet Union's first explosion of an atomic bomb and the creation of the Communist Peoples Republic of China. The Philadelphia region felt the impact as jobs returned to the Navy Yard. A new radiological decontamination training facility distributed manuals for ship decontamination in the event of an air burst of atomic bombs.

The fear of nuclear attack loomed large for civilians too. In 1952, Pennsylvania's Civil Air Patrol dropped leaflets in Bucks and Chester Counties that warned of potential bombs. By the 1950s, the Philadelphia District of the Corps of Engineers supervised construction of twelve NIKE/AJAX surface-to-air missile sites at locations averaging twenty-five miles from Center City. Regular U.S. Army and Pennsylvania National Guard manned the batteries with command-and-control functions located at a facility in Pedricktown, Salem County, New Jersey. Missile sites in New Jersey protected the New York area in the north and the Philadelphia area in the south.

As nuclear espionage dominated national news, in May 1950 authorities arrested a South Philadelphia man, Harry Gold, on espionage charges. A South Philadelphia High School graduate, Gold had studied chemical engineering at Drexel Institute and by the 1930s had begun to provide the Soviets with documents about industrial solvents and manufacturing processes from the Pennsylvania Sugar Company, the Fishtown refinery where he worked. At that time one of the largest sugar refineries in the world, Pennsylvania Sugar had subsidiaries that produced everything from Quaker brand antifreeze to solvents, lacquers, and rum.

Following his arrest, Gold confessed to acting as a courier to pass information for the Soviets about the Manhattan Project, which produced the atomic bomb, to atomic spy Klaus Fuchs. This led to the arrest of David Greenglass, a Manhattan Project machinist whose testimony resulted in the espionage arrest, trial, and execution of Greenglass's sister Ethel Rosenberg and her husband, Julius. Gold served fifteen years of the thirty-year sentence he received before his parole from the federal penitentiary in Lewisburg, Pennsylvania, in May 1966.

Reflecting continuing anxiety about Communist activity within the United States, organizers of Pennsylvania Week activities in 1951 chose "Defense" as their theme. Philadelphia's Civil Defense Council, citing a shipment of purported sabotage manuals allegedly unloaded from a ship at the Philadelphia docks, warned of the need to detect subversive threats. The region's desire to expose potential Communist subversives manifested in the adoption of statewide loyalty oaths in Pennsylvania (1951) and New Jersey (1949). Delaware remained one of only seven states to resist adopting such legislation. Locally, meanwhile, in 1955 the Philadelphia School District dismissed twenty-six teachers for refusing to answer questions about Communist affiliations on the

**FIGURE 92.** Independence Hall in a civil defense exercise, 1953. The Cold War made Greater Philadelphia a potential target for Soviet attack. In October 1953, a state-wide exercise saw two B-36 bombers simulate the dropping of a nuclear bomb on the city. Smoke grenades and burning pans of oil increased the realism. Officials estimated the attack would have killed 140,000 residents of the region and obliterated Independence Mall. SPECIAL COLLECTIONS RESEARCH CENTER, TEMPLE UNIVERSITY LIBRARIES.

basis of their Fifth Amendment rights. In the suburbs, the Bucks County Bar rejected an applicant based on his association with a Marxist fellow student at the Pennsylvania State University. An appeal eventually overturned the decision.

The Cold War elevated the importance of universities to national security. As centers of scientific production, the federal government provided campuses with unprecedented funding. Philadelphia's campuses benefited from the Section 112 program, a 1959 revision to the Housing Act that responded to the Soviet Union's launch of its satellite *Sputnik 1* two years before. This enabled urban universities in selected cities, including Philadelphia, to undertake massive expansion projects at little or no cost to the universities.

Because of their perceived importance and the federal dollars they received, universities came under the scrutiny of authorities early and often. Barrows Dunham, a professor of philosophy and department head at Temple University, attracted interest from the Federal Bureau of Investigation (FBI) because of his former membership in the Communist Party. Subpoenaed to appear before the U.S. House Un-American Affairs Committee in October 1952, Dunham ultimately sought protection under the Fifth Amendment and refused to answer questions. Cited for standing in contempt of Congress in May 1954, Dunham secured an acquittal a year later. Temple officials dismissed Dunham and continued to cooperate with the FBI. In July 1981 Temple's trustees acknowledged Dunham's dismissal as an error and reinstated him as professor emeritus entitled to a lifetime pension.

The Cold War further revitalized the Philadelphia Naval Yard during the Vietnam War, when the facility entered its most active period of operations and highest level of employment since World War II. Its annual payroll reached nearly $90 million. Activity diminished after Vietnam, but the naval base remained vital to national defense throughout the Cold War. Most notably, the Jimmy Carter presidential administration awarded Philadelphia $500 million to fulfill the first Carrier Service Life Extension Program (SLEP) contract for the sixty thousand–ton attack carrier *Saratoga*. Continued SLEP contracts employed thousands of Delaware Valley residents and brought hundreds of millions of dollars to the region over the next twenty years.

While often engulfed in Cold War tensions, Philadelphians also sought ways to alleviate them. In 1958, the Philadelphia Orchestra departed for its first tour of the Soviet Union and Eastern Europe. In 1973, the orchestra embarked on another first, a trip to the Peoples Republic of China that preceded by six years official U.S. recognition of the country's Communist government. This type of exchange also extended to sport. In July 1959, Philadelphia hosted the first in a series of track meets between American and Soviet athletes at the University of Pennsylvania's Franklin Field. While Soviet athletes largely prevailed over their American counterparts, almost twenty years later the defending Stanley Cup champion Philadelphia Flyers scored a convincing 4–1 victory over Moscow's Central Hockey Club at the Spectrum on January 11, 1976. Even Philadelphia's fictional heavyweight champion, Rocky Balboa, enlisted as an athletic diplomat, with *Rocky IV* (1985) featuring him winning over a hostile Soviet crowd in the boxing ring.

The region also offered the site for the 1967 summit meeting between President Johnson and Soviet Premier Kosygin. The two met June 23–24 at Hollybush Mansion, the residence of Glassboro State College (later Rowan University) president Thomas E. Robinson. The choice of site, with only two days' notice, derived from a disagreement about whether the meeting should take place in Washington or in New York, where Kosygin was attending an emergency United Nations Security Council meeting to discuss the recently concluded Six-Day War. Both sides agreed on Glassboro, located exactly at the midpoint between New York and Washington. Johnson considered the site ideal for its relatively rural location, removed from the growing protests on Philadelphia's campuses against the Vietnam War. The summit failed to produce any agreements, notably on the limitation of antiballistic missile systems, and the Soviet invasion of Czechoslovakia in August 1968 delayed further serious discussion between

**FIGURE 93.** Miss Liberty and the Freedom Bell, 1950. The reigning Miss Pennsylvania—Emilie Longacre, from Chester County—receives the Miss Liberty crown from a representative of the Crusade for Freedom, a Korean War-era propaganda campaign that used the "Freedom Bell"—inspired by the Liberty Bell—to win hearts and minds at home and abroad. As part of the campaign, the United States presented a ten-ton Freedom Bell (ironically, made in Britain) to West Berlin. SPECIAL COLLECTIONS RESEARCH CENTER, TEMPLE UNIVERSITY LIBRARIES.

American and Soviet officials until 1972. However, the Glassboro meeting's spontaneity and its spirit of cooperation resonated widely at the time. This helped pave the way for a period of thawed relations between the Cold War adversaries referred to as détente.

Philadelphia continued to serve as an important site for the nation's expression of patriotism. As the Cold War varied in intensity, the city hosted America's Bicentennial celebration in 1976 and the bicentennial anniversary of the Constitution in 1987. It also rewarded the pursuit of freedom globally, awarding the inaugural Liberty Medal in 1989 to Lech Walesa of Poland, the leader of Solidarity, the Soviet bloc's first independent trade union.

The Cold War concluded in 1991 with the internal collapse of the Soviet Union. The tensions of the era served to revitalize the military establishment in Greater Philadelphia, injecting the economy with money and jobs. The cost, however, included an anti-communist hysteria that occurred throughout the nation. Thousands of area residents lost their lives in Cold War–era military conflicts. While the region contributed markedly to the nation's defense, through its missile defense initiative and operations at the Philadelphia Naval Shipyard, its sacrifices proved more substantial.

## Korean War

**Levi Fox**

Although active hostilities during the Korean War lasted for little more than three years (1950–53), the conflict had a lasting impact on the Philadelphia area. The war provided a boost for the shipbuilding industry on both sides of the Delaware River, and area military bases played a major role in preparing soldiers and supplies for deployment. The sizable human toll in southeastern Pennsylvania, South Jersey, and Delaware, however, helped to encourage an antiwar movement in Philadelphia and attempts by students to circumvent the draft. In the aftermath, fatalities also motivated monuments to local citizens who served in the Korean War.

The Korean War resulted from conflict that followed the division of the Korean peninsula after World War II into two political units, north (supported by communist Soviet Union and China) and south (backed by the United States). During the late 1940s, at the same time that similar ideological conflicts led to the "Iron Curtain" dividing Europe, these divisions as well as the Chinese Civil War fostered the advent of the Cold War in East Asia. The Korean War began on June 25, 1950, when the North Korean military invaded South Korea, and the internal conflict became international in the fall of 1950 after the United States persuaded the United Nations to send troops to stop the spread of communism by defending the South. While American public opinion supported the Korean War during the early months of the conflict, by January 1951 as the Chinese and North Koreans captured the southern capital, Seoul, for the second time, nearly half of those polled opposed American involvement, and support never fully rebounded.

For Philadelphia and the surrounding region, the onset of the Korean War brought about a spike in local employment. The Philadelphia Navy Yard experienced a temporary upsurge of 3,700 new jobs by the end of 1951, which increased its total workforce to more than 12,500 people. Primarily preparing United Nations ships for service in the Pacific Ocean, Navy Yard workers also modified seaplanes and submarines from World War II with modern technologies. The return of vessels from the front kept Navy Yard workers employed through the mid-1950s. The New York Shipbuilding Corporation in Camden experienced a similar surge in employment for constructing new ships and converting existing vessels.

Military bases in New Jersey, Delaware, and eastern Pennsylvania also played a major role in the Korean War. Soldiers from across the northeastern United States reported to Fort Dix in New Jersey for basic training. During the first two years of the Korean War, jet fighter squadrons trained for combat at Delaware's Dover Air Force Base, which also became the location for Air Mobility Command support services and strategic aerial defense of Washington, D.C. North of Philadelphia, the United States Naval Air Station Joint Reserve Base Willow Grove was home to the 111th Fighter Wing of the Pennsylvania Air National Guard, which trained on bombers such as the B-29 Superfortress before being assigned to the Strategic Air Command and deployed to Korea. The Philadelphia region also felt the human toll of the war. More than six hundred deaths in the war, over one-fourth the total for Pennsylvania, came from Bucks, Chester, Delaware, Montgomery, and Philadelphia Counties. In addition, forty-three Delawareans and nearly eight hundred New Jerseyans died in Korea.

The region's sizable local sacrifice, along with the presence of a socialist community that had supported Progressive Party candidate Henry Wallace for president in 1948, helps to explain why Philadelphia became one of the centers of organized protest against the Korean War. The protest movement also drew strength from the longstanding local influence of Quakers and other pacifist denominations, such as the Mennonites, as well as from the large number of universities in the area. Throughout the Korean War the Philadelphia-based Central Committee for Conscientious Objectors (CCCO) counseled young people about their rights under the Selective Service System to avoid active combat for religious reasons, a protection not available for politically motivated pacifism. In order to be able to choose their branch of service, such as the navy or air force rather than the army, many Philadelphia-area college students volunteered to serve in the Korean War rather than wait to be drafted.

Doylestown native James Michener, who covered the war for the *Saturday Evening Post*, was one of the first people to use the term "Forgotten War" because he believed that by the latter half of the conflict the American public was wholly ignoring Korea. Although armistice negotiations to end the Korean conflict began in mid-1951, they took two years to conclude in part due to disagreements over the repatriation of prisoners of war who claimed that they did not wish to return to the Chinese or North Korean militaries. The war formally ceased on July 27, 1953, with the signing of an armistice ending active hostilities, but no permanent peace treaty was ever negotiated.

## Vietnam War

**Nicholas Trajano Molnar**

The Vietnam War had a significant impact on the Philadelphia region. During the height of open American involvement in the war from 1965 to 1968, thousands from the area were drafted or volunteered for the armed forces, and hundreds lost their lives. Other citizens participated in antiwar or peace protests. While the war created employment in defense industries, it limited economic opportunity in other ways, especially in the postwar period. Among the most lasting of the war's impacts, the region gained a more diverse population from an influx of political and economic migrants from war-torn countries in Southeast Asia.

In the early 1960s, few people were fully informed about the events that had transpired in Vietnam since the end of World War II. The United States had been involved in the region for decades, initially supporting France with billions of dollars of aid against anticolonial Vietnamese nationals. After the departure of the French in the mid-1950s, the United States remained in the region and supported anti-communist forces there as part of larger Cold War against the Soviet Union, lending support to the Republic of Vietnam (South Vietnam) while opposing the Democratic Republic of Vietnam (North Vietnam).

Young men from Pennsylvania, New Jersey, and Delaware became drawn into the Vietnam War in large numbers between 1962 and 1968 as American troop levels in South Vietnam escalated from 10,000 to nearly 550,000, the vast majority added after the 1964 Gulf of Tonkin incident. By the end of the war in 1975, when the North Vietnamese captured Saigon and the United States withdrew its last contingent of regular military forces, more than 3,100 Pennsylvanians had been killed as a result of the conflict. Of these, 646 (20 percent of all the Keystone State's war dead) came from the city of Philadelphia alone. Philadelphia's Edison High School lost sixty-six alumni, more than any other high school in the United States. The city of Camden and Camden County accounted for nearly 6 percent of New Jersey's nearly 1,500 killed, while Wilmington and New Castle County accounted for 68 percent of 122 men from Delaware who perished.

The enormous manpower needs and the increased "credibility gap" between the federal government's rationale for the war versus the realities conveyed through television and soldiers' accounts led to the development of what one scholar has called the "largest and most effective antiwar movement in American history." While not limited to college students, antiwar activism in the Philadelphia region drew strength from increased enrollments on many of the region's campuses, due in part to the awarding of educational deferments from the draft. In 1966, students and faculty at the Quaker-founded colleges of Haverford, Bryn Mawr, and Swarthmore Colleges went on an extended hunger strike to protest American involvement in the conflict, an action eventually joined by students at Friends Select High School. By 1967, mass demonstrations, teach-ins, petitions, and civil disobedience spread beyond locations and groups traditionally associated with pacifism, extending to Temple University, the University of Pennsylvania, and other campuses. As a result of nearly two years of campus protests and debates, Penn's board of trustees overwhelmingly decided to cancel its chemical and biological warfare contracts with the Pentagon.

As in other metropolitan areas across the country, most people were not directly involved in fighting the war, but they experienced its divisive impact nonetheless. Debates about the Vietnam War and American involvement took many forms on college campuses, at federal facilities, and in public spaces. Philadelphians demonstrated in support of the war as well as against it. The Liberty Bell and Independence Hall, symbols of American democracy, became contested sites for demonstrations by those who supported the war as a crucial element of the Cold War against communism as well as those who believed the war immoral or simply a waste of taxpayer money. In this heated political climate, acts of open defiance toward the American government occurred, such as the "Camden 28" raid of one of the

**FIGURE 94.** Vietnam veterans carrying a replica of the Liberty Bell at an Independence Hall peace protest, 1971. SPECIAL COLLECTIONS RESEARCH CENTER, TEMPLE UNIVERSITY LIBRARIES.

city's draft boards and the theft of classified documents from an FBI office in Media, Pennsylvania.

When young men were drafted or enlisted, their absence from the workforce opened opportunities for others. Philadelphians benefited by working in defense industries such as local shipyards, arsenals, and private companies that supplied matériel and weapons to the military. In 1968, economists estimated that without the Vietnam War, local employment in federal government agencies related to the war effort would have dropped 10.2 percent, amounting to thousands of people, and total federal expenditures in the Philadelphia region would have dropped 42.3 percent, amounting to nearly $2.5 billion.

After the war, the region and the nation as a whole experienced starkly negative economic impacts. Because the Vietnam War and the Great Society domestic programs of President Lyndon B. Johnson had been financed simultaneously without any significant increases in taxes, the ensuing effects of runaway double-digit inflation and mounting federal debt ravaged the economy. Although veterans had opportunities for education through the GI Bill, the poor state of the American economy compounded with declining industry in the region meant that many would not have the same economic opportunities as previous generations of veterans. In addition to the challenges of a deindustrializing economy, the smooth reintegration of Vietnam veterans was further complicated by postwar health and addiction issues. These included the debilitating effects of exposure to the toxic herbicide "Agent Orange" (the Veterans Administration presumes that anyone who served in Vietnam between January 9, 1962, and May 7, 1975, was exposed and therefore eligible for benefits), drug abuse, homelessness, and post-traumatic stress disorder.

America's longest war in the twentieth century also led to one of the most dramatic and visible demographic changes in the region's history. Although not always welcomed—a study by the Philadelphia Commission on Human Relations revealed that the new arrivals were disproportionately victims of interracial violence in the late 1980s—a surge in refugees in the aftermath of the Vietnam War led significant numbers of Southeast Asian migrants to resettle in the region. This influx, combined with a post-1965 American immigration policy that emphasized family reunification and encouraged chain migration, made Philadelphia home to one of the largest Vietnamese communities and the second-largest Cambodian community in the United States.

By the turn of the twenty-first century, the Vietnamese were the largest foreign-born population in Philadelphia, numbering nearly 12,000. South Philadelphia and Elmwood, neighborhoods for migrants from European countries in previous times, became spaces where these newcomers resided and congregated. Vietnamese refugees, especially those who could speak Chinese, initially frequented Chinatown and proved a boon to shop owners there, but by the twenty-first century they had carved out a neighborhood that became colloquially known as "Little Saigon" in South Philadelphia. By 2015, the combined Philadelphia-Camden-Wilmington Metropolitan Statistical Area had a population of 34,507 Vietnamese, with the highest concentrations in the outskirts of the city of Philadelphia and nearby towns like Pennsauken, Egg Harbor, and Atlantic City; Camden County had become home to 4,260 Vietnamese, the largest number in any county of New Jersey. The influx of these new Americans from Vietnam, Cambodia, and Laos introduced a polyglot of cultures, foodways, and traditions into the already diverse region, reinvigorating the region just as previous generations of immigrants before them.

## Gulf Wars

**Andrew Heath**

Between 1991 and 2011 the United States waged two wars in Iraq. With the first coming at the end of the Cold War (1991) and the second (2003–11) forming one front in a wider post-9/11 "War of Terror," the conflicts reverberated in the Greater Philadelphia region. Fewer military personnel from the Delaware Valley lost their lives in combat than in previous foreign wars, but the impact proved considerable for service people and their communities, local Arab American and Jewish populations, and the region's residents who rallied to cries of "No Blood for Oil" and "Support the Troops."

The origins of the two Gulf Wars go back to earlier upheavals in the Middle East. Saddam Hussein, the murderous head of Iraq's Ba'ath Party who built his leadership around a cult of personality, launched an invasion of Iran in 1980 that won tacit support from the United States, which opposed an anti-American Iranian regime. The costly war of attrition finally petered out in 1988. A heavily indebted Iraq then turned its attention to Kuwait, which Saddam accused of exceeding its oil production quota. In August 1990 he ordered Iraqi troops across the Kuwaiti border and subdued the emirate within a couple of days. Aware of the impact instability in the region would have on gas prices, and eager to show United States leadership as part of a post–Cold War "new world order," President George H. W. Bush began to assemble an international coalition, initially to protect neighboring Saudi Arabia from Iraqi incursion (Operation Desert Shield) and then to liberate Kuwait (Operation Desert Storm). U.S.-led combat operations began on January 16, 1991, and concluded with the rout of Iraq's retreating forces from Kuwait at the end of February.

In the Philadelphia region the conflict took place amid the prospect of cuts to local military installations. With the Soviet threat receding and modernizers in the Pentagon eager to build a leaner, more efficient armed forces, the federal Base Realignment and Closure (BRAC) commission had proposed closing Fort Dix in New Jersey's Burlington County in 1988. The local congressman lobbied successfully to prevent closure, but other sites soon came under scrutiny, including the Philadelphia Navy Yard, which had helped to equip the U.S. Navy since the time of the early republic. As tensions in the Persian Gulf heightened, defenders of the Navy Yard noted how one battleship (USS *Wisconsin*) and two of the carriers (USS *Saratoga* and USS *Independence*) dispatched to the Persian Gulf region had been retrofitted at the facility. Despite the shipyard's role in modernizing the fleet, however, Secretary of Defense Richard B. Cheney recommended shutting it down along with Fort Dix just weeks after the Gulf War's conclusion in April 1991. Fort Dix, which had trained Kuwaitis over the preceding months and had sent thirty units to the Middle East, was once again saved, but the Navy Yard closed in 1996.

As some of the region's residents wondered how the conflict would impact economic life, others took stands for or against the war. With no prospect of a draft for young people, relatively few American casualties, and little public sympathy for the brutal Iraqi dictator, peace campaigners struggled to mobilize on anything approaching the scale they had managed during the Vietnam War two decades earlier. With the war underway, 400 Philadelphians boarded buses for an antiwar march in Washington, D.C., while a later rally in the capital drew 140 residents on buses organized by the South Jersey Coalition for Peace and Justice. Alongside these pockets of dissent came professions of support for the troops. In Camden, schoolchildren wearing yellow ribbons and American flags as lapels paraded through the streets. Similar events took place across the region. One thousand people turned out in Haddonfield, for instance, to show support for men and women in uniform.

For Philadelphians with ties of faith and family to the Middle East, the war proved a troubling time. Saddam's retaliatory missile attacks on Israel spurred a surge in attendance at synagogues across the region. At the University of Pennsylvania students gathered in front of Van Pelt Library to express sympathy with Israelis under attack. The estimated four thousand Arab Americans in the Philadelphia vicinity, meanwhile, fell under suspicion, with some facing arson, death threats, and FBI questioning.

While the war itself did not last long, its aftereffects lingered for the Greater Philadelphians who fought in it. The U.S.-led coalition, which established almost total air superiority in the early days of the conflict, inflicted catastrophic losses on Iraqi forces. When the ground invasion commenced in late February it quickly overcame resistance. While tens of thousands of Iraqis perished, only around three hundred American service personnel lost their lives. Over the following years, however, more than one in three veterans reported a range of debilitating symptoms including pain, tiredness, and cognitive dysfunction. The multi-symptomatic condition became known as Gulf War syndrome, and while the causes remained a mystery, suspicion centered on exposure to chemicals and prophylactic treatments during service in the Middle East. One American Legion post in South Philadelphia grew its membership from thirty-four to over one thousand as veterans struggling with the condition sought support in their dealings with the federal Department of Veterans Affairs.

While veterans battled Gulf War syndrome over the following decade, Saddam remained in power, despite ongoing U.S. economic and military pressure. After the September 11, 2001, attacks on New York and Washington, however, the opportunity to depose the Iraqi leader as part of a broader "war on terror" presented itself. A prolonged military buildup set the stage for a March 2003 full-scale invasion, which quickly toppled the Ba'athist Party government and forced Saddam into hiding. After disbanding the Iraqi army, however, the U.S.-led occupation struggled to subdue a widespread insurgency, especially in Baghdad and the Sunni-majority provinces to the north. Having handed over power to Iraqi authorities, the United States completed its withdrawal in 2011.

Delaware Valley military installations once more supplied personnel and provisions to the war effort. South Jersey bases, having faced the threat of closure over the 1990s, prospered from the war on terror and conflict in Iraq, benefiting from over $200 million in investment between 2000 and 2003. McGuire Air Force Base, which merged with Fort Dix and the Naval Engineering Station Lakehurst (the site of the 1937 Hindenburg disaster) during the conflict, became a crucial staging post. As war loomed in March 2003, its 305th Air Mobility Wing forwarded seven thousand tons of cargo to the Middle East, four times the usual monthly average. The increased activity provided a boon to the Burlington County economy, which drew an estimated $700 million a year from the bases' presence, but McGuire's personnel had reminders on site of the risks of combat. Theirs was one of just two bases in the United States that had the facilities to ship blood and plasma to troops overseas.

Whether those troops belonged in the Middle East split residents of the Delaware Valley. The second Gulf War proved far more divisive in the region than the first. Saddam's invasion of Kuwait had provided a clear pretext for intervention in 1991, but the basis for war in 2003 appeared far less obvious, resting heavily on questionable intelligence regarding weapons of mass destruction and spurious links between Iraq and Al-Qaeda. Peace activists had been organizing against the potential for war since President George W. Bush signaled a desire to overthrow Saddam during his 2002 State of the Union address proclaiming an "axis of evil" linking Iraq with Iran and North Korea. In fall 2002 the Pennsylvania Region Anti-War Network (PRAWN) came together and began to stage small protests outside military recruitment centers alongside larger rallies. With war clouds gathering the following February, a crowd of approximately ten thousand Philadelphians marched from Spring Garden Street, along Broad and Market Streets, and to the Liberty Bell. The antiwar march, one of the largest in the city's history, occurred on the same day as rallies around the globe against the impending military action and included more than fifty organizations, among them veterans, high schoolers, college students, and labor unions.

For all the strength of the peace movement, however, the war initially proved popular with the wider public. As in the Gulf War of 1991, Delaware Valley residents organized to support the troops. In Feasterville, Pennsylvania, between three hundred and five hundred residents—including servicepeople's families—gathered to raise money for armed services relief funds at Willow Grove's Naval Air Station Joint Reserve Base. The same day several World War II veterans gathered in Campbell Square in the Richmond section of Philadelphia to honor Americans in service. The Second Street Irish Society organized a rally in early April as a riposte to antiwar protests. Across the region bumper stickers proclaimed support for military action.

Such patriotic fervor sometimes spilled over into harassment of the region's Muslim and Arab American communities. Only around six hundred Philadelphians hailed from Iraq, and many of them had fled Saddam's regime. One Iraqi American estimated 99 percent of his compatriots in the city hated the dictator. But a much larger population in the Delaware Valley with Middle Eastern roots, already regarded with suspicion after the September 11 attacks, came to be seen by some as an internal threat. Wary of the risks, the national Council on American Islamic Relations urged Arab Americans to stockpile food in case another terrorist attack on U.S. soil left them exposed to reprisals, although few residents of Philadelphia appear to have taken the council's advice. Law enforcement kept a watchful eye on the community. The FBI, aided by local police, rounded up around two hundred local Iraqis, along with a handful of other residents of Middle Eastern descent, for questioning as part of Operation Liberty

**FIGURE 95.** Philadelphia Veterans Day Parade, 2017. Although the kilts and bagpipes evoke the ancient clans of the Scottish Highlands, the Philadelphia Police and Fire Pipes and Drums band dates to 1996. The Veterans Day Parade in Philadelphia is younger still, with the first taking place in 2015. PHOTOGRAPH BY DONALD D. GROFF.

Shield. Assurances that the interviews were voluntary and would not be used in immigration proceedings did little to assuage fears. And the conflict in the Middle East made it harder for Muslims in the region to find places to worship. A proposal to turn a property into a mosque in Voorhees, New Jersey, prompted anonymous flyers warning that the site might become a sanctuary for terrorists. In response, the Coalition for Multi-Faith Democracy formed in fall 2003 to support the project, which won approval in November. Even then, one opponent called the prospective site "an insult to every soldier" who had died in Iraq.

From 2006 a trickle of refugees from the conflict began to settle in the Delaware Valley. With the help of the Catholic Diocese of Camden, a small number of Iraqis found homes in Atlantic City, Somers Point, Cherry Hill, and other communities, and a thousand displaced Iraqis arrived in Philadelphia prior to 2018, almost doubling the size of the existing community. Many hailed from middle-class backgrounds; some had worked for U.S. forces and found their families endangered as a result. Philadelphia's reputation as a sanctuary city for immigrants, longstanding African American connections to Islam in the metropolis, and the help offered by the wider Arab American population eased the pain of relocation, despite the backdrop of growing hostility to Muslim immigration in national politics.

As in 1991, far more Iraqis than Americans lost their lives in the conflict, and the numbers of displaced people seeking sanctuary in the Philadelphia region hints at the toll the war took on the civilian population. The long insurgency that followed Saddam's overthrow became much costlier to U.S. forces than the invasion itself. Of the 4,500 or so U.S. troops killed in Iraq between 2003 and 2011, 198 hailed from Pennsylvania, 82 from New Jersey, and 14 from Delaware. Of these, about 90—mostly young men in their twenties—hailed from Philadelphia and its surroundings. Suicide after returning to the United States proved deadlier to combatants than the Iraqi army or their irregular successors. Nevertheless, Iraq remained a dangerous place for Americans, with U.S. civilians working in the country especially vulnerable. Nick Berg, a resident of Chester County, provides a tragic example. He traveled to Iraq in March 2004 in search of work for his communications company. After running into trouble with the authorities he disappeared in April; troops found his headless body (soon accompanied by a gruesome execution video) in Baghdad in early May.

The inability of the U.S.-led occupation to stop such insurgent violence, coupled with the failure to find any weapons of mass destruction, diminished support for the war. As midterm elections approached in 2006, over half the Pennsylvania voters polled wanted to either reduce troop numbers in Iraq or withdraw from the region altogether. The swing away from Bush's Republican Party propelled Democrat Patrick Murphy to victory in the race to represent Pennsylvania's Eighth Congressional District, which then encompassed parts of Philadelphia, Bucks, and Montgomery Counties. In doing so Murphy became the first Iraq War veteran in Congress.

Neither war in the Gulf claimed anything like the number of American lives of previous conflicts involving the United States. Between 2001 and 2011, indeed, roughly as many Philadelphians died from homicide in their own city as American troops died in Iraq. In this respect the conflicts heralded a new way in warfare in which overwhelming technological superiority, backed by the might of the world's largest economy, would deliver victory without the kind of losses that had eaten away at support for military intervention in Vietnam. Nevertheless, casualties in both conflicts came from across the region, and many more suffered from the aftereffects of combat. Moreover, the wars in the Gulf—especially the more controversial and longer-lived second installment—sparked intense disputes at home over what it meant to support the troops.

## War in Afghanistan

**Robert J. Kodosky**

Greater Philadelphia contributed substantially to the U.S. war effort in Afghanistan (2001–21). Its defense industry and military bases, which had expanded in the Cold War, supported combat operations with both matériel and personnel, providing the region with a considerable economic boost. A wave of voluntary organizing aided troops, helped veterans, and provided humanitarian relief to Afghans. In contrast to other post-1945 wars, the conflict, launched in response to the terror attacks of 9/11, elicited little widespread dissent. The war also precipitated incidents of Islamophobia in the area, however, that prompted educational outreach to non-Muslims by Philadelphia's Muslim community.

On September 11, 2001, Al-Qaeda ("the Base"), founded by Osama bin Laden in 1988, executed four coordinated attacks on the United States. Three hijacked commercial airliners crashed into targets in Washington, D.C., and New York City; a fourth plane went down in a field near Shanksville, Pennsylvania after its passengers fought the hijackers. The attacks claimed nearly 3,000 lives, including 750 from New Jersey and 30 from Pennsylvania. Dozens of the victims resided in the Philadelphia region.

The United States responded to the attacks by initiating Operation Enduring Freedom on October 2, 2001. This targeted Al-Qaeda and the Taliban government that harbored it in Afghanistan. The 111th Fighter Wing, Pennsylvania Air National Guard, assisted in loading ordinance for the first combat sorties into Afghanistan. It operated from Kuwait where it had deployed from the Naval Air Station Joint Reserve Base Willow Grove in Montgomery County immediately after the September 11 attacks. Its personnel later moved to Afghanistan, in 2002 and in 2008, as the 103rd Expeditionary Fighter Squadron.

As the war wore on, thousands of service people trained and mobilized at an expanded Joint Base

McGuire-Dix-Lakehurst, which included a new urban warfare training center and housing for military families. The Burlington County base became, after state government, the second largest employer in New Jersey. Over forty thousand service personnel, civilians, and their families contributed to base operations. It also served as home to the Sixth Airlift Squadron, nicknamed during World War II as the "Bully Beef Express," which routinely made multiple-day flights to Afghanistan in support of combat operations.

The War in Afghanistan rejuvenated Greater Philadelphia's defense industry, which after rapidly expanding during the Cold War had declined due to a round of base closures in the 1990s that included the Philadelphia Naval Shipyard. Defense Logistics Agency Troop Support in Northeast Philadelphia provided more than $14.5 billion annually in food, clothing, medicine, and other supplies. The Delaware Valley chapter of the National Defense Industrial Association, an organization with over one thousand members, generated $4.5 billion in 2005 to provision troops. By 2012, Boeing's campus in Ridley Park, Pennsylvania, grew its workforce to 6,200, and delivered five Chinook troop transport craft and three V-22 Ospreys each month. In the suburbs, Alloy Surfaces added hundreds of workers to its plants in Delaware County where it produced expendable antimissile decoys. The Campbell Soup Company, which remained headquartered in Camden, New Jersey, despite shutting down its factory there in 1991, delivered over $70 million in grocery products to the military in 2005.

Compared to other wars, the region's casualties in Afghanistan remained low. Seven Philadelphians serving in the military lost their lives in Afghanistan, joining over 80 others killed there from the rest of Pennsylvania. While 3 from Delaware did not return home from Afghanistan, the 48 who died there from New Jersey included 2 from Philadelphia's neighboring city, Camden. America's military, in total, experienced 3,590 fatalities in the twenty years it spent in Afghanistan. Less quantifiable was the toll exacted on veterans and their families from post-traumatic stress disorder, a condition that impacted nearly 16 percent of those who deployed. By the war's conclusion, suicide had claimed four times as many lives of American service personnel than had hostilities.

Regional institutions supported combatants' physical and mental rehabilitation. The Philadelphia Veterans Affairs Medical Center treated injured troops while area veterans pioneered programming in the arts to help process their wartime experience. Philadelphia's Warrior Writers, founded in 2007, developed writer workshops for veterans while the Rosenbach Museum bridged home and war fronts through its 2012–13 exhibit *War Stories*.

The Philadelphia region supported those deployed in myriad other ways. The United Service Organizations (USO) of Pennsylvania and New Jersey, the Liberty USO, helped to usher troops in and out of Philadelphia International Airport and the area's military bases. State and city governments, including Philadelphia's, reinstated Gulf War–era policies to grant reservists and guardsmen pay differentials and health benefits not provided by the military during active duty. Civic and religious organizations extended support to the people of Afghanistan. The Mennonite Central Committee, the Muslim Peace Fellowship, and Catholic Relief Services worked to deliver items such as food and blankets to Afghans. The American Friends Service Committee additionally led initiatives to aid Afghan refugees and pursue peaceful alternatives to war.

Only a few hundred of the tens of thousands of Afghans in America resided in Greater Philadelphia during the war. They constituted a small part of Greater Philadelphia's Muslim community whose members, in the aftermath of the 9/11 attacks, were occasionally targeted with acts of violence, including a suspected arson attack against a Syrian-owned convenience store in Bucks County. Organizations such as the Foundation of Islamic Education on Montgomery Road and the Islamic Family Center on Old York Road responded to Islamophobia with open house educational initiatives.

The long hunt for Osama bin Laden culminated in a raid of his compound in Pakistan that resulted in his death on May 2, 2011. As the news spread through social media, spontaneous celebrations erupted throughout Philadelphia, including at Citizens Bank Park where Phillies fans began chanting "U.S.A." during a nationally televised game against the New York Mets. The jubilation resulted in a heightened alert issued by the Philadelphia Police Department to monitor the safety of the city's mosques.

But Bin Laden's death did not end America's military presence in Afghanistan. When troops did withdraw, over the spring and summer of 2021, the Taliban rapidly regained control of much of the country. Philadelphia became the second American city to welcome Afghan refugees when over 250 arrived at Philadelphia International Airport on August 30, 2021. As Joint Base McGuire-Dix-Lakehurst launched Operation Task Force Liberty, an effort to house ten thousand Afghans for up to a year, Camden provided a staging area by converting a Pier 5 warehouse into a temporary shelter.

The Philadelphia area's defense industry and its military bases built from their Cold War foundations to contribute matériel and personnel to the War in Afghanistan. The conflict benefited the region economically while generating tension between its Muslim and non-Muslim communities. Greater Philadelphia evidenced little protest against the War in Afghanistan as a response to the 9/11 attacks while providing essential humanitarian support and caring for its participants on all sides.

## EXPLORE MORE

The region's connections to foreign conflicts and revolutionary struggles can be glimpsed in landscapes of memory, museums and heritage sites, and the calendar of parades that honor veterans of the United States and their comrades who did not return. War memorials commemorating local people's heroism and sacrifice in foreign conflicts dot the region. In Philadelphia itself, the tomb of the unknown soldier (though it may not hold the remains of a soldier at all) sits on the old potter's field of Washington Square. Amid other commemorations of the Revolutionary War, the statue of the Polish nobleman and Patriot General Casimir Pulaski at the west entrance to the Philadelphia Museum of Art is particularly notable for its acknowledgment of foreign support in the battle for independence. Another European to assist the Continental army, the Prussian Baron von Steuben, has a statue at Valley Forge. World War I is commemorated in the statue of a "Tenderloin Doughboy" at Second and Spring Garden Streets and, via a bronze globe, at the *Aero Memorial* (1948) at Aviator Park facing the Franklin Institute on Logan Square. One of the most striking memorials to World War II is Walter Hancock's 1952 bronze sculpture of the Archangel Michael at Thirtieth Street Station, which remembers the Pennsylvania Railroad workers who lost their lives in the fight against the Axis powers. For later wars, Penn's Landing has served as a site of remembrance. The Korean War Memorial in Foglietta Plaza at Front and Spruce Streets sits a short walk from the Vietnam Veterans Memorial, dedicated in 1987. Other memorials sanctify the role of different groups. Women's willingness to sacrifice their sons on the altar of the nation is immortalized in the 1928 sculpture *American War Mother and Her Sons*, Belfield Avenue and Twenty-First Street, Germantown, while Black soldiers and sailors who fought for the republic are remembered in the 1934 *All Wars Memorial to Colored Soldiers and Sailors*, which relocated from Fairmount Park to Logan Square in 1994.

Other memorials are scattered around the region, sometimes humble and hidden away, sometimes hard to miss. Camden's Eighth Ward World War II Memorial, located in Memorial Park on Broadway, provides an example of the former; so too does a memorial to the same conflict in Newton Lake Park, Haddon Township, N.J., which honors the dead who had worked for the R.M. Hollingshead Corporation. Crossing the Brandywine Creek in Wilmington, Del., Baynard Boulevard provides a more prominent site of remembrance. Flanked by monuments to Delaware's World War I and Black servicemen, the avenue also has the city's Vietnam War memorial. Erected in 1983 as one of the earliest to mark that conflict, it takes the form of a poignant sculpture of a Black GI carrying his white comrade. Trenton's World War I memorial, completed in 1930 on West Lafayette Street, is now the city's Patriots Theater. The nation's twenty-first-century wars have, as of the early 2020s, made less of an imprint, but they have not been forgotten entirely. The Victims of Terrorism memorial in Cooper River Park, Merchantville, N.J., honors those who lost their lives on September 11, 2001, as well as in other terrorist attacks.

The region's warriors are interred across the Delaware Valley's cemeteries. Commodore David Porter, a naval officer in the Quasi-War and War of 1812, is buried in the Woodlands Cemetery in West Philadelphia. The Naval Plot and Soldiers' Lot in Mount Moriah Cemetery, at Sixty-Second Street and Kingsessing Avenue, provides a resting place for over two thousand navy officers and seamen. One of the nation's first military resting places, the Philadelphia National Cemetery, is on Limekiln Pike in West Oak Lane, and has been a final home for service people from 1862. It includes a monument to those who fought in the Mexican-American War. Much newer is the Washington Crossing National Cemetery in Newtown, Pa., which opened in 2009.

Greater Philadelphia is well-served by military museums. The Museum of the American Revolution at 101 S. Third Street and the visitor center at Valley Forge National Historical Park in King of Prussia illuminate the region's involvement in the break with Britain. New Hall, at 320 Chestnut Street, served as the Department of War in the early national era and was reconstructed to serve as small museum. The American Helicopter Museum and Education Center is located in West Chester. Other regional museums include the Pennsylvania Veterans

Museum, Media, Delaware County; the National Guard Militia Museum of New Jersey in Lawrenceville; and the Naval Air Station Wildwood Aviation Museum in Lower Township, Cape May County.

With the Delaware River the incubator of U.S. sea power, naval heritage is particularly prominent. On the Philadelphia riverfront, the Independence Seaport Museum at 211 S. Columbus Boulevard counts among its exhibits the USS *Olympia*, a steel cruiser from the Spanish-American War that served as the flagship at the Battle of Manila Bay, and a World War II–era submarine, the USS *Becuna*. Across the river in Camden lies the Battleship New Jersey Museum and Memorial. Fortifications to protect Philadelphia and its shipping from attack still line the river. Guarding the entrance to the Delaware River at Cape May stands the World War II Lookout Tower. Farther upstream, Fort Delaware State Park has a history that spans the Civil War to World War II. And closer to Philadelphia still is Fort Mifflin, first occupied in 1771 and still in use by the Army Corps of Engineers as of 2024. Memorial Day in late May and Veterans Day in early November are marked across the region. The former features parades in Trenton and Wilmington. In Philadelphia a Veterans Day parade, inaugurated in 2015, marches along Market Street. Posts of the American Legion can be found throughout the Delaware Valley.

The region's military history is amply documented. Prominent bases that served the nation in its wars with foreign powers are covered in Jeffery M. Dorwart, *Fort Mifflin of Philadelphia: An Illustrated History* (University of Pennsylvania Press, 1998); Daniel W. Zimmerman, *Fort Dix* (Arcadia Publishing, 2001); and Kevin Pace, Ronald Montgomery, and Rick Zitarosa, *Naval Air Station Lakehurst* (Arcadia Publishing, 2003). The Delaware Valley's importance to the U.S. Navy is explored in Jeffery M. Dorwart and Jean K. Wolf, *The Philadelphia Navy Yard: From the Birth of the U.S. Navy to the Nuclear Age* (University of Pennsylvania Press, 2001); Thomas Heinrich, *Ships for the Seven Seas: Philadelphia Shipbuilding in the Age of Industrial Capitalism* (Johns Hopkins University Press, 1997); and Joseph-James Ahern, *Philadelphia Naval Shipyard* (Arcadia Publishing, 1997). On the region's armaments production, see James J. Farley, *Making Arms in the Machine Age: Philadelphia's Frankford Arsenal, 1816–1870* (Pennsylvania State University Press, 1994); and Margaret M. Mulrooney, *Black Powder, White Lace: The du Pont Irish and Cultural Identity in Nineteenth-Century America* (University of New Hampshire Press, 2002).

For work on the regional impact of individual wars and revolution prior to the twentieth century, see Kevin Kenny, *Peaceable Kingdom Lost: The Paxton Boys and the Destruction of William Penn's Holy Experiment* (Oxford University Press, 2009); Catherine Hebert, "The French Element in Pennsylvania in the 1790s: The Francophone Immigrants' Impact," *Pennsylvania Magazine of History and Biography* 108, no. 4 (October 1984): 451–69; Gary Nash, "Reverberations of Haiti in the American North: Black Saint Dominguans in Philadelphia," in "Explorations in Early American Culture," Supplement, *Pennsylvania History* 65, no. 5 (1998): 44–73; Victor A. Sapio, *Pennsylvania & the War of 1812* (University Press of Kentucky, 1970); and Randy W. Hackenberg, *Pennsylvania in the War With Mexico: The Volunteer Regiments* (White Mane Publishing Co., 1992).

Conflicts after 1900 are treated in Peter John Williams, *Philadelphia: The World War I Years* (Arcadia Publishing, 2013); Margaret B. Tinkcom, "Depression and War, 1929–1946," in Russell F. Weigley, ed., *Philadelphia: A 300-Year History* (W. W. Norton, 1982); Marston A. Mischlich and Gail Mischlich, *Southern New Jersey: Pulling Together During World War II* (Dorrance Publishing, 2022); Michael Morgan, *World War II and the Delaware Coast* (History Press, 2016); Peter F. Slavin and Timothy A. Slavin, *Delaware in World War II* (Arcadia Publishing, 2004); Philip Jenkins, *The Cold War at Home: The Red Scare in Pennsylvania, 1945–1960* (University of North Carolina Press, 1999); Paul Lyons, *Philadelphia Communists, 1936–1956* (Temple University Press, 1982); Sherman Labovitz, *Being Red in Philadelphia: A Memoir of the McCarthy Era* (Camino Books, 1998); Paul Lyons, *The People of This Generation: The Rise and Fall of the New Left in Philadelphia* (University of Pennsylvania Press, 2003). These works capture some of the domestic conflicts that the nation's foreign wars have provoked, while showing how the Delaware Valley has contributed to American military might.

# Contributors

**Guy Aiken** has a Ph.D. in religious studies from the University of Virginia, where he is currently a lecturer in interdisciplinary studies.

**Elizabeth Hayes Alvarez,** Ph.D., received her degree in religion from the University of Chicago. She heads the Learning Fellows Program and facilitates meaningful learning across a range of classrooms.

**Daniel Amsterdam** is a professor of history at the Georgia Institute of Technology.

**Annie Anderson** is an American studies Ph.D. student at Rutgers–Newark. She has worked for Eastern State Penitentiary Historic Site and the Rikers Public Memory Project.

**William V. Bartleson** is an independent scholar of military history who has worked with the New Jersey National Guard Militia Museum and the Center for Veterans Oral History.

**James M. Bergquist** was Professor Emeritus of History, Villanova University.

**Gretchen E. Boger** is Director of Curriculum and Instruction and an upper-school history teacher at the Baldwin School in Bryn Mawr, Pennsylvania.

**Paul Campbell** works for the National Park Service as special events coordinator at Independence National Historical Park. He has an M.A. in history from Temple University.

**Augustin Cerveaux** is an independent scholar and former fellow of the Chemical Heritage Foundation.

**Sarah Chesney** completed her Ph.D. in anthropology in 2014 and is currently the staff archaeologist at San Felipe de Austin State Historic Site in San Felipe, Texas.

**Peter Cole** is a professor of history at Western Illinois University and a research associate in the Society, Work & Politics Institute, University of the Witwatersrand.

**Nathaniel Conley** received his Ph.D. from the University of Arkansas. His research focuses on Maryland and Pennsylvania with emphasis on the lower class and the border between slavery and freedom.

**Danielle Podwats D'Amelio** is an educator with an M.A. in English and media studies from Rutgers University–Camden and a B.A. in both English and education from Rowan University.

**Saanika Jeet Dhillon** is a graduate fellow at Syracuse University studying museum studies. She received an M.A. in American history and a B.A. in history.

**Jeffery M. Dorwart** is Professor Emeritus of History, Rutgers University, and has authored many works on local, military, and naval history in the Greater Philadelphia region.

**Jacob Downs** was born and raised in Philadelphia's Far Northeast. He holds degrees in American history and political science and earned his master's in gender perception during Philadelphia's industrial past.

**Christian DuComb,** Ph.D., is an associate professor of theater at Colgate University and author of *Haunted City: Three Centuries of Racial Impersonation in Philadelphia* (2017).

**Lance Eisenhower** is a public history professional in the Greater Philadelphia region and has a master's degree in history from Villanova University.

**David Elesh** is emeritus faculty in sociology at Temple University. He has written widely on industrial change and its consequences.

**Herbert Ershkowitz** was Professor of History Emeritus at Temple University.

**Simon Finger** is author of *The Contagious City: The Politics of Public Health in Early Philadelphia* (2012) and teaches the history of colonial North America and the history of medicine at The College of New Jersey.

**Levi Fox,** Ph.D., is an assistant professor of history in the Department of Civic Engagement at Immaculata University and the owner of Jersey Shore Tours.

**Gail Friedman** is a writer and city planner and earned a master's degree in public history at Temple University.

**Reena Sigman Friedman,** Ph.D., is an associate professor of modern Jewish history at Reconstructionist Rabbinical College and an adjunct professor at Gratz College.

**Michael Goode** is an associate professor of history at Utah Valley University. His teaching and research focus on early American history in an Atlantic World and indigenous context.

**Patrick Grubbs** is Associate Dean of Arts, Humanities, and Social Sciences and a professor of history at Northampton Community College in Bethlehem, Pennsylvania.

**R. Scott Hanson** is a senior scholar in urban history and material culture in the Department of History and Lenfest Center for Cultural Partnerships at Drexel University.

**Charles Hardy III** is a former professor of history at West Chester University of Pennsylvania and supervising historian of ExplorePAhistory.com.

**Christina Afia Harris** earned her Ph.D. from the Department of Africology and Africana Studies at Temple University. Her essay is derived from her research and her personal experience as an ODUNDE participant.

**Andrew Heath** studied in London and Philadelphia and now teaches at the University of Sheffield in the United Kingdom. He is the author of *In Union There Is Strength: Philadelphia in the Age of Urban Consolidation* (2019).

**Carola Hein** is a professor of history of architecture and urban planning, Delft University of Technology, a professor at Leiden and Erasmus University, and UNESCO Chair in Water, Ports and Historic Cities.

**Monica Henry** is Associate Professor Emerita at Université Paris Est-Créteil. She is currently co-project director and editor of *The Papers of William Short.*

**John Hepp** is Professor of History Emeritus at Wilkes University, and his focus is urban cultural history in the period 1600 to the present.

**Timothy Kent Holliday** is an early American historian of the body. He teaches in the Critical Writing Program at the University of Pennsylvania.

**Mark Jaffe** is a journalist focused on energy and environmental issues. He has worked for the *Philadelphia Inquirer*, Bloomberg News, *Denver Post*, and *Colorado Sun.*

**Hillary S. Kativa** is an archivist in the Greater Philadelphia region and holds graduate degrees in history and library science from Villanova and Rutgers University.

**Lawrence H. Kessler** holds a Ph.D. in history from Temple University and is a postdoctoral fellow at the Consortium for History of Science, Technology, and Medicine.

**Robert J. Kodosky,** Ph.D., is a history professor at West Chester University and author of *Tuskegee in Philadelphia: Rising to the Challenge* (2020).

**Paul A. Kopacz** was employed by United Parcel Service for thirty years. He received his B.A. from Temple University in 2004 and his M.A. in history from Villanova University in 2016.

**James Kopaczewski** received his Ph.D. in United States history from Temple University in 2022.

**Julianne Kornacki** is a doctoral student in political science with an interest in the history of municipal and neighborhood politics in Philadelphia.

**David M. Krueger** earned his Ph.D. in religion from Temple University and is a historian of American religion serving as executive director of the Dialogue Institute.

**Anne E. Krulikowski,** Ph.D., teaches American history and public history at West Chester University. She has published a history of West Chester University and on urban topics.

**Christina Larocco** is editor of the *Pennsylvania Magazine of History and Biography* and scholarly programs manager at the Historical Society of Pennsylvania.

**Demian Larry** is a Ph.D. candidate in American history at Temple University. His dissertation is about the politics and economics of airport development in Philadelphia.

**Jessica Linker** is an assistant professor of history at Northeastern University and co-director of Huskiana Press.

**Tehyun Ma** is a lecturer in global history at the University of Sheffield. She previously studied at the University of Pennsylvania and Bristol University.

**Dianna Marder** retired in 2012 after twenty-seven years as a staff writer at the *Philadelphia Inquirer,* where she wrote about the courts, crime, and the cultural impact of food.

**Isaac Barnes May** is a student at Yale Law School. He earned his Ph.D. in religious studies from the University of Virginia.

**Jack McCarthy** is an archivist and historian specializing in Philadelphia music, industry, and Northeast Philadelphia. He regularly writes, lectures, gives tours, curates exhibits, and directs projects on these topics.

**Marie Basile McDaniel** is an associate professor of history at Southern Connecticut State University. Her essay was based on her dissertation, "'We Shall Not Differ in Heaven': Marriage, Order and Identity in Eighteenth-Century Philadelphia" (2010).

**James R. McIntyre** has been researching and writing on the Seven Years' War and American War of Independence for over twenty years.

**Andrew McNally** received his Ph.D. from the University of Minnesota in 2017. His dissertation explored the history of the international understanding movement in U.S. education.

**Charlene Mires** is a professor of history at Rutgers–Camden and editor-in-chief of *The Encyclopedia of Greater Philadelphia.*

**Nicholas Trajano Molnar** teaches history in Philadelphia and is author of *American Mestizos, the Philippines, and the Malleability of Race, 1898–1961* (2017).

**Molly Nebiolo** is an assistant professor of history at Butler University. Her book project examines health and city spaces in the colonial Anglo-Atlantic world.

**Stephen Nepa** teaches history at Temple University and Moore College of Art and Design. A contributor to numerous books and journals, he lives in Philadelphia.

**Dael A. Norwood** is a historian and the author of *Trading Freedom: How Trade with China Defined Early America* (2022).

**John B. Osborne,** Ph.D., is Emeritus Professor of History at Millersville State University of Pennsylvania and founding director of the University Honors Program.

**Steven J. Peitzman** is a professor of medicine at Drexel University. His historical work includes *A New and Untried Course: Woman's Medical College and Medical College of Pennsylvania, 1850–1998* (2000).

**Leonard Norman Primiano** was a professor of religious studies at Cabrini University. He codeveloped "The Father Divine Project," an online research database and multimedia interpretive documentary about the Peace Mission Movement.

**David Reader** is a history teacher at Haddonfield Memorial High School in New Jersey and volunteers at the Historical Society of Pennsylvania and the Historical Society of Haddonfield.

**Mary Rizzo** is an associate professor of history at Rutgers University–Newark. She is the author of two books and a founder of the Chicory Revitalization Project.

**Mabel Rosenheck** is Director of Education and Exhibition Planning at LancasterHistory.

**Molly Roth** was a nonprofit administrator in Philadelphia with an interest in the cultural anthropology of Mande West Africa. She was founding executive director of the Global Philadelphia Association.

**Evan Rothera** is an associate professor of history at the University of Arkansas–Fort Smith and author of *Civil Wars and Reconstructions in the Americas* (2022).

**Dan Royles** is an associate professor of history at Florida International University. He is the author of *To Make the Wounded Whole: The African American Struggle against HIV/AIDS* (2021).

**Francis Ryan** is a labor educator at Rutgers University's School of Management and Labor Relations. He has written extensively on Philadelphia labor and working-class history.

**Rosina McAvoy Ryan** teaches in the Department of History at La Salle University. She earned her Ph.D. at Temple University, where her dissertation examined the College Settlement of Philadelphia.

**John Saillant** is a professor of English and history at Western Michigan University. His writings have appeared as essays, books, and edited documents since 1992.

**Barbara Klaczynska Schmidt,** Ph.D., has degrees from Holy Family University, University of Wisconsin–Milwaukee, and Temple University. She studies women, ethnic, and urban history with a particular focus on Philadelphia.

**Zachary M. Schrag** is the author of *The Fires of Philadelphia: Citizen-Soldiers, Nativists, and the 1844 Riots Over the Soul of a Nation* (2021).

**Grace Schultz** earned an M.A. in history with a concentration in public history from Temple University and is an archives technician at the National Archives at Philadelphia.

**Philip Scranton** is Emeritus Board of Governors Professor, History of Industry and Technology, at Rutgers University–Camden.

**Peter Seibert** is the president of the Independence Seaport Museum located in Philadelphia. He has served as a CEO for museums across the United States.

**Daniel Sidorick** teaches labor history at Rutgers University. He is the author of *Condensed Capitalism: Campbell Soup and the Pursuit of Cheap Production* (2016), winner of the Richard P. McCormick Prize.

**John Kenly Smith Jr.** is Associate Professor Emeritus of History at Lehigh University. Initially a chemical engineer, he specialized in the history of industrial R&D.

**Robert F. Smith** is Provost at Valley Forge Military College and author of the book *Manufacturing Independence: Industrial Innovation in the American Revolution* (2016).

**Alexandra L. Straub** received her Ph.D. in history at Temple University, where she studied American environmental history, and works at the University of Pittsburgh as a research coordinator.

**Helen Tangires,** Ph.D., is the administrator of the Center for Advanced Study in the Visual Arts at the National Gallery of Art in Washington, D.C., and the author of multiple works.

**Theresa Altieri Taplin** earned an M.A. in history from Villanova University. She is a certified archivist and museum professional in Philadelphia.

**Domenic Vitiello** is a professor of city planning and urban studies at the University of Pennsylvania. His essay is based on collaborative work on the Philadelphia Migration Project at University of Pennsylvania.

**Matthew A. White** received his Ph.D. in history from the University of Florida and is Director of Education at the Smithsonian Institution's National Postal Museum.

**Luke Willert** received a graduate degree in history at Harvard University. He writes about the American West and environmental history.

**Christopher Willoughby,** Ph.D., is the author of *Masters of Health: Racial Science and Slavery in U.S. Medical Schools* (2022).

**Kathryn Wilson** is an associate professor of history at Georgia State University. She is the author of *Ethnic Renewal in Philadelphia's Chinatown: Space, Place and Struggle* (2015).

**Thomas Wirth** serves as a lecturer in the history department at the State University of New York College at Cortland.

**Megan C. McGee Yinger** earned her American studies degrees from La Salle University (B.A.) and Penn State Harrisburg (M.A., Ph.D.).

# Subject Index

## A

## B



## C

## D



## E

## F



## G



## H

## I



## J



## K



## L

## M

## N



## O



## P

## Q



## R



## S

## T

## U



## V



## W

## Y

# Place Index

## A



## B



## C

## D



## E



## F

## G



## H



## I



## J



## K

## L



## M



## N

## O



## P



## Q



## R



## S

## T



## U



## V



## W



## Y

# Biographical Index

## C



## D



## E



## F

## G



## H



## I



## J

## K



## L



## M

## N



## O



## P



## R

## S



## T



## V



## W

## Y



## Z

Acknowledgments

This book would not be possible without the many years of effort by individuals, associations, and funders associated with *The Encyclopedia of Greater Philadelphia* project. Preliminary plans for an encyclopedia of Philadelphia were discussed at the University of Pennsylvania Press as early as 2000. Then conceived as a print volume, the idea revived during 2007 among individuals involved in commemorating the twenty-fifth anniversary of *Philadelphia: A 300-Year History* with a special issue of the *Pennsylvania Magazine of History and Biography* (October 2007) and an event at the Historical Society of Pennsylvania (HSP). *PMHB* editor Tamara Gaskell and the special issue guest editor, Charlene Mires, worked together to initiate these projects, with the cooperation of the Barra Foundation and HSP. Mires encouraged historian Gary Nash to mention the prospect of an encyclopedia as a new initiative for Philadelphia history in his historiographical essay in the special issue, a call he amplified in his featured address at the HSP event.

The University of Pennsylvania Press subsequently enlisted three Philadelphia-area scholars to serve as general editors and leaders of the project: Charlene Mires, then of Villanova University; Howard Gillette of Rutgers University–Camden, then the director of the Mid-Atlantic Regional Center for the Humanities (MARCH); and Randall Miller of Saint Joseph's University. Gillette's influence broadened the project's focus from the city of Philadelphia to the region at large. The project began in earnest in April 2009 with a two-day Civic Partnership and Planning Workshop, and public engagement continued through a series of Greater Philadelphia Roundtable discussion programs, thematic essays copublished with WHYY and the *Philadelphia Inquirer*, teachers' workshops in collaboration with public history partners, and an online invitation for nomination of topics.

In 2010, the Mid-Atlantic Regional Center for the Humanities at Rutgers–Camden became the project's home after Mires succeeded Gillette as the center's director. Guided by public input and advice from potential funders, the project evolved from the concept of a book with companion website (the model of The Encyclopedia of Chicago, 2004) to a digital platform envisioned as aggregating and disseminating knowledge in a variety of ways. The project grew topic by topic online, making possible the set of thematic books now published with the University of Pennsylvania Press. Readers are encouraged to visit the digital encyclopedia, https://philadelphiaencyclopedia.org/, to explore topics beyond the scope of the present volume and to read new topics as they appear.

*The Encyclopedia of Greater Philadelphia Team*, 2009–23
(CUMULATIVE LIST)

EDITOR-IN-CHIEF: Charlene Mires.

CO-EDITORS: Howard Gillette, Randall Miller, Tamara Gaskell.

CONSULTING EDITORS: Gary Nash, Emma Lapsansky-Werner.

ASSOCIATE EDITORS: Carolyn Adams, William W. Cutler III, Andrew Heath, Tyler Hoffman, Hillary Kativa, Cyril Reade, Nancy Rosoff, Philip Scranton, Jean R. Soderlund, Domenic Vitiello, Stephanie Grauman Wolf.

EDITORIAL, TECHNICAL, AND EDUCATIONAL ADVISERS: Eugenie Birch, Vibiana Bowman Cvetkovic, Richardson Dilworth, Travis DuBose, Charles Hardy, Amy Hillier, Ken Hohing, Guian McKee, Alexis Moore, Elizabeth Nash, Richard Newman, Daniel Richter, Mary Rizzo, Lori Shorr, George Thomas, Zara Wilkinson, Kathryn Wilson, Rebecca Yamin.

MANAGING EDITORS: Donald D. Groff, Hillary Kativa (books).

PRODUCTION EDITORS: Lucy Davis, Luther Hoheisel.

EDITORIAL ASSISTANTS: Tia Antonelli, Lucy Davis, Joshua DiPrima, Luther Hoheisel, Hannah Lee, Mikaela Maria, Gina Torres.

COPY EDITORS: Donald D. Groff, Lauren Cooper, Lucy Davis.

DIGITAL MEDIA COORDINATORS: Sharece Blakney, McKenna Britton, Audrey Johnson, Scott Hearn, Jennifer Long Levy, Amy Osterhout.

ADMINISTRATIVE COORDINATOR: Sharon Smith.

RESEARCH, DIGITAL PUBLISHING, AND FACT-CHECKING ASSISTANTS: Tia Antonelli, Kelly Banks, William Bartleson, Sharece Blakney, Brandon Borrelli, McKenna Britton, Melissa Bryson, Melissa Callahan, Vincent Cammarota, Kimberly Coulter, Amanda Cross, Lucy Davis, Joshua DiPrima, Elizabeth Eimer, Olivia Errico, Sabrina Gonzalez-Morabito, Scott Hearn, Luther Hoheisel, Fatima Ijaz, Audrey Johnson, William Krakower, Sebastian LaVergne, Hannah Lee, Joshua Lisowski, Mandi Magnuson-Hung, Mikaela Maria, Daniel Marren, Thomas McPherson, Maggie Montalto, Arthur Murphy, Andin Ncho, Darragh Nolan, Alaina Noland, Miriam Parrotto, Victoria Scannella, Nicole Skalenko, Benjamin Thompson, Gina Torres, Kevin Wakefield, Quincy Wansel, Mariam Williams, Emily Winters, Victoria Wroblewski, and additional students in publishing and editing seminars taught by Carol Singley at Rutgers–Camden.

WEBSITE DEVELOPMENT: Azavea (Brian T. Jacobs), Roy Rosenzweig Center for History and New Media (Ken Albers), Rutgers Web Consulting Services (Ivanok Tavarez, Bart Grebowiec).

CIVIC AND ARCHIVAL PARTNERS: African American Museum in Philadelphia, American Philosophical Society, Association of Philadelphia Tour Guides, Athenaeum of Philadelphia, Avenging the Ancestors Coalition, Camden County Historical Society, City of Philadelphia Department of Records, City of Philadelphia Mural Arts Program, Eastern State Penitentiary Historic Site, Economy League of Greater Philadelphia, Fels Institute of Government, Foundations of the Union League, Free Library of Philadelphia, Friends of Laurel Hill Cemetery, Global Philadelphia Association, Greater Philadelphia Tourism Marketing Corporation (Visit Philadelphia), Historic Germantown, Historical Society of Pennsylvania, Independence Hall Association, Independence National Historical Park, Independence Seaport Museum, International Visitors Council, Library Company of Philadelphia, National Archives–Mid-Atlantic Region, National Constitution Center, National Museum of American Jewish History, Philadelphia Consortium of Special Collections Libraries, Philadelphia History Museum, Philadelphia Museum of Art, Preservation Alliance for Greater Philadelphia, Temple University Libraries, WHYY, Young Involved Philadelphia.

FUNDERS: Barra Foundation, Mayor's Fund for Philadelphia, Mid-Atlantic Regional Center for the Humanities, National Endowment for the Humanities, Pennsylvania Humanities Council, Pew Center for Arts and Heritage, Poor Richard's Charitable Trust, Rutgers–Camden Dean of Arts and Sciences, Rutgers–Camden Digital Studies Center, Rutgers Research Council, William Penn Foundation, University of Pennsylvania Press, and generous individual donors.